COMPARATIVE BUSINESS-GOVERNMENT RELATIONS

COMPARATIVE BUSINESS-GOVERNMENT RELATIONS

George Cabot Lodge

Harvard University Graduate School of Business Administration

PRENTICE HALL, Englewood Cliffs, New Jersey 07632

Library of Congress Cataloging-in-Publication Data

Lodge, George C.
    Comparative business-government relations / George Cabot Lodge.
      p.   cm.
    Includes bibliographical references.
    ISBN 0-13-171299-3
    1. Industry and state. 2. Business and politics. 3. Comparative
government.   I. Title.
HD3611.L58   1990
338.9--dc20   90-6731

338.9
L822c

Editorial/production supervision: *Edith Riker/Sally Ann Bailey*
Interior design: *Edith Riker*
Cover design: *Photo Plus Art*
Manufacturing buyer: *Peter Havens*

© 1990 by Prentice-Hall, Inc.
A Division of Simon & Schuster
Englewood Cliffs, New Jersey 07632

Printed in the United States of America

10 9 8 7 6 5 4 3 2 1

ISBN   0-13-171299-3

Prentice-Hall International (UK) Limited, *London*
Prentice-Hall of Australia Pty. Limited, *Sydney*
Prentice-Hall Canada Inc., *Toronto*
Prentice-Hall Hispanoamericana, S.A., *Mexico*
Prentice-Hall of India Private Limited, *New Delhi*
Prentice-Hall of Japan, Inc., *Tokyo*
Simon & Schuster Asia Pte. Ltd., *Singapore*
Editora Prentice-Hall do Brasil, Ltda., *Rio de Janeiro*

CONTENTS

CHAPTER 2

GOVERNMENT TARGETING AND THE U.S. RESPONSE

CHAPTER 3

CHAPTER 5

ENSURING ECONOMIC JUSTICE

BOOKS RECOMMENDED FOR FURTHER STUDY

PREFACE

The cases and articles in this book were written or selected for a Harvard Business School course, Comparative Business-Government Relations, first offered in the spring of 1989. The students included candidates for the master's degree in business as well as those from the Kennedy School of Government with an eye on public administration. This mix brought exceptional excitement to the classroom discussions, which makes me believe that the material is useful to a wide range of students interested not only in busines and government, but also in political science, political economy, and sociology.

OBJECTIVES

The book has three educational objectives:

- To provide an understanding of the different roles and relationships of business and government in key countries of Asia, Europe, and the Americas; of how and why these are changing; and what choices managers have as a result of the changes.
- To facilitate the students' ability to inspect their assumptions about government-business relations so as to open the way for more effective decision making.
- To place students at the interface of government and business in different national settings so as to provide an opportunity to deal realistically not only with policy questions but with the hurly-burly of implementation.

The book focuses on a few countries, principally Japan, the United States, Brazil, and France, and Europe as a region, and on a few industries, principally steel, computers, semiconductors, telecommunications, health equipment, and earth imaging from space. It concentrates on those issues which are most controversial and politically charged, affecting the lifeblood of nations and stability of regimes, as well as the fortunes of great corporations. Some of the issues concern substance, such as industrial policy and government targeting to promote a predetermined definition of the national interest. Others relate to process: how decisions are made and how control is exerted. Still others concern behavior: the actors in government, for example, who they are, what motivates them, what their relationship is to one another and to business.

The comparative approach helps students to keep an open mind as they seek the ingredients of effective management of government-business relations. It helps them to recognize and respect how the history of different countries has shaped those relations. It expands their field of choice as they look for what works best. It reminds them that increasingly the relationships of government and business in one country affect those in others and that as a consequence new forms of transnational government, such as the European Commission and Parliament, are emerging.

To deal effectively with the material in this book, students must think systematically. The institutions of government and business are in themselves complex systems. Each is fraught with internal divisions reflecting the interests of different constituencies. Together they are part of larger systems which are at once political, social, economic, and cultural. Effective management requires perception and understanding of how these systems work and interact.

This book also provides a way for students to refine their moral understanding. Government-business relations and the purposes that drive them lie at the heart of the public spirit in different communities: they are intimately tied to that community's definition of morality. Both sets of institutions depend for their legitimacy on a framework of ideas, an ideology. Effective managers are sensitive to what those ideas are and how they may be changing.

ORGANIZATION

The book is divided into five chapters. The first, Roles and Relationships of Business and Government, is an essay, an overview of the subject, that sets forth several conceptual frameworks for the comparative analysis of different patterns of roles and relationships of business and government. These include two ideological prototypes, individualism and communitarianism; the notion of community need, together with the questions of relevant community, who decides community need, and how business is aligned with it; different sources of management authority; and the concept of the legitimacy gap between practice and preachment.

The second, Government Targeting and the U.S. Response, begins with an introductory case on the steel industry, which demonstrates the importance of government policies to that industry in Europe and the United States. The chapter goes on to examine industrial policies in Japan and Brazil, the challenges the policies pose to the U.S. government and industry, and the response taken. It is designed to reveal different purposes and structures of business-government relations, to allow analysis of how they came to be and discussion of which way they are likely to go.

The third chapter, Managing the Government Affairs Function, provides an opportunity to discuss the design, organization, and management of the government affairs function in multinational corporations, as well as the role of industry associations. This segment should be seen against the conceptual backdrop of Chapter 1.

The fourth, Managing at the Interface, combines the first three. Focused on telecommunications and earth imaging in Japan, France, and the United States, the readings explore the nature of the governmental decision-making apparatus—bureaucracies and the like—and the relationship of firms to that apparatus.

The fifth chapter, Ensuring Economic Justice, compares how four countries go about saving ailing industrial giants who are too important to die. It also examines how the United States approaches problems of minorities and small business. Finally, there is a bibliography with brief descriptions of books that may be useful.

ACKNOWLEDGMENTS

In 26 years of teaching I have accumulated a heavy burden of gratitutde for all that I have learned from students in Harvard's executive and MBA programs, from my generous faculty colleagues, and from scores of executives and academics outside Harvard who have helped me write cases and books. All of them deserve credit for what is useful in this book.

I should like to thank especially the professors, research assistants, and MBA students who wrote or helped to write many of the cases which follow: Visiting Fellow Paul M. Achleitner, who worked with me on the European–U.S. Steel Dispute; Professor Marie Anchordoguy, who while she was a research associate at Harvard Business School, wrote the paper from which the Japanese computer case is drawn; Professor Joseph Badaracco, who as a research assistant worked with me on the Allied Chemical case; Professor Joseph L. Bower, who with Dr. William J. Murphy and Professor Kosei Furakawa, Keio University, wrote Cooperation for Competition; Charles H. Ferguson, research fellow at MIT, author of Sources and Implications of Strategic Decline; Professor J. Ronald Fox, author of the Note on U.S. Decision Making; Professor Barbara Jenkins of Carlton College, Ontario, who while a postdoctoral fellow at HBS, worked with me on the French telecommunications cases; Professor Chalmers Johnson of the University of California, San Diego, author of the paper describing the Japanese telecom wars; Charles E. McKittrick, vice president of IBM for governmental programs, author of the IBM case; Andrew Regan, author of the Government Redress case; Professor Robert B. Reich of the Kennedy School of Government who wrote Bailout; Joel Szabat and Frits van

Paasschen, who worked with me on the Brazil informatics cases; and Associates Fellow Robert S. Williams, whose brilliant efforts resulted in Sematech, JESSI, and Sensing the Earth from Space.

I am deeply grateful for the help and encouragement of Harvard Business School Dean John H. McArthur and Research Director Michael Y. Yoshino. Rose Giacobbe and her staff in Word Processing did wonders with countless drafts and revisions of these cases. Thanks also to the Research Division, especially its graphics department, and to Barbara Feinberg, for her very special editorial skills.

I am very grateful also to Lois Smith for her great help in keeping all facets of this book on track and organized, for typing, revising, and checking.

ROLES AND RELATIONSHIPS OF BUSINESS AND GOVERNMENT

This essay attempts to provide a way for managers to think about worldwide government-business relations and some of the issues which will be affecting those relations in the 1990s. Largely a synthesis of the work of leading scholars, it compares the roles and relationships of government and business in a variety of different nations in Asia, Europe, and the Americas. It suggests some analytical frameworks which may be helpful in managing relations with governments more effectively, concluding with a brief and partial list of questions on which to focus.

Throughout history, government and business have been engaged in trying to define and fulfill the needs of communities. They have worked toward that goal—together and separately—in relationships marked by both suspicion and trust, conflict and cooperation.

During the late Middle Ages, when the merchants, bankers, and artisans of Europe's cities were exploring the paths that have led to today's corporations, they encountered from church and state what one historian called "a furious chorus of invectives against cupidity and avarice."[1] Indeed, the only socially acceptable purpose of business in feudal times was the service of the bishops and the knights.

Then, with the Reformation, the Enlightenment, and the Industrial Revolution, business in the West burst this communitarian mold and with revolutionary fervor proclaimed itself free. Business became the lead horse in an economic troika composed of its own efforts, government's encouragement and protection, and religion's invention of new conceptions of God to justify its ascendancy.[2] The

Professor George C. Lodge wrote this essay and gratefully acknowledges the helpful comments of colleages at the Harvard Business School, Professors Joseph L. Bower, John B. Goodman, J. Ronald Fox, Thomas K. McGraw, Michael G. Rukstad, Bruce R. Scott, Richard H. K. Vietor, Richard E. Walton, and Michael Y. Yoshino; Research Fellows Marie Anchordoguy and Barbara Jenkins; and Charles E. McKittrick, Jr., vice president of IBM.

excesses of business provoked a backlash of regulatory antagonism, especially where its growth preceded the development of government's will and capacity to control it, as in the United States.[3] Economic power had separated from political authority, and government retaliated. The retaliation, however, was muted by the power of organized interest groups, including business. In America, where faith in pluralism flourished, the policies of government were shaped by whichever combination of interest groups held sway at a particular time.

In other countries, such as Japan and Germany, where feudalism lasted even into the twentieth century, government was in place and endowed with authority to shape the growth of business and to control the power of interest groups by giving them public status and responsibility. Thus, the sense of mutuality of interest between government and business, cemented perhaps with coercion, was perforce greater.

In the 1940s, business and government combined for war throughout the industrial world. In the United States, they created "the arsenal of democracy," and a decade later in Japan and Germany, they launched spectacular economic growth. However, in America, the cooperative spirit between business and government that had prevailed during wartime was short-lived, having been primarily a function of unifying crisis. With peace came a return to the normalcy of ambivalence, a preoccupation with domestic priorities, and the ascendancy of domestic interest group pressures. In Japan and Germany, the cooperative spirit, rooted deep in the structures of the system, allowed a focus of national effort on regaining strength in the world economy.

Three phenomena central to business-government relations have marked the 1980s. The first was the extraordinary performance of those countries—such as Japan, Korea, Taiwan, and Germany—whose national strategies were characterized by close cooperation between business and government to gain world market share in selected industries. Those countries whose strategies were more inward-looking, marked by incoherent, rigid, or antagonistic business-government relations were less successful.

The second phenomenon was the globalization of business, the formation of intricate coalitions of multinational enterprises, often aided by governments. These coalitions appeared to be challenging the ability of nation-states—especially those who were losing world market share—to control business or even their own territories.[4] The second phenomenon, unlike the first, was eroding governmental power. Indeed, Professor Michael Porter could refer to nation-states as mere "platforms" on which the multinational corporations play, exploiting the strengths of some states and the weaknesses of others.[5]

The third phenomenon, an outgrowth of the other two, was the increased importance of technology to the political as well as economic development of countries. While technology itself ensured its own speedy spread throughout the world, the ability to tame and exploit it varied country by country. Business, through globalization, might capture its benefits, but nations and their governments risked being left behind with declining living standards. The speed of technological development, and the learning required to exploit it, meant that once behind, nations found it difficult if not impossible to catch up. Many governments were assisting, directing, guiding, or controlling business to make sure that their particular nation had a technological edge: Brazil in minicomputers, for example, Japan and the United States in microelectronics.

In the face of these phenomena—intensified world competition, the globalization of business, and the politicization of technology—governments generally were anxious. Jacques Dondoux, head of the French government's Direction Générale des Télécommunications in 1986, for example, put the case this way:

> If we want to retain our identity as Frenchmen, in the context of Europe, of course, the state really must intervene. There comes a point when the state must take risks so that on the vast world economic scene, Frenchmen can get a small piece of the action.[6]

National security, indeed sovereignty itself, was at stake. Although in 1987 there were approximately 160 sovereign states in the world, the meaning of *sovereignty* was far from clear. It refers to an ancient notion, juridical in nature, implying certain rights recognized in international law to self-determination and equality in such bodies as the General Assembly of the United Nations. Although cherished politically, its economic meaning and feasibility are confused and uncertain. The nations of the world seem increasingly less able to manifest their autonomy because of their dependence on one another for goods, technology, markets, and credit.

Is national sovereignty likely to die as a realistic concept? Will the political issues which are its chief concern require attention from transnational governmental bodies such as the General Agreement on Tariffs and Trade, the International Monetary Fund, the European Community, and the Organization for Economic Cooperation and Development? Will those issues—employment, incomes, skill development, welfare, pollution—become the responsibility of multinational corporations? Such a drift of authority away from the nation-state, if it occurs, is, of course, unlikely to occur without a fight even though the global corporation has undeniably useful attributes which are as political as they are economic. DuPont demonstrated this in the early 1980s, for example, when it assembled the 40 or so producers of freon in the world and secured an agreement to limit production so as not to damage further the ozone layer over Antarctica.

To think intelligently about the management of business-government relations within and among the nations of the world requires an understanding of the sharp differences both in the behavior of government and business in different countries as well as in prevailing views about how they are supposed to behave. So we shall examine a range of roles and purposes of government and business in selected countries, and we shall see that these seem to be accompanied by comparable forms of organization and structure in each. Those nations whose governments have an efficient assignment to think coherently over time about the nation's priorities, for example, tend to be centralized and dominated by a prestigious and powerful bureaucracy. They are invariably related in a more or less cooperative way to business which itself is organized into influential industry associations.

On the other hand, those national governments whose function is as much as anything to protect the individual, tend to be more fragmented and decentralized and accompanied by loosely organized business groups with which it has distant, if not adversarial, relations. Along with an analysis of roles, purposes, and structures, we shall also compare some of the more important tasks which governments perform and the tools they use.

THE ROLES OF GOVERNMENT

There are two ideological paradigms concerning the role of government, one of which we shall call *individualistic* since it stresses the individual rather than the community, and the other we shall call *communitarian* because it reverses the stress. National practices exemplify some mix of these two types.

In an individualistic society, the role of government is limited. Government's fundamental purpose is to protect property, enforce contract, and keep the marketplace open so that competition among firms may be as vigorous and as free as possible. Government is essentially separate from business. It should intervene into the affairs of business only when the national health and safety requires it. Its intervention thus hinges on crisis—epidemics, pollution, economic disaster, war—and it should be temporary, an exception to the normal state of individual and business autonomy. The purpose and direction of government should be left to the play of interest groups, which fix government's priorities. An individualistic society is inherently suspicious of government, anxious about centralized power, reluctant to allow government to plan—especially over a long time span.

The role of government in a communitarian society is quite different. Here, government is prestigious and authoritative, sometimes authoritarian. Its function is to define the needs of the community over the long as well as the short term, and to see that those needs are met, albeit not necessarily through its own offices. It is a vision setter for the community; it defines and ensures the rights and duties of community membership; it plays a central role in creating—sometimes imposing—consensus to support the direction in which it decides the community should move. Consensus-making often requires coercion of one sort or another, which occurs in either a centralized or decentralized fashion, that is, either flowing down from an elite or up from the grass roots. Communitarian societies may be either hierarchical or egalitarian. If the former, the nature of the hierarchy may vary from meritocratic to oligarchic, ethnocratic, theocratic, or aristocratic.

To oversimplify, among so-called capitalist countries the United States has tended traditionally to occupy the position furthest in the direction of individualism, Japan furthest toward communitarianism. Other nations can be placed somewhere along a continuum in between the extremes. Germany is more communitarian than the United Kingdom, but less than Japan. France is a complex mix under which a communitarian president and a more individualistic prime minister could, in the 1980s, share power effectively. Brazil and Mexico are also ideological mixtures, but less well integrated than France.[8] Mikhail Gorbachev's USSR may, with luck, move out of its dark ages to a more Japanese-like version of communitarianism if *perestroika* succeeds in removing "the rust of bureaucratism from the values and ideals of socialism."[9]

Individualism tends to produce what Professor Chalmers Johnson of Berkeley calls a "regulatory" state in which the market shapes business activity and government regulates business so as to achieve ends that the market cannot meet. Communitarianism, on the other hand, is characterized by a "developmental" state in which government's task is to define the nation's priorities and to see that they are met. The developmental state is associated with such historical patterns as economic nationalism and mercantilism.[10] The role of government in individualistic societies is invariably democratic, whereas communitarian government may be democratic or autocratic. We shall consider later the variety of governmental structures that are associated with these different roles.

These broad categories may be further distinguished by the strategies that governments pursue and the priorities that they set. For example, they may be inward looking, focused on domestic considerations, or outward looking, aimed at achieving global position politically or economically.[11]

Traditional western economics is rooted in individualism, holding that free trade among independent firms uncontaminated by the hand of government would result in the best outcome for all concerned. Firms benefit from their country's natural endowments or its comparative advantage.

The dramatic success of Japan and other Asian countries in the last 20 years has, however, thrown this theory into question. These nations have greatly benefited themselves and their companies by proceeding contrary to the tenets of individualism. Their governments and companies practice neither free trade nor free enterprise, as they are traditionally conceived, and they are quite prepared to restrict the freedom of the market if it serves their purposes. Furthermore, they are unwilling to accept comparative advantage as a static notion, deriving from nature's gifts. Rather, they are determined to *create* their comparative advantage so as to suit their national goals.[12] Indeed, Pat Choate of TRW has estimated that "nearly 75% of world commerce is conducted by economic systems operating with principles at odds with" American individualism.[13]

It has taken a long time for western economists to realize this discrepancy between U.S. theory and the global reality, but by the mid-1980s, the stars were in line. Some nations, MIT's Paul Krugman said, notably Japan, had clearly advanced their interests by adopting a national strategy in which government acted in concert with business to encourage certain industries. "At least under some circumstances," wrote Krugman, "a government by supporting firms in international competition, can raise national welfare at another country's expense."[14] This support, he found, took the form of promoting exports in a variety of ways, while protecting, more or less discreetly, certain domestic markets.

He went on to caution that industry "targeting" by government for the purpose of promoting the national interest succeeds only under certain conditions: the government must know what its national interest is, its definition of that interest must be economically beneficial, key actors—business and labor—must be willing or be coerced to abide by its definition, and the community must in general be prepared to make the sacrifices entailed by the national strategy to achieve it. He pointed to many instances in the West where government, for political reasons, sustained ailing industries—coal, steel, shipbuilding, autos, textiles—with questionable results for the economy as a whole. Other countries, he acknowledged, have allowed uneconomic industries to decline while encouraging new ones—computers, semiconductors, and aircraft, for example—thereby helping those industries to acquire world leadership in technology and in manufacturing processes. These countries have thus acquired world market share in the industries of the future, earned substantial incomes from exports, and achieved high growth rates.

However, Krugman pointed to a variety of problems with government intervention on behalf of domestic industry:

- There are no models with which to measure—that is, quantify—the benefits and costs of such strategies. "Will a dollar of R&D in the semiconductor industry convey ten cents worth of benefits, or ten dollars?" Krugman asked. "Nobody really knows."[15]
- The political risks outweigh possible economic gains. Interest group pressures in a pluralist democracy are likely to tilt government policy away from long-run future benefits and toward the short-run preservation of the status quo. "A country cannot protect everything and subsidize everything."[16] So some industries must suffer for others to prosper and in a democracy this does not occur easily.
- Government lacks the competence to understand all industries in the economy and to be able to measure accurately the costs and benefits of a strategy to benefit particular ones. "Suppose the glamorous high-technology sectors yield less external benefit than the government thinks, and boring sectors more. Then a policy aimed at encouraging external economies may prove actually counterproductive."[17]

Japanese planners have argued that these difficulties could be overcome and that it was clearly the role of government to do so. Myohei Shinohara, an architect of Japan's postwar development, wrote that during Japan's miracle growth period, the Ministry of International Trade and Industry (MITI) applied two consistent criteria in selecting particular industry sectors for promotion and protection: "an income elasticity criterion" and "a comparative technical progress criterion." He wrote, "MITI's industrial policies were expected to foster the industries in which demand growth and technical progress were comparatively high."[18]

Japan believed that it was "a function of the state . . . to induce, guide, and accelerate the structural changes needed for long-term growth. Japanese industrial policy thus involves a commitment to long-term planning and programming of the nation's economy."[19] While the role of MITI had softened by the late 1980s, industry leaders in Japan acknowledged that the role of government as described by Shinohara had not changed.[20] Western economists have looked toward the Japanese trend with growing interest. Chalmers Johnson's opinion was that foreign enterprises "haven't a chance unless foreign nations compete with Japan on the level of government-business relations."[21]

It should be quickly noted that this notion of government as a strategist and as a partner with business for global competition has nothing necessarily to do either with the size of government or with government ownership. In both categories, Japan and the United States are well below other major industrial countries (see Figures 1–4). Nor is the issue one of state intervention in the economy per se. All governments intervene for one reason or another. What is important is the purpose and the method of intervention. Johnson says, "There could be no more devastating weakness for any major nation in the 1980s than the inability to define the role of government in the economy."[22]

James C. McGroddy, an IBM group executive in manufacturing, spoke of this role at the Harvard Business School in 1987 in connection with the difficulties of the American semiconductor industry: "When it comes to emerging technologies, where lead times are short, results uncertain, and capital investment required is very big, there are problems which are beyond the powers of business." He gave as an example the use of X rays in lithography for the manufacture of semiconductors, a long-range, high-risk project: "Whoever gets it will have a definite advantage. Government help in these areas is important to coordinate industry competition for research and development and to provide funds. America needs such a national effort, but it is not on the agenda. Defense Department programs for military needs are fine, but they are irrelevant to global competitiveness. We need sharing and subsidies."[23]

Figure 1   Extent of State Ownership in Seven Countries

	Posts	Telecommunications	Electricity	Gas	Oil Production	Coal	Railways	Airlines	Motor Industry	Steel	Shipbuilding
Brazil	●	●	●	●	●	●	●	◕	○	◕	○
Britain	●	●	●	●	◔	●	●	◕	◑	◕	●
France	●	●	●	●	NA	●	●	◕	◑	◕	○
West Germany	●	●	◕	◑	◕	◑	●	●	◕	○	◕
India	●	●	●	●	●	●	●	●	○	◕	●
Japan	●	○	○	○	NA	○	◕	◔	○	○	○
United States	●	○	◔	○	○	○	◔	○	○	○	○

Legend: Privately owned all or nearly all ○   Publicly owned all or nearly all ●   75% ◕   50% ◑   25% ◔

NA–Not applicable or negligible production.

Source: Adapted from a chart in *The Econmist* (London), December 30, 1978, and reprinted with special permission as used in Thomas K. McCraw. "From Partners to Competitors: An Overview of the Period Since World War II," in *America Versus Japan* (Boston: Harvard Business School Press, 1986), p. 12.

Figure 2   Central Government Expenditures, Selected Years 1880–1980
(percentage of GNP for selected years)

	1880	1900	1920	1940	1960	1980
Japan	7.2%	15.9%	23.5%	40.0%	28.7%	30.2%
United States	3.0	2.4	8.5	9.6	18.3	33.0

Source: Koichi Emi, *Government Fiscal Activity and Economic Growth in Japan, 1868–1960* (Tokyo: Kenkyusha, 1963); Appendix A-1, U.S. Department of Commerce, *Historical Statistics of the United States, 1975,* Series F. IMF; *World Economic Outlook* (April 1985), p. 109, as used in Michael G. Rukstad, "Fiscal Policy and Business-Government Relations," in *America Versus Japan,* Thomas K. McGraw, ed. (Boston: Havard Business School Press, 1986), p. 311.
Note: General expenditures for Japan include all general account and special account expenditures less duplications between accounts.

Figure 3   Major Industrial Countries: General Government Expenditures, Selected Years 1965–1985
(percentage of gross domestic product)

	1965	1970	1975	1979	1985
Japan	18.5%	18.2%	25.9%	30.2%	32.6%
United States	28.1	32.8	36.0	33.0	36.7
United Kingdom	33.8	36.6	44.5	41.4	46.0
Canada	29.9	36.4	41.3	40.2	48.5
West Germany	33.8	39.1	49.5	48.0	48.5
France	37.5	38.2	42.5	45.4	52.4
Italy	32.8	32.5	41.0	42.9	54.6

Source: International Monetary Fund, *World Economic Outlook* (April 1985), p. 109, as used in Michael G. Rukstad, "Fiscal Policy and Business-Government Relations," in *American Versus Japan,* Thomas K. McCraw. ed. (Boston: Haravd Business School Press, 1986), p. 300.
Note: Between 1965 and 1979, 60 percent of the increase in the ratio of government expenditures to gross domestic product (GDP) was attributable, on average, to increases in transfer payments. If the period from 1979 to 1985 is examined, one finds that interest payments and transfer payments each account for about 40 percent of the increase in the ratio, on average, while purchases of goods and services account for the remaining 20 percent.

In Johnson's terms, if Japan's government is developmental in nature, that of the United States is regulatory.[24] If Japan's purpose is to use marketplace competition as only one of several procedures for ensuring that business activity serves the needs of the community as determined by government, the United States tends to suppose that a market kept open by antitrust laws will, for the most part, both define and fulfill community needs single-handedly.

We can imagine four ways in which governments can bring business activity into line with the needs of the community: (1) promoting marketplace competition, a route that has the unique virtue of both defining and fulfilling community need, (2) regulating the marketplace in those instances where competition by itself is unreliable or unacceptable, (3) establishing a partnership with business, and (4) manipulating the birth certificate that the community gives the corporation, that is, the corporate charter. Individualistic communities tend to prefer 1, and 2; communitarian communities, 3 and 4. One of the Japanese government's most striking features—and the one that distinguishes it from old-fashioned European socialism—is its heavy use of 1 and almost total nonuse of 4. But 3 is the prevalent

Figure 4   Government Outlays as a Percentage of GNP, 1975 Versus 1985a

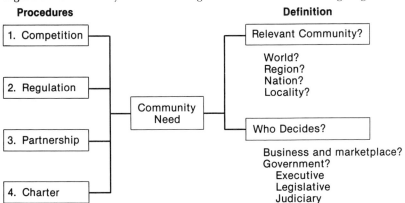

Source: OECD, as used in "Battening Down the Hatches: Survey the Dutch Economy," *The Economist*, September 12, 1987, p. 7.

means in Japan, because it has proven most efficient in meeting community need (see Figure 5).

   Government's selection of an appropriate choice among these four requires a clear definition of community need. Here a critical question is, "Who decides? What is the role of government in deciding, and what is the role of business?"

Figure 5   Community Need: Defining It and Procedures for Aligning Business with It

Procedures		Definition
1. Competition		Relevant Community?
		World? Region? Nation? Locality?
2. Regulation	Community Need	
3. Partnership		Who Decides?
		Business and marketplace? Government? Executive Legislative Judiciary
4. Charter		

Source: George C. Lodge, *The American Disease* (New York: Alfred A. Knopf, 1984), p. 66.

The Purposes of Government

To the extent that communities rely on government—not the marketplace—to define community needs, government's role is shaped by that definition. In post–World War II, Japan and Germany, for example, the purpose of government was clearly to strengthen the economy to compete in the world. That of the United States was to build geopolitical strength against the Soviet Union, a purpose augmented in the 1960s and 1970s by a preoccupation with eliminating poverty, preventing ecological degradation, promoting consumption, and sustaining pluralistic democracy. The roles of all three governments were shaped by these purposes.

To examine the point in somewhat greater detail, consider welfare. Virtually every government is concerned in one way or another with the welfare of its people. But this concern takes different forms. The tradition in the West has been to focus on income security, which has meant a governmental role embodied in unemployment insurance, assistance to families, and social security. In Japan, the focus has been on employment security which has reflected itself in distinctly different roles for both government and business in providing jobs and job tenure. By 1985, as the value of the yen soared, it appeared that income security, even in Japan, was becoming more important. (See Figure 6.) This change in purpose will inevitably affect roles.

The success of different nations in meeting their welfare objectives depends a good deal on their ability to adapt quickly to external changes which require

Figure 6   Social Security Transfers as a Percentage of GNP, 1975 Versus 1985

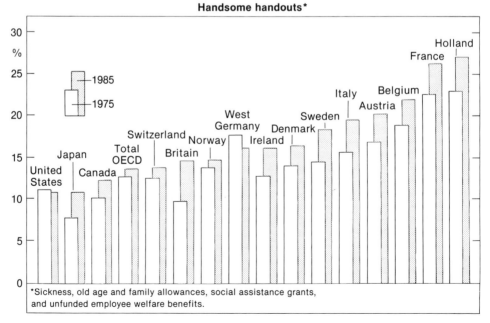

Source: OECD, as used in "Welfare Paradise: Survey the Dutch Economy," *The Economist,* September 12, 1987, p. 10.

choices among competing community needs. Income transfers must be balanced against other needs such as current account surpluses, the availability of capital for business investment, the acquisition and application of new technology, education, and access to world markets.[25]

Oxford Professor Andrew Shonfield, looking back at the postwar policies of the United Kingdom in which a commitment to a strong currency was combined with an equal commitment to the "abolition of want, disease, ignorance and squalor," remarked:[26]

> One of the strangest aspects of British politics now appears to be the mood of insouciance in which a whole series of political decisions was taken, regardless of their effect in adding to the existing overload of economic burdens on the country. The politicians and even more the officials responsible, just assumed grandly that "a way would be found" of paying for the decisions that were taken in the interest of the nation.[27]

Britain's lingering desire to defend the pound, even though doing so resulted in a disastrous outflow of investment capital, led Sam Brittan to write that "the position of sterling as an international currency, with all the risks to which it exposed Britain, was regarded as desirable in itself, like a prisoner kissing the rod with which he is being beaten."[28]

Professor Jorge Domínguez of Harvard, considering the gap between the Mexican government's purposes as set during its revolutionary period and the country's needs in the 1980s—for competitive enterprise, foreign investment, and a skilled and motivated work force—writes,

> Mexico's central dilemma is the conflict between the Revolution's goals and the performance of those who have ruled in its name. Because so much can be justified in the Revolution's name, the country's once-central legitimating myth no longer serves as the criterion for choosing among plausible alternatives.[29]

In France, too, the need for a reevaluation of policy became clear. French policies of the early 1980s, which involved nationalizing major industries while at the same time promoting the rights of French labor in pursuit of both grandeur and income distribution, had to change in 1983, because of world competition.

By the late 1980s, the West generally had come to appreciate that if government had an obligation to assure citizens' rights, it had, partly as a consequence, as much of an obligation to insist that those citizens perform certain duties. The Asian nations, long preoccupied with duties more than with rights, were forcing this appreciation in the West.

Sweden, with one of the lowest unemployment and highest participation rates in the world, is a good example of this new focus on citizen's duties (see Figure 7). In Sweden, more than 80 percent of the working-age population is in the labor force, and the objective of government is to provide a job to everyone who wants one. The policy begins with a prohibition of all private employment agencies. This means that all job information is in one place. Both job seekers and managers in search of workers are put in touch with one another through centrally collected data that is available in local offices throughout the country. Unemployed persons

Figure 7   Selected Unemployment and Participation Rates, 1986

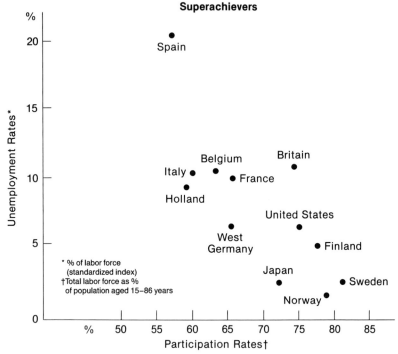

Source: *The Economist*, November 21, 1987, as used in "A Job for Everyone Who Wants
One: The Nordic Three Survey," p. 5.

must report to a local office within a few weeks for "intensive consultation," after
which, if no job can be found, they must enroll in a training program. If they remain
unemployed after training, the jobless must work for municipalities doing public
work, for example, as hospital orderlies or construction workers. The government
also subsidizes retraining within companies to smooth over adjustment to new
competitive pressures. For Sweden, competitiveness is critical since more than 40
percent of the country's industrial production is exported.[30]

In 1988, even in the traditionally individualistic United States, there was an
increasing preoccupation with the communitarian notion of citizens' duties. Some
30 states had some form of "workfare," requiring those on welfare to work or train
for a job. Increasing authority was concentrated in the Office of Management and
Budget so as to give greater direction and purpose to executive policies. And the
"Reagan revolution" would be felt long after his departure in the nation's federal
courtrooms. He appointed 334 federal judges, 45 percent of the total. They were, in
the words of *The Wall Street Journal*, "transforming the courts, which not long ago
were seen as paramount protectors of individual liberties and minority rights, into
stern enforcers of criminal law, narrow interpreters of the Constitution, and
defenders of executive authority."[31]

Government and Global Industries

As governments are being forced to adapt their roles and purposes to the new reality of global competition, so they are competing among themselves to attract foreign firms and to make those within their borders more competitive. Between 1980 and 1985, the number of global agreements—joint ventures, partnerships, and alliances among firms across national borders—increased a hundredfold.[32] Global industries thus gained substantial leverage over nation-states. No longer were firms bound to a country or two. They could shop around and did so, seeking the most inviting "platforms" on which to do their work.

Michael Porter writes,

> A country is a desirable global platform in an industry if it provides an environment yielding firms domiciled in that country an advantage in competing globally in that particular industry....An essential element of this definition is that it hinges on success outside the country, and not merely country conditions that allow firms to successfully manage domestic competition.[33]

Some of the factors that make platforms attractive are low-cost labor and natural resources, of course, but more importantly, skilled scientific talent, advanced infrastructure, and local markets.[34] Other enticements include tax breaks, subsidies, tariff protection, and government procurement agreements.

As countries compete to receive the blessings of global industries, governments that have clearly defined their community's needs will do better than those that are less certain. Also, there may be a convergence—even collusion—among countries in terms of the package of inducements they are prepared to offer, and international organization may be seen by nation-states as a way to protect themselves from being whipsawed by global firms. Politics, in any case, will play an increasingly important role.

The French government's negotiations with German, Swedish, and American telecommunications firms in the mid-1980s are an example. The competing firms had roughly similar technological capabilities. The French government provided inducements, but it also had a complex package of needs, including some which were political. Both the German and the French government were loath to help a gigantic American firm—AT&T—increase its global power. In addition, both wanted to bolster Europe's economic strength against Japan and the United States. The Americans resented German moves to get the contract. Outcome: the Swedes got the nod.[35]

For the global firm, an obvious need emerges to manage governmental relations in a far more sophisticated way than in the old days when government was regarded as merely an obstacle to be hurdled. Today, government relations can be an important competitive advantage.[36] And a company's relations with one government can have a profound impact on its relations with others.

THE STRUCTURES OF GOVERNMENT

Neither the state, a nation's ultimate political authority, nor the government, the changing collection of institutions which manages its affairs, are unitary concepts. They are not monoliths. Governments everywhere, in fact, are a warring, competing collection of executive agencies, legislative bodies, and courts being played upon by countless interest groups at home and from abroad. To understand what they do, it is necessary to look inside and see the structures, the people who work them, the networks that influence them, and the tensions that separate them. In the United States, the interests of the departments of State and Commerce are often at odds, the former worrying about foreign policy, the latter about access to foreign markets. Similarly, the German Foreign Office has argued that foreign economic policy is an instrument of foreign policy and should not be sacrificed on the altar of free trade, an ideology which is dear to the Economics Ministry.[37] And in Japan, consensualism scarcely mutes the disputes between MITI and the Ministry of Finance.[38]

Furthermore, effective government rarely rules by fiat; it listens carefully to the voices of business, labor, and other interest groups and then seeks to compose a harmonious synthesis between those voices and its own views. And whatever the formalities may be, personalities are important in shaping the behavior of government. As President Nixon's one-time assistant, John D. Ehrlichman, put it, "The presidency is, of course, a constitutional institution, but it is also a baggy suit of clothes that molds itself to the man [sic] who is sitting in the chair and the kind of staff he has."[39]

The Paradigms Revisited

The two polar paradigms of individualism and communitarianism that were mentioned earlier also provide a way to begin to think about the structures of government: where power lies, how it is used, and who uses it. The communitarian state, with its planning and vision-setting functions, tends to be relatively powerful, coherent, and centralized. The executive bureaucracy is more important than the legislature, and that bureaucracy attracts to its ranks society's best and brightest and therefore commands respect from business and the public generally. Communitarian systems are often characterized by strong political parties, with one party or a coalition of parties retaining control over a long period of time. Some examples are the various party coalitions that have governed Germany since World War II, the Liberal Democratic Party in Japan, and the Social Democratic Party in Sweden. More authoritarian variations of one-party rule have prevailed in South Korea, Taiwan, and Singapore. Communitarian government's structure is thus consistent with its overriding role: to establish a consensus behind a coherent strategy for the nation's development.

There are, of course, examples of communitarian states where some of these characteristics are not clearly in evidence. Mexico has long had strong one-party rule, yet its government bureaucrats often do not command the same respect as those of Japan or Sweden. Its consensus-making capabilities are weakened. Indeed, when one element of a communitarian system is weak, the whole is disproportionately weakened.

In contrast, individualism carries with it an essentially limited role for government. As exemplified by the United States under this structure, power is widely dispersed, checked, and balanced, that of the legislature being at least as great and perhaps greater than that of the executive or the judiciary. This follows the intent of the nation's founders. Federalist Paper No. 51 spoke in the 1780s, for example, of the need to design controls over the power of government so "that the private interests of every individual may be a sentinel over the public rights."[40] Samuel Huntington echoed that sentiment when he wrote, "Because of the inherently anti-government character of the American Creed, government that is strong is illegitimate, government that is legitimate is weak."[41] The exploits of CIA Director William Casey and Lt. Col. Oliver North in the early 1980s were only one of many examples of executive impatience with this creed.[42]

Communitarian governmental structures evolved from those of feudalism. Those structures associated with individualism either emerged from the feudal forms and were affected by them, or grew fresh in soil virtually uncontaminated by old forms. Since the United States stands alone in the world in terms of its degree of independence from feudal traditions, individualism and its governmental structures exist there in their purest form. That is not to say that U.S. practice does not from time to time depart from its ideal. It does so frequently, especially in times of crisis. The National Recovery Administration during the Great Depression sought to convert the structures of government into something capable of industrial planning in cooperation with big business. The quick and ignominious death of the NRA at the hands of the Supreme Court serves for many as a reminder that such ventures are not for America. American departures from the individualistic mode are regarded as suspect, illegitimate, and almost doomed to fail (see Figure 8). When such a gap occurs between ideology and practice, authority falters and the community faces two choices: pull the wayward institutions back into line, and practice what you preach; or install a new ideology and preach what you practice, perhaps using some traditional institutions and fine-tuning them. Either way tends to cause ambivalence on the part of decision makers in both government and business, exemplified in 1987 and 1988 by the uncertain efforts of the U.S. government to encourage national competitiveness in certain key industries, especially semiconductors, superconductivity, and biotechnology.

Harvard Professor Steven Kelman in his study of government regulation in Sweden and the United States elaborated on the distinction between these governmental structures:

> Out of the Swedish tradition grew dominant values encouraging individuals to defer to the wishes of government and encouraging leaders to be self-confident in charting a course of how people should behave. Out of the American tradition grew values encouraging self-assertion and refusal to bow before the desires of rulers.

It was this difference which made agreement between government and business about health and safety regulation so much more difficult in the United States than in Sweden. Kelman explained further,

> Contemporary Swedish society, like many European societies, emerged from a history of brutally sharp distinctions between ruler and ruled. The Swedish word

overhet is a generic term for those on top of society, seen as an undifferentiated presence by those at the bottom...It translates literally as "those over us" and consisted [sic] of those—kings, aristocrats, bishops—born to rule over others.[43]

Mixed with Sweden's contemporary democratic structures, elements of *overhet* are recognizable even today in the deference that citizens show to government. This is not unlike the respect that Japanese have for the young "summa cum laudes" who run the Ministry of Finance or the Ministry of Trade and Industry. In both Japan and Sweden, the words of the Swedish poet that mark the entrance to Uppsala University ring a responsive chord: "To think freely is great, to think correctly is greater." Such thoughts are not found in America, where the emphasis on individual rights versus rights of the state was driven deep into the governmental system. With about 2,000 lawyers per million population, the United States has the world's record for litigation, whereas Sweden with 440 lawyers per million has one of the lowest rates of litigation, lower (by half) than that of Japan.[44]

Figure 8   The Legitimacy Gap

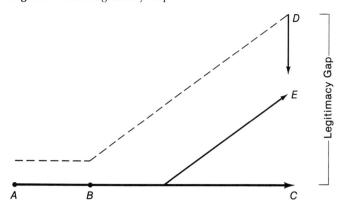

The solid line ABC in Figure 8 represents a traditional ideology proceeding through time. The dashed line represents institutional practice—that is, what government, business, and labor are actually doing and how they are related to one another. During time period *AB*, institutional practice conforms to the prevailing ideology and, after that, departs: changes in the real world compel the institutions to behave differently than they did. By time *C*, institutional practice is very different from what the ideology presumed: the old hymns are being sung, but they are not being practiced. There is a gap, *DC*, which may be called a "legitimacy gap." There is an ideological schizophrenia: the new practice brings forth a new ideology to justify itself, but loyalty to the old ways discourages its articulation. As the legitimacy gap widens, two conflicting pressures converge on managers: one seeks to force errant institutions back into conformity with the *ABC* ideology; the other argues for a more forceful and articulate expression of the new ideology, which is the only means of legitimizing what is actually occurring *(ABE)*.

Source: George C. Lodge, *The American Disease* (New York: Alfred A. Knopf, 1984), p. 34.

Strong and Weak States

In such places as Japan and Sweden, a strong government is associated with virtue. In the United States, as Huntington pointed out, it is at least reason for suspicion if not an outright sign of evil. Other countries, it would seem, are arrayed between these polar extremes.

We cannot simply say that communitarian governments are strong and individualistic ones weak. Such is clearly not the case. For example, no one would attribute strength to Lebanon's communitarian government. We must look further for traits consistent with strength and weakness.

We might say that a government is strong if it can (1) create a consensus in society that is sufficient to allow government to design and implement goals for the community as a whole, (2) change the behavior of important groups such as business in order to further its policies, and (3) change the structure of society—the nature of ownership, the degree of industrial concentration, and the importance of particular sectors—in pursuit of its goals.[45]

Japan

Let us take Japan as an example of a country in which a government has, since World War II, shown its capacity to meet all three of the criteria listed. Until recently we might have selected MITI as the most dramatic exemplar of governmental power in Japan. With a staff of fewer than 10,000 employees, it has done what the much larger Commerce Department, United States Trade Representative, and Small Business Administration in the United States are supposed to do.[46] Today, however, without denying MITI's continuing influence, it is probably the Ministry of Finance (MOF) that has the lead in Japanese governmental power. It is the MOF that attracts the University of Tokyo's top graduates today.

Following is an excerpt from *The Economist* describing the work of "Japan's men [never women] of MOF":[47]

> Japan's most powerful economic policymaker is not a politician, but a civil servant—the top career bureaucrat in the Ministry of Finance..."
>
> It suits the Japanese pursuits of harmony and consensus to see policy disputes as politically neutral technicalities. It suits the economic bureaucrats, drawn from the top graduates of the best universities, even more. MOF, which is legally responsible for the financial management of Japan's central government, is thereby granted great power. It raises the government's money and decides how it will be spent. Policy initiatives, big or small, from any other part of the government have to win the approval of MOF.
>
> *THE GUIDING HAND*
>
> Within Japan, the ministry's role is often likened to that of a village elder who decides the shape of the annual harvest and then shares it in the way that is best for the village as a whole so as to preserve social order and cohesion. This perception gives it an authority far beyond its legal responsibility and makes its guidance— channelled through a network of informal instructions to financial institutions—a policy instrument in its own right.

This is not to say that the process is simple. Far from it. Three factors complicate things:

• **Internal organisation.** The ministry is composed of different parts which compete with each other for influence and resources. Its various bureaus are responsible for MOF's day-to-day operations, and directors of these bureaus have considerable autonomy....

It is the responsibility of the **civil-service vice-minister** to coordinate these often-conflicting interests. That role is what makes him (and his secretariat) so powerful—much more so than the corresponding **political vice-minister,** and probably more so even than his minister. The civil-service vice-minister is always a career bureaucrat. Customarily, the head of the Budget Bureau gets the job when it falls vacant. Once a new vice-minister is appointed, all the other senior officials of his "year"—i.e., those who entered the ministry in the same intake—retire to jobs outside the ministry. As a result, none of his peers remains to challenge his authority.

• **Relations with other ministries.** MOF has to deal with all the other ministries and official agencies. Each of these has its own economic divisions. Some occasionally bid for parts of the finance ministry's power over economic policy. The Ministry of International Trade and Industry, for instance, sets industrial policy; it controls some useful instruments of economic policy such as the Export-Import Bank and the Japan Development Bank. It also has some responsibilities concerning foreign exchange....

• **Relations with parliament.** Bureaucrats have long been accustomed to primacy over politicians. (MOF was established in 1870, and is therefore an older institution than the cabinet.) Only in recent years has the pendulum started to swing towards the parliament.

Japanese politics remains more a matter of horse-trading between interest groups than of policy debate. Academic studies have suggested that the governing Liberal Democratic party shields economic policy from political pressures; the party's main interest is in securing pork-barrel projects for its members that help keep their voters happy. The shield has been strengthened by the way a conservative coalition has held power for the past 30 years and protected existing economic policies against anything so inconvenient as a change of the party in power.

However, MOF cannot push through policies which arouse broad opposition among politicians. For example, the ministry has been trying since the late 1970s to introduce a new indirect tax. So far it has failed. Earlier this year a planned sales tax was torpedoed. It was opposed for varying reasons by a broad coalition that encompassed some of the governing party's core supporters as well as the opposition parties. This opposition was sufficient to kill it.

OLD PALS

However, the fate of MOF's tax reform effort is the exception rather than the rule. There are many other institutional reasons why politicians rarely present a challenge to the authority of the bureaucrats. Both the leaders of the Liberal Democratic party and senior officials at the finance ministry tend to come from the same highly educated elite, which gives them a similar outlook.

Senior bureaucrats usually retire in their 50s to take second jobs in companies or with influential industry associations and quasi-official business research organisations. This means that much of the outside advice offered on economic policy remains heavily influenced by the finance ministry's old boys. As a back-up, some 40 former MOF officials who are now members of parliament act as a cabal on economic-policy issues, irrespective of the faction of the party that they belong to.

Germany

What we see in Japan is an interministerial apparatus, closely tied to big business, and presided over by senior civil servants who descend to companies at about the age of 50; it is an apparatus that surpasses parliament in power and influence. It is important to note that in a real sense, business generally is a part of government— perhaps even a controlling part. Much the same can be said of Germany, where, as Peter Katzenstein has pointed out, "Parliament is more or less eclipsed by the direct cooperation between interest groups and the ministerial bureaucracy."[48] The interest groups include the country's major banks, which are the "quarterbacks" of the German system because of their pervasive presence at all major decision-making points, holding in proxy 85 percent of all privately held shares.[49] They are early-warning systems, identifying weaknesses in German industry and, on occasion, organizing rescue operations.[50] Interest groups also include the numerous, well-organized, and powerful German business associations, which—like similar associations in Japan—have intimate relationships at all levels of the bureaucracy. In both Germany and Japan, labor organizations are also powerful and well represented in government decision-making bodies (see Figures 9 and 10.) The power of business in the governance of both these countries has led one observer to apply to them the term, *nonstatist communitarianism.*[51]

The "commanding heights" of state power are occupied in both countries by carefully selected individuals who are widely respected. "The state thus offers to a particular class of people a mechanism of political organization and control which it denies to others."[52] This does not mean that government policy will necessarily reflect the narrow concerns of this group, but it does mean that this group can define the national interest, relatively confident that their definition will be backed by a national consensus.

The structure of government in Germany differs from that of Japan in one important respect. It is more decentralized. Policy-making involves a constant struggle between three main rivals: the federal government in Bonn, the governments of the regional states (the *Länder*), and the independent central bank (*Bundesbank*).[53] The federal budget represents less than half of total public spending. The federal government and the regions try to coordinate their policies through advisory bodies, but Bonn's capacity to control Germany depends upon the cooperation of the *Länder.* And the *Länder* have power through their own 45-member chamber (the *Bundesrat*) in the Bonn parliament. In matters involving their own interests, such as taxes, the *Länder* have veto power. The *Bundesbank* has control, too, though its sole authority over monetary policy and its great prestige as the principal bulwark against the inflation, which Germans dread most of all.[54]

France

French governmental structures, dominated by a well-respected, relatively autonomous, and strong (sometimes autocratic) bureaucracy, reflect what is perhaps the world's most sophisticated mixture of individualism and communitarianism. Professor Janice McCormick of Harvard Business School finds two versions of each

Figure 9   Selected Countries' Trade Union Membership as a Percentage of the Labor Force, 1985–1986

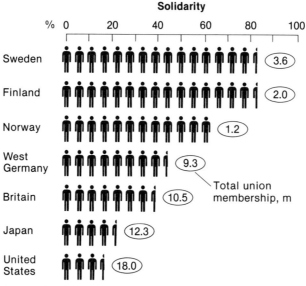

Source: European Trade Union Institute; national statistics.

Source: "Drifting Off Course: The Nordic Three Survey," *The Economist,* November 21, 1987, p. 8.

Figure 10   Selected Countries' Trade Union Membership as a Percentage of the Labor Force, 1979 Versus 1986

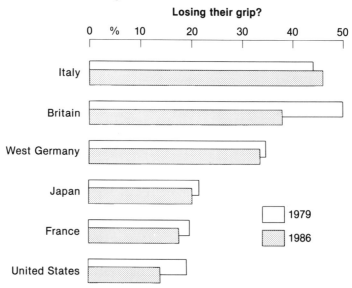

Source: European Trade Union Institute; national statistics; OECD, as used in "World Business," *The Economist,* November 28, 1987, p. 68.

structure, which she labels liberalism, jacobinism, authoritarianism, and social democracy.[55] The common element around which all parties can rally, however, is the belief that government is "the reflection of the general will," as defined by Jean-Jacques Rousseau, "a will that is superior to that of any business or individual interest."[56] Until the early 1980s, that "will" was permeated by a desire to keep France uncontaminated by the world. More recently, it has been informed by the reality that competitiveness in the world economy is a prerequisite for all else. Toward this end, the state becomes the partner of business.

Professor John Zysman of Berkeley sees the French state (*l'état*) as "an almost metaphysical notion..., the unified authority of the society." The bureaucracy, created by kings to control unruly nobles, retains its power today as an instrument of collective power, insulated from interest groups, and administered by the Grands Corps, which is composed of the top-ranking graduates of the two Grands Ecoles, the Ecole Nationale d'Administration (l'ENA) and the Polytechnique.[57] "At the heart of this centralized system is the Direction du Tresor in the Ministry of Finance, what more than one ranking official has called the sanctuary in the temple, the holy of holies." Here is centered the control of capital markets, credit allocation, public enterprise financial policy, and lending to private firms. In exercising its control, the French state uses three sets of tools. The first is direct state action, what Zysman calls *faire*. The second is incitement to others to act (*faire faire*). And the third is simply to leave be (the traditional *laissez faire*).[58] In government's attempts to equip France for growth in the industries of the future—electronics, computers, telecommunications—all three tools have been used. The role and structure of government in France in the 1980s was thus being shaped by the need to link domestic economic management to the international economy.

Britain and the United States

In attempting to link nations by governmental roles, Katzenstein has noted that Japan, Germany, and France are quite distinct from the United States and Britain. The former to varying degrees, pursue their objectives using a wide range of relatively sharp instruments with which they can operate on particular sectors of the economy and even on individual firms.[59] The latter, the offspring of individualism, rely on a limited number of relatively blunt policy instruments that affect the entire economy rather than particular sectors or firms. From the end of World War II to the early 1960s, government policymakers in Britain, for example,

> tried to minimize government's role in the entire range of decisions affecting investment, the determination of wages and the conditions of work, and industrial relations. They attempted to limit the government's economic policy instruments to global mechanisms which would minimize administrative discretion. [Fiscal and monetary policy, for example.] Government's economic policies, it was widely believed, should function globally as simply and as automatically as possible. It was this dramatic reassertion of the liberal state...that prompted Andrew Shonfield to remark...that "The striking thing about Britain is the extraordinary tenacity of older attitudes toward the role of the state."[60]

When in the 1960s the British government sought to collaborate with business and labor to formulate something like an industrial policy, neither the institutions, the instruments, the personnel, nor the ideology were there to make it work. Furthermore, the policy itself was flawed in that it *assumed* the competitiveness of British exports, persisting in defending the value of sterling in world markets.

Among the most important factors explaining Britain's planning failures is the role of organized labor, the Trades Union Council. The TUC has had a very different mission than have the union movements of Germany, Japan, and the United States. Traditionally, it has seen itself as a leader of the working class pitted against the capitalist owning class, "the enemy within." Not only has the TUC been loath to share decisions with business and government, important segments of it have perceived the destruction of business and government as a patriotic duty. In Germany and Japan, on the other hand, the interests of labor unions are tied inexorably to the competitiveness of firms and to the economy as a whole. In the United States, the role of unions in the 1980s was uncertain. The old adversarial role embodied in the idea of the collective contract was being challenged by a new role in corporate governance not unlike that of Japan and Germany.

In terms of planning impediments for the U.S. government, the responsibility for linking domestic economic management with the international economy is scarcely even considered an appropriate role for government. But to the extent that such linking nevertheless occurs, it does so with little if any coordination among a disparate group of departments and agencies, including, for example, the Departments of Commerce, State, Defense, Treasury, and Agriculture; the White House Offices of the United States Trade Representative and Management and Budget, and the Council of Economic Advisers; and a welter of congressional committees and subcommittees. Fundamentally, the link is considered to evolve automatically from the interplay of market forces in a world of free trade and free enterprise. That is to say, it is taken for granted. It is significant that during the three years that the 1986 Tax Bill was being framed, the inner circles of government never discussed its effect on national competitiveness in the world.[61]

Inaction and budgetary pressures in Washington forced increased activity at the state level during the 1980s. States hard hit by foreign competition such as Michigan developed strategies for competitiveness, working with business and labor. Interest groups also went to the states seeking action on a variety of fronts, including boycotts of companies doing business in South Africa, plant closing, and antilayoff restrictions, pay based on "comparable worth," and safety and health regulations.

Strategy Versus Structure.   In government, as in the world of business, strategy often dictates structures.[62] But the reverse may also occur. The structure—embodied for example, by the young men of Japan's MOF or by the traditional economists of the President's Council of Economic Advisers—conditions and constrains strategy. Furthermore, in both business and government, different structures may serve the same strategy, some more efficiently than others. The governments of both the United States and Japan promote exports, but they employ quite different structures and tools.

Finally, there is the question of what happens when old structures meet new challenges. Japan's emphasis on employment security, respect for seniors, and consensualism through bottom-up decision-making may have been fine for periods of rapid growth. But will it serve as well the needs of contraction, conversion, and restructuring that the nation faced in the late 1980s? "There is no harmonious way to move 3,000 jobs offshore," wrote Bernard Wysocki, Jr., *The Wall Street Journal's* Tokyo bureau chief. Furthermore, pushing decision-making control down to the level of assistant section chiefs may have given government offices *esprit de corps* and an atmosphere of collegiality, "but it also has produced ministries that are highly turf-conscious, inbred, and inflexible...". When a nation confronts tough choices about which there is no consensus—taxes, land prices, and the like—does it not need strong, tough, quick leadership? In this regard, Wysocki likens Japan's prime minister to the king in a game of chess. "He is surely important, but his own power is limited. He can only move one space at a time. To succeed, he has to persuade other, more powerful and agile players to move on his behalf."[63]

THE ROLES AND STRUCTURES OF BUSINESS

Comprehension of the relations between government and business requires not only an awareness of how the roles and structures of governments vary throughout the world, but also an appreciation of similar variations in the roles and structures of business. For the purposes of this essay, we shall concentrate on the large, publicly held companies that have increasingly allied themselves not only with other firms like themselves through joint ventures of one sort or another, but also with governments both at home and abroad.

Again, our ideological paradigms—individualism and communitarianism—will be helpful. But let us first denude the corporation of any ideology and see what it looks like. It is a collection of people and material brought together to complete a process: it gathers resources, designs and produces goods or services, and distributes them to the communities that it serves. To do this, it must develop skills among its employees, provide motivation to them, and exert organizational control over them. It should do this as efficiently as possible, maximizing benefits and minimizing costs.

Now let us introduce ideology. Externally, what goods does the corporation make? What resources does it use? What are the effects of its functions on the communities around it? Who decides these external issues? Internally, what are acceptable and effective methods for providing motivation and control? In the organizational hierarchy, who is admitted? Who succeeds, and how? Who decides these internal issues? Finally, how are costs and benefits defined? What happens to the surplus of benefits that it is the corporation's purpose to accrue? Again, who decides?[64]

The Roles of Business

The answers to these questions depend upon the role that the corporation plays in society and the sources from which it derives its legitimacy. Considering the various national communities we have been observing, there are four possible sources of

Figure 11   Sources of Management Authority

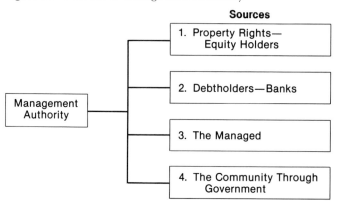

Source: George C. Lodge, *The American Disease* (New York: Alfred A. Knopf, 1984), p. 71. (See Figure 5.)

legitimacy—four sources of authority for corporation managers (see Figure 11): (1) the owners, that is, the shareholders who obtain authority via the idea of property rights, which in individualistic communities, is semisacred; (2) the banks or other debtholders, who have an interest in safeguarding their loans; (3) the managed, that is, the corporate membership; and (4) the community, as represented by its government.

Corporate raiders, like T. Boone Pickens, argue forcefully that it is source 1 that counts. Indeed, many American managers would agree with him in thought as well as deed that the fundamental purpose of the corporation is the satisfaction of shareholders. Incentive systems, corporate allocation of resources, market strategies, and personnel policies are tied to this overriding purpose. It is indeed the source of authority that emerges naturally from the individualistic paradigm. Debtholders have a secondary position. Employees are to be hired and fired insofar as they are needed to maximize return to shareholders. And government is an adversary to be kept at arm's length, avoided entirely if possible.

Other American managers, however, especially those who have felt the fierce bite of Asian competition, are not so sure. In fact, General Motors entered into a joint venture with Toyota partly to learn a different conception of the corporation, one in which the authority of the managers derives from the managed.[65] It turns out that employee motivation, productivity, and efficiency are greater when employees participate in decisions that affect their work and when they have the degree of employment security required to make sensible a sacrifice today for gains tomorrow. And the U.S. semiconductor industry, on the ropes in its contest with Japan, is moving toward industry cooperation in partnership with government in hopes of attracting several billion dollars of subsidies which are presumably in the national interest.

Even the Business Roundtable has had reservations about connecting corporations too closely to shareholders. In a statement issued in 1978, during the heyday of talk about "shareholder democracy," the Roundtable said, "Proposals to enlarge materially shareowner participation in corporate governance all run into...stubborn practical difficulties, and are likely to be of interest only to a very small and unrepresentative group of corporate critics."[66]

So in America, there is doubt and even conflict about corporate purpose.* In Germany, however, corporate purpose springs from a well-ordered combination of all four sources. Banks, which have a dominant position on corporate boards of directors, exert their control both as holders of shares and of debt. Employees participate in corporate decision making through codetermination. Unions, banks, and corporate executives are informed about and responsive to the national interest as defined in numerous governmental forums in which all four are well represented.

Similarly, in Japan, corporate legitimacy has always derived from a clear combination of all sources. An executive of Mitsui, Japan's giant *soga shosha*—with sales of $120 billion in 1986, the largest non-U.S. company in the world—described Mitsui's purpose as follows, emphasizing the order: (1) to contribute to Japanese society, to serve the greater glory of Japan; (2) to realize profit for the company so as to promote the welfare and happiness of its employees; and (3) to foster and strengthen the spirit of Mitsui for the future, as that spirit is set forth in the company logo, "Ten, Chi, Jen" [heaven, earth, and human beings]. The satisfaction of shareholders, he said, is but a means to these ends (see Figure 12). The sources of authority are thus clearly 3 and 4 from our previous list, as well as a spiritual something beyond 4, which requires a bit of history to understand.

Mitsui was founded in 1671 as a merchant house in feudal Japan at a time when society was controlled by the local *shogun* and his government bureaucracy. The population was ranked in order: *samurai* (retainers of the feudal lord) came first, then peasants, followed by artisans, and, finally, merchants. The highest value was placed on learning albeit of a sort restricted by Confucian orthodoxy.

Mitsui managers of the day made no bones about their desire for profits, but it was in a spirit of ancestral obedience and loyalty in the knowledge that the stuff of this world was not theirs (or anyone else's) personal property, but had to be handed over, increased, to future generations of Mitsui men. Furthermore, being of a lowly order in the scheme of things, the justification for their activities had to be sanctioned by government.

When the Meiji modernization came in 1868, Mitsui's purpose was to serve the interests of government and to acquire knowledge toward that end. The

---

*There is nothing new about this conflict as the following quotations from *The Modern Corporation and Private Property* by Adolf Berle and Gardiner Means, published in 1932 reveals:[67]

> Power over industrial property has been cut off from the...legal right to enjoy its fruits....The explosion of the atom of property destroys the basis of the old assumption that the quest for profits will spur the owner of industrial property to its effective use...the very foundation on which the economic order of the past three centuries has rested.
>
> ...
>
> The rise of the modern corporation has brought a concentration of economic power which can compete on equal terms with the modern state—economic power versus political power, each strong in its own field ....The future may see the economic organism, now typified by the corporation, not only on an equal plane with the state, but possibly even superseding it as the dominant form of social organization
>
> ...
>
> The net result of stripping the stockholder of virtually all of his power within the corporation is to throw him upon an agency lying outside the corporation itself—the public market....The fact appears to be that liquid property obtains a set of values...represented by market prices, which are not immediately dependent upon the underlying values of the properties themselves.

Figure 12   Ranking of Corporate Objectives: United States and Japan, 1981

	United States	**Japan**
Return on investment	8.1	4.1 (2)
Share price increase	3.8	0.1
Market share	2.4	4.8 (1)
Improve product portfolio	1.7	2.3
Rationalization of production and distribution	1.5	2.4
Increase equity ratio	1.3	2.0
Ratio of new products	0.7	3.5 (3)
Improve company's image	0.2	0.7
Improve working conditions	0.1	0.3

Source: Adapted from Economic Planning Agency, Japanese Government, "Economic Survey of Japan 1980/1981" (Tokyo: *Japan Times*, 1982), p. 196, as used in James C. Abegglen and George Stalk, Jr., *Kaisha, The Japanese Corporation* (New York: Basic Books, 1985), p. 177.

Note: Two hundred and ninety-one Japanese companies and 277 U.S. companies ranked factors weighted 10, for first importance, to 1, for least importance.

industrialization of Japan was in no sense marked by a flourishing of individualism. It was indeed carried out "for the sake of tradition itself, because, in the Japanese context, tradition had divine meaning and was symbolized in the Emperor." The modernization was necessary to protect Japan from foreign predators and to preserve its "innate superiority to any other nation."

The legitimacy and purpose of Mitsui and the other great *zaibatsus* was thus closely tied to the purposes of government and government provided both protection and prestige. Mitsui operated the Osaka mint for the government, established banks, managed factories and mines. This conception of the firm was not only necessitated by the social and political context, it was also essential to the company's ability to attract top-notch young talent who sought prestigious careers.[68]

Strains

We can immediately sense some strain. As Japanese, American, and European companies intensify their alliances—as they merge, invade one another's territories, and globalize, what happens to the old moorings? Mitsui's internationalization brings strain to their relationship with the Japanese government, strain with Japanese employees, strain with Japanese ways. Similar strains affect General Motors, the United Automobile Workers, and the governments of both Michigan and the United States for which GM's globalization is a cost.

The sources of authority for the corporation in communitarian countries, at least those such as Japan, Germany, Sweden, and—to a lesser degree—France, have been clear: a well-organized combination of banks, employees, and government. In both the United Kingdom and the United States, there has been considerable doubt and confusion, a gap between ideology and what seems necessary and practical. In both countries, managers are therefore uncertain, torn by conflict between and among the four sources. The future seems likely to spread and intensify the confusion as the well-understood principles enunciated by the Mitsui executive and Mr. Pickens collide and change—of necessity.

The Structures of Business

Structure tends to follow purpose. Again, the United States and Japan appear to be polar extremes with European countries ranged on the spectrum in between.

Starting with the internal structure of the factory and the firm and extending out to the general structure of industries and business in the nation, we see a pattern: the United States individualistic, Japan communitarian; United States participants—managers and managed, suppliers and supplied, buyers and sellers— tied by contract, Japan's tied by consensus; United States' relations among competitors competitive, Japan's a mixture of rivalry and cooperation. For example, Japan's lead in semiconductors can be attributed to the cooperation, as well as the competition, among its major computer companies. Furthermore, this cooperation was directed and subsidized by MITI. Such behavior would have been diametrically opposed to U.S. business philosophy at the time, and a clear violation of the antitrust laws. The U.S. semiconductor industry was composed of relatively small, entrepreneurial, fiercely competitive firms, whose driving ambition was to use their relatively thin capital resources to maximize returns to shareholders. Only in 1987 on the brink of disaster did the American semiconductor companies move to change their structure.

Clearly, Japanese business is structured in a radically different way from that of the United States.[69] This is true at all levels: the *keiretsu*, the groups of affiliated companies such as Mitsubishi or Mitsui; the industry associations; and the Keidanren, which brings all business together for joint planning with government. Germany, France, Sweden, and even Britain are also characterized by much stronger and more important industry organizations than those of the United States. These European associations work closely and cooperatively with government on hun- dreds of issues, ranging from occupational health and safety to tax laws and environmental regulation.

There can be no doubt, however, that in recent years, some American industries are moving toward a different pattern—around such issues as toxic substances and pharmaceuticals, for example. The pressure of foreign competition is forcing cooperation among domestic competitors in the United States, and the antitrust laws have been loosened to allow some collaboration (the National Cooperative Research Act of 1984). Competitive pressure is also forcing the global alliances that we have mentioned before. These are profoundly changing the domestic national structures of industries; indeed, when the smoke clears, there may well be very different structures of business the world over. Does this mean convergence toward some common pattern? If so, how much drag will different national traditions present? How will that friction be overcome? Perhaps most interesting, can the structures of business and industries change without their roles and purposes also changing and without changes in their relationships to government?[70] Are we, in fact, dealing here not with discrete institutions, but with whole systems?

BUSINESS-GOVERNMENT RELATIONSHIPS

Various kinds of relationships between government and business flow from the different roles and structures we have described. Broadly speaking, these relationships can be characterized in terms of process, and in terms of substance.

Process

At one end of the business-government relationships spectrum in matters regarding process, are the widely used and continuing forums of such countries as Japan, Germany, and Sweden. Organized through industry associations as well as through so-called peak organizations, these forums often include formal representation from other interest groups, such as labor unions, environmentalists, academics, and consumers. The purpose of these networks is to define community priorities and to agree on policies to fulfill them.

At the other end of this same spectrum are the more ad hoc, adversarial, litigious procedures, characteristic of the United States.[71]

We know, however, that the United States does not always behave according to its founders' most rigid guidelines, as the example of the National Recovery Administration given earlier, indicates. Time and again in American history, business—railroads, oil, agriculture—and government have collaborated. Loans and loan guarantees to America's housing industry totaled nearly $160 billion in 1980, while housing and real estate receive more tax subsidies than all other industries combined. The nation's 18,000 sugar growers receive about $2 billion a year, and the defense industry enjoys a more or less symbiotic relationship with government. In 1985, for example, the Department of Defense spent $35 billion for research and development on new technologies, which was about one-third of all such expenditures in the United States.[72] Indeed, the ability of those with political influence to secure governmental support prompted Theodore Lowi, professor of American Institutions at Cornell University, to characterize the American system as "socialism for the organized, capitalism for the unorganized."[73] And yet, generally, along with the collaboration has come denial of partnership, protestation of autonomy, and insistence upon noncontamination. Because of the desire to maintain this appearance of business autonomy, there have not evolved in the United States the ongoing, formal, and respected mechanisms of cooperation that prevail in other countries. Their creation would suggest an acceptance of business-government cooperation, which is ideologically forbidden.

Substance

Scores of issues concerning substance lie at the interface between government and business—taxation, public spending, environment, health, safety, tariffs, and many more. Two general issues, related to substance, will be focused on here: (1) the competition among governments to attract foreign investment with corporate favors and (2) the growing alliance between business and government to foster national competitiveness.

The Hunt for Foreign Investment

Research by Louis T. Wells, Jr., and Dennis Encarnation has established that

> competition among governments for foreign investment appears to be on the rise. Whether the context pits Ohio against Tennessee, Scotland against Ireland, Singapore against Taiwan, the story remains the same: numerous governments, at all levels and on all continents are actively vying for the opportunity to serve as hosts for foreign firms.[74]

The reasons are straightforward: countries need to earn foreign exchange with which to pay increasingly anxious lenders, they want access to world technology and markets to grow and improve their standard of living, and they want to press their own business managers into becoming more competitive. The rules of admission of course differ widely. Albania and Burma, for example, exclude virtually all foreign investment. The rest seek it, offering varying terms and conditions, carrots and sticks, in a variety of different ways.

Certain of the conditions for investment relate to the idiosyncrasies of ownership philosophy. The Mexican government, by virtue of its revolutionary norms, has steadfastly opposed foreign investment as a threat to its sovereignty. In recent years, however, this opposition has substantially softened, if not in law, in practice and especially, it appears, with regard to Japanese investors. (It was not the Japanese, after all, who stormed Chapultapec.) In the 1970s, the Indian government wanted to develop a domestic computer industry. It felt the need for help from foreign firms, but insisted on Indian participation in ownership. IBM was unwilling to alter its policy of 100 percent ownership of subsidiaries, mindful of the precedent it would set elsewhere. There were a number of other multinationals to which the Indian government could—and did—turn.[76]

"When MNCs and host governments face each other at the bargaining table," writes Benjamin Gomes-Casseres, "each brings a series of needs, resources, and options that to a great extent determine the outcome of negotiations." Success, whether for the government or for the firm, depends upon the skill with which each organizes itself "to exploit its strengths and defend against its weaknesses."[77] High among the skills necessary for the firm is the ability to collaborate with other companies to develop technologies or to integrate manufacturing operations. U.S. antitrust laws, and the practices that they encourage, have caused U.S. firms to be less experienced in cooperative ventures than are their Japanese and European rivals.[78]

Another necessary skill for firms involves coordination of foreign subsidiaries by the headquarters management. The importance of governmental relations in subsidiary management affects the extent to which each subsidiary is coordinated centrally versus managed locally. In the latter approach, each subsidiary is responsible for its own interface with government. IBM has moved in the direction of coordinated management because, as Jacques Maisonrouge, former CEO of IBM World Trade said, "The control issue was critical. Optimization of the whole system was not equal to optimization of each of the subparts."[79] Amir Mahini and Louis Wells cite the example of Xerox: "The first steps toward coordination in governmental relations began in a region where a common market had threatened the independence of decisions in different countries. One of the issues that had influenced the change in approach (away from diffusion of focus) involved conflicting positions in different subsidiaries with respect to tariffs."[80] As European governments have cooperated to develop a regional strategy with regard to computers and telecommunications, firms likewise have had to coordinate their national governmental strategies within a regional context.

Partnerships for National Competitiveness

Japan. Government-business collaboration to achieve national competitiveness has reached its most sophisticated form in Japan. The process has four components:

1. Forums.   In 1987 there were 213 Japanese government-business councils. MITI sponsored 20, the Ministry of Finance 14, with others attached to other ministries. Some were attached directly to the office of the prime minister, as was the case, for example, with the Advisory Group on Economic Structural Adjustment for International Harmony, chaired by Haruo Maekawa. In April 1987, the Maekawa Commission recommended a national goal of "steadily reducing the nation's current account imbalance to one consistent with international harmony." To achieve this goal, the report spoke of the "urgent need" to "seek to transform the Japanese economic structure into one oriented toward international coordination" by making efforts to "enhance the quality of the nation's standard of living."

The membership of these councils included scholars, industrial leaders, union leaders, and government officials. They meet about 12 times a year, with each meeting lasting about two hours. Although some councils are more or less permanent, most expire after two years. Each council has many subcommittees composed of junior people who meet often and are responsible for drafting.

The purpose of the council reports is, in the words of one participant, "to shape a context for action" by business and government, to define "a vague image," to "establish the basis for consensus."[81]

Although the councils are useful, some observers perceive drawbacks. Membership tends to be stagnant. "Old-fashioned" thinkers tend to dominate. MITI's council on energy policy, for example, has changed little over the last 20 years.[82]

2. Administrative Guidance.   "Administrative guidance" means government action, usually by MITI, which encourages companies to act so as to achieve an administrative aim. It is rarely, if ever, imposed by law. Indeed, law in Japan is notoriously weak. "It is like an heirloom samurai sword," writes Kawashima Takeyoshi. "It is to be treasured, but not used." In more than 30 years of antitrust enforcement, for example, there have been only six prosecutions and three of these were begun in 1949.[83] MITI's legal powers are unimportant. Its influence derives from: its ability to obtain funds and to channel them for research and development in areas which are critical to national competitiveness; the respect it enjoys in both government and business which derives partly from its habit of careful consultation with industry leaders before making a decision—arm-twisting is most undesirable; and its skill at securing the cooperation of industry rivals for the achievement of joint projects.

For example, to encourage the use of robots by small and medium-sized firms and to build a large domestic market to allow scale economies for its robot manufacturers, MITI in 1980 encouraged the establishment of the Japan Robot Leasing Company Ltd. (JAROL). It was a joint venture between 24 robot manufacturers and 10 insurance companies. The Japan Development Bank provided JAROL with low-interest loans to allow for easy leasing terms. By 1982 Japan had 31,900 industrial robots in place; the United States had 7,232.[84]

MITI is also useful in limiting excessive competition. It accomplishes this both by mediating among Japanese firms—stabilizing prices and minimizing price wars—and by protecting Japanese firms against the pressures of foreign governments. On the other hand, its guidelines are sometimes unreliable and inconsistent. For example, before the Toshiba Machine Company, a member of the Mitsui Group, was caught violating regulations of COCOM (the coordinating Committee for Multilateral Export Controls) by selling eight computer-guided milling machines to the Soviet Union, MITI guidelines had emphasized ways in which Japanese companies could overcome COCOM rules.* After the event, MITI guidance changed completely, becoming much more stringent.[86]

The Toshiba matter was a cause célèbre in the United States and even more in Japan where TV viewers in July 1987 watched nine members of the U.S. Congress smashing a small Toshiba radio with sledgehammers during a press conference on Capitol Hill. The Congress members were expressing their anger over the fact that the Toshiba equipment would allow the Soviets to mass-produce a more silent propeller for their submarines and thus avoid detection by the United States. This was especially galling to those who felt that Japan was not paying full fare for U.S. protection. One Pentagon official estimated that it would cost some $30 billion for the United States to regain its technological lead.[87] (Although Toshiba's chairman resigned after a meeting of the Mitsui Group chairmen, some Japanese wondered why the Congress members had not smashed any Norwegian products, since a Norwegian state-controlled enterprise, Kongsberg Vaapenfabrikk, was equally guilty of violating COCOM regulations.)

Furthermore, as Japanese companies have become global in their reach, with many foreign partners and alliances, MITI's guidelines often appear irrelevant or counterproductive. To quote Jitsuu Terashima of Mitsui: "We are always fighting MITI guidelines."[88]

3. The Government Banks. The Industrial Bank of Japan, the Japanese Development Bank, and other banks have a limited influence on business today compared to the important role they played in the 1960s and early 1970s. Nevertheless, while they are not used to sustain doomed industries, they are still a source of low-cost credit to help promote those vigorous industries that are important to Japan's future.

---

*There is no law against espionage in Japan. Foreigners caught doing it are simply put on a plane home.[85]

4. Management Personnel. Many big Japanese companies have ex-vice ministers of MITI or MOF in their top management. For example, Eme Yamashita, executive vice president of Mitsui Co., had been a career vice minister of MITI. This is very helpful in ensuring good relations and understanding between government and business.[89]

United States

The Conference Board reports that more than one-third of 185 CEOs it surveyed spent 25 percent to 50 percent of their time "dealing with various government agencies (legislative and executive) to influence legislation and policy and to assure their own compliance with government regulation."[90] This movement has been exacerbated by the pressures of international competition. Quick action by the Food and Drug Administration is critical to pharmaceutical companies seeking to place their innovations on the market. A respite from Japanese competition was essential to allow Harley-Davidson to regain at least some portion of the U.S. motorcycle business. Retaliatory action against the Brazilian government's computer strategy which involved protecting its home market was sought by some U.S. manufacturers.

Andrew S. Grove, president of Intel, one of America's leading manufacturers of semiconductors, has decried the deterioration of the U.S. information processing industry in the face of Japanese strategy, a strategy which includes initial home market protection, followed by a highly focused "laser-beam" attack to acquire market share at whatever the cost, followed by the proclamation of free market principles. To remedy the situation, he wrote that America needs "a new vision of competitive behavior." And then he continued, "Even though our preference and value system lean toward the individual, we need to think in terms of national entrepreneurship."[91] He went on to advocate a "manufacturing-development consortium" and "coordinated action" with government.

The obstacles in the way of such an achievement are well exemplified in the study of the worldwide automobile industry made by Davis Dyer, Malcolm S. Salter, and Alan M. Webber. The automobile industry is the world's largest; it is a leading source of jobs and investment; and far from being a stodgy smokestack business, it is at the cutting edge of high technology, "creating not only the car of the future, but the factory of the future."[92] It is an industry, like information processing, in which government policies are strategically critical. "In Germany," says Salter, "the government is financing major automotive R&D programs; in France, the government provides major funding for Renault and a restructuring of the auto and parts industries; and in Japan, the government enacted special depreciation schedules for auto companies and provides...R&D assistance and export incentives."[93] (See Exhibit 1 for a summary of comparative government policies toward the industry.)

There can be no doubting the importance of government policy to the industry in the United States: loan guarantees to save Chrysler, energy policy in the 1970s that kept gas prices low, federal fuel economy, pollution and safety standards, the promise of "deregulation" by President Reagan, voluntary restraint agreements to protect the industry from the Japanese, Federal Trade Commission permission to allow General Motors to enter into a joint venture with Toyota, and a ballooning federal budget deficit that raised interest rates and, thus, the value of the dollar, cheapening imports, and hurting exports.[94] An observer from Mars might conclude that the U.S. Government and the industry must be in close touch if not cooperating, but nothing could be further from the truth. "Instead, both government and management have continued to espouse the philosophy of the past, of separate responsibilities, separate authority, and separate interests, while settling into the practice of business as usual in handling day-to-day regulatory matters and ignoring long-term questions of strategic thinking."[95] And this behavior is not a function of a "rogue bureaucracy" or of a particular political party. It is very much a matter of the system.

Howard Paster, a United Autoworkers lobbyist, said, "The administration is willing to let the marketplace determine whether there is an auto industry and if so, what size and what level."[96] An OMB official in charge of regulation supported Paster's criticism, saying, "In the case of regulation, I almost never know how it will affect the different companies." Furthermore, in spite of the talk of deregulation, the evidence is that virtually none took place. Paster continues, "We have no ongoing auto policy in this country. There is no institutional continuity or capability in the government, no industry-driven consensus, no long-term thinking, and no congressional authority or capacity to look long range at autos."[97]

And the industry doesn't want any. Said James Johnston, GM's vice president for industry-government relations, "GM is strongly in favor of the market. We believe we're better off if the government doesn't direct or impede where we're going, but sets a climate where the market can decide."[98]

Nevertheless, the FTC approval of the joint venture with Toyota (New United Motors Manufacturing, Inc.–NUMMI) dictated how many cars the venture could make, how the price should be set, how long the venture could last (12 years), and how the two partners could communicate.[99]

So the government continued, as it always had, to play a critical role in the industry's development while at the same time both sides vigorously denied it. Ideology and practice were far apart. Furthermore, when government intervention was acknowledged, it had its critics.

Don Campbell, assistant to Senator Donald Riegle (D., Mich.) boasted, "In the eyes of the auto companies, government is neither capable nor desirable as a partner for business."[100]

Robert Lighthizer, a former deputy in the Reagan administration's Office of the United States Trade Representative (USTR), complained, "There really is no United States trade strategy. We simply lurch from crisis to crisis."[101]

Trade restrictions were negotiated with the Japanese with no quid pro quos, no agreement or understandings concerning investment, wages, management bonuses, work rules, training, or plant locations—either in the United States or abroad.[102] Finally, when management gave itself large pay hikes, said one official, "the trust was busted."

William Krist, also a former assistant USTR, commented cryptically, "The debate in the United States is between chaos and industry policy, and those aren't the only options."

In 1988, however, there were some signs of change. Robert J. Eaton, vice president in charge of General Motors' technical staffs, spoke of the cooperative research efforts of companies and governments in Japan and Europe in automotive electronics. "If we in the United States are to gain and preserve a technological edge in this area, the time to make the commitment is now...Building government and private sector consensus and cooperation...is always difficult, but we know it can be done once we all acknowledge that it should be done."[103]

Also, at the state level new models were being created, not too different from those of Japan: investment incentives, special allocations for training and education, linkages among firms and with research centers or universities, infrastructure development—all this to help the state compete against other states and nations.

Whatever the attitude of American corporate executives may be about the role of state and federal governments in the United States and about the most desirable relationships between business and those governments, there has been a dramatic increase in the time, money, and effort which business is investing in managing those relationships. As power in Washington has proliferated and dispersed, moving from the Executive branch to several hundred congressional subcommittees, the decisions which Washington makes can affect the lifeblood of companies. As a result, by 1987 there were 23,011 lobbyists registered with the secretary of the Senate (a ratio of 43 to 1 for each member of the House and Senate). This compares with only 365 in 1961. During the same period the number of lawyers listed with the District of Columbia Bar Association climbed from 12,564 to 46,000, and the journalists accredited to Congress or the White House from 1,522 to 5,250. Some 1,300 corporations were listed as maintaining Washington offices in 1986 compared to only 100 in 1968 and the number of trade associations headquarters had tripled to 3,500 with a work force of about 80,000.[104]

At the same time business, labor and other interest groups have become more aggressively involved in the funding of political campaigns. Hedrick Smith, Pulitzer Prize–winning reporter for *The New York Times* in his book *The Power Game*, recorded "the skyrocketing growth of corporate political action committees" (PACs) to raise money and contribute to candidates of their choice. In 1974, there were 89 corporate PACs. Ten years later they numbered 1,682. Overall PACs increased their donations from $8.5 million in 1974 to $132.2 million in 1986.[105]

ISSUES FOR MANAGERS

Managers of a corporation that has had a particular pattern of relationships with government, rooted in a certain set of assumptions about authority and purpose, may have a difficult time adapting to a different pattern. Even though it may be plainly rational to do so, old mindsets may get in the way.

Take, for example, a hypothetical example of an American telecommunications company intent upon increasing its global market share. Its managers for years have dealt with Washington as a customer, a rate setter, a law enforcer: in general, either as a contractor or a setter of constraints, but in either case as an adversary to be held at a distance in order to allow maneuvering room within which the corporation and its allies can organize to achieve its objectives. Lawyers and political infighters are prominent in the Washington office. Their principal task is to keep government out of the company's way, insulating the decision-making apparatus in headquarters from interference. But the Washington office is only marginally connected to that apparatus. Headquarters sets the strategy which the government affairs people are supposed to protect from governmental attack.

Now let us say that this company is seeking to sell its services elsewhere in the world where government is a major player in determining the shape and purpose of the telecommunications market. It faces competitors who have long been intimately tied to their respective governments, sharing their purposes, conditioned to working with governmental bureaucracies. The American company may have superior products and services which the world wants and needs, but if it does not know how to establish appropriate new relationships with governments, it will fail. It may need the assistance of the U.S. government in conducting the political and diplomatic negotiations which are often inherent in telecommunications decisions. It will need also to understand the ways in which foreign governments act as partners and players in the telecommunications business. Furthermore, it will need practice in understanding the bureaucratic power game which is at the heart of all government decision making. Without this understanding and practice it will find itself at a disadvantage against competitors who have always thought in terms of government as a partner and a player.

It might even happen that its friends in foreign governments, respecting its superior products and mindful of its habits of mind, might seek to advise the American company about its shortcomings in, for example, choosing local allies or designing its market offerings. It would be natural for such advisers to approach the company through its Washington office since they would suppose that it would be the appropriate place to speak of governmental affairs. But the Washington office, while perhaps understanding and sympathetic, would be poorly positioned in the corporate hierarchy to influence decisions at headquarters.

All the foregoing raises a variety of questions for corporate mangers:

Information and Intelligence.   What is the best way to collect and analyze global data for application to corporate decisions, and how is the product of such analysis best transmitted to corporate decision makers? In this respect, how are old mindsets about government and business inspected and renovated so that there is a timely perception of reality?

Transition and Transformation.   How can firms originating in "individualistic" settings reorient themselves to manage government relations in "communitarian" ones? And vice versa. In the same vein, how can firms in "individualistic" countries prevent themselves from being exploited by those from "communitarian" countries?

Organization.   What is the most effective way for firms within an industry to organize themselves for governmental relations? Is it better to go it alone or to proceed jointly and cooperatively with others?

Nationalism Versus Internationalism.   In the face of seemingly inevitable global alliances among major corporations, how do firms manage the costs to particular nations? Are new and more vigorous transnational governmental bodies necessary to provide more reliable standards of adjustment for those adversely affected by global competition?

Exhibit 1   Auto Sector Policies of Major Producing Countries, 1985

	France	**Germany**	**Japan**	**United States**	**United Kingdom**
Ownership	100% of Renault.	40% of VW; 5% of BMW.	None.	None.	99% of BL.
Trade	10.3% of EEC tariff; unofficial OMA with Japan (3% of market); alleged NTBs.	10.3% of EEC tariff.	Tariff on parts, but not cars; alleged NTBs; monitors exports.	3% tariff. VER program from 1981 to 1985. After lifting VER, Japanese imports closely monitored.	11% of EEC tariff; OMA with Japan (11% of market).
Investment	Major funding for Renault, restructuring of auto and parts industries; actively promoting investment in distressed regions; monitors foreign investment.	Economy-wide incentives; regional development program; open door to foreign investors.	Economy-wide incentives; special depreciation schedules for autos; monitors foreign investment.	States offer large subsidies for plant consideration.	Major funding for BL; actively promotes investment in distressed regions (Ford engine plant).
Competition	Encouraged collaboration in auto, components, and machine tool sectors.	Cartel office regularly challenges price hikes, but allows extensive cooperation.	MITI encouraged collaboration in parts; successful in components industry.	Traditionally strong antitrust oversight; FTC investigation.	Monopoly commissioned approved BL merger. Chrysler U.K. takeover by Peugeot.

Financial Assistance	Small-scale R&D; regional and restructuring grants.	Small R&D programs under way in advanced automotive technology.	Some R&D assistance.	Major loan guarantees to Chrysler in 1979.	Small-scale R&D; regional grants.
Regulation Safety/Design	EEC directives and local regulations; lukewarm on EEC harmonization.	EEC directions and local standards; strict inspections; favors strict, harmonized EEC standards.	Extensive MOT standards; strict inspections.	Very extensive NHTSA standards; slowdown in new standards.	EEC directives and local regulations.
Emissions	EEC regulations in force since late 1970s. Resisting reforms.	EEC regulations in force since late 1970s. Lead-free gas mandatory by 1986.	Standard as strict as or stricter than those of the United States.	Very extensive standards since 1970; slowdown in implementation.	EEC regulations in force since late 1970s.
Fuel Economy	Voluntary agreement between industry and government (1979).	Voluntary agreement between industry and government (1979); methanol law.	Voluntary guidelines (12% reduction by 1985).	Mandated CAFE standards since 1975.	Voluntary agreement between industry and government (1979).
Fiscal	Progressive auto tax; high VAT; high gas tax.	VAT and progressive use tax on cards; high gas tax.	Numerous auto taxes; moderate gas tax.	Auto tax in state hands; very low gas tax.	VAT; progressive use tax; low gas tax.

OMA—Orderly marketing agreement. NTB—Nontariff barrier. VAT—Value-added tax. VER—Voluntary export restraint.

Source: Mark B. Fuller, "Note on World Auto Industry in Transition," case #9-385-332 (Boston: Harvard Business School, 1985), as used in Davis Dyer, Malcolm S. Salter, and Alan M. Webber, *Changing Alliances* (Boston: Harvard Business School Press, 1987), pp. 309–310.

ENDNOTES

1. J. Huizinga, *The Waning of the Middle Ages: A Study of the Forms of Life, Thought and Art in France and the Netherlands in the XIVth and XVth Centuries* (London: Edward Arnold, 1924), p. 18.
2. George C. Lodge, *The New American Ideology* (New York: Alfred A. Knopf, 1976), p. 70, and Karl Polanyi, *The Great Transformation* (Boston: Beacon Press Paperback, 1944), p. 195.

3. Alfred D. Chandler, Jr., notes that in "1929 the government's working force in Washington was still a good bit smaller than that of United States Steel, General Motors, or Standard Oil. Then the change began. By 1940, a million civilians worked in the federal government; by 1970s, nearly three million did." Two administrative hierarchies with different cultures grew at different periods. Unlike in Japan and Germany, the public hierarchy in the United States came on the scene after the private one was fully developed. The public protest against big business which marked the early part of the twentieth century in American thus took a long time to receive governmental recognition. Alfred D. Chandler, Jr., "Business and Public Policy," *Harvard Business Review* November–December 1979.
4. Raymond Vernon, *Sovereignty at Bay: The Multinational Spread of U.S. Enterprises* (New York: Basic Books, 1971).
5. Michael E. Porter, "Competition in Global Industries: A Conceptual Framework," in Michael E. Porter, ed., *Competition in Global Industries* (Boston: Harvard Business School Press, 1986), pp. 39–42.
6. Interviewed for BBC Television, *Horizon*, March 10, 1986, quoted in Stephen Wilks and Maurice Wright, eds., *Comparative Government-Industry Relations* (New York: Clarendon Press, Oxford University Press, 1987), p. 10.
7. For a more elaborate explanation of these paradigms, see George C. Lodge and Ezra F. Vogel, eds., *Ideology and National Competitiveness* (Boston: Harvard Business School Press, 1987), Chap. 1.
8. Ibid., Chaps. 3–10.
9. Gorbachev quoted in *The New York Times*, February 19, 1988, p. 1.
10. Chalmers Johnson, *MITI and the Japanese Miracle: The Growth of Industrial Policy, 1925–1975* (Stanford, Calif.: Stanford University Press, 1982), pp. 17–19.
11. The concept of "inward-looking" and "outward-looking" strategies was developed by Bela Belassa of the World Bank and is explained in Bruce R. Scott, *U.S. Competitiveness in the World Economy. An Update* (Boston: President and Fellows of Harvard College, 1987). Scott also has a useful description of neomercantilism in that chapter.
12. John Zysman, Stephen Cohen, and Laura Tyson at the University of California at Berkeley must get credit for inventing the notion of "created" comparative advantage. See, for example, John Zysman and Laura Tyson, *American Industry in International Competition* (Ithaca, N.Y.: Cornell University Press, 1983), pp. 422–427.
13. Pat Choate and Jayne Linger, "Tailored Trade: Dealing with the World as It Is," *Harvard Business Review* (January–February 1988), p. 86.
14. Paul R. Krugman, "Is Free Trade Passé?" *Economic Perspectives*, Vol. 1, no. 2 (Fall 1987), p. 136.
15. Ibid., p. 139.
16. Ibid., p. 140.
17. Ibid., p. 141.
18. Quoted in Bruce R. Scott, *Japan as Number One?* Harvard Business School case 9-387-005, Boston, p. 10.
19. Johnson, *MITI and the Japanese Miracle*, p. 28.
20. Yoshiro Ikeda, former chairman of the board of Mitsui and Co. Ltd., quoted in Scott, *Japan as Number One?* p. 8; the point was confirmed by the author in an interview with Yotaro Kobayashi, president of Fuji Xerox Co. Ltd. in December 1987.
21. Quoted in Scott, *Japan as Number One?* p. 9.
22. Johnson, *MITI and the Japanese Miracle*, pp. 16 and 18.
23. James McGroddy, speech to participants in the Advanced Management Program, Harvard Business School, Cambridge, Mass., October 31, 1987.
24. Johnson, *MITI and the Japanese Miracle*, p. 17.
25. For a comparison of the industrial policies of Japan, France, Germany, Brazil, and Taiwan, see Jack N. Behrman, *Industrial Policies: International Restructuring and Transnationals* (Lexington, Mass.: D. C. Heath, 1984), Chaps. 1–3.
26. Quoting report of the Beveridge Commission, in Bruce R. Scott, *The Beveridge Plan and the Welfare State* (Harvard Business School case 0-388-032), Boston, p. 6.
27. Andrew Shonfield, *British Economic Policy Since the War* (London: Penguin Books, 1958), p. 89, quoted in Stephen Blank, "Britain: The Politics of Foreign Economic Policy," in Peter J. Katzenstein, ed., *Between Power and Plenty: Foreign Economic Policies of Advanced Industrial States* (Madison: The University of Wisconsin Press, 1978), p. 97.
28. Blank, *"Britain,"* p. 122.
29. Jorge I. Domínguez, "Revolution and Flexibility in Mexico," in Lodge and Vogel, eds., *Ideology and National Competitiveness,* p. 271.
30. "The Nordic Survey," *The Economist*, November 21, 1987, pp. 6 and 7.
31. Stephen Wermiel, "Reagan Choices Alter the Makeup and Views of the Federal Courts," *The Wall Street Journal*, February 1, 1988, p. 1.
32. Barbara Jenkins, LAREA/CEREM surveys.

33. Porter, *Competition in Global Industries,* p. 39.
34. Ibid, pp. 39–40.
35. See Barbara Jenkins, *Compagnie Générale des Constructions Téléphoniques,* unpublished.
36. Porter, *Competition in Global Industries,* p. 53, and Amir Mahini and Louis T. Wells, Jr., "Government Relations in the Global Firm," in ibid., p. 291.
37. Michael Kreile, "West Germany The Dynamics of Expansion," in Katzenstein, ed., *Between Power and Plenty,* p. 199. See Clyde V. Prestowitz, Jr., *Trading Places* (New York: Basic Books, 1988), for an insightful account of interagency dispute on trade matters in the United States.
38. Thomas K. McCraw, "From Partners to Competitors," Chapter 1 in Thomas K. McCraw, ed., *America Versus Japan* (Boston: Harvard Business School Press, 1986), p. 25.
39. *Proceedings,* Institute of Politics, John F. Kennedy School of Government, Harvard University, Cambridge, Mass., 1986, 1987.
40. Quoted in Lodge, *The New American Ideology,* p. 116.
41. Samuel P. Huntington, *American Politics: The Promise of Disharmony* (Cambridge, Mass.: Harvard University Press, 1981), p. 39.
42. See Bob Woodward, *Veil: The Secret Wars of the CIA, 1981–1987* (New York: Simon & Schuster, 1987).
43. Steven Kelman, *Regulating America, Regulating Sweden: A Comparative Study of Occupational Safety and Health Policy* (Cambridge, Mass.: MIT Press, 1981), p. 119.
44. Ibid., p. 115.
45. This is a modification of criteria for a strong government suggested by Stephen D. Krasner, in Katzenstein, ed., *Between Power and Plenty,* p. 60.
46. McCraw, *America Versus Japan,* "From Partners to Competitors."
47. *The Economist,* November 28, 1987, p. 72.
48. Katzenstein, *Between Power and Plenty,* p. 200.
49. John Zysman, *Governments, Markets and Growth* (Oxford: Martin Robertson, 1983), p. 256.
50. K. Dyson, "The Politics of Economic Recession in West Germany," in A. Cox, ed., *Politics, Policy and the European Recession* (London: Macmillan, 1982), p. 39, quoted in Wilks and Wright, eds., *Comparative Government-Industry Relations,* p. 40.
51. See Christopher S. Allen, in Lodge and Vogel, eds., *Ideology and National Competitiveness,* p. 80.
52. Katzenstein, *Between Power and Plenty,* p. 17.
53. *The Economist,* December 5, 1987, p. 76.
54. Ibid., p. 77.
55. Janice McCormick, "France: Ideological Divisions and the Global Reality," in Lodge, and Vogel, eds., *Ideology and National Competitiveness,* Chap. 3.
56. Ibid., p. 56.
57. Zysman in Katzenstein, *Between Power and Plenty,* p. 267.
58. Ibid., p. 269.
59. Ibid., p. 20.
60. Andrew Shonfield, *Modern Capitalism* (Oxford: Oxford University Press, 1965), p. 88, quoted in ibid., p. 101.
61. Richard Darman, undersecretary of the Treasury, speech at Harvard Business School.
62. Alfred D. Chandler, *Strategy and Structure: Chapters in the History of American Industrial Enterprise* (Cambridge, Mass.: MIT Press, 1962).
63. "Manager's Journal," *The Wall Street Journal,* December 14, 1987, Op/Ed page.
64. See Lodge, *The American Disease,* pp. 283–284, for an elaboration of these questions.
65. See Davis Dyer, Malcolm S. Salter, and Alan M. Webber, *Changing Alliances* (Boston: Harvard Business School Press, 1987), pp. 242–243, for a description of the Toyota-GM plant at Fremont, California, and its innovative human resource management practices.
66. Quoted in Lodge, *The American Disease,* p. 286.
67. *The New York Times,* February 19, 1988, editorial page.
68. J. Hirschmier and T. Yui, *The Development of Japanese Business, 1600–1980,* 2nd ed. (London: George Allen and Unwin, 1981), pp. 11, 19, 41, and 123.
69. McCraw, "From Partners to Competitors," pp. 79–86, and Michael Y. Yoshino and Thomas B. Lifson, *The Invisible Link: Japan's Sogo Shosha and the Organization of Trade* (Cambridge, Mass.: MIT Press, 1986). See also, Alfred D. Chandler, Jr., and Herman Daems, eds., *Managerial Hierarchies: Comparative Perspectives on the Rise of the Modern Industrial Enterprise* (Cambridge, Mass.: Harvard University Press, 1980).
70. See Joseph L. Bower, *When Markets Quake* (Boston: Harvard Business School Press, 1987), for an informative discussion of the desirability if not necessity of industry collaboration in the face of worldwide overcapacity such as that faced by chemicals, automobiles, and semiconductors.
71. Joseph L. Badaracco, Jr., *Loading the Dice: A Five-Country Study of Vinyl Chloride Regulation* (Boston: Harvard Business School Press, 1985).

72. See Richard H. K. Victor, *Energy Policy in American Since 1945: A Study of Business-Government Relations* (Cambridge: Cambridge University Press, 1984), for an analysis of government-business relations in the energy industry, and David Vogel, "Government-Industry Relations in the United States: An Overview," in Wilks and Wright, eds., *Comparative Government-Industry Relations*, p. 91.

73. Theodore J. Lowi, *The End of Liberalism: The Second Republic of the United States*, 2nd ed. (New York: W. W. Norton, 1969), p. 279.

74. Dennis J. Encarnation and Louis T. Wells, Jr., "Sovereignty En Garde: Negotiating with Foreign Investors," *International Organization* (Winter 1985) p. 47.

75. Ibid., p. 55.

76. Benjamin Gomes-Casseres, "Ownership Negotiations Between MNCs and Host Governments," Harvard Business School working paper 88-019, Boston, p. 8.

77. Ibid., p. 3.

78. Benjamin Gomes-Casseres, "Competing Abroad: Jointly or Alone?" Harvard Business School working paper 88-018, Boston, p. 4.

79. Ibid., p. 24.

80. Amir Mahinia and Louis T. Wells, Jr., "Government Relations in the Global Firms," in Porter, ed., *Competition in Global Industries*, p. 307.

81. Interview with Jitsuro Terashima of Mitsui USA, in New York City, December 9, 1987.

82. Ibid.

83. John O. Haley, "Sheathing the Sword of Justice in Japan: An Essay on Law Without Sanctions," *Journal of Japanese Studies* (Summer 1982), pp. 265 and 269.

84. George C. Lodge and Richard E. Walton, "The American Corporation and Its New Relationships," 1987, p. 16. unpublished.

85. C. Johnson, "Japanese-Soviet Relations in the Early Gorbachev Era," *Asian Survey* (November 1987), p. 1159.

86. Terashima interview.

87. George R. Packard, "The Coming U.S.-Japan Crisis," *Foreign Affairs* (Winter 1987/88), p. 248.

88. Terashima interview.

89. Ibid.

90. Gordon Donaldson and Jay Lorsch, *Decision-Making at the Top* (New York: Basic Books, 1983), p. 13.

91. "Forum," *The New York Times*, December 13, 1987.

92. Davis Dyer, Malcolm S. Salter, and Alan M. Webber, *Changing Alliances* (Boston: Harvard Business School Press, 1987), p. x).

93. Malcolm S. Salter, *Negotiating Corporate Strategy in Politically Salient Industries*, Harvard Business School case 1-384-141, Boston, p. 7.

94. Dyer, Salter, and Webber, *Changing Alliances*, pp. 211–212.

95. Ibid., p. 212.

96. Ibid., p. 213.

97. Ibid., p. 217.

98. Ibid., p. 216.

99. Ibid., p. 221.

100. Ibid., p. 223.

101. Ibid., p. 224.

102. Ibid., p. 225.

103. GM Press Release, May 3, 1988, p. 3.

104. Hedrick Smith, *The Power Game: How Washington Works* (New York: Random House, 1988), pp. 29–31.

105. Ibid., p. 32.

GOVERNMENT TARGETING AND THE U.S. RESPONSE

The European-U.S. Steel Dispute of 1982

The year 1982 brought economic problems to the U.S steel industry, which were more severe than any since the Depression of the 1930s. Capacity utilization averaged less than 50 percent, roughly 45 percent of the labor force or 175,000 employees were laid off or on short week by the end of the year, and industry losses exceeded $3.5 billion. Steel was, however, still the fourth largest industry in the United States, with sales of roughly $44 billion in 1981, $12 billion in wages and salaries, and plants in 39 states and some 300 communities.

In 1980, President Ronald Reagan had committed his administration to maintaining "a modern, world-class steel industry" in America,[1] but had also emphasized his staunch commitment to free trade. In March 1982, his chief spokesman on trade, Ambassador William E. Brock, U.S. trade representative (USTR), told the Senate Finance Subcommittee on Trade that "free trade, based on

This case was written by Paul M. Achleitner, Visiting Fellow, under the supervision of Professor George C. Lodge, as the basis for classroom discussion. The cooperation of Hans van der Ven, Senior Research Associate, is gratefully acknowledged. Copyright © by the President and Fellows of Harvard College.

mutually acceptable trading relations, is essential to the pursuit of our goal [a healthy U.S. economy]. We will strongly resist protectionist pressures . . . (and) . . . strictly enforce United States laws, and international agreements."[2]

On October 21, 1982, Secretary of Commerce Malcolm Baldrige signed an agreement with Viscount Etienne Davignon, commissioner of the European Community (EEC), limiting steel imports into the United States from Europe for three years. The deal was struck only hours before U.S. laws would have required punitive actions against the imports, following countervailing duty and antidumping suits filed by the U.S. industry. Baldrige told Congress that the agreement was "a step toward free trade" and that failure to reach an agreement would have been a "giant step toward protectionism."[3]

INDUSTRY BACKGROUND

Because steel is a key component of most sectors in an industrial economy— especially manufacturing, construction, power generation, mining, and transportation—there is substantial government involvement in the industry, characterized by nationalization in most European and developing countries, government-directed financing and cartels in Japan, and periodic interference in the United States.

The United States clearly dominated the world steel business in 1950, accounting for 57 percent of free world raw steel production, but its share dropped to roughly 24 percent in 1981. The European Community's share dropped slightly from 32 percent to 28 percent, while Japan's rose from 3 percent in 1950 to 22 percent in 1981. The rest of the non-Communist world, mainly Spain, Brazil, and South Korea, accounted for 26 percent of world production in 1981 versus 8 percent in 1950.[4]

The Japanese strategy of building greenfield plants in excess of domestic need to gain economies of scale and cost advantages for exports was increasingly adopted by developing countries in the early 1970s.* Brazil, for example, expanded its crude steel capacity by 160 percent from 6.5 million metric tons in 1970 to 16.7 million in 1980.† Like many other developing countries—such as Korea, Taiwan, and Mexico—Brazil built capacity ahead of anticipated market growth and in excess of domestic need, encouraging steel exports to earn foreign exchange. Crude steel imports for all developing countries, therefore, dropped from roughly 59 percent in 1960 to 41 percent in 1980.[5]

Technology and Resources

Governments in Europe and Japan since World War II encouraged and assisted their industries to modernize. The basic oxygen process for making steel, which yields substantial cost advantages over the traditional open hearth process, was

---

*A greenfield plant is a new plant on a new site as opposed to a refurbished plant or a new facility on an old "brownfield" site.

†Steel is measured in short or net tons or in metric tonnes. One net ton = 0.91 metric tonne; 1 metric tonne = 1.1 net tons.

widely used in Europe and Japan long before its general adoption in the United States. For example, it accounted for only 17.5 percent of U.S. raw steel production in 1965, compared with 55 percent in Japan. A more recent innovation was continuous casting accompanied by process computerization. These and other technological developments enhanced the optimum capacity of an integrated steel plant to between 6 and 7 million tons, according to Robert Crandall of the Brookings Institution.[6] The average capacity of integrated plants in Japan in 1982 was 7 million net tons. In the United States it was about 3 million; most plants were more than 27 years old, and only two integrated greenfield plants had been built since World War II.

There were, of course, sound economic reasons for the comparative deterioration of American plant and equipment. Space and cost constraints made construction of new integrated steel plants in the United States exceptionally expensive. High construction and capital costs in particular made the marginal cost of producing a ton of steel in the older, smaller U.S. facilities generally less than the average cost in newer, larger, more efficient units.[7] In contrast, in many Asian and Latin American countries land near shipping channels was cheap and plentiful, labor was inexpensive, and governments were eager to help.

The U.S. industry's difficulties were exacerbated by changes in the sources of iron ore and new transportation developments. Iron ore and metallurgical coal prices fell substantially through the 1960s, as did shipping costs. Steel plants on coastal sites benefited. At the same time, surface transportation costs rose, punishing landlocked U.S. and European producers, often situated near deteriorating ore deposits. For example, the cost of shipping iron ore from Brazil to Japan fell 60 percent from 1957 to 1968. In 1957 American steelmakers paid $9.63 c.i.f. (cost, insurance, and freight) per net ton of iron ore in comparison to $16.69 for Japanese producers; in 1976 it was $27.62 for the United States versus $15.81 for Japan.[8]

Labor Costs

Labor costs also weighed heavily on the U.S. steel industry. Hourly employment costs reached $22.69 by early 1982, 89 percent above the all-manufacturing average, compared with 33 percent above the average in 1970.[9] In Germany hourly employment costs in the steel industry were $13.18 in 1981, a mere 12 percent above the all-manufacturing average. (See Exhibit 1.)

The increased U.S. labor cost largely arose from the Experimental Negotiation Agreement (ENA) of 1973. Steel labor contracts in the United States traditionally ran for three years and the possibility of a strike during contract negotiations regularly induced inventory buildups with vast stockpiling and surging imports. Strongly influenced by the bitter 116-day national strike of 1959 and in their desire to stabilize markets and avoid such disruptions, management and the United Steel Workers of America signed the ENA, which prohibited industrywide strikes, called for binding arbitration of disputes, and guaranteed at least 3 percent a year wage increases plus automatic cost-of-living adjustments on top of whatever might be agreed to in contract negotiations. The ENA was renewed in 1977 and 1980, but canceled by the industry for 1983.

The ENA wage gains were partially responsible for declines in industry employment from 512,000 in 1975 to 391,000 in 1981. These were matched by reductions in the European steel work force from 792,000 to under 600,000. However, labor productivity rose substantially higher in the EEC and Japan than in the United States, so U.S. unit labor costs per ton shipped in 1981 equaled $171.19 versus $98.73 in Japan and $131.60 in West Germany (see Exhibit 1).

The cost advantage of the most efficient European mills over their American counterparts was estimated in 1982 to be $85 per ton of steel. (Japan's advantage was more than $100 per ton.)[10] This was largely due to the considerable appreciation in the value of the U.S. dollar in comparison with the yen and most European currencies in the early 1980s. Peter Marcus, steel analyst for Paine Webber Mitchell Hutchins, Inc., estimated that West German pretax costs per ton shipped in U.S. dollars were lowered 23.8 percent in exchange rate fluctuations in 1981 compared with the 1978–1979 exchange rate average.[11]

Capacity Utilization Rates

The high fixed costs of steel production, aggravated in Europe and Japan by high debt ratios and the commitment to maintain stable employment, made high and stable utilization rates desirable. But steel as a basic industrial commodity was strongly affected by economic downturns. As a producer's good characterized by relatively inelastic demand, steel was subject to severe price cutting during slack periods, but price wars do not increase overall sales, so producers traditionally sought stable markets with stable prices.

The "incremental ton" of steel disproportionately affects profitability as additional tonnage reduces fixed costs. An increase in capacity utilization from 80 percent to 85 percent, for example, will generally boost profits by a much greater percentage and make further investment more attractive. When demand falls in home markets, therefore, producers try to improve lagging utilization rates by selling abroad at any price they can obtain, as long as it helps cover fixed costs.*

Potential economies of scale quickly become liabilities when demand is lacking, however, and sagging demand has haunted the world steel industry since the boom years of 1973 and 1974. Steel use in developed nations actually declined relative to GNP by about 21 percent between 1970 and 1981. The world's aggregate capacity utilization rate has not exceeded 75 percent since 1974; in 1981 raw steel production capacity in the free world was 665 million tons, but only 455 million tons were produced.[12]

Financial Situation

Profitability of major steel firms all over the world was strongly affected; European producers were especially hard hit. Between 1975 and 1981, 52 international

---

*European and Japanese producers often regard labor as a fixed cost.

steelmakers incurred at least $7 billion of losses, received $15 billion of subsidies, and increased long-term debt by at least $40 billion. (See Exhibit 2.) Although comparing favorably with their European competitors, the big seven integrated steel producers of the United States—U.S. Steel, Bethlehem, Armco, Inland, Jones & Laughlin (LTV), National, and Republic—faced a grim financial situation in 1982. Annual real income after taxes between 1975 and 1980 was about half what it had been during the previous decade. An average steel company share sold for less than 40% of book value.[13] Return on equity (ROE) averaged 6.8% in the late 1970s, compared with 15.6% for manufacturing generally. The industry estimated that it needed between $4 billion and $5 billion a year to maintain and modernize its plants; however, aggregate cash flow averaged only $3.1 billion a year between 1975 and 1980, all but once failing to meet capital expenditures.[14] In 1981, however, the leasing provisions of the Economic Recovery Tax Act (ERTA), which enabled profitable companies to acquire tax benefits from profitless ones, improved the situation.

The disastrous financial performance of European producers can be partly explained by strong price wars within the EEC, prompted by attempts to improve individual utilization rate by cutting prices. During 1980–1981 EEC steel prices lagged some 15 percent to 20 percent below prices on the Japanese and American markets, where producers avoided cutthroat competition. (See Exhibit 3.)

SUPRANATIONAL INDUSTRY REGULATION IN EUROPE

The concentration of the European steel industry in already depressed areas with rapidly rising unemployment (such as the Walloon part of Belgium) led to increased public intervention to preserve employment. Ailing companies received public support in return for providing employment because spreading the costs of the economic and social adjustment of one exceptionally hard-hit sector over the whole economy was generally considered a positive achievement of the modern European welfare state. This support ranged from direct compensation by governments for operating losses to loans at reduced interest rates, loan guarantees, tax rebates and incentives, and such nonfinancial measures as import protection, buy-domestic rules, and the tying of foreign aid to domestic steel purchases.

European governments overcame their general reluctance to relinquish authority to a supranational body in the steel sector.* In 1951, the European Coal and Steel Community (ECSC) was founded as a forerunner of the European Community. It was to establish control over the steel sector to ensure peace and prevent a renewal of German military power at a time when war without a strong

---

*This case emphasizes the European Community as a whole and the policy of the European Commission. However, steel industries in individual countries and national policies toward them differ widely. Also, average statistical figures about the community tend to hide the enormous problems of a country like Belgium, with large concentrations of steel production in certain areas, as compared with the Netherlands, for example, which has a more diversified industrial base.

steel industry was unthinkable. The European Commission, arising from the original ECSC treaty, therefore, held powers in the steel sector beyond those in any other sector of the community.

Economic Measures

In 1977, when its plight became clear, the European Commission adopted a coordinated plan for restructuring the European steel industry. The Davignon Plan, named after Viscount Etienne Davignon, the commissioner responsible for industrial policy, was designed to dismantle overcapacity, reorganize the industry financially, restore international competitiveness by reducing production costs, and spread the costs of these adjustments over time and among producers so bankruptcies of large integrated firms with unacceptable social costs could be prevented. The scheme consisted of voluntary restrictions on production along with a system of mandatory and recommended minimum prices for steel products established through Eurofer, the Association of European Iron and Steel Producing Industries, which represented all large integrated producers in the EEC countries.

To reinforce these internal mechanisms and raise steel prices, the commission established reference prices and persuaded some 15 European and non-European exporting countries to conclude self-limiting agreements with the EEC, keeping steel exports to "traditional levels" and respecting EEC price schedules. However, although restructuring efforts centered on better output techniques and higher productivity, they almost inevitably led to increases in production capacities, therefore aggravating the problem of excess capacity further. (See Exhibit 4.)

In the late spring of 1980, the market, and with it the cartel arrangement, virtually collapsed. Prices fell by as much as 30 percent, and the German manufacturer Kloeckner withdrew from Eurofer after it was refused a higher production quota. To prevent the volatile market situation from triggering large bankruptcies, which would require national government measures, the European Commission on October 6, 1980, declared a "state of manifest crisis" and imposed strictly monitored compulsory production quotas on the 350 leading steel firms. Cutbacks in production for the fourth quarter of 1980 and the first half of 1981 ranged between 12 percent and 25 percent, according to product. Imports were to be controlled even more strictly, and the "unofficial import quotas" were lowered 15 percent from the 1980 level. These measures only led to a modest price increase—between 5 percent and 10 percent according to most estimates—while raw material prices kept climbing. By July 1981, when the crisis manifesto expired, a new, partly voluntary, partly mandatory system of production and sales restrictions was set up (Eurofer 2). It was complemented by an EEC price policy, effectively a European steel cartel.

Social Plan and Aid Code

The EEC Council of Ministers also adopted a "social plan" and an "aid code" on June 25, 1981. Under the social plan, about $200 million dollars of EEC funds were made available to member states to finance early retirements and extra costs of short-time work prompted by restructuring. Under the aid code or subsidy rules, governments were obliged to report their subsidies of national steelmakers to the European Commission. Investment, closure, developments, and emergency aid had to be related to a restructuring program including financial reorganization to facilitate a return to profitability. The basic requirements were a reduction in production capacity and progressive reduction in subsidies, with all aid to be phased out no later than December 31, 1985. This was expected to put severe pressure on national governments to speed up their steel industry restructuring plans.

INDUSTRY-GOVERNMENT RELATIONS IN THE UNITED STATES

The relations between the U.S. government and big steel contrasted sharply with those of other countries. Except during wartime, they were characterized by either distance or conflict. At first, government respected the industry's power and importance. Preoccupied with the need to stabilize world markets for their products, Andrew Carnegie and J. P. Morgan created the U.S. Steel Corporation in 1901. The value of the gigantic merger was nearly three times the entire federal budget at that time. By 1913, U.S. Steel had 265 agencies in 60 countries; exports accounted for 17 percent of its revenues. (Its aggressive export drives led Canada in 1904 to adopt the world's first antidumping law.) An antitrust suit was brought against the company, which controlled some 65 percent of the domestic market, but it was set aside in 1920 mainly because the company's role in world trade substantially benefited the national interest.

If building capacity and gaining markets was the challenge of the 1920s, the Great Depression brought problems of glut. The steel industry successfully lobbied for the Smoot-Hawley Tariff Act of 1930, which established the highest tariffs in American history. World War II brought increased demand, and the industry worked closely with government to meet the nation's military needs. With peace, however, the industry cut back on investment, fearing excess capacity. President Truman, in view of the Korean conflict, demanded further expansion; the industry—still horrified by the experience of the 1930s and restless under government price controls—was reluctant to comply. When the industry declined to settle with the United Steel Workers of America without governmental assurance of large price increases, Truman attempted to seize it, although he was thwarted by the Supreme Court.[15] In 1962 President Kennedy assailed the industry for raising prices after what he considered a modest wage settlement and virtually forced Roger M. Blough, chairman of U.S. Steel, to rescind the increase.

The United States had become a net importer of European and Japanese steel after the lengthy national industry strike of 1959. In 1968, President Johnson applied "jawboning pressure" to persuade the industry to reduce prices, but shortly after the industry obtained major relief from imports. The State Department negotiated a set of "voluntary restraint agreements" (VRAs) in 1969 with European and Japanese producers, limiting steel exports to the United States to an annual target of 14 million tons.[16] The agreements held until 1972. Crandall estimates that although the VRAs raised import prices by 9.3 percent to 8.3 percent, domestic prices were only increased by 1.2 percent to 3.5 percent.[17] However, serious side effects resulted as foreign exporters shifted to higher valued products such as specialty steel or, as did Japan, to steel-using products such as automobiles to maximize profits under the quantitative restrictions.

The 1977 Confrontation

Strong world steel demand in 1973 and 1974 reduced the importance of the import issue for the U.S. steel industry, which was operating at nearly full capacity. By 1977, however, capacity utilization had plummeted to less than 79 percent, and ROE reached the all-time low of 0.1 percent, a profit margin on sales of 0.06 percent. Alan Wood Steel Company filed for bankruptcy; Youngstown Sheet and Tube and Bethlehem Steel partially closed three plants, laying off some 17,000 employees.

World demand also leveled off, causing substantial price reductions in Europe, where producers tried to secure market shares. United States steel imports rose to a 17.8 percent market penetration (compared with 13.4 percent in 1974) and were widely perceived as contributing to industry deterioration. In the fall of 1977, therefore, the industry filed 11 antidumping complaints accusing European and Japanese steelmakers of selling below cost. (For a more complete explanation of U.S. trade laws and policies, see Appendices A and B to this chapter.)

The legal process for handling these suits was extremely cumbersome, often taking 13 months or more, and they were bitterly resented by the European allies. But pressure was mounting on the Carter administration from the congressional steel caucus, which included more than 200 members. By November 2, 13 bills calling for various forms of quotas were before Congress. A White House Council on Wage and Price Stability study showed that Japanese firms enjoyed a real cost advantage over U.S. producers; the antidumping complaints in their case were unjustified. The European industry, however, was clearly selling below unit costs in the U.S. market.

The administration faced a major dilemma. Implementation of antidumping duties on European steel would poison U.S.-European relations and virtually assure the failure of the Tokyo Round trade negotiations, concerned with these very problems, while Japanese low-cost producers could fill any gap left by the Europeans. President Carter asked Undersecretary of the Treasury Anthony Solomon, to develop a policy quickly. In December the president accepted Solomon's recommendations in full, but implementation was slow and spotty.

Aware that steel companies would not be able to meet the $4 billion annually required to modernize, the Solomon report recommended a reduction in the depreciation schedule for them from 18 to 15 years and loan guarantees by the Economic Development Administration (EDA) of the Department of Commerce to afflicted companies and communities. Although the report did not recommend reduction of pollution standards, it suggested better coordination between the Environmental Protection Agency and the Occupational Safety and Health Administration. It recommended easing antitrust provisions to promote more cost-efficient joint ventures and federal funds to supplement a suggested 3 percent of sales to be used for research and development.

The report also recommended that a steel advisory committee representing government, industry, and labor deal with the industry's ongoing problems. The committee met regularly between 1977 and 1980, but was abandoned by the Reagan administration. The tax burden was lowered in 1978, but it took until 1981 to get relief on the environmental front through the Steel Industry Compliance Extension Act.

The Trigger Price Mechanism

The recommendation of the Solomon task force with the greatest impact was a reference price system, made effective in March 1978, to discourage illegal dumping of low-cost foreign steel in the U.S. market. American officials would gather information from foreign and domestic sources to construct the average costs, including 8 percent profit, of Japanese steelmakers, assumed to be the world's lowest-cost producers. Costs would be computed c.i.f., and four U.S. regional markets (Great Lakes, East, Gulf, and Pacific) would allow for different transportation costs. Invoices would be required, and when the import price was below the reference price, the trigger price mechanism (TPM) would initiate an investigation, speeding up the laborious legal process and relieving complainants of the burden of proof. Claiming insufficient resources both to administer the TPM and to investigate independent dumping complaints, the Treasury Department warned the industry that the TPM would be maintained only if it refrained from filing antidumping petitions.[18] Eventually, the industry withdrew its complaint, but there was widespread apprehension that the government had obtained another club over both industry and labor in its battle to keep prices and wages down. Lloyd McBride, president of the United Steelworkers Union, claimed that the TPM was virtually a "license to dump" for the Europeans because EEC producers could still undersell Americans below European cost without going under the Japanese-based trigger price.

Any success the TPM might have had was short-lived as the value of the dollar climbed against the yen, lowering the trigger price in dollar terms. U.S. Steel took the lead in demanding higher trigger prices or import quotas and threatened to file antidumping suits. Again, the problem of steel imports became involved in domestic and international politics. President Carter did not want to alienate his European allies and was also reluctant to raise trigger prices, fearing inflation and charges of protectionism.

On March 21, 1980, U.S. Steel filed 23 antidumping petitions against 16 companies in seven European countries. The government suspended the TPM. After intense negotiations, the industry withdrew the suits in October 1980, and the administration reinstated an improved TPM.

At the time, David Roderick, president of U.S. Steel, summarized his views of the role of governments:

I am a free trader. I am an Adam Smith man. If everyone is operating under the free enterprise system, free trade can work very well. Enter the government....Incidentally, I think 45 percent of the free world steel capacity outside the United States is government-owned. The government says we are going to sell our steel $40 to $45 dollars [sic] under the cost of making it. They do it for one year. They do it for 10 or 20 years. The system doesn't correct itself. They are going to take tax dollars...to subsidize losses in steel...as a matter of national priorities instead of building two battleships. That abuse can stay in the market indefinitely.[19]

Economist Milton Friedman, also a free trader, argued on the other hand that U.S. consumers benefited from cheap subsidized foreign steel and the country benefited from imports, which allowed foreigners to buy U.S. exports. "It makes no sense to provide a financial hothouse for the steel industry."[20]

The Collapse of the TPM

When Malcolm Baldrige became secretary of commerce early in 1981, he found himself at the center of yet a new conflict about steel imports and the TPM.* Demand for basic carbon steel products had dropped rapidly because of the overall recession, which had especially hit car producers and construction. Domestic market prices in the United States actually fell below the trigger prices, virtually cutting off European imports, which dropped to their lowest level since World War II, 22 percent of total imports. (See Exhibit 5).

At the same time, however, the European currency values dropped significantly vis-à-vis the yen and the U.S. dollar. Because these two currencies were used to calculate the trigger prices, European exports became more profitable at trigger price level, and it became easier for some European producers to meet constructed value criteria (see Appendix A) below the trigger price. Therefore, in March 1981, two European producers filed for preclearance.

Under TPM provisions, preclearance to sell below trigger price could be granted to any producer that could prove it was more cost efficient than the assumed Japanese cost leader on whose costs the trigger prices were calculated. Preclearance had been granted to Canadian producers for the Great Lakes area who successfully claimed that short transportation made them more cost efficient than the distant Japanese. Overall, Canadian steel imports rose 33.0 percent from the first quarter of 1980 through the first quarter of 1981, while EEC imports fell 40.3 percent. Roderick made it clear, however, that the U.S. industry would revive antidumping suits against EEC companies should any substantial TPM concessions be made. This would bring down the delicate TPM structure and create strong tensions between precleared and other European exporters.[21]

During the summer of 1981, imports from Europe were rising substantially (see Exhibit 5), and trigger prices were increasingly disregarded by EEC exporters.

---

*Following complaints of the industry that the Treasury Department was too concerned with international cooperation, Congress, in 1979, transferred responsibility for administering the antidumping and countervailing duty statutes to the Commerce Department, which was expected to take a view similar to that of the domestic industry. (See Appendix C to this chapter.)

On October 5, 1981, *American Metal Market* reported that imported cold-rolled carbon steel in the Great Lakes area was available at $403 per ton. The domestic producer list price was $493 per ton, and the trigger price was $495.

A number of factors were contributing to this situation. European applicants for preclearance anticipated receiving it and priced accordingly. Others felt that trigger prices did not reflect the profound exchange rate differences and expected to be able to prove in an investigation that they were exporting at a price well above their costs. Prices in Europe were depressed, and the strong dollar made export margins even more enticing. Apart from that, if TPM collapse and replacement with quantitative restrictions were imminent, one could actually be penalized tomorrow for compliance today. The influx of European imports was increased by Independent American Steel Distributors, which throughout 1981 had set up offices in Europe and purchased cheap European steel for sale at home at the higher American prices.

In October 1981, when August import data became available, it was clear that something must be done—steel imports were 34 percent above those of the previous month and 62 percent higher than in August 1980. In early November, Baldrige announced that he was eliminating preclearance completely because the "Department of Commerce's limited resources can be better used to examine unfair trade practices." He said the department would maintain the TPM only for "as long as it is in the interest of all parties: Europe, Japan, and the American steelmakers." Therefore, "if the American industry filed massive cases, I think that would mean the demise of the Trigger Price Mechanism." To prove his concern for the industry and determination to enforce the trade laws, he announced that the Commerce Department would itself initiate five antidumping and countervailing duty complaints against steel products from Belgium, France, Brazil, South Africa, and Rumania, despite the delicate political implications. "Since I have been here, we have always been ready to self-initiate when the industry can show injury," Mr. Baldrige added.[22]

On November 19, the chairman of the Executive Committee of the House Steel Caucus, Representative Adam Benjamin (D., Ind.), demanded a meeting between the president and industry, labor, cabinet, and caucus officials to develop a comprehensive solution to the import problem, requesting a "quantitative restriction which would be correlated to the growth or contraction of the American economy, thereby protecting domestic companies and workers during recessionary periods."[23]

The industry's support in Congress suffered a serious setback, however, when U.S. Steel announced its $6.4 billion bid for Marathon Oil. As Representative Sam N. Gibbons (D., Fla) put it, "U.S. Steel cries that they did not have the capital to modernize their plants, they could not compete. I think they can fool us once, but fool us twice? Shame on us."[24]

In the first week of December, President Reagan and industry leaders met for the first time. Steel caucus members were not invited. A White House spokesperson announced that the administration had agreed to ask the EEC to restrain steel shipments voluntarily. Hours later, however, the announcement was denied by the Commerce Department; Secretary Baldrige would only seek

European compliance with U.S. Trade laws and warn of the consequences of flouting the TPM.[25]

The EEC as a whole, unlike some individual producers, was eager to keep the TPM alive, despite its shortcomings. It provided all European producers a safe way to export without being sued for dumping or for accepting government subsidies (see Appendix A). The predictability of the TPM was preferred over the uncertainty of antidumping and countervailing duty actions. On December 15, Baldrige and Davignon met in London and agreed "to try to achieve peace by amending the TPM and by leaning hard on their own producers."[26]

THE 1982 DISPUTE

However, on January 11, 1982, U.S. Steel, Bethlehem, and five other companies sought antidumping duties in 38 cases and, for the first time, countervailing duties to offset foreign government subsidies in 94 cases. The petitions covered 70 percent of all imported carbon steel items from seven EEC countries, Spain, Brazil, Rumania, and South Africa. The prospects for the complaints looked promising to the industry because it could show injury and, further, on January 8, the European Commission had approved large new national subsidy programs for the steel industries in France, Belgium, and Italy. For the U.S. government, the timing was less fortunate; the petitions came at a time when it was also prodding the EEC to liberalize trade in services and to reduce agricultural subsidies. Baldrige immediately abolished the TPM as he had said he would. Imports in January reached their highest level ever, with a market penetration of 26.6 percent. Of the 132 suits, 7 were dismissed immediately because of lack of evidence, 16 were withdrawn by the industry, and on February 18 the International Trade Commission (ITC) determined insufficient evidence of injury in 54 other cases. The Commerce Department, therefore, had to investigate 55 suits and a preliminary decision on the amount of illegal subsidies was due by June 10 (see Appendix A).

In the meantime, Baldrige declared that he wanted to see these investigations through to establish once and for all if there really were reasons for substantial countervailing duty claims. "Our determination will not be influenced by appeals from foreign governments, but will reflect our adherence to U.S. trade laws and international obligations," he stated on March 29, adding that "no emotional reaction by the U.S. government can help the U.S. industry over the long run. The reasoned judicious policy now being implemented which confines domestic economic actions and protection from unfair foreign trade is the proper course."[27]

Baldrige promised that negotiated settlements would not be sought unless the domestic steel industry favored them and that the Commerce Department, not the State or Treasury departments, would dictate any talks with foreign countries regarding these complaints. He also recommended the reestablishment of the defunct Tripartite Advisory Steel Committee. "I can't do that unilaterally. I have to get the administration to go along with that, but I am going to recommend personally that we do that."[28] (As of January 1982, the Tripartite Committee had not been recalled.) On May 7, U.S. Steel filed further countervailing duty suits on welded pipes from West Germany, France, Italy, Brazil, and South Korea, increasing the coverage of the suits to some 85 percent to 90 percent of EEC steel export products, or about $2 billion of total imports.

Protectionism or Fair Trade

On May 24 Representative Benjamin introduced the Fair Trade in Steel Act of 1982, which would have imposed specified steel quotas for five years, beginning with the second half of 1982. He asserted that "it is important that the American steel industry be freed from the political tradeoffs, international quid pro quos, and foreign policy give-aways which have persuaded administration after administration to ignore and flaunt enforcement of U.S. trade laws."[29]

Although the bill pleased steel executives, it was not expected to reach the House floor because committee members from agricultural constituencies feared European retaliation against such a protectionist measure. (In 1981, the United States had an overall trade surplus with the EEC of $16 billion.) Others opposed the bill, stating that standard arguments for trade protection did not—or should not—apply to the steel industry. These arguments included changing income distribution—protection would, for example, transfer income from consumers to steelworkers, increasing domestic employment; improving the balance of payments; and promoting national defense.

The Europeans had made it clear that imposition of countervailing duties would be regarded as an extremely hostile act. Davignon commented that the Americans not only "risked a protectionist move in Europe, but made it a probability."[30] European producers pointed out that the American antidumping law actually required them to raise prices during periods of falling demand to meet the law's "constructed value criteria" (see Appendix A). The question of subsidies was even more disputed. Not only was the definition of the term itself in doubt, but it was also extremely difficult to prove—as the law required— that the subsidies directly affected exports.

Tension was heightened by other simultaneous discussions about coordinated Western trade policies with Eastern Europe. During May, Baldrige and Davignon had a number of "informal" meetings at which steel trade was "discussed." The intensity of these discussions increased dramatically in early June, just before the Commerce Department's preliminary findings on foreign subsidies were due. On June 8, Mr. Baldrige met with steel executives in New York, as he had done before, submitting a European proposal for a voluntary restraint agreement limiting European carbon steel exports to roughly 6 percent of the U.S. market (versus 6.3 percent in 1981). The industry, however, sought a level closer to 4.3 percent of flat-rolled products and inclusion of pipe and tube products, so no agreement was reached.[31]

Preliminary Commerce Department Findings

On June 11 the department announced preliminary findings that nine foreign governments (seven from the EEC) had unfairly subsidized exports to the United

States: 40.4 percent for some products of British Steel Corporation, 20.6 percent to 30 percent for French steel products, as little as 3.6 percent for West German products, and even smaller margins for exports from Luxembourg and the Netherlands. As a result, U.S. importers were obliged to post cash or bonds equivalent to these estimated subsidies to cover eventual countervailing duties, which could range from less than $3 to more than $200 a ton. In a dozen instances, insufficient evidence was found. Final findings were due August 24.

All parties reacted forcefully. Roderick felt the rulings were "encouraging" but expressed "disappointment" over some findings. (U.S. Steel had charged in its petitions that subsidies ranged between $50 and $300 a ton.) "If a better mechanism presents itself to deal with the import problems that is less disruptive than the trade cases but which arrives at an equally equitable solution, we would, of course, be open to considering it," he added.[32]

American importers announced that they would change their buying patterns. "We would have to shift from those with high margins to those with low margins. That's the ABC of our business," Ferdinand Lamesch, president of Trade Arbed Incorporated, said. He emphasized that despite the provisional 3.6 percent duty on West German flat-rolled products, for instance, the West German price would still be about $40 a ton below prices of U.S. producers.[33]

Within the EEC, the findings created strong tensions between producers who would be virtually excluded from the U.S. market and those more or less cleared of wrongdoing. Davignon attacked the United States for a "dangerous political mistake" and said that it interpreted the General Agreement on Tariffs and Trade (GATT) unilaterally. He announced a formal complaint against the U.S. subsidy interpretations of GATT and another against the U.S. Domestic International Sales Corporation (DISC) program, which provided tax subsidies for U.S. exporters.

Later in June, the ITC released a study showing that the 1969–1974 voluntary restraint agreements worked efficiently, saved 19,117 jobs per year on average, and reduced imports 20.1 percent from before 1969.[23] While the pressure for a negotiated settlement was mounting, United States–EEC relations were deteriorating. When Baldrige traveled to Brussels in July to discuss the steel dispute, he found the Europeans too preoccupied with U.S. sanctions against companies selling gas pipeline equipment to the Soviet Union even to discuss steel seriously. On July 30, the American Iron and Steel Institute released its newest statistics, showing that imports accounted for 22.6 percent of supply in the first half of 1982, but were up to 25.6 percent in June.

Viscount Davignon reached an agreement with Baldrige on August 5. The EEC would issue export licenses for carbon steel products to the United States, voluntarily restricting the market penetration to an average of 5.75 percent. At the same time, negotiations about pipe and tube exports to the United States would be started. The next day, however, top executives of the U.S. industry rejected the agreement, embarrassing Baldrige and angering the Europeans. The industry refused to withdraw its petitions, and there was no way to stop the legal proceedings underway. (Until July 23, the Commerce Department could have suspended the suits if an equally beneficial settlement were negotiated, but the EEC did not seize that opportunity, unlike the Brazilian government, which agreed to collect an "export tax" to offset the subsidies.)

The U.S. producers insisted on a lower market penetration and inclusion of alloys, pipes, and tubes in an agreement that would then cover some 90 percent of produce as opposed to the 45 percent affected by the Commerce Department findings. Because of the structure of the ECSC, pipes and tubes were, however, not under the jurisdiction of the European Commission; further, they were mainly produced by German companies largely cleared of subsidy violations.

On August 10 the Commerce Department announced its preliminary findings in the antidumping cases, ruling that producers from five EEC countries and Rumania sold steel in the U.S. market between 0.5 percent and 41.0 percent below fair value (18.8 percent for British Steel plate, 40.7 percent for cold-rolled sheet from Italy's Tecsid, and 27.7 percent from Sacilor in France). While acquitting producers from the Netherlands and Luxembourg, the department found that six of eight German companies were dumping at margins between 2.4 percent and 19.1 percent. These margins were cumulative over the subsidy findings; importers were to post bonds (up to $145 a ton). But the department emphasized that the findings were only preliminary and subject to change. Baldrige, expressing disappointment over the rejection of the August 5 agreement, said he would not attempt to "jawbone" the industry. He would allow the cases to proceed, although he felt that an agreement would be significantly better, given the "productivity problem of the industry."[35]

The Approaching Deadline

On August 24 the Commerce Department announced its final determination of subsidies and subsequent countervailing duties. These findings were generally significantly lower than the preliminary estimates, but would still have excluded British, French, and Italian steel products from the U.S. market (for British Steel, they reduced the margin from 40.4 percent to 20.3 percent). In part, they reflected European arguments about the methods used to calculate subsidies.* Baldrige, hinting at the original agreement, asserted that "it is up to the producers themselves to evaluate what method of relief from unfair trade is in their best interest before the ITC final injury determination in October."[36]

Roderick, in turn, announced that the industry would appeal most of the rulings to the Court of International Trade, but submitted new conditions for an accord, asking for an expanded agreement covering alloys and coated products and a system for an expanded agreement covering alloys and coated products and a system of permanent consultations between the United States and the EEC.[37] However, despite intensive negotiations, no agreement was reached by October 15, when the ITC made its final decision that the U.S. industry was injured in 14 of the remaining 16 cases, rejecting, however, injury in the case of West German hot-rolled

---

*Commerce Department officials assured that it was standard procedure that preliminary determinations would be higher than final ones, because higher duties could not be collected retroactively, but importers could be reimbursed.

plate and cold-rolled sheet and strip, which accounted for about 40 percent of the volume in question.

The commission would submit its findings to the Commerce Department by Thursday, October 21, at 5 P.M., at which time the law requried imposition of countervailing duties. Over the weekend, Baldrige, in consultation with the U.S. industry and Davignon, agreed to include certain alloy steel goods and coated products in the EEC export licensing system, limiting shipment to the United States to an average of 5.44 percent of consumption. The U.S. Customs Service would monitor licenses and reject imported shipments without proper EEC papers. Pipe and tube products would be monitored separately with consultations if they rose above 5.9 percent market penetration. The agreement, therefore, covered some 90 percent of European exports to the United States in comparison to the roughly 45 percent affected by the countervailing duty suits. It was expected to reduce the EEC tonnage to the United States by roughly 13 percent from the 1981 level.

However, on October 20, the new conservative German government rejected the pipe and tube accord. After Davignon received word from Washington "no pipes, no deal," a cabinet-level EEC meeting was held on the morning of October 21. When the Germans were guaranteed an additional 17,000 tons a year out of the "European share" and exposed to considerable peer pressure, they agreed to the deal. By 11 A.M., Washington time, the arrangement was confirmed, and by 4:40 P.M. the U.S. industry had withdrawn its suits.

Reaction to the Agreement

President Reagan announced the agreement while campaigning, and Baldrige said, "The agreement will be a shot in the arm to employment in the U.S. Steel industry." He estimated that had it been in effect in 1981, some 25,000–30,000 jobs could have been saved. "You cannot have free trade unless you have some recourse if you are being unfairly traded against," Baldrige said. "You can't simply have free trade and let other people take advantage of you by subsidizing."[38]

Roderick estimated that the agreement could mean 15,000 to 20,000 more jobs for U.S. steelworkers, but added, "If we eliminated all imports, we would not have any unemployed steelworkers."[39] At a news conference in Pittsburgh, he asserted that "with the European agreement, we have addressed ourselves to one-third of the problem. We recognize the other two-thirds is still there, and we intend to aggressively pursue trade actions against those import sources." He announced that U.S. Steel would formally file a complaint under Section 301 of the Trade Act of 1974 with the U.S. Trade Representative (see Appendices A and C) against Japan, because an existing Japanese-European accord, which limited Japanese steel exports to the EEC, represented an attempt to divert Japanese steel to the U.S. market. "Nothing is guaranteed, but we think we have a very compelling case," Roderick said.[40]

APPENDIX A
U.S. Trade Laws

The Antidumping Act of 1921

Traditionally, dumping occurs if a producer sells its goods in the United States at prices lower than those in its home market. The 1974 Trade Act, however, extended the law for cases in which home market prices are—for an extended period of time—below cost of production. For them, a "constructed value" (or "fair value") is compared with the U.S. price, consisting of direct and indirect average production costs plus an imputed 8 percent profit. If this value is above the U.S. price, dumping occurs. According to the GATT agreement, as implemented by the 1979 Trade Act, duties can be imposed to make up for the difference, but only if the imports cause "material" injury to the domestic industry.

An antidumping suit must be filed simultaneously with the Commerce Department and the International Trade Commission (ITC). The ITC determines if there is enough evidence of injury (preliminary injury test). If so, the Commerce Department must determine within defined time limits, first preliminarily, and then finally, the duties to be imposed. After the department's final decision, the ITC makes a conclusive injury determination. The Customs Office is then responsible for collecting the duties. Throughout the process, the office of the United States Trade Representative (USTR) is responsible for "policy oversight."

The Countervailing Duty Law

Section 303 of the Tariff Act of 1930 is meant to counteract a foreign government's subsidization of exports to the United States. Under GATT rules export subsidies are generally prohibited, but domestic subsidies are legitimate. If domestic subsidies spill over to exports and injure the industry of the importing country, countervailing measures (generally in the form of duties) can be imposed on the products. An expedited settlement process for such disputes was set up under the GATT.

According to the amendment of the 1979 Trade Act, the ITC must determine preliminary and final injury and the Commerce Department must calculate the amount of the alleged subsidies, that is, the countervailing duties. As for antidumping cases, the law sets precise time frames for this process. Although the law tries to define subsidy (bounty or grant), considerable discretion is left to the Commerce Department. According to Section 704(c) of the act, the department can suspend its investigation until 30 days before the final determination of countervailing duties is due if it can reach a negotiated settlement equally beneficial to the plaintiff. After that, countervailing duties can only be avoided if the plaintiff withdraws its suit or the ITC determines no injury.

All Commerce Department and ITC decisions can be appealed to the U.S. Court of International Trade, part of the federal court system, in New York.

Relief from Unfair Import Competition

Section 337 of the Tariff Act of 1930, as amended, declares unlawful "unfair methods of competition" (such as price fixing, predatory pricing, deceptive advertising, infringement of patents, and so on) that cause substantial injury to the domestic industry. Complaints must be filed with the ITC which, in case of violation, can embargo the articles and impose civil penalties. The president may, however for policy reasons, void the ITC's rulings.

Relief from Injury Caused by Fair Import Competition

Section 201 of the 1974 Trade Act, the so-called escape clause, provides for relief if an article is being imported into the United States in such increased quantities, that it is a substantial cause of serious injury to the domestic industry. If it finds injury, the ITC recommends a remedy to the president. The president, with advice from the USTR, can impose tariffs or quotas, negotiate orderly marketing agreements with other nations to limit their exports, or decide not to grant relief. If the president's decision differs from the ITC recommendations, Congress may override it.

Relief from Foreign Discrimination Against U.S. Commerce

Section 301 of the 1974 Trade Act authorizes the president to take all appropriate actions, including retaliation, against foreign restrictions that hinder U.S. commerce. The USTR administers investigations of such restrictions.

APPENDIX B

U.S. TRADE POLICY*

The international trading system was revolutionized after World War II, when global exports and imports far outpaced the growth in production of goods and services. From 1950 to 1980 the arithmetic sum of imports and exports rose from 8.4 percent of GNP to 21.2 percent for the United States, from 25.4 percent to 57.3 percent for West Germany, and from 20.1 percent to 31.2 percent for Japan.

The explosion of world trade can be largely attributed to strong U.S. advocacy of free trade. It was widely recognized that uncontrolled rounds of tariffs and countervailing tariffs (known as beggar-thy-neighbor policies) had significantly

---

*This section is excerpted from the note "International Trade" by Assistant Professor David Yoffie, 0-382-107.

contributed to the economic disaster of the 1930s. To avoid this, the United States constantly encouraged other countries to reduce tariffs and other barriers to trade.*

The United States was the driving force behind the General Agreement on Tariffs and Trade (GATT), which in 1947 largely set the stage for world trade expansion. After years of laborious bilateral negotiations to lower tariffs, President Kennedy, in the Trade Expansion Act of 1962, obtained the authority for multilateral trade negotiations from Congress and initiated the first round of GATT talks. This "Kennedy Round" was a resounding success. Duties on two-thirds of industrial countries' products were cut by 50 percent or more; average reductions on manufactures were about 33 percent.

The subsequent explosion in world trade, however, triggered more subtle protectionism as countries experienced problems in adapting to changing world markets and increasing interdependence. Authorized by the Trade Act of 1974, the United States initiated the Tokyo Round of Multilateral Trade Negotiations. By 1979 they had made substantial progress in limiting the impact of nontariff barriers, but as all participants seemed more interested in trade surpluses than a Ricardian world of maximum aggregate welfare, the vague, nonbinding, language left many questions for the 1980s.

Although the U.S. government could be regarded as the principal advocate of free trade, it frequently had to yield to protectionist demands from domestic industry which, supported by Congress, claimed to be injured by unfair competition (including voluntary restraint agreements in textiles and apparel, orderly marketing agreements for footwear and color televisions, and the multifiber agreement). One of the most powerful industries persistently claiming harm by unfair imports and demanding government action was the U.S. steel industry.

APPENDIX C

U.S. GOVERNMENT JURISDICTION OVER FOREIGN TRADE†

According to the U.S. Constitution, the basic authority and power to "regulate commerce with foreign nations" as well as to "pay and collect duties" is vested in Congress, which has, therefore, historically played a key role in foreign trade. Under the Trade Agreement Act of 1934, although not relinquishing its basic constitutional powers, Congress delegated to the president the authority to conduct tariff negotiations with other countries. Until the Trade Expansion Act of 1962, the State Department was largely responsible for these. Setting the stage for the Kennedy Round, Congress authorized a special representative for trade negotiations (STR) in the White House, responding to industry complaints that the State

*According to the theory of comparative advantage, all countries would benefit if every nation produced what it excelled at producing and traded it on a world market without barriers.

†This section is based on Congressional Research Service Report No. 81–193E.

Department emphasized foreign policy over domestic economic interest. In the 1974 Trade Act, which authorized U.S. participation in the Tokyo Round, the STR was elevated to cabinet level and equipped with a number of formal business and labor advisory committees. In the 1979 Trade Agreement Act, which implemented the results of the Tokyo Round, the office was further strengthened and renamed the United States Trade Representative (USTR). Its advisory committees (numbering 45 by 1982) were made permanent.

In addition, in 1979 responsibility for administering the antidumping and countervailing duty statutes was transferred to the Commerce Department from the Treasury Department, which was felt to be more interested in international monetary cooperation than enforcement of potentially disruptive legal actions. To ensure "objective treatment" of antidumping and countervailing duty suits, the act also provided judicial review of the decisions by the U.S. Court of International Trade.

In 1981, 25 executive branch departments and independent agencies were involved at some level in formulating and implementing U.S. foreign trade and investment policy. Some of the more relevant are outlined below.

Office of the United States Trade Representative

In 1979 the USTR was given "the lead role for representing the United States on trade matters abroad and for developing and coordinating the effective implementation of U.S. trade policy." The USTR is the principal adviser to the president (his or her office is located in the White House) on international trade policy and quasi-ex officio the foremost advocate of free trade. He or she is also supposed to coordinate development of U.S. trade policy.

The Commerce Department

The Commerce Department includes an undersecretary for international trade, who heads the International Trade Administration, set up by the secretary of commerce to promote world trade and strengthen the international trade and investment position of the United States. The department is also responsible for the Import Administration (which administers antidumping and countervailing duty laws) and the Export Administration (which oversees export controls and antiboycott provisions).

United States International Trade Commission

The ITC is an independent governmental agency with a wide range of international trade responsibilities that include advising the president on the domestic effects of trade agreements, determining injury to domestic industry alleged in antidumping and countervailing duty cases, and investigating unfair trade practices.

Other agencies with traditional interests in trade include the *Agriculture Department* (mainly dealing with promoting agricultural exports), the *State Department* (focusing on the foreign policy perspective), the *Treasury Department* (handling international monetary affairs), the *Justice Department* (together with the *Federal Trade Commission*, administering antitrust laws), and the *Labor Department* (administering Trade Adjustment Assistance Programs to workers).

ENDNOTES

1. Reagan-Bush Campaign Committee press release, September 16, 1980.
2. Testimony before the Senate Finance Subcommittee on Trade, March 24, 1982.
3. Report of Senate Steel Caucus Hearing, October 25, 1982.
4. American Iron and Steel Institute (AISI) annual reports.
5. Central Intelligence Agency, The Burgeoning LDC Steel Industry (Washington, D.C.: Government Printing Office, July 1979), and AISI.
6. Robert W. Crandall, *U.S. Steel Industry in Recurrent Crisis* (Washington, D.C.: Brookings Institution, 1981), 11.
7. Ibid., p. 72.
8. Ibid., p. 23.
9. *U.S. Steel News*, July 1982.
10. Hans Mueller and Hans van der Ven, "Perils in the Brussels-Washington Steel Pact of 1982," Vol. 5, no. 3, *The World Economy*, (London, 1982), p. 271.
11. Peter Marcus and and Karlis Kirsis, *The Steel Strategist No. 6* (New York: Paine Webber, 1982).
12. Larry Oppenheimer, *Steel Industry in Transition*, Congressional Budget Office Staff Working Paper (Washington, D.C.: Government Printing Office, 1982), p. 8.
13. Ibid., p. 2.
14. *Steel at the Crossroads, One Year Later* (Washington, D.C.: AISI, 1981).
15. Crandall, *U.S. Steel Industry*, p. 18.
16. Ibid., p. 91.
17. Ibid., p. 105.
18. Barry Eichengreen and Hans van der Ven, *United States Antidumping Policies: The Case of Steel* (Cambridge, Mass.: Bureau of Economic Research, November 1982), p. 6.
19. *Iron Age*, January 2, 1978.
20. *Newsweek*, February 20, 1978.
21. *The Economist*, May 18, 1981.
22. *American Metal Market*, November 6, 1981.
23. *Congressional Record*, 97th Congress, House 8635, November 19, 1981.
24. Ibid., House 8671, November 20, 1981.
25. Ibid., House 9054, December 9, 1981.
26. *The Economist*, December 19, 1981.
27. *American Metal Market*, March 30, 1982.
28. Ibid.
29. *Congressional Record*, 97th Congress, House, Vol. 128, no. 64, May 24, 1982.
30. *The Wall Street Journal*, January 12, 1982.
31. Ibid., June 9 and 10, 1982.
32. *American Metal Market*, June 15, 1982.
33. *The Wall Street Journal*, June 14, 1982.
34. *American Metal Market*, June 24, 1982.
35. Ibid., August 12, 1982.
36. Ibid., August 25, 1982.
37. *The Wall Street Journal*, August 30, 1982.
38. *The Boston Globe*, October 22, 1982.
39. *Business Week*, November 8, 1982.
40. *The Wall Street Journal*, October 22, 1982.

Exhibit 1 International Competitiveness of Steel, 1976 Versus 1981

		United States	Japan	West Germany	United Kingdom
Labor Productivity	1981	8.27	8.57	9.91	13.5
(work-hours per ton shipped)	1976–1981 annual % rate of improvement	1.2	3.4	3.3	7.3
Unit Labor Costs	1981	171.19	98.73	131.60	129.87
(dollars per ton shipped)	1976–1981 annual % rate of increase	9.8	6.7	4.4	5.4
Hourly employment costs	1981	20.70	11.52	13.28	9.62
(dollars)	1976–1981 annual % rate of increase	8.5	10.8	7.9	12.0
Steel employment costs (as %	1970	133	167	125	N/A
of all-manufacturing average)	1982	189	175	112	115
Capacity Utilization					
(net shipments as % of reported	1981	76.80	59.60	63.10	61.90
capability)	1976–1981 average	80.40	67.00	62.60	71.60
Break-even operating rate	1976–1980 average	73.2	56.5	60.5	111.2
Percentage yield	1976	71.00	74.00	74.00	72.00
(shipments/raw steel prod.)	1981	73.00	85.00	75.00	73.00
Iron cost	1976	42.71	35.22	36.17	35.82
($ per ton of steel shipped)	1981	70.86	54.75	49.02	60.14
Coal/coke cost	1976	42.68	53.76	58.85	55.05
($ per ton of steel shipped)	1981	56.08	65.06	82.23	97.45
Energy cost (excl. coke)	1976	22.47	25.69	28.66	26.96
($ per ton of steel shipped)	1981	59.07	50.57	47.34	84.02
Total pretax cost (% of U.S. costs on dollar basis)	1981	100	89	87	108
Final pretax profit	1976	2.45	15.15	16.06	31.03
(dollars per ton shipped)	1981	7.98	9.98	44.00	139.71
Marginal profit	1976	79.29	93.62	109.68	99.97
(dollars per extra ton shipped)	1981	137.07	197.49	127.46	93.53

Note: All measures based on a ctual operating rates of major producers.

Source: Based on information from *World Steel Dynamics* and American Iron and Steel Institute.

Exhibit 2 Financial Rations of Major Steel Producers, Selected Years 1972–1980 (%)

Steel sector results	1974					1977					1980					1972–1980 Average				
	U.S.	EEC	W. Ger.	U.K.	Japan	U.S.	EEC	W. Ger.	U.K.	Japan	U.S.	EEC	W. Ger.	U.K.	Japan	U.S.	EEC	W. Ger.	U.K.	Japan
Pretax income to sales	10.6	3.0	3.7	3.4	3.5	0.6	10.6	0.8	-17.4	1.1	0.2	-7.9	2.0	-22.4	7.4	3.8	-3.6	1.9	-8.5	3.8
Pretax income to assets	13.3	2.8	4.7	2.8	2.6	-0.6	7.2	0.8	-10.7	0.6	0.2	-6.4	2.2	-18.3	5.2	4.7	-2.5	2.1	-6.2	2.5
Operating profit to sales	15.5	14.1	11.6	12.0	16.6	5.3	2.2	9.7	-7.0	18.8	5.4	4.3	10.9	-11.8	23.1	9.3	8.1	10.6	1.3	19.6
Consolidated results*																				
Return on shareholders' equity	15.1	8.1	10.1	8.3	10.9	1.0	18.5	0.3	-28.5	3.9	8.5	-35.6	3.4	-101.2	16.0	7.5	-13.6	4.2	-46.5	9.8
Debt to shareholders' equity	39.9	149.5	95.5	106.5	379.1	56.9	228.2	99.4	134.1	549.2	52.0	216.2	111.8	147.5	337.6	49.4	180.4	98.5	125.0	420.7
Dividends to net income	26.0	43.4	53.3	9.8	60.5	325.6	2.2	519.5	0.0	127.8	32.6	-1.3	32.5	0.0	29.9	71.9	-146.2	104.5	4.6	86.9
Net income to sales	6.0	2.1	2.0	3.2	1.6	0.4	-7.4	0.1	-14.1	0.6	3.0	-7.8	0.6	-34.5	2.9	3.2	-3.4	0.9	-13.7	1.7
Labor costs to sales	32.1	24.1	24.2	30.7	12.4	35.6	30.2	28.3	34.1	14.2	36.1	28.0	27.5	37.7	12.7	35.5	28.1	27.8	33.9	13.0
Capital outlays to sales	5.5	7.3	4.3	13.8	12.7	7.1	7.1	5.4	15.1	9.8	6.2	5.6	5.3	6.3	5.5	6.5	8.9	5.8	13.3	11.2

*Includes nonsteel activities of steel producers.
Source: Based on data provided by *World Steel Dynamics* (for 15 companies in the United States, 8 companies in Japan, 15 companies in the EEC, 6 companies in West Germany, and 1 company in the United Kingdom).

Exhibit 3 Steel Prices, 1977–1982

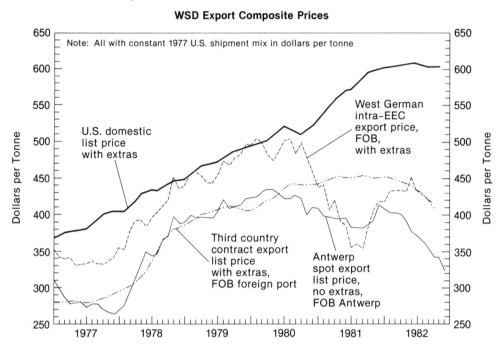

WSD Export Composite Prices

Note: All with constant 1977 U.S. shipment mix in dollars per tonne

U.S. domestic list price with extras

West German intra-EEC export price, FOB, with extras

Third country contract export list price with extras, FOB foreign port

Antwerp spot export list price, no extras, FOB Antwerp

Dollars per Tonne

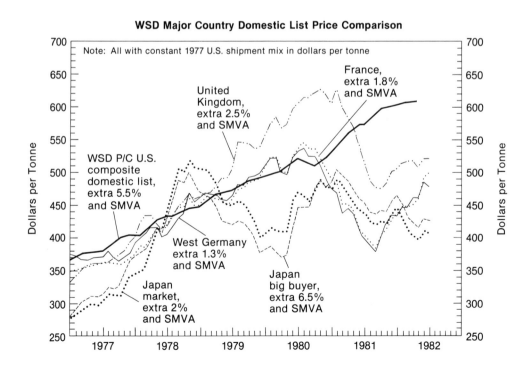

WSD Major Country Domestic List Price Comparison

Note: All with constant 1977 U.S. shipment mix in dollars per tonne

France, extra 1.8% and SMVA

United Kingdom, extra 2.5% and SMVA

WSD P/C U.S. composite domestic list, extra 5.5% and SMVA

West Germany extra 1.3% and SMVA

Japan market, extra 2% and SMVA

Japan big buyer, extra 6.5% and SMVA

Dollars per Tonne

Exhibit 4   Steel Investment Expenditures at Constant Dollar Prices for Alternate Years, 1970–1980, in the United States, European Community, and Japan (in billions of U.S. dollar equivalents, 1970 prices)

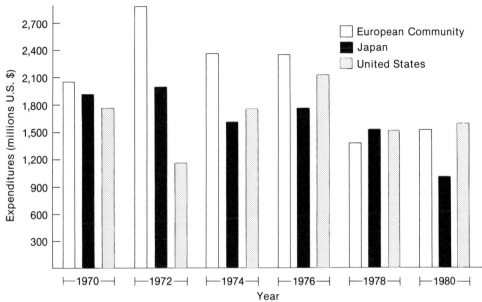

Source: Organization for Economic Cooperation and Development.

The Relative Attractiveness of Investment:
Replacement Capacity Versus Expansion Capacity

Initial Price/Cost Relationship

Price/ton	= $500
Fixed costs/ton	= $150
Operating costs/ton	= $300
Gross profit	= $ 50
Return on sales	= 10%

Assume that a project costs $100 million and takes three years to build. It lasts for 25 years and reduces operating costs by $25 per ton. The benefits of the project will differ greatly, depending on whether it provides replacement or incremental tonnage.

Effects of New Technology on Overall Costs

If Replacement		50% Incremental Tonnage
$500	Price/ton	$500
$150	Fixed costs/ton	$75
$275	Operating costs/ton	$275
$75	Gross profit/ton	$150
15%	Return on sales	30%
$45.8 million	Present value of investment (gross, at a 15% interest rate)	$355.9 million
23%	Internal rate of return (gross)	51%
13%	Internal rate of return (net)	30%

*Assuming that sufficient capacity exists in other facilities to permit expansion without major capital expenditures and/or that the investment provides significant yield improvements.

Exhibit 5   Steel Imports into United States, 1975–1982 (thousands of net tons)

Year	Japan	EEC	Canada	Other	Total		Import % of Apparent Supply	
			Imports					
1975	5,844	4,118	1,009	1,041	12,012		13.5	
1976	7,984	3,188	1,304	1,809	14,285		14.1	
1977	7,820	6,833	1,892	2,762	19,307		17.8	
1978	6,487	7,463	2,364	4,821	21,135		18.1	
1979	6,336	5,405	2,354	3,423	17,158		15.2	
1980	6,005	3,887	2,368	3,235	15,495		16.3	
1981	6,220	6,482	2,899	4,297	19,898		19.1	
1982	5,185	5,597	1,844	4,037	16,663		22.3	
						Year to Date		**Year to Date**
1981								
Jan.	403	298	235	346	1,281	—	14.8	—
Feb.	434	264	283	253	1,234	2,515	14.7	14.7
Mar.	328	238	293	283	1,142	3,657	12.3	13.9
Apr.	513	568	329	351	1,761	5,418	18.4	15.1
May	606	513	291	362	1,722	7,191	18.8	15.8
June	562	524	268	311	1,665	8,856	17.5	16.1
July	464	531	292	376	1,663	10,519	19.4	16.6
Aug.	705	857	209	455	2,226	12,745	24.6	17.6
Sept.	544	648	180	376	1,748	14,493	20.4	17.8
Oct.	501	544	218	454	1,872	16.364	22.4	18.3
Nov.	642	724	174	381	1,921	18,285	25.8	18.8
Dec.	517	618	127	351	1,613	19,898	22.9	19.1
1982								
Jan.	581	744	164	480	1,969	—	26.6	—
Feb.	682	411	145	363	1,600	3,569	23.2	25.0
Mar.	418	372	186	360	1,336	4,905	18.5	22.8
Apr.	354	319	141	215	1,029	5,934	16.2	21.3
May	589	564	157	386	1,696	7,630	25.5	22.1
June	455	747	184	397	1,784	9,413	25.6	22.6
July	359	395	135	224	1,113	10,526	20.7	22.4
Aug.	531	364	155	400	1,451	11,977	24.1	22.6
Sept.	353	386	177	274	1,191	13,168	20.6	22.4
Oct.	314	346	153	332	1,146	14,314	21.5	22.3
Nov.	274	493	151	341	1,258	15,572	24.0	22.4
Dec.	273	455	96	267	1,090	16,663	20.9	22.3

Source: American Iron and Steel Institute

Mastering the Market: Japanese Government Targeting of the Computer Industry*

To explore how government policies influence corporate decisions in an industry, I have analyzed the effects of Japan's persistent efforts to nurture a computer industry. Computers is a useful case for several reasons. Since the government viewed it as strategic to long-term economic growth, intervention has been extensive, providing ample opportunity to evaluate the ways that the Ministry of International Trade and Industry (MITI), which creates and implements Japan's industrial policies, has influenced private sector decisions in the computer industry.

The Japanese computer industry's development has been remarkable by any measure. Enormous capital requirements and the rapid obsolescence of products make the computer industry among the most difficult industries to enter. With IBM holding a 70 percent share of the world computer market in the early 1960s, any firm interested in moving into the computer field faced tremendous odds. General Electric and RCA both gave up in the early 1970s. Honeywell recently broke off its computer division and merged it into Honeywell Bull, a joint venture with NEC of Japan and Machine Bull of France; Sperry and Burroughs have merged in an effort to survive in the competitive market. European companies, despite an early lead, have also struggled to stay competitive.

The United States, with the world's largest computer market, the most advanced computer scientists, and heavy aid from the Defense Department, has always maintained a large lead over the rest of the world in the computer field. Yet Japan, with little defense spending and far behind the United States in technical computer training, has managed to sustain three major computer companies and several small ones. Only in Japan have local firms been able to roll back IBM's market share to below 30 percent. Six years ago, Fujitsu became the first firm to overtake IBM in a national market. While there is no danger that Japanese firms will take over the world mainframe computer market in the foreseeable future, they have steadily increased their share. Fujitsu, once a tiny communications maker, supplies mainframes and supercomputers to ICL of Britain, Siemens of Germany, and Amdahl of the United States; Hitachi exports mainframes to BASF of Germany and National Advanced Systems of the United States; NEC, once an importer of Honeywell technology, has been supplying technology and mainframes to Honey-

*Excerpted from an article with the same title by Marie Anchordoguy, Research Fellow, Harvard Business School. *International Organization* Vol. 43, no. 3 (Summer 1988). ©1988 by the World Peace Foundation and the Massachusetts Institute of Technology. Reprinted with permission from MIT Press.

well for the past five years and is the primary supplier of technology for the recently established joint venture between Honeywell, NEC, and France's Machine Bull.

What were the key elements in the development of Japan's computer industry? I suggest that the government, through various microeconomic policies, created a market environment conducive to the industry's development. More specifically, by using protection and promotion policies to reduce the costs and risks of operating in the computer market and to limit the number of players in each market segment, the government altered profit expectations in ways that provided firms with market incentives to enter the industry, increase investment, improve quality and technology, and reduce costs. They primarily used heavy protectionism, a quasi-governmental computer rental company, substantial financial assistance, and consolidation of the industry in government-sponsored cooperative R&D projects.

PROTECTIONISM

MITI had its heaviest hand in the computer market in the 1960s, when it used powerful protectionist policies to keep out foreign firms and computers. In 1960, when the government and businesses agreed to nurture a domestic industry, the government raised the tariff on computers from 15 to 25 percent.[1] Even more effective than tariffs were import quotas, which were easy to enforce because importing a computer required an import license from MITI. "Why do you have to use a foreign computer?" was the greeting users faced when they came to MITI to apply for a computer import. Pressure tactics were not uncommon. "There were even cases when we had to make it compulsory for them to change their minds from a foreign to a domestic computer," recalls MITI's Hiramatsu Morihiko, who became known as the "Devil Hiramatsu."[2]

Some firms complained bitterly about policies that forced them to use low-quality, unreliable domestic computers. MITI's pressure was particularly resented in the 1960s, when domestic machines were substantially inferior to their foreign counterparts. In 1961, responding to MITI pressure to buy domestic machines, a group of firms explained that they were sorry to apply for imports but they did not want to be the guinea pigs for domestic computer makers.[3] Other firms criticized MITI policy, saying that domestic computers were "obstructions to the promotion of rationalization efficiency."[4]

Government institutions were also expected to buy domestic machines, although exceptions were made, such as for Japan Telegraph and Telephone Company (NTT), when inferior domestic machines would have hindered the nation's communications system. Dependence on the Ministry of Finance for funds and interdependence with other government agencies also made it very difficult for MITI to reject all government import requests. Still, such approvals were exceptions; the government clearly favored domestic machines. In 1982, 91 percent of the computers used by the government were domestic machines, 9 percent foreign; in comparison 56 percent of all the computers in use in Japan at the time were domestic machines, 44 percent were foreign.[5] Favoritism toward domestic machines is all the more dramatic because the government primarily used very large computers, a market that even today is dominated by IBM. The government provided a huge market for domestic makers: the government purchased or rented 25 percent of all domestic computers during the 1960s and 1970s; by the early 1980s, this share had increased to 30 percent.[6]

In addition to limiting imports, several laws gave the Japanese government tight control over foreign investment in the Japanese market. These laws allowed the government to use access to the Japanese market as leverage for acquiring foreign technology cheaply and for pressuring foreign companies to make joint ventures with Japanese companies.

The most dramatic example of government control over a foreign computer company was MITI's web of regulations over IBM, which first entered Japan in 1937 as the Japan Watson Tōkei Kikai Company. In 1949, the company was reestablished as Nihon (Japan) International Business Machines. This was just one year before the Foreign Capital Law was enacted, enabling IBM Japan to avoid being forced by Japanese law to join hands with a Japanese firm.[7] Still, however, laws prevented IBM from producing in Japan or repatriating earnings. MITI used these laws in the late 1950s to obstruct IBM's attempts to supply the capital and technology IBM Japan needed to produce in Japan.[8] But blocking IBM Japan from producing in Japan did not stop Japanese firms from flooding MITI with import applications for IBM's very popular 1401 computer. Heavy demand for the foreign machine made the Japanese makers and the government keenly aware of the giant gap between domestic and IBM machines.

The Japanese government faced a dilemma: Japan could not develop a computer industry without IBM's basic patents, but IBM would not license its patents unless it was given the right to produce in Japan. While Japan needed the patents, it did not want to allow IBM to produce in Japan because it would reduce its control of IBM's sales. To acquire the patents while giving in as little as possible to IBM's demands for local production, long and sometimes bitter negotiations took place between IBM and MITI, which represented the firms.

In 1960, when J.W. Birkenstock of IBM requested permission to produce in Japan and remit profits to its U.S. parent in exchange for giving Japanese companies access to IBM patents, Hiramatsu Morihiko of MITI demanded that IBM, in addition, make a joint venture with a Japanese firm.[9] But Birkenstock did not budge; in fact, he got tougher announcing that IBM would not give access to its patents unless MITI allowed IBM Japan to manufacture its popular 1401 small computer in Japan. Angry about the introduction of a new condition, MITI abruptly broke off the negotiations. MITI knew, however, that without IBM's patents, domestic firms could not produce computers. Sabashi Shigeru, head of MITI's Heavy Industries Bureau, finally agreed to allow IBM to produce in Japan, but politely warned IBM not to go too far: "Japanese makers are mosquitoes, IBM is an elephant. I would appreciate it if IBM does not do anything to crush the mosquito under its feet."[10]

Sabashi not only got the patents; IBM also reduced the royalty cost by 20 percent from what had originally been negotiated.[11] The makers paid IBM a 5 percent royalty of sales on systems and machines and 1 percent on parts. MITI let

IBM Japan pay its parent 10 percent of sales in royalties despite strict foreign exchange regulations that restricted such large transfers.[12] MITI made sure IBM's technology was spread widely; 15 firms signed the five-year contract. Although the contract went into effect January 1, 1961, the government did not allow IBM Japan to start production until 1963. Moreover, MITI kept its strings tightly wrapped around IBM by placing conditions on the volume it exported and the type of machines it sold in Japan.[13] MITI was particularly concerned that IBM Japan not produce small- and medium-scale machines that would, free from the high tariff on imports, threaten the sales of domestic ones.[14] IBM generally cooperated. MITI's Hiramatsu praised IBM's cooperation with the Japanese government: "Without using any political power, it (IBM) is trying to tie a loyal relationship with MITI."[15]

Because they needed IBM patents, the Japanese government could not force IBM to make a joint venture with a local firm, but it succeeded in doing so with other U.S. makers. Sperry Rand, which makes UNIVAC computers, was forced to make a joint venture with Oki to gain access to the Japanese computer market. In this way, Japanese firms gained relatively easy and cheap access to foreign technology, machinery, and R&D. By the mid-1960s, all the Japanese computer firms except Fujitsu had made technological licensing agreements with foreign firms: Hitachi with RCA, Toshiba with General Electric, Mitsubishi with TRW, and NEC with Honeywell.

Limiting imports and foreign investment shifted demand to domestic machines, which in turn stimulated supply. By raising the prices of foreign machines, protectionism helped the firms price lower than their foreign counterparts. Indeed, despite inferior computers, dependence on imports dropped from 80 percent in 1959 to 20 percent by 1968;[16] sales of foreign computers declined from 93 percent in 1958 to 42.5 percent by 1969.[17] By the late 1960s, foreign firms only dominated the large-scale computer market. The foreign share increased in the early 1970s when IBM introduced a new, far more advanced series of computers, but by late 1975, when the market was officially liberalized and the Japanese started to bring out machines competitive with IBM's, the foreign share was whittled down to about 44 percent of the market; the foreign share has decreased gradually up to the present to about 40 percent (see Table 1).

One might expect that this heavy government protection would lead to gross inefficiency and technological sluggishness. In the short run, there certainly were inefficiencies, and Japanese users sometimes complained in the 1960s about being forced to use inferior domestic computers. But protectionism did not lead to sluggish growth in the long run. A key reason is because, while domestic companies were buffered from foreign firms, they were not protected from one another; indeed, the government promoted competition among several domestic firms. Moreover, the government constantly compared Japanese machines to those of IBM. With the government using IBM as a threat to domestic firms, coupled with foreign pressure for Japan to open up its high-technology markets, the companies realized that without competitive machines, they would not be able to survive in the long run.

Table 1 Japanese and Foreign Shares of the Japanese Computer Market, 1958.nd1982 (in billions of yen, %)

Year[a]		1958	1959	1960	1961	1962	1963	1964	1965	1966	1967	1968
Japanese	Amount	0.07	0.52	1.83	2.42	7.35	12.87	17.85	26.89	35.81	51.25	91.23
	Growth (%)	—	619.3	250.6	32.6	203.3	75.1	38.7	50.7	33.2	43.1	78.0
	Market share (%)	7	21.5	27.3	18.3	33.2	29.7	42.8	52.2	53.6	47.2	56.5
Foreign (primarily IBM)	Amount	0.94	1.9	4.87	10.85	14.76	30.44	23.82	24.63	31.01	57.4	70.14
	Growth (%)	—	102.6	156	122.7	36	106	(-21.9)	3.4	25.9	85.1	21.8
	Market share (%)	93	78.5	72.7	81.7	66.8	70.3	57.2	47.8	46.4	52.8	43.5
Total	Amount	1.01	2.42	6.7	13.27	22.11	43.31	41.6	51.52	66.82	108.7	161.4
	Growth (%)	—	139.5	176.3	98.1	66.6	95.9	(-3.9)	23.7	29.7	62.6	48.3
	Market share (%)	100	100	100	100	100	100	100	100	100	100	100

Year[a]		1969	1970	1971	1972	1973	1974	1975	1976	1977	1978	1979	1980	1981	1982
Japanese	Amount	122.0	197.4	206	222.7	271.4	310.3	342.7	415.1	882.8	970	1,076.8	1,211.5	1,372	1,563.4
	Growth (%)	33.7	61.8	4.3	8.1	21.9	14.3	10.4	21.1	—	9.9	11	12.5	13.3	14
	Market share (%)	57.5	60	59	53	51	48	56	57	54.2	52.1	53	52.5	54.8	55.9
Foreign (primarily IBM)	Amount	90.4	133.5	144.1	196	256.9	330.6	271.3	316.4	745.1	890	953.2	1,099.2	1,134.1	1,233.4
	Growth (%)	28.8	47.8	7.9	36	31	28.6	(-17.9)	16.6	—	19.5	7.1	15.3	3.2	8.8
	Market share (%)	42.5	40	41	47	49	52	44	43	45.8	47.9	47	47.5	45.2	44.1
Total	Amount	212.4	330.9	350.1	418.7	528.3	640.9	614	731.5	1,628	1,860	2,030	2,310.3	2,506.1	2,796.8
	Growth (%)	31.6	55.8	5.8	19.6	26.2	21.3	(-4.2)	19.1	—	14.3	9.1	13.8	8.5	11.6
	Market share (%)	100	100	100	100	100	100	100	100	100	100	100	100	100	100

a 1958–1976: Share of annual deliveries (rental/purchase) of general purpose computers; 1977–1982: share of installed base.

Source: JECC Kompyūtā Nōto (JECC Computer Notes), 1979, pp. 10–11; Kompyūtopia (Computopia), January 1981, 1983, and other January issues.

Note: Some discrepanices may occur due to rounding.

THE JAPAN ELECTRONIC COMPUTER COMPANY

Despite the importance of protectionism in allowing MITI to bargain for the necessary patents and to control foreign imports and investment, these policies alone would not nurture a domestic industry. A key problem was that to compete with IBM, which was renting its machines, the Japanese also needed to offer rentals; to rent, they needed capital. Japanese users could not afford to buy Japanese computers, yet Japanese computer firms could not afford to rent them.

Renting computers is costly and risky. It not only involves huge amounts of capital to finance rentals, but also the risk that users may trade in a computer after a short time for a newer model. Indeed, the huge sum of capital needed to rent computers and invest heavily in R&D is a major barrier to entering the computer industry. To reduce this barrier, MITI helped establish the Japan Electronic Computer Company (JECC) in 1961. With no sales division, only a couple hundred employees, and profits of, at best $1–2 million a year, it is not surprising that few Japanese have ever heard of JECC. Yet this quasi-private computer rental company played a critical role in nurturing the industry's development. To the all-star team of Japanese computer makers that jointly owned JECC—Hitachi, Fugitsu, NEC, Mitsubishi, Toshiba, and Oki—the company served as a funnel for a generous flow of government low-interest loans. Between 1961 and 1981, the government channeled about $2 billion in loans into JECC to help the company buy computers from member firms and rent them to the public for low monthly fees.[18] Through JECC, the makers were able to borrow funds from banks to which they would not otherwise have had access.[19] For MITI, which placed its retired officials into top management positions at JECC, the rental company provided an institution through which to guide the industry. Through JECC, MITI quelled price wars and stimulated the demand and supply of domestic computers.

Only seven companies joined JECC even though 15 had made contracts to use IBM's basic patents. A MITI committee of people from government, industry, and academia decided that success in the computer industry would require huge sums of money—amounts that only the seven large and experienced electric and telecommunications firms could generate.[20] The JECC system was set up to work as follows: when a user asked to rent a computer, JECC purchased it from the maker and rented it to the user at a monthly rate decided by JECC; the rental rate could not be changed.[21] Users were required to keep a computer at least 15 months. Afterward they could trade it in for a new one without penalty. When a computer was returned, the maker had to buy it back from JECC at the remaining book value.

One of JECC's major functions was to enlarge the market for domestic computers by offering them at low monthly rental fees. In 1960, the year before JECC's establishment, only 4 percent of Japanese computers were rented; within two years, this had jumped to 46 percent and by 1965, to 78 percent.[22] The market for domestic machines grew much faster than that for foreign machines, even though foreign computers were considered far better than Japanese ones until the mid-1970s.[23] With overall growth of 67 percent in computer sales from 1961 to 1962, domestic makers enjoyed a 203 percent increase, while foreign firms increased only 36 percent. By 1965, the Japanese firms overtook foreign firms, increasing sales 51 percent to gain a 52.2 percent share of the domestic market. That same year, foreign firms' sales grew by a mere 3.4 percent to 24.6 billion yen; they watched their share slide under the 50 percent mark for the first time (see Table 1).

JECC not only stimulated the demand and supply of domestic computers, it also funneled huge amounts of relatively invisible government funds to the firms. Since JECC carried the burden of financing rentals, the computer firms did not need to acquire large loans to provide rentals themselves. JECC also gave them an immediate return on investment; if the firms had had to finance their own rentals, they would have received their return in small monthly payments spread over 3.7 years per machine.[24] In the meantime, they would have had to provide financing for the user. Receiving their return immediately through JECC not only provided the companies with vital up-front cash, it also enabled them to focus their scarce resources on production, technology, quality, and cost. JECC accelerated the market forces driving the development of low-cost, technologically sophisticated computers.

While it is impossible to calculate definitively the importance of JECC to the firms, an estimate suggests that they received substantial benefits. By receiving their return in advance through JECC, the firms got the benefit of $269.44 million in up-front cash in the period 1961–1969 and $495 million from 1970–1981.[25] This up-front cash—an interest-free loan—represented a subsidy of $22.5 million in the 1961–1969 period and $45.12 million from 1970 to 1981.[26] Low-interest JDB loans to JECC also provided the computer makers with a subsidy of $178.2 million during the 1961–1981 period.[27]

While absolute numbers are important, it is the amounts relative to the firms' other resources that help us more critically evaluate their importance to the firms. From 1961 to 1969, the firms would have had a cash flow of 120.3 billion yen if they had run their own rental system, compared to the flow of 217.3 billion yen they received under the JECC system.[28] With only 120.3 billion yen, they would have had difficulty renting their own computers in addition to investing 103.9 billion yen in R&D and plant and equipment during the 1960s. A mere 16.4 billion yen would have remained to cover production and overhead cost.

The real question, however, is whether the firms could have acquired enough loans from private sources to finance their own rentals, and, if they could have, whether they would have been willing to invest heavily in computers. While it cannot be proved, the evidence suggests that it would have been very difficult, if not impossible, for the firms to have gotten enough loans, with the possible exception of Hitachi. Indeed, even the government-backed JECC found it difficult to attract enough funds from private banks. In the early 1960s, private banks were only willing to match JDB loans to JECC; later, the JDB supplied about 40 percent of the loans, private banks 60 percent. But each bank only lent a small amount to JECC. A high-ranking JDB official explained that, in order to get private banks to lend to JECC in the 1960s, the JDB had to guarantee the loans.[29]

Since banks required a JDB guarantee to induce them to lend to the government-backed JECC in the 1960s, it is highly unlikely that they would have made the necessary loans to the computer firms, especially since such loans would have tightly pinched the firms' finances. JECC borrowed a total of 140.4 billion yen from 1961 to 1969;[30] in comparison, the industry as a whole only invested a total of 103.9 billion yen in plant and equipment and R&D during this period. Thus, to rent their computers during the 1960s, the firms would have needed a sum of money more than the amount they were already investing in R&D and plant and equipment. It is highly improbable that they could have borrowed that much money, and, even if they could, that they would have been willing to invest that much in a computer rental system. Indeed, one of JECC's major functions was to manipulate the market so that the firms would view entry as profitable in the long run. Without JECC and its government backing, it is highly unlikely that they would have entered; if they had, they, like RCA and GE, would have been under heavy pressure to withdraw from the market.

JECC's financial backing was undoubtedly critical to the firms. But direct financial benefits were not the only way that JECC assisted the firms. By acting as the manager of a price cartel, JECC assured the firms a reasonable return on their machines. This price cartel was particularly important in the early years when the firms were already selling at a loss to compete with IBM and to promote the diffusion of domestic machines. As the computer makers became more competitive, JECC gradually reduced, in relative terms, its support of the industry and shifted the burden to the private sector's shoulders. In the 1960s, 65 percent of the domestic computers were rented through JECC; this dipped to about 30 percent of the machines in the 1970s and only 11 percent by the early 1980s.[31]

One might suspect that the computer companies used JECC as a dumping ground for computers they could not sell on the open market. But the government only allowed JECC to buy computers that users wanted to rent. There was a direct link to the market; if no one applied to rent a computer JECC did not buy it. Those with the best machines got the most benefit from JECC.

GOVERNMENTAL FINANCIAL ASSISTANCE

Protectionism and JECC were key ingredients to nurturing a domestic computer industry. But the firms needed funds so that they could invest heavily to make better computers. A variety of subsidies, low-interest loans, tax benefits, and loan guarantees lowered costs and risks and raised profit expectations in the computer industry, thereby inducing increased investment in R&D and plant and equipment.

Contrary to the conclusions of some studies of Japan's industrial policy,[32] I found that government financial aid to the computer industry was relatively large in proportion to what the firms were investing. From 1961 through 1969, estimated subsidies and tax benefits ($132.6 million) were equivalent to 46 percent of what the private sector was investing in R&D and plant and equipment; if we include government loans, total aid ($542.8 million) was equal to 188 percent of what the firms were investing; indeed, the government was also giving loans for use as working capital. From 1970 to 1975, subsidies and tax benefits ($636.55 million) were equivalent to 57 percent of what the firms were investing, and with government loans, total aid ($1.8 billion) was 169 percent the firms' investment.

From 1976 to 1981, subsidies and tax benefits ($10.3 billion) declined to 25.2 percent of what the firms were investing, but with government loans, aid ($3.74 billion) was still equal to 91.6 percent of what the firms were investing.

In addition to analyzing the absolute and relative amount of aid, we must also look at the context in which the aid was given. Aid was particularly critical in periods following an IBM announcement of a new computer. During these periods, MITI would group the firms together in cooperative R&D projects to develop machines to compete with IBM's new models. In the early 1970s, for example, IBM came out with its 370 series, which had several times the power of Japanese computers at the time. The IBM 370 shocked the world computer market and led to the withdrawal of RCA and GE from the industry. The Japanese were particularly shocked because the 370 was introduced before they had even finished an R&D project to develop a machine to match IBM's earlier computer series. Moreover, the oil shock and sharp revaluations of the yen in the early 1970s had plunged the Japanese economy into a recession, and the United States was pressuring Japan to open up its computer market. The introduction of the 370 at the time threatened to destroy Japan's computer industry once and for all.

The firms knew this and would not have continued to pour resources into such a risky venture without some assurance of support and protection. MITI stepped in with $213 million for the "New Series" project to build machines that would counter IBM's 370 series. The money was contingent on the six computer firms consolidating into three groups. The government hoped that with groups focusing on different sizes of computers, the industry would be able to compete with IBM's full line of computers, even though no single firm could have done so.

Some would argue that, by U.S. standards, $213 million was a small amount. But it was a relatively large amount for the Japanese companies—equivalent to 30 percent of what they invested in R&D for computers themselves during that same period.[35] Moreover, it was concentrated on a high-risk research project that the firms were unlikely, and perhaps unable, to undertake on their own, although it was nonetheless critical to their survival. As one former high-level MITI official explained: "Government financial aid in the seventies was critical to the firms' survival...the firms cooperated in the New Series Project because of the fear of bankruptcy."[34] Kobayashi Taiyū, Fujitsu's chairman, also attributed the survival of the Japanese industry at this critical juncture to government subsidies for cooperative R&D.[35] Indeed, the infusion of government aid helped the industry develop machines to counter the IBM 370 series, bringing them neck-to-neck with IBM in computer hardware. When the IBM 370 was introduced in 1970–1971, the foreign share of the Japanese market increased until the results of the "New Series" project started coming out in 1975; then the Japanese share rose (see Table 1).

The impact of government aid on a firm during this risky period is shown by comparing government aid to Fujitsu in 1975 with its profits and investment that year. A conservative estimate is that Fujitsu received $32.59 million in government subsidies and tax benefits in 1975, equivalent to 36 percent of what Fujitsu invested in R&D and plant and equipment in the computer industry that year. Including low-interest government loans of $75.25 million to Fujitsu that year, total government benefits were equal to the total of Fujitsu's investment in plant and equipment and

R&D that year and half of its profits. This tremendous amount of aid helped Fujitsu maintain its computer operations during this very risky period.

NTT, a government monopoly until April 1985 and still under government control, also funneled large, but relatively invisible, sums of money into the computer industry. Its huge R&D and procurement budgets provide heavy support to Hitachi, NEC, Fujitsu, and Oki. As the fields of computers and data communications started to blur in the late 1960s and early 1970s, NTT channeled profits from its telephone operations into data communications R&D. Most of the funds were consigned to Fujitsu, Hitachi, and NEC—the same firms that MITI consistently promoted. By favoring these firms, NTT lowered the barriers for their entry into the field and substantially reduced their costs and risks of operating in the industry.

Honoki Minoru, director of NTT's data communications division, explained why NTT got into the field of computers and data communication:

> Behind NTT's aggressive entry into data communication, was, frankly, a view of it as a policy to counter IBM. If our computer makers had only been a bit stronger, it would have been okay for NTT not to do the DIPS Project (a cooperative project among NTT, Fujitsu, Hitachi, and NEC to develop computers for data communications use). But five or six years ago, our national (computer) technology and IBM's were on different levels. Because of this, NTT had to take the lead and do it (develop computers for use in data communications). Also, with regard to liberalization of communications circuits, the reason was the same. The reason we hesitated for many years was because we were waiting until domestic technology got up to that (IBM's) level.[36]

Despite its archrivalry with the Ministry of Post and Telecommunications (MPT), which supervises NTT, MITI cooperated with the MPT to gain more aid for the computer industry.[37] Indeed, while MITI could not get as much money from the Ministry of Finance (MOF) as it wanted for the industry, NTT was a gold mine, flush with funds from high-priced telephone services. As an "independent" entity, NTT was relatively free to subsidize data communications with profits from telephones. NTT also received other government funds annually. For example, from 1964–1971 NTT received $436.1 million in low-interest loans from the FILP budget—largely composed of citizens' savings in post office accounts— and $1.4 billion in grants from the general budget.[38]

NTT's dependence on private firms for all of its equipment and much of its R&D gave those firms in the "NTT family" a guarantee of substantial R&D grants and heavy procurement of their products. NEC's president Kobayashi Kōji said:

> ...if we are to start doing an on-line information service, it will take a substantial amount of money, so if a large firm like NTT doesn't start it for us...it cannot be done...so I want NTT to put all its power into it for us and invest in it. I look forward to NTT doing the same as America's Department of Defense.[39]

Indeed, firms in the so-called "NTT family" not only got NTT to finance a substantial part of their research, they also, by producing what NTT wanted, were essentially guaranteed a large part of the NTT market, which totaled approximately $13.3 billion from 1965–1975.[40] As of 1968, 70 percent of all NTT purchases were from Fujitsu, NEC, Oki, and Hitachi; NTT bought 60 percent of each of these firms' telecommunications production.[41] NTT spent 170 billion yen ($472.2 million) on data communications over the five-year period starting in 1968.[42]

One might suspect that the funds the firms received through NTT, JECC, and MITI were used to support inefficient operations. While the firms' operations were clearly inefficient in the early years, aid was generally given in ways that encouraged efficiency over the long run. Firms often had to match subsidies. Tax benefits increased with marginal increases in investment. Strings were tightly attached to subsidies and loans; they had to be used for specific R&D or machinery. Most important, aid was closely tied to results. A firm that was not competitive could expect to be cut off from future subsidized R&D.

COOPERATIVE RESEARCH PROJECTS

Protectionism, JECC, and financial aid were all critical to creating an environment for computer industry growth, but the firms were far behind IBM when they launched their computer efforts and would never catch up without rapidly improving their technology. The government helped narrow the technological gap by using cooperative projects to reduce redundant research, to accelerate technological advancement, and to encourage the firms to specialize so that they could achieve the economies of scale necessary to compete with IBM. "Cooperation" usually meant that labor was divided, with resulting patents open to all participants at low cost. In some cases, firms took different approaches to the same problem; in a few cases, firms researched the same topic together.

In the first major government–private sector computer research project, called "1966 Super High-Performance Computer Project," the government concentrated the entire computer industry on the development of one system: the prototype of a machine to counter IBM's 360 series, which was the world's first third-generation computer, characterized by integrated circuits, a series of compatible machines ranging from small to large, and a buffer memory. A 12 billion yen ($33.33 million) grant supported the project, which continued until 1972. While 12 billion yen may seem like a small amount today, it was relatively large then. Indeed, the firms had only invested 11.2 billion yen ($31.11 million) of their own funds on R&D related to computers between 1961 and 1965.[43]

Hitachi, Fujitsu, and NEC researched mainframe architecture and integrated circuits; Mitsubishi, Toshiba, and Oki were to work on peripheral equipment. Each firm worked separately. Hitachi, by submitting the best design proposal, was made the leader of the project and given responsibility for creating the final prototype computer. The government, by fully funding the project, owned the resulting patents, which it offered at low cost to participating firms.

While the project fell short of its goals (the resulting prototype did not match IBM's most advanced 360 series models, let alone the advanced 370 series of computers IBM announced in the early 1970s), the effort nonetheless helped the industry make critical technological advances in integrated circuits, buffer memories, and mainframe architecture. It also established a standard for the interface between peripherals and mainframes.[44] Hitachi, NEC, and Fujitsu incorporated these advances in their subsequent mainframe computers,[45] which, while not competitive with IBM, sold well because of import restrictions and government procurement; the results were also used in a subsequent NTT project to develop computers for use in data communications.[46]

In the early 1970s, when IBM introduced its revolutionary 370 series, the Japanese government and industry panicked. IBM was pulling even further ahead of the Japanese. While RCA and GE withdrew from the computer industry after the IBM announcement, the Japanese took drastic measures to survive. MITI tried to persuade the six firms to merge into two or three. The Ministry of Finance also pushed for mergers. According to one MOF official, "If we are going to promote the computer industry, six firms should not be selfishly competing; we should reduce the industry to about three firms in order to gain international competitiveness."[47] But the firms were not willing to merge. In the end, they compromised and reorganized into three groups for the "New Series" project to develop computers to counter IBM's new series.

Fujitsu vice president Kiyomiya Hiro explained the importance of cooperation between Fujitsu and Hitachi in the "New Series" project to his employees:

> To explain our cooperation with Hitachi, the important thing is "cooperation and competition." Frankly speaking, if we do not do this, we cannot confront our American competitors. For example, if Japanese makers in the domestic market did not cooperate and only competed, before we knew it, we would be taken over by the American firms; there is a danger that every maker would be dealt a fatal blow. On the other hand, if we only cooperate and do not compete at all, we will all slide into stagnant waters, which also would be bad. The British and French computer industries are examples of this. Thus, using cooperative relations during the early stages of development as a case, we will then compete on commercializing the product; as a whole we must oppose the threat posed by foreign capital. Thus we will cooperate on R&D but in sales and production we will compete fiercely as we have in the past . . . Finally, I would like to add that in the background of this move is the earnest guidance of MITI and the deep understanding of NTT. In regards to the big problem created by the decision to liberalize the computer industry in three years, both NTT and MITI have been serious and forward-looking in considering what form our computer industry should take in order to oppose the giant power of American capital.[48]

The "New Series" project was different in type and degree from earlier cooperative efforts. First, financial backing was greater; the government gave $213 million for the five-year "New Series" project compared to $33.33 million in subsidies given for the six-year "1966 project." Second, the firms were expected to cooperate more closely; Fujitsu and Hitachi developed large IBM-compatible computers, NEC and Toshiba medium and small Honeywell-compatible computers, and Oki and Mitsubishi small specialized computers. By having each group focus on certain technologies and models, the project produced competition and redundant research and helped the industry to develop a full series of computers to compete with IBM's 370 series, even though no single firm had the resources to do so.

The computers developed in this project made the Japanese computer makers competitive with their foreign counterparts in hardware. Indeed, according to Fujitsu chairman Kobayashi Taiyū, the reason the Japanese makers were able to survive when IBM brought out the 370 series, even though RCA and General Electric left the industry, was "because MITI started providing research grants and made different companies get together for cooperative development of new machines; for the first time, Japanese makers were ready for battle."[49]

In the "1966" and "New Series" R&D projects, it was easy to determine the research goal–to match existing IBM computers. But as the firms caught up with IBM in hardware in the mid-1970s and became stronger and more independent, cooperation among competitors became increasingly difficult. It became necessary to focus cooperation on basic or production technology that was one step removed from product development. "If R&D content is too close to commercialization, cooperation will not go far," explained Shimizu Sakae, senior managing director of Toshiba.[50]

The next challenge fit the bill. IBM was expected to use very large integrated circuits (VLSI) in its next generation of computers. If Japan were to remain competitive, it needed the capability to produce those advanced integrated circuits. To receive subsidies to study VLSI production technology, MITI required that the firms reorganize into two groups. Mitsubishi, Fujitsu, and Hitachi set up one group lab; Toshiba and NEC formed another. NTT, which had its own VLSI project involving Fujitsu, Hitachi, and NEC, had a separate lab but exchanged information with the MITI project labs. The four-year project started in 1976 and cost 72 billion yen ($360 million), 30 billion yen of which was funded by the government. The firms each contributed an equal amount to cover the remaining 42 billion yen.[51]

The division of labor varied according to the research theme. The most important research topic—the electron beam and X-ray beam exposure devices for drawing narrower lines on wafers—were studied in three parallel research groups. Each took a different approach in hopes that at least one would succeed. The project members tried a total of seven different ways to get the electron beam to draw narrower patterns on the wafer. Each of the three groups was led by one firm but included members from other firms. Tarui Yasuo, head of the project, said that it would have been difficult to mix equal numbers of people from rival firms for R&D on the most important devices.[52] In contrast, the different research groups worked together to develop ways to reduce defects in silicon crystals.

The project helped the firms in several key ways. It induced them to take the risky step of committing themselves to VLSI. According to Nishimura Taizo, general manager of Toshiba's International Operations: "That a project is assigned by the government is a clear sign that if you are not on the bandwagon, you will miss something important."[53] Another was to reduce the cost of R&D: "Because of the limited R&D resources of a private firm, we cannot allow a failure; we cannot deny that this participation in MITI's VLSI project is a big hedge against risk."[54]

The project achieved most of its technical goals. They developed technologies to draw narrower patterns on silicon wafers and found ways to decrease defects in silicon crystals.[55] Shimizu of Toshiba said the project was very important in helping the firms produce 64K RAM and ultimately the one megabit chip. Toshiba and NEC jointly developed an electron beam device in the project and are using it today in their VLSI efforts. Shimizu noted that "the timing of the project was critical; there was no electron beam and we needed a breakthrough to get ahead. The firms did not have any of the equipment for producing VLSIs, such as the electron beam or testing equipment."[56] The project resulted in about a thousand patents; 59 percent were held by one person, 25 percent by one company with a few members from other companies, and 16 percent by groups consisting of several members of various firms.[57] The different groups also exchanged information, and patents were open to all the members.

The VLSI project helped the makers produce low-cost, high-quality VLSI, thereby boosting their computer sales at home and abroad. Indeed, advances in VLSI, which helped increase the processing speed and memory capacity of Japanese machines, were key in the Japanese makers' ability to keep up with IBM hardware in the late 1970s. More recently, they have helped the Japanese come out with mainframes that exceed IBM's top machines in performance but that are lower in price.[58] Today, eight years after the project ended, the technology from this project is playing an important role in the mass production of one-megabit chips.[59]

R&D in new areas is risky, inevitably involving some failures. Joint research projects reduced costs and risks by dividing firms into teams to take different approaches to a problem, to focus on different parts of a computer system, or to work on completely different systems. To encourage specialization, the firms were generally assigned research in specific market segments. NEC, Fujitsu, and Hitachi have always been assigned the mainframes and integrated circuits, and Mitsubishi, Oki, and Toshiba the less sophisticated peripheral equipment. Not surprisingly, Fujitsu, Hitachi, and NEC are Japan's primary mainframe producers today and the other three its major producers of peripherals.

Indeed, the ability of the government to influence the actions of private companies was far greater than one might suppose from the subsidies. First, in most cases, the government required that the firms match R&D subsidies and commit engineers to the projects. The government used subsidies as leverage to get the firms to invest more. Second, the threat of being dropped from future government-sponsored projects, as Oki was when it did not commercialize the results of the "New Series" project, also pushed the companies to work hard, advance technologically in the projects, and commercialize their results.

CASES OF INEFFECTIVE POLICIES

Discussion thus far has focused on the successful cases of government intervention, but policies have not always been effective. In general, failures occurred when the government did not incorporate market incentives into its policies. For example, the government sponsored the creation of a special software company—the Japan Software Company—in the mid-1960s to develop the software for a government–private sector cooperative R&D project. The company, a joint venture among Fujitsu, Hitachi, NEC, and the Industrial Bank of Japan, was also expected to take orders from private companies for software development.

The software goals for the project were far too ambitious: to make a "common language" software that could run on Fujitsu, Hitachi, and NEC mainframes. Lagging far behind IBM, and with scant experience in developing software, the company was not able to even come close to meeting the goals. Soon after the project ended, the firm went bankrupt; it had not developed enough outside orders to support its existence once the project subsidies ended. It had become an organization with all the characteristics of a bureaucracy—slow, clumsy, and inefficient.

The primary factor involved in the downfall of Japan Software was its insulation from the market. Once they were guaranteed financing for the project, managers of the company had little incentive to compete in the market or attract outside orders.[60] Confident that the government would not allow the company to go bankrupt, the managers ignored the financial health of the company. This contrasts sharply with JECC, the computer rental company: computer makers were required to buy back from JECC the machines that had been traded in; JECC was prohibited from losing money by a requirement that the computer makers bear any losses; and JECC was never guaranteed any money—it had to negotiate annually for new loans. With software that was inferior and more expensive than that of its competitors, it was not surprising that Japan Software received few outside orders.[61] When the project ended, the subsidies stopped, leaving the firm with no option but to fold.

Another case of ineffective targeting policies is the Information Processing Promotion Association (IPA), established in 1970 to promote the diffusion of general-purpose software programs. The idea was perfectly reasonable: by having the IPA fund the development of software packages and rent them for low monthly rental fees, the government hoped to change the Japanese habit of using custom-made software, which was draining the productivity of the nation's small pool of software engineers. Firms applied to the IPA for funds to develop software packages. The IPA, after approving an application, funded the software package development. Once again, the problem was that the institution operated without the constraints of market competition; there was no effort to match the software developed with market needs. Not surprisingly, few of the packages have ever been rented.[62] In contrast to JECC, which only bought a computer when a user specifically asked for it, the IPA bought software and then tried to persuade firms to use it.

The fundamental flaws in Japan Software and IPA were partly because of deeper problems in Japan's software industry. First, Japan Software's products were the nation's first major efforts to develop advanced software. The government and the firms had little experience to draw from and the reverse engineering that worked so well in hardware was ineffective in software, which must be tailored to differences in language and business practices. The IPA was also given a formidable task: to change the Japanese preference for custom-made software, a preference deeply rooted in a belief that custom-made programs give the user an edge over competitors who use mass-produced packaged software. The key defects of these two institutions—the lack of ties to the marketplace and the existence of only vague, overly ambitious goals—thus in part resulted from the government and businesses failing to understand the software market. With reverse engineering impossible, and few trained software engineers, the tasks that were given to these institutions were completely unrealistic.

ENDNOTES

1. *Denshi Kōgyō Nenkan* (Electronics Industry Yearbook), (Tōkyō: Dempa Shimbunsha, 1962), p. 161. Rate was reduced to 15 percent for GATT members in 1964, when Japan changed its status in GATT and joined the OECD. *Genkū Yunyu Seido Ichiran* (A Summary of the Current Import System), (Tōkyō: MITI Chōsa Kai, annual).
2. "JECC Monogatari" (The JECC Story), segment 19 in *Kokusan Denshi Keisanki Nyūzu* (Domestic Computer News), no. 135 (Tokyo: JECC), April 1, 1981, p. 8.
3. *Asahi Shimbun* (Asahi News), June 6, 1961.
4. *Yomiuri Shimbun* (Yomiuri News), September 14, 1961.
5. Percent in monetary value. *Kompyūtopia* (Computopia), (Tōkyō: Kompyūtā Eiji Sha), January 1983, pp. 92 and 95.
6. Estimated using data on computers in general at government institutions. In the 1960s, about 25 percent of domestic computers were used in government offices, thus the assumption that the government bought or rented about 25 percent of Japanese computers annually. *Kōmpyūtāa Jitsudō Tōkyō Chōsa* (Survey of Computers Currently in Use), (Tokyo: JECC, annual); *Kompyutopia*, January issues.
7. *Denshi Kogyo Nenkan*, 1976, p. 683. The Foreign Capital Law is sometimes translated as the Foreign Investment Law.
8. "JECC Monogatari," segment 3, no. 119, December 1, 1979; Matsuo Hiroshi, *IBM Okoku o Obiyakasu Fujitsu* (Fujitsu Threatening the *IBM Okoku o Obiyakasu* Monarchy), (Tōkyō: Asahi Somorama, 1980), p. 152.
9. "JECC Monogatari." segment 3, no. 119, December 1, 1979.
10. Ibid., segment 4, no. 120, January 1, 1980, p. 6.
11. *Kompyūtopia*, December 1973, p. 24.
12. "JECC Monogatari," segment 5, February 1, 1980, p. 3.
13. Ekonomisuto Board, ed., *Sengo Sangyō Shi e no Shōgen* (Interviews for a History of Postwar Industry), Vol. 1 (Tōkyō: Mainichi Shimbunsha, 1977), pp. 142–143.
14. "JECC Monogatari," segment 5, February 1, 1980, p. 3.
15. "JECC Monogatari" segment 4, no. 120, January 1, 1980.
16. *Denshi Kōgyō Nenkan*, 1971–1972, p. 172.
17. *JECC Kompyūtā Nōto* (JECC Computer Notes), (Tokyo: JECC, 1979), p. 10.
18. *JECC 10 Nenshi* (Ten-Year History of JECC), (Tokyo: JECC, 1973), pp. 50–51, 59; *JECC Kompyuta Noto*, annual.
19. Interview with Ishiguro Ryūji, director of the JDB's Center for Research on Investment in Plant and Equipment, November 12, 1984.
20. "JECC Monogatari," segment 9, June 1, 1980, p. 2.
21. Interview with Ishii Yoshiaki, general manager, JECC's Research Division, July 19, 1984; various discussions with Hirose Kōichi of JECC in 1984.
22. *Denshi Kōgyō Nenkan*, 1970–1971, p. 180.
23. Interview with Hirose Kōichi of JECC.
24. JECC's monthly fee is one-forty-fourth of the sales price; 44 months equal 3.7 years.
25. Marie Anchordoguy, "The Role of Public Corporations in Japan's Industrial Development: The Japan Electronic Computer Company," *Political Science Quarterly*, Winter 1988–1989.
26. Ibid.
27. Marie Anchordoguy, "The State and the Market: Industrial Policy Towards Japan's Computer Industry," Ph.D. dissertation, University of California, Berkeley, pp. 382–383. Subsidy is the difference between the interest JECC paid on JDB loans and the estimate of what the firms would have to pay if they had borrowed the money at the prime rate from private banks.
28. Anchordoguy, "The Role of Public Corporations."
29. Interview with Ishiguro Ryuji, November 12, 1984.
30. *JECC 10 Nenshi*, pp. 50–51, 59.
31. Calculated using data from *JECC Kōmpyūtā Nōto*, 1979, pp. 10–11, 377; *Denshi Kōgyō Nenkan*,1979, p. 447; Dokusen Bunseki Kenkyukai, ed., *Nihon no Dokusen Kōgyō* (Japan's Monopolistic Enterprises), Vol. 1 (Tōkyō: Shin Nihon Shuppankai, 1969), p. 292; *Kompyuta Warudo* (Computer World), May 31, 1982, p. 21.
32. See Jimmy Wheeler, Merit E. Janow, and Thomas Pepper, *Japanese Industrial Development Policies in the 1980s* (New York: Hudson Institute, 1982).
33. They invested $708.8 million.
34. Interview with Maeda Norihiko, February 28, 1986.
35. Interview in *Bungeishunjū*, September 1982, p. 101.

36. Cited in *Kompyūtopia*, October 1973, p. 43.
37. See Anchordoguy, "The State and the Market," pp. 120–121.
38. Calculated at 360 yen to the dollar *Nihon Kaihatsu Ginkō Tōkei Yōran* (JDB Summary of Statistics), (Tōkyō: JDB, annual); *Hojokin Benran* (Handbook of Subsidies), (Tōkyō: Nihon Densan Kikaku Kabushiki Gaisha, annual).
39. *Kompyūtopia*, April 1969, p. 30.
40. Nihon Denshin Denwa Kōsha 25 Neshi Iinkai, ed., *Nihon Denshin Denwa Kōsha 25 Nenshi* (25-Year History of NTT), Vol. 3 (Tōkyō Denki Tsūshin Kyōkai, 1978), p. 249.
41. Nihon Chōki Shinyō Ginkō Sangyō Kenkyūkai, *Shin Jidai ni Chōsen suru Nihon no Sangyō* (Japan's Industries: Challenging the New Era), (Tōkyō: Mainichi Shimbun Sha, 1968), pp. 230–233.
42. Ibid., p. 10.
43. *Denshi Kōgyō 30 Nenshi* (Thirty Year History of the Electronics Industry), (Tōkyō: Nihon Denshi Kikai Kogyo Kai, 1979), pp. 82, 108.
44. *Kōgyō Gijutsu In, Ogata Purojekotu ni yoru Chōkō Seinō Denshi Keisanki* (The Super High-Performance Computer Project of the Large-Scale Program), (Tōkyō: Nihon Sangyō Gijutsu Shinkō Kyōkai), July 1972, pp. 9–10, 17; Kompyutopia, June 1973, pp. 15–17; *Electronics*, 24 May 1971, pp. 42–49; Ibid., 24 April 1971, pp. 42–43; *Denshi Kogyo Nenkan*, 1973, pp. 312–315.
45. *Kompyutopia*, June 1973, p. 15.
46. *Ogata Purojekuto ni yoru Chōkō Seinō Denshi Keisanki*, p. 202.
47. *Toyo Keizai Shukan* (Oriental Economist Weekly), January 24, 1970, p. 42.
48. Letter from 1971 reprinted in *Fujitsu Shashi*, Vol 2 (Tōkyō: Jyoban Shoin, 1977), pp. 134–136. (A History of Fujitsu).
49. Interview with Kobyashi in *Bungeishunju*, September 1982, p. 101.
50. Interview the Shimizu Sakae, February 3, 1986.
51. *Denshi* (Electronics), (Tōkyō: Nihon Denshi Kikai Kōgyōkai, July 1976), pp. 9, 14.
52. Tarui Yasuo, *IC no Hanashi, Toranjisuta kara Cho LSI made* (The Story of ICs, from Transistors to LSI), (Tōkyō: Nihon Hōsō Shuppan Kyokai, 1984), pp. 147, 156.
53. Interview with Nishimura Taizo, general manager of Toshiba's International Operations Electronic Components Division, February 3, 1986.
54. Quotation from a participant in VLSI project, cited in Uozumi Toru, *Komptūtā Sensō* (The Computer War), (Tōkyō: Aoya Shoten, 1979), p. 156.
55. *Tarui, IC no Hanashi, Toranjisuta kara Cho LSI made*, pp. 168–170; *Japan Computer News*, September 1977, p. 7; *EDP in Japan* (Tōkyō: JECC, 1977), pp. 53–54; *JECC Kompyūtā Noto*, 1981, p. 183.
56. Interview with Shimizu, February 3, 1986.
57. Tarui, p. 149.
58. *Electronics*, November 25, 1985, pp. 20–21.
59. Discussion with Todoriki Itaru, director general of MITI's Agency for Industrial Science and Technology, January 23, 1986.
60. Interview the Yamamoto Kinko, managing director of the Japan Information Processing Development Center, February 28, 1986.
61. *Kompyūtopia*, February 1973, pp. 27–30.
62. Minamisawa Noburō, *Nihon Kompyūtā Hatten Shi* (The History of the Development of Japanese Computers), (Tōkyō: Nihon Keizai Shimbunsha, 1978), p. 173–174.

Cooperation for Competition:
United States and Japan

George M. Scalise, senior vice president and chief administrative officer for Advanced Micro Devices, Inc., of Sunnyvale, California, thumbed through the ever-increasing pile of papers he was collecting on the Microelectronics and Computer Technology Corporation, a cooperative research effort just incorporated. Whether AMD should join in the venture or not was the question of immediate importance to Mr. Scalise on that August day in 1982.

ADVANCED MICRO DEVICES

From its inception in 1969 with eight employees, two rented rooms, no products, no manufacturing facilities, and $50,000, AMD had grown in 13 years to a company employing over 10,000 people with sales in the 1983 fiscal year expected to be more than $300 million (see Exhibit 1 for salient financial data).

Headquartered in Sunnyvale, the company designed, developed, and manufactured complex monolithic integrated circuits for sale to original equipment manufacturers of computation, communication, and instrumentation equipment. AMD endeavored to offer standard or catalog items of high-quality rather than custom-designed products for a single customer. To market its products, it operated 34 field offices throughout the world (primarily in the United States, Western Europe, and Japan). The direct sales force of 118 sales representatives supported by 32 field applications engineers was assisted by independent sales representatives.

From its original product focus as an alternative-source manufacturer of other suppliers' circuits, AMD evolved an ability to design and develop proprietary products. By 1982, those products represented nearly 50 percent of the company's total revenues from sales.

There are two process technologies associated with integrated circuit manufacturing, bipolar and metaloxide semiconductor (commonly referred to as MOS) technologies. AMD offered a broad range of products utilizing both that afforded the company a great amount of design flexibility. The split of bipolar and MOS products was fairly even as the following indicates:

This case combines one on MCC prepared by William J. Murphy, Research Assistant, under the supervision of Professor Joseph L. Bower, and a note on Japan's VLSI project prepared by Professor Bower and Professor Kosei Furakawa of Keio University. It is designed to serve as the basis for class discussion rather than to illustrate either effective or ineffective handling of an administrative situation. Copyright © 1986 by the President and Fellows of Harvard College.

	1980	1981	1982
Bipolar	48%	52%	55%
MOS	50	45	42
Other	2	3	3

AMD's competitors in the integrated circuit marketplace were a varied lot, some large firms for which integrated circuits were only a small portion of sales, and other foreign-based companies receiving various forms of direct and indirect government assistance. Original equipment manufacturers also had significant captive business.

THE MICROELECTRONICS AND COMPUTER TECHNOLOGY CORPORATION

At the heart of integrated circuitry is the semiconductor, a thin wafer fabricated from silicon into which a microscopic maze of circuit elements has been added. As an industry, semiconductor manufacture was the pride of American capitalism. For many it embodied an entrepreneurial spirit that had arguably grown weak in other sectors of the economy. It was an industry that had invented new technologies and had developed products and markets to take advantage of these innovations. A key ingredient of modern industrialized society and the promise of a prosperous economic future, both in the United States and abroad, semiconductors were seen as critical to national defense as well as to industrial progress.

Despite its "champion" status the domestic semiconductor industry began to raise a chorus of alarm as the 1980s unfolded. The success of the industry and its importance to all industrialized nations (and those who aspired to that status) was at the root of its problems. The manufacture of integrated circuits to add "smarts" to everything from highly complex and sophisticated machine tools to household toasters and military hardware was evolving into a feverish and highly competitive worldwide business with an astonishing rate of new technological development.

One industry leader who decided to act on his concerns was William Norris, chairman and CEO of Control Data Corporation (CDC) of Minneapolis, Minnestoa. In describing his efforts to launch a broad-based, cooperative venture in the highly competitive computer business, Norris noted the initial resistance he encountered:

> I felt discouraged about launching such a venture here in the U.S., so, in 1979, I went back to Europe where I had been on four previous occasions regarding cooperation among the industry. It was obvious that Europe was not going to be able to make it competitively in the computer industry, so I thought the participants would be able to see the merits of a cooperative effort. But again, they were not really interested. They could see their problems, but thought they could solve them alone. About this time the Japanese thrust in microelectronics had become more apparent so we decided, "Well, this is the time to go back around the Horn again and get broad-base cooperation started in the United States. The result was MCC."

Control Data had a history of cooperating on technical matters with other industry members, in part inspired by the difficulties of competing against the industry giant IBM. In the early 1970s CDC and National Cash Register Company were able to form a successful joint venture regarding magnetic peripherals. Later in the decade CDC joined with Honeywell and others in projects aimed at magnetic recording media—some joint projects involved 15 or more organizations.

Mr. Norris's initial efforts to whip up enthusiasm for the Microelectronics and Computer Technology Corporation (MCC) met with a lukewarm reception when initially proposed in the spring of 1981. Industry sentiments were fairly well captured by H. Glen Haney, vice president for strategic planning and development at Sperry Univac, quoted in an *Electronic News* article (June 15, 1981) on the Control Data proposal: "the very essence of our business technology is the chips and microelectronics. To willingly put the core of your R&D thrust outside your own control and share it with competitors is basically unattractive."

Despite such initial reservations, 16 companies met in Orlando, Florida, on February 19, 1982 to further explore the possibilities of cooperative research (see Exhibit 2). In his remarks to that group, Norris was explicit about the perceived threat that had galvanized the companies into action:

> The extent and nature of the Japanese challenge in microelectronics and computer industries has been widely discussed and documented in recent months. We have seen the U.S. semiconductor industry's preeminent position in semiconductor memories eroded in a few short years and, just a few months ago, through the vehicle of the conference on fifth-generation computer systems, the Japanese announced their intent to continue their market momentum in microelectronics while they mount a parallel effort to become the world's leader in computing by the end of this decade.
>
> Japanese industry has the advantages of (1) government-promoted cooperation between industry members at the base technology level, (2) preferential market treatment accorded their industry members as a result of tariff and nontariff barriers to outside entry into their domestic markets, (3) partitioning of products and product lines between their companies in world markets, (4) the willingness of their investors to provide low-cost capital and to take the long view with respect to company profitability.[1]

Norris then turned to some of the constraints facing domestic firms in trying to formulate a response to the Japanese threat:

> Microelectronics and computer firms in the United States are suffering from a combination of scarce capital resources, high capital costs, and a rapidly growing need for capital to develop and exploit appropriate new technological possibilities. We are also faced with a critical shortage of relevant scientific and engineering talent.

He pointed out that there was enormous duplication of research and development efforts, a situation, he argued, that represented waste not only to the corporations conducting the R&D but also to society as a whole. (Exhibit 3 lists MCC benefits.)

On August 12, 1982, MCC was formally incorporated and began the task of organizing staff and setting up the research projects.

HOW MCC WOULD WORK

Although generally characterized as highly competitive, the microelectronics and computer industries had witnessed a number of cooperative efforts over the years including the cross-licensing of patents, a common practice. Trade associations and technical conferences served as mechanisms for the exchange of ideas and joint ventures; they were not uncommon, although they were for the most part short-lived and limited in scope.

But MCC was to be a significant departure from prior practices. In the first place, the projected scope of MCC's endeavors was large: annual expenditures of a $100 million or more were anticipated. The first year of the venture was expected to cost nearly $20 million; by the third year, that amount would triple.

MCC would be established as a for-profit organization. Each sponsoring company would be a shareholder and have a member on the board of directors. Norris was characteristically candid about MCC's structure:

> I don't know how to manage a nonprofit organization, and I do not think many other people do it well....So many of the nonprofits I know start out with enthusiasm and dedication, but when the original group or founder...leaves, then survival of the organization becomes the objective....Also, I think that a nonprofit entity that would be as significant as the one we are talking about here would get a lot of political attention, possibly adverse....One further reason for the structure is that I believe in the profit system and therefore operate that way.

MCC MEMBERSHIP

MCC participation was limited to U.S.-based private sector companies either in the computer or microelectronics industries. This eligibility requirement targeted domestic producers and users of microelectronic components and devices, as well as their trade associations.

Even though all "public sector entities" were precluded from MCC membership and equity participation, it was recognized that government actions and policies would be of importance to MCC. The Defense Department in fact took a keen interest in MCC and sent representatives to the February 1982 meeting in Florida.

The MCC proposal called for members to commit to (1) equity ownership, (2) the enhancement of competition for computing and microelectronics products and services, (3) active involvement in MCC governance, (4) the assignment of appropriate personnel to MCC duties, and (5) the sharing of funding for relevant projects.

HOW MCC WOULD BE ORGANIZED

MCC's principal governing body had as its first duty the selection and recruitment of a president for the corporation. The president also held the title of chief executive officer, and was a member of the board of directors and of the Research and Development Advisory Committee (RDAC). A number of candidates were being considered, for the job, including Admiral Bobby Inman (see Exhibit 3 for a biography). RDAC was composed of a member from each shareholder company, and MCC's president and Research and Development Division (RDD) manager; its function was to identify the most promising research and development projects. The president would have all authority over MCC personnel, including hiring and firing.

RDD actually managed the research and development projects of MCC. Organized on a project basis as needed, it had two permanent departments that supported all the projects and would be funded out of MCC's general funds—the Prototype Support Department and the Design Tools Department.

The Prototype Support Department was to set up and run a "foundry" to produce microelectronic parts designed by the project teams. Similarly, the Design Tools Department was to develop computer-aided design (CAD) tools for the use of the project teams; CAD software was of particular interest. It was hoped that both departments could sell services and products outside of MCC to help offset costs.

In addition to the two Research and Development Division departments, MCC had four permanent service elements reporting directly to the president: (1) Education Services Section (ESS), to develop training materials; (2) Applications

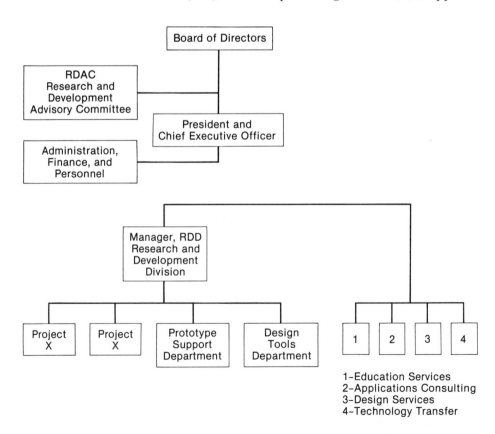

Consulting Section (ACS), to assist firms incorporating microelectronics into their products; (3) Design Services Section (DSS), to provide computer-aided design (CAD) services as opposed to providing CAD tools; and (4) Technology Transfer Section (TTS), to help facilitate the transfer of MCC-generated technology to shareholders, although direct participation in projects by shareholder personnel was expected to cover most technology transfer.

PROJECT SELECTION

Upon receiving a project suggestion by a member company or on its own initiative, RDAC undertook an evaluation of the suggested research effort (see Exhibit 4 for projected activities). If RDAC found that the project under scrutiny was promising, it was referred to RDD for development of a formal research proposal. The proposal was then sent back to RDAC for its approval. Passing that, it was recommended to MCC's board of directors which then decided whether to proceed.

Since a shareholder's support obligation to MCC was largely made on a project-by-project basis, those shareholders interested in a particular project met to determine exact funding and personnel. Once this had been determined, the final step was authorization by the board to RDD to proceed.

MCC's BENEFITS AND COSTS TO AMD

AMD's George Scalise put aside his stack of papers and spoke on the pros and cons of association with MCC:

> On the positive side, we see MCC as an opportunity to share the costs of some vital and expensive projects, the results of which would provide us with the means to deal with design and process problems. It will enhance our opportunity to innovate using our own design concepts and product selection. Thus, we are not compromising our competitive posture.

Elaborating on this point, he said:

> In some ways it is analogous to buying a commercial piece of equipment for your processing line. All your competitors may buy the same piece of equipment, but there are a lot of ways of utilizing that machinery—some more effective than others.
> We also feel that because MCC involves both the computer hardware people and the component people, there is an opportunity for developing projects that will better satisfy our mutual needs. Coordination is an important issue here.

He continued:

> Looking at MCC from these standpoints, the association is very appealing...in very broad terms they are the most important positive aspects of MCC. On the other side are our concerns, one of which is project definition. Does a project get defined in such a way that it is going to result in a completed satisfactory program, one that is really going to do the job that we perceive needs to be done?

Our second question about MCC is, "Are we going to be spending a lot of funds on getting something started that would be diluting our efforts in the long term?" It must be remembered that we could use the funds to extend and expand what is already going on inside AMD. We are concerned that the savings from shared expenses might get washed away by start-up costs.

Reflecting on how AMD and its potential partners might balance the pros and cons, Scalise noted:

The companies have already made substantial investments in research projects that parallel those being proposed by MCC. Their decision to participate in MCC will be determined by the cost of participating in the program and their assessment of the extent to which the MCC projects will complement and enhance the results of their in-house programs.

George Scalise was conscious that Japan had organized its cooperative microelectronic research effort somewhat differently from MCC.

THE VLSI TECHNOLOGY RESEARCH ASSOCIATION

In 1980, Japan announced to the world that a prototype 256K RAM chip had been produced in a laboratory of the VLSI (very-large-scale integrated circuits) Research Association. Concurrent reports that Hewlett-Packard had found U.S. chips less reliable and that the Japanese had a head start in the 64K chip market seemed to indicate that Japan would succeed with semiconductors the way it had with automobiles, despite the presence in the industry of leading U.S. manufacturer's such as IBM, Intel, and Texas Instruments. Somehow, the Japanese had caught up in a field that the United States had invented, and, since the achievements of Shockley and his colleagues at Bell Labs in the early 1950s, dominated with strong, forward-looking companies.

Companies such as Fujitsu, Hitachi, and Nippon Electric (NEC) had managed to establish themselves as effective competitors in the computer and semiconductor markets. And those three companies, with Mitsubishi Electric, Toshiba, and the Ministry of International Trade and Industry (MITI), had joined together to do advanced VLSI-related research. Although such cooperation conformed to the notion of "Japan, Inc.," and the reality of behavior in some fields of Japanese economic life such as steel or raw material purchasing, it seemed uncharacteristic of the way these samurai companies had competed with each other in the past. As interesting as the question of "what happened?," the question of *how* it happened seemed more intriguing.

The Beginnings

Until the announcement of the IBM 360 in 1964, the Japanese government's efforts to stimulate the development of the computer industry had been modest. Nonetheless, the groundwork was laid through a series of business/government research committees, new legislation, limited subsidies to the emerging mainframe companies, and several government-initiated joint ventures—one, a special-tax-status leasing corporation. (For a more complete account, see Appendix A to this case.)

Following IBM's announcement, the level of government initiated or coordinated activity rose dramatically. A MITI manager involved in the early efforts at stimulating computer development stated it this way: "MITI took the initiative through informal pressure…and used financial measures to guide these companies."[2]

According to Julian Gressler, "between 1965 and 1975 the government worked closely with the industry to develop 'target' technologies."[3] One important result was the "super/high-performance" computer produced jointly by the six mainframe manufacturers—Hitachi, Fujitsu, NEC, Toshiba, Oki, and Mitsubishi under MITI's Electronic Technology Laboratory (ETL) and funded at ¥10 billion. A spin-off of MITI's Electric Machinery Laboratory and begun in 1957 when the importance of the computer was first recognized, ETL was, until the 1970s, Japan's leading research center on computers and transistors.

MITI also led a ¥22 billion Pattern Information Processing (PIPs) system project aimed at optical and oral character recognition and a ¥720 million software promotion effort was organized under a new Information Technology Promotion Agency. Nippon Telephone and Telegraph, Japan's government-owned communication company, sponsored a project to improve the use of computer time sharing in electronic exchange and transmission systems.

While these projects involved cooperation among participating companies, the management format usually resembled U.S. defense contracting with parts of a system assigned to different subcontractors all managed by a prime contractor. The nature of activity changed, however, with the advent of the IBM System 370, which coincided with the first major "liberalization" of Japan's trade. Convinced that Japanese manufacturers would be vulnerable to this new competition, the electronics industry section of MITI took the lead in exploiting the companies' desire for assistance. With the support of a study group of Liberal Democratic Party (LDP) representatives in the Information Industry Congressman's Association, MITI moved to realign the industry.

Strong pressure was exerted to force the six fiercely independent competitors into three groups that would pursue different, complementary lines of development. Hitachi and Fujitsu were to build IBM-compatible systems; Toshiba and NEC were to use GE and Honeywell technology; and Oki and Mitsubishi, Xerox Data Systems technology. The results were not nearly as neat. Hitachi and Fujitsu eventually competed head on with rival IBM-compatible systems, although they did create Nippon Peripherals Ltd., a joint venture. The Oki-Mitsubishi team produced the COSMOS series of computers, but Oki withdrew from the mainframe business. NEC and Toshiba produced the ACOS series of computers and organized NEC–Toshiba Information Systems (NTIS) to market and distribute the line jointly.

This was the situation when the next stage of trade liberalization was implemented in 1975. (Coincidentally, transcripts from the antitrust cases against IBM revealed IBM's plans for a future system of computers to be introduced in the 1980s.) MITI's electronics policy section anticipated new problems. Said one MITI manager, active at the time, "The computer industry has a special problem because of the large market share in Japan of IBM [60%]...total market share of all Japanese manufacturers might be 5%. And after full liberalization IBM might cause heavy damage to the Japanese infant industry...they might need a little assistance."[4]

One result of this line of thought was a cabinet decision on the occasion of import liberalization that "the government [will continue to] cherish the independence and future growth of Japan's computer industry, and will keep an eye on movements in the computer market so that liberalization will not adversely affect domestic producers."[5]

The Idea of a Cooperative Project

Government argument focused on the threat of IBM's R&D capability and the likelihood of creating an effective rival through cooperation of the five Japanese manufacturers. A series of discussions among personnel at MITI, NTT, and in the industry began in 1974 and gathered intensity in 1975. The same year, NTT commissioned its traditional suppliers, NEC, Fujitsu, and Hitachi to develop a very large-scale integrated circuit chip as an ingredient of future telecommunication development.

In MITI's view this was too narrow an approach as one MITI manager explained:

> ...actually the two projects proceeded separately. MITI's VLSI project was intended for the computer industry. We thought that VLSI would be the key component for the future system of computers, which IBM was intending to develop.
>
> MITI's projects were mainly designed for the fundamental technology of the semiconductor industry, especially in the field of microfabrication of the semiconductors' microcrystal technology...such fundamental technology would be very useful all over the computer industry and in other fields of the semiconductor industry.

The computer industry was organized into two groups, the Electronic Industry Promotion Association consisting of some 70 or 80 companies, and a subgroup consisting of the five mainframe manufacturers, each of whom selected partners from the larger group. The LDP wanted to concentrate government resources on the five partnerships: it opposed subsidies to individual companies.

A senior officer of one of the "Big Five" discussed the choice of partner companies:

> There were many discussions with industry companies. MITI indicated the final proposal and the companies followed it. And I should say the final decision [was] based on the fact that the member companies should have the ability and intention to develop similar methods....[and] to make big large-scale computers, to utilize those technologies. That was the case for their combining.

Extensive consultation began in 1974 among scientists in the companies and at ETL, and among company lab directors, managers, and NTT. The Ministry of Finance and the Ministry of Post Telecommunications were also deeply involved.

Although from the beginning MITI had sought a pooling of resources rather than conventional constructing out of the related pieces, managers at MITI commented: "Industrial firms do not like cooperation because all the manufacturers are competitors with each other."

One company manager said:

> All the member companies had some sense of crisis. When we looked at the IBM Future System concept, we saw we would not be able to meet the threat without the kind of cooperation MITI wanted.
>
> Basically, none of the companies were opposed. They were afraid of losing their freedom. There was also some hesitation, some concern about whether or not the result of the union would be successful.

Another manager noted:

> Some companies wanted to limit the project—for example, to the inspection of imported equipment and value analysis. It was nearly half a year before they discussed what might be possible if a lab were established. But my feeling was that if we did not [try] the process of making a VLSI cooperative lab, there would be no government money.

Eventually, after a year of intensive discussion, it was decided to establish a VLSI Technology Research Association (VLSI/TRA) whose members would be the five mainframe computer manufacturers. The VLSI/TRA was formally established in April of 1976 with "Mr. M. Sato" as executive director and "Dr. Suzuki" as director of the cooperative lab.* Mr. Sato had served MITI as head of the Electronics Industry Section and later as leader of several large government-sponsored development projects. Dr. Suzuki was a distinguished researcher at ETL, known for his work on MITI's Sunshine (solar energy) Project.

Organization

According to Mr. Sato:

> The VLSI Technology Research Association differed from other comparable research associations in two aspects. First, [it] had affiliate cooperative laboratories in fact as well as name...the staff were on loan from each member company...second, the partner companies [were in the] identical business...they were competitors.
>
> [If they had been] from different businesses, the division of labor could have been easy. In contrast, an association of competitors involved assigning responsibility among members.

The association was governed by a board of directors chaired in rotation for a year by one of the company presidents; Mr. Sato ran the meetings. As shown below, the association consisted of six cooperative labs, two others, a secretariat, and a number of advisory boards and committees. The choice of Mr. Sato as

---

*These are disguised names.

executive director was apparently obvious to all except Mr. Sato himself, who at first turned the job down but was selected nonetheless.

In a paper prepared by Mr. Sato to describe the project, he emphasized the importance of the early discussion: "We began discussing the research systems and themes under the framework of this joint project in 1975, one year before the association started....[proceeding] in three groups. The top group was composed of managing directors or vice presidents of the five companies. Below this, a research group headed by Dr. Suzuki and an administrative group met frequently."

The discussions produced ground rules summarized in two pages of text. The budget was not exact, but it would be set annually; MITI's contribution had a ceiling and would be no more than 50 percent. The total number of participants was set. Should the project succeed and the companies develop computers with VLSI components, the companies would have to return the subsidy from profits. A critical research policy was established: "The research activities should concentrate on fundamental technology of VLSI, on research that was different from research which each member had in its own labs."

From the government's point of view, it was critical that the research be applicable; assuring the government on this score was to be the role of CDL and NTIS. The labs created by these older, established joint ventures were assigned tasks of prototype development and testing and evaluation that were specific to the needs of the members.

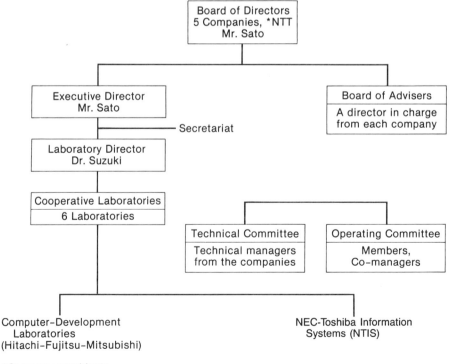

*Company presidents.

The cooperative labs were organized to study microfabrication technology, crystal technology, process technology, test and evaluation technology, and device technology. The crystal work, led by an ETL researcher in one lab, was estimated to require virtually all the limited talent available in the five companies; it was of basic interest to all VLSI technologies. Three approaches to microfabrication were pursued in three separate labs, while testing and evaluation and device technology were studied in two cooperative labs and at NTIS and CDL. All chip design work was performed at NTIS and CDL.

Mr. Sato described the work on the project in its early phases:

> After much discussion [in 1975], the companies had already decided to locate the Cooperative Laboratories in space available in the newly built NEC Central Research Laboratory Building in Kawasaki.
>
> ....[next] was how to lay out laboratory facilities. Parts of the Kasumigaseki Building were rented and about 20 officials, including R&D directors, the assistants, and designers from the partner companies, began to produce concrete plans to construct the facilities for the Cooperative Laboratories. The discussions were centered on the objectives of R&D, year-to-year R&D schedules, and then ways of promoting mutual understanding among researchers whose knowledge and backgrounds were diversified.
>
> Financially, the association was managed on a yearly basis, so the budget for the year 1976 was to be balanced by the end of the year. Purchasing of machinery equipment was the top priority issue. As we depended on U.S. manufacturers for most parts of the machinery installed in the Cooperative Laboratory, the layout and listing of such equipment were seriously discussed.
>
> ...the laboratory was transferred to Kawasaki in August 1976, and from then the number of research staffs loaned from the member firms was increased. Some of them started on R&D, and others were engaged in the studies of related documents and research papers.
>
> Most [people on the] Cooperative Laboratory staffs were on loan from the five member companies. Some particular posts, including the laboratory director [Dr. Yasuo Suzuki], planning chiefs, and several others, were taken by officials from the Electronics Technology Research Laboratory, a research institute affiliated with the Ministry of International Trade and Industry.
>
> Six sections were established, based on objectives of R&D efforts. Three of them were assigned to the research on microfabrication, one of the most sophisticated of our themes. The remaining three sections were for the study of crystals, processes, and devices.
>
> The closest attention was needed in our effort to assign staff members to each section. Chiefs of the six sections came from the five [companies] and the MITI. For other positions, however, staffs from those [companies] were deliberately mingled because of the nature of this laboratory.

Dr. Suzuki's selection of researchers was based on his prior knowledge of their work. As one manager noted, "Of course there was much negotiation, but basically Dr. Suzuki said, 'NEC should join this laboratory, and here are the qualifications for members.' We discussed and chose people accordingly." This approach was not universal. One company explained, "We have three grades of researchers—excellent leader quality, an assistant leader group, and a worker group. It was difficult to send our top class people, so we sent our good people from the second group."

Asked how the wishes of the employees were factored into the assignment pattern, one lab director said that assignments were "our decision not their wishes. This is Japan." Sato described the staffing activity: "one of the most imperative problems was whether each of the five [companies] would successfully bring the results of our joint studies back [to the mother company]."

Mixing research staffs from the various companies might cause the forest to be overlooked for the trees. To avert this potential problem, each section was staffed with a preponderance of people from head researcher's company.

> One lab director said that this pattern had certain benefits:
> Dr. Suzuki organized the three microfabrication laboratories in competition. When we started, we had no unique solution, so we would compete with each other. [On the surface], we were not secretive. We smiled at each other. But even one or two years after, it was very rare to visit among the three laboratories.
> This pattern also helped with the recruiting, for once a man was primarily identified with a lab, its director felt visible and wanted to succeed. In the final stages, however, life changed.
> Mr. Sato is a very nice man, as you know. Every month he opened the bar in the evening and called up many people—scientists here—and discussed everything, not only technical matters, cultural things or social things. This improved things very much. Also, in the later stage... the atmosphere... changed, because the target was so high and all new information came up in the laboratories, not from mother companies. So, just two years after the laboratories were established, the members ... were very interested mutually... and in the final stage there were no barriers among the labs. And still they competed.

Returning to the early days, as described in Mr. Sato's paper:

> ...researchers assigned to each section would not mingle easily with those from different member companies and diverse backgrounds. The six sections especially would stick to [their own specialties], being careful [not to leak] secrets on R&D work done individually. One section ran to an extreme by installing some machinery equipment at the door leading to the other section to keep the door shut. Instructions against such behavior were issued in fear of fires or other types of accidents involving laboratory buildings and facilities but [they] failed to work.
> It was quite often that I deplored over the difficulties in exchanging scientific studies or works. The laboratory director held control of what was being studied and it is the way any laboratory should function.
> I, as executive director, never interfered with the subject or content of any research work done by the staffs. I sought to step up the exchange of any studies and hoped each member researcher would be just outspoken as to his engaged work. What I actually did the last four years was nothing but to chat with the staff over sake. By that, I believed I could help them express complaints or concerns over their jobs and other problems and then dispel such worries.

Supporting Staff, Treatment of Loaned Researchers

He continued with his description of the association:

> Cooperative Laboratories stretched over 3,300 square meters of land, and had about 100 including the secretariat staff on the payroll. However, the laboratory, hastily constructed and formed, was devoid of backup staffers.

At ordinary companies, malfunctioning machinery can be repaired by concerned departments. We at the laboratory had no such divisions or staff responsible for the equipment out of order or maintenance services. As a countermeasure then, I called on each member firm to provide us with a crew of maintenance and control experts...

The secretariat was responsible for general affairs concerning not merely the laboratories, but the association as a whole. These circumstances also forced me to call on the partners to send increased female work forces in order to lessen the researchers burden of processing miscellaneous duties.

Also demanding was how to treat the researchers loaned from the partner firms and to cope with their labor union. Payment systems or standards employed by their parent companies were applied without any amendment, and their salaries were calculated by each of their employers. The secretariat [took care of matters] covering working schedules and salary payment.

Personnel evaluation was done by a sectional committee which was based on a system we originally introduced. Data for evaluating the staffs then were submitted to the employer companies and the personnel-affairs departments of their head offices.

...when the Electrical Workers' Union went on a strike, Nippon Electric, a union member, followed suit, and so our labor union resorted to NEC's tactics of struggle.

Library was an urgent issue, too. The new laboratory had no reference books or data in stock. In order to tide it over, NEC's library was opened to us. When our staff used the library, those from NEC deliberately kept as much separate from NEC employees using the institution as possible.

At the beginning, the companies expected little from the cooperative laboratories; their skepticism was reflected in the budgeting process, where they sought to narrow the scope of the work. Eventually, as results proved exciting, money flowed easily, exceeding the companies' original target by 50 percent. During their operations other problems that developed included constraints on costs, lab budget overruns, the difficulties of less successful researchers, and, particularly, patents.

What to do with patents was a perpetual problem not settled until the last year of the project. The companies, MITI, and even individuals wanted final ownership, and from the beginning IBM wanted access to them. One company wanted total ownership of its work. Another company took the view that the project was so important that shared progress was worth the costs, so they urged their scientists to patent as many things as possible, reasoning the reward would eventually return to the company.

The final decision was (1) the association would receive 100 percent ownership of patents; (2) each member of the association would have access to the patents; (3) if a member had a cross-licensing agreement with a third party, for example, IBM, only the patents invented by that member's researchers would be available; and (4) if there was no cross-licensing, licenses would be available through the association. "Know-how" was to be transferred to members through announcements, the presentation of papers, visits, and discussions and to nonmembers through academic symposia.

Related to patents was the visits by members of the association to mother companies. Said one lab director:

Once in the very early stage, the MITI officers visited the lab. No laboratory head was there except me. After that, people who wanted to visit mother companies had to register or report to Dr. Suzuki. Sato and Suzuki did not want people visiting so frequently. The most nervous company was NEC because our lab was in their yard.

The question of visits tied in a way to the problem of patents and know-how.

Small-scale prototype work was done cooperatively in microfabrication (E-beam lithography) and crystal technology. Discoveries were reported in detail, making the information available to each company. Devices were then developed within each company laboratory out of the common knowledge.

The result created a subtle problem of disclosure. While working on a device back at the mother computer company, researchers would learn something that might be considered relevant to the cooperative lab. Debates would ensue as to what should be shared.

The evaluation and testing phase was shared. Whatever information and equipment it took to test the findings were included in the agreement and shared. Beyond that data was not to be disclosed.

It was a soft line, a delicate line. The Japanese people are quite experienced in working on soft line problems like this... experience teaches everyone how to deal with things. This is a particular point that just about every person visiting from abroad raises, and this is the one point that apparently is the most difficult [for them] to understand...

A company manager gave an example of the relationship among the cooperative labs, NTIS, CDL, and the companies:

In February 1980, NTIS announced in the press the development of a 256 RAM. But the actual chip that NEC is now manufacturing is quite different from the prototype. What was announced was only an assurance... to assure the government in the form of a working chip.

In dealing with disputes that arose, Mr. Sato was described as very effective in his use of sake, and he joked, "Sometimes I felt as if I spent days doing nothing but drinking sake."

During the course of the project, there was extensive reporting back to the companies—Mr. Sato briefed the company presidents, while Dr. Suzuki, the managing directors—and regular meetings of the participating scientists were held. In the first phase, there were extensive discussions of the literature and what ought to be done; thereafter, regular reports were made on progress in the labs. More than 300 papers were presented and 50 announcement meetings were held. Commenting on the cooperative experience, managers of the participating companies reflected several perspectives. One thought it critical that the research target had been well chosen:

If we had chosen today's technology or tomorrow's then maybe we would not [have been] successful but we chose to focus on the future. We were not familiar with E-Beam technology or electrolithography. Today, I think it would be very difficult to develop such cooperation because we are now going to very different concepts.

I think they [the managers] had a very nice experience in the labs. They were able to meet researchers from other companies.

Another manager rated the project as "70 out of 100":

First, secrecy prevented disclosure in full. Second, the mental pressures on researchers were great. But so much was gained...The R&D outcomes were disclosed so the company gained much knowledge it did not have before.

The disclosure interested Americans too. But our company also gave things that they did not wish to. The weakest gained the most [and] became relatively strong; the relative position of the big firms changed. We are more careful about what to do jointly and what to do ourselves.

Every researcher told people from the mother company that pressure was very high at the laboratories. They gained from the personal experience of companies that had different atmospheres. But they knew that the company reputation was at stake.

A manager who directed the lab led by Company B said:

The cooperative lab was so special. The reason why the companies were so isolated from each other was because of the poor technology. We didn't want to open our research studies to other companies, simply because we were anxious about how far we were behind other companies. But right now the Japanese technology is coming up so nicely, so we talked more freely with other people from other companies. [The cooperative laboratories were] a great implement for future national projects. In every national project, the question is now...should we make a joint laboratory or not? ...We have joint laboratories for the fifth generation of computers. The fact is we were forced to participate...We are impressed by the results of cooperation, but I would say that nowadays in our company and other companies, we have many, many things to do and many projects. We need plenty of good engineers to do these things ourselves...so unless we are the ones to recognize that a kind of joint laboratory is necessary, we have to be forced to participate.

Reflecting on the strategic implications of the project, he noted:

I do not think the competition problem was so great simply because the cooperative laboratories were so small, time was so limited, and the subject limited. So I do not know what was going on in other companies. But my unique experience was to know the people in the other companies... That was a very nice experience.

Each lab was different. Laboratory one, two, and three had a most serious target, so we did work hard overnight, the weekend...at a later stage near termination, all the people did hard work. There was something else that was interesting. If a scientist worked in Company C, they always had many kinds of meetings and had to write documents. But there was no such [busy] work in the cooperative laboratories ...they concentrated on the research, just like the American industrial laboratories. In Japanese research laboratories there are many things to do [laughter]. In Company C, if we want scientists to work more than 40 hours we have to negotiate with the union.

We had a joke—if we were free to decide or make a choice, to which company would we move [laughter]? We had very interesting discussions.

An interesting factor for the manager was that compensation was from the mother company. So even in the same job at the laboratory, they did not know each other's salary. This was nice...even the bonus would come on a different day. But the problem in a certain sense at the cooperative laboratory is if a company is really ignoring the work that someone is doing there. Actually, we did not work for Suzuki. We worked for Company C…in the end I worked for Company C and myself.

The results of the projects were dramatic: 1,000 patents were applied for in VLSI process technology. (See Exhibit 6.) At the second conference on VLSI held in 1982, the number of papers from Japan equaled those from the United States.

Mr. Sato's assessment of the project provides some insight into what it meant to manage such a venture:

Recalling the past four years, I wonder what factors added up to make this joint project successful.

First of all, I believe that the association was able to start the study to develop VLSI at a very good time. In the process of the study, all the research staff of the association, from the top to bottom, clearly understood at least the meaning of this research project.

Secondly, we cannot ignore that we sufficiently considered what we were going to do before actually starting on the project. The subjects and contents of this project had been discussed for nearly one year before the association launched it. As a matter of fact, in a series of assessment meetings, childish arguments and verbal attacks of others were repeated. But I would say that such arguments were very effective to bring eventual success to our project. I think we could produce outstanding results because we could argue frankly, stressing each position and the [desire] to seek corporate profits. Over the last three months, we held meetings to decide on ways of redistributing the use of machinery and equipment to the members…many high performance machines [the members] were friendly enough to provide chances for rival firms to receive the items they hoped for…

What concerned me most was each event which rocked the period, rather than reports of many fruitful results of the study. All of the events, I am sure, would be very important [to examine] for the future equivalent of this joint study.

The contribution by research workers is the third point I would like to stress. The themes of the studies done were all of the first grade. In the first half…an important researcher attended scientific meetings as one of the audience, but in the latter half he presented the data of the research as a team member. This might have largely encouraged other members of each section or other research workers. This project is significant in that the joint project team could afford to spend large amounts of funds, several times greater than a single enterprise can do on R&D. And the team could conduct a broader spectrum of research with the huge amounts of money. [And] it was found out that we proved that it was possible even for an institution made up of competitors to be successful, depending upon the "boundary condition."…

However, a joint-study association cannot always be successful. Without favorable conditions, it is doubtful that it can do well…one of the factors for our success [might be] that our association was managed and operated on a four-year basis. We were forced to work overnight and overtime because our project period was set to four years. It would be…reasonable to limit a project period to a certain period.

By the way, research staffs of the association…became "friends," and a "graduates' group" was organized. The get-togethers of this sort are really welcome.

It [is] one of the greatest pleasures for me to have witnessed and managed the world's first successful joint research project by rivalling companies.

APPENDIX A
COOPERATION FOR COMPETITION: UNITED STATES AND JAPAN
THE DEVELOPMENT OF THE JAPANESE COMPUTER AND
SEMICONDUCTER INDUSTRY IN THE POST–WORLD WAR II
PERIOD

The history of the Japanese computer industry in the post–World War II period may be divided into three periods. In the first period (1951–1963), the industry received modest governmental attention and grew slowly. In the second period (1964–1975), it gained increasing strategic importance, received extensive governmental protection and support, and grew rapidly. And in the current period, beginning with trade liberalization in 1976, the industry has become the guiding force for Japan's industrial development. Although the government's postliberalization program simply extends the policies of an earlier era, there is now a critical difference: the semiconductor and computer industry is repositioned to be the center of a matrix of new "flagship" industries.

THE EARLY YEARS, 1951–1963

Japan's interest in the computer arose from its desire to avert technological domination by the United States. The first projects began in the early 1950s (approximately ten years after development of the Mark I digital computer in the United States) and were based at the universities. In 1951, Tokyo University scientists and the Tokyo Shibaura Co. Ltd. (Toshiba) began full-scale computer development using a large number of vacuum tubes. In 1954, the parametron was invented by Dr. Eiichi Goto of Tokyo University, an event that greatly encouraged government support.

Shortly thereafter, two new projects were launched that laid the foundation for Japan's first commercial computer products. One project, under the auspices of the Agency for Industrial Science and Technology, sought to formulate computer logic using transistors. A second was located at Tokyo University, the Communications Research Laboratory at Nippon Telephone and Telegraph (NTT), and at NTT's international affiliate, the Kokusai Denshin Denwa Co. (KDD). NTT focused on electronic switching using the parametron; KDD began developing code conversion equipment.

The arrival in 1954 of the first American computer exports underscored for many Japanese observers the need to develop an independent industry. In 1955, MITI organized a research committee at the behest of the principal transistor manufacturers (Nippon Electric [NEC], Fujitsu, Hitachi, Matsushita, and Toshiba), to consider the future of the computer industry. Members included MITT and NTT officials, prospective manufacturers, and various scientists; budget for the first year was $2,200.

The committee's conclusions sketched the course of future policy: (1) industrial growth should be encouraged, (2) foreign technology should be acquired, and (3) imports of computers should be limited.

Implementation of these objectives soon began. Japan's Electronics Industry Provisional Development Act of 1957 authorized direct subsidies for the research and development of promising technology; loans to products just entering commercial production; accelerated tax depreciation on plant and equipment and a special tax credit for research and development; and selective exemptions from the antitrust laws to permit cartels for the control and allocation of raw materials, production, and joint research. A new electronics industry division was established within MITI's Heavy Industry Bureau, and an Electronics Industry Deliberation Council was created to serve as a liaison with the industry.

Although the government's program was principally under MITI's jurisdiction, MITI did not attempt to regulate directly; instead, market forces, lubricated by government support, were to drive the industry's development. Moreover, the approximate $1 million in total subsidies awarded the computer industry during 1957–1961 were extremely modest. Total subsidies, tax savings, and loans from the Japan Development Bank (a long-term credit institution under the jurisdiction of the Ministry of Finance) were less than $25 million.

The period 1957–1960 marked the introduction of the first Japanese commercial computer projects. In 1957, both NEC and Hitachi began marketing a series of small business computers (known as the NEAC1200 and HIPAC1 series, respectively) using the parametron. Soon, however, IBM introduced its IBM 1401 model, launching the second generation of computers.

Despite Japan's progress, many of its industry leaders still feared a foreign takeover. By 1960, foreign imports claimed 70 percent of the Japanese digital computer market, and IBM (and to a lesser extent Sperry Rand) controlled the basic patents to electronic data processing equipment. IBM, it was feared, would unduly influence the development of Japan's computer industry. To repel this threat, the Japanese government raised the basic tariff rate from 15 percent to 25 percent, toughened allocations of foreign exchange for imported computers, and inaugurated vigorous "buy-Japan" procurement policies. MITI conditioned IBM's right to manufacture in Japan and remit profits on that company's agreement to license its basic patents to all interested Japanese manufacturers.

Financing remained a problem. Although the six domestic manufacturers enjoyed easy access to commercial credit and a special "strategic industry" tax exemption, development of the computer was an expensive and risky undertaking. MITI encouraged the industry to pool its resources; the three-year FONTAC project, sponsored by the Agency for Industrial Science and Technology, served as a prototype for later cooperative efforts. Under the project, Fujitsu took responsibility for software and Oki and Nipon Electrtic shared the burden of hardware development.

In 1961, MITI also persuaded the industry to establish a $3 million joint venture called the Japan Electronic Computer Corp. (JECC), financed by private industry and loans from the Japan Development Bank. JECC purchased computers from manufacturers and rented them to end users; the manufacturer agreed to repurchase obsolete equipment. Losses resulting from the repurchase of obsolete equipment could then be partially set off against a special tax reserve fund.

Particularly in the early years, the establishment of JECC gave substantial relief to the Japanese industry. IBM and the other foreign firms had been renting their machines at one-fortieth to one-sixtieth of the purchase price (including maintenance costs) per month, and this practice had enticed many Japanese firms to purchase these machines. JECC thus served two functions: it met the financial needs of its Japanese members and it discouraged foreign competition. IBM and other foreign manufacturers were excluded from JECC, but more important, Japanese systems containing more than an established percentage of foreign made components (approximately 25 percent) were made ineligible for JECC financing.

THE RISE OF THE INFORMATION INDUSTRY, 1964–1975

In 1964, IBM introduced its new System 360, acclaimed as the third generation of computers. IBM's announcement coincided more or less with General Electric's acquisition in Europe of the largest French manufacturer, Machines Bull. Despite its efforts, Japan was falling farther behind.

The government's first action was to request that the Electronic Industry Deliberation Council, prepare a report setting forth the basic elements of the response required: to achieve independent technological excellence, increase domestic market share, expand government industry cooperation, initiate development of a "super" computer, strengthen JECC, rationalize production of peripheral equipment, and educate new technicians.

Institutional change was also needed. MITI established a data analysis center within its bureau for intelligence and policy, and organized a subcommittee on the information industry in the Industrial Structure Deliberation Council. The six computer manufacturers and JECC were also encouraged to establish a private institute, the Japan Information Processing Development Center, and in 1965 the Japan Federation of Economic Organizations (Keidanren) formed its own computer policy review committee.

Between 1966 and 1975, the government worked closely with the industry to develop "target" technologies. One important effort (1966–1971) was the development of a "super/high performance" (high speed) computer, a ¥10 billion project under MITI's Electro-Technical Laboratory (ETL). Hitachi was the prime contractor; Fujitsu and NEC took computer mainframes; and Toshiba, Oki, and Mitsubishi had responsibility for optical character recognition (OCR), kanji display and graphic cathode ray tube (CRT) displays. Hitachi and Fujitsu developed disk drives; NEC and Hitachi developed computer language compilers, operating systems and utility programs; and Tokyo University began researching high-speed logic circuits.

A second effort was the NTT (Dendenksha) Information Processing System (DIPS) project initiated in 1968 by NTT in collaboration with Fujitsu, Hitachi, and

NEC. Its purpose was to connect large-scale, on-line (timesharing) computer systems to electronic exchange and transmission systems. In 1973, NTT announced that the project had developed a model with three times the power of other existing Japanese systems.

The ¥35 billion PIPS (Pattern Information Processing System) project (197180) continuing the work of the earlier superhigh-speed performance project, was charged with developing a "fourth-generation pattern information" system that could recognize Japanese characters, three-dimensional objects, and human speech.

These three programs contributed to closing the hardware gap with IBM.

Although hardware remained the most important priority during the 1960s, MITI also recognized a need to perfect software and train personnel. In 1970, the Information Technology Promotion Agency was organized to marshal $720 million through the government's and manufacturers' financial investment and loan program with the majority of funds used to guarantee loans to private software companies and the remainder to develop and diffuse advanced software. This effort and the Information Technology Institute, a research center established within the Japan Information Processing Development Center that inaugurated regional programs to train systems analysts, senior programmers, and other specialists contributed directly to the rise of the Japanese software industry in the next years.

Although the government gave priority to the development of the computer industry, semiconductors also became increasingly important after 1960. From the outset, government policies toward the semiconductor industry were linked to the computer because the major computer manufacturers were also the major semiconductor producers. In semiconductors, MITI's overriding objective was to limit foreign competition and acquire foreign know-how and technology. The government discouraged foreign purchases of stock in Japanese semiconductor firms, and rejected all foreign requests to establish wholly owned manufacturing subsidiaries and joint ventures with over 50 percent foreign equity.

A well-known case was Texas Instruments' effort to form a wholly owned manufacturing outlet in Japan. After years of negotiation, Texas Instruments at last reached a settlement with the Japanese government. In exchange for MITI's permission to establish a 50–50 joint manufacturing venture with Sony, Texas Instruments reportedly agreed to license its vital integrated circuit patents to Nippon Electric, Hitachi, Mitsubishi, Toshiba, and Sony, and to limit its production to 10 percent or less of the Japanese integrated circuit market.

By 1969, it was obvious that the six major computer and semiconductor manufacturers were operating inefficiently. MITI well understood that, despite generous government assistance, if the Japanese firms continued to produce similar systems for a domestic market a fraction of the size of the U.S. market, the industry would not be able to compete internationally. MITI therefore decided to expedite the development of core technologies and realign the industry.

The 1971 Law for Provisional Measures to Promote Specific Electronic and Machinery Industries (Kidenho) provided legal authority for targeting "state-of-the-art" technologies. Designed as strategically important were (1) technologies demanding a special R&D investment (including all technology where Japan was substantially behind the United States, e.g., digital computers, integrated circuits, (2) technologies where it was thought a large volume of production would yield economies of scale (magnetic disks and facsimile equipment); and (3) technologies where modernized production techniques were becoming increasingly necessary to improve quality and performance and to reduce production costs.

MITI's realignment policy had two objectives: first, to reduce the risk of foreign takeovers once capital liberalization began (in 1969, deemed inevitable), and second, to expand production and encourage specialization in order to increase exports and diversify markets.

Realignment, however, did not please the industry. Independent, proud, and fiercely competitive, each of the manufacturers resisted relinquishing auton-omy. There were other impediments: the companies' inability or unwillingness to dismiss lifetime employees, the difficulty of restructuring relations with commercial banks, rigidities of vertical integration that inhibited mergers and spin-offs, and the restraints imposed by licensing arrangements with American producers.

But MITI's policies eventually prevailed. In 1969, exercising its authority under the 1957 Electronics Act, MITI cartelized the production and design of some peripheral equipment believing that further innovation in this sector was unlikely. The cartel was directed through a steering committee of the major manufacturers under MITI's supervision.

In 1971, the six major manufacturers agreed to form three groups: (1) Hitachi and Fujitsu, (2) NEC and Toshiba, and (3) Mitsubishi Electric and Oki. During 1972–1976, each group received subsidies totaling ¥57.47 billion for research and development; an additional ¥4.63 billion was paid to the peripheral equipment manufacturers (including the six major companies). On the eve of liberalization, the industry again regrouped. Mitsubishi joined Fujitsu and Hitachi, and Oki Electric split off to specialize as a terminal manufacturer.

The Hitachi-Fujitsu association paired two technically and financially strong companies. In the NEC-Toshiba alignment, the relationship of the American cross-licensees may have been more important than the financial strength of the companies. In the United States the computer division of General Electric, the Toshiba licensee, had merged with Honeywell, NEC's licensee. The Mitsubishi-Oki arrangement linked the financially strongest company (Mitsubishi) to the firm with perhaps the closest ties with the United States via its joint venture, Oki-Univac.

The alliance also produced a shakeout. Although the Oki-Mitsubishi collaboration produced the COSMOS computer series, Oki decided to withdraw in 1975 as noted. It has since concentrated on peripherals. Some observers viewed Mitsubishi's pairing with Hitachi and Fujitsu to be temporary and limited to the purposes of the VLSI project. The NEC-Toshiba alliance produced the ACOS computer series (100, 200, 700, 900).

Fujitsu's and Hitachi's attempt to build the "M" series reveals the conflicts that have at times attended MITI's efforts to promote intraindustry cooperation. Initially, Fujitsu was to be responsible for the "M"-160 and "M"-190, and Hitachi, the "M"-170 and "M"-180 models. The arrangement, however, collapsed when Fujitsu announced its new M-1802 model and Hitachi retaliated with two models of its own.

Yet Fujitsu and Hitachi's cooperation has not been entirely fruitless. In September 1973, the two companies formed a 50–50 joint venture, the Nippon Peripherals Ltd. (NPL), to conduct R&D, and manufacture and market peripherals and terminals. NPL has signed agreements on an OEM basis with Memorex, NCR Japan, Mitsubishi Electric, and other domestic Japanese manufacturers, and in recent years has greatly expanded its overseas sales.

LIBERALIZATION AND ITS AFTERMATH

On December 24, 1975, the Japanese government inaugurated a new round of trade liberalization. Foreign capital investment was greatly expedited and the burdensome import quota system was eliminated. Trade and investment in computers were completely liberalized on schedule by April 1976. On the eve of its new policy the cabinet released the following statement:

> Because the computer industry is becoming increasingly important to the future of our economy, society, and the people's daily life, we have tried to foster and strengthen this industry. On the occasion of the import liberalization...the government [will continue to] cherish the independence and future growth of Japan's computer industry, and will keep an eye on movements in the computer market so that liberalization will not adversely affect domestic producers nor produce confusion. The government and the local public organizations, industrial and financial circles shall endeavor to recognize and understand this situation correctly.

That resolution set the tone for the government's liberalization "counter-measures" policies that continue today.

To mitigate liberalization, the government expanded its support for research and development of "core" technologies, and foreign penetration of the Japanese market was checked, principally by limiting foreign procurement opportunities and by administrative restraints. Japanese planners reasoned that these restraints could be relaxed, gradually because market forces would limit foreign participation naturally, when Japanese industry became more competitive. It was hoped that, by the early 1980s, Japan's industry could begin its own drive on the world market.

Exhibit 1 AMD, Inc., Financial Summary—For the Ten Years Ending March 28, 1982 (thousands of $ except per share amounts)

	1973	1974	1975	1976	1977	1978	1979	1980	1981	1982
Net sales	$ 11,199	$ 26,429	$ 25,815	$ 34,387	$ 62,116	$ 92,331	$148,276	$225,593	$309,391	$281,580
Expenses:										
Cost of Sales	6,531	15,959	18,292	20,491	35,565	58,728	90,541	115,967	171,113	167,617
Research and development	751	1,485	1,715	2,132	5,529	6,960	10,886	28,309	35,136	44,557
Marketing, general and administrative	2,576	4,702	6,511	8,953	12,435	17,331	27,044	43,910	64,723	64,405
	9,858	22,146	26,518	31,576	53,529	83,019	128,471	188,186	270,972	276,579
Operating income (loss)	1,341	4,283	(703)	2,811	8,587	9,312	19,805	37,407	38,419	5,001
Interest expense (income), net	(202)	(365)	707	577	413	627	(200)	159	1,844	1,651
Income (loss) before items listed below	1,543	4,648	(1,410)	2,234	8,174	8,685	20,005	37,248	36,575	3,350
Provision (credit) for taxes on income	797	2,219	(421)	800	3,700	3,648	9,050	13,971	11,891	(5,600)
Cumulative effect of change in deferred income accounting in 1975 and benefits of NOL carry-forwards in 1973	(577)	—	1,483							
Net income (loss)	$ 1,323	$ 2,429	$ (2,472)	$ 1,434	$ 4,474	$ 5,037	$ 10,955	$ 23,277	$ 24,684	$ 8,950
Net income (loss) per share	$ 0.14	$ 0.22	$ (0.23)	$ 0.13	$ 0.38	$ 0.41	$ 0.76	$ 1.53	$ 1.55	$ 0.55
Shares used in per share calculations	9,610	10,938	10,766	11,416	11,672	12,302	14,342	15,177	15,894	16,291
Long-term debt	$ 44	$ 161	$ 7,062	$ 4,172	$ 8,560	$ 6,788	$ 6,417	$ 14,517	$ 28,954	$ 36,820
Depreciation and amortization	122	703	1,668	2,087	2,334	3,158	5,806	10,087	16,399	22,516
Total assets	$ 12,850	$ 20,735	$ 23,370	$ 27,041	$ 40,774	$ 74,768	$109,477	$164,756	$224,694	$243,523

Exhibit 2   Attending Organizations

The Microelectronics and Computer Technology Corporation
Meeting in Orlando, Florida
February 19, 1982

- Advanced Micro Devices, Inc.
- Burroughs Corporation
- Computer and Business Equipment Manufacturers Association
- Control Data Corporation
- Department of Defense
- Digital Equipment Corporation
- Electronic Industries Association
- Gellman Research Associates
- Harris Corporation
- Honeywell, Inc.
- Massachusetts Institute of Technology
- Mostek Corporation
- Motorola Corporation
- National Cash Register Corporation
- National Semiconductor Corporation
- Rockwell International
- Signetics Corporation
- Sperry Corporation
- Texas Instruments
- United Technologies Corporation
- Xerox Corporation

Exhibit 3   Biographical Sketch of Bobby Ray Inman

Bobby Ray Inman was born in Rhonesboro, Texas, in 1928. He graduated from the University of Texas with a Bachelor of Arts degree in 1950. In 1951, he entered the Naval Reserve; he was commissioned as an ensign in 1952.

Admiral Inman served in the Korean and Vietnam conflicts. He was graduated from the Naval War College in 1972 and, from that year until 1977, was director of Naval Intelligence. He became director of the National Security Agency in July 1977 and served in that capacity until March 1981, when he was promoted to admiral—he was the first naval intelligence specialist to attain four-star rank. At the same time as that appointment, he was also assigned the post of deputy director of the Central Intelligence Agency.

Admiral Inman retired from government service on July 1, 1982, with the permanent rank of admiral.

Currently, he is a director of the Federal Reserve Bank of Dallas, Science Applications, Inc., Texas Eastern Co., and Tracor, Inc. He also serves in a volunteer status as director of the Arms Control Association and the Rickover Foundation. He is a trustee of the Brookings Institution, Southwestern University, and the St. James School. He is a senior fellow at the Hoover Institution of War,

Peace, and Revolution at Stanford University and is a member of the Defense Science Board, Governor's Science and Technology Advisory Council of the State of Texas.

Exhibit 4   Summary of MCC Benefits

Benefits will flow primarily to MCC shareholders and secondarily to other firms in the U.S. microelectronics-based industries.
Benefits to MCC's shareholders include

– The broadened scope of research and development.
– The reduced duplication of research and development.
– The more rapid integration of vertically related technologies.
– The reduction in the ratio of invested capital to value of research and development results.
– The joint development and availability of commonly needed tools and services (such as training and CAD tools).
– The heightened awareness of technology needs and traps.
– Optimum utilization of scarce technical talent.

These benefits, in combination, will serve dramatically to enhance the competitive position of MCC shareholders as well as the rest of U.S. microelectronics-based industry in its markets at home and abroad.
Without MCC, many of these benefits will be denied MCC shareholders and the nation as a whole. MCC is appropriately viewed in a "but for" context: It will be possible in years to come to advance such conclusions as, "But for MCC, the U.S. economy would not be deriving all the benefits it is now enjoying through the exploitation of microelectronics technology in both domestic and worldwide markets."

Exhibit 5   Projected MCC Activities

Activities related to microelectronics and computers to be carried out by MCC include

– Basic research.
– Applied research.
– Instrumentation development.
– Process development and testing.
– Packaging technology.
– Prototype or pilot plant operation.
– Software development, related to the microelectronics design and production processes.
– Computer architecture research.
– Artificial intelligence research.

 – Training and education in microelectronics and computer science.
 – Liasion with university and other research facilities.
 – Liaison with industry and trade associations.

   The scope of MCC's activities will be determined by its overriding objective: to enable the United States to compete vigorously and successfully in all markets for computing systems and microelectronics components, devices, and products.

Exhibit 6   The Work of the Project

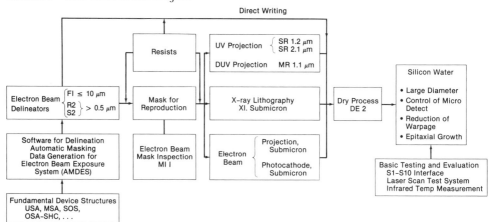

Important accomplishments as summarized by one non–Japanese competitor:

Development	Date	Manufacturer	Description
1. Electron Beam Exposure Systems			
a. Model S–2	3/80	Fujitsu	Minimum 0.5 μm line width; 9–15 min. to draw 1 M–bit chip
b. Model VL–R2	2/80	Toshiba	Minimum 0.5 μm line width; 12 min. to draw 5″ mask
c. Model F	5/79	Hitachi	Minimum 0.5 μm line width for 1 M–bit VLSI production
2. X-ray Exposure Unit	12/79	Joint Development	1 μm pattern drawing Maximum 50 4″ wafers (negative resist) per hour
3. Dry Etching Unit	3/80	N E C	Minimum 0.5 μm reproduction 40 wafers per hour
4. Automatic Masking Data Generation for Electron Beam Exposure System (AMDES)	3/80	Joint Development	Software system for submicron electron beam lithography

Source: From a non-Japanese company.

ENDNOTES

1. Julian Gressler, *High Technology and Japanese Industrial Policy*, Subcommittee on Trade of the Ways and Means Committee, U.S. House of Representatives, October 1, 1980.
2. Interviews at MITI, Tokyo, August 1982.

3. Gressler, *High Technology and Japanese Industrial Policy.*
4. Interviews at MITI.
5. Gressler, *High Technology.*

Sources and Implications of Strategic Decline: The Case of Japanese–American Competition in Microelectronics

Charles H. Ferguson Center for Technology, Policy, and Industrial Development Massachusetts Institute of Technology

ABSTRACT

The past decade has seen severe erosion of America's technological and competitive position in a number of areas critical to future economic growth and military power—robotics, microelectronics, and advanced materials, among others. One symptom of (and contributor to) the erosion of U.S. leadership has been the decline of the U.S. semiconductor industry in the face of Japanese competition. Between 1978 and the present, Japan's share of the world semiconductor market (now about $30 billion) rose from 28 percent to nearly 50 percent, the American industry's world market share declined rapidly (from 60 percent to 40 percent, approximately), and the United States became a large net importer of advanced semiconductors.

Close analysis of the semiconductor industry's decline calls into question the adequacy of several frequently advocated policies, as well the conventional economic models upon which some recommendations are based. Japanese–American semiconductor competition has fundamentally been driven by strategic and institutional forces, and is a contest between two sectoral systems (including relevant governmental components) more than market competition of the sort typically described by economic theory.

The Japanese industry succeeded because its strategic regime encouraged external predation and rewarded investments in future productivity while simultaneously restraining consumption and unproductive distributional conflict. Conversely the American regime encouraged short-term calculations, distributional conflict, and consumption relative to investment. Moreover, in the presence of external challenges, U.S. firms practiced lifeboat diplomacy, betraying each other, their customers, and their suppliers rather than improving collective, long-run productivity.

Whether the American regime can now be changed sufficiently to preserve a competitive industry is unclear. However, policy measures which do not recognize the strategic deadlocks facing the industry will be ineffective or even detrimental. Policy interventions must lengthen the time horizons of U.S. actors, encourage vertical integration, and ensure that assistance yields enduring productivity gains rather than short-term profits. Otherwise the industry will waste government support just as it wasted the superiority it once enjoyed.

Revised, June 30, 1987. Reprinted with permission by the author.

INTRODUCTION

The crisis of the American semiconductor industry represents the first public appearance of an issue likely to assume great prominence in the years ahead. The past decade has seen severe erosion of America's technological and competitive position in a number of areas critical to future economic growth and military power—robotics, microelectronics, and advanced materials, among others.[1] The ultimate effects of continued decline, though impossible to predict in detail, could be quite large. They may include lower living standards for the American people; a major increase in Japan's leverage in American, and indeed global, affairs; and rising tension over relationships between government policies and national economic performance.

One symptom of, and contributor to, the erosion of U.S. economic and technological hegemony has been the decline of the U.S. semiconductor industry in the face of Japanese competition. Between 1978 and the present, Japan's share of the world semiconductor market (now about $30 billion) rose from 28 to 50 percent, the American industry's world market share declined rapidly, and the United States became a large net importer of advanced semiconductors.[2] Japan now leads in several technologies and continues to progress more rapidly than the United States.[3]

Microelectronics is a rapidly growing sector increasingly critical to the computer, telecommunications, aerospace, robotics, automobile, and defense industries.[4] Hence—and as recent political events demonstrate—it is not an arena in which U.S. failure, and/or Japanese hegemony, will be taken lightly. But the significance of U.S. decline, and the optimal policy for reversing it, depend upon the forces which underly the industry's competitive dynamics. And here, the semiconductor industry offers some interesting cautionary lessons. Many analyses of U.S. industrial difficulties have focused upon mature, concentrated, and unionized sectors, citing attendant rigidities and/or macroeconomic forces as the causes of U.S. decline. Yet the semiconductor case shows that American troubles extend to an entrepreneurial, fragmented, nonunionized high-technology industry. Furthermore, close analysis of this industry calls into question the adequacy of several frequently advocated policies, as well the economic models of markets, firm-level behavior, and international trade upon which some recommendations are based.

In particular, Japanese–American semiconductor competition has fundamentally been driven by strategic and institutional forces, and accordingly must be understood as a contest between two sectoral systems (including relevant governmental components) more than as market competition of the sort typically described by economic theory. Although traditional economic variables (such as national market access or closure, exchange rates, industry structure, and the costs of capital and labor) certainly played a role, they were often the consequence of strategic processes and institutional performance as much as their cause. Hence to understand U.S. decline, we will need to consider the institutional system which shaped the decisions and performance of the U.S. industry. Both in the United States and Japan, successive actions by employees, firms, and government policymakers reflected and continuously reinforced systemic incentives. Their result is the international contrast in industrial structure, conduct, and competitive success which confronts us today.

The Japanese industry succeeded because its strategic regime encouraged external predation, rewarded investments in future productivity, and provided rigorous competitive discipline, while simultaneously restraining consumption and unproductive distributional conflict. Conversely the American regime encouraged short-term calculations, distributional conflict, and consumption relative to investment, so that in the long run Americans were collectively inefficient relative to Japanese producers. Moreover, the American regime was not only chronically inefficient, it was also inflexible and self-destructive when placed under stress. In the presence of external challenges, U.S. firms faced incentives to practice lifeboat diplomacy—to betray each other, their customers, and their suppliers rather than to improve the sector's collective, long-run productivity.

Hence when Japan entered global competition, the resulting American decline was largely predetermined. Whether the American regime can now be changed enough to preserve a competitive industry remains unclear. However, policy measures which do not recognize the strategic deadlocks facing the industry will be ineffective or even detrimental. Successful policy interventions must lengthen the time horizons of industrial actors and ensure that assistance yields enduring productivity gains, rather than short-term profits, inflationary wage spirals, or zero-sum distributional competitions. Otherwise, the industry will waste or consume government support just as it wasted the technological superiority it once enjoyed.

THE DEVELOPMENT AND COMPARATIVE STRUCTURE OF THE U.S. AND JAPANESE INDUSTRIES

Until the late 1970s, the U.S. and Japanese semiconductor industries evolved quasi-independently. Japan imported U.S. technology and capital equipment,[5] restricted both import penetration and direct foreign investment by U.S. semiconductor firms,[6] produced for its domestic market (particularly the consumer electronics industry), but largely refrained from export drives directed at the United States.[7] The U.S. industry sold technology to Japan, generally acquiesced to closure of the Japanese market, but also controlled the rest of the world market. At the height of its success in the mid-1970s, the U.S. industry held 95 percent of its domestic market, half of Europe's, and 60 percent of the world market—though less than a third of Japan's.[8]

The Japanese and U.S. national industries also diverged structurally. The Japanese industry became a relatively stable oligopoly[9] protected by the national government from foreign competition. Imports were controlled, and direct foreign investment was effectively prohibited. Semiconductor production was dominated by diversified, vertically integrated firms such as Nippon Electric Corp. (NEC) and Hitachi, for whom semiconductors accounted for 10 to 25 percent of total revenues.[10] These firms used roughly a quarter of their semiconductor production internally in the electronics products which constituted their principal businesses. They also maintained close, enduring relationships with their suppliers, the Tokyo city banks, the national government, and sometimes each other.[11] Entry into the Japanese industry came only through the diversification efforts of other large industrial complexes (Kawasaki, Sanyo, Sharp, Sony) rather than through the creation of new firms confined to semiconductor production. The industry's major firms also followed typical Japanese personnel practices such as lifetime employment, so employee turnover was consequently low.

In the United States, by contrast, there evolved a two-part industry, divided into "captives" and "merchants." The few major and relatively stable "captives," such as IBM and AT&T, produced for their internal use but refrained from market competition. Conversely the open-market "merchant" industry, which at its peak accounted for 70 percent of U.S. production and dominated the world market,[12] evolved into a structurally unstable, fragmented, highly entrepreneurial arena.[13] Most U.S. merchant producers were young, relatively small firms whose semiconductor sales represented at least 40 percent, and often the entirety, of their total revenue.[14] Market leadership, employee loyalties, and supplier relationships were transitory; many semiconductor and capital equipment producers rose and fell rapidly, and employee turnover averaged 20 percent across the industry.[15] For 20 years this pattern of instability, frequent mobility, and new venture formation was considered a critical factor in the industry's success,[16] though by the mid-1970s the performance of IBM, AT&T, and the Japanese industry should have suggested otherwise.[17]

Equally striking, and analogous, is the contrast between the two nations' semiconductor capital equipment, materials, and services sectors. Once again, the Japanese industry is dominated by relatively large diversified firms, either semiconductor producers themselves or major firms with experience in relevant optical, chemical, mechanical, or construction technologies. And where the equipment producers themselves are small, they are linked to larger firms which consume much of their output.[18] For example, Fujitsu owns 22 percent of Advantest (test equipment); NEC owns 50 percent of Ando (testers); Hitachi owns Hitachi Electronic Engineering (various products); Hitachi and Matsushita manufacture their own automated assembly equipment; Toshiba and Hitachi produce electron beam machines used to make masks, the blueprints for integrated circuits; Nikon and Canon produce advanced lithography equipment; and Shimizu, a large construction firm, builds clean room facilities.[19]

The American capital equipment and services industry, in contrast, resembles its semiconductor-producing counterpart in its extreme fragmentation and entrepreneurialism.[20] A few stable, relatively large, established equipment firms (e.g., Teradyne and Perkin-Elmer) coexist and compete with innumerable "start-ups"—newly founded ventures such as Trillium, Master Images, Zycad, and hundreds of others. As of 1986, 55 percent of U.S. equipment and services vendors had annual sales of less than $5 million.[21] Nearly half are less than ten years old;[22] many are already failing. And even the established firms are having difficulties; for like its domestic clientele, the U.S. semiconductor equipment and services sector is decaying rapidly.

THE ONSET AND EXTENT OF AMERICAN DECLINE

American decline began roughly a decade ago and coincided with the transformation of semiconductor production from an artisanal endeavor to a complex, large-scale, capital-intensive activity. With the advent of very-large-scale integration (VLSI) in the late 1970s, microelectronics came of age. Capital-intensive, automated production became essential, as did large initial investments in product design, a wide technology base, large R&D efforts, and close relationships to equipment suppliers and final systems producers. As integrated circuits became in effect complete systems, they became strategically critical to a wide range of major industries including consumer electronics, computers, and weapons systems.[23]

These developments offered a potentially large advantage to Japanese semiconductor producers as a consequence of their technical diversification, large resources, and vertically integrated structure. This structural advantage, together with the rising strategic value of semiconductors, also offered the possibility of large future rewards in downstream industries based upon leadership in microelectronics. Beginning in the mid-1970s, the Japanese industry, in part assisted by its national government through such means as the VLSI Project sponsored by the Minsitry of International Trade and Industry (MITI), acted accordingly.

The ensuing decline of the American industry, which had previously dominated all advanced semiconductor markets, was noteworthy for its rapidity. Japanese firms now hold 75 percent of world markets for dynamic random access memories (DRAMs), 50 percent of world microprocessor markets, 70 percent of world microcontroller markets, and 40 percent of the world market for application-specific integrated circuits (ASICs).[24] Japan's share of the total world market nearly doubled to 50 percent in less than a decade, while the U.S. industry's world market share shrank by 20 percent. Six of the world's ten largest open market semiconductor producers are now Japanese, the United States is a major net importer of semiconductors, Japanese capital spending has surpassed that of the U.S. merchant industry, and the Japanese domestic semiconductor market is now larger than that of the United States.[25]

Less widely appreciated, but probably equally important, is the concomitant and similar decline of U.S. capital equipment, materials, and services technology. Over the past decade, the Japanese equipment industry's world market share has more than doubled to over 30 percent, primarily at the expense of U.S. firms.[26] Moreover, Japanese suppliers have reached parity or even superiority in major technologies, including packaging, automated assembly equipment, various ultrapure materials, some categories of fabrication equipment, and specialized procedures such as maskmaking.[27] For example, Hoya and Shin-Etsu now hold 90 percent of the world market for mask-quality glass and quartz; IBM's new East Fishkill facility is being built by Shimizu; and Japanese firms supply nearly half of Intel's masks.[28]

Relative R&D performance has changed as dramatically. While the United States still leads in many areas of theoretical research, it now trails in applied R&D. Between 1975 and 1982 the U.S.' share of world integrated circuit patent activity declined from 43 percent to 27 percent, while Japan's share rose from 18 percent to

48 percent.[29] By the mid-1980s, over 40 percent of papers presented at the IEEE Solid State Circuits Conference came from Japan, as did over 20 percent of all semicondctor technical publications worldwide.[30] Japanese efforts in X-ray lithography, which will probably dominate semiconductor production by the mid-1990s, appear to be far larger than those of the United States. NTT and its largest suppliers have embarked upon major programs for cooperative R&D, while among U.S. firms only IBM has a comparable effort.[31] Japan leads the United States in gallium arsenide research and appears to have reached at least parity in laser systems, optoelectronics, and several other major technologies.[32]

Absent major structural, behavioral, and policy changes, then, the prospect is for continued decline within the relevant American industries, and for Japanese dominance of most semiconductor technologies and markets by the mid-1990s. This prognosis is strongly reinforced by consideration of the structural sources of U.S. decline.

THE SOURCES OF THE U.S. INSTITUTIONAL REGIME

The American industry's decay was the result of a systemic pattern involving a number of interrelated forces, of which three are particularly salient. They are (1) chronic failures of government policy; (2) persistent disadvantages in the costs of capital and skilled labor; and (3) an entrenched sectoral regime whose member firms were unstable, immature, and shortsighted. The result was an industry incapable of developing the technologies, institutions, and skills required in global markets, and the creation of strong incentives to maximize immediate cash flow rather than long-run productivity. Moreover, each failure reinforced the others. The resulting institutional regime reduced the American industry's efficiency, perpetuated the perverse incentives shaping corporate strategy, and blocked productive responses to macroeconomic, political, and competitive problems. Let us therefore consider this regime's principal ingredients, and then how they combined to form a strategically inferior sectoral regime.

Government Policy Decisions

Government actions affecting the semiconductor industry, to the extent they exhibit any systematic pattern, have tended to fragment the industry and to shorten its time horizons, while failing to supply adequate levels of the resources, such as engineering education, required for long-run growth.

Although many early semiconductor innovations came from AT&T and General Electric,[33] by the 1970s the industry was dominated by smaller, entrepreneurial firms. In retrospect, this change appears partly to have been a byproduct of government actions focused on other issues—albeit one permitted by the initial small scale of early production and markets. In 1956 AT&T, then the dominant presence in semiconductor technology, agreed as part of an antitrust settlement to license upon demand its patents and to refrain from open market competition.[34] In effect, the history of the industry started over. There followed a rising flow of defectors from established, large firms such as AT&T and GE, into dozens of small, relatively new firms which sought to fill the vacuum left by AT&T's departure.[35] Hence, antitrust policy favored fragmentation over either concentration or industrywide cooperation. Until the early 1980s, when the 1969 IBM case and the 1976 AT&T case were both resolved and new legislation exempted cooperative research from antitrust constraints, antitrust policy was clearly antagonistic to the industry's concentration and/or rationalization.

In the 1960s this trend was furthered by Defense Department procurement policies at a time when the military dominated U.S. semiconductor markets. Throughout the 1960s, defense procurement demanded technology more advanced than commercial uses, was cost-insensitive, often paid for R&D and early production experience, but also often required firms to license second sources.[36] These policies, too, favored new firms over large established ones, and tended to fragment the industry. They may also have contributed to the industry's emphasis upon product R&D to the neglect of manufacturing efficiency. Thus early military procurement policy probably contributed to the industry's later structural problems. But it also performed valuable functions by reducing firm-level risk and funding generic R&D.

Unfortunately, these positive contributions largely ended in the 1970s, while new negative effects appeared. By the mid-1970s, the military ceased to provide substantial, commercially useful industrial support via its R&D and procurement spending. The military's share of total demand declined from 50 percent of U.S. consumption in 1965 to about 15 percent a decade later, and for several reasons military demand came to lag severely, rather than lead, commercial technology.[37] Concomitantly, in the 1970s defense procurement policies shifted away from support of generic R&D and toward specifically military technology, reducing commercial spin-off and drawing resources from commercial efforts, while remaining insensitive to manufacturing costs.[38] No commercial policy replaced the void left by the relative decline and changing nature of defense purchasing, so the industry's growing requirements for skilled labor, long-term capital investment, structural change, and Japanese market access remained unmet.

Other, nonmilitary, policies contributed seriously to the industry's fragmentation. The creation of new ventures through employee defections from established firms was subsidized by tax expenditures. Capital gains differentials, the tax treatment of losses, and the R&D tax credit favored new start-ups by making venture capital available on favorable terms, and lowered the capital costs of start-ups relative to those of established firms.[39] Worse, tax and regulatory changes greatly increased venture capital flows in the early 1980s, just as the industry's rising strategic importance and scale requirements made stability more important. In addition, the taxation of individual income—particularly of capital gains and incentive stock options—permitted start-ups to offer higher effective compensation than more mature firms.[40]

Capital and Labor Market Effects

Macroeconomic forces and national differentials in factor costs (for both capital and professional labor) certainly seem to have played a significant role in the industry's competitiveness. For decades prior to the recent rise of the yen and of Japanese living standards, American salaries for professionals and managers were perhaps double those in Japan. Several studies have indicated that capital costs were substantially higher as well.[41] Altogether, these disadvantages probably constituted a significant drag on the U.S. industry's competitiveness.

But economywide factor costs are not, by themselves, the principal source of the industry's problems. Even where factor cost differences were important, their effect upon the semicondctor industry was substantially worsened by problems whose basic causes lay elsewhere. High U.S. professional labor costs, for example, were raised further by the need to use wage increases to reduce personnel turnover, and high turnover also discouraged training which would have alleviated skilled labor shortages. U.S. microelectronics firms also faced higher effective capital costs as a result of their instability, through their obligation to pay risk premiums for debt and to maintain greater relative liquidity to cushion against external shocks such as recessions or exchange rate changes.

Even including these effects, however, factor cost differences cannot fully explain the American problem. The U.S. industry already showed signs of decline at a time when its aggregate R&D, capital spending, and resources still dwarfed Japan's, and prior to the dollar's rise in the early 1980s. As early as 1978, Japanese producers captured 40 percent of the world market for 16K memories, and Japanese products were judged superior in quality to those of the U.S. merchant industry.[42]

Nor do factor costs explain why the U.S. industry maintained its fragmented structure and entrepreneurial behavior despite steep, technogically driven increases in capital intensity, scale economies, and vertical integration requirements. By the early 1980s an efficient-scale semiconductor factory cost well over $100 million, and efficient production demanded both organizational sophistication and computer systems expertise. Similar forces were transforming capital equipment and materials technologies. Yet U.S. start-up creation actually accelerated in the early 1980s,[43] and sectoral rationalization is coming only through competitive decline, rather than through foresighted strategic decisions.

The Institutional Regime of the U.S. Industry

The forces acting upon the industry during its seminal period, then, included antitrust policies and decisions, the evolution of defense procurement, incentives for new ventures derived from tax effects, high capital and labor costs, and a few accidents of history. These conditions gave rise, perhaps somewhat by chance, to a rather unusual set of corporate structures and strategies. But once in place, this industrial regime was quite stable. It was systematically perpetuated, defects included, not only by the larger economic and policy environment, but also through the structure and practices of the merchant industry. The most striking of these factors were entrepreneurialism, structural instability, short life cycles for firms as well as products, high personnel turnover, wide use of incentive stock options (ISOs) vesting over four-year periods, and an extreme emphasis upon short-term, individual optimization. In short, the most stable feature of the system was the instability and turbulence of its individual elements.

Once corporate instability, high turnover, and the continuous formation of new ventures became accepted facts within the American industry, subsequent activity came to assume and thereby reinforce them. In Silicon Valley, a large infrastructure of venture capitalists, consultants, headhunters, subcontractors, equipment producers, service firms, and leasing companies arose in response to an industry constituted of young, unstable, cash-limited, entrepreneurial firms. Business practices came to assume instability, discouraging long-term commitments. Firms paid thousand-dollar rewards to employees who recruited personnel from other firms, including their previous employers. Stock options became essential to the recruiting and retention of talented employees until a public offering made founders, venture capitalists, and valued employees wealthy. (Thereafter, performance incentives and loyalty often waned considerably, and firms frequently became net victims of headhunting rather than predators.) Regional concentrations of high-technology firms, factor markets, and infrastructure—such as Silicon Valley—grew rapidly, reinforcing fragmentation by providing locally the ingredients for new ventures.[44] But as the regime reinforced and perpetuated itself, it also crippled the industry's long-run productivity and competitiveness.

THE INSTITUTIONAL SOURCES OF AMERICAN DECLINE

The U.S. industry's counterproductive behavior, and its decline, derived from elements of its strategic regime which encouraged shortsightedness, distributional conflict, and consumption relative to collective, long-run productivity growth. Hence, the industry gradually consumed and wasted rather than reinvested the fruits of its initially superior technological position and resources. When Japan reached technical parity and entered global competition, these same weaknesses worsened U.S. competitive difficulties. Rather than merging and/or increasing joint domestic R&D efforts, for example, U.S. firms exited markets, reduced long-term R&D, switched to Japanese suppliers, sold technology to foreign competitors, and sought protectionist measures at the expense of their own customers, including the U.S. computer industry. These problems were not incidental; they were deeply rooted in the organizational and strategic patterns of the industry.

Consider first some concomitants of the fact that the industry, particularly in Silicon Valley, consisted of shifting networks of entrepreneurial, small firms. The flexibility, market responsiveness, shared infastructure, and informational benefits of such networks have been much discussed. However, these benefits are accompanied by costs, one of which is vulnerability to predation. Even if networks of small-scale firms are highly productive, in the long run many of their benefits may accrue primarily to predators, and come at the expense of larger U.S. firms, future productivity gains, and/or the larger economy. Moreover, in the merchant industry's case, instability fed by unchecked entrepreneurialism led to inflationary spirals, shortened corporate planning horizons drastically, and slowed the increases in capital intensity and vertical integration implied by the direction of technological change. So the system was also incompatible with the industry's optimal growth path.

The fragmentation and instability of the industry left its member firms in poor bargaining positions vis-á-vis those with longer time horizons, better information, superior financial or organizational assets, or scarce talents. Hence whatever the system's productivity benefits, a high proportion of them were redistributed to others not likely to reinvest in the long-term welfare of the industry or the nation. If the accounting could ever be done, we might find that among the largest beneficiaries of the merchant industry's growth period were Japanese and South Korean technology buyers, Silicon Valley landholders, and several thousand of the nation's youngest Porsche and Lamborghini owners.[45] And in part because the industry's regime left it open to both external and internal predation, it was also a rather inefficient way to organize semiconductor production.

Consider, for example, the relationships among personnel turnover, firm life cycles, and long-run productivity. Turnover has averaged 20 percent industry-wide in American electronics, versus less than 5 percent in the Japanese industry and a few highly stable U.S. firms such as IBM and AT&T. One source of turnover is defection to new ventures; start-ups are typically founded and populated by experienced defectors from more established firms. Another source of turnover is failure; layoffs without notice have been common in many Silicon Valley firms, and they do not breed employee loyalty.

Excessive turnover through layoffs and defections reduces an industry's long run productivity.[46] Major defections severely disrupt important R&D efforts, customer relationships, or organizations. In some cases, entire R&D groups or design teams have defected in the midst of important projects. AT&T, General Electric, Motorola, Fairchild, and Intel among others have been the victims of mass defections which have caused severe operational disruptions. More generally, learning effects of several kinds are widely considered critical to competitive advantage in the semiconductor industry. Under conditions of high turnover, many learning opportunities are lost.

In the merchant industry the prevalence of defection reduced firms' time horizons, raised their costs, and reduced their propensity to make risky and/or long-payback investments. If training benefits future competitors rather than current employers, firms will rationally decline to invest in their employees.[47] Conversely, they will be incented to raid other firms to obtain needed skills. They will similarly be less inclined to invest in long term R&D likely to diffuse to competitors through turnover. And they will be forced into inflationary bidding spirals, raising compensation for important employees in order to keep turnover to acceptable levels. There is increasing agreement within the industry that these phenomena have major effects upon corporate policy and operational efficiency.[48]

Instability at the industry level—the rapid ascent and decline of firms—both reflected and aggravated high turnover levels, and also produced other large-scale pathologies. Long-term cooperation between semiconductor producers and their customers or suppliers was unsustainable and, therefore, was rarely practiced. Instead leasing, subcontracting, lenient second-sourcing and technology licensing, low-wage offshore assembly, and external sourcing were widely used by merchant firms to maximize cash flow and reduce capital requirements.[49]

These practices symptomized and worsened U.S. firms' inability to manufacture efficiently, to cooperate with suppliers, to trust and invest in their employees, to plan for future technological requirements, and to invest at efficient scale. Successive waves of young merchant and capital equipment firms thus fell victim to new technologies, and later Japanese competitors, because their narrow product lines, insufficient capitalization, and underinvestment in long-term R&D left them vulnerable to sudden change in a single technology or market. Worse, this pattern led U.S. firms to undervalue the retention of proprietary technology and the development of managerial skills.

The sale of technology—through second sourcing or similar arrangements—was encouraged by the weakness of legal protection, by the high rate of technology leakage through imitation and personnel turnover, by merchants' inefficiency at manufacturing relative to development, and by the industry's fragmentation. Technology leakage and manufacturing inadequacies lowered the expected future value to the developer of declining to license a technology. Conversely, instability and cash flow pressure increased the propensity to license widely, since licensing relieved otherwise unacceptable capital requirements and market risk. In a rapily changing industry which was fragmented both horizontally and vertically, technology and capital equipment sales seemingly benefited the seller while primarily damaging competitors. Even if the practice damaged the firm in the long run, the combination of executive personnel mobility and the industry's collective growth implied that such damage had little personal relevance to decision makers unless it became visible quite rapidly—say, in less than five years.

Moreover, since the Japanese market was effectively closed to direct U.S. penetration in any case, the alternative to royalty revenue was often no revenue at all. Since the diffusion of the technology (through theft, imitation, or licensing by other suppliers) was regarded as inevitable, declining to sell it seemed senseless. But given the different structures, planning horizons, and manufacturing abilities of the Japanese and U.S. industries, such sales constituted gradual industrial suicide.[50]

In part, then, such practices were traceable to real and individually rational, albeit collectively destructive, strategic incentives facing firms and executives as a consequence of their arena's fragmentation, instability, and lack of cooperation. As one senior merchant executive told me, "One does not accumulate vast personal wealth by trying to swim upstream." But such decisions also derived from, and again reinforced, a wider managerial failure to appreciate long-run technology trends, the importance of manufacturing, and the competitive strength of the Japanese industry. The industry was parochial, rather inbred, inexperienced with the large-scale manufacturing and systems considerations emerging as critical to the industry's future, and habituated to both chronic instability and unquestioned collective dominance. Its executives therefore lacked experience with mass manufacturing, failed to monitor Japanese progress, and assumed that merchants could generate new technology faster than Japanese firms could use it against them.[51]

Consequently Intel, Texas Instruments, Motorola, LSI Logic, and other merchants neglected their own manufacturing efficiency while repeatedly licensing their technology to Japanese firms. These same Japanese firms then predictably used their manufacturing skills, increasing technical prowess, and vastly superior resources to turn upon their U.S. benefactors, rapidly becoming their strongest global competitors. Although Japanese firms have used exceptionally aggressive and sometimes legally dubious tactics,[52] a large fraction of the merchants' ensuing problems derived from their own faulty decisions. For example authorized Japanese second sources hold almost half the world market for Intel microprocessors;[53] Toshiba now competes directly with its contractual technology supplier, LSI Logic;[54] and Hitachi and NEC first licensed, and then reverse engineered, Motorola and Intel microprocessors, respectively.[55]

This behavior, in combination with the persistent fragmentation of the industry through new venture formation, imply that to a large extent the U.S. merchant sector functions as a laboratory for research, development, and market testing as much as it functions as a productive industry. Unfortunately the laboratory is globally accessible to all large, integrated firms, while its large strategic and economic costs are borne by the United States alone.

The contrast with the Japanese industry's behavior is instructive, and suggests how it overcame the merchants' first-mover advantages. As in other electronics sectors, large vertically integrated Japanese producers began by purchasing technology and refining their manufacturing skills, but did so with an eye to the future. While in the late 1970s, 80 percent of merchant-produced semiconductors were still assembled in low-wage Asian facilities, nearly 90 percent of Japanese production was assembled domestically.[56] Japanese semiconductor producers were leaders in both developing and using automated assembly technology, a fact which partly accounts for the quality and cost advantages enjoyed by the Japanese industry in commodity markets. Japanese R&D and capital spending grew rapidly, both as a percentage of revenues and in absolute terms, and now exceeds the merchant industry's.[57] And, finally, Japanese firms invested heavily in their employees and used highly skilled workers, including many degreed engineers, in their manufacturing operations.[58]

In the Japanese industry, furthermore, independent venture formation and hostile acquisitions are strongly discouraged, industry entry occurs nearly entirely through the internal diversification of large firms,[59] and no organized venture capital market exists.[60] Supplier relations appear to be stable, of long duration, to involve extensive technology interchange, and frequently to include equity holdings.[61] Personnel raiding is rare and considered unethical;[62] defection is also discouraged by the compensation structure (for example, its relationships with social life and its dependence upon seniority).[63] Salary costs can be controlled, and investments in R&D, training, and diversification can be made with some assurance that their returns accrue to the employer and parent firm rather than to predators.

The large-scale structure of the Japanese industry also sugggests how its partial strategic coordination (e.g., with respect to American imports and abstinence from personnel raiding) can coexist with competitive discipline. First, there exists a significant and efficient central authority (the Japanese government) which provides public goods and prevents undue disruption from imports, predatory startups, and other sources of strategic disarray. Second, Japanese semiconductor producers are highly export dependent—both in the semiconductor market and in their other electronics businesses, for which semiconductors are one major input.[64] Third, they are both producers and consumers; the internal capacity of each deters others from overcharging. And finally, their low capital costs, long time horizons, and vertical integration provide incentives for them to continue their pursuit of technological leadership, because potential future rewards in downstream industries are far larger than those obtainable directly from semiconductor markets.

CONSEQUENCES

The foregoing analysis suggests that a technologically competitive semiconductor industry is important to the United States, and that conventional policy measures may be inadequate to sustain it. First, consider the practical matter of what continued decline would mean.

Through the growing use of digital information processing, industrial activity is entering a deep revolution driven in large measure by the remarkable progress of semiconductor technology. The technical and economic evidence suggest that this progress will continue for another 20 years or more. Concomitantly the world semiconductor industry will grow from $30 billion currently to perhaps $200 billion by the year 2000. Hence even if its decline had no effect upon other industries or upon national security, it would merit some concern. But, to the contrary, semiconductor production is strategically important in virtually every conceivable sense. Other industries ever more strongly dependent upon competitive semiconductor technology include computers, digital communications, automotive electronics, industrial instruments, numerically controlled machine tools, and aerospace products. The semiconductor content of these goods now ranges from 3 percent to 10 percent, and is increasing rapidly.

Collectively, these industries will gradually come to represent a substantial fraction of U.S. and world GNP; by the turn of the century, world computer production alone will exceed $500 billion. Some of these sectors, such as computers and industrial instruments, are among the few remaining net U.S. exporters.[65] Moreover, they contribute disproportionately to American living standards. In 1984, for example, U.S. private sector wages averaged $350 per week; manufacturing sector wages were higher, $434 per week. But weekly wages in the U.S. semiconductor industry were $516; in the computer industry, $552; and in the entire office equipment sector, $546.[66] Competitive decline in these sectors would therefore reduce U.S. GNP, living standards, and tax receipts by changing the mix of economic activity toward industries with lower growth, skill levels, and productivity gains. Decline could also cause welfare losses through trade effects, since these sectors are highly competitive.

In short, the strategic importance of semiconductor technology to industrial growth suggests that, quite apart from geopolitical or military issues, Japanese dominance would be cause for concern. The Japanese industry is a vertically integrated oligopoly of large multinational electronics firms. The four largest Japanese semiconductor producers are also Japan's four largest computer producers, accounting for 80 percent of all computer production by Japan-based firms,[67] and they are major semiconductor capital equipment manufacturers as well. These companies possess close, enduring relationships with their capital equipment suppliers and customers. They, and the national government which supports them, are strongly committed to success in industries dependent upon microelectronics. Additionally, all these firms have a history of aggressive, legally questionable behavior,[68] and Japanese markets have long been closed or at least restricted to Americans. For all these reasons, it is overwhelmingly likely that if Japanese firms collectively dominate advanced semiconductor technology, they will deny their best technology to their U.S. competitors to gain advantage in downstream markets. Indeed, there is some evidence that this process is already underway.[69]

This suggests a troublesome conclusion. The U.S. industry has locked itself into institutions and strategic practices which generate behavior contrary to its own, and the nation's, long-term interests. These strategic problems imply that market forces alone will not reverse the industry's decline. To the contrary, merchants, capital equipment firms, stockholders, and executives will continue their distributional struggles while the industry collectively disinvests, voluntarily or otherwise. Concomitantly, the Japanese industry will continue its progress to penetrate even larger industries, again at American expense.

But unpleasant as this conclusion may be, it suggests another which is more troubling still. The existing stock of economic theory (even including newer models of strategic international trade) is largely irrelevant to the semiconductor industry's problems and their solution. Conventional economic analysis would not predict that two national sectors would evolve such completely different structures and practices as did the American and Japanese semiconductor industries. Nor would neoclassical economic models predict that such differences would entrench themselves, persisting even in the face of strong technological and competitive forces. Were such structural and strategic divergence to arise, economics would not predict that the highly competitive industry with flexible markets and large initial advantages would prove the less adaptable, and that it would be systematically defeated by the stable, government protected oligopoly in which capital rationing and strategic coordination limited personnel mobility and market entry. And, finally, the traditional economic prescriptions for such a troubled industry would range from laissez-faire to a generic infusion of resources (capital, skilled labor, and/or R&D); explicit strategic intervention would be rejected. So would efforts to reduce the pressures of market competition, for example, through vertical integration, horizontal coordination, or disincentives to personnel mobility.[70]

Yet it would seem that economic theory accords rather poorly with the semiconductor industry's past behavior. And on the analysis I have suggested, its usual remedial prescriptions would fare little better. For example, support in the form of generic resources alone—for example, through industrywide R&D funding, tax credits, or guaranteed procurement—would be largely wasted via the strategic processes described (distributional conflict, inflationary spirals) and indeed might impede necessary structural rationalization by propping up the current system. If resources are to be used effectively, then, policy must focus upon the industry's specific problems, assist in developing efficient public and private institutions, and change the incentives that these institutions both face and generate. The emphasis must be upon lengthening their time horizons and increasing the profitability of productive investment relative to liquidation, consumption, or zero-sum conflicts which produce redundant efforts and mutual betrayal. Structural rationalization, vertical coordination, technology sharing, decreased personnel turnover, and increasing governmental responsiveness would necessarily be simultaneously instruments and consequences of these changes.

ECONOMIC ANALYSIS AND SEMICONDUCTOR INDUSTRY POLICY

The inability of contemporary economic theory to illuminate the semiconductor industry's condition or aid in its improvement flows, I believe, from four related issues in economic analysis—and in economic activity. The first is the significance of learning and institutional performance, relative to competitive markets, as determinants of long-run industrial efficiency. The second is the importance of an industry's norms of strategic interaction—so that is, the industrywide patterns of cooperation, competition, and reciprocity prevailing in the various economic and political markets which make up industrial arena. (For example, in seeking government assistance firms may compete in seeking individual gains at each other's expense, or agree to cooperate in seeking industrywide support, or reciprocally support each other's requests for individual benefits.) The third issue is the importance of externalities and industry-level public goods in determining economic efficiency. And the fourth issue is that of the time horizons of economic actors, which are affected by the strategic environment and which have a profound effect upon long-run efficiency. Hence the common thread linking these issues is the interplay between strategic choice, the evolution of industrywide behaviors and incentives, and finally their implications for long-run efficiency.

Models combining these considerations are relatively new to economic theory. Such models are not yet fully amenable to the mathematical formalism or stylized assumptions which have come to dominate the discipline of economics. They also, however, cast serious doubt upon the relevance of traditional competitive market theory to actual industrial behavior, and upon its utility as a guide to economic policy. Indeed, the theoretical results thus far obtained for evolutionary and/or strategically driven processes (e.g., through the analyses of Arthur and Axelrod)[71] have inverted or bypassed many of the results of neoclassical economic theory.

But these forces are critical to the actual dynamics of high-technology industries—and quite possibly to other sectors as well. Learning and technological progress are important to long-term industrial efficiency. Often, their maximal exploitation requires the development of effective and enduring institutions; therefore the forces shaping these institutions are critical. The same can be said of the patterns of cooperation and competition between these institutions.

In economic competition, firms and industries institutionalize themselves and interact (with each other and with governments) in significant measure through successive decisions to cooperate or compete—in factor markets, inputs, product markets, and in the political markets affecting government policies. These repeated strategic interactions, in the form of other firms' expected and actual responses to each generation of technology, politics, and market behavior, in turn constitute a large fraction of the environmental forces affecting corporate efficiency and strategy. The time horizons of firms, and therefore their long-run productivity growth, will be both a causal force and a consequence of the strategic norms of the various arenas in which they act.

For example, Silicon Valley firms came to feel that they could not appropriate benefits from long-term investments and that they could not trust their employees, their suppliers, or each other. Hence fewer long-term investments were made, fewer public goods were provided, less cooperation was undertaken, mutual betrayal became normal, and future strength received less attention than current profits. Over time, the industry's shortsightedness, internecine warfare, and inefficiency became entrenched in an equilibrium of chronic entrepreneurialism which corroded subsequent decision making and precluded the development of farsighted, effective, efficient-scale institutions.

To the extent that such forces as these are at the core of the industry's behavior, there is no particular reason to suppose that "the market," that is, the long-run outcome of these various strategic interactions, will supply a result satisfactory to the U.S. economy at large, future generations, domestic semiconductor users, our military allies, or even the semiconductor industry's current employees. There may be efficient markets for many products, but there is no reason to suppose an efficient market for national industrial systems. Nor is there reason to have confidence in the ability of the semiconductor industry itself, in its current state, to use productively any assistance provided to it, unless such assistance is tied to conditions which change incentive structures for the better.

Semiconductor industry policy, therefore, must combine the provision of resources with mechanisms which both encourage long-run efficiency and weed out those who cannot or do not practice it. Essential provisions in such a policy would be measures to reduce personnel turnover, dampen current cost growth from professional wage increases, rationalize the industry, encourage technical information exchanges, increase the linkage between compensation and long-run success, and support major investment programs by large users of semiconductors and/or capital equipment. Only in the presence of such changes to the U.S. incentive structure would large commitments for engineering education, manufacturing technology development, semiconductor capital investment, and/or government procurement yield enduring productivity gains.

A number of policy instruments are potentially useful in effecting such incentive changes. For example, support programs (such as R&D grants or low-interest loans) might disburse aid over long time periods and might require collateral, long-term commitments by the employees and executives of supported firms. Support might, for example, be restricted to firms which possess pension funds meeting specified criteria in order to maximize incentives for stability. Defaulters, individual and corporate, could be forgiven their debts but then barred from subsequent further assistance. Subsidy programs might also impose requirements for long-term profit sharing or equity grants to employees of recipient firms.

Support for small firms might require matching participation by a firm in the downstream industry, say, equity investment obligatorily phased over a five to ten-year period. Alternatively, support might be allocated to groups of firms with the requirement that they commit to purchase a portion of each other's output, and of each other's stock. Funding should also be open to foreign firms, perhaps up to some maximum percentage, but all recipients should be required to invest a minimum fraction of their funds within the United States.

Such programs might be administered, and government-provided funds allocated, by boards of directors drawn from industry, relevant government agencies, and universities. If so, their tenure should be sufficiently long, and their terms arranged, so as to insulate the system from disruptions caused by electoral or other political shifts, and their activities should be exempted, statutorily if possible, from operational oversight by Congress and from legal constraints such as the antitrust laws of stockholders' claims. More conventional assistance—educational loans, university grants, national laboratories—could then proceed in parallel with industrial growth oriented toward long-term productivity gains.

In such a policy context, the recommendations of the Defense Science Board and the U.S. industry's attempt to institutionalize joint manufacturing technology development (i.e., Sematech) represent small but encouraging developments in a generally bleak picture. They also represent an opportunity for precisely the forms of institutional change and collective learning required for the future health of American high technology, for the education of American policymakers, and for reassessment of relationships between academic policy analysis and the real economic choices which confront us.

ENDNOTES

1. See, for example, the report of the Defense Science Board (DSB) Task Force on Foreign Semiconductor Dependence (1987); Charles H. Ferguson, "American Microelectronics in Decline: Evidence, Analysis, and Alternatives," VLSI Memo 85–284, MIT Dept. of Electrical Engineering, Cambridge, Mass., 1985 National Academy of Sciences, "Advanced Processing of Electronic Materials," 1986; and the Japanese Technology Evaluation (JTECH) reports compiled by the Commerce Department and the National Science Foundation.
2. Unless otherwise indicated, semiconductor production and market share estimates are from Dataquest Corporation's Semiconductor Industry Service. Trade data are primarily from the U.S. Commerce Department; some of the principal statistics are summarized in the Commerce Department's annual U.S. Industrial Outlook. The semiconductor market as defined here excludes "captive" production (i.e., for internal use only) of U.S. firms such as IBM, AT&T, and GM. This exclusion changes absolute statistics somewhat, but not the general picture of American decline. Captive production accounts for roughly 40 percent of U.S. production. It must be emphasized, however, that semiconductor economic statistics should be considered approximate.
3. The DSB Task Force concluded that the United States now maintains a lead in only three of more than a dozen technologies it surveyed. Similar conclusions have been reached by a number of other assessments, both public (e.g., NAS, JTECH) and proprietary. The consensus is that the United States leads in design and software but lags in most other areas, particularly those related to manufacturing.
4. The long-run growth trend (since the late 1950s) of world semiconductor production is roughly 15 percent annually. Cost/performance has improved approximately 40 percent annually. Semiconductor technology improvements account for a significant and growing fraction of the productivity improvements of these other industries, all of whose semiconductor content is growing steadily.

5. As recently as 1980, Japan imported two-thirds of its capital equipment requirements, at a time when imports of semiconductors themselves had already declined to less than a quarter of Japanese consumption.

6. Semiconductor imports were subject to severe formal restrictions until 1975 and are still restricted in practice through a combination of government and industrial practices. Direct foreign investment, once explicitly prohibited, is now increasingly common, though a joint venture with a local producer is usually a practical necessity. Texas Instruments was granted exceptional permission to establish a wholly owned Japanese subsidiary, at a time when TI had leverage through its possession of critical patents. As a condition for entry, TI was required by MITI to license its patents to the entire Japanese industry, which it did, and to restrict itself to a small fraction of the Japanese market. This latter condition proved very easy for TI to meet.

7. According to the U.S. integrated circuit imports from Japan were less than $50 million in 1977. In 1984, they were over $1.1 billion. U.S. Department of Commerce, *U.S. Industrial Outlook*, various years.

8. Dataquest Corp. For Japanese data, see BA Asia Ltd., "The Japanese Semiconductor Industry," 1980 and 1982.

9. The identities and rank order of the principal Japanese semiconductor producers have remained extremely stable. In contrast, market leadership changed hands repeatedly in the U.S. industry. For market share data, see Dataquest and BA Asia Ltd.

10. BA Asia Ltd., "The Japanese Semiconductor Industry." See also M. Borrus, J. Millstein, and J. Zysman, "Trade and Development in the Semiconductor Industry," in J. Zysman and L. Tyson, (eds.), *American Industry in International Competition*, Ithaca, N.Y.: Cornell University Press, 1983.

11. Company annual reports; Dodwell Marketing Company, "Industrial Groupings in Japan" and "Key Players in the Japanese Electronics Industry," various years; Japan Company Handbook, various years.

12. Semiconductor industry statistics are notoriously uncertain, and captive production is difficult to estimate precisely because captives rarely disclose production information and because their production is not sold competitively. However, fairly reliable estimates of captive production have been constructed. IBM is the largest captive by far with, worldwide production of $4 billion. Other major captives are AT&T, GM/Delco, Hewlett-Packard, and DEC. Estimates for captive production are those of Dataquest, ICE Corp., and the author. Estimates for merchant production are those of Dataquest.

13. For extended descriptions of U.S. merchant industry behavior, see Ferguson and E. Braun and S. Macdonald, *Revolution in Miniature*, 2nd ed, "American Microelectronics in Decline," (Cambridge University Press, 1984), particularly Chapter. 10

14. Dataquest; company annual reports. See also Chase Econometrics, "The U.S. and Japanese Semiconductor Industries: A Financial comparison," commissioned by the U.S. Semiconductor Industry Assocaition, 1980.

15. For information regarding turnover in the U.S. industry, see Braun and Macdonald, *Revolution in Miniature*, particularly pp. 132 ff.; for industrywide statistics, see the surveys of the American Electronics Association. The author has also gathered proprietary information from industry sources.

16. For discussion of the U.S. industry's fragmentation and instability, see Braun and Macdonald, op cit,. particularly p. 123 for the evanescence of market leadership; Ferguson, and, for concentration ratios, *U.S. Industrial Outlook* (1986), pp. 32–33.

17. IBM was among the first, if not the first, to produce semiconductor memories and use memories (of its own manufacture) in computers in the early 1970s, and also developed elaborate testing and packaging technologies in the same decade—for example, Level Sensitive Scan Design (LSSD) and Thermal Conduction Modules. AT&T has been a technology leader throughout the industry's history And as early as 1971, there existed a public study. See J. Tilton, *The International Diffusion of Technology: The Case of Semiconductors* (Washington, D.C.; Brooking, 1971), which suggested that the Japanese industry was institute, rapidly closing on the U.S. industry. By the mid-1970s, Japanese practice was less than a year behind the U.S. industry in most technologies..

18. Statistical data are taken from company reports; Dodwell; VLSI Research, a U.S. market research firm covering the semiconductor equipment industry; the U.S. Dept. of Commerce, *A Competitive Assessment of the U.S. Semiconductor Manufacturing Equipment Industry* (1985). Assessments of supplier-customer relationships and comparative technological strength are derived from confidential industry and government sources. Considerable effort has been devoted to these questions.

19. See "Industrial Groupings in Japan;" company annual reports; VLSI Research.

20. VLSI Research; Semiconductor Equipment and Materials Institute (SEMI); Dataquest; and company reports.

21. SEMI membership data.
22. Ibid.
23. For example, single-chip microprocessors now available contain 100,000 to 500,000 devices, sell for $100 to $500, and possess more functionality and speed than the largest computer CPUs in existence 25 years ago. Such 1960 machines required thousands of small-scale semiconductor devices and cost over $1 million.
24. Dataquest.
25. Dataquest Corp., except for trade data from the U.S. Department of Commerce.
26. VLSI Research; industry and government sources.
27. Confidential industry and government sources; for a public assessment, see the report of the DSB Task Force on Foreign Semiconductor Dependency (1987).
28. Confidential industry and government sources. One major U.S. firm stated that it now stockpiles certain materials as a consequence of the domination of world supply by a single Japanese firm. It was remarked, however, that stockpiling is of limited utility in high-technology areas because such stockpiles rapidly become obsolete.
29. National Science Foundation, *Science Indicators* (1985). Appendix Table 1–20, p. 205.
30. Damian Saccocio, "Publish or Perish? An Analysis of Semiconductor Papers in the U.S., Japan, and Europe," unpublished manuscript, MIT Dept. of Political Science, Cambridge Mass., 1986.
31. Confidential industry and government sources.
32. See the DSB Task Force report, as well as the JTECH report on Opto- and Microelectronics, May 1985.
33. See, for example, Braun and Macdonald, *Revolution in Miniature*, Chaps. 4–6, and Christopher Freeman, "The Economics of Industrial Innovation, 2nd ed., (Cambridge, Mass.: MIT Press, 1982), particularly Table 4.6b, p. 95, of the paperbound edition.
34. See Gerald Brock, *The Telecommunications Industry* (Cambridge, Mass.: Harvard University Press, 1981), Chap. 7.
35. See Freeman, *"American Microelectronics in Decline,"* pp. 96–99; Braun and Macdonald, *Revolution in Miniature,* Chaps. 6 and 10; Ferguson, *"American Microelectronics in Decline,"* D. Okimoto, in D. Okimoto, T. Sugano, and F. Weinstein, eds., *Competitive Edge: The Semiconductor Industry in the U.S. and Japan,* Ch 4, (Stanford, Calif.: Stanford University Press, 1984).
36. See Braun and Macdonald, *Revolution in Miniature,* Chaps. 6 and 8; Ferguson, *"American Microelectronics in Decline,"* D. Okimoto, in d. Okimoto, T. Sungano, and F. Weinstein, eds., *Competitive Edge: The Semiconductor Industry in the U.S. and Japan,* Ch 4 (Stanford University Press, 1984).
37. R. Wilson, P. Ashton, and T. Egan, "Innovation, Competition, and Government Policy in the Semiconductor Industry," Charles River Associates, Cambridge, Mass., 1980, p. 146.
38. Industry interviews. See also the DSB Task Force report and Okimoto" pp. 84–89.
39. Changes in capital gains tax rates have been strongly correlated to the size of venture capital flows into the semiconductor industry. Venture capital flows have in turn been correlated with levels of start-up activity, most spectacularly in the early 1980s. See Ferguson, *"American Microelectronics in Decline,"* p. 53, and Braun and Macdonald, *Revolution in Miniature,* pp. 132–137. The capital gains differential may also have increased the relative attractiveness of stock offered in initial public offerings (IPOs), since the returns to these stocks came primarily through capital growth rather than fully taxable dividend income.
40. Incentive stock options (ISOs) can be granted in amounts up to $100,000 per employee. Under pre-1987 tax laws, they offered both lower effective rates (because taxed as capital gains) and income deferral (because taxed at the time of stock sale, not at the time the options are granted or exercised).
41. See the Chase Econometrics report for an analysis specific to the semiconductor industry. For more general treatments, see, for example, Data Resources, Inc., *The DRI Report on U.S. Manufacturing Industries* (New York: McGraw-Hill, 1984), pp. 28–34.
42. For market shares, the source is Dataquest. For quality data, see, for example, U.S. Office of Technology Assessment, "International Competitiveness in Electronics," 1983, pp. 247–249, for data drawn both from Hewlett-Packard and from OTA consultants.
43. Dataquest. See also Ferguson, *"American Microelectronics in Decline,"* pp. 19–28, and Braun and Macdonald, *Revolution in Miniature,* pp. 124–128.
44. See Ferguson, "American Microelectronics in Decline," 2 and 3, and Braun and Macdonald, *Revolution in Miniature,* Chaps. 7, 8, 9.
45. See Braun and Macdonald, *Revolution in Miniature,* pp. 128–130. I am indebted to an IBM executive and to a Stanford professor for the unusual form of growth accounting exhibited here. Confidential industry interviews have also indicated the significance of inflationary spirals in land, housing, construction, and wage costs.

46. To indicate the feelings held by some regarding venture capital–based start-ups and their effect upon turnover, let me quote the CEO of one of the industry's largest firms: "The best thing that could happen to this industry would be if every tenth venture capitalist were arbitrarily shot."

47. See the OTA report, Chaps. 6 and 8, for discussion of many of these issues, including the relationship between turnover, training levels, and product quality.

48. Confidential industry interviews.

49. For the use of leasing, see company annual reports; for the absence of long-term obligations, company reports and industry interviews; for the absence of long-term investments (e.g., equity holdings) in suppliers, company annual reports; for offshore assembly, see BA Asia Ltd., U.S. Dept. of Commerce trade statistics for semifinished versus finished semiconductors, and Dataquest.

50. For a compilation of Japan–U.S. licensing arrangements (without, however, an evaluation of their relative importance), see Carmela S. Haklisch, *The Technical Alliances in the Semiconductor Industry* (New York: New York University Graduate School of Business Administration, 1986). For a highly critical account, see Borrus, Millstein, and Zysman. "Trade and Development in the Semiconductor Industry." For aggregate Japan-U.S. technology trade balances in technology and license fees versus products, see *Science Indicators* (1985), p. 15, and Tables 1–16 and 1–17, pp. 201–202.

51. Confidential industry interviews. I am particularly indebted to one extended series of interviews, the subject of which was one firm's rationale for technology licensing to Japanese competitors, for assisting in my understanding of this issue.

52. For example, alleged dumping and predatory pricing, NEC's alleged violations of copyright law in connection with its reverse engineering of Intel's microprocessors, and alleged patent infringements by several firms.

53. Dataquest; confidential industry sources.

54. Company annual reports and product literature describe the products and technologies made available to Toshiba by LSI Logic, particularly the LDS computer-aided design system. Toshiba supplies process technology in return, but not processing hardware or training. Confidential industry interviews have indicated that the competition between the two companies is quite fierce.

55. Company annual reports; Dataquest. Confidential interviews and press reports indicate that the ensuing rivalries have significantly damaged the U.S. firms in question.

56. BA Asia Ltd., various years; OTA Electronics report, p. 136.

57. Dataquest; confidential industry estimates.

58. Industry and government sources. Statistics are difficult to come by, but there is near unanimity in regard to the high educational and skill levels of Japanese plant-floor workers.

59. See Dataquest for ranked listings of Japanese producers over time; Dodwell's for their general financial characteristics.

60. See, for example, M. Flaherty and H. Itami, "Finance," in Okimoto, Sugano, and Weinstein, eds., *Competitive Edge.*

61. Dodwell, *"Industrial Groupings in Japan,"* BA Asia Ltd, various years; confidential interviews.

62. Industry interviews.

63. Industry interviews. For general accounts, see, for example, Rodney Clark, *The Japanese Company,* (New Haven, Conn.: Yale University Press, 1979). See also the work of Ronald Dore and Ezra Vogel. For aggregate turnover levels and variation of wages with seniority, see for example, *Japan Statistical Yearbook,* 1985.

64. The major semiconductor and electronics firms export from 25 percent to 75 percent of their total output. Usually semiconductor exports are a small refraction. See Dodwell's and company annual reports.

65. Commerce Department statistics.

66. Source for all U.S. salary statistics is U.S. Bureau of Labor Statistics, 1985.

67. *Japan Electronics Almanac,* 1986, pp. 85 ff.

68. Such allegedly irregular behavior is not confined to the practices noted specifically in connection with the semiconductor industry. For example, Fujitsu has allegedly engaged in large-scale software piracy. IBM has submitted its claims against Fujitsu to binding arbitration. Hitachi employees were found allegedly seeking to bribe IBM employees, and Hitachi reportedly paid IBM $300 million and permitted IBM to inspect its products for five years, to prevent litigation. Both Fujitsu and Hitachi have paid IBM substantial compensation as a consequence of unauthorized use of IBM system software. A Toshiba subsidiary was recently implicated in major export controls violations involving the sale of advanced machine tools to the Soviet Union, and Toshiba is now negotiating with National Semiconductor regarding alleged copyright infringement associated with microcode for a communications circuit used in IBM personal computers.

69. Confidential industry and government interviews. The process is apparently not confined to captive Japanese production of equipment, materials, and semiconductor products, but also seems

to extend to major Japanese equipment suppliers with particularly close relationships to their domestic Japanese customers.

70. Such conventional economic thinking has been very much in evidence in recent discussions within the federal government, though it is not always heeded.

71. W. Brian Arthur, *Competing Technologies and Lock-in by Historical Small Events: The Dynamics of Allocation Under Increasing Returns* (Stanford, Calif.: Stanford University Center for Economic Policy Research, 1985); Robert Axelrod, *The Evolution of Cooperation*, (New York: Basic Books, 1984); and Robert Axelrod, "An Evolutionary Approach to Norms," *American Political Science Review* (December 1986).

Sematech

Robert N. Noyce, the new CEO of Sematech and coinventor of the integrated circuit, looked out his office window in August 1988 at construction crews scurrying about the facilities. He hoped that on this tightly guarded site there would soon be the most advanced semiconductor factory in the world. He smiled with approval at the red, white, and blue band of bricks that had been built into the new fab building as a permanent testimonial to the patriotic fervor that surrounded Sematech.

For the first eight months of its existence, however, Sematech did not have a CEO. This was the most likely reason for the delay in obtaining fiscal 1989 money from the government. Lack of leadership had also caused Sematech personnel problems, clashes among its disparate member companies, and delays. Some insiders termed it "internal chaos."

It was now up to Noyce to get Sematech going. He had to devise a technical agenda, secure cooperation among the 14 members (Exhibit 1) and begin developing closer relationships with suppliers, end users, and Washington officials.

IN THE BEGINNING

In 1947, William B. Shockley and a team of Bell Laboratory engineers devised the solid-state transistor, thus giving birth to the semiconductor industry—one of the most dynamic industries of modern times. Over the next 40 years, semiconductor products would shrink in size, grow in power, and diminish in price. They had become so pervasive that they were being called the "crude oil of the 1980s."[1]

INDUSTRY STRUCTURE

Three distinct parts, sometimes referred to as a "food chain," made up the semiconductor industry ecosystem: the chip makers, the materials and equipment companies, and the end users of chips (i.e., manufacturers of computers, consumer electronics).

Semiconductor companies were divided into "merchants" that produced for external markets and "captives" that produced semiconductors primarily for internal consumption.[2] There were close to 200 U.S. merchant semiconductor manufacturers. In 1987 they employed over 250,000 people in the United States. Total worldwide sales of semiconductors were about $46 billion in 1987.

Upstream were materials and equipment makers. They were about a third the size of the device manufacturers with worldwide sales of about $9 billion in 1987. Their products ranged from X-ray lithography machines to silicon. There

Associates Fellow Robert S. Williams prepared this case under the supervision of Professor Geroge C. Lodge as the basis for class discussion rather than to illustrate either effective or ineffective handling of an administrative situation.

were over 700 U.S. firms with roughly two-thirds having sales of less than $10 million and more than 500 Japanese firms. U.S. companies relied heavily on international markets because less than 50 percent of the world market was domestic. While in Japan close relationships between the device makers and equipment firms allowed partnerships to develop that enabled them to share proprietary information and cooperate, long-term U.S. relationships were often marked by mistrust and antagonism.

On the downstream side, semiconductors were core components of computers, telecommunications, consumer electronics, industrial electronics, and defense electronics. Chips were only a small part of the total cost of these products; however, their contribution to performance was disproportionate to their cost. In 1986, the U.S. electronics industry accounted for approximately $230 billion in annual sales and 2½ million jobs. Worldwide sales were $400 billion.[3]

U.S. electronics and computer firms, including the captives like IBM and AT&T, bought chips from independent producers in the United States and, increasingly, Japan. In contrast Japanese chip users like Hitachi and Toshiba not only made all their own but were major exporters. In Europe, also, the large electronics companies like Philips, Siemens, and Thomson were producers of chips for internal use as well as export.

The technical development of dynamic random access memory (DRAM) chips set the pace for progress in semiconductor technology because the key components of these commodity devices permitted feature reduction more readily, thus increasing the chip's power more easily as compared to complex logic chips. The Japanese semiconductor strategy was based on large-scale DRAM production. From 1975 to 1986, the U.S. share of the merchant DRAM business declined from nearly 100 percent to less than 5 percent, most taken away by Japanese firms like NEC and Toshiba. All but two U.S. manufacturers had abandoned the DRAM business by 1987.[4]

Although most industry observers thought that Japan had made a killing on DRAMs, a report by Montgomery Securities said that the top five Japanese DRAM producers had invested $5 billion in DRAMs since 1980, but had only made a return of $1.5 billion by the end of 1987. Some experts said that the Japanese were willing to take these losses because their semiconductor strategy was part of a much larger strategy, which was to dominate the major end-user areas, such as telecommunications and computers. A DRAM shortage in early 1988 made U.S. companies dangerously dependent on their Japanese competitors for critical components and was providing windfall profits to the Japanese.

Upstream U.S. industries were also affected by the loss of U.S. DRAM production. By 1986, Japanese companies commanded 40 percent of the world market for semiconductor capital equipment, an industry the United States had dominated only a few years before.

Market Share.   The United States and Japan traded places for dominance in the global semiconductor market in 1986. The U.S. share of the worldwide merchant semiconductor market had been declining for over a decade—from nearly 60 percent in 1975 to 39 percent in 1987. Over the same period, Japan's share of the market rose from 20 percent to 48 percent. Six Japanese merchant firms held top ten market positions in 1987, including the top three spots, as opposed to four in 1982.

By 1987, Korea had managed to secure about 6 percent of the global merchant market for semiconductors. With the support of the Korean government as well as low labor and overhead costs, Korea had become a low-cost leader in the production of commodity chips. European producers supplied about 11 percent of the world market in 1987, about the same as in 1984.[5] European producers had avoided commodity chips because they saw opportunity for improved margins in lower-volume ICs aimed at specific markets.

GOVERNMENT-INDUSTRY RELATIONS IN JAPAN AND THE UNITED STATES

Besides the fundamental differences between the United States and Japan in industry structure, capital equipment investment, and R&D spending, Japanese companies displaced the Americans by utilizing a focused combination of government support and forced coordination toward the electronics industry. Japan's joint R&D projects were supported by MITI and Nippon Telegraph and Telephone (NTT).

The very-large-scale integrated circuit (VLSI) project had been instrumental in propelling the Japanese forward in semiconductors. It lasted four years (1976–1980), cost ¥71 billion ($360 million), and yielded over 1,000 patents. The Japanese were actively engaged in several other ongoing programs designed to foster the development of the computer and electronics industries. (See Exhibit 2.)

Although the U.S. government had no official policy toward any industry, it had played a critical role in the U.S. electronics industry's development. In fact, over the years it had provided more support for semiconductor-related research and development than the Japanese government. Its support, however, did not go to chip makers but to defense contractors. Japanese research assistance, on the other hand, went to commercial semiconductor firms, and was aimed at exploiting commercial applications. In 1987, the United States spent approximately $4 billion on semiconductor research: $3 billion came from the semiconductor device industry, and half a billion each came from the equipment and materials industry, and the federal government. The amount spent on manufacturing research, however, was only $350 million.

There were two major differences in the way government R&D dollars were spent in the two countries: (1) U.S. corporate R&D concentrated heavily on specific product design while Japanese companies devoted more of their effort to broadly applicable process technology, and (2) Japanese companies cooperated more with each other on longer-term technology research.[6]

A number of U.S. agencies besides the Department of Defense (DoD) were involved in government-sponsored R&D, including the National Science Foundation (NSF), National Aeronautics and Space Administration (NASA), the National Institutes of Health, the National Bureau of Standards, and the National Labs.

Unlike DoD, NSF did not focus its funding on any particular end uses; it responded to proposals from the research community. Although NSF's semiconductor research budget was small ($23 million) when compared to DoD's, NSF did help to build a base of qualified scientists and engineers. The National Bureau of Standards research concentrated on the science of measurement. Under the Department of Energy (DoE), the National Labs helped facilitate coordination of basic research in semiconductors and developed engineering talent. Very few commercial applications originated there. NASA did not work on semiconductor manufacturing or silicon technology.[7]

Within the DoD, various branches funded basic research in microelectronics. The Defense Advanced Research Projects Agency (DARPA), which was separate from the services, supported long-term research for military applications, including microelectronics.

Even by the late 1970s, however, DoD realized that commercial application usually preceded military application by as much as ten years. Military systems were becoming technologically obsolete before completing their expected life span. To remedy this situation, in 1978 DoD initiated the very-high-speed integrated circuit (VHSIC) program to reduce the delay experienced in getting advanced, state-of-the-art ICs into military usage. The VHSIC program was originally conceived as a seven-year $339 million project to conclude in 1989. The estimate ballooned to over $1 billion over a ten-year period. In April of 1987, a report for the House Armed Services Committee gave the VHSIC program little credit for contribution to commercial technology.[8] One reason was that very few chip makers were involved. (See Exhibit 3.)

U.S. PRIVATE SECTOR INITIATIVES

Semiconductor Industry Association (SIA).

In 1977, five companies founded SIA (it had 48 members in 1988) to coordinate the political action of the semiconductor industry. Its agenda included trade concerns, export controls, intellectual property rights, capital formation, research and development, and antitrust issues.

Throughout the 1980s a variety of allegations about Japanese trade practices emanated from SIA. In 1985, three member companies filed two major antidumping suits. In July 1986, an agreement was reached whereby the suits against Japan would be suspended if they stopped dumping EPROMs and DRAMs. The Japanese also had to increase access to their domestic market, allowing U.S. market share to rise from 9½ percent to 20 percent by 1990.[9]

In March of 1987, the United States Trade Representative (USTR) found that the Japanese were not complying with the trade agreement, so President Reagan, acting under Section 301 of the Trade Act, imposed a 100 percent duty on $300 million of Japanese exports to the United States. In June 1987, the United

States agreed to lift some of the sanctions in response to the progress the Japanese had made in eliminating dumping in third markets.

Although the falling value of the dollar had improved the sales of U.S. products generally, penetration of the Japanese semiconductor market in 1988 was still only 9.8 percent. In addition, sanctions and trade agreements accelerated the Japanese move to increase sales of 256K, one-megabit DRAMs and application-specific integrated circuits (ASICs). By June of 1988, there was a shortage of DRAMs. Their selling price skyrocketed to 3 to 5 times of what the floor price set by the 1986 agreement had been. Many end users of chips claimed the chip agreement had forced Japanese producers to raise prices and cut back supply. Others claimed it was simply a result of inadequate capacity.

Although the American Electronics Association (AEA), which represented the U.S. end users, firmly believed a healthy U.S. semiconductor industry was in their best interest, Ralph Thomson, senior vice president at AEA said, "Our members were willing to pay a premium (10–25 percent) for chips to protect our semiconductor industry, but we expected a reentry to the DRAM market.[10] My members are upset! In June 1988, ten major companies petitioned our membership to get rid of the FMV system, or they would leave AEA."[11]

The Microelectronics and Computer Technology Corporation (MCC)

MCC was a precedent-setting, privately funded, for-profit research venture formed in 1982. Its purpose was to counter Japan's high-tech invasion and preserve U.S. leadership in electronics. There were 21 members supporting the organization with $65 million in 1986. Two major differences marked MCC from Japan's VLSI project: the biggest U.S. player, IBM, was absent from MCC; and the government provided no funding or guidance. The government did, however, legislate specific exemptions to the U.S. antitrust laws, without which MCC would have been illegal. The National Cooperative Research Act of 1984 was passed by Congress "to promote research and development, encourage innovation, stimulate trade, and make necessary and appropriate modifications in the operations of the antitrust laws." The act provided that a joint R&D venture "shall not be deemed illegal per se under the antitrust laws." MCC became the first joint venture to clear antitrust review under this law, in 1986.[12]

In 1988, however, there were questions about how effectively MCC was working. It had difficulty attracting as many researchers from member companies as planned and some programs were behind schedule.

Semiconductor Research Corporation (SRC).

SRC was another consortium composed of most of the U.S. semiconductor firms.[13] Headed by Larry Sumney, its goal was to improve basic research in universities and help develop young engineers.

U.S. GOVERNMENT PARTICIPATION: A CHANGE IN COURSE

The DoD Task Force.

In December 1985, the deputy undersecretary of defense for research and engineering requested that a task force of the Defense Science Board (DSB) be established to assess the importance of recent trends in the semiconductor industry. The report of the task force, released in February 1987, concluded that U.S. military forces depend heavily on technological superiority; semiconductors were the key to leadership in electronics; competitive, high-volume production was the key to leadership in semiconductors; high-volume production was supported by the commercial market; leadership in commercial volume production was in jeopardy; and U.S. defense will soon depend on foreign sources for state-of-the-art technology in semiconductors.

Claiming that "the existence of a healthy U.S. semiconductor industry was critical to the national defense," the task force said, "DoD should encourage and actively support with contract funding (approximately $200 million per year) the establishment of a U.S. Semiconductor Manufacturing Institute formed as a consortium of U.S. manufacturers."[14]

Outside DoD, the DSB report was controversial. A DoD insider said, "The defense contractors didn't want to be in the chip business, and yet VHSIC was leading them down that path. They knew they couldn't make any money on chips so they were hoping that they could get the chip folks involved so that defense contractors could go back to making military equipment."[15]

SIA proposed Sematech immediately following the DSB report. Charles Sporck, president of National Semiconductor, said, "That was purely coincidental. There was a problem and DoD recognized it at about the same time that we did."

THE SEMATECH INITIATIVE

The SRC formed a Manufacturing Competitiveness Panel (MCP) in 1984 to provide a forum to help define the Sematech initiative. In that year, however, firms were enjoying high profits, so the idea of collaborating did not have much appeal.

In July 1985, a workshop of manufacturing experts was held and the concept of an industry-government cooperative was introduced, and in January 1986, MCP discussed the concept more thoroughly. Still it attracted little support from industry leaders, who doubted that a productive working relationship with government could be achieved.

At the same time, in late 1985, IBM came up with an alarming report about the status of the U.S. semiconductor industry and decided in early 1986 to share it with industry and government. According to Sanford L. Kane, vice president of IBM who was responsible for the project, "All the data we used was publicly available, but it was amazing to see that no one was aware of how bad the situation had gotten."

Many in industry asked why IBM was doing this. Kane responded, "The survival of the U.S. semiconductor industry was critical to us for several reasons. Number one, we were one of the largest purchasers of chips in the world. We liked to source locally, and we didn't want to lose the option of buying U.S. chips. Besides, since most Japanese companies were both competitors of ours and suppliers of chips, we didn't want to be in a position where we had no choice but to be dependent on our competitor. Second, IBM was the largest manufacturer of chips in the world. We produced in-house those chips that gave us a technological edge. To stay state-of-the-art, we needed to have sophisticated equipment to make the semiconductors. If the U.S. chip makers go, so would the U.S. equipment companies. We knew it would be difficult to establish close relationships with the Japanese, especially since most of their firms are associated with chip companies. We would be forced to share information and it would be doubtful whether we could get access to state-of-the-art equipment as quickly as our Japanese counterparts. Thus, when we analyzed the numbers and saw that the industry was dying, we knew we had to do something about it."

At the time, Kane had devised a possible solution similar to Sematech. Government was not part of the plan, Kane said. "We thought the industry could do it alone and we were concerned about the strings that would be attached to the money. But I soon discovered industry was in no position to fund it alone."

At an SIA board meeting in June 1986, George Scalise, chairman of the SIA Public Policy Committee, gave a rousing speech about the need for manufacturing excellence. Charles Sporck volunteered to see what could be done. His goal was to forge a consensus on what the industry needed among suppliers, chip manufacturers, end users, and government officials. Sporck said at the time, "Our system creates design excellence, but nothing in regards to manufacturing."

Organizing Sematech Members

In September, Sporck presented his findings to the SIA board, which then created an eight-person task force to define objectives and create an organizational framework for Sematech. In November 1986, at another SIA board meeting, dissension arose over a number of items including whether Sematech should be simply a research facility or a production facility as well. A few merchant companies wanted Sematech to be a source of chips, but captives like IBM and AT&T thought that would be too complicated and would have major antitrust implications. They also did not want to be pressured into buying the chips.

"Issues of membership and the balance of power were resolved rather easily," said Kane. "We carefully set it up so that no one firm could dominate."

The area of intellectual property was another difficult subject. It was eventually decided that technology could only be transferred to overseas subsidiaries and joint ventures that had a minimum of 51 percent U.S. control.

The issue of foreign involvement split some participants. Clearly, if DoD was participating, foreign members would be excluded, but even IBM had some trepidation. Kane said, "We were schizophrenic. We were involved in Europe's ESPRIT project and were participating in MITI's superconductivity project."

Although support was growing throughout 1986, there were still reservations. T. J. Rodgers, president of Cypress Semiconductors, a small firm in Silicon Valley said, "Sematech is a patriotic subsidy for large semiconductor companies. Although they say anyone can join, the fee structure (1 percent of total semiconductor sales) is set up in such a way that it is proportionally 2.6 times more expensive for companies with less than $500 million in sales. The government should at least support the industry more broadly." (The minimum admissions fee was $1 million.)

By early 1987 there was a game plan. Sematech would concentrate on advanced manufacturing techniques to counter the competitive forays of the Japanese. Emphasis would be placed on manufacturing process development.

On March 3, 1987, the SIA board approved what the task force had put together. The SRC gave Sematech a $100,000 grant to cover start-up costs. On May 12, 1987, the SIA board approved a five-year plans and created site and CEO selection committees. A legal staff was added and temporary offices were set up in Santa Clara, CA. A working group was established, which became Sematech's first employees. Member companies put up their pledges. Larry Sumney, president of SRC, was made managing director. He spent most of his time lobbying for Sematech in Washington.

Getting the Upstream Companies Involved

The SIA knew it was essential to get the equipment and material firms involved, but the firms were highly fragmented and had their own objectives. In addition, the only trade association that represented them was SEMI (Semiconductor Equipment and Materials Institute), which was an international organization. Although SEMI supported many of the SIA's activities, SEMI executives had difficulties with trade sanctions since many of their members were Japanese. But in concept, SEMI supported Sematech, and agreed to help set up a separate organization called SEMI/Sematech. In this way, SEMI could keep its distance from the project. SEMI/Sematech, created in September 1987, became an independent organization to ensure that U.S. suppliers had every opportunity to benefit from Sematech.

SEMI held several meetings in 1987 to resolve a number of issues: the smaller SEMI members were concerned that the big players would get all the contracts. Who would be allowed to join? What would the dues be? Could it be structured to give equal status to all U.S. players? Large SEMI companies, like Perkin-Elmer and General Signal, were afraid they would be forced to subsidize smaller companies. Who would get the technology and how fast and what could you do with it once you got it. This last point was especially complicated because at least 50 percent of the market for SEMI companies was overseas.

By August 1988, 144 companies had joined SEMI/Sematech. Each had the opportunity to bid on a project. Once a company was awarded a contract, the results of the project would be shared among all companies, but the details would be kept proprietary. Sam Harrell, president of SEMI/Sematech, expected "over half the annual Sematech budget to filter down to the equipment and materials companies in the first couple of years. However, this is only a small percentage of the total R&D

spent in these industries. The real benefit will come from greater cooperation and improved relationships with chip makers."

Selling the Government

Charles Sporck, chairman of SIA's steering committee on Sematech, spearheaded the lobbying movement in Washington. In February 1987, the industry coalition set out to convince the government that the need for their support outweighed reluctance to increase federal spending. Opponents also felt that Sematech would not perform as advertised and that the government had no business funding it. Lobbying efforts were coordinated by the law firm of Dewey, Ballantine, Bushby, Palmer & Wood, and included numerous presentations by key industry executives to key supporters and opponents on Capitol Hill and government agencies.

Bob Noyce, testifying before a congressional hearing on Sematech, spelled out why government should be a part of it. "We are asking that the government assume a role common for most of our major industrial rivals and which gives our competitors a large advantage. That is, to encourage the health and competitiveness of the most crucial and productive industries for national economic well-being. The advantage of this project is that government's role is temporary and the money is to be spent only on research [after the fifth year, Sematech would be funded only by its members]...To optimize the benefits of the funds we receive, we hope that the government will give maximum operational discretion to Sematech. The project will offer significant benefits to the nation as a whole. First, it will ensure the viability of the U.S. electronics industry...and second, it will maintain a domestic source of supply for the critical microelectronic products that are vital for our national defense."[16]

The Government Process

A successful lobbying campaign required understanding the intricate network of relationships in Washington. The lack of coordination between the many government groups resulted in government decision making in smaller systems. In general, 80 percent to 90 percent of operational decisions in Washington are made in subsystems—by a few relatively low-level people in the executive and congressional branches.[17]

Sematech lobbyists had to locate the most favorable subsystems for their cause. The Semiconductor Congressional Support Group (SCSG) was a bipartisan forum of 28 House and Senate members who were champions of the chip industry. Started by industry in September of 1985 in response to the recently filed 301 case, SCSG was designed to inform key members in Congress about chip issues so as to get their help to back legislation and to apply pressure on the administration.

Since that time, the industry had staged regular triennial meetings where approximately 300 government officials attended a two-hour session on the industry. In addition, a monthly newsletter was sent to key government decisions makers.

This group included key players from many governmental entities including the White House, executive departments, congress and interagency groups, all of whom had power to influence Sematech's future. Sematech had to gather enough support on the Hill to get through two rounds of congressional legislation—in both the House and Senate—(1) authorization: the approval for the program; and (2) appropriations: the actual allocation of funds—before it could receive government funding. Even then it came one year at a time.

GOVERNMENT POSITIONS TOWARD SEMATECH

The Interagency Working Group Report

In 1986, prior to the chip agreement with Japan, the National Security Council (NSC) commissioned an interagency study of the semiconductor industry. The NSC had hoped that commissioning the report would mollify the SIA and reduce the pressure which the association was putting on the administration to make trade sanctions against Japan. One month later, however, the chip agreement was reached. The NSC maneuver had failed, yet, the commission to do the report remained.[18]

In early 1987, NSC passed control to Charles H. Herz, general counsel for the National Science Foundation (NSF). Herz said: "I wanted to find a promising mechanism for national science policy where the government, universities, and industry could play constructive roles together. We had precedents for government participation in basic generic research. But application-oriented research was different."

The report examined the status of the industry and possible government roles to assist it, including funding Sematech. Herz finally achieved consensus among a diverse group of people, but said, "It took us too long (the report was never formally released). It didn't have the influence it could have had. The biggest difficulty was not so much conflict between agencies, but the communication gap between economists and engineers."

The NSF report gave three justifications for government support of Sematech: national security, national economic interest, and several "market externalities," which legitimized government intervention.

The report warned that Sematech could not be the whole answer to the industry's woes and raised a set of critical questions the group felt industry—not government—should answer:

- How effectively could such vigorous, independent, and hitherto secretive competitors collaborate in work so closely bearing on competitive advantage?
- How would all be assured that each was fairly providing its share of know-how and technical information, fairly paying its share of support, and benefiting in proportion to that share?
- How well could such a consortium hold together in the face of centrifugal forces inherent when competitors try to cooperate?

- Would such a venture, independent of the existing firms, with all the attendant problems, add enough to justify its cost and the diversion of talents and attentions it would entail?

There was also concern that since all members would have access to the technologies, they would all tend to compete prices down and so weaken even their collective ability to appropriate the benefits from their R&D investments. "Sematech might make a good candidate for an experiment," the report concluded, "but care should be taken that it doesn't turn into political pork."

The Congressional Research Services (CRS) Report

In March 1987, the House Armed Services Committee requested a report on Sematech and the industry to help them in determining whether to fund the project. It suggested several alternatives to Sematech and raised concerns about federal involvement, specifically DoD participation.

The Congressional Budget Office (CBO) Report

The CBO issued a report for the Senate Commerce Committee entitled, "The Benefits and Risks of Federal Funding for Sematech," in September 1987. It echoed many of the concerns raised in the NSF and CRS reports. Although the CBO report did not formally endorse the Sematech plan, it recognized that this was a potential opportunity for the federal government to provide assistance to an industry that had large impact on the economic health of the United States and possibly national security as well.

The Debate in Congress

The issues debated in Congress included national security, the importance of semiconductors to other industries, and the industry's ability to deal effectively with its problems with or without government support. The rationale for direct government support for the venture was based on industry claims that it had insufficient funds to invest in a facility of this magnitude, that government was a major consumer of chips, and that a strong industry was in the national interest.

Although many of the questions raised in the government reports were unanswered, Sematech seemed to pass through the legislative process unscathed. According to Glenn McLoughlin, coauthor of the CRS report on Sematech, "It appeared that by April of 1987, the issue was already a *fait accompli*. The real question was where other money would come from. There seemed to be very little discussion of the alternatives or concerns raised in the report. It isn't that surprising. Thirty-seven states plus Puerto Rico submitted proposals for Sematech, why would any one be against it?"

One Senate insider said, "Timing was critical for Sematech; they had three things going for them: the proposal came at a time when competitiveness was in vogue, it was a high-tech industry, and the trade bill was a major agenda item. Everyone wanted to be associated with doing something for U.S. competitiveness, and then here comes the Sematech proposal. It fit the bill." Congressional supporters prepared for the tough questions, but as one Senate staffer put it, "Nobody pressed us."

Justice Department

The loosening of the antitrust laws regarding cooperative research made it probable that Sematech would receive Justice's blessing. However, there were several differences between Sematech and MCC. First and most important, IBM and AT&T were members. Second, Sematech's commercial application goals provided a greater opportunity for potential market abuses. Finally, with substantial government involvement, Justice would be forced to draw the line between cooperative research and antitrust violation carefully.

SIA was faced with a complication. Both IBM and AT&T had battled the Justice Department before and had no desire to do so again. Both wanted to be confident Sematech would pass antitrust review.[19] SIA and Dewey, Ballantine had several meetings with Justice and concluded that antitrust concerns could be met if Sematech was set up as a nonprofit corporation, did not sell any product on the open market, gave U.S. firms first opportunity to supply the products, did not have any foreign-based members, was not dominated by a few large companies, conducted business in a way that could easily reveal that no collusion regarding price and competitive actions took place, and treated all U.S. suppliers equally and fairly.

USTR

There also appeared to be general support for Sematech from several civilian agencies, but none felt it was a high enough priority to put funding behind it. The USTR was divided: Ambassador Clayton Yeutter took no position; but Michael Smith, Deputy USTR, was a strong advocate.

Commerce

Malcolm Baldrige, secretary of Commerce, liked the idea of Sematech, but thought the program was too big. He told the SIA he was fighting too many other battles and that he just could not "carry the ball" on this one.[20] Nevertheless, within Commerce many people were frustrated by their inability to halt Japanese dumping and increase U.S penetration of the Japanese market. This group thought Sematech might be a step in the right direction.

Office of Management and Budget

Dr. Tom Dorsey, an economist for OMB, did not buy the SIA pitch. He said, "After the 301 agreement, there was nothing left for SIA to do, so they pushed Sematech.

"Once the DSB report came out," Dorsey continued, "the SIA was jumping all over us to fund Sematech. SIA had hired a consultant to work with DoD on that report, so of course the report would say 'help the industry.'"

Dorsey and other government objectors didn't buy claims that the DRAM was a technology driver either: "When you look at the history of the industry, only a couple of U.S. device makers were ever in DRAMs and yet most have been successful. Look at the Europeans, they aren't in DRAMs and they're making money."[21]

Dorsey continued: "The total aggregate R&D budget for these semiconductor firms is over $4.5 billion. They claim Sematech is critical to their success; yet unless government puts in $100 million a year, it won't fly. Where are their priorities? If Sematech is so important, why did they have such a hard time finding a CEO? No one wanted the job; they know it's going to be a disaster."

He said further, "There is a real danger of politicization here, a risk that this won't be done for scientific reasons, but instead evolve into a giant entitlement program. Government shouldn't be allocating resources and making priorities, the market should. If public money was the answer, then why aren't the French doing well? They throw a ton of money at their industries."

In the end, government opponents concluded that there was no national economic problem. However, on the national security issue, Dorsey said, "If DoD says there is a national security problem, we can't argue with them."

Treasury and Council of Economic Advisers

Both supported the main thrusts of Dorsey's arguments. Treasury's difficulty was spending scarce money. It also felt that the semiconductor industry's decline was a simple case of the dollar being too strong, and that when the exchange rates began to favor the United States, the industry would return to profitability.

The Reagan White House

Bill Graham, the president's science adviser, was also opposed; he could not bring himself to spend money on what he perceived to be a robust industry when the development of new technologies, particularly superconductivity, was so important. Graham commissioned a study group, called the "White House Council Panel on Semiconductors." Although he tried to keep its findings from the rest of the administration, results came out in August 1987. Much to Graham's chagrin, the report concluded that possibly the government should back Sematech but the funds should not come out of civilian agencies.

Once the tide appeared to turn in Sematech's favor, the office of Dewey, Ballantine attempted to sway the president. Although officially, the administration had not taken a position, it was clear on ideological grounds that they were against it. Dewey, Ballantine appealed to the political interests of the Reagan camp by saying, "Look it's going to pass in Congress, you might as well get some political mileage out of it." But the president never embraced the program.

The Debate Within Defense

While Sematech was being discussed in Congress, DoD was attempting to draft an industrial plan that could identify and prioritize industries critical to national security. But it was not ready for the Sematech decision. A DoD insider said, "Steel, textiles, boots, chemicals, semiconductors, they are all important, but we can't afford to give $100 million to each. The key to remember here is that DoD's goal is to protect national security, not to protect or save ailing U.S. industries. When industry can't save itself and its absence threatens national security, then DoD steps in."

According to one Washington observer, "The Defense Department was divided into two camps: (1) the research and development side composed of more aggressive and innovative people, and (2) the procurement, logistics, and manufacturing technology side which was considered to be more traditional and bureaucratic. The procurement side was against Sematech, while the R&D people were generally for it."

In January 1987, DoD created a $50 million place holder for Sematech in the 1988 and 1989 budget as a result of the DSB report. According to Ed McGaffigan, staff assistant to Senator Jeff Bingaman (D. N. Mex.), "DoD made the move without even knowing what Sematech was going to be. This made the Armed Services Committee the dominant player in the Sematech proceedings. We held a hearing in March 1978, and by April we had decided that $100 million a year would be appropriate."

The initial Sematech legislation, however, was introduced March 23, 1987, sponsored by James Florio (D., N.J.) and Don Ritter (R., Pa.), both members of the Semiconductor Support Group. Florio was chair of the subcommittee on Commerce, Consumer Protection and Competitiveness, and Ritter was the cochair of the Republican High-Tech task force. Other supporters in the House included Jake Pickle (D., Tex.), Les Aspin (D., Wis.), Vic Fazio (D., Calif.), and Don Edwards (D., Calif.). In the Senate, Jeff Bingaman (D., N. Mex.), Pete Domenici (R., N. Mex.), Lawton Chiles (D., Fla.), Lloyd Bentsen (D., Tex.), and Alan Cranston (D., Calif.), were supporters.

Florio had attached the legislation to the omnibus trade bill, which after years of debate appeared to be reaching a vote. Industry, however, was not moving as fast as the legislation. In the spring of 1987, Sematech had not resolved many issues including where in government the money would come from. DoD or Commerce were two logical places to seek funding. However, debate over which one was dividing some congressional Sematech supporters. SIA was in a delicate position, because it did not want to alienate any of its allies. Those who supported Defense did so because they realized that it was the only department with the budget, the expertise and the votes to fund Sematech. Commerce supporters were afraid that DoD would dictate the research agenda. For practical reasons Sematech leaders leaned toward DoD; they were confident that they could set the research agenda. However, the possibility of using the Commerce channel was not formally dismissed.

By the summer of 1987, the trade bill was blowing down (it did not receive a presidential signature until August 1988). Lawton Chiles (D., Fla.), chair of the

Senate Budget Committee and a member of the Defense Appropriations subcommittee where Sematech would ultimately receive its money introduced the Senate's
version of Sematech legislation as part o the defense bill. Jeff Bingaman, a member
of the Armed Services Committee, responsible for authorizing all Defense R&D
budgets, co-sponsored the bill. The Chiles-Bingaman legislation reflected the
progmatic rationale of having DoD fund Sematech. McGaffigan said, "It was
important because it created a framework for the relationship between DoD and
industry. Senate staffers acted as brokers during the summer of 1987. Funding—
50/50 split and the Arms Export Control Act—the ability to export Sematech
knowledge, were two of the major issues the legislation resolved."

In September, amendments to Chile's proposal were made in both the
Senate and House. By October, the Senate had authorized $100 million a year for
fiscal 1988 and 1989 through the DoD budget in the form of a grant.[22] The House
authorized only $25 million. (See Exhibit 4.)

Sanford Kane of IBM said, "Part of the problem was site selection. Funding
was supposed to have been completed in September. We never expected it to drag
on to December. It forced us to not select a site until after funding was completed.
We tried to keep the issues separate, but we couldn't."

To dramatize Kane's dilemma, Senator Chiles, the sponsor of the Sematech
bill in the Senate, in November advocated only $35 million for Sematech. "Chiles
was playing hardball," said a House aide. "He called the Sematech people in and
told them if Florida was not chosen for the project he would try to zero out the
money."[23]

NSF Funding

In November of 1987, NSF proposed a $3 million grant to Sematech through the
Semiconductor Research Corporation. The purpose of the grant was to help
sponsor workshops to help with the technical planning effort. The workshops were
designed to bring together experts from industry, government, academia, and the
broad technical and scientific community of the United States. Kane said, "We
opted not to take the money. There were too many strings attached. We funded the
workshops with industry money."

Congressional Approval

On December 18 in conference, Congress agreed to give Sematech $100 million for
fiscal 1988.[24] The bill was signed by President Reagan, December 22.

Texas Wins the Sematech Sweepstakes

Austin took the coveted Sematech site prize on January 6, 1988, surviving a long,
grueling battle between 12 other finalists, beating out 134 proposals. The Texas
package had included a variety of financial and other tangible benefits including a
rent-free facility, free supercomputer time, employee move-in assistance, and season
tickets to sporting and cultural events. The 11 other finalists received a $50,000
planning grant to submit proposals for University Centers of Excellence.

With site selection behind them, Sematech board members and the SIA lobbyists quickly began to garner congressional support for fiscal 1989 funding. Key Texas legislators, led by Jake Pickle, were important to this effort. Pickle said, "It became my job to hold hands and guide the legislation."[25]

DARPA

In February 1988, Sematech was assigned to DARPA, a specialized unit within the R&D side of DoD. Craig Fields, deputy director of research for DARPA, would be the point man for DoD. Although there was some concern that this transfer would affect the management of Sematech, many in the industry believed DARPA's sponsorship would ensure that some of the best scientists, engineers, and technicians in microelectronics, currently working at DARPA, would be called on to help evaluate and subsequently assist in the development of the initiative.[26]

Craig Fields (who had not been a participant in the earlier negotiations with Sematech) rejected the first operating plan submitted by the Sematech board in February 1988. A DoD insider said, "We were surprised that they had left out so many basic things that to us seemed obvious. They handed us a very detailed list of all the inputs required (people and equipment), but absolutely nothing on the outputs, no milestones, no dates, no lists of deliverables or dollars associated with any projects. They have to remember, if they screw up, it's our heads that will roll, we're the ones that have to protect national security."

Kane felt that Sematech had not managed DARPA's expectations well, but went on to say, "We knew the plan wouldn't have passed the scrutiny of Sematech's member company boards; however, DARPA had unrealistic expectations of what the plan would include. At the time we still weren't sure if the government was going to fund this. Thus, our commitment was only on a part-time basis."

Fields remarked, "I kick back all operating plans; that's the way this business works, it's an iterative process. It really was no big deal. Our relationship with industry has been warm from the start. We're all agreed on the importance, relevance, and goals of Sematech."

Once Sematech and DARPA understood each other better, there were still several major areas to resolve. According to Kane, "Fields was concerned that Sematech would turn into an expensive finishing school for process engineers. DARPA was opposed to a central facility. They thought we should only fund projects. They had never done manufacturing science before. They didn't understand why we would be spending money on what IBM already knew." Fields was also concerned about the level of cooperation among the Sematech members. He told Kane, "As companies, you have submitted advanced research projects for DARPA funding that you haven't shared with each other. You've told us more than you have told each other."

In April 1988, Fields requested a meeting with the Sematech board in Dallas to iron out their differences and to get things back on track. In the April meeting Fields pressed for influence on the research agenda. Sematech did not want DARPA in the management decision chain but felt obligated to give Fields something, so they set up a six-person team to manage 20 percent of the annual Sematech budget for research with outside vendors. According to Sporck, "The six-person team had advisory capacity only on how the $40 million would be spent (three would come from Sematech and three from DARPA)."

"DARPA isn't worried who has what vote," Fields said. "We know the smarter ideas will be the ones that get endorsed, and that's all we care about."

Dr. Bill Bandy, project manager at DARPA, assumed the operational responsibilities for DARPA's interaction with Sematech. Bandy saw his role as, "dealing with technical issues, planning and making sure they are heading in the right direction."

Bandy had several meetings with both Sematech and SEMI members. "My sense is Sematech wants DARPA there. We are helping with the process and they appreciate our feedback. I'm also there to help them avoid land mines. So far there have been three major problems. Not having a permanent CEO has meant a lack of leadership. The other two problem areas could have been dealt with more effectively if a CEO had been there. First—member companies are not sending the quality of personnel at the rate promised. Sematech has actually rejected some of the people they've sent. Both fit and skills are important. And second, the working structure has been a bit chaotic. They have had people in positions that weren't right for the job."

On whether DARPA would dictate the research agenda, Bandy stated, "We won't, because Sematech will be producing at a level of quality that is commensurate with military requirements."

John Reilly, vice president of Temple, Barker & Sloane, and an Information Technology expert, felt Sematech was being naive. "DARPA has the power to cut Sematech off whenever they like. In a bureaucracy power is all negative. I've never known one DoD program that they ultimately haven't directed."

Kane said, "If we don't spend the money, DARPA doesn't get it, so they'll want to work with us." Fields did not think it was an issue. "The fact is we are in complete agreement on 98 percent of what Sematech is doing. Unfortunately, the press only focuses in on the 2 percent."

DoD Delay of Fiscal 1988 Funding

Although the Congress had approved $100 million for Sematech in December 1987, there was some difficulty in getting the funds. Before an actual check could be cut, Sematech had to sign a Memorandum of Understanding (MOU) with DoD.

On May 12, 1988, the MOU was signed. Federal funding began.[27]. Sporck said, "We can now direct our efforts to the achievement of Sematech's unique goal to restore global competitiveness to the U.S. semiconductor industry."[28]

The MOU stated the justification for federal funding as being that:

> Congress had found that it is in the national economic and security interest of the United States to provide financial assistance to Sematech for research and development activities in the field of semiconductor manufacturing. In order to further this finding, Congress appropriated funds to be used for grants for the purpose of encouraging the semiconductor industry in the United States to:

1. Conduct research on advanced semiconductor manufacturing techniques.
2. Develop techniques to use manufacturing expertise for the manufacture of a variety of semiconductor products.

People involved with Sematech were asked what "the national economic and security interest" meant in the MOU. According to Charles Sporck:

> The U.S. industrial base is in deep trouble. We have ignored it or done damage to it for years. Some industries are more important, and the semiconductor industry is one of them. If we allowed semiconductors to erode, serious damage to the U.S. could occur. Our members and some in government believe this. On the other hand, some government economists don't even think we need an industrial base.

Another industry official said:

> We (SIA and the government) made a collective jump from understanding that the industry had a problem to the realization that Sematech was part of the answer. We did not, however, spend much time on the intellectual rationale on why it was a good idea. In retrospect we created the justification, but never discussed in depth the details of why we were doing it. We think there is a national economic problem, but it is difficult to label Sematech as addressing that because of the political ramifications.

A Senate staffer from a key office involved in Sematech said:

> The economic interest really doesn't mean much. It was just put in to demonstrate that it is not strictly a military project.

An issue brief by the Congressional Research Service on Sematech in July 1988 questioned the economic justification:

> Although the DSB report emphasized that a Sematech-like plan was vital for national security, subsequent reasons for defending the plan have emphasized national economic security. Many in government, academia, and the defense community have questioned whether this broadening of the federal interest is valid.[29]

On the other hand, Dick Elkus, chairman of Prometrix Co., said:

> The nation which controls the development and production of semiconductor devices and equipment will have achieved a major step toward technological domination and economic and political leadership in the world.

Further Delay in Congressional Support for FY 1989

In the president's FY 1989 budget, $44 million was requested for Sematech. Both the House and Senate authorized $100 million in the spring of 1988 for fiscal 1989, but in the appropriations process the Senate appropriations Committee only allocated

$44 million to Sematech. It was thought since Sematech just received the first $100 million, it could not spend it all, so six-month funding for fiscal 1989 would make better sense.

A congressional staffer from Texas felt, "Politically Sematech has been naive. Our office worked very hard to get federal and state support for Sematech. Once Austin was selected, we didn't get a call from them. They didn't realize that it is important to do that, even if it's after hours."

McGaffigan, Senator Bingaman's staffer disagreed, "There's a remarkable connection between the Centers of Excellence and where Armed Service Committee members are from, that's political savvy."

Noyce is Chosen CEO

Although Sematech had pledged to Congress that a CEO would be named by March 31, 1988, it took until July 27. According to Sporck, "It certainly took longer than we thought, but that is the nature of consortia. Our problem was we were looking for a 40-year-old Bob Noyce and they just don't make those candidates."

Paul Castrucci, a 32-year veteran of IBM was named the COO. He brought more than 30 years of experience to his new post. Observers said, "As head of IBM's semiconductor plant in Vermont, he had run one of American's premier manufacturing facilities."

The Technology

Member companies had held ongoing workshops to hammer out objectives throughout 1978. The following issues had already been settled:

- Sematech would focus on the manufacture of both DRAMs and fast SRAMs. IBM donated its 0.8-micron, 4Mb DRAM process, while AT&T contributed its 0.7-micron, 64K fast SRAM process.[30]
- Fabrication operations wold begin by late 1988.
- Equipment would be geared to high-volume production, but on a small scale.
- Working devices produced by Sematech would not be sold.

According to Dataquest, an industry market research firm, Sematech's targets (assuming they hit them) would give its members a lead of one to one and one-half years over of the rest of the merchant semiconductor industry.

Some experts were concerned about whether Sematech would address the more holistic issue of manufacturing science. Without the pressure of the marketplace, would Sematech be able to simulate the entire manufacturing process from equipment to personnel organization and human resource management issues? Kane responded, "IBM has had experience demonstrating processes without being at actual scale. We are confidence we can simulate high-volume production."

VHSIC Director Sonny Maynard said another objective in Sematech was obtaining zero setup time. "This would mean no test wafers would be required and changing product on the line would only involve changing the programs in the computers." Maynard was concerned, however, about whether they had the proper spending algorithem and whether the SEMI people would see enough money to develop new equipment. "Is $250 million a year enough?"

Decisions Facing Sematech

Culture Clashes. Noyce felt merging 14 different management approaches into one was one of his biggest challenges. "I have to devise a culture that is not like any of the member companies. It has to be more appropriate for a consortium." What specific things must Noyce do to create a unique culture and get the Sematech work force productive?

Dealing with Washington. Sematech had to get annual operating plans approved and government funds appropriated each year. Keeping a high profile in Washington would be important. Noyce said, "We have to cover our bases because there exists a highly diversified set of agendas in Washington." What should Noyce do?

Small Company Participation. There were close to 200 U.S. semiconductor firms, and yet, Sematech's 14 members were all large. Was there a role for the start-up or very small company in Sematech? If so, why and what would be the best way to get them involved.?

Maximizing Technology Transfer. What could Noyce do to ensure an efficient way to transfer what went on in Austin to the member companies? How could it be set up to maximize the members' growth, competitiveness, and return on the investment in Sematech?

Noyce: Spokesperson for the Industry? Should Bob Noyce become the spokesperson for the semiconductor industry? Should he become the focal point for all semiconductor efforts in Washington? Although there were many advantages to having one spokesperson, was the CEO of Sematech the appropriate choice?

National Advisory Committee for Semiconductor Research. Legislation to establish a national advisory committee on semiconductors had been written in the trade bill before the president. The committee would analyze current efforts and help legislators develop a national semiconductor R&D strategy. (See Exhibit 7.)

The committee would consist of industry and government people. Having a governmental structure in place would provide the industry with an inside track to Washington. Noyce had to decide if he should support such a committee and whether he should become involved.

A final thought: As Noyce reflected on the past two years and what lay ahead, he recalled what Machiavelli had pointed out almost 500 years ago in *The Prince*:

There is nothing more difficult to plan, more doubtful of success, nor more dangerous to manage, than the creation of a new system. For the initiator has the enmity of all who would profit by the preservation of the old institutions and merely lukewarm defenders in those who would gain by the new.

Exhibit 1   Sematech Members and B.O.D. Representatives

Advanced Micro Devices, Inc., W. J. Sanders, III
American Telephone and Telegraph, Michael A. Turk
Digital Equipment Corporation, Robert B. Palmer
Harris Corporation, Jon E. Cornell
Hewlett-Packard Company, George E. Bodway
Intel Corporation, George Schneer
International Business Machines Corporation, S. L. Kane
LSI Logic Corporation, Wilfred J. Corrigan
Micron Technology, Inc., Joseph L. Parkinson
Motorola, James A. Norling
National Semiconductor Corporation, Charles E. Sporck
NCR Corporation, J. H. Van Tassel
Rockwell International Corporation, Gilbert F. Amelio
Texas Instruments Incorporated, George H. Heilmeier

Exhibit 2 Foreign Government Supported Joint R&D Programs in Commercial Microelectronics

Country	Project	Companies	Technical Focus	Time Frame	Government Funds ($ Millions)
Japan	MITI VLSI	5	VLSI Manufacturing	1975–1979	$112
Japan	NIT VLSI	3	VLSI Device	1975–1979	309
Japan	New Function Elements	12	VLSI Device & Mfg.	1980–1990	140
Japan	Supercomputer	6	High Speed Devices	1981–1989	135
Japan	Optoelectronics	13	Optical Semiconductors	1979–1986	80
Japan	Sortec	13	Synotron Litography	1986–1996	62[a]
Japan	Optical ICs	13	Optical Semiconductors	1986–1996	42[a]
Korea	ETRI 4M DRAM	4	Develop 4M DRAM	N.A.	80
EEC	ESPRIT	Many	Commercial Computing	1984–1994	675
Britain	Alvey Project	—	Commercial Computing	1983–1987	—
Germany-Netherlands	Mega Project	2	1M SRAM/4M DRAM	1984–1989	150

Source: Bureau of National Affairs.
[a]Funding from the Key Technology Center includes some private contributions.
N.A.–Not available.

Exhibit 3   Federal Spending for Semiconductor Research in Fiscal 1987

Agency	Outlays
Department of Defense	
Office of the Secretary of Defense	
Very-High-Speed Integrated Circuits	122
Strategic Defense Initiative Organization	60
Defense Advanced Research Projects Agency	16
Manufacturing Technology	14
Microwave and Millimeter-Wave Monolithic Integrated Circuits	10
Defense Nuclear Agency	7
Armed Services	
U.S. Air Force	60
U.S. Navy	28
U.S. Army	25
Independent Research and Development	[a]
Department of Energy	
National Laboratories	
Sandia	55[b]
Lawrence Berkeley	4
Brookhaven	2
Other	2[c]
Photovoltaic Research	15
National Science Foundation	30
National Bureau of Standards	4
Subtotal	454
Incremental R&D Tax Credit	75[d]
Total	529

Source: Congressional Budget Office.
[a]Cannot be estimated; see text.
[b]Excludes work performed at Sandia but reimbursed by the Department of Defense.
[c]Includes Oak Ridge, Lawrence, Livermore, Ames, and Argonne.
[d]Average of 50 and 100. See text for details.

Exhibit 4 Funding Status Report, Fiscal 1988–1989 (millions)

Year	President's Budget Request	Defense Authorization			Defense Appropriations			Concurrent Budget Resolution
		HASC	SASC	Conference	NAC	SAC	Conference	
1988	$50	$10	$100	$100	$100	$65	$100	Conference Report Budget Assumptions for Sematech adopted
	Program Element $54 6377390d	Raised to $25 M on H. Floor M.R. 1748	S.1174 S. Rept. 100–57	H. Rept. 100–446 P.L. 100–180	H.R. 3576 H. Rept. 100–410	S.1423 S. Rept. 100–235	H.J. Res. 395 H. Rept. 100–498 P.L. 100–202	H. Con. Res. 93 H. Rept. 100–175
	M. REPT. 100–58							
1989	$44.785	$100	$100	Pending	$100	June		Conference Report Budget Assumptions for Sematech adopted
	Program Element #65 0603739d	H.R. 4264 H. Rept. 100–563	S. 2355 S. Rept. 100–236		H.R. _____	M. Rept. 100.____		H. Con. Res. 268 H. Rept. 100–658

Source: SIA.

Note: Government participation in Sematech began in 1988.

Key: HASC = House Armed Services Committee.
SASC = Senate Armed Services Committee.
HAC = House Appropriations Committee.
SAC = Senate Appropriations Committee.

Exhibit 5   Sematech Objectives

DEFINE the Competitive Position

DEVELOP with U.S. Vendors a Self-Sustaining, World-Competitive Support Infrastructure for Leading Edge Equipment and Materials

DEVELOP with Member Companies, Universities and Government Labs Leading Edge Processes and Manufacturing System Methodology
  – Phase 1: .8 micron (baseline)
  – Phase 2: .5 micron (parity)
  – Phase 3: .35 micron (leadership)

DEMONSTRATE Performance of these Manufacturing Capabilities in an Integrated and Flexible Environment
  – New Equipment
  – New Processes
  – Manufacturing Systems

TRANSFER the Technology to Member Companies

Exhibit 6   Sematech Organizational Relationships

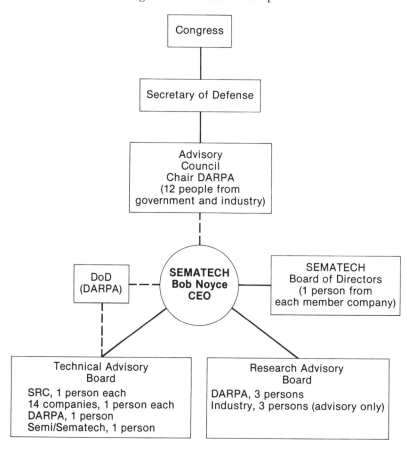

Exhibit 7   National Advisory Committee on Semiconductors

Background

The concept of a National Advisory Committee on Semiconductors (NASC) was first put forward by the SRC in 1986 and was endorsed by the SRC Board of Directors and the Semiconductor Industry Association Board of Directors in 1987. The NACS, with a membership of five high-level federal officials, four semiconductor industry officials, and four "who are eminent in the fields of technology, defense, and economic development," will evolve a national semiconductor research and development strategy to assure continued U.S. leadership in semiconductor technology and will advise government officials, legislators, and others on the needs and priorities that address this goal. The focus of the NACS is R&D and its structure and functions provide for strong industry input. With an objective of maximizing our resources, the NACS would be an industry-government partnership to address a national priority.

The NACS legislation calls for administrative support from "an appropriate agency or organization" to acquire the data and perform the analyses required. The SRC is considered an organization that can provide this support. Funding is authorized, but no appropriation is provided. Under the legislation, funds may be obtained from federal agencies or from private sector companies or organizations.

Exhibit 8

BIOGRAPHY: ROBERT N. NOYCE

Chief Executive Officer Robert N. Noyce is a widely known leader in the electronics industry and also is vice chairman of Intel Corporation, a firm he cofounded.

Dr. Noyce cofounded Fairchild Semiconductor Corporation in 1957 and coinvented with Jack Kilby the integrated circuit, enabling Fairchild to produce the first commercial integrated circuit. In 1968, he cofounded Intel with long-time associate Gordon E. Moore.

Dr. Noyce is a long-time board member of the Semiconductor Industry Association, which he helped found and served as its first president. He also was a member of the President's Committee on Industrial Competitiveness.

Biography: Paul P. Castrucci

Chief Operating Officer Paul P. Castrucci joined Sematech after a 32-year career with International Business Machines Corp., where he was the senior member of IBM's Corporate Technical Committee. In his former job, he was responsible for conducting special analyses of advanced manufacturing and process development activities in semiconductor integrated circuits.

Prior to being appointed to IBM's Corporate Technical Committee in 1987, he managed all production operations at IBM's state-of-the-art, 5,000-employee semiconductor facility in Burlington, Vermont. Accomplishments included deliver of 1 million bit DRAM, a 6,000 gate CMOS gate array, a RISC microprocessor, the industry's first 8-inch wafer production line, and transfer of CMOS gate array technology to Intel Corporation. He also organized joint equipment development programs with vendors to accelerate the advancement of submicron processing capability.

Mr. Castrucci has been granted 24 U.S. patents, including basic patents for integrated circuit memory devices, semiconductor process manufacturing and the smart card, plus a total of 131 patents in semiconductor technology worldwide.

Dr. Craig I. Fields

Dr. Craig I. Fields received his B.S. degree from the Massachusetts Institute of Technology and his Ph.D. from the Rockefeller University. After serving on the faculty of Harvard University, he joined the Defense Advanced Research Projects Agency (DARPA) in 1974.

While at DARPA, Dr. Fields has been responsible for managing and transferring research programs, primarily in the area of advance computer technology. He is currently the deputy director for research at DARPA.

Exhibit 9 Key Dates in Sematech History

1982

SRC formed in North Carolina.
MCC formed in Austin, Texas.

1984

National Cooperative Research Act.
SRC formed Manufacturing Competitiveness Panel.

1985

Antidumping suits filed.
Semiconductor Congressional Support Group formed.
IBM analyzed the U.S. semiconductor industry. Report shown to IBM top management. IBM decided to share information with rest of the industry.

1986

February–May—IBM presented data on industry to most U.S. semiconductor firms and key government officials.
June—Sporck assigned task to travel the country to forge consensus among industry food chain and government.
September—Chip agreement with Japan signed.
     —SIA board created task force to define objectives and derive a framework for Sematech (Sept.–Mar. 1987).
November—SIA board meeting with press—discussion among members created controversy and bad publicity about the Sematech effort.

1987

February—DSB report stated a Sematech project is needed in the name of national security

March—SIA unanimously approved Sematech concept. A 14-member working group is created to develop a five-year business and operating plan. SRC gave Sematech $100,000 to cover start-up costs.

First Sematech legislation proposed under the National Defense Authorization Act.

Sanctions levied against Japan.

April—CRS report issued.

May—SIA approved Sematech concept. Voted SIA as interim board of directors. Formed site and CEO selection committees. Working group stayed together to become first official Sematech staff. SIA members agreed to fund start-up costs.

Letters sent to all 50 governors requesting proposals for the Sematech site.

June—Larry Sumney chosen as interim CEO of Sematech.

Congressional hearings held on Sematech.

Member companies began to come to consensus on what Sematech should be.

Technical workshops began to discuss Sematech (several were held across the country throughout 1987 and early 1988).

Reagan lifted some sanctions on Japanese goods.

August—Sematech incorporated in Delaware.

September—Founding companies committed money to Sematech.

Semi/Sematech formed.

CBO report issued.

White House report on semiconductors issued.

November—NSF report published but not distributed.

NSF $3 million grant is turned down by Sematech.

December—In conference the House and Senate agreed to fund Sematech $100 million for Fiscal Year 1988.

President Reagan signed Sematech funding into law.

1988

January—Austin selected as site for Sematech.

Meeting held between SIA and AEA member CEOs to work out differences.

IBM and AT&T announced they would donate 4-megabyte DRAM and a 64K SRAM, respectively, to SEMATECH.

SEMATECH had 50–60 full-time employees.

February—DARPA received jurisdiction for Sematech within DoD.

Craig Fields of DARPA rejected first operating plan.

NCR joined Sematech.

March—SIA board meeting dealt with problem of CEO-created troika of Sandy Kane (IBM), George Schneer (Intel), and Jim Peterman (TI) to act as CEO and COO.

March 31 was the deadline given to government on when a CEO

> would be named. Sematech provision that members could quit if not
> satisfied with its progress on March 31, 1988 is pushed back to June 1,
> 1988.
> April—Sematech employees moved to Austin.
>   Fields met with Sematech officials in Dallas to work out differences.
> May—Memorandum of Understanding is signed with DoD.
>   First funds from government are received.
>   Five universities received a $0.5–1.5 million for Centers of Excellence
>   programs.
> June—Deadline for consortium to break up Sematech if not far enough along.
>   AEA and SIA reached consensus on modifications of the chip agree-
>   ment and proposed them to USTR and Commerce.
>   Senate approved only $44 million for Fiscal Year 1989 Sematech
>   funding (House approved $100).
>   Sematech Congressional Support Group formed.
> July—Bob Noyce and Paul Castrucci chosen as CEO and COO of Sematech.
>   Fiscal Year 1989 government fund still pending.

ENDNOTES

1. David Yoffie, "The Global Semiconductor Industry, 1987" (Boston: Harvard Business School, 9-388-052, 1987).
2. Captive firms included such companies as IBM, AT&T, DEC, HP, and DELCO Electronics. Although production numbers for captives were not available, industry experts believed captives to represent one-third to one quarter of the total U.S. market.
3. Cited from testimony of C. Scott Kulicke before the Subcommittee on Commerce, Consumer Protection and Competitiveness, of the Committee on Energy and Commerce, U.S. House of Representatives, June 7, 1987.
4. Texas Instruments and Micron Technology were the only U.S. producers of DRAMs in 1987. In early 1988 Motorola reentered DRAM production.
5. Four companies—Philips, Siemens, Thomson-SGS, and Telefunken—accounted for over 80 percent of semiconductor production by firms based in Europe.
6. *National Science Foundation Report on the Semiconductor Industry*, November 1987, p. 40.
7. Semiconductors could be divided into two basic categories: silicon based and compound based. Compound-based materials were primarily used in specialty products. Silicon was by far the predominant semiconductor material for the 1980s and 1990s. All Sematech work was focused on silicon-based chips.
8. Glenn J. McLoughlin and Nancy R. Miller, "The U.S. Semiconductor Industry and the SEMATECH Proposal," the Congressional Research Service, the Library of Congress, *April 23, 1987*, p. 10.
9. David Yoffie, "The Semiconductor Industry Association and the Trade Dispute with Japan," (A) #9-387-205, (B) #9-387-195, (C) #9-388-049, and (D) #9-388-104, 1987.
10. Required investment for a minimum efficient-scale DRAM plant was $250 million to $450 million and would take approximatley 18 months to get up and running. In addition, a workable design must be available.
11. FMVs were the established floor price for chips as determined by the Department of Commerce.
12. "Research Venture Gets U.S. Approval on Computer Work," *The Wall Street Journal*, March 5, 1985.
13. SRC was formed in 1982. The government did not participate financially until 1986 when it made a $1.2 million grant. In 1987 four agencies—NSF, DoD, National Bureau of Standards, and NSC—were funding $2.4 million of the SRC's $20 million budget.
14. From a letter written to Charles Fowler, chairman of the Defense Science Board (DoD), from Normal Augustine, president, Martin Marietta Corporation.

15. The DSB report was headed by Norm Augustine, president and CEO of Martin Marietta, a large defense contractor that was a key participant in VHSIC. Several semiconductor executives, also participated in the report.

16. Congressional testimony before the subcommittee on Commerce, Consumer Protection, and Competitiveness, June 7, 1987.

17. A. Lee Fritschler and Bernard H. Ross, *How Washington Works* (Cambridge, Mass.:, Ballinger, 1987), Chap. 6.

18. The agencies involved included the CIA, Commerce, State, National Security Agency, National Science Foundation, Justice, OMB, Office of Science and Technology Policy, U.S.T.R., Council of Economic Advisers, Energy, and Defense.

19. Sematech lawyers never asked Justice for a business review. Although they were confident of a favorable decision, it could have delayed the project six months.

20. Baldridge had played a key role during this time in the Fujitsu/Fairchild attempted takeover. He was adamantly opposed to the takeover on grounds that access to Fairchild's U.S. distribution system would enable Fujitsu to dominate the U.S. semiconductor industry.

21. Like most American chip producers, the Europeans concentrated on ASICs and other more specialized microprocessors.

22. By using the form of a grant, Sematech could avoid the complex defense contracting requirements. To ensure proper use of the funds, an amendment was passed to create a 12-member advisory board that would report annually to Congress on Sematech progress. Membership would be composed of industry and government officials.

23. Mark Nelson, "Texans Flexed Political Muscle," *Dallas Texas News*, January 7, 1988.

24. When the House and Senate approve different amounts for a line item, the two resolve the difference via a conference made up of key representatives from both sides.

25. Nelson, "Texans Flexed Political Muscle."

26. Ibid.

27. Almost immediately, an initial federal contribution of $15 million was sent to Sematech. The remaining federal monies would be made periodically as Sematech certified that member companies matching funds had been received.

28. Quoted from Sematech press release, May 12, 1988.

29. Glenn J. McLoughlin, "Semiconductor Manufacturing Technology Proposal: Sematech," Congressional Research Service Issue Brief, pp. 8–9, July 15, 1988.

30. DRAMs stored data that could be erased from memory by interrupting the flow of electrical current. DRAMs performed similar functions more quickly but cost more and had less memory than similar sized DRAMS. EPROMs (electrical programmable read-only memory), could be reprogrammed and erased by exposure to ultraviolet light. ASICs were customized chips for specific application uses.

Semiconductor Statistical Supplement

Equipment and Materials
Semiconductors
End Users
R&D
United States versus Japan
European Semiconductors

Exhibit 1 Worldwide Equipment and Materials Sales, 1987

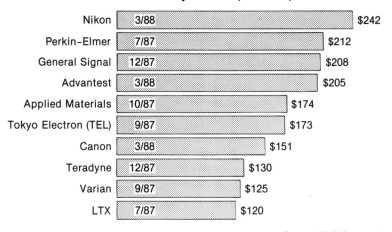

Worldwide fiscal year sales ($ millions)

Company	Date	Sales
Nikon	3/88	$242
Perkin-Elmer	7/87	$212
General Signal	12/87	$208
Advantest	3/88	$205
Applied Materials	10/87	$174
Tokyo Electron (TEL)	9/87	$173
Canon	3/88	$151
Teradyne	12/87	$130
Varian	9/87	$125
LTX	7/87	$120

Source: VLSI Research

Exhibit 2

	Volume	Market Share in United States	Market Share in Japan	Worldwide Market Share
United States	$2.591	77.2%	34.8%	59.3%
Japan	1.865	18.3	52.8	30.6
Rest of world (Row)	0.950	4.6	2.9	6.8

Equipment Sales, 1987

[a]Numbers do not add because of joint ventures.

Materials, 1987 (Silicon Only)

Volume[a]

United States	$542.73
Japan	744.33
Rest of World	307.95

Source: VLSI Research. Total equipment, world volume: $5.4 billion
Total materials, world volume: $7.8 billion (all materials)
Total U.S. employment equipment: 45,000

Exhibit 3 Semiconductor Equipment Sales Demographics, 1982–1987 (in millions of dollars)

	1982	1983	1984	1985	1986	1987
U.S. purchases	$1,555.5	$2,100.8	$3,250.9	$3,103.6	$2,541.8	$2,591.0
U.S. sales	1,378.5	1,812.8	2,741.0	2,517.2	2,016.7	2,000.2
Japan sales	127.0	218.7	394.8	442.7	406.9	472.9
ROW sales	50.0	69.3	115.1	143.7	118.2	117.9
Japan purchases	907.8	1,295.4	2,172.5	1,867.9	1,664.3	1,865.4
U.S. sales	373.1	454.3	767.6	768.9	475.8	648.5
Joint ventures	86.9	139.3	241.5	278.9	194.9	177.8
Japan sales	412.2	651.1	1,092.0	749.7	942.1	985.7
ROW sales	35.6	50.7	71.4	70.4	51.5	53.4
ROW purchases	276.2	381.1	798.1	1,155.1	835.1	957.7
U.S. sales	152.3	229.6	510.4	677.8	481.8	561.8
Japan sales	31.3	40.9	125.7	256.4	165.0	198.9
ROW sales	92.6	110.6	162.0	220.9	188.3	197.0
Total purchases	2,739.5	3,777.3	6,221.5	6,126.6	5,041.2	5,414.1
U.S. sales	1,903.9	2,496.7	4,019.0	3,963.9	2,974.3	3,210.5
Joint ventures	86.9	139.3	241.5	278.9	194.9	177.8
Japan sales	570.5	910.7	1,612.5	1,448.8	1,514.0	1,657.5
ROW sales	178.2	230.4	348.5	435.0	358.0	368.3

Semiconductor Equipment Sales Demographics, 1982–1987 (in percent)

	1982	1983	1984	1985	1986	1987
U.S. purchase	100.0%	100.0%	100.0%	100.0%	100.0%	100.0%
U.S. sales	88.6	86.3	84.3	81.1	79.3	77.2
Japan sales	8.2	10.4	12.1	14.3	16.0	18.3
ROW sales	3.2	3.3	3.5	4.6	4.7	4.6
Japan purchases	100.0	100.0	100.0	100.0	100.0	100.0
U.S. sales	41.1	35.1	35.3	41.2	28.6	34.8
Joint ventures	9.6	10.8	11.1	14.9	11.7	9.5
Japan sales	45.4	50.3	50.3	40.1	56.6	52.8
ROW sales	3.9	3.9	3.3	3.8	3.1	2.9
ROW purchases	100.0	100.0	100.0	100.0	100.0	100.0
U.S. sales	55.1	60.2	64.0	58.7	57.7	58.7
Japan sales	11.3	10.7	15.7	22.2	19.8	20.8
ROW sales	33.5	29.0	20.3	19.1	22.5	20.6
Total purchases	100.0	100.0	100.0	100.0	100.0	100.0
U.S. sales	69.5	66.1	64.6	64.7	59.0	59.3
Joint ventures	3.2	3.7	3.9	4.6	3.9	3.3
Japan sales	20.8	24.1	25.9	23.6	30.0	30.6
ROW sales	6.5	6.1	5.6	7.1	7.1	6.8

Source: VLSI Research Inc.

Exhibit 4   U.S. Semiconductor Companies, 1987

Total Worldwide Sales
$46.837 billion

Total Worldwide Captive Volume
$14.6 billion (estimated)

Total Worldwide Merchant Volume
$32.237 billion

Top Five US. Captives	Top Five U.S. Merchants	Top Five U.S. ASIC Producers
IBM	Motorola	AMD
AT&T	Texas Instruments	LST Logic
DEC	Intel	AT&T
Hewlett-Packard	National/Fairchild	Texas Instruments
Delco Electronics	AMD/MNI	Motorola

Semiconductors, 1987

	Volume[a]	Market Share in U.S. (%)	Market Share in Japan (%)	Worldwide Market Share (%)
United States	21.295	80.1%	9.3%	48%
Japan	20.021	9.3	90.5	39
Europe	1.197	2.0	1.0	11
Rest of world	1.197	—	—	2

Total U.S. employment: 267,820

Sources: *Dataquest* and VLSI Research.
[a]Includes captive and merchant sales, in billions.

Exhibit 5   Capacity Utilization—World Semiconductor Industry, 1973–1987

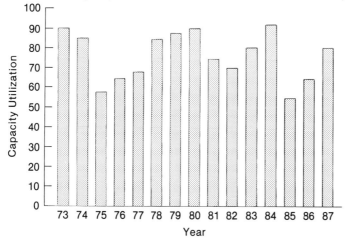

Source: VLSI Research.

Exhibit 6   Price Versus Cost for 64K-Bit DRAMs, 1981–1989

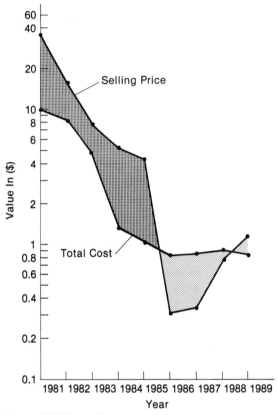

Source: VLSI Research.

Exhibit 7   Estimated Semiconductor Sales, 1982–1987 (Worldwide in $ millions—including captives)

	1982	1983	1984	1985	1986	1987	1982–1987 CAGR
North America	$10,482	$12,793	$18,726	$16,319	$17,599	$21,295	15.2%
Japan	6,660	8,660	12,344	10,863	16,546	20,021	24.6
Europe	2,347	3,702	3,640	1,104	3,574	4,324	13.0
Rest of world	127	205	387	675	989	1,198	56.6

Source: VLSI Research.

Exhibit 8   Worldwide Semiconductor Market, 1984–1987 (Percentage of market share, excludes captives)

Regional Companies	1984	1985	1986	1987
Japanese companies	40%	42%	46%	48%
North American companies	48	45	42	39
European companies	11	12	11	11
Rest of world companies	1	1	2	2
Total	100%	100%	100%	100%

Source: *Dataquest.*

Exhibit 9   Worldwide Semiconductor Market Share, 1986–1987 (Top 10 companies)

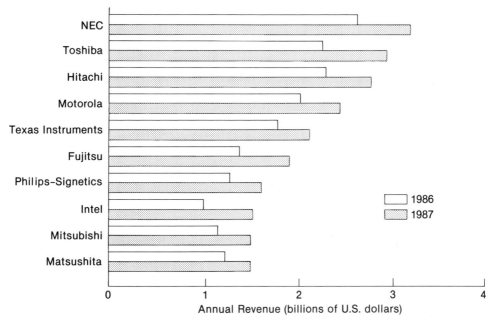

Source: *Dataquest.*

Exhibit 10   Worldwide Semiconductor Production by Region, 1986–1992 Est.

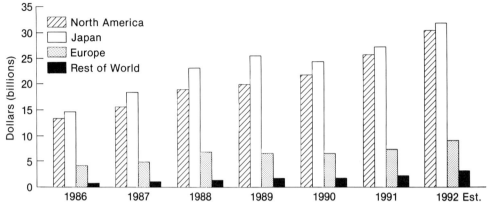

Source: *Dataquest,* June 1988.

Table 1   Worldwide Semiconductor Production
by Region, 1984 Versus 1992 Est.

	1984	1992 Est.
North America	49.8%	40.9%
Japan	38.3	42.8
Europe/Rest of world	11.9	16.3
Total	100.0%	100.0%

Source: *Dataquest,* June 1988.

Exhibit 11   Worldwide MOS EPROM Market Share, 1984–1986

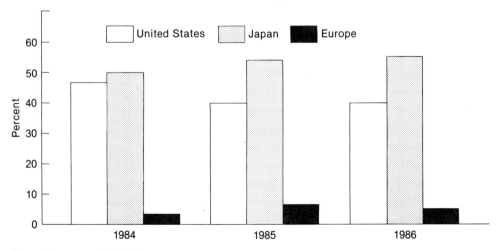

Source: Dataquest, July 1988.

Exhibit 12   Worldwide ASIC Suppliers by
Region, 1987

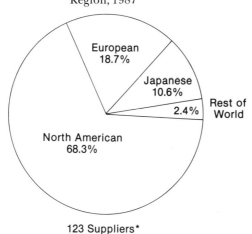

123 Suppliers*

*Excludes full-custom ICs.

Source: *Dataquest,* June 1987.

Exhibit 13   Worldwide Electronic Equipment Market by Electronics Segment, 1986–1988

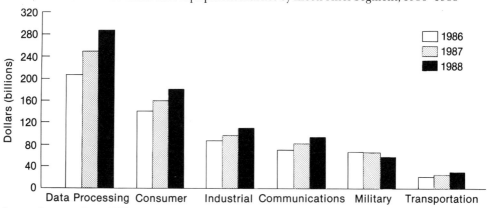

Source: *Dataquest,* June 1988.

Exhibit 14   Worldwide Semiconductor Consumption by Electronics Segment, 1986–1988

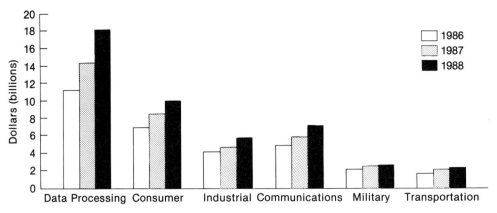

Source: *Dataquest,* June 1988.

Exhibit 15   **Electronics, 1987**

Markets	**Volume (billions)**
United States	$210.5
Japan	108.7
Europe	103.6
Rest of World	53
Total U.S. employment: 2.5 million	

Source: VLSI Research.

Exhibit 16   Semiconductor End Uses, 1986

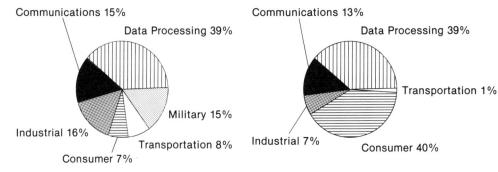

Source: *Dataquest.*

Exhibit 17   Electronics in America's Largest Industry, 1987

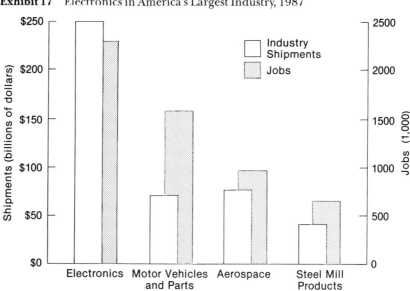

Source: Semiconductor Industry Association.

Exhibit 18   Semiconductors Are the Leverage Point in Electronics

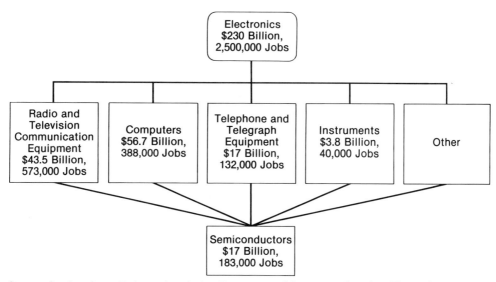

Sources: Semiconductor Industry Association, Department of Commerce, American Electronics Association.

Exhibit 19   U.S. Semiconductor R&D, 1988 ($4 billion)

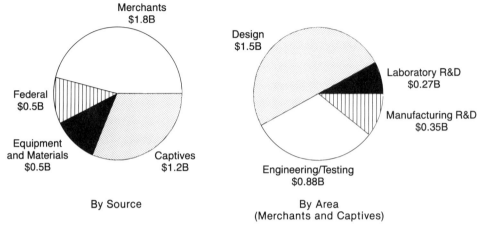

By Source

By Area
(Merchants and Captives)

Source: Department of Defense.

Exhibit 20   Federal Funding, 1987–1993 Est. Silicon R&D

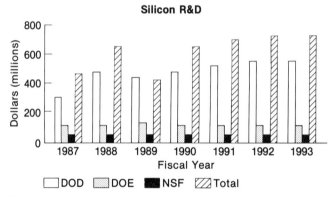

Source: Department of Defense.

Exhibit 21   Rankings for Percent of Sales on
R&D, 1986–1987

	1987	1986
Semiconductors	9.6%	12.2%
Information Processing	7.6	7.9
Pharmaceuticals	9.5	7.8
Telecommunications	5.5	5.1
Aerospace	4.4	4.5
Automotive (and parts)	3.5	3.6
All-Industry Average	3.4	3.5
Machinery	NA	
Steel	NA	

Source: Adapted from *Business Week*.

Exhibit 22   R&D Spending, United States and Japan, Selected
                  Years 1976–1984

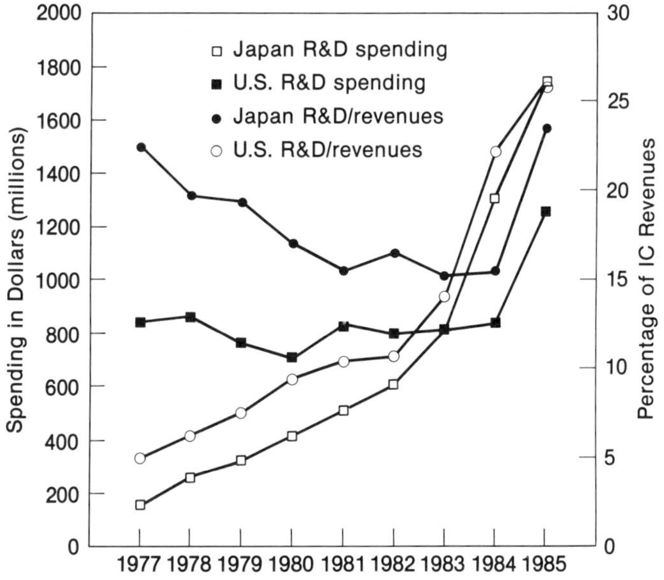

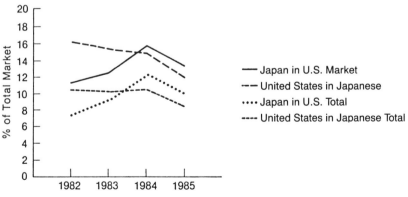

Source: *Dataquest* (excludes U.S. captives).

Exhibit 23   U.S. and Japanese Shares in the Other's Markets, 1982–1985

Source: *Dataquest.*

Exhibit 24   DRAM Market Shares, United States Versus Japan, 1975–1986

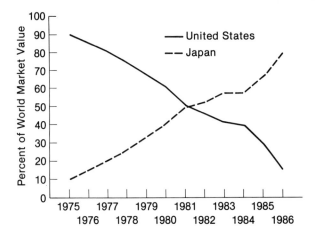

Source: *Dataquest.*

Exhibit 25   Semiconductor Statistical Supplement

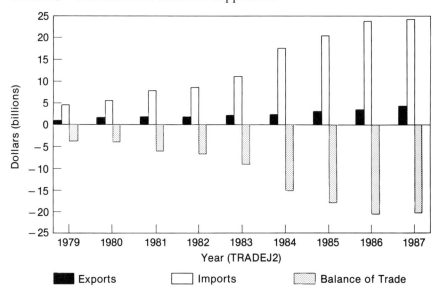

Source: American Electronics Association.

Exhibit 26   Comparison of U.S. and Japanese Trade Environments

This is a synopsis from a report sponsored by the White House Science Council Panel on Semiconductors conducted in 1987.

INDUSTRIAL

United States	**Japan**
Emphasis on short-term performance makes long-term investment difficult. Industry, especially the manufacturing equipment industry, is fragmented—resulting in cutbacks in R&D during down periods of business cycle.	Strong vertical and horizontal structure of industry supports firms, even in down cycles: alliances with banks provide low-cost finances. Operating near- or below-cost facilities market penetration.

MANUFACTURING

Manufacturing not adequately emphasized. Product design and differentiation used for comparative advantage. Industry slow to apply new technology to manufacturing. Lack of emphasis on quality resulted in lower yield and higher cost. R&D and financial management considered the best careers.	Industry strives for highest-quality, lowest-cost manufacturing. Fundamentals critical to yield have been mastered. Manufacturing a respected career.

TRADE

Export controls sometimes put U.S. firms at a competitive disadvantage. Government perceived oriented toward export control—not promotion.	Government oriented to export promotion, import control. U.S. firms excluded from market.

TECHNOLOGY

U.S. firms emphasize design technology. Product differentiation preferred over product quality. Many innovations in manufacturing equipment were pioneered here but utilized first in Japan because of the short-term profit mindset of U.S. companies.	Japanese are often first to accept new manufacturing equipment. New equipment developed in Japan goes to Japanese industry first. Japanese firms spend heavily on R&D, even in adverse economic periods.

EDUCATION

Too little stress on mathematics and science in education. Fewer high school graduates prepared for engineering curricula. Work force less skilled. Outstanding research-level scientific education.	Science, math, and technology emphasized at all levels; precollege graduates are some two years ahead of U.S. students. System produces more engineers many used in manufacturing. Strong continuing education in industry.

GOVERNMENT POLICY

Adversarial relationship exists between government and industry. Government policies concerning mandatory benefits, product liability, tax incentives, and antitrust levy cost on U.S. firms experienced less in other countries.	Government has *created* a comparative advantage in semiconductors by protectionism at home, targeting U.S. industry, market penetration, dumping, and government funding and direction of R&D. (Laboratories have *commercial* assigned missions.)

FINANCIAL

Cost of capital nearly twice that in Japan. Lower savings rate. Greater defense share of GNP (6 percent). Japanese defense is only 1 percent, leading to $80 billion advantage. Equity market focused on short-term performance.

Companies have close relationship with banks—get substantial funding at low interest rates. Capital cost less and almost unlimited funds available for long-term development, modernization, and "buying" market share through losses. High savings rate.

OTHER COMPARISONS

Antitrust laws do not recognize that many markets are worldwide. Government actions breed high caution, prevent companies from jointly working global markets. Product liability law fosters excessive litigation, create excessive risks. Ineffective means for U.S. companies to redress foreign piracy of patented processes.

Government and culture support industry cooperation. Semiconductor companies are members of large corporate families with $100–200 billion annual revenues, centered around large banks. Firms have ready sources of finance.

Exhibit 27   Distribution of European Semiconductor Fabricators, 1988

Top Semiconductor Companies in Europe*		
	Sales 1968 $m	% increase over 1987
Philips (Holland)	1,002	7.7
SGS Thomson (France/Italy)	650	21.0
Texas Instruments (United States)	636	29.3
Motorola (United States)	616	28.9
Siemens (W. Germany)	571	20.2
Intel (United States)	485	71.4
National Semi- conductor (United States)	390	13.0
NEC (Japan)	370	48.6
Toshiba (Japan)	349	85.6
AMD (United States)	279	18.7
*By European sales.		

Source: *Dataquest.*

Exhibit 28   European Chip Makers Sales, 1986

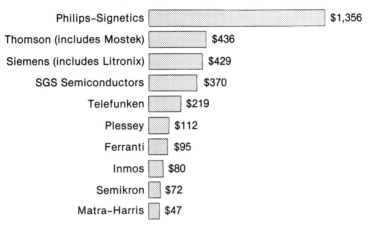

Estimated 1986 Results for the 10 Leading European Suppliers
(millions of U.S. dollars)

Philips–Signetics	$1,356
Thomson (includes Mostek)	$436
Siemens (includes Litronix)	$429
SGS Semiconductors	$370
Telefunken	$219
Plessey	$112
Ferranti	$95
Inmos	$80
Semikron	$72
Matra–Harris	$47

Source: *Dataquest.*

Note on the Structure of the U.S. Government Decision-Making Process

"The constitutional convention of 1787," wrote Richard Neustadt,[1] "is supposed to have created a government of 'separated powers.' It did nothing of the sort. Rather, it created a government of separate institutions that share powers." Despite the apparent conflict that often characterizes relations between the administration and Congress, then, there is nevertheless a very real interdependence and need for mutual compromise.

Public policy in the United States is obstensibly made by Congress and the administration. But as the responsibilities assumed by the federal government have grown and the problems it deals with have become more complex, decisions are more often made, not by the Congress as a whole or by the president and his staff, but by subcommittees of Congress, independent agencies, and bureaus of the Executive branch. The leading members of these subunits are the major and the constant participants in the process through which legislation and programs are shaped.[2] That power is now also shared by an increasing number of people who are not part of government at all, but who choose to become involved in the process through participation in "subsystems" of the government decision-making process.

SUBSYSTEMS

The term "subsystems," as used here, refers to the pattern of interaction among the various groups who influence or make the decisions in any particular area of public policy.[3] The participants are drawn from several interrelated institutions: a government agency or bureau, congressional subcommittees, parts of the relevant state or local governments, and any special interest groups that care to involve themselves. In the federal system the numerous subsystems then interact with one another to form public policy.

Some researchers[4] point out that the subsystems are organized around specific government programs that may number as many as 800 to 1,000, and that any business manager wishing to enter a subsystem has only to identify the specific program he wishes to monitor, support, or change. A manager in the field of agribusiness, for example, should concentrate on price support, soil bank, or food inspection programs rather than try to influence the broader issue of agricultural policy. Comparable programs he might enter to influence health policy would include hospital construction, cancer research, medical education, drug licensing, or communicable disease control.[5]

CONGRESSIONAL SUBCOMMITTEES

In Congress, four subcommittees, two in the House and two in the Senate, are responsible for each government program. Every program of the federal government actually goes through the whole legislative cycle twice. On the first cycle the program is authorized or created (depending upon the program, this happens once every one, two, or three years) and often an expenditure ceiling is set. No money can be spent, however, until the legislative wheel turns again and an annual appropriation bill becomes law.[6]

Congressional subcommittees are responsible for making recommendations concerning both the resources and the authority to be allocated to an agency or bureau. Their influence therefore often extends beyond the legislative enactment of policies, into the interpretation, refinement, and application of laws. Since all bureau leaders and agency heads know they depend on the committees for renewals of their funds and for any needed modification of their authority they try to follow, within reason, what they think the committee members who shaped a given law want of them.[7]

The demand on a committee member's time and attention, the limits of his or her knowledge, and therefore his or her dependence on others for information, judgment, and even action, contribute to the sizeable influence of the committee staff. Staff members often control communications between their superiors and those outside, draft committee reports, and, as committee agents, inject their views into the subsystem in ways and to degrees far beyond the limits of their formal roles.[8] As agents of committees they also have the power to investigate bureau policies and organization, and here again inject their views into bureau affairs.[9]

The chairman of the pertinent congressional subcommittees, two or three members of each subcommittee, and a corresponding number of subcommittee staff are the direct participants in a policy-making decision. The participants from the executive branch usually include agency or bureau heads along with individuals at lower levels of the bureaucracy.

The White House staff participates in policy decisions, but on most issues the president himself rarely becomes involved. Although he sits at the center of the administration, his decisions are usually the product of numerous individual influences and many pressures having little in common with his own inclinations.[10] The risk to his prestige that failure and controversy pose usually outweigh any benefits that might accrue from his involvement. Too frequent intervention can lower the prestige of the president' office and dissipate the reserve of power needed to push through major policy initiatives.[11]

Since most domestic federal programs are actually administered by state and local governments, the state and local bureaucrats are also part of the subsystems. Housing, welfare, education, highways, mass transit, and airport programs, for example, are funded in part by the federal government, but are run almost wholly by state and local government.[12]

Lobbyists are yet another group, this time representing whatever special interest is affected by legislation and government regulation. but their number and their constituency vary from one program to another. Finally, political party members, the media, and occasionally the courts are participants.

Since the administration and Congress are not cohesive units, interest groups frequently find it both more profitable and more immediately effective to cultivate those subunits of Congress and the administration dealing directly with their special interest, rather than to try to influence an entire agency. This is accomplished not just by lobbying in Washington, but by working at the grass-roots among the clientele of the bureaus, exerting pressure through the constituencies of a subcommittee's members, and by working with local press and television.[13]

The key participants in subsystems are several levels below the top of their respective hierarchies. This is especially true in the federal bureaucracy, where power and responsibility in government departments and agencies typically flow from the bottom up, except in cases of major national concern.[14] In the executive branch, the bureau leaders who are near the bottom of the administrative ladder are the most involved in policy-making. A cabinet secretary and his or her immediate deputies seldom play a major role in most policy decisions. Similarly, subcommittees are at the bottom of the congressional hierarchy and control most of the legislation. Congress as a whole seldom makes decisions. Most, perhaps 95 percent, of all subcommittee decisions are upheld by full committees. Full-committee decisions are upheld nearly 90 percent of the time on the floor of the House or the Senate. This means that one has about a 90 percent chance of predicting a decision in Congress once one knows how a subcommittee is likely to vote.[15]

The approximately 100 participants in any one subsystem represent a tiny fraction of the federal bureaucracy. There are usually 25 from Congress (including staff members), 6 to 10 from agencies or bureaus, 6 to 10 from the White House, and 30 to 50 from special interest groups. Frequently they all know each other, often well enough to be familiar with each other's views on the policy in question, making the policy decision even more predictable.[16]

The number and configuration of participants change from time to time and from program to program, as do their roles relative to each other and to the outcome of the debate. Since all participants have concerns and objectives that must be accommodated in the process, a set of checks and balances is maintained to limit the influence of any particular power center. The most successful participants are those who are experts on current issues and who exact the broadest support from the greatest number of other participants by adjusting their goals to include the needs of others. They build alliances through bargaining and compromise. These alliances are continually being formed and re-formed, since no one set of participants can achieve its goals without the help of others. Alliances are formed, for example, between bureau chiefs and legislators, journalists and interest groups, congressmen and lobbyists.

In politics bargaining involves a process of accumulating favors that can be recalled at a later date. The support of a power center in solving one particular problem implies the obligation to return the help in solving another. The decisions that result from alliance building, trading favors, and bargaining often reflect the compromises made by the interested parties. Although compromise is necessary for consensus, it frequently dilutes the effectiveness of the legislation involved.

GOVERNMENT BUREAUS

A bureau is an administrative unit large enough to execute policy (e.g., make rules, prepare budgets, and write legislative proposals) and also still small enough to pay attention to administrative details.[17] Some examples of bureaus are the Office of Toxic Substances within the U.S. Environmental Protection Agency; the Economic Regulatory administration within the Department of Energy; the Bureau for Indian Affairs within the Department of Interior; the Office of Tariff Affairs within the Treasury Department, and the Office of the Special Representative for Trade Negotiations within the Executive Office of the President. The bureau is often the unit that provides both continuity and specialization in a specific area of policy. To a considerable extent, departments and agencies are assemblages of, or holding companies for, bureaus.[18] Because of the fact that a government agency or bureau is the focal point for implementing government programs, some political theorists hold that the bureau leader has the most significant power in a subsystem.

There are approximately 400 bureau leaders in the federal government.[19] Most of them are high-ranking career executives; a minority are political appointees. As career bureaucrats, the great majority remain at their jobs when administrations change and politically appointed department heads move on. They are fairly secure in their jobs because they are judged on their technical performance, rather than political affiliation. Bureau leaders function as staff experts to politically appointed superiors and as general managers to subordinates. They have authority to administer federal programs. They are active policymakers as well. The president and his administration can exert influence on them by using mechanisms such as budgetary controls, clearance requirements for proposed legislation, staffing controls, and departmental organization and supervision.[20]

IRON TRIANGLES

A similar long-standing description[21] of government decision making suggests that the policy-making process consists of a series of informal but enduring "iron triangles," whose three sides are made up of people from executive bureaus, congressional committees, and interest groups. The congressional committees and their chairs who form one side of the triangle operate, for the most part, independently of other members of Congress, congressional leadership, and party pressures. They, along with their staff, develop expertise and familiarity with the issues, individuals, groups, and federal agencies involved in the policy matters they handle. Further, they often develop close relationships that cross party lines. The results are numerous minibureaucracies in Congress that mirror the characteristics of stability, endurance, and cohesion found in their federal counterparts.[22]

Lobbyists and other interest group leaders form another side of the triangle. They are specialists in the areas for which they lobby, and one of their functions is to participate in deliberations between the bureaus and committees handling the policy decisions that affect their clients.

The third side of the iron triangle is formed by bureau leaders whose ability to influence congressional committees is an important part of their power. They have several strategies for achieving their goals; they can anticipate the expectations of congressional committees and other groups, or play one committee off against another (for example, exploit the Senate appropriations committee's tendency to countermand decisions of its counterpart in the House).

While committee hearings provide opportunities for all participants in a system to influence policy-making, bureau leaders and interest group representatives are particularly adept at using hearings to build an impressive case for their side; they can document their viewpoint for the record, and win over neutral or indifferent committee members. Their presentations can also leave a favorable impression that can have a lasting and controlling effect on subsequent committee decisions.[23]

Some bureau leaders are adept at using publicity to achieve their goals, and opportunities to do so abound. Press releases can keep the activities of a bureau and its officials before the public; radio and television can be used for the same purpose. Official publications and reports can also be used to support the bureau's policies and goals.[24]

Another bureau strategy is to seek the endorsement of high-ranking administrators. This is especially effective when the policies under consideration are crucial to the administration and when the bureau's existence is under attack, for example, from a hostile congressional committee. To strengthen contacts with congressional committees, many bureaus maintain liaison units that employ top-level officials and legal and political talent to handle requests from Congress for information and other routine work that might impinge on bureau-committee relations.

Relations among bureau leaders, subcommittee chairmen, and interest group leaders can also affect policy-making within subsystems as studies of congressional records indicate.[25] Bureau leaders maintain friendly relations with interest group leaders in particular because they frequently represent a bureau's clientele and therefore can provide support for, or opposition to, rulemaking and policy changes as they are needed. A bureau leader also uses clientele, interest groups, and other interested parties as consultants or advisers, to share in the study, planning, discussion, promotion, or application of its policies.[26] This is not only a way of sharing policy-making with people who are affected by it, but also of building political support for a bureau and its programs. Today the use of advisory groups and consultants is common throughout the bureaucracy.

ISSUE NETWORKS

Sometimes observers become so preoccupied with trying to find the power centers in configurations such as the iron triangles that they miss the larger open networks of people who are having increasing influence on policy-making today.[27] Subsystems that Hugh Heclo calls "issue networks" are composed of shared-knowledge groups that deal with broader public policy issues (e.g., health care, nuclear power, gun control, consumer protection, and energy) rather than specific programs. They analyze and refine political strategies through which they, too, can shape public policy and determine government decisions. They have varying degree of commitment to or dependence on other participants, but a great deal of commitment to issues. Frequently, their interest in material or financial benefits to themselves is secondary to their ideological commitment to issues. The price of buying into one or another issue network is watching, reading, talking about, and trying to act on particular policy problems.[28]

Issue networks share information about people as well as policies. Reputations are established by word of mouth and, as a result of those recommendations, participants move from one part of a network into another. In that fashion policy experts from academia or business often move into government, and vice versa. This movement, together with the fluidity of issue networks both inside and outside government, often leads to the appointment at a very high level in government of people who first established their reputations as specialists in particular areas of public policy. Both political parties use these outside advisers as federal appointees and in the process create a new political bureaucracy which coexists alongside the permanent one in government.

Issue networks occasionally clash with the more traditional iron triangles, but one is not likely to replace the other. Instead the issue networks are likely to continue to overlay the existing political structure, decreasing its predictability and in the process imposing an additional strain on government leaders. For example, confrontations between issue networks and iron triangles in the area of public health have caused the disintegration of the once mighty Public Health Service and its corps by reducing its funding and assigning its responsibilities to other agencies.

Issue networks were formed over the past 25 years in response to a number of changes in the political system. The tremendous growth in the scope of activity of the federal government, coupled with a virtually nonexpanding bureaucracy was one of them. Although both federal regulations and federal spending increased sixfold between 1950 and 1975, the bureaucracy only grew by one-fifth.[29] Partly because of its relatively small bureaucracy, the federal government relies heavily for the administration of its programs on third-party intermediaries such as state and local governments and both public and private institutions such as schools, hospitals and social service agencies, thus fostering "government by remote control." Increasing numbers of federal regulations are also largely administered through third parties. One result of this remote-control government is that the American people have come to expect that government will solve their problems without being obtrusive.

The strategy of responding to increased public aspirations for government aid administered through third parties has saved the federal government from coping with the vast bureaucracies found in many European countries, but it has also complicated the relationship between administration and politics in Washington. More and more policy concerns have been pushed out of the traditional power centers of the federal government and into the hands of numerous intermediary issue networks. Many specialized groups, including trade and professional associations, have sprung up to join the ranks. Government policy has increased the incentive for formerly cohesive groups to divide up and to re-form around particular issues. The once monolithic system of medical representation, for example, has become increasingly fragmented over differences in attitude toward federal funding and regulation of health care. The extent to which interest groups influence public policy depends upon the demands of their constituents, but they all seem to express the same desire for "compensatory politics," that is, government assistance to compensate for a particular disadvantage vis-á-vis the general population.

While size of the federal bureaucracy generally has increased relatively little, the upper and upper-middle levels of the agencies, where technical and supervisory skills are required, has expanded considerably. This creates pressure on the system for more experts, or policy professionals able to understand and interpret the complex federal environment created by the legislators and bureaucrats. These experts are selected more for their knowledge of the government decision-making process and the substance of the issues than for their professional training and experience. They constitute a professional-bureaucratic subgroup of policymakers in the issue networks.

Issue networks have replaced the bond between Congress and the executive branch that was formerly forged by political parties. The information exchange that once was expected of a disciplined national party system is now provided by specialized issue networks. Information sharing, technical language, and an analyctic repertory for coping with the issues provide a common framework for political debate and decision making in both the legislative and executive branches of government.

ENDNOTES

1. Richard E. Neustadt, *Presidential Power* (New York: John Wiley, 1963), p. 22.
2. "Policy-Making is the formulation, adoption, and application of legal courses of action." From J. Leiper Freeman, *The Political Process; Executive Bureau-Legislative Committee Relations* (New York: Random House, 1965), pp. 15 and 120.
3. Freeman, *The Political Process*, p. 11. See also A. Lee Fritschler and Bernard H. Ross, *Business Regulation and Government Decision-Making* (Cambridge, Mass.: Winthrop, 1980), pp. 73–81.
4. Fritschler and Ross, *Business Regulation and Government Decision-Making*, p. 74.
5. Ibid., p. 74
6. Ibid., p. 75.
7. Freeman, *The Political Process*, p. 96.
8. Ibid., p. 128.
9. Ibid., p. 112.
10. Ibid., p. 68.
11. Ibid., p. 42.
12. Fritschler and Ross, *Business Regulation and Government Decision-Making*, p. 77.
13. Freeman, *The Political Process*, p. 58.
14. Ibid., p. 22
15. Randall, B. Riley, *Congress: Process and Policy*, 2nd ed. (New York: W. W. Norton, 1975), pp. 190.–193. See also Fritschler and Ross, *Business Regulation and Government Decision-Making*, p. 80.
16. Fritschler and Ross, *Business Regulation and Government Decision-Making*, p. 78.
17. Walter G. Held, *Decision-Making in the Federal Government*, (Washington, D.C.: Brookings Institution, 1979), p. 4.
18. Freeman, *The Political Process*, p. 23.
19. Held, *Decision-Making in the Federal Government*, p. 4.
20. Freeman, *The Political Process*, p. 62.

21. Woodrow Wilson was one of the first political theorists to describe the "iron triangle" relationship. See Woodrow Wilson, *Congressional Government* (Boston: Houghton Mifflin Co. 1885). Others include Douglas Cater, *Power in Washington* (New York: Random House, 1964), Freeman, *The Political Process*, and Held, *Decision-Making in the Federal Government*.
22. Freeman, *The Political Process*, p. 28.
23. Ibid., p. 83.
24. Ibid., p. 85.
25. Ibid., p. 78.
26. Ibid., p. 94.
27. Hugh Heclo, "Issue Networks and the Executive Establishment," in *The New American Political System*, Anthony King (ed.) (Washington, D.C.: American Enterprise Institute, 1978), pp. 87–123.
28. Ibid., p. 102.
29. Ibid., pp. 89, 90.

Brazil's Informatics Policy: 1970–1984

In the summer of 1984 Brazil's military government was debating how best to acquire the technology required to produce the new 32-bit "superminicomputer." Since 1975 the government had prohibited any company not 100 percent Brazilian owned from doing business in smaller computers—micros and minis—as well as in a wide range of related products: software, terminals, and semiconductores. But supermini technology appeared to be beyond the reach of Brazilian firms. The military had seized power in 1975 to save Brazil from what it perceived to be a "leftist" takeover. Now, 10 years later the presidency was to pass, in a few months, to a newly elected civilian, Tancredo Neves.

The government's so-called "informatics" policy had been highly controversial. Colonel Edison Dytz, chairman of the Special Secretariat of Informatics (SEI), which would make the decision about superminis, saw reserving market share for the domestic industry as the only way, over the long run, for Brazil to gain the technological capability to compete in the world economy. He and other supporters of the policy were determined to liberate Brazil from what they considered "the colonialism of the multinationals." They argued that the policy had helped to create a thriving industry of 140 local computer companies, growing by about 30 new companies a year. Since 1979 the multinationals' share of Brazil's computer market, worth an overall $1.5 billion, had dropped from 77 percent to 54 percent.

Opponents saw the market reserve policy as inevitably widening the technological gap between Brazil and the rest of the world. Senator Roberto Campos claimed that Brazil was "seriously behind in terms of computer production." He submitted legislation to abolish SEI and open the country's computer markets to anyone. N. Knowlton King, president of the São Paulo chapter of the American Chamber of Commerce, believed that Brazil risked "finding itself among the second-class countries." Robeli Libero, president of IBM do Brasil (established in 1924), said that his company's exports from Brazil in the next four years would be only $1 billion, half of what they might have been without the government's policies. At the same time IBM's investments in Brazil were falling—from $176 million in 1982 to $80 million in 1983. IBM's official policy in Brazil as elsewhere was to avoid shared ownership and joint manufacturing ventures. Burroughs, too, was cutting back, and Ford had been forced to sell its Philco integrated circuit plant in the city of Belo Horizonte.

The Brazilian business community was divided. Some official of ABICOMP, the Brazilian Association of Computer and Peripheral Manufacturers, noted that their members' prices were an average of 2.6 times higher than those charged for similar equipment on world markets. Indeed, a healthy black market in smuggled computer equipment was flourishing. Others defended the policy. Edison Fregni, president of ABICOMP, for example, rejected Campos's notion of a technology gap: "A nation is advanced or behind technologically depending on its ability to respond adequately to the growing needs of its society." Arnon Schreiber, president of

Professor George C. Lodge prepared this case as the basis for class discussion rather than to illustrate either effective or ineffective handling of an administrative situation.

Digirede, the leading manufacturer of bank automation equipment, said that no multinational computer maker had ever developed a product designed specifically to meet Brazilian needs. And Congresswoman Cristina Tavares observed that "Brazilians will have to pay a price to attain international control of computer technology."[1]

SEI's decision about superminis would be made at a time when the Brazilian Congress was debating whether to enact into national law—to be in effect for eight years—the collection of market reserve policies that had evolved since 1975. Foreign multinationals were not the only active participants in this debate; the U.S. government was increasingly hostile to what it perceived to be Brazil's flagrant violation of the principles of free trade.

The following analysis of the history of Brazil's informatics policy is excerpted from a paper by Emanuel Adler, who at the time, was a researcher with the Institute of International Studies at Berkeley.[2]

BRAZIL'S COMPUTER MARKET AND THE GROWTH OF ITS DOMESTIC COMPUTER INDUSTRY

In the early 1970s the Brazilian computer market was already the twelfth largest in the world. While the world market was growing at a rate of about 20 percent a year, the Brazilian data processing market was growing at a rate of 30 percent to 40 percent, second only to Japan. Growth rates were still high in the mid-1970s, between 20 percent and 30 percent. By 1975, when the national computer policy went into effect, Brazil had become the tenth largest data processing market; by 1976 the market was worth about $1.4 billion, or 1% of the Gross Domestic Product (GDP).[3]

By 1982 the value of installed computers in Brazil had reached $2.8 billion.[4] In dollar terms the computer industry grew 64% between 1979 and 1980, 26% between 1980 and 1981, and 51% between 1981 and 1982 (the latter after adjusting for 100% inflation). Growth for 1979–1980 reflects the entrance of new domestic enterprises into the market; the 1981–1982 figure represents a real growth in sales. The market is expected to reach $5 billion by 1985.[5]

The growth in the number of installed computers between 1970 and 1982 is set forth in Table 1, which is broken down into six categories adopted by the Brazilian Special Secretariat of Informatics.[6]

Between 1970 and the appearance of the first Brazilian computers in the marketplace in 1978, the number of computers in the country grew almost fourteenfold. Even discounting microcomputers, the number of computers increased 270 percent between 1973 and 1978, and 673 percent between 1973 and 1982. The number of installed computers grew 71 percent in 1981–1982 alone.

The data indicate a very dramatic change in the market between 1970, when small- and medium-sized computers accounted for 99 percent of all computers, and 1978, when the micro- and minicomputers made up 71 percent of the total. By 1982 this latter figure had jumped to 87 percent. Large computers also grew at a high rate: 346 percent, between 1977 and 1982, with 51 percent between 1980 and 1981 alone[7]. Because by 1982 mini- and microcomputers were doing what small- and medium-sized computers had done in the past, and since the power and speed of large and very large computers were unmatched, the market for medium-sized computers was compressed while the extremes grew significantly.

Before Brazil formulated a computer policy the country's computer requirements were met by MNCs such as IBM, Burroughs, Hewlett-Packard, Honeywell Bull, Data General, Digital, and Olivetti. Brazil's computer imports increased from $13.3 million in 1969 to $99.8 million in 1974 and to $111.9 million in 1975.[8] IBM,

Table 1

Number of Installed Computers in Brazil, 1970–1982 by Size

Class	1970	1971	1972	1973	1974	1975	1976	1977	1978	1979	1980	1981	1982
Micro	a	a	a	586	1,514	2,143	3,131	3,846	4,290	4,791	4,722	8,756	17,702
(%)				(38)	(54)	(56)	(60)	(64)	(62)	(60)	(53)	(61)	(73)
Mini	a	a	a	19	81	173	265	356	656	1,015	1,675	2,719	3,571
(%)				(1)	(3)	(4)	(5)	(6)	(10)	(13)	(19)	(19)	(14)
Small	378	403	454	639	775	1,057	1,309	1,296	1,378	1,494	1,688	1,858	1,950
(%)	(75)	(70)	(68)	(40)	(27)	(27)	(25)	(21)	(20)	(18)	(19)	(13)	(8)
Medium	122	163	184	250	288	327	228	353	370	377	388	408	400
(%)	(24)	(28)	(28)	(16)	(11)	(9)	(7)	(6)	(5)	(5)	(5)	(3)	(2)
Large	2	2	10	45	72	82	99	122	166	226	248	374	544
(%)	(0)	(0)	(1)	(3)	(3)	(2)	(2)	(2)	(2)	(3)	(3)	(3)	(2)
Very Large	4	10	19	33	42	61	72	87	93	97	123	143	172
(%)	(1)	(2)	(3)	(2)	(2)	(2)	(1)	(1)	(1)	(1)	(1)	(1)	(1)
Total excluding microcomputers	506	578	667	986	1,258	1,700	2,083	2,214	2,663	3,209	4,122	5,493	6,637
Total	506	578	667	1,572	2,772	3,843	5,214	6,060	6,953	8,000	8,844	14,249	24,339

Source: SEI, *Boletim Informativo*, Vol. 1 (August–October 1981), p. 9; Vol. 2 (July–September 1982), p. 4; and Vol. 3 (June–September 1983), p. 6.

Burroughs, and Hewlett-Packard manufactured computers in Brazil to meet domestic as well as global requirements. By 1980 IBM do Brasil, the largest computer company in Brazil, held 53.8 percent of the total value of installed computers and was IBM's fastest-growing subsidiary, generating about 50 percent of the company's Latin American business with the medium-sized and large computers, tape drives, terminals, printers, and data-entry equipment produced in its Sumaré plant.[9] Burroughs, the second largest company with approximately 15 percent of the total value of installed computers in 1980, manufactured medium-sized, large, and very large computers.[10]

Once Brazil decided to enter the domestic computer market, the industry developed rapidly. Only two years after that decision, domestic companies were producing hardware and software, peripheral devices, terminals, modems, and special ("intelligent") terminals. The dollar value of installed domestic computers grew from 2 percent of the total value of installed computers in Brazil in 1978, to 19 percent by 1982, by which time 67 percent of installed computers had been produced by domestic companies. Figure 1 shows the growth of domestic installed computers between 1980 and 1982, by number and value.

By 1983 Brazil had about 100 domestic computer companies, which employed 18,000 individuals; gross sales amounted to $687 million or 46 percent of total gross sales.[11] Most had been founded after 1976 under the guidance of the national computer policy. In 1982 they accounted for 67 percent, 91 percent, 13 percent, and 1 percent of the value of installed micro-, mini-, small-, and medium-sized computers, respectively.[12] The largest company, Cobra SA (a state-owned company) ranked third in sales, with about 36.2 percent of the total value of installed minicomputers by June 1982. At that time the other large national companies important in this segment of the market were Labo, with 18.4 percent; SID, 7.6 percent; Edisa, 23.3 percent; and Sisco, 5.0 percent. Cobra, Dismac, Edisa, and Prológica held approximately 72 percent of the value of installed microcomputers.[13]

Domestic computer companies invest a relatively high share of their sales in research and development. In 1980 domestic firms producing computers with indigenous technology spent an average of 14.4 percent of their sales on R&D, while national firms working under foreign licenses spent an average of 7.9 percent. The

Figure 1   Number and Value of Installed Domestic (Shaded Sections) and Foreign Computers, 1980–1982 (in thousands)

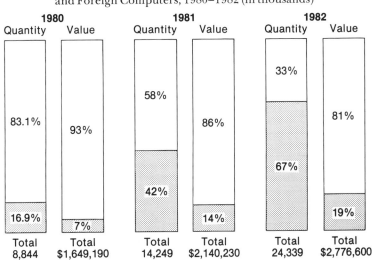

1980		1981		1982	
Quantity	Value	Quantity	Value	Quantity	Value
83.1%	93%	58% / 42%	86% / 14%	33% / 67%	81% / 19%
16.9%	7%				
Total 8,844	Total $1,649,190	Total 14,249	Total $2,140,230	Total 24,339	Total $2,776,600

Source: SEI, Boletim Informativo, Vol. 3 (June–September 1983), p. 10.

total Brazilian domestic computer industry's R&D average was 8.7 percent, which is more than 6.1 percent spent by the American computer industry during the same year.[14]

The reduction of domestic industry imports—they fell from $81 million in 1981 (26.6 percent of the total computer import) to $49 million in 1983 (21.4 percent of the total computer import)[15]—is one indicator of the success achieved by the pragmatic antidependency policy and its emphasis on R&D. Shares in sales of products based on local technology (technology not obtained under licensing agreements or for which such agreements have recently expired and only minor improvements made since) have risen dramatically between 1979 and 1981, while those of imports have declined during the same period (see Table 2). Domestic systems rose from 28 percent in 1979 to 60 percent in 1981, and imports fell from 29 percent to 7 percent. Although all terminals are now manufactured entirely domestically, peripheral devices still depend on foreign technology. Totaling the five categories shown in Table 2, we find domestic technology increased from 31 percent in 1979 to 53 percent in 1981, while imports decreased by a factor of almost four. During the same period the MNC import content of total sales rose from 28 percent to 40 percent.[16]

Finally, it should be pointed out that some domestic computer companies have now reached a level of technological sophistication and economic efficiency which allows them to produce for export. Cobra, Microdigital, Prológica, and Elebra have been the domestic export leaders (Elebra has even exported components to the United States).

ECONOMIC GROWTH, TECHNOLOGY, AND THE INTERNATIONAL COMPUTER INDUSTRY

From 1968 to 1973— the period of Brazil's economic miracle—Brazil's GDP grew at an average yearly rate of 10.1 percent. Industrial production grew even faster, so that by 1975 the Brazilian manufactured value added was about 25 percent of the Brazilian GDP, representing almost 20 percent of the value added of all the developing countries combined. Even more remarkable was Brazil's real growth in capital goods manufacturing output, which average 20.8 percent a year between 1968 and 1973.[17] This growth rate produced the capital necessary for Brazil's industrial and technological development and kindled expectations that Brazil had at last found the road to self-sustained growth.

Buttressing the economic progress was the relative stability and continuity of Brazil's political regime, which began with the coup in 1964 that overthrew João

Table 2   Dollar Share of Sales for Equipment Manufactured With Local Technology and of Imports, 1969–1981

	1979		1980		1981	
	Technology	Imports	Technology	Imports	Technology	Imports
Systems	28%	29%	41%	18%	60%	7%
Peripheral devices	—	111	4	48	6	36
Terminals	100	8	100	8	100	3
Modems	10	21	37	22	50	13
Special terminals	100	6	100	22	100	14
Total	31	29	39	20	53	8

Source: UNCTC. *Transborder Data Flows and Brazil* (New York: United Nations, 1983), pp. 223–25.

Notes: Figures for sales include exports. Imports for a given year appear as percentages of sales during that year. Since corporations may improt to increase inventories, percentages may be higher than 100.

Goulart and continued until the 1984 elections. Economic leadership during this period was also remarkably stable: minister of planning, João Paulo dos Reis Velloso, a key figure in the development of Brazil's computer industry, held this position (later changed to secretary of planning) from 1969 to 1979.

Emboldened by its economic growth, Brazil became involved in large infrastructure and industrial projects: during this period Brazil built Itaipú, the biggest hydroelectric plant in the world, implemented a policy to run cars with alcohol, and established a huge nuclear energy program.[18] The evolution of computer technology and of the international computer industry came at an opportune time for Brazil. Searching for new ways to develop domestic technology, Brazil took advantage of the rise of mini- and microcomputers and of the progress in semiconductor technology.

Semiconductor technology received a boost when the transistor invented by Bell Laboratories in 1947 was integrated, along with other necessary components, into a single silicon base, or "chip." This integration reduced manufacturing costs, increased efficiency, and enlarged information storage capacities.[19] The price per bit of storage fell from about 1.000 cent per bit in 1970 to 0.050 cent per bit in 1979,[20] and it is expected to fall to 0.001 cent per bit by 1989.[21]

The revolution in semiconductor technology was responsible for the development of minicomputers, which appeared for the first time in 1965 when Digital Equipment Corporation introduced its PDP-8 model. The minicomputer industry has since become fiercely competitive. At the beginning of the 1970s, approximately forty new companies were created to manufacture minicomputers.[22] Since then minicomputers "have experienced price declines of at least five while at the same time their main memory capacities have increased by factors of two to four times, and processing speeds have increased by perhaps a factor of 1,000....[By] the middle of the 1970s technological innovations were leading minisystems to be so powerful as to challenge the lower range of the mainframe computer market." By 1980, before the appearance of 32-bit superminicomputers or "superminis," the minicomputer market was estimated at $15 billion—roughly one-fourth of the world computer market.[23]

Probably the most important technological jump in semiconductor technology to date occurred in 1971, when Intel introduced a chip known as the microprocessor, which can be programmed to carry out information processing and control functions[24]—in essence, a computer-on-a-chip. After several generations, processing power of the chip has increased tremendously, while cost per function has decreased.[25] The microprocessors were built into microcomputers almost as powerful as minicomputers, at a fraction of their cost, and are increasingly finding their way into homes as "personal computers."

When Brazilian technocrats first discussed developing a domestic computer industry in 1971, these advances in computer technology did not escape them. However, their ideas of the state-of-the-art at that time were based on computer technology of the late 1960s; they were not aware of the advantages they would later receive from advances in the technology of microprocessors and microcomputers. By 1977, when the crucial political decisions were made, those responsible for domestic computer policy were fully aware of the importance of these developments. Timing was not irrelevant. That MNCs, in particular IBM, had not yet begun manufacturing mini- and microcomputers in Brazil when the national endeavor was first considered constituted an opportunity. For had the MNCs already established a niche in Brazil with these systems, the cost and difficulty of pushing them out of the market might have proved too high.

The new technological developments generated a very dynamic world semiconductor market characterized by the entry of companies from several nations and capable of supplying millions of computers-on-a-chip every year. The worldwide worth of semiconductors increased from about $400 million in 1959 to $5.4 billion in 1974, and to approximately $20 billion in 1983. The growth of this market spawned many additional firms in the United States as well as in Japan and Europe, which began to compete for the production market for integrated circuits. For example, Japan sold 70 percent of all the 64K chips in 1982 and is now aggressively involved in the production and sale of 256K chips;[26] and today (1986) six out of the ten largest manufacturers of chips are Japanese. By 1982, Japan, Western Europe, and the United States controlled 30 percent, 17 percent, and 50 percent, respectively, of the production of integrated circuits.[27]

These technological and market changes have partially transformed the highly concentrated and oligopolized international computer industry. In the 1970s this industry grew at a rate of between 10 percent and 15 percent annually; correspondingly the number of computers in use worldwide has doubled every few years.[28] One giant, IBM, controlled 60 percent of the computer market (valued at $11.7 billion). By the end of the decade this lead had narrowed to a still impressive 40 percent of the $53.5 billion market.[29] IBM's gross sales were worth $46 billion in 1984.[30]

Today U.S. companies hold 80 percent of the computer market. Seven of the industry's top ten companies are American: IBM, Burroughs, Texas Instruments, Motorola, Digital, NCR, and Control Data. But Japan, which has been making large inroads, holds close to 10 percent, or about $9 billion, of that market. In 1983 Japan's computer equipment exports amounted to $3.9 billion, with Nippon, Fujitsu, and Hitachi listing among the ten largest computer companies worldwide.[31] Smaller Japanese companies are supplying computer hardware to U.S. firms and, together with Taiwanese and Korean companies, selling components and personal computers on world markets. In all, 500 computer hardware manufacturers, 5,000 software companies, and about 430 producers of communication equipment currently sell $268 billion worth of products. With the present compound annual growth of 20 percent, data processing revenues are expected to reach $1 trillion by 1990.[32]

DEVELOPMENT OF A BRAZILIAN COMPUTER INDUSTRY

Encouraged by the changes that were taking place in the international computer industry, and anxious to promote industrialization and domestic technological development, as early as 1971 Brazil's technocrats decided to invest the capital made available by the economic miracle in a domestic computer industry. The availability of inexpensive chips, along with the possibility of obtaining technology under license helped Brazil shift its technological dependence from the older computer hardware market dominated by market giants to the dynamic semiconductor market dominated by foreign components, and software know-how available from small new companies. The domestic computer industry development was thus an ideological, institutional, and political outgrowth of the general science and technology policy that Brazil implemented at the end of the 1960s.

A group of economists working for the National Bank for Economic and Social Development (BNDES), headed by José Pelúcio, identified the source of Brazil's underdevelopment as technological dependency. Their diagnosis assumed that economic development was linked not only to growth rates but also to an increased capacitiy for understanding and perceiving the impact of forces of modernization. This diagnosis found partial support from the military; the diagnosis received strong support from planning institutions, which were staffed largely by economists trained by the Economic Commission for Latin America, and from the scientific and technological community, many of whom had been involved in setting up the National Research Council (CNPq) and the nuclear independence policy at the beginning of the 1950s. Adherents of the dependency diagnosis believed Brazil would achieve autonomy not by rejecting foreign technology but by attaining the ability to make technological decisions.

The dependency diagnosis may be considered pragmatic because it did not accent the structuralist view that the world capitalist system necessarily leads to stagnation and to eternal dependence. Instead, it attempted to identify Brazil's weaknesses in order to effect reforms. To achieve the objective of technological autonomy, Brazil developed an indigenous technological capacity guided by a national strategy of selective interdependence, possibilities of importing technology, local comparative advantage, and possibilities of exporting the resultant technology.[33]

The strong relationship that developed between Pelúcio, the guiding force behind the science and technology policy during the 1970s, and Velloso, was crucial to the implementation of such a policy. Velloso was a powerful advocate for technological antidependency ideas and their realization. A strong supporter of a market economy and interdependence, he nonetheless believed that the key to an economically sound future lay in developing a domestic technological potential including strategic sectors such as computers.

The government established the Studies and Projects Financing Agency (FINEP) in order to support national technological development and to link the domestic technological infrastructure to national industry; Pelúcio headed FINEP for most of the 1970s. The National Science and Technology Development Fund, which operated under the jurisdiction of FINEP, became the main financial instrument for scientific and technological development. The National Research Council, currently the National Council of Science and Technology, became the central organism for planning, coordinating, and implementing scientific and technological policy. The Industrial Technology Secretariat was charged with promoting and developing domestic technology. Further, technological funds were made available within the framework of research institutes and banks; technology foundations and companies were attached to research institutes to work in priority areas; the university system was reformed and a graduate studies plan issued; and fellowships and grants for scientific and technological training increased significantly.

The share of the national budget earmarked for science and technology, which had been .84 percent in 1970, rose to 3.64 percent in 1982, R&D expenditures as a percentage of Gross National Product almost tripled between 1971 and 1979, from .24 percent to .65 percent, and the percentage of scientists and engineers engaged in R&D increased from .8 to 2.1 for every 10,000 people between 1974 and 1978.[34] Brazil also issued the strong Industrial Property Code and related acts aimed at opening "technological packages" so that indigenous technologies would be used when possible.

Pelúcio, the BNDES, and other autonomy-oriented science and technology institutions and planners also provided the means to train computer science professionals. The improvements in the scientific and technological infrastructure in the sector produced a critical mass of experts sufficient for "the government to adopt an aggressive policy of technological independence in the sector."[35]

FINEP supported development of hardware, software, and process-control uses in addition to financing several university projects and establishing computers in Brazilian universities. The CPNq provided fellowship and research support to institutions, assisted in a microelectronics project, and organized a task force to coordinate the policy of future data processing technology.

By the mid-1970s, when the computer policy began to take shape, those graduates sent abroad to study were beginning to return, strengthening their institutions and universities. Although prior to 1972 professional training depended heavily on MNCs and their "free courses," by 1977 forty undergraduate and graduate university courses were being offered.[36] Universities in São Paulo, Minas Gerais, and Rio Grande do Sul offered graduate programs in computer science. By 1982 Brazil had 19 universities, 450 research scientists organized into 74 groups, and 12 government research centers working on computer technology. Total human resources available in the data processing equipment industry were 14,646 in 1981, 31.5% of whom were university graduates.[37] (See Table 3.)

Table 3   Employment of University-Trained Personnel by Activity in Foreign Subsidiaries and Brazilian-Owned Firms in 1979 and 1982 by Percentage

Activities	Subsidiaries		Brazilian Owned	
	1979	1982	1979	1982
Marketing	44%	40%	27%	31%
Suport services	8	7	5	11
R&D	3	4	31	27
Production	11	15	14	14
Others	34	34	23	17
Total	100%	100%	100%	100%
(Quantity)	(2,521)	(2,697)	(1,531)	(4,027)

Source: SEI, elaboration by Instituto de Economí Industrial. (From Fabio Stefano Erber, "The Development of the 'Electronics Complex' and Government Policies in Brazil," *World Development*, Vol. 13, no. 3, p. 302.)

Cobra: The Early Days

Early in 1971, when the Brazilian navy decided to equip its vessels with English Ferranti computers, it also initiated a project to plan, develop, and manufacture a domestic computer prototype suitable for naval operations, preferably one that could interface with Ferranti.[38] The navy's Communications and Electronic Directorate contacted Pelúcio at the BNDES Science and Technology Fund. The Guaranys Project grew out of this relationship (naval officer José Luis Guaranys became more involved in this project than anyone else) as did a special working group (GTE/FUNTEC 111) established to formulate goals for the project. The Guaranys Project had two primary objectives: establish a three-sided (tripé) partnership of Brazilian state and private enterprises with MNCs[39]—with the foreign partner agreeing to transfer its technology to the company; and promote and finance the development of a domestic minicomputer prototype.

The selection in April 1973 of the private Brazilian company, E.E. Electrônica, and the creation of a holding company called Brazilian Digital Electronics initiated the first course of action. One year later Brazilian Digital Electronics became Digibrás, in effect an industrial promotion agency set up to study the market, provide consulting services and support for national firms, identify R&D needs, and organize the necessary supporting companies.

Digibrás was originally supposed to create two computer companies, one in association with Ferranti mainly to meet military requirements, and the other in association with either Japanese Fujitsu or West German Nixdorf to produce computers for the civilian markets. The first company, founded in 1974, was Cobra, a joint venture between the state, E.E. Electronica, and Ferranti (which held only about 3 percent of the capital shares and acceded to Cobra's demand to transfer its technology). The venture resulted in the first Brazilian-assembled minicomputers, the 700 Series.

When the attempt to create a second company failed, Cobra began a search for the foreign technology that would allow Brazil to produce a minicomputer for commerce and industry by itself. Although Data General seemed the most likely candidate to transfer minicomputer technology to Cobra, the American company was not willing to accept Brazil's conditions that patents, blueprints, and general know-how be transferred to Cobra at the end of the licensing period. A small American company, Sycor, Inc., did, however, accede to Cobra's terms, and in 1976 Cobra and Sycor signed agreements to effect technology transfer, provide technical assistance and training, ad purchase certain products. Sycor was exempted from import controls and thus gained almost exclusive access to a fastgrowing market, while Cobra obtained the necessary technology to develop what became its 400 Series.[40]

Cobra relied on foreign technology while the development of the domestically designed minicomputer and peripheral devices were still in the making but remained committed to absorbing this technology. The use of foreign technology was relatively successful because "it substantially reduced the time required to begin local production of minicomputers and helped to avoid mistakes both in product and process designs that would probably have occurred had Cobra relied initially on local technological sources only."[41] The 400 Series became Cobra's main product until its domestically designed minicomputer, the G-10 came of age.

The hardware for Brazil's first domestic computer was developed at the University of São Paulo, while the software was worked on at the Pontifical Catholic University of Rio de Janeiro. First planned as a solely scientific computer, the G-10 was then transferred to Cobra, which broadened its scope. Cobra received another boost when the Federal Data Processing Service, the largest Brazilian data processing enterprise, and the University of Rio de Janeiro transferred terminals they had developed to Cobra. With these additions the G-10 minicomputer became Cobra's 500, a computer designed in Brazil and using almost entirely locally developed components.

Cobra's financial situation in 1976 did not match its relative success in R&D and technology transfer. Lacking purchase requests from the private market, Cobra initially sold only to government institutions and the armed forces. Assistance for the failing enterprise came from two quarters. IBM's help was inadvertent: its plan to introduce its minicomputer System 32, which would have killed Brazil's domestic minicomputer industry even before it was born, mobilized Cobra's allies. More positive help came from a consortium of eleven banks, including such giants as Bradesco and Itaú. Foreseeing the need for electronic automation in banking, these banks decided to purchase 39 percent of Cobra's shares.[42]

The government's determination to keep Cobra alive was based on the belief that only a state-owned company could lead the effort to absorb foreign technology, develop local technology, and satisfy Brazil's growing need for domestic computers. Cobra had thus become a means to achieve a national goal that was more significant than market efficiency and even import substitution. By setting up Cobra, Brazil was following in the footsteps of India, which had established a "national champion," the Electronics Corporation of India Limited,[43] in order to develop its domestic computer industry. But equally influential to Brazil's ultimate success in reducing dependency in the computer field was CAPRE.

CAPRE AND THE GUERILLAS' AUTONOMY MODEL

The government created the Commission for the Coordination of Electronic Processing Activities (CAPRE) on April 5, 1972 to manage development of a domestic computer. CAPRE undertook to gather available information about the computer market and the human resources, as well as to provide incentives for scientific and technological development in this sector. CAPRE also endeavored to prevent unnecessary imports and to prevent government agencies from using data processing equipment inefficiently. CAPRE's subordination to the Planning Ministry, under Velloso, was crucial for its ultimate success. The ministry's transformation into a secretariat with direct links to the president and assumption of responsibility for Brazil's scientific and technological network became a source of political power for CAPRE and a shelter for the guerillas involved.

The pragmatic antidependency ideology unified the Planning Secretariat, the scientific technological institutions, the universities and their scientists, and

CAPRE. While Pelúcio set up the groundwork and Velloso provided cautious support, Ricardo Saur, CAPRE's executive secretary, engaged in direct action to turn this ideology into industrial reality.

CAPRE became more than the institution entrusted by presidential decree to develop a specific technology: it became the home for an ideologically assertive group—a "guerilla headquarters" of sorts—that set itself up to sell ideas, raise consciousness, and use political power to achieve its goals. While CAPRE took its first formal actions—creating national programs for data processing centers and computer training, identifying the strengths and liabilities of the scientific and technological infrastructure[44]—the pragmatic antidependency guerrillas began their intellectual and political "attacks." Although most of the guerrillas came from CAPRE, some worked in institutions such as the Federal Data Processing Service and Cobra. The core, known among each other as the Group, included Saur, Ivan de Costa Marques, Mário Ripper, Arthur Pereira Nuñes, and Claudio Zamitti Mammana. They began by formulating in their own minds a doctrine that became known as the National Model.

The model had two key features: only national companies would participate in Brazil's computer industry; and each piece of foreign technology could be purchased only once. The group infused the scientific and technological community and the political system with optimism, insisting that "the thing could be done." As teachers at universities and as technocrats at government agencies, they emphasized Brazil's few but significant technological successes in order to generate a positive feedback effect. Computers, industry, politics, and academia became interwoven upon the creation of the Seminars of Computation at the University, which became another forum for airing the guerrillas' ideas: market protection, national enterprises, and technological autonomy.[45] *Dados e Idéias*, a monthly data processing magazine issued by the Federal Data Processing Service, also provided pressure for instituting economic controls on the computer market. Besides publishing technical material, *Dados a Idéias* became a forum for commentary and criticism on the government's computer policy and on the dangers of technological dependency.

It is interesting to note that a similar phenomenon seems to have occurred in India. Grieco hinted at the existence of guerrillas and guerrilla "attacks" when he discussed the political actions of the Atomic Energy Commission (referred to as a "network").

This gave the atomic energy policy "network" a strong incentive to break its stalemate with Defence and, building upon national dissatisfaction over the country's progress in electronics, this network waged a campaign in 1969 and 1970 that led to a victory over Defence for control of national electronics policy. New policy units were created—the Electronics Commission and the Department of Electronics—which were supposed to be neutral but which were, in fact, heavily staffed by key members of the atomic energy network.[46]

As it is widely known, India's Atomic Energy Commission has been one of the country's ideological leaders in the push for technological independence.

In December 1975 CAPRE acquired new power through Resolution 104, which held that all imports of computer parts, accessories, and components require CAPRE's prior authorization. CAPRE raised import duties, required deposits without interest for the value of imports, and set import quotas. In addition it established an import limit: $110 million in 1976, $100 million in 1977, and $130 million in 1978.[47] Its formal power grew when it was charged with imposing further import control measures and with studying the state-of-the-art and proposing a national informatics policy. CAPRE thereby became the "guardian of the gate," freeing the guerrillas to act as they chose.

Brazil's deteriorating balance-of-payments situation after 1974 played into the need for import control which gave CAPRE increasing authority over the computer market. But CAPRE'S concerns were "... much broader than the simple objective of controlling imports so as to rectify the country's balance-of-payments problems. The government was convinced that informatics was strategically important to the nation and that, therefore, Brazil needed a policy which would enable it to acquire the technical capability necessary to reduce its dependence."[48] From the guerrillas' perspective, the balance-of-payments crisis was a blessing.

CAPRE's power stemmed from its ability to set guidelines and policies without much high-level interference. Despite CAPRE's position, however, Velloso and other high-level policymakers did not envision a totally domestic computer industry. The government still wanted to exploit the MNCs' technology, although "the multinationals here," according to Saur, "including the biggest, IBM, declared their lack of interest in this effort."[49]

CAPRE made two decisions in July 1976 which created the basis for reserving the mini- and microcomputer markets for Brazilian enterprises and reflected the government's pragmatic approach vis-à-vis the MNCs. Decision #1 divided the market and the industry into two sections. While it recommended that "the national informatics policy for medium and large computer markets be based on investment rationalization and optimization of installed resources" (i.e., on the market, namely, foreign industry), it also recommended that when feasible mini- and microcomputers and peripheral devices be reserved for the domestic industry.[50] Decision #2 gave CAPRE the power to control the purchase of software and data processing services by government agencies and enterprises.

Decision #1 continued the policy initiated in the early 1970s but also represented a response to IBM's announcement, made in a blitz advertising campaign that attracted almost 400 potential buyers,[51] that its minicomputer System 32 would be assembled in Brazil from parts brought in under its import quotas.

These two policy decisions reflected CAPRE's efforts to protect a weak national industry without giving the MNCs the impression that Brazil was enforcing a protectionist policy. Because high-level government officials continued to hope that IBM and other MNCs would enter into joint ventures with domestic companies, they would not agree to reserving the entire mini- and microcomputer market for domestic companies.

CAPRE's strategy was determined by its council; however, the decision to have two "containment lines"—allowing only Brazilian companies to produce domestic computers and accepting joint ventures with the MNCs was strictly a guerrilla strategy.

The Economic Development Council's Decision of January 12, 1977 aided the CAPRE guerrillas by establishing the following criteria for fiscal incentives in the data processing industry: extent of nationalization; export potential; extent of technology transfer; analysis of enterprises already in the market; and domestic capital majority. CAPRE used these criteria to select "winners" from among the domestic and foreign companies invited under Decision 01 of June 1977 to present proposals for the production of minicomputers in Brazil.[52] Among the sixteen companies that submitted proposals were seven MNCs, but only joint ventures.

As the time for a decision approached, Velloso was under heavy fire from two camps. Ministers and high-level government officials outside the Planning Secretariat and the science and technology institutional network, and industrial elites, mainly from São Paulo, pointing out Cobra's ailing condition, remained unconvinced that Brazil could successfully challenge IBM. Further, IBM and other MNCs were pressuring the highest echelons of Brazil's political power structure to prevent a decision that would leave them outside the market. The media put CAPRE's case on the front pages, playing up the tough MNC line regarding joint ventures and IBM's attempt to use System 32 to undermine Cobra. The subject of MNCs, which had traditionally aroused nationalist feelings, generated outrage once the facts became public knowledge. The government found it increasingly difficult to do anything that indicated it was bending under pressure from the MNCs. That the powerful banking consortia which had invested money in Cobra were pressing for the domestic alternative and that key military actors at the armed forces high command favored domestic companies and market closure also worked in CAPRE's favor.

The critical decision was made in mid-April 1977, at an informal meeting of the CAPRE council and the ministers directly and indirectly involved in the data processing sector. Although the ministers tended to prefer joint ventures because they feared that the movement toward a national computer industry was based on enthusiasm alone, they nevertheless decided that any interested company could present a bid and that final decisions would be based on the conditions specified by the Economic Development Council.

The ministers told CAPRE informally that nationals should be preferred only if their bids were as good as those of MNCs; if not, CAPRE should accept IBM's proposal. However, because according to one of the Economic Development Council's criteria for investment in computers, MNCs had to be willing to engage in joint ventures, it would have been almost impossible for CAPRE to choose IBM. Thus, the CAPRE council decision of June 1977 calling for bids from domestic and foreign firms to produce minicomputers was in fact a cover-up; a decision had already been reached.

CAPRE's blow to the MNCs came at the end of 1977. It chose four companies, rather than the anticipated three: Cobra and three private domestic consortia that had just been or were still in the process of being created and that were developing minicomputers under foreign licenses: SID, Labo, and Edias. CAPRE later approved a fifth company, Sisco, which developed minicomputers with its own technology.[53] Under the terms agreed to by the companies involved, technology transfer had to be completed by 1982, and payment for this technology was not to exceed 3 percent of net sales. Local firms could purchase foreign technology only once and had to develop further models locally.

This choice represented a strategic victory for CAPRE and Saur, as it allowed the market reserve policy to be implemented. In addition, it permitted government policy makers to say: "We play according to the rules, we asked for bids from everyone, and we let the best bid win."

Velloso played his cards very diplomatically, assuring the MNCs that the joint venture condition was not mandatory and that CAPRE would judge the proposals by additional criteria. The MNCs, taking Velloso's words as a genuine indication that the door was open to them, felt that although Brazil would prefer to have local equity—even control—it was prepared to waive this condition if other factors proved more compelling.[54] However, while Velloso was telling the MNCs that everything was fine, CAPRE was telling IBM's vice president the opposite. Although some domestic companies among the bidders had yet to begin operation, CAPRE decided to favor them anyway as a result of its strong determination to exclude MNCs from the minicomputer market and the green light signaled by the ministers' decision.

After winning the minicomputer battle, CAPRE began to eye the medium-sized computer market. Fearing that the MNCs might scale down medium-sized computers and use them to compete with Brazilian minicomputers, and/or that the domestic industry once in operation might not be able to compete in the market, CAPRE in December 1978 issued new criteria for the manufacture of central processing units and peripheral devices beyond the minicomputer range. These criteria included assurances that such projects would not interfere with mini- and microcomputers, and that there would be local decision making, the possibility of technology transfer, a growing nationalization index, and export potential.[55] CAPRE thereby prohibited IBM and Burroughs from manufacturing medium-sized computers in Brazil.

SEI: THE EVOLUTION OF THE MODEL AND ITS STRUGGLE TO SURVIVE

CAPRE's responsibilities increased as new domestic computer companies appeared on the scene. The military, which, except for the navy, had not shown any particular interest in the process, was impressed by the successful challenge to IBM. By the end of 1978, they realized that the data processing sector was too strategically important to leave in the hands of a Planning Secretariat that, after the 1979 elections, might be led by "internationalists" (as actually happened when first Mário Henrique Simonsen and then Antônio Delfim Netto became planning secretary) who might retreat from the antidependency policy and again fall prey to the MNCs.

Heading the military's interests was the National Intelligence Service (SNI), from whose ranks came João Batista Figueiredo, elected president of Brazil in March 1979. In January 1979 the SNI initiated an inquiry commission, headed by Ambassador Paulo Cotrim, whose findings criticized CAPRE. According to the commission, CAPRE lacked a policy aimed at reducing dependency on foreign sources of software and microelectronics. With the Figueiredo government posed to take office, and the SNI's mistrust of CAPRE's "leftist" technocrats, CAPRE began to lose its power base, and the architects of the autonomy policy were edged out.

When the Cotrim commission was turned into a presidential committee, it decided to abolish CAPRE and to place data processing policy under the jurisdiction of the National Security Council (CSN). Following the commission's guidelines, the committee recommended increasing incentives for domestic techno-logical development and establishing a policy to nationalize development of semiconductors. The Special Secretariat of Informatics (SEI) replaced CAPRE in December 1979, and the cooperation between government technocrats and the scientific community which had characterized the mid-1970s eroded. SEI was attached to the CSN and reported directly to the president.

SEI's main tasks were to advise the CSN on informatics and to formulate a national informatics plan and policy. It was also charged with stimulating and assisting the development of technology, components, equipment, programs, and services, and with protecting the technical and commercial viability of domestic companies producing systems and components.[56] In addition, SEI was to try to coordinate real time control systems, microelectronics, and national software policy.

SEI marked a new stage in the politics associated with Brazil's domestic computer industry and policy. Economic elites and consumer associations opposed the protectionist policy on efficiency grounds and, encouraged by the prevailing atmosphere of *abertura*, or political openness, also objected to CSN's control over policy matters. Furthermore, some members of the new cabinet strongly opposed CAPRE's model and explicitly desired to enter into joint ventures with MNCs.

Also opposed to the changes were the guerrillas, the scientific and technical communities, and a majority of the computer associations created after CAPRE began to implement its policy—essentially the model's watchdogs. Institutions such as the Brazilian Association of Computer and Peripherals Equipment Industries, the Association of Data Processing Professionals, the Association of Data Processing Service Enterprises, and the Brazilian Computation Society feared that SEI would, in time, ally themselves to the MNCs, approve joint ventures, and eventually erode the model.

Thus, SEI had to begin by rowing against not one but two streams. It had succeeded, and even prospered, by operating under the CSN's shield. But it had also strengthened its position by promising opponents of the model that the market reserve would soon be watered down or even eliminated and promising watchdogs of the model that the reserve would be not only maintained but strengthened.

SEI's first actions evidenced determination to keep the market reserve, to control the data processing sector, and to deal with the MNCs firmly yet pragmatically. Its first Normative Act (March 1980) set guidelines for data processing imports, stipulating that preference be given to "the national alternative" and that software be developed domestically. Later that year, SEI ordered that all data processing equipment be registered, that both domestic and foreign federal government purchases receive prior permission, and that the government favor domestic data processing services.[57] It also stated that approval for new projects aimed at manufacturing data processing equipment and parts, and the import of components would depend on the extent to which they used locally developed technology and were directed by Brazilians.

The first major test for the new policy came in August 1980, when SEI gave IBM permission to manufacture limited quantities of its medium-sized Model 4331 computers in Brazil. At that time the market for medium-sized computers was growing by 10% a year, and SEI preferred locally made equipment over imports.[58] Domestic producers, scientists, and guerrillas feared that this decision would prevent the domestic development of medium-sized and large computers, and would suffocate local industry. A permanent commission was therefore set up to oversee and protect the national computer industry's actions. The commission also decided to regard SEI's permission to IBM as inconclusive.[59]

SEI was slightly restructured in 1981: the Advisory Council consisting of private- and public-sector representatives was created. SEI's scope was broadened, and incentives were established for Brazilian firms only. The Advisory Council represented a major gain for supporters of the market reserve because it provided them with an additional forum in which to advance their ideology. For example, when SEI's secretary general Octavio Gennari Netto announced that the market reserve for computers would be maintained for only another three years,[60] supporters of the model protested so strongly that the idea was never mentioned again; the SEI eventually passed Normative Act 016 of July 1981, which made permission to manufacture reserved products increasingly difficult to obtain. SEI grew even stronger in 1982 when it took over some of the Digibrás' functions. (This take over led subsequently to Digibrás' demise in 1983.)

More recently (1984) SEI has announced that it must approve all R&D performed in the informatics sector and that the federal government can contract informatics services from foreign firms only when no national company is qualified to render that service. SEI has also broadened the market reserve to include digital machinery used in measurements and in biomedical work, and has created a section to register all domestic and foreign software programs marketed in Brazil. Although the registry is not obligatory, SEI will not approve any unregistered imports or manufacturing projects.

Aiming to correct a major bottleneck that had prevented Brazil from producing genuine domestic systems and to promote development of domestic 16-bit software, Normative Act 027 of November 1983 states that SEI will approve only those microcomputer manufacturing projects whose software is developed locally. In 1984 the Special Software Commission was set up to establish the juridical basis for a Software Law.

SEI leaders have also confronted the problem of developing their own chips; currently Brazil purchases these from abroad or from foreign companies located in Brazil. In the 1970s the Ministries of Industry and Commerce and of Communications tried to get a foothold in the semiconductor industry; FINEP and the CNPq helped by training appropriate personnel and promoting relevant R&D. But these efforts did not bear fruit, and a semiconductor company set up by the state was shut down in 1980 because of financial difficulties.

When SEI began dictating Brazilian microelectronics policy in 1981, it established a component import control policy and began to coordinate the R&D activities of various institutions. In order to carry out these activities, SEI created a microelectronics research institute. The Informatics Technological Center (CTI) opened in May 1984 in Campinas, near São Paulo, and two private domestic firms,

Itaú and Doças de Santos, were chosen to locate near CTI and open plants to manufacture microelectronic products.

The development abroad of the superminicomputer reopened the technological gap between the Brazilian data processing industry and foreign competitors. This new development, which has fueled consumer and political opposition to domestic computer policy, has sent both SEI and domestic manufacturers back to the drawing board. In an effort to close the gap, SEI decided to encourage the development of the superminicomputer in Brazil. Its call was answered by eight domestic companies: three committed themselves to develop the superminicomputer with local technology, another five requested permission to manufacture them with imported technology. These companies have committed themselves to effect technology transfer and a high nationalization index.

SEI had to choose among several alternatives: local production of superminicomputers with foreign technology; local production with local technology; joint ventures with MNCs. Some prominent senators, members of Congress, and industrialists, including Minister of Industry and Commerce João Camilo Penna,[61] called for joint ventures. SEI policy makers were in favor of acquiring foreign technology but rejected joint ventures. But supporters of the model held out for total local control over the industry.

Exhibit 1   Some of the Key Players

José Pelúcio, head of the National Bank for
Economic and Social Development (BNDES).

Col. Edison Dytz, chairman of the
Special Secretariat of Informatics (SEI).

João Paulo dos Reis Velloso, Minister
of Planning, 1969–1979.

Sen. Roberto Campos, opposed to informatics policy,
a friend of MNCs and the United States.

Ricardo Saur, executive secretary of
the Commission of the Coordination of
Electronic Processing Activities (CAPRE)

ENDNOTES

1. *International Management*, September 1984, pp. 83 and 84.
2. "Ideological 'Guerrillas' and the Quest for Technological Autonomy: Brazil's Domestic Computer Industry," *International Organization*, Vol. 40, 3, (Summer 1986), pp. 678–699.
3. Wando Pereira Borges, president of Digibrás, *Hearings Before the Parliament* (Cámara dos Deputados) Mimeo, Brazil, D.F., August 31, 1977; Joseph M. Grieco, *Between Dependency and Autonomy*, p. 158; Indin's Experience with the International Computer Industry" *International Organization*, no. 36 (Summer 1982), p. 158; Paulo Bastos Tigre, "Industria de Computadores e Dependència

Tecnológica do Brasil," Master's thesis, University of Rio de Janeiro, 1978, p. 75; CAPRE, Boletim Técnico 1 (January–March 1979), pp. 38–39; and G. B. Levine, "Brazil 1976—Another Japan?" *Datamation* 21 (December 1975).

4. SEI, *Boletim Informativo,* 3 (June–September 1983), p. 10.

5. *Data News,* May 3, 1983, p. 9; and *Brazil Trade and Industry,* May 1982, p. 11.

6. The SEI (which has been in charge of computer policy since 1979) classifies computers according to their mean value: Class 1, $20,000; Class 2, $90,000; Class 3, $180,000; Class 4, $670,000; Class 5, $1,900,000; and Class 6, $3,000,000. SEI, *Boletim Informativo,* 8 (July–September 1982), p. 5. Roughly, the six classes stand for microcomputers, minicomputers, small-, medium-, large-, and very-large-sized computers. The microcomputer category includes electronic accounting machines and desktop models.

7. SEI, *Boletim Informativo,* p. 7.

8. *Dados e Idéias,* 5 (April–May 1977), p. 30.

9. Robert A. Bennett, "IBM in Latin America," in Jon P. Gunneman, ed., *The Nation-State and Transnational Corporations in Conflict: With Special Reference to Latin America* (New York: Praeger, 1975), Appendix B, p. 225.

10. United Nations Center on Transnational Corporations (UNCTC), *Transborder Data Flows and Brazil* (New York: United Nations, 1983), p. 80; *Brazil Trade and Industry,* May 1982, p. 12; and information provided to me by IBM do Brasil.

11. *Data News,* May 15, 1984, p. 4.

12. SEI, *Boletim Informativo,* p. 11.

13. Ibid., pp. 13, 18.

14. Paulo Bastos Tigre, *Technology and Competition in the Brazilian Computer Industry* (New York: St. Martin's, 1983), p. 94.

15. *Data News,* November 6, 1984, p. 6.

16. UNCTC, *Transborder Data Flows and Brazil,* p. 98.

17. Pedro S. Malan and Regis Bonelli, "The Brazilian Economy in the Seventies: Old and New Development," *World Development,* 5 (January–February 1977), pp. 36 and 38, and United Nations Industrial Development Organization (UNIDO), *Industrial Priorities in Developing Countries* (New York: United Nations, 1979), pp. 2–3.

18. Success eluded Brazil's attempt to master the nuclear fuel cycle and set up a large number of nuclear plants, despite the agreement signed with West Germany to effect the largest technology transfer in history and despite spending billions of dollars. For an analysis of the Brazilian-West German deal see Normal Gall, "Atoms for Brazil, Dangers for All," *Foreign Policy,* 23 (Summer 1976). For a description of the Brazilian nuclear power industry and its problems, see Margarete K. Luddeman, "Nuclear Power in Latin America: An Overview of Its Present Status," *Journal of Interamerican Studies and World Affairs,* 25 (August 1983).

19. Atul Wad, "Microelectronics: Implications and Strategies for the Third World," *Third World Quarterly* (October 1982), p. 629.

20. Michael Borrus, James Millstein, and John Zysman, with the assistance of Aeton Arbisser and Daniel O'Neill, *International Competition in Advanced Industrial Sectors: Trade and Development in the Semiconductor Industry,* Joint Economic Committee, 97th Congress, 2nd sess., February 1982, p. 34.

21. Dimitri Ypsilanti, "The Semiconductor Industry," *OECD Observer,* issue 132 (January 1985), p. 14.

22. *Business Week,* August 2, 1982, p. 55.

23. Grieco, *"Between Dependency and Autonomy,"* p. 58; *World Business Weekly,* April 21, 1980, p. 35.

24. Wad, "Microelectronics," p. 679.

25. For example, a 32-bit microprocessor with the power of a mainframe computer can execute one million or more instructions per second; analysts predict it will cost no more than twenty dollars by the end of the 1980s. *Business Week.* July 30, 1984, p. 56.

26. *Business Week,* May 23, 1983, p. 53.

27. Borrus et al., *International Competition in Advanced Industrial Sectors,* p. 123; and Ypsilanti, "The Semiconductor Industry," p. 15.

28. *World Business Weekly,* April 20, 1981, p. 30.

29. *Time,* July 11, 1983, p. 45, and *Business Week,* June 8, 1981, p. 84.

30. *The New York Times,* January 20, 1985, p. D-5.

31. *Business Week,* July 16, 1984, p. 61, and *Data News,* November 6, 1984.

32. *Business Week,* July 16, 1984, pp. 62 and 49.

33. See Francisco R. Sagasti, "A Framework for the Formulation and Implementation of Technology Policies: A Case Study of ITINTEC in Peru," in Earl Ingerson and Wayne G. Bragg, eds., *Science, Government, and Industry for Development,* The Texas Forum (Austin: University of Texas Institute of Latin American Studies, 1975), pp. 207–210.

34. Seriado Estatístico, *Revista Brasileria de Tecnologia*, 13 (April–May 1982), p. 61; United Nations Educational, Scientific, and Cultural Organization, *Statistical Yearbook 1975* (Paris: UNESCO, 1975), p. 527, and ibid., 1978–79, p. 845.
35. National Council of Science and Technology (CNPq), *Avaliação e Perspectivas*, Vol. 3 (1978), p. 47.
36. Ricardo A. C. Saur, *Hearings Before the Parliament (Câmara dos Deputados)*, Mimeo, Brazil, D. F., 1977), p. 17.
37. CNPq, *Avaliação a Perspectivas*, p. 47; UNCTC, *Transborder Data Flows and Brazil*, pp. 91 and 97.
38. Ferranti built a general-purpose and real-time 16-bit computer design for use in data communications networks, real-time information systems, and process control. Steve Yolan, "Computer Production Prospects in Brazil Brighten," *Electronic News*, June 7, 1976, p. 32.
39. Evans developed the tripé thesis in *Dependent Development*.
40. See Jack Baranson, *North-South Technology Transfer: Financing and Institutional Building* (Mt. Airy, Md: Lomand, 1981), pp. 38–42.
41. Paulo Bastos Tigre, "Brasil: A Future in Homemade Hardware," *South* (February 1982), p. 99.
42. Silvia Helena, "Os Banqueiros e ar COBRA," *Dados e Idéias*, 5 (April–May 1977), p. 35
43. Grieco, *Between Dependency and Autonomy*, p. 625.
44. Saur, *Hearings*, p. 16
45. See, for example, Seminario sobre Computação na Universidade, *Recomendaçóes, Florianópolis*, September 29, 1977.
46. Grieco, *Between Dependency and Autonomy*, even identified the main "guerrilleros" when he wrote: "In 1971, the individual selected to head both the Commission and the Department was M. G. K. Menon, who was until then director of the Tata Institute for Fundamental Research, which is under the Atomic Energy Commission. His key deputy in the department was A. Parthasarathi, who had been a principal officer in the AEC. An important analyst for the AEC, N. Seshagiri, was chosen to head the Electronic Commission's intelligence-gathering and analysis unit" (p. 627).
47. *Dados e Idéias*, 1 (April–May 1980), p. 8. For example, in 1976 CAPRE examined 2,000 requests and granted only $115 million of the $250 million requested.
48. UNCTC, *Transborder Data Flows and Brazil*, p. 63.
49. Saur, *Hearings*, p. 4.
50. CAPRE, *Boletim Informativo*, 4 (July–September 1976), p. 53.
51. Marília Rosa Millan and João Lizardo Hermes de Araújo, "Na Palavra dos Técnicos, um Ponto de Vista Nacional," *Cadernos de Techologia e Ciência*, Vol. 1 (December 1975–January 1976), p. 36.
52. CAPRE, *Boletim Informativo*, 4 (July–September 1979), p. 53.
53. Silvia Helena, "Minis: A Decisão Final," *Dados e Idéias*, 2 (October–November 1977), pp. 34–35.
54. *Business in Latin America*, October 19, 1977, p. 331.
55. *Conjuntura Econômica*, February 1979, p. 95.
56. UNCTC, *Transborder Data Flows and Brazil*, p. 69.
57. SEI, "Ato Normativo," Mimeo, March 1980, June 1980.
58. But SEI made certain that Model 4331 remained a medium-sized computer by stipulating that its minimum memory power had to be 2 million bytes, that the nationalization index would be set at the 85% level established by the Industrial Development Council, and for each two units sold in Brazil, three had to be exported. *Business Latin America*, October 22, 1980, p. 344.
59. Coordination of Entities for the Defense of an Informatics National Industry, "Anál.is da Decisão da SEI de 6 de Agôsto de 1980," Mimeo, Gennari Netto, the decision to allow IBM to manufacture its Model 4331 did not undermine the model because at the time Brazil did not have the potential to manufacture a computer that size. He stated that the permit was not the result of pressure by IBM but of an understanding at SEI that the market would gain (customers were unattended at that size level) and the model would not lose.
60. Gennari confided that the statements attributed to him regarding the market reserve were the result of selective editing by the media in order to inflame the controversy between those for and against the market reserve. SEI may also have used these remarks to frighten the domestic industry into becoming more competitive.
61. *Data News*, July 26, 1983, p. 2.

The USTR and Brazil: 1985–1988

> If we are going to let the market dictate the structural adjustment of the economy (in the United States) and not protect industries which are not competitive in the international market, such as shoes, we have to let the market also dictate our access to the markets of other countries in those sectors in which we are competitive, such as hi-technology products. (John Rosenbaum, USTR spokesman, September 10, 1985)
>
> Whether the Informatics Law is good or bad, it is now a question of national sovereignty. (*Gazeta Mercantil*, September 10, 1985)

In April 1988, Clayton Yeutter, the United States trade representative (USTR), had to decide what action to recommend to President Ronald Reagan in response to the latest concessions made by Brazil on their informatics law. Reagan's previous move, in November, had been successful in causing Brazil to ease some of its barriers against hardware and software. Upon the USTR's request, the president had imposed tariffs on certain Brazilian manufactured goods, along with a ban on Brazilian electronics products, which had forced Brazil to back down, at least for the moment. The U.S. sanctions were suspended until April, affording Brazil time to comply fully with U.S. grievances. Anticipating that Brazil would not yield on every point, Yeutter had to consider three alternatives: (1) to recommend reinstating trade sanctions until Brazil completely opened its computer market, (2) to continue negotiations with Brazil while rewarding it for recent concessions by indefinitely suspending Reagan's retaliation, or (3) to be satisfied with Brazil's progress and recommend lifting sanctions permanently.

Yeutter had to consider the reaction of the U.S. computer industry. He recalled the experience of Data General, which had fought for so long for action in the late 1970s and early 1980s. Finally, 1985 Data General had struck its own technology transfer agreement with Brazil's state-run computer firm, COBRA. While the agreement resulted in only a trickle of royalty payments, Data General had clearly opted to negotiate with Brazil on its own, rather than to seek help from the U.S. Trade Representative's Office for support. On the other hand, Yeutter knew that computer software manufacturers such as Microsoft wanted more severe action.

Yeutter also knew that companies in other industries which could be affected by a Brazilian retaliation might feel differently about trade sanctions. Moreover, the growing U.S. trade deficit had become a serious issue in Congress, where days earlier the House of Representatives had overwhelmingly approved a trade bill that Reagan had vowed to veto.

Frits van Paasschen, MBA, 1988, and Joel Szabat, MBA, 1988, prepared this case under the supervision of Professor George C. Lodge as the basis for class discussion rather than to illustrate either effective or ineffective handling of an administrative situation.

The United States Trade Representative

The USTR is a part of the Executive Office and reports directly to the president, similar to the Office of the Management of the Budget (OMB) or the Council of Economic Advisers (CEA). It as created by Congress in 1962. Before that time no one cabinet department had been responsible for all aspects of foreign trade. State, Treasury, and Commerce each had substantial personnel and resources devoted to monitoring various aspects of trade, and developing trade policy.

USTR's role and influence were expanded in the early 1970s. The Trade Act of 1974 spelled out the extent of the USTR's new power. Under Section 301 of the act, whenever the president suspected that a foreign country might be violating the precepts of fair trade, he could authorize an investigation into that nation's trade practices and if they were found "unreasonable" he could authorize economic sanctions.

A separate investigating body, termed the 301 Committee, was formed for each suspected trade violation. Each committee consisted of subcabinet-level representatives from State, Treasury, Commerce, Justice, Agriculture, Labor, CEA, and OMB. A member of the USTR's office chaired each 301 Committee, and all hearings and negotiations for the investigations were conducted by USTR personnel.

Investigations were time consuming, ranging from two to six years. The committee had to quantify the extent to which a U.S. industry was being damaged by the targeted trade restriction; and it had to determine whether the trade restrictions were "unreasonable," which was rarely easy given the conflicting goals among the departments and the ever-changing foreign trade policies of the international community. Hence, 301 investigations were usually kept tightly focused. The broader in scope an investigation was, the harder it was to quantify results and the more difficult to develop an interagency consensus.

Although the president could self-initiate a 301 investigation through the USTR, normally, an industry would investigate perceived unfair trade practices, then contact the USTR and request a full-blown 301 investigation. If the USTR felt that the complaints were justified, he or she would then forward them to the president, who would authorize a 301 investigation to begin.

Typically, U.S. exporters who alleged that they were being victimized by restrictive trade policies would rally their industry associations. The USTR benefited from this procedure. First, by requesting a 301 investigation, industry associations signaled when they had a serious trade problem; this saved the USTR the time and resources needed to track and identify foreign trade barriers. Second, in requesting the 301 action, the associations normally provided valuable background data. Finally, an industry push for 301 action assured the USTR's office of strong lobbying support of retaliatory action were recommended to the administration and Congress.

If a trade practice was found to be unreasonable and economic sanctions were imposed, the retaliation had to be roughly equal in value to the damages caused by the unreasonable practice. The 301 Committee tried to ensure that possible sanctions would not hurt U.S. companies located in the targeted nation.

The trade representative would recommend options to the president, who had the authority to impose any form of retaliation deemed appropriate.

Within the USTR and the White House, "decisions to retaliate are taken with great reluctance," according to a USTR negotiator. She likened sanctions to a blunt instrument whose effects were difficult to calibrate with precision. Apart from Brazil, the United States had imposed sanctions on only one other country. During 1985, the United States determined that Japanese manufacturers were dumping semiconductors in the market, and the Reagan administration had responded by limiting certain Japanese imports.

There were opportunities for creative forms of retaliation, however. "We handled one (301) case where the actual damages were small, only $2–3 million, but it was important due to the precedent it set," commented one USTR official. "We could hardly impose a $3 million increase in tariffs—they'd never notice it! So instead we sent a message by processing their mail more slowly through customs."

By 1985, foreign trade issues had become highly controversial in the United States. The nation had recovered from the worldwide recession of 1981–1982 more quickly than others. Domestic demand increased rapidly, while at the same time, the value of the dollar climbed. Consequently, imports flooded the U.S. market and exports declined, as U.S. manufacturers were burdened with overpriced products and sluggish overseas markets. Record trade deficits resulted. Between 1979 and 1985 total U.S. exports to Brazil, for example, felt by 10 percent as a result of Brazil's import substitution and the recession that hit the country in the early 1980s. At the same time Brazil's exports to the United States had more than doubled during the same period, causing its trade balance to shift from a deficit to a surplus of more than $5 billion. (See Exhibit 2 for computer-related trade with Brazil.)

Trade worries set the stage for a partisan clash. The Congress, controlled by Democrats, wanted U.S. companies and jobs protected. "Japan bashing" and "Buy American" became popular themes among business and labor groups. The textile industry introduced an advertising campaign with the slogan "It matters to me— Made in the U.S.A," which featured celebrities such as Bob Hope and Don Johnson. Representative Richard Gephart of Missouri first entered the national spotlight by proposing legislation that would mandate U.S. retaliation whenever the balance of trade with another nation dropped below certain levels. Both Republicans and Democrats decried the loss of 600,000 manufacturing jobs since the beginning of the Reagan administration.

The Reagan White House was committed to "free trade," seeking to reduce trade barriers through the GATT and bilateral talks. Reagan officials feared that new protectionist legislation would undercut these efforts and provoke a trade war.

Brazil Since March 1985

On March 15, 1985, Jose Sarney of the Brazilian Democratic Movement Party (PMDB), became the first civilian president since the military coup in 1964. As vice president–elect, Sarney replaced the immensely popular President-elect Tancredo Neves who had died suddenly just prior to inauguration. Although he had spent 25 years in the National Congress, Sarney lacked both Neves's political skill and his clout with the military. Sarney even said of himself:

> My political transition to the coalition of Tancredo Neves had been the subject of criticism. After all, I was placed on the ticket because I represented factions that would provide the required electoral vote. I was not a candidate of hope, or even of change. I was a device, a chess pawn in the political strategy. There was no lack of confidants who whispered in my ear that...people were saying "Sarney is only a piece in the game. If anything goes wrong, he'll never take office."...The greatest optimists thought I might last 90 days at most, as Brazil slid back into institutional instability. The question was whether we would return to a harsh military regime and total dictatorship, or if we were on the road to civil war.[1]

When Sarney took office, inflation was running at 250 percent and rising, unemployment was at an all-time high, and the country was in the deepest recession of its history. Event though the Brazilian economy had boomed at various times during the previous 21 years of military rule, many Brazilians had not shared in the prosperity—the richest 1 percent owned as much as the poorest 50 percent.

By November 1985, political instability eased after direct elections for national and state offices, which were part of the move toward greater democracy. Eventually, a constitutional assembly was formed to begin drafting Brazil's eighth constitution. Two years later, the first draft called for greater privatization and deregulation, increased popular participation in state matters, more state responsibility for education and health, and stronger individual and minority rights.

Sarney initiated the Cruzado Plan on February 28, 1986, to fight runaway inflation and to begin to reduce income disparities. It froze wages and prices and introduced a new currency, the cruzado, to replace the cruzeiro. In addition, the complex indexing system, a key contributor to inflation, was abolished. According to Sarney, "The prompt reaction of the people to price controls aroused a popular movement without precedent in Brazilian history."[2] Later in 1986, the Cruzado Plan showed its first signs of success, as inflation dropped to less than 1 percent per month. Wholesale prices only rose 50 percent in 1986, far lower than the rates of 220 percent in 1984 and 1985. Real GDP rebounded in 1984 after floundering in the early 1980s. The economy grew 8 percent and 11 percent in 1985 and 1986, respectively.

On February 19, 1987, Sarney declared a moratorium on two-thirds of Brazil's $112 billion foreign debt, an action Sarney supporters hailed as a way of ensuring Brazil's growth. In practice, however, the moratorium made it nearly impossible for commerce to finance imports and exports. By early 1988, the moratorium had shriveled into a temporary accord with creditors. More ominously, observers predicted that the burden of servicing the debt would soon bring Brazil back into confrontation with its creditors.

By the end of 1987, inflation had returned with a vengeance, projected to end the year at 330 percent; even Brazil's robust trade surplus was down $3 billion from the previous year. Sarney's popularity plummeted amid growing concern over rising foreign debt and talk of political corruption. On November 15, the constitutional assembly voted 48 to 45 to reject Sarney's bid to have the presidential term, including his own, extended from four years to five years. This meant that elections would be held in 1988. According to one Brazilian party official, the vote was "a political disaster for the president." A former editor of the *Journal do Brasil,* the center-left newspaper, stated that "There is deeper disillusionment than I have ever seen in this country." Public opinion polls indicated that 65 percent to 75 percent of Brazilians favored an election in 1988.[3]

In a remarkable turnaround, Sarney received heavy support from the military in influencing the legislature to reconsider a five-year term for all future presidents. This was accomplished through "a flurry of favours from the government and of threats from the armed forces."[4] According to the nation's top military commanders, the five-year term was "fundamental in order to secure the country's tranquility." This statement was construed by assembly members as a threat of military intervention. Sarney's close aide and communications minister, Antonio Carlos Magalhaes, linked almost all federal spending to pledges of loyalty to Sarney. Although the new legislation did not guarantee Sarney a five-year term, observers were confident that he would receive a one-year extension in April 1988. Brazil's first direct presidential election since 1960 would, therefore, take place in November 1989.

The Informatics Policy and the Reagan Administration, 1985–1987

In March 1985, Data General came to terms with COBRA on a technology transfer agreement.[5] COBRA would be allowed to manufacture and sell two models of superminicomputers that Data General had introduced in the United States three years earlier. Under the terms of the contract COBRA could not resell or lease the technology until five years after it began to produce the computer models. Data General had no equity position but received royalty payments.

Rebuffed in the GATT talks of January 1985, the United States Trade Representatives' Office requested in June that Brazil enter into formal consultations on its informatics law. The Brazilian government refused, stressing that the nature of Brazilian laws was an internal matter and that the informatics law did not violate the provisions of GATT. The Brazilians also maintained that computer sales by U.S. firms to Brazil had increased from $533 million to $1 billion between 1979 and 1985, concluding that the United States could not claim that Informatics was unfair to U.S. exporters.

During the first week of September 1985, President Reagan received a trade bill from Congress. The administration objected to several "protectionist" measures in the bill. Protectionist sentiment was mounting in Congress—over 300 proposals for restricting trade were pending—and there was no guarantee that a presidential veto would be sustained. He also rejected a congressional request to ban Brazilian shoes from the United States market. Simultaneously, however, the administration announced that the USTR would investigate unfair trade practices in Japan, the European Economic Community, and Brazil in accordance with section 301 of the Trade Act of 1974. This was the second time in the history of the Trade Act that 301 action had been "self-initiated" by the USTR's office.

President Reagan chose September 7, Brazil's independence day (the local equivalent of the fourth of July), to devote some of his weekly radio broadcast to Brazil. He said, "I am directing the U.S. trade representative to start proceedings ... against a Brazilian law that has restricted U.S. exports of computers and related products and squeezed out some American computer firms operating there."[6]

There was much speculation about the reasons for the president's action. Was it concern about America's trade deficit, especially with Brazil? Was he angered by the threat posed by Brazil's policy for American companies operating in Brazil, or was he merely defending free trade principles?

Some suggested that President Reagan was trying to impress Congress more than Brazil. As one U.S. computer industry executive put it:

> The president was trying to prove to key members of Congress that the U.S. did in fact have a viable trade policy—he self-initiated a series of unfair trade practices cases—and since everyone thought that a Latin American country was necessary and since Brazil was known to have very restrictive import policies, Brazil was chosen as a test case.

The USTR invited briefs from all interested parties. In response, the two major U.S. computer industry associations submitted short letters that offered lukewarm support for the 301 action. According to one association, the American Electronics Association (AEA):

> We support efforts to negotiate mutually acceptable changes to the Brazilian informatics policies. Our member companies welcome the opportunity to work closely with you in negotiations with Brazil. We are also exploring the possibility of initiating industry-to-industry discussions with our Brazilian counterparts on these questions. Our hope is that these efforts will lead to expanded, rather than contracted, trade relations between our two nations.[7]

The Computer and Business Equipment Manufacturers Association (CBEMA) wrote:

> The overwhelming margin by which the Informatics Law passed in Brazil attests to the strong political support for this law. For this reason CBEMA feels that the fundamental objective of U.S. negotiations should be to improve the way the law is implemented and to assure the timely phase-out of its provisions.[8]

Several corporate members of the two associations pushed for stronger support of the 301. However, companies with ongoing business in Brazil, such as IBM, Burroughs, and now Data General, resisted a harsh line. According to an AEA officer, "Before the administration unveiled the 301, the USTR approached the industry for our support. Almost unanimously we advised against it."

The 301 action stirred a response in Brazil. One Brazilian businessman said that "it probably elected 40 leftist congressmen and if retaliation ensues it will be 80."[9] On September 23, President Sarney defended the informatics law in a speech before the United Nations.

The administration had difficulty in developing a consensus in Washington. State and Treasury opposed putting pressure on Brazil when delicate negotiations on Brazil's repayment of its debt to U.S. banks were underway. (A year later, indeed, the U.S. ambassador to Brazil was to denounce the 301 action as "a stupid policy.")[10]

By March 1986, the U.S. computer industry finally reached a consensus. According to an industry executive,

> Most of the activity concerning trying to define an industry position occurred in the association and industry groups. Eventually, everyone realized that none of us were going to get what each of us individually would have liked . . . in the end, although the issue of copyright protection was not the ideal one to choose, given domestic concerns and the present U.S. international trade agenda. intellectual property rights became the key issue in the Brazil 301 case.

A USTR negotiator called the agreement to concentrate on copyright protection, "the lowest common denominator." Software copyright protection was chosen because all the U.S. hardware and software manufacturers were concerned about the possible loss of their proprietary technology. It was also important to the Reagan administration, which had recently persuaded Japan and other countries to adopt strict intellectual property rights laws, and was trying to get these protections included in the GATT.

In October 1986, the Brazilian Computer Industry Association (ABICOMP) filed a brief with the USTR, defending the Informatics policy and summarizing supporters' rationale for the restrictions. The ABICOMP statement argued that the informatics law was justified under the terms of two GATT articles: Article XVIII, which allowed import restrictions to accomplish balance of payment objectives and to protect infant industries, and Article XXI, national security considerations. Similar grounds were used by the U.S. government in rejecting Fujitsu's application to acquire Fairchild, a U.S. semiconductor manufacturer.

Despite frequent U.S. requests for bilateral meetings, Brazil was loath to negotiate any trade concessions with U.S. representatives. The Foreign Ministry agreed to talks only after a series of public hearings in Washington in March 1986 demonstrated strong administration, industry, and congressional support for the 301 investigation.

The industry endeavored to resolve the conflict on its own. In two meetings, one held in the United States in May 1986 and the other in Brazil six months later, representatives of the countries' computer firms and trade associations failed to reach a consensus.

The USTR Findings

No progress was made in the July and August 1986 meetings between the U.S. negotiators and their Brazilian counterparts, either. Consequently, the United States decided to "up the ante," in the words of one official. In October, only months since proceedings began, the Section 301 Committee concluded its investigation and found that the Informatics Law unreasonably, "burdens and restricts U.S. commerce."[11] The estimated annual damages to U.S. manufacturers from loss of sales was placed at $105 million.

The 301 findings cited four areas which the U.S. negotiators felt constituted unfair trade practices:

1. *Intellectual Property Rights.* Through GATT and bilateral talks the United States was pushing for worldwide copyright protection for software and other "intellectual" properties. Brazil offered no such legal protection. U.S. firms could only protect proprietary software by entering into technology transfer agreements, which would have to stipulate that the Brazilian company could not license or sell the software to other firms for a period of three to five years. Any Brazilian company that could "pirate" proprietary software was free to manufacture, sell, and export it.

2. *Investment.* The Brazilian law combined tariff and quota barriers with unique restrictions on foreign investment and production inside the country. By law, foreigners were restricted to a 30 percent equity stake in any Brazilian computer company and could have no equity in any company that participated in a technology transfer agreement. As the U.S. negotiators saw it, this was a de facto bar to joints ventures.

3. *Administration.* The United States complained that the Special Secretariat of Informatics (SEI) had no explicit criteria or appeals process to guide decisions on foreign applications to produce, sell, or enter into joint ventures and technology transfer agreements.

4. *Market Access.* Informatics was broadly and loosely defined. The United States wanted a clear statement of what was covered by the market reserve restriction of informatics. The United States further requested an established sunset date for the market reserve.

As the Brazilians had begun direct negotiations, the United States suspended any retaliatory action until December 1986. Reluctantly, the Brazilians bent under U.S. and internal pressure. Less than 24 hours before the U.S. deadline expired, President Sarney proposed legislation that would provide copyright protection for software. Sarney also offered guarantees that the market reserve policy would not be renewed when it expired in 1992, and that the market reserve would not be extended to other areas of U.S. concern, such as pharmaceuticals. The Brazilians refused the U.S. request to define the area encompassed by the informatics laws, on the grounds that this was a rapidly changing, high-technology field. Administratively, the Sarney regime restructured SEI, established a formal appeals process to CONIN,[12] and proposed an "ad hoc group" of Brazilian and U.S. government representatives that would meet to discuss problems that U.S. companies had with SEI or the market reserve policy.

The 301 Committee was not completely satisfied with the provisions of the copyright protection bill or Sarney's response to objections about the market reserve. Moreover, the issue of investment restrictions had not yet been addressed. Nonetheless, Yeutter was pleased with the negotiations' progress and hoped that the copyright protection bill might be favorably amended in the legislative process. On Yeutter's recommendation, President Reagan extended the suspension of 301 retaliatory action until the end of June 1987. Yeutter was charged with personally monitoring Brazilian actions and the progress of the negotiations.

In June, the Brazilian Chamber of Deputies narrowly passed legislation that provided copyright protection for software. The bill was still subject to approval by the Senate. Although Yeutter felt that the bill contained important loopholes weakening protection for intellectual property, he remained satisfied with the general course of negotiations. Sarney's administrative changes appeared to be working. CONIN overturned several SEI decisions that had been unfavorable to U.S. firms; also, U.S. companies were not using the Ad Hoc Group in applying to manufacture and sell computer-related equipment. But there was still no progress on the issue of investment. According to several officials, the USTR understood Sarney's difficult position. "We had gone to the brink" to get copyright protection, said one official. The general belief was that a few more months of negotiations would produce an acceptable agreement. In view of this progress, Reagan again suspended 301 action, from June until December of 1987. Speaking on behalf of the AEA's 3300 corporate members, R. Wayne Sayer said:

> The government of Brazil is to be commended for pushing this bill in the current domestic political environment... in light of this progress we supported the administration's decision to suspend the 301 proceedings.[31]

Confrontation: December 1987 to April 1988

By the end of 1987 negotiations had once again soured. Henry Kissinger told the *Los Angeles Times* that if the U.S.-Brazil conflict continued "populist, antimarket, anti-U.S. forces will be dangerously strengthened just when a democratic constitution is being drafted."[14] The U.S. negotiators were mindful of the need to maintain a domestic constituency so that they would be clearly "defending American interests." They had to keep the U.S. computer industry on board, it being clear that there was no other domestic constituency. The USTR file on the case revealed only one letter from a domestic manufacturer in another industry, hoping to benefit from the case. This was a small Massachusetts producer of disposable paint filters expressing the hope that if the United States retaliated against the informatics law, it would do so by raising tariffs on imported Brazilian paint filters.[15]

In September, Microsoft Corporation negotiated a deal to license a disk operating system (DOS) to six Brazilian hardware manufacturers. SEI refused to approve the agreement, ruling that a Brazilian firm, Scopus, already manufactured a similar system. This ruling extended the scope of the "rule of similars" to include, for the first time, software. U.S. industry and government officials contended that the Scopus system was far inferior to Microsoft's DOS. Just as Data General's CEO Edson De Castro had done 10 years earlier, Bill Gates, CEO of Microsoft, tried to rally U.S. industry and the USTR against SEI's ruling.

Gates asked Yeutter to persuade the Ministry of Science or President Sarney to overturn SEI's ruling.[16] Should that fail, he wanted the Reagan administration to take action under the 301 finding. Gates argued that the new software protection bill pending in Brazil's Senate might increase software protection, but that the functional equivalency preference as applied by SEI to software amounted to, "an insurmountable barrier," that would keep U.S. software companies out of the Brazilian market.

Two of the Brazilian companies planning to license Microsoft's DOS appealed to CONIN to reverse SEI's ruling. Scopus and other Brazilian companies argued forcefully in support of the functional equivalency rule, claiming they could not compete if Brazil opened its markets to U.S. software; Brazil would be forever dependent on foreign software. In further support of Scopus's case were indications that SEI had initially pressured Scopus to develop a DOS that would rival imports. Moreover, the Brazilian computer market and peripheral manufacturers turning a profit. Against heavy U.S. pressure, CONIN and the Ministry of Science refused to overrule SEI.

During this time, U.S. negotiators realized that the Brazilian Senate was unlikely to pass an acceptable software protection bill. Although the copyright protection was considered adequate, the bill gave SEI "vaguely worded discretionary authority to define functional equivalence (for hardware and software) and levy a 200 percent tax," according to a USTR salesman. The tax was to be used to fund the development of the Brazilian computer industry.

During 1987, major U.S. microcomputer manufacturers, already shut out of Brazil by the market reserve, had become alarmed by the increasing number of low-cost clones being produced in Brazil. Brazil's Unitron applied to SEI for permission to manufacture what Apple executives saw as a reverse-engineered clone of its Macintosh microcomputer, using pirated software. These firms, rankled at being locked out of Brazil, feared Brazilian exports that might undercut their won foreign sales. They thus intensified pressure on Congress and the administration for some form of retaliation.

This pressure along with Yeutter's report that negotiations had again deadlocked set the stage for President Reagan to act. On November 13, he announced that the United States would impose $100 million worth of tariffs on Brazilian shoes, aircraft, and earthenware, and prohibit the importation of any Brazilian data processing products. Reagan stated that he would remove the tariffs if Brazil reversed its policy. This was the first retaliation taken against a debtor country.

Within two days of Reagan's announcement the Brazilian Congress voted to allow Sarney discretionary authority to retaliate against the United States. Sarney stated that he would prefer to have GATT mediate a settlement. In the United States, firms such as Microsoft and Apple, along with CBEMA and the AEA, enthusiastically endorsed the sanctions. In testimony before the Section 301 Committee in December, R. Wayne Sayer said:

> While we hope that Brazil will recognize legitimate U.S. interests, if this does not occur then sanctions are critical to emphasize to other countries that international trade rules and agreements must be respected.... We strongly support the President's decision to impose sanctions if SEI's decision on Microsoft is not immediately overturned, and if the problems associated with the software protection law are not corrected.[17]

William Krist, vice president of AEA for international trade affairs, spoke out forcefully against Brazil's Informatics policy:

> A great deal of effort has gone into developing a set of international agreements to assure a measure of free trade, free markets, and property rights protection. These agreements constitute a global guidelines which national governments can use to

resist the pressure of special interest groups for special treatment and thus they promote the general interests of the country as a whole. Brazil's policies fly in the face of these international agreements and guidelines. I believe that the government was captured by an extremely narrow interest group which is running inefficient plants at enormous profit.

We would like to see Brazil have a strong Informatic capability, but it must be part of the world system. Their go-it-alone, reinventing the wheel strategy doesn't make sense. I must say that in recent years the policy has been moving in the right direction but it has a long way to go.[18]

Between November and January 1987, a rapid succession of events ensued. On November 27, the director of SEI announced, "Brazil is no longer interested in protecting or simulating basic computer programs similar to those produced by Microsoft."[19] On November 30, Sarney formally requested that GATT mediate the U.S.-Brazilian dispute. Brazil pledged to step up enforcement action against software pirates on December 10. Eleven days later, Sarney used a line-item veto to strike down the 200 percent tariff in the Software Protection Bill, on the grounds that the taxing mechanisms were unconstitutional.

CONIN issued a clarification of the functional equivalency rule in January, following more bilateral talks and direct negotiation between Yeutter and CONIN directors. CONIN declared that Microsoft would not be allowed to sell its DOS 3.2 in Brazil, but would be allowed to license to sell its newer DOS 3.3, on the grounds that no functional equivalent existed. Microsoft executives announced that they were skeptical of the ruling, calling it "a PR move" and "a token concession that doesn't mean anything."[20]

Also in January, executives of Brazil's major exporters issued a public statement, after a month of behind-the-scenes pressure on the Brazilian government to ease restrictions that the United States found objectionable. The executives termed CONIN's action, "a great demonstration of [Brazil's] good faith."[21] The former head of the Brazil Exporters Association claimed that U.S. importers had already postponed $500 million worth of Brazilian orders. The group requested that Reagan resolve the trade conflict with Brazil.

More meetings between Brazilian representatives and the 301 Committee took place between January and March. CONIN appeared ready to retreat from the plan to license Unitron's Apple clone. Sarney stated that SEI would reformulate its operating guidelines concerning software regulation. Informed by Yeutter that negotiations were again progressing, on March 1, 1988, Reagan lifted the sanctions until the end of April.

Exhibit 1   Significant Events, 1985–1988

1985		
	March	President Sarney takes office in Brazil. Data General signs agreement with COBRA.
	June	United States requests consultations with Brazilian government on the informatics law.
	September	Sarney defends the law at the United Nations. Reagan initiates a 301 action against Brazil in the face of

		protectionist sentiment in Congress.
1986		
	February	Sarney introduces Cruzado Plan to fight inflation.
	March–August	U.S. industry and governen search for a consensus with Brazil.
	October	ABICOMP files brief with USTR before December deadline.
1987		Debt moratorium declared by Brazil.
		Inflation up to 330 percent. Sarney's popularity falls. Negotiaitons with U.S. sour.
1988		Elections scheduled for November 1989 in Brazil. Sarney's term extended. Inflation at 600 percent.

Exhibit 2   U.S. Exports and the Brazilian Market, 1979–1985 (amounts in $U.S. millions)

	1979–1985		
	1979	**1985**	**% Growth**
All U.S. Exports			
World	178,578	206,925	+ 16%
Brazil	3,407	3,070	− 10
Computer-Related Exports			
Computers[a]			
World	3,442	7,230	+ 110
Brazil	47	86	+ 83
Parts[b]			
World	2,716	7,337	+ 170
Brazil	62	175	+ 182
Integrated circuits[c]			
World	767	1,930	+ 152
Brazil	5	19	+ 280
Total Computer Related			
World	6,925	16,497	+ 138
Brazil	114	280	+ 146

Sources: U.S. exports to world from *United Nations Yearbook of International Trade Statistics, 1980 and 1985* U.S. exports to Brazil from U.S. Census Bureau, U.S. Exports, World Area, and Commodity Groupings (Schedule E). Taken from Peter B. Evans "Declining Hegemony and Assertive Industrialization: U.S.–Brazilian Conflicts in the Computer Industry," unpublished manuscript, October 1988, p.8.

[a]Computers-automatic data processing equipment.

[b]Parts-parts for automatic data processing equipment office machines.

[c]Integrated circuits-integrated circuits of electronic microcircuits.

ENDNOTES

1. José Sarney, "Brazil: A President's Story," *Foreign Affairs* (Fall 1986), p. 103.
2. Ibid., p. 112.
3. *The Wall Street Journal*, November 16, 1987, p. 27.
4. *The Economist*, March 26, 1988.
5. Interview: Wayne Fitzsimmons, vice president, Data General, March 1988.
6. Peter B. Evans, "Declining Hegemony and Assertive Industrialization: U.S.-Brazilian Conflicts in the Computer Industry," unpublished manuscript, October 1988, p. 1.
7. AEA letter filed with USTR, Case 301-49, October 11, 1985.
8. CBEHA letter filed with USTR, Case 301-49, October 11, 1985.
9. Evans, "Declining Hegemony and Assertive Industrialization," p. 19.
10. *Journal Mercantil do Brasil*, Mercantile Journal of Brazil October 20, 1985.
11. USTR-Brazil 301 Trade Case," printed by USTR, October 1985.
12. National Council on Informatics and Automation. See Brazil's Informatics Policy: 1970–1984— Supplement: *Outcome and Retrospect*, N2-389-045, Rev. November 1988.
13. Testimony by R. Wayne Sayer to 301 Committee, December 17, 1987.
14. Evans, "Declining Hegemony and Assertive Industrialization," p. 19.
15. Ibid., p. 25.
16. Letter from Gates to Yeutter, September 24, 1987.
17. Sayer, testimony.
18. Interview, March 1988.
19. *The Journal of Commerce*, November 27, 1987, p. 3A.
20. Interview with Martin Taucher, Microsoft, May 1988; also *Seattle Times*, January 15, 1988, p. 1c, and *Financial Times*, January 21, 1988, p. 8.
21. *Journal of Commerce*, January 25, 1988, p. 3A.

3

Managing the Government Affairs Function

Governmental Programs at IBM*

Among corporations of comparable size, IBM was a relative latecomer to government relations as a separate function. Until the 1960s, IBM was guided in the governmental sphere by the view that (1) the corporation was normally little affected by government policies and could live with them, whatever they were and (2) when there were occasionally government policies that might indeed have a material impact on corporate interests, it was the job of top management in the United States and country managers abroad to deal with those issues. Government relations had, of course, been a way of life abroad from the very beginning but country general managers were expected to handle the task themselves.

The first major step toward altering this traditional view was proposed U.S. tax legislation which would—inadvertently—have had devastating consequences for IBM's standard practice at that time of renting equipment to users rather than selling it. Congress was about ready to adopt that legislation before it came to IBM's attention. That near miss convinced Tom Watson, Jr., IBM's chief executive officer, that it was essential to track Washington developments much more closely than had formerly been the case. Monitoring, without any form of active representation, was begun through a small office in Washington operating under the direction of the IBM Communications Department.

Two events, one in the United States and one in Europe, brought IBM across the threshold into a much more active role. The institutionalization of the function began in Europe during the mid-1960s.[1] It resulted from a serious controversy over

*This statement and the remarks that follow were presented by Charles E. McKittrick, Jr., vice president, governmental programs, IBM, at the Harvard Business School Colloquium on Comparative Business-Government Relations, July 8, 1988.

denial by the United States of a license for exportation of a non-IBM computer on national security grounds. The management of IBM World Trade, as the international operations are called, recognized in the ensuing debate over "extraterritoriality" an issue that could cause European governments to regard U.S.-based companies, and therefore, IBM, as unreliable suppliers. Management concluded that country general managers would be unable to devote the time or resources needed to deal with a governmental problem of this magnitude.

In the United States, the trigger event was a trade and tax bill that, had it been adopted, would have repealed the U.S. foreign tax credit. Had that happened, it would have been extremely difficult for U.S. companies to compete in world markets. The proposed legislation would also have made it far more difficult to import into the United States, greatly increasing the probability of foreign retaliation against U.S. exports. IBM, along with most other companies heavily involved in international trade and investment, believed the proposal had the potential to disastrously change the environment in which we conducted our business. Jane Cahill Pfeiffer, who was the IBM vice president for communications at that time, recommended to Frank Cary, then the chief executive officer, the establishment of a greatly expanded government relations function at the corporate level.

An IBMer with nearly 25 years of marketing experience, who currently was a vice president of the Data Processing Division, was selected as the first head of the expanded function. In choosing him, Mrs. Pfeiffer and Mr. Cary had already answered one of the four central questions that had to be decided. That first question was whether to have the corporate Governmental Programs function headed by someone whose main contribution was knowledge of government and government processes or, alternatively, to choose someone based primarily on his knowledge of the company and its business. His skills certainly belonged to the second category rather than the first.

The second, third, and fourth questions were equally important. They were (2) whether to locate the head of corporate Governmental Programs in Washington or at headquarters, (3) whether to unite or separate the staff that should interface with the government and the staff responsible for public affairs (i.e., the group devoted to determining corporate positions and watching longer-term public policy trends), and (4) whether to people the organization with experienced Washington hands or with employees from within the corporation. Our decisions—not necessarily graven in stone for all time—were to lodge corporate Governmental Programs in Washington, to combine government relations and public affairs staff in a single organization and to house them together, and for the most part to staff internally rather than hiring from the outside.

Those decisions meant a lot of time on airplanes to corporate headquarters in Westchester County, N.Y., for me and my staff, endless briefing sessions plus a massive job of coordinating positions with corporate line and other staff functions, and a need to learn Washington from the ground up (and to repeat that learning periodically as some people move on to other jobs and new people come aboard). Nevertheless, we have not had cause to regret any of those decisions.

While it might be different in another corporation, at IBM a detailed knowledge of the computer business and an instinctive understanding of the corporate culture have been indispensable both for me personally and for my principal staff. Like other government relations functions, we are inevitably driven by legislative and regulatory issues. But we steer, to the extent we can, according to fundamental business objectives. Growing up in "the business of the business" is what equips us to understand those objectives in an industry whose technology, whose competitive focus, whose very boundaries are subject to constant change.

As to the choice between Washington and headquarters, our view—derived from the marketing experience which I and my colleagues share—is that we have "clients" at headquarters interested in certain issues and outcomes and government officials in Washington to whom we must explain IBM's point of view. It's certainly essential to stay in close touch with the client to understand his needs and integrate his views and yours, but you need to *live* with the government people if you are to know their requirements and to make our policy story successful. Our value added to IBM is our knowledge of the government for IBM's information, advice, and advocacy.

Of all the decisions that we made, colocating government relations and public affairs was arguably the most significant. It has resulted in an almost seamless relationship between government relations and "issue management." While we do have some people who mainly lobby and others who mainly monitor issues and refine positions and strategies, their presence in the same organization brings greater balance to both functions. In addition, Governmental Programs also attempts to track emerging issues—subjects in the early stages of political and intellectual discussion that could rise to the top of tomorrow's political agenda. That gives us, we think, a creative mixture, a capacity to both do and think, to act on today's issues while preparing ourselves for the next series of debates.

Thus, for example, we have been following the debates on "industrial policy" and "international competitiveness" from their inception. We managed two projects on those topics on behalf of the Business Roundtable—for John Opel, during his term as IBM's chief executive officer, and then for John Akers, our current CEO. Our corporate views were greatly sharpened by these efforts, and we participated actively, and we believe effectively, in the legislative debate on U.S. trade and competitiveness legislation during the 100th Congress. We are prepared, we think, for the next stages in that discussion in the next U.S. administration.

IBM Governmental Programs—my function—is a corporate department with responsibility for coordinating government relations activities worldwide. (We also have an apparatus managed out of my office which covers the U.S. states in which IBM has substantial operations.) I report through the vice president for external relations, Kenneth W. Dam, the former U.S. deputy secretary of state, who is officed at corporate headquarters in Armonk, N.Y.

Outside the U.S. regional functions are lodged in Brussels (headquarters of the European Community) for IBM's Paris-based Europe/Middle East/Africa Corporation, in Tokyo for the Asia/Pacific Group, and in New York for the Americas Group (which covers Canada as well as Latin America). In addition, there are individual external programs offices in most of the countries where IBM has a major presence.

Where the issues are unique to the country, the responsibility lies with the country's external programs managers with guidance from the region. However, issues increasingly cross national borders and transcend regional groupings. Indeed, a startlingly large number of issues are global in character. Trade policy actions in the United States—to take only the most obvious example—reverberate not only in Japan, Europe, and Canada but among the newly industrialized countries (Brazil, Hong Kong, Korea, Mexico, Singapore, Taiwan), the less developed countries (including China) and even the COMECON countries.

Coordinating corporate responses to these transcendent international issues is the responsibility of my department, carried out with the close cooperation of my colleagues in World Trade. The Council on Public Affairs, which is chaired by the IBM director of Public Affairs (corporate), a key member of my staff, and which includes his counterparts from the regional functions meets quarterly to exchange briefings and to formulate strategic recommendations. These meetings are supplemented by regular visits between managers and staff of functions here and abroad and by a staggering amount of information and advice which moves daily over our internal computer communications network. That network permits virtually instantaneous communication between terminals anywhere within the system, allowing those who have charge of the issues to ask questions and receive answers without worrying about time zones. Those responsible for strategy—often the same people asking and answering the questions—are able to talk more frequently (and, in some cases, more interactively) than they could if they depended exclusively on the telephone.

A number of programs have been initiated in our effort to weld worldwide governmental/external programs functions into a cohesive unit. Meetings of public affairs managers from major countries are held approximately every 18 months to talk policy, discuss common problems, and exchange ideas. Corporate Governmental Programs—my organization—runs regular educational programs through our "Public Affairs Institute" to build the skills of government relations professionals around the world (as well as staff executives with public affairs responsibilities in other functions). Like other corporate departments, we established a policy of bringing external programs staff from overseas on assignment to the United States and sending key U.S. governmental programs staff out to the regions. Such out-of-area assignments normally run two to three years. While this rotation system exacts a price in learning time, the benefit is a far more sophisticated understanding of the global environment in which IBM must do business to be successful. By now a substantial number of IBM governmental/external programs professionals have had experience not only in their own countries and regions but in areas of the world where the political and business situations are very different. They bring to bear a more spacious understanding of issues and a larger armory of techniques than do many with more parochial backgrounds. Synergism is an overused word but it is what we seek to achieve: a creative mix of people and professional experience that is greater than the sum of the parts.

Apart—perhaps—from the degree of emphasis placed on coordinating and establishing corporate positions on public policy issues and apart also—perhaps—from the extent to which the function has been internationalized, IBM does more or less what everyone else does:

- We identify issues of potential concern to IBM and consult with our "clients" within the corporation as to their effects.
- We work with the client functions to establish policies and strategies.
- We track the issues and report to clients and to corporate management on developments (in greater or lesser detail, depending on the extent of their interest and involvement).
- We seek to develop and maintain contacts with public officials and private groups that are part of the policy decision-making network on any given issue.
- We develop, recommend, and carry out action programs designed to achieve a desired policy result.
- We earn our keep by the results we achieve.

In general, IBM's experience is that success in the public policy arena depends on ensuring that what IBM wants to achieve is generally compatible with *the government's* priorities. To that end, we make a conscientious effort in shaping our policies and strategies to understand what each government is seeking to achieve. We tell officials, because we firmly believe, that IBM's presence in our country (or region) is an asset for them. Support of country and community institutions is one means of demonstrating that. We maintain active programs of philanthropy, grant sabbaticals to our employees for teaching and other community service roles, occasionally assign employees to a requesting institution to perform special tasks, and sometimes lend our technological expertise to assist particular projects such as the hurricane-warning system in Antigua intended to serve all the countries of the Caribbean.

In pursuing our government relations objectives, we try very hard to have a consistent philosophy. In practice, that means that we seek to advocate policies in one country that are related, or at least not diametrically opposed, to the policies we are advocating in other countries. A useful example is provided by our strategy on telecommunications policy, which has a U.S. federal aspect, a U.S. state and local dimension, an international component, and policy corollaries at regional and national levels throughout the world.

The connecting policy thread is our firm belief that a private, deregulated, transparent network, allowing easy and relatively inexpensive access to value added systems, serves the best interests of users (as well as equipment and service providers). A competitive communications system, responsive to market signals instead of to bureauctratic directives, serves the best interests, we believe, of citizens and of their governments. This is the position we have taken in support of deregulation in the United States and in urging that revenues from monopoly services not be permitted to subsidize competitive operations. It lies behind the argument we have made abroad for dismantling government communications monopolies and for providing market access to IBM and other suppliers of equipment and services.

We make those arguments not just to government officials but to the user community, which stands to benefit greatly from cheaper, more plentiful and more technologically sophisticated services. Realizing the full benefits of modern information technology is not possible, in our opinion, without an efficient and competitive worldwide communications network. To be sure, we are serving IBM's interest; but we think these policies also serve the best interests of the regions and countries that implement them. Against what some considered to be heavy odds a few short years ago, we are making steady progress because, in my view, we have the right side of the argument from a public policy perspective and because, objectively, technological developments are moving in a direction which makes competition an ever more attractive option.

What has been described in this paper may sound ambitious—and it is. But it is accomplished with approximately a couple of hundred professionals world-wide, about one-twentieth of 1 percent of the total number of IBM employees. Our people work hard. But they have high esprit de corps. They are a select group, the best we can recruit. And they are rewarded for achievement, are given promotions inside the function, and are able to move on if they wish after a time to other functions in the corporation. In general, those who have gone on to jobs elsewhere in the corporation have been valued additions because of their experience in Governmental Programs.

On the day after the NCAA basketball finals where his underdog University of Kansas team had upset the University of Oklahoma for the championship, Danny Manning, the Kansas star, was asked on the CBS News whether he felt Kansas had been lucky. His answer: "Luck is preparation meeting opportunity." I offer that—and its converse, that bad luck is mainly lack of preparedness meeting risk—as a slogan for all public affairs professionals.

Questions and Answers

Q: What is your agenda in July 1988?

A: The most important thing right now is a broad effort to analyze and understand the issues that will affect IBM in the next decade. At a recent international IBM meeting in Madrid, we found that most people, irrespective of their country, were working on a similar set of issues. Thus, an important dimension of the issues for the 1990s is their international character. How do we manage issues on an international basis? Which of these issues are only of interest to IBM, which affect our whole industry, which are of general concern to business? Do we adopt different strategies or approaches based on the potential impact of the issue? These are the kinds of questions we are wrestling with as we look at the next decade.

I expect Public Affairs activity to grow exponentially over the next five years. Frankly I'm concerned that what has been beneficial for our company in the last half of the 1980s may not necessarily prove useful in the first half of the 1990s. You may recall the children's game where you put six dots in two lines on a piece of paper and then ask how you can connect all six dots in three straight lines. The solution, of course, is to draw one of the lines far outside the box formed by the six dots. I am challenging our people, as we look into the next decade, to think outside the box.

Q: You said, "What IBM wants is to be compatible with government priorities." It sounds like a terrific statement, but it leaves two questions that I'd like you to address: Who determines government priorities? And what if they conflict with IBM's interests?

A: The government determines its priorities through the budget process, through the appropriations process, and through other formal and informal decision-making forums. IBM expresses its opinion on what those priorities should be as do other interested parties in business, labor, consumer groups, and many, many others. In a broader sense, we would like to believe that our interests and priorities often are the same as those of the government, but we fully understand that this cannot always be the case. When government priorities conflict with our interests, we would like those making the particular decision to understand our viewpoint first. And we are not shy in expressing that viewpoint. The final decision, however, is very clearly left up to those with responsibility for it.

I can think of a country where we were having considerable difficulty doing business. Our interests and those of the country seemed, to some, to be at cross purposes. In this instance, we worked very hard to demonstrate that telecommunications liberalization, intellectual property protection, and a fairly open market were not simply IBM interests. They were policies that would benefit that country. Today, that country pursues such open policies not because they benefit IBM, which they do, but because they are judged to benefit the whole country.

Q: The next question closely related to that is sometimes the U.S. government and other governments that you are dealing with will disagree in terms of what a particular policy might be, and therefore, is it impossible to be compatible to both the home and host government?

A: We have had instances where the policies of the United States have been in direct conflict with those of another country. The most notable example related to U.S. actions against foreign companies who were judged to be supportive of the Soviet oil pipeline. In such cases, our interest is to get the matter resolved as fairly, quickly, and completely as possible. We want to be respected citizens wherever we do business and that is made more difficult when we get caught in between differing aims of two governments.

We think because of the breadth of our international business and the way in which our technology supports national goals and programs in many countries, that we represent a unique asset in countries where we operate—and we are able to demonstrate it. However, it is clear that because we are a U.S.-owned company, we understand that our motives and actions are sometimes questioned overseas. We can only remove such doubts by demonstrating, on a daily basis, the interaction of interests and goals between us and the countries where we do business.

ENDNOTE

1. In IBM's vocabulary, Governmental Programs is the broad function in the United States that deals with government issues. It includes both the government relations function and a public affairs department, which handles issue management. Activities outside the United States are conducted through External Programs, which is responsible for some other activities besides government relations.

Allied Chemical Corporation (A)

In June 1976 Richard Wagner, president of the Specialty Chemicals Division at Allied Chemical, faced two difficult decisions. He had to recommend whether Allied should support passage of the Toxic Substances Control Act then pending before Congress. He also had to decide whether to implement a proposed new program, called Total Product Responsibility, in his division.

Wagner found these decisions especially difficult because of the variety of factors he had to consider, including Allied's business prospects, recent developments in the chemical industry, and the increasing public and government concern about the health, safety, and environmental effects of chemical production. Another important factor was the set of problems related to Kepone, a pesticide produced until 1974 by Allied and afterward by an outside contractor.

ALLIED CHEMICAL

Allied Chemical was a major producer of chemicals, fibers and fabricated products, and energy. With headquarters in Morristown, New Jersey, the company operated over 150 plants, research labs, quarries, and other facilities in the United States and overseas. In 1975 Allied earned $116 million on sales of $2.3 billion. (See Figure A and Tables A and B for Allied's organization and recent financial performance.)

During the late 1960s and early 1970s, Allied had changed dramatically. One company official said Allied was run as "a loose feudal barony" in the 1960s. *Forbes* called the company "a slow-moving, low-growth, low-profit producer of basic inorganic chemicals, fertilizers, and dyestuffs."[1] Changes began in 1967 when John T. Connor resigned as secretary of commerce and became chairman of Allied. Over the course of several years, Connor brought in 250 new executives, pruned failing businesses, established systematic planning and tight cost control, and increased corporate supervision of the divisions. At the same time, he stressed decentralized decision making and said that innovation and flexibility were crucial to Allied's future.

Connor's most important step was an $800 million commitment to find and develop oil and gas supplies throughout the world. According to Connor, this strategy would be financed with new capital and with funds "from existing businesses that were losing, had poor prospects, or had severe environmental risks."[2] The largest investments were in Indonesian gas fields and North Sea oil fields. In Indonesia, Allied had a 35 percent interest in a joint venture with Pertamina, the Indonesian government petroleum agency. The British government

Joseph L. Badaracco, Research Assistant, prepared this case under the supervision of Professor George C. Lodge as a basis for class discussion rather than to illustrate either effective or ineffective handling of an administrative situation. It is not intended to provide a full account of any of the situations described. Most names and position titles for Allied personnel have been disguised.

had announced its intention to obtain a voluntary 51 percent participation in the North Sea oil fields, but the form that participation might take had not been determined them.

This energy investment was very risky. Finding and developing new reserves was highly competitive, technically difficult, and very costly. Changes in government regulations or tax laws, either domestic or foreign, could cut profits. And problems with weather, technology, or politics in host countries could delay the start of production. These risks seemed justified as shortages of energy and chemical feedstocks occurred during the 1970s and as the potential payoff from the investment grew. Connor stated that energy could provide as much as half of Allied's profits by the early 1980s.

In mid-1976, however, the return on the energy investment was still small. In fact, it appeared that Allied's energy businesses, taken altogether, would just about break even in 1976. Allied's U.S. natural gas pipelines lost money because of federal price controls on interstate gas shipments. Its coal and coke business had chronic operating problems and, following a plea of no contest, the company had been fined approximately $100,000 for allegedly failing to meet the Environmental Protection Agency (EPA) air pollution requirements. Finally, obtaining government approval to operate Allied's nuclear fuel reprocessing plant could prove difficult. Company officials then hoped that 1977 would bring the first profits from North Sea oil, and they expected profits from Indonesian gas sales in 1978.

Table A   Financial Performance, 1972–1975
             ($ in millions except per share data and ratios)

	1975	**1974**	**1973**	**1972**
Sales	$2,333	$2,216	$1,665	$1,501
After-tax income	116	144	90	64
EPS	4.17	5.19	3.27	2.30
Debt/equity	0.59	0.45	0.49	0.54
Gross margin/sales	22%	23.3%	24.6%	24.3%
R&D/sales	4.51%	1.39%	1.73%	1.89%
Pollution control facilities cost	$34.4	$29.0	$28.0	$25.0

Table B   Line of Business Performance, 1974–1975 ($ millions)

Line of Business	**1975**		**1974**	
	Sales	**Income from Operations**	**Sales**	**Income from Operations**
Energy (petroleum, nuclear, coal, and coke)	$ 581	$ 28	$ 511	$ 32
Fibers and fabricated products	504	46	484	81
Chemicals (inorganic, plastics, organic, and agricultural)	1,248	144	1,221	135
Total	$2,333	$218	$2,216	$248

While Allied had invested heavily in energy, chemicals provided the foundation of company earnings. In 1976, for example, chemicals most likely produced 75 percent of company profits, even though they were only 50 percent of total company sales. Allied produced approximately 1,500 chemicals and sold them to all major industries. These sales were primarily to other chemical manufacturers for use in making their products. Other sales were to dealers, who sometimes resold them under their own names, and ultimately to consumers. The two best years in the history of Allied's chemical business were 1974 and 1975. Sales were expected to weaken later in 1976, however, as a result of the recession that began in 1975.

Allied's fiber and fabricated products had been a steady contributor to company profits. On average, this business accounted for one-fifth of total sales and profits during the early 1970s. Allied made fibers for clothing, carpeting, and auto tires. The company was also the world's largest manufacturer of auto seat belts and shoulder harnesses.

Overall, Allied's record in the early 1970s did not compare favorably with chemical industry standards. Between 1971 and 1975, Allied's return on equity, sales growth, and return on total assets were the second lowest among the 13 major diversified U.S. chemical companies. EPS growth was exactly the average of the 13 companies. On the positive side, Allied improved its relative performance in 1974 and 1975, and its energy investment offered the prospect of major improvements in the future.

Figure A   Company Organizational Chart

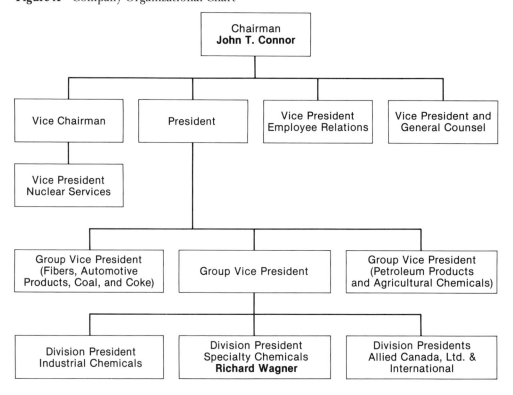

THE CHEMICAL INDUSTRY

In 1976 chemicals was one of the largest U.S. industries, with annual sales of more than $100 billion. In the 20 years after World War II, chemicals became a high-profit, glamor industry that often grew twice as fast as the GNP. From the mid-1960s to the mid-1970s, however, industry growth had slower and financial performance dimmed. Among the reasons were higher raw material costs, increased government regulation, the slowdown in U.S. economic growth, and what many considered the maturity of major segments of the industry. Nevertheless, the industry continued to contribute $3–5 billion per year to the U.S. balance of payments.

Roughly 80,000 chemical compounds are sold in the United States and 500 to 1,000 new ones are added each year. More than 12,000 companies manufacture these chemicals and most of these companies have sales of less than $5 million per year. The major customer for chemical products is the chemical industry itself. A typical chemical company will buy the product of one chemical company, process it, and sell its products to yet another chemical company. In most cases, a long chain of intermediate processors connects a chemical raw material with its ultimate consumer.

The industry is highly competitive. Many chemicals are commodities and compete on price. Competition comes from both natural products (such as cotton fabric) and close chemical substitutes. Chemical firms also face competition from suppliers—especially oil companies—that integrate forward, and from customers integrating backward. For a highly capital-intensive industry, chemicals have a low degree of concentration. The 10 largest chemical companies account for roughly 35 percent of industry shipments. Low concentration encourages competition by limiting oligopolistic pricing. The industry is also highly cyclical, lagging the business cycle by a few months, and vigorous price cutting usually occurs during recessions.

In the past, successful chemical companies tended to follow a basic pattern of growth. They made large investments in research and development, resulting in new products or better processes. These innovations lowered prices and took markets from other chemicals and from natural products. In turn, new markets permitted larger-scale operations, further economies, and further R&D. The R&D investments were the key to successful performance. The importance of innovation to the industry is indicated by the fact that half of all chemical products sold in 1970 were not produced commercially in the 1940s. Ammonia fertilizers, sulfa drugs, Dacron, and nylon are some of the results of chemical industry R&D.

Industry prospects were especially uncertain in 1976. The industry earned record profits in 1974 and 1975—an abrupt change from its sagging performance from 1967 to 1973. In response to these profits and to shortages in 1974, a $25 billion capital spending boom took place. This new capacity raised the specter of industrywide overcapacity and renewed price cutting. In fact, the new capacity came on line just as the economic slowdown affected chemical sales in 1976.

At the same time, costs were rising. Environmental laws and high construc-tion costs raised the price of new plant and equipment. Companies were testing more of their products and raw materials for harmful effects, and testing costs were escalating. It was not unusual then for tests on just one substance to take several years and cost $500,000. Most important, the days of cheap and plentiful oil and natural gas had ended. Chemical companies are disproportionate users of fossil fuels because they need energy to run plants and to use as feedstock for their products. Higher energy costs meant that chemical products in general lost some of their price competitiveness against non-chemical products.

Industry executives were also concerned about an "innovation shrinkage." R&D spending in 1976 would be roughly $1.4 billion, up from $800 million 10 years before. But a higher percentage of this spending was going to modify products already on the market or into government-required health and safety research. Reduced R&D seemed to threaten future industry growth.

KEPONE

Wagner had to make his decisions at a time when Allied was in the middle of the Kepone affair. Problems related to Kepone had preoccupied Allied executives for nearly a year and seemed to be growing rather than subsiding. Kepone was a DDT-like pesticide used in ant and roach bait in the U.S. and as a banana pest killer abroad. It looked like fine, white dust and was toxic. Between 1966 and 1973, Allied made Kepone at its Hopewell, Virginia, plant or had Kepone made for it by outside contractors. Profits were under $600,000 a year, and Allied had no health or safety problems with its Kepone production.

In early 1973 Allied needed more capacity at Hopewell for other products, so it sought bids from companies willing to produce Kepone for Allied. This was not unusual: twice before, outside contractors had made Kepone for resale by Allied. The lowest bid by far was submitted by Life Science Products (LSP), a new company owned by two former Allied employees. Both of them had been involved in the development and manufacture of Kepone. LSP leased a former gas station near the Hopewell plant, converted it, and began making Kepone in March 1974.

For 16 months, LSP produced Kepone under conditions that might have shocked Charles Dickens, according to most accounts. Brian Kelly, a reporter for the *Washington Post,* described the plant as "an incredible mess. Dust flying through the air...saturating the workers' clothing, getting into their hair, even into sandwiches they munched in production areas.... The Kepone dust sometimes blew...in clouds. A gas station operator across the street said it obscured his view of the Life Science plant.... Two firemen in a station behind Life Science say there were times when they wondered if they could see well enough to wheel their engines out in response to a fire alarm."[3]

Two months after LSP started operations, Hopewell's sewage treatment plant broke down because Kepone allegedly killed the bacteria that digested sewage. LSP employees soon developed the "Kepone shakes"; some saw doctors provided by "informal agreement"[4] with LSP, but they were diagnosed as hypertensive. This continued until July 1975, when one worker saw a Taiwanese doctor, who sent blood and urine samples to the Center for Disease Control (CDC) in Atlanta. The Kepone levels in the samples were so high that the CDC toxicologists wondered whether the samples had been contaminated in transit. The CDC notified the Virginia State epidemiologist.

Five days later, the epidemiologist examined several workers at LSP. He later said, "The first man I saw was a 23-year-old who was so sick, he was unable to stand due to unsteadiness, was suffering severe chest pains...had severe tremor, abnormal eye movements, was disoriented. . . ."[5] The next day LSP was closed by the Virginia State Health Authorities.

In early 1976 a federal grand jury in Richmond, Virginia, was called to consider the Kepone events. In May it indicted Allied, LSP, the two owners of LSP, four supervisors at Allied, and the City of Hopewell on a total of 1,104 counts. Most of the counts were misdemeanor charges. Hopewell was indicted for failing to report the massive Kepone discharges and for aiding and abetting LSP, for violating federal water pollution laws by dumping Kepone and non-Kepone wastes into the James River before 1974, and for conspiring to conceal the dumping. These cases would then be prosecuted by William B. Cummings, U.S. attorney for Virginia. Allied faced penalties of more than $17 million if convicted.

By the end of June there had been several more legal developments. Allied had publicly denied any wrongdoing. The City of Hopewell had pleaded no contest to the charges against it. Allied's attorneys favored a no contest plea on the pre-1974 dumping charges, but they were confident the company would be found innocent of the other charges. The case would not come to trial until the early fall. Allied also expected suits from the LSP workers, local fishermen, and seafood companies, as well as a large class action suit. These suits would claim damages of astronomical proportions—more than $8 billion.

The Kepone toll had been mounting week by week. The LSP workers were now out of the hospital, but more than 60 of them still reported symptoms of Kepone poisoning. (Mice fed high levels of Kepone had developed tumors that were characterized as cancerous.) The James River was closed to fishing because Kepone tends to accumulate in many species caught for seafood. The James had tens of thousands of pounds of Kepone in its bed, and sales of seafood from the Chesapeake Bay (into which the James flows) were hurt badly. A "60 Minutes" TV report on Kepone damaged Allied's image and reinforced a growing public view that chemicals equaled cancer. Finally, publicity about the Kepone incident increased the likelihood that the Toxic Substances Act would become law.

The impact of Kepone on Allied was traumatic. The company's reputation for environmental safety and responsibility seemed shattered. Settling the court cases could have a significant effect on earnings, and uncertainty about this cost would result in a qualified auditors' statement. Morale was low, and hiring had become difficult. Problems also developed in Allied's dealings with federal regulatory agencies, such as the EPA and Occupational Safety and Health Administration (OSHA). These relations depended on good faith bargaining, and Allied met with increasing skepticism and even suspicion. Costly delays resulted in getting permits for new construction. Officials feared the cost of new oxime productions facilities at Hopewell would rise more than $10 million because of these delays. (Oximes were organic chemicals used to produce biologically degradable pesticides.)

Allied management felt a strong sense of moral responsibility to the LSP workers, their families, and the Hopewell community. The company already funded research aimed at finding a way to eliminate Kepone from the bodies of the LSP workers. Allied also planned to establish a multimillion-dollar foundation to help with the Kepone cleanup and make grants for other environmental improvements.

Wagner found it hard to understand how the Kepone affair happened in the first place. Allied had made Kepone without any health or safety problems, and the LSP owners should have been able to do the same. Hopewell officials knew about the discharges when the sewage facility began having trouble, yet they took no action. The Virginia Air Quality Resources Board had an air-monitoring filter within a quarter of a mile of LSP, but it was not checking Kepone emissions. Virginia's Water Quality Control Board knew there was a serious problem in October 1974. The board did not use its authority to shut down the LSP plant but tried to use persuasion to get changes.

Federal agencies were also involved. In autumn 1974 the Occupational Safety and Health Administration received a letter from a former LSP employee, who claimed he was fired for refusing to work under unsafe conditions. OSHA responded by writing to the LSP owners. They, in turn, wrote back that there was no problem and OSHA accepted their assurances. The Environmental Protection Agency had sent an inspector to LSP in March 1975. The inspector was uncertain whether the EPA had jurisdiction over pesticides. His letter of inquiry to the EPA regional office in Philadelphia was unanswered in July when LSP was closed.

TOXIC SUBSTANCES CONTROL ACT

In less than a week, Wagner would report to Allied's executive committee on the Toxic Substances Control Act (TSCA). He had to recommend company support for the act, or opposition, or continued neutrality. A neutral stand meant Allied would keep a low profile and issue public statements saying the company supported some features of the Act and opposed others.

TSCA was a new approach to government regulation of harmful chemicals. Past legislation aimed at remedial action, while TSCA aimed at prevention. Senator James B. Pearson (R., Kansas) made this distinction:

> Existing legislation simply does not provide the means by which adverse effects on human health and the environment can be ascertained and appropriate action taken before chemical substances are first manufactured and introduced into the marketplace. At present, the only remedy available under such Federal statutes as the Clean Air Act, the Federal Water Pollution Control Act, the Occupational Safety and Health Act, and the Consumer Product Safety Act, is to impose restrictions on toxic substances after they have first been manufactured.[6]

TSCA was intended to *prevent* unreasonable risks to health and the environment. It gave the Environmental Protection Agency two new powers. The EPA could compel companies to provide information on the production, composition, uses, and health effects of the chemicals they made or processed. Using this data, the EPA could then regulate the manufacture, processing, commercial distribution, use, and disposal of the chemicals.

TSCA had three key provisions. Section 4 (testing) authorized the EPA to require testing of a chemical for any of several reasons. The reasons included clarification of health effects, toxicity, and carcinogenicity. Before requiring tests, the EPA had to show that (1) the chemical could pose an unreasonable risk to health or the environment, or that human or environmental exposure to the chemical would be substantial; (2) there was insufficient data for determining the health and environmental effects of the chemical; and (3) the only way to develop this data would be by testing the chemical. The manufacturer would pay for the testing.

The most controversial provision of TSCA was section 5—premarket notification. This required a manufacturer to report its intent to produce any new chemical to the EPA 90 days before doing so. A manufacturer had to make similar notice of plans to produce a chemical for a "significant new use." These reports had to disclose the chemical's name, chemical identity and molecular structure, its proposed categories of use, the amount to be made, its manufacturing by-products, and its disposal. The manufacturer was also required to submit available data on health and environmental effects.

If the EPA found that there was not enough information to judge the health or environmental effects, it could prohibit or limit the manufacture, distribution, or use of the chemical until adequate information was provided. This was the third key provision of TSCA. It gave the EPA broad new powers to regulate the operations of more than 115,000 establishments that made or processed chemicals. TSCA also directed the EPA to weigh the costs and benefits of the testing and regulations that it required under these new powers.

Wagner had to sort out a number of complicated issues to make his decision. He had to ask whether, as a citizen, he thought TSCA was in the public interest. As an Allied executive, he had to consider how support for TSCA would affect Allied's image and how the Act itself would affect Allied's chemical business. This last question was especially difficult since TSCA could help business in some ways and hurt it in others. For example, TSCA might cut the chances of another Kepone incident. The costs of testing and reporting might give large chemical companies, like Allied, a competitive edge over smaller firms. But these costs would also hurt Allied's bottom line and make chemical products, particularly new ones, less competitive with natural products. Wagner had his assistant, a recent graduate of a leading eastern business school, summarize the major arguments for and against TSCA. The assistant's report is presented in the following two sections.

For TSCA

1. TSCA closes gaps in current laws. The act will require testing *before* exposure, so workers and communities will not be used as guinea pigs.
2. TSCA's cost will be low. The EPA and the General Services Administration estimate total costs to industry of $100–200 million a year. Industry sales exceed $100 billion a year.
3. TSCA will reduce national health care costs by preventing some of the health effects of harmful chemicals. Care for cancer patients alone now costs more than $18 billion per year.

4. Under current laws, the incidence of cancer has been rising and many chemical disasters and near-disasters have occurred.
5. The act offers protection for the interests of chemical companies. When companies disagree with EPA regulations, they can file a timely law suit and seek a court injunction.
6. TSCA may reduce the risks of doing business in chemicals. The act may, in effect, put a "government seal of approval" on hazardous chemicals. It could also cut the risk of a company being sued because a customer used its products in a dangerous way.
7. Public support for the act will help restore Allied's image as a responsible community-minded company.
8. The act is likely to pass this year, so Allied might as well get on the bandwagon. The Senate has already passed the act and the current version lacks several features that caused House opposition in past years. Public pressure for passage is building, especially in the wake of the Kepone headlines. The membership of the Manufacturing Chemists Association, the major industry trade group, is split over the act.

Against TSCA

1. The industry is already sufficiently regulated. Twenty-seven major federal laws now cover almost every aspect of company operations. Large chemical companies like Allied already deal with more than 70 government agencies.
2. Companies already do extensive testing of chemicals before marketing them. The tests sometimes cost several hundred thousand dollars and take several years. They are performed by highly trained scientists working in the most modern labs. Furthermore, companies have a strong incentive to do sufficient testing: they want to avoid the many heavy costs imposed by incidents like Kepone.
3. TSCA will be extremely costly. Dow puts the cost at $2 billion annually; the Manufacturing Chemists Association estimates $800 million to $1.3 billion. There will be less innovation because of excessive testing burdens on new chemicals. U.S. chemical exports will become more costly and less competitive, U.S. jobs will move overseas, and the testing and reporting requirements will hurt or even close many small companies. This will also affect large companies like Allied. We rely on small companies as suppliers, and Allied itself is basically a composite of 60 or 70 small specialty chemical companies.
4. The act is dangerously vague. The EPA gets very broad powers with few restrictions.
5. Reporting to the EPA under TSCA will require us to disclose trade secrets and other confidential data.
6. Supporting the act to aid our image or get on a bandwagon won't fool many people. It will be taken as a public relations move and could raise even more suspicions about Allied's motives.
7. It's not even clear there's a bandwagon. The Senate passed the act in 1972 and 1973 and the House killed it both times. Even though the EPA is lobbying hard for TSCA, the Commerce Department and the Office of Management and Budget oppose it. There is as yet no indication whether President Ford will sign or veto the act.
8. Many of the reports of chemical "disasters" have been exaggerated by the media and by environmental groups. We should not give in to pressures based on this sort of misinformation.

TOTAL PRODUCT RESPONSIBILITY

Wagner also had to decide whether to implement a new program called Total Product Responsibility (TPR). This program had been developed in 1975 by the engineering and operations services unit in the Specialty Chemicals Division. This 17-person staff unit developed policies and procedures related to health, safety, maintenance, and quality control (see Figure B). TPR would use "tools of policy, procedure, control, and review" to help Allied "properly discharge its legal and moral responsibility to protect its employees, customers, the public, and the environment from harm."

TPR was first proposed in 1975 by R. L. Merrill, vice president of engineering and operations services. Merrill had come to Allied after several years with Dow Chemical and was impressed by Dow's Product Stewardship Program. According to *Business Week,* product stewardship meant Dow would assume "total responsibility for how its products affect people" and Dow's products would carry "a virtual guarantee of harmlessness."[7] Dow had 600 people involved in setting up product stewardship in 1972. They prepared environmental and safety profiles for all 1,100 of Dow's products. Then film cassettes were made for presentations to Dow employees, customers, and distributors. In its first year, product stewardship cost $1 million.

Merrill's original proposal was not for a program as extensive as Dow's. Merrill had suggested a survey of information currently available to Allied on the health and environmental effects of its products. This survey would then be followed by whatever tests were needed to supplement existing information. But during 1975 and early 1976, an expanded TPR slowly took shape around this original suggestion. If it was important to get complete health and safety information about Allied's products, it also seemed important to get similar information on raw materials, processes, and customer uses of Allied products. And, in turn, it seemed important to make sure all this information was reflected in Allied's everyday operating procedures.

The first step in implementing TPR would be for Wagner to issue a 25-page memorandum on TPR to all management personnel in his division. The memo would set out standards of operating and business practice that covered virtually every aspect of division operations. Line management would then have to make sure that operating procedures conformed to these standards. The following excerpts are from the TPR memorandum.

Specifications: Specifications should exist for every raw material...and every finished product.... No specifications may be changed without the approval of the director of operations/general manager after review with operations services.

Testing: All of the division's products will be reviewed on a priority basis, as determined by our toxicology specialists, to determine the known or suspected undesirable toxic effects which those products may have on our employees, customers, the public, and the environment.

Plant SOPs: Standard operating procedures will be developed by plants for each product area. Procedures will be designed by engineering, technical, and operations groups to provide capability of producing uniform product quality and to ensure process continuity. Use of approved procedures will be mandatory and

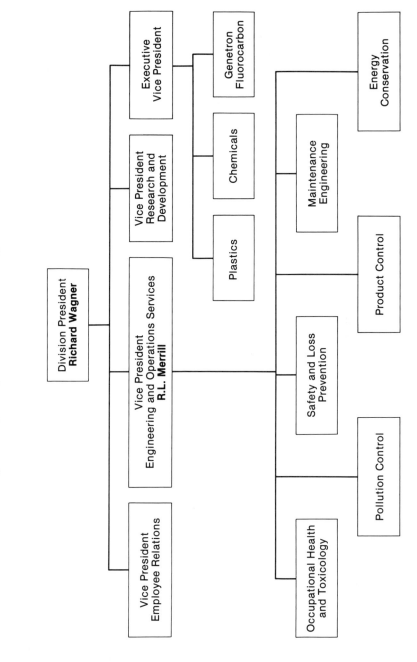

Figure B   Specialty Chemicals Division Organization Chart

revisions to accepted methods will require approval of preestablished authority levels.

Equipment Testing: Testing procedures and frequencies are to be developed to insure reliability of equipment at the 95 percent confidence level to minimize the possibility of unforeseen problems arising.

Change Procedure: Changes in R&D, product development, manufacturing, distribution, and marketing that may adversely affect the process, employees, product, customer, the public, or the environment should not be made without the approval of the director of operations, director of marketing, or research laboratory director, as appropriate, and after review with operations services.

Technical Bulletins: Technical literature and bulletins should include all safety and environmental statements necessary to protect employees, customers, the public, and the environment. Operations services is to receive, edit, and approve all literature and bulletins to assure that all such proper statements are included.

Advertising: Advertising copy should reflect true and accurate statements about our products. Advertising copy should be reviewed by operations services to prevent misleading statements concerning claims in the areas of environmental products' safety, health, and quality assurance.

Product End Use: Marketing departments should make every effort to determine the end-user application of each product sold. Consideration should be given to the desirability of using the product in that application and the customers's understanding of the effect of such use on the operation.... A product should not be sold to a customer where it is known that the end-use application is not proper.

Capability of Existing Customers: Marketing departments have the responsibility to establish the capability of our customers concerning their competency to handle our products in a manner that protects the customers' process, employees, the public, and the environment. Hazardous products should not be sold to customers whose capability is deemed inadequate. If it is determined that an application or end use of the product is improper... the sales of this product to that customer should be discontinued immediately.

New Customers: Hazardous products should not be sold to new customers until the capability of that customer is deemed adequate.

Outside Contractors: When outside contractors are to be used to process, reprocess, repackage, or manufacture materials for us, the review should include a determination of the toxicity and hazards of the materials to be handled, and an in-depth study of the contractor's capability to perform the work such as not to endanger the contractor's employees, the public, or the environment.... When a contractor is retained, it is the responsibility of the appropriate business area to arrange for periodic inspections and reviews of that contractor's operations by the operations services department.

Wagner had distributed the draft memo within the Specialty Chemicals Division and discussed the program with a variety of line and staff personnel. Reaction was mixed. Leonard Warren, director of marketing services, said:

> I don't know where I come down on this. I know that chemical companies are getting burned in the newspapers and in court, and the result is more and more government people telling us how to do business. We've got to stop this, but we've also got to make money. As I read TPR, it says we're going to say "no" to some people who want to buy from us. We'll also be harrassing our current customers and prospects by asking them how they use our products, who they sell to, and what their customers do with their products. Some of them are going to tell us to keep our noses out of their businesses. A lot of our products are virtually commodities and they're already hard enough to sell without the burdens of TPR paperwork, TPR costs, and the mixed signals we'll be giving to our reps.
>
> Now I'm not completely opposed to TPR in some form. After Kepone, it will make Allied's reputation a little better. There are probably some customers that we shouldn't sell to, because they're too risky, and this program will help us get rid of them. In some cases, it might even help sales because it would be a reason for our reps to have even further contacts with customers, and more information about uses of our products could be a useful kind of market research for us.

Another hesitant view came from Joe DeStefano, a production manager at the Hopewell complex:

> My first reaction is that we already do a lot of the things in the TPR memo. The difference is that our current procedures are not formalized and we don't have to get as much clearance before making changes. I can't help wondering whether TPR isn't going to make business a lot more bureaucratic. It seems to me that the government already does enough of that. Under TPR, we would have to go through operations services to do almost anything. We could end up with more paperwork, buck-passing, and bureaucracy. Sometimes I'm not sure what's more important: getting a good product out the door at a profit or complying with a thousand rules and restrictions.

Janet Baker, an associate corporate counsel who handled environmental cases, supported TPR:

> Allied has to do something like TPR. Kepone costs are skyrocketing and we can't afford to let another Kepone happen. TPR sends a clear message throughout the division that health and safety are top priority. We've sent the message before, but it needs vigorous emphasis. If we don't take steps to run our business as safely as possible, the government will do it for us.
>
> But there are problems. Customers and suppliers could well resent our sanctimonious attitude when we poke our noses into their businesses. Refusals to deal have to be handled unilaterally and without publicity or else we may be liable for conspiracy allegations, antitrust, trade disparagement, or libel suits.

Despite these objections and misgivings, Merrill remained enthusiastic about TPR; he argued:

Of course TPR won't be free of problems, but it does much more good than harm. It will help our image and cut our risk of environmental and safety problems. Besides the government is likely to require most of what's in TPR in just a few years. By starting now, Allied can learn to do business under these inevitable new conditions.

  It's also absolutely essential that the attitude of Allied managers and workers toward the government start to change. The government is going to be a major factor in the chemical industry for the indefinite future. We can either take an adversary approach and comply with regulations in a minimal, grudging way or we can recognize that the government is here to stay, learn to cooperate with federal agencies and, as a result, get better results in regulatory proceedings and lower our risks of future Kepones.

In making his decision, Wagner also had to consider the views of Allied's chairman and the executive committee. There was strong support among these executives for "some concrete steps" that would prevent another Kepone and change company attitudes toward government health and environmental rules. At the same time, Wagner could not ignore his division's earnings and performance. In the summer of 1976, sales were weakening as a result of the recession that began in 1975. Wagner wondered if this was the right time to divert managerial time and attention from the chemical business. He was also concerned about the possible impact of TPR on the flexibility, decentralized decision making, and innovation he had been trying to encourage in his division. He also wondered whether TPR would have kept the Kepone problem from happening in the first place.

FURTHER DEVELOPMENTS

Since 1976 was an election year, Wagner had been paying some attention to the positions candidates took on regulation in general and the chemical industry in particular. Senator Vance Hartke (D., Indiana), who then faced a serious reelection challenge, campaigned hard for greater regulation of chemicals. One of his speeches included the following remarks:

> The hazards associated with chemicals like PCB's, vinyl chloride, BCME, and asbestos have all dramatically illustrated how important it is to get early warning with respect to new chemical substances. . . .
> During this (last) five-year period, there have been in excess of one million deaths in this country from cancer. Over a million infants have been born with physical or mental damage. . . . While many of the grave health risks to human beings have declined in recent years, cancer statistics have done just the opposite. In fact, the incidence of cancer was estimated in 1975 to be some $2\frac{1}{2}$ percent above the previous year. . . .
> It is no accident that the hot spots for cancer in this country are in close proximity to those locations where the chemical industry is most highly concentrated.
> . . . It is tragic that those who rely upon the industry for jobs have essentially become guinea pigs for discovering the adverse effects of chemical substances. It is also tragic that much of the information which has shown the cancer-producing potential of many chemicals has come from death records of employees. For example, of one million current and former American asbestos workers who still

survive, fully 300,000 have been projected to die of cancer. This death rate is 50 percent higher than that of the U.S. population at large.[8]

At the same time, Wagner was also aware of growing opposition to government regulation. The leading presidential contenders then—Ford, Carter, and Reagan—all sounded the theme of "too much government interference." Academic studies had documented the large indirect costs of regulation and even reformers like Ralph Nader were very critical of agencies such as the FTC, which Nader said was basically a captive of the industries it regulated. Industry also joined this movement against regulation. Dow Chemical, for example, announced completion of its own "catalogue of regulatory horrors" and claimed it had spent $50 million in 1975 to meet regulations it considered excessive.[9]

ENDNOTES

1. "Risk Rewarded," *Forbes*, March 15, 1977, p. 101.
2. Ibid.
3. Christopher D. Stone, "A Slap on the Wrist for the Kepone Mob," *Business and Society Review* (Summer 1977), p. 4.
4. Ibid., p. 5.
5. Ibid., p. 6.
6. Library of Congress, *Legislative History of the Toxic Substances Control Act* (Washington, D.C.: Government Printing Office, 1976), p. 215
7. "Dow's Big Push for Product Safety," *Business Week*, April 21, 1973, p. 82.
8. Library of Congress, *Legislative History of the Toxic Substances Act,* p. 216.
9. "Dow Chemical's Catalogue of Regulatory Horrors," *Business Week*, April 4, 1977, p. 50.

The Health Industry Manufacturers Association

Burton A. Dole, Jr., chief executive officer of Puritan-Bennett Corporation of Kansas City, Missouri, would shortly become chairman of the board of the Health Industry Manufacturers Association (HIMA) in March 1989. The Washington-based industry association represented some 300 members (see Exhibit 1). Dole had a long interest and involvement in public affairs, especially in efforts to reduce the soaring costs of product liability suits. His company specialized in the manufacture of anesthesia equipment and medical ventilators.

Dole wondered what HIMA's strategy should be in the years ahead. Although he had high regard for Frank Samuel, the association's innovative president, he was concerned that Samuel's cooperative approach to government relations might be losing support among the membership. He also feared that it might be in trouble in Congress, where HIMA had agreed to the passage of a crucial piece of regulatory legislation only to be repudiated by three of its most powerful members. The consequence appeared to be stringent new controls in the near future. Relations with the principal government regulatory agencies in the health field appeared to be cooperative at the top, but relations at the working level were somewhat chilly.

Could a group of companies as varied as HIMA's members combine effectively for *any* useful purpose? Could HIMA have a strategy worthy of the name? If the answer to that was possibly yes, then what should it be? Who should determine it and how should it be implemented? Dole believed that the success of the industry depended significantly on how it answered these questions. Clearly the future was going to be even more difficult than the past. Intensifying foreign competition would see to that.

These were the thoughts that were going through Dole's head as he prepared for his first meeting as chairman of HIMA's board. (See Exhibit 2 for list of board members.)

THE ASSOCIATION

The Health Industry Manufacturers Association represented a wide range of companies that developed and manufactured more than 90 percent of the medical devices, diagnostics, and health care information systems in the United States. Their products ranged from Band-Aids and tongue depressors to dialysis machines and artificial hearts—in short, from bedpans to brainscans. Member companies included billion-dollar giants like Johnson & Johnson, Pfizer, IBM, and General Electric. Eighty percent of the membership, however, consisted of smaller compan-

Professor George C. Lodge prepared this case as the basis for class discussion rather than to illustrate either effective or ineffective handling of an administrative situation.

ies with less than $20 million in domestic sales. Most of the large companies had their own Washington offices that handled relations with the federal government, but for the smaller members HIMA was their only conduit. Membership dues were structured by sales and large companies essentially controlled HIMA's board of directors.

HIMA consistently sought cooperative relationships with government, especially with the Food and Drug Administration (FDA), the Health Care Financing Administration (HCFA), and the House and Senate committees on health. The association began in 1976, when the Food, Drug, and Cosmetic Act was amended to extend FDA regulation in the medical area beyond drugs to "devices." (The former metabolize in the body while the latter do not.) The FDA determined what was safe and effective; the HCFA decided what would be paid for under Medicare, the government's $80 billion-a-year health plan for elderly and disabled Americans. These two government agencies thus played a central role in the health industry's development. HIMA was concerned that the ability of its membership to compete effectively in the world economy might be threatened by the actions of the two agencies unless they were carefully coordinated and managed and unless both agencies were fully aware of and sensitive to the problems and capabilities of the industry.

Dr. Richard W. Young, CEO of Mentor O & O, Inc., a manufacturer of diagnostic and surgical equipment for eye care with $12 million in sales, was chairman of HIMA's Smaller Company Advisory Committee and a member of the board of directors. "Small companies in particular get a great deal of help from HIMA. It's impossible for us to keep up with the latest HCFA regulations, for example. We have to rely on HIMA experts. Somebody calls me up from California, let's say, and tells me that a piece of our equipment has been rejected for payments under Medicare. I wouldn't know where to go, but the HIMA people can make a few quick phone calls and get an answer."

ORGANIZATION AND PURPOSE

In 1984 HIMA's board of directors chose Frank E. Samuel, Jr., to serve as president. A graduate of Harvard Law School (1965), Samuel came to work for the Agency for International Development in the Kennedy administration, part of a new generation committed to the ideals of more effective government. In 1968 he moved to a private law firm, and then on to a four-year stint at the Department of Health, Education, and Welfare. He joined HIMA as general counsel in 1975.

As president, Samuel increased HIMA's staff from 39 to 51, recruiting some highly skilled and experienced talent from government, such as Ted R. Mannen, senior vice president for policy, who had been legislative assistant to Sen. Adlai Stevenson (D., Ill.) (See Exhibit 3 for list of staff and area assignments.) Samuel was given high marks from many of the government officials with whom he worked. One House aide said: "He's put together a top-notch staff . . . not just competent, but free from the 'obnoxiousities' typical of most trade groups." Another added: "He is effective because he is honest and straightforward and presents information for my use that is helpful." Helen Darling, health staff assistant to Sen. David Durenberger (R., Minn.), called Samuel "a true leader—intelligent, knows the field, has style and insight. He has made HIMA a model Washington trade association."

Samuel believed that the U.S. regulatory system needed "retooling to meet certain agreed-upon national objectives. One goal of the regulatory framework should be to get new medical technology products to patients as quickly as possible consistent with public safety. Second, the medical device and diagnostics industry contributes to U.S. international competitiveness and should be encouraged."

Acknowledging the contribution of "the FDA imprimatur" to public confidence in a product, he felt that the time which the agency takes to approve new products could be greatly shortened. (In 1988 it was nine months, four months shorter than in 1986.) "But what's really needed," he said, "is a basic change in the philosophical concept of the regulatory relationship between device manufacturers and the FDA."

He called for a radical change in attitude. "The FDA has to get off its high horse; it's not morally or scientifically superior to industry. Congress needs to act responsibly; headlines do not improve health unless they reward innovation. And the industry has to give up its dolls and needles and do a better job of working closely with the FDA regulators. Industry should be prepared from the CEO level down to cooperate and initiate, not just react and complain."[1]

John A. Gilmartin, CEO of Millipore and another HIMA board member, endorsed Frank Samuel's approach to government relations but was pessimistic about its chances of prevailing.

> It's the only sensible way to go, but look at what he's up against. First there is the diversity of HIMA's membership. The big pharmaceutical companies have long had adversarial relations with FDA over drugs, and that extends into devices even though the two are very different. A drug doesn't change. New ones come along but the old ones remain. Devices change all the time; they evolve. The pacemaker of today is very different from the one 10 years ago. So with devices ongoing cooperation is essential. But old habits change slowly and the big companies have their own Washington offices—lobbyists. These company representatives are kind of a Bedouin tribe in Washington. They are pros trying to get done what the boss wants. They may have some influence back at headquarters but not much. They are generally not in on the strategy making. They are implementers. They may have good relations with HIMA's staff but they still have to obey headquarters where the old assumptions are often still very much intact. So they run around HIMA anytime they want.

B. Kristine Johnson, vice president for public affairs, public relations, and corporate planning of Medtronic, had this to say:

> What Frank has really brought to HIMA is the realization that the industry must be involved in a broad array of issues which go well beyond—but eventually affect— short-term, narrow interests of particular companies. If the industry is going to have a place at the policy table, we have to be interested in and knowledgeable about the big picture—reducing the federal deficit, health policy generally, United States competitiveness. Company interests, after all, are but a subset of these larger questions.

Leah Schroeder, HIMA vice president for government affairs and a former congressional administrative assistant, added: "Our goal is to ensure that any time a health policy issue is being considered in the White House, the Office of Management and Budget, the Department of Health and Human Services, or the Congress, we will get a call at HIMA to come and help."

On the other hand, some like Robert M. Moliter, manager of government programs for GE's Medical Systems group, felt that Samuel "fails to recognize the inherent tensions between the regulators and regulated which are quite proper and which are designed into the system." He also questioned whether HIMA was "really as macro as it should be. Take Medicare, for example, I think we should be out there with the hospitals lobbying against excessive cuts." Moliter was chairman of HIMA's government and public affairs section, composed of representatives of 24 association members (see Exhibit 2).

Samuel estimated that about 30 percent of his membership agreed with his call for a more cooperative approach, some because they were genuinely enthusiastic, and others because "you attract flies with honey." About 20 percent, he thought, were negative, "feeling that things are fine as they are, don't rock the boat. If we were more forthcoming we would give the government new ideas about how to regulate us and would be forced to disclose our secrets. Let sleeping dogs lie. We also have antitrust fears, and believe that in general government equals grief—the less we have to do with it the better." The remaining 50 percent were, he felt, essentially indifferent.

Among the enthusiasts was HIMA's long-time board member Ben L. Holmes, vice president/general manager, Hewlett-Packard Medical Products Group, which had 4,000 employees manufacturing electromedical devices such as monitors, ultrasound imaging equipment, electrocardiographs, and advanced computer systems for medical use. HP had an exemplary record with the FDA. Holmes explained why his company needed HIMA.

> First, it imposes discipline on us. It's sort of like school. You have to read the studies HIMA prepares. You have to prepare for the meetings, seminars, and conferences. That keeps us on our toes and up to date.
>
> Second, Hewlett-Packard benefits when the industry standards are high—the higher the better for us. HIMA membership includes all the major players. It imposes pressure on all its members to do their very best. That's good for us. It protects us from fly-by-nights.

THE FOOD AND DRUG ADMINISTRATION

The FDA regulated safety standards for all drugs, most of the food that was eaten, cosmetics, health equipment, and devices and materials ranging from gauze bandages to pacemakers. Products under FDA regulation came from 90,000 companies and represented $550 billion, or one-quarter of the U.S. gross national product. FDA spent $550 million a year—$2 per American—and had 7,000 employees. Like HCFA, it was part of the Department of Health and Human Services (HHS) and had two functions imposed by Congress: product approval and ensuring good manufacturing practices.

Medical device regulation was first authorized in the Federal Food, Drug, and Cosmetic Act of 1938, but was greatly strengthened by amendments to that act passed in 1976. These amendments were the result of numerous injuries reported in the early 1970s as a result of fraudulent and hazardous use of medical devices. They required medical device manufacturers to register and list their products annually, to submit to regular inspections of their manufacturing practices, to make periodic reports on product experience, and to submit new devices for premarket approval (PMA). According to Section 510(k) of the amendments, "new" devices could not be marketed until they had received a PMA or had been classified as Class I or II products, meaning that they were less risky than those placed in the Class III category. Firms were required to notify the FDA 90 days before marketing a device that was not sold prior to the enactment of the 1976 amendments. There was considerable controversy over the meaning of the word "new" in Section 510(k).

To obtain a PMA, a manufacturer had to satisfy the FDA that its product was both safe and effective. (In 1986, 5,153 PMA and 510(k) submissions were filed with FDA, double the number filed in 1977.) The manufacturer could contend and the FDA could agree that a product was not new, in that it was substantially the same as a product manufactured before the amendments were passed. In such a case FDA approval was not required. (Original PMAs were reviewed in an average of 337 days during 1987, down from 395 days in 1986.)

HIMA worked hard to help the FDA be more effective. In 1986, for example, the association lobbied Congress to provide the FDA with an additional $800,000 that the Office of Management and Budget had not allowed it to request. The funds were earmarked for product approval. Again in 1987 HIMA was instrumental in Congress appropriating an extra $2 million above the OMB-imposed FDA limit. The following year it supported an FDA request for an additional $1.3 million, and also sought to recover for FDA regulatory authority which during the Reagan years had slipped to the states.

In 1988 James Benson was acting deputy commissioner of FDA. Before that he had been deputy director of FDA's Center for Devices and Radiological Health, HIMA's interface with the agency. He said:

> Samuel is a good man and I'm in favor of the concept he is advocating [emphasizing the word concept]. Take, for example, home blood-glucose monitors which allow diabetics to regulate the flow of insulin they are taking. This device required the most intimate cooperation between our people and the industry. Its safety and effectiveness depend not only on the device itself, but also on how well the patients using the device are educated. We have to be concerned and involved in both areas.
>
> But there are serious problems. Right now we're being investigated by Congressman John Dingell's Oversight Committee[2] and by the inspector general of HHS for the alleged misbehavior of an employee in the generic drug area. The employee is suspected of arranging for a company to be moved up on the waiting list for approval in return for a gift. This is a serious offense. It's taken half my time for the past two weeks. If Dingell holds hearings on this, the whole agency will tend to increase its distance from companies. Our integrity is absolutely critical; we cherish our reputation. We must.
>
> There are 3,000 FDA inspectors in the field. They see themselves as cops. They are concerned that cooperation with industry might taint their integrity. I believe much more can be accomplished by working with business as partners but it takes a

while to change the old practices. If we don't do better, frankly I'm worried that our industry will go down the tubes in the face of competition from countries such as Japan where industry and government work much more closely together. Their approval times are much shorter than ours and their products are often better. I don't know how they do it but it sure works well.

Benson accused the industry—including HIMA—of sometimes being excessively rigid and legalistic. "One-half of the product recalls we find are due to bad design, not manufacture. So we put out guidelines—just guidelines, nothing more—on product design. HIMA complained that there had been no due process, no industry participation in drafting the guidelines, no hearings, and so on."

On the other hand, he spoke approvingly of HIMA's educational programs for its membership and the numerous workshops, seminars and conferences where FDA regulators and industry people get together to discuss common problems. "They have been very helpful. They serve as a useful clearinghouse for information. HIMA has also helped us a great deal on the Hill with our appropriations. They realize that if we are to give them timely PMAs, we need the staff to do the work."

Regarding FDA's relationship with the other government agency critical to the health industry's future, HCFA, Benson admitted that they did not work closely together. "It's a turf problem. We should be much more involved in each other's decision making. I wish industry would help us here but I find that particularly the big companies are unwilling to use their clout for such bureaucratic purposes. I guess they fear a backlash."

Dr. Kshitij Mohan, director of the Office of Device Evaluation, said:

Samuel is reaching for a team approach. There's nothing wrong with that, but it's kind of nebulous. Do we have a common goal with industry? If so, what is it? Our goal is public health. What's industry's? It's profits and often quick profits. Let's face it, we have different roles.

The United States is not like Japan. The medical device regulatory group in the Japanese government has fewer than a dozen people; we have 800. But in Japan government and industry are synergistic. Business respects government, looks to government for standards and even leadership, helps government, and government respects business. They are extensions of one another. Here we believe in a separation of roles, due process, adversary proceedings, and the rest. Our society is distrustful of collaboration between government and business. Congress would never allow close collaboration, neither would consumer groups. So we must maintain an essential tension between the FDA and the industry. But having said that I think there is substantial room for more cooperation and interaction. Here I agree with Samuel.

He cited a number of steps which he thought should be taken:

We should get together with the company earlier. As soon as a company starts to think about a new product, they should involve us. When they are designing prototypes, they should know our requirements. Quality should be built in. And we can learn from them as well.

Companies, especially the small ones, are so eager to hit the market that they don't pay enough attention to quality. Here again the Japanese are impressive.

If a company has a failed device, they should admit it straightaway and get it off the market. They shouldn't pretend and try to squeak by. That wastes everybody's time and erodes trust.

Walter E. Gundaker, director of the Office of Compliance, Center for Devices and Radiological Health, oversaw 75 field investigators whose task was to assure good manufacturing practices among HIMA members. "We see three kind of companies," he said. "Those who are way out of line, those who are always good, and then a middle group that may swing one way or the other. Our job is to get the violators. We are cops, let's face it. How close do you want us to get to those whom we are supposed to police?"

He continued:

We want companies to monitor their failures and to analyze the trends which the data show. They argue that that's not part of the regulations and we can't force them to do it. Some companies are, of course, outstanding. They do what they're supposed to do and we have good relations, but many fight us every inch.

HIMA has been very helpful, but there's lots of room for more cooperation. Take defibrillators, those pads used to shock heart attack victims. Often they malfunction because of bad batteries. They lie around the fire house or somewhere and nobody checks the batteries. It's not the manufacturer's fault, but they often get the blame. Here we need an education program for users which should involve the manufacturers as well as us.

THE HEALTH CARE FINANCING ADMINISTRATION

At the same time as federal regulation of medical devices increased, the government also became more actively involved in deciding which health services would be paid for through Medicare and Medicaid.[3] For HIMA "these programs symbolized a national commitment to assuring quality health care for all Americans. And they encouraged investment in research that led to advances in medical technology and practice virtually unimaginable two decades ago."[4]

In the early 1980s, however, this commitment was threatened by rising costs[5] and federal budget constraints. By 1987 these costs had reached an estimated $496.6 billion, or about $5 a day for each American. The most dramatic cost containment effort was Medicare's shift in 1983 to a "prospective payment system" (PPS), setting the payment rates for hospitals before treatment was provided instead of paying for the actual costs afterwards. The payment system was administered by HCFA, which placed all medical problems into "diagnosis-related groups" (DRGs), establishing a fixed payment for each group. This payment covered *all* services and supplies provided to Medicare patients.

Robert Streimer, HCFA associate administrator, explained some of the complexities:

Adjustment to the PPS rates went well beyond HCFA just saying "yes" or "no" to a particular device. HCFA could say, for example, "Yes, this new artificial hip is covered. It goes to the DRG 210, but the payment rate for that DRG will not change." It might take anywhere from 18 to 24 months before the PPS rate formulas would recognize that a new and presumably more expensive hip was being routinely used in DRG 210. In some cases, a service or device might be so unique that it didn't fit into a DRG, in which case a separate pricing judgment would have to be made. Cochlear implants or heart transplants for example.

HCFA decided what medical devices could be paid for by Medicare, and increasingly HCFA's policies were being followed by other Medicare contractors such as Blue Cross/Blue Shield and commercial insurers. As a consequence, those policies were a significant factor in determining hospitals' decisions concerning expensive medical equipment. Recent coverage review times varied from about nine months for an implantable automatic defibrillator to five and a half years for a phrenic nerve stimulator.

HIMA was concerned that budget pressures on Medicare might discourage or delay innovation in medical technology. In 1986 Medicare consumed about 7 percent of the federal budget; in 1988, however, it was 8 percent, and by 1993 it would be more than 10 percent even if no new benefits were added.[6] (See Table 1.)

Table 1   Medicare Outlays, 1968–1992 Proj.

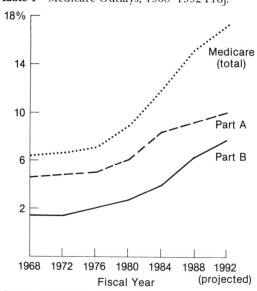

Source: Congressional Budget Office.

Medicare's Growth

This chart shows Medicare outlays as a percentage of all federal nondefense spending except interest payments on the national debt. Medicare outlays are shown in total, as well as broken down into outlays for Part A, the hospital program, and Part B, the outpatient program. Most Part B outlays go for doctors' services. (Totals may not add up because of rounding.)

HIMA negotiated with HCFA on whether and how to incorporate new technologies into the payments system. This was a complex and subtle process that had to take into account the range of possible technologies, and balance their short- and long-run costs and benefits, their social and economic value, and the interests of patients, taxpayers, and the economy in general.

Dr. William Roper, administrator of HCFA, said, "We have to ask how cost effective a particular device is." HCFA would not, for example, cover an experimental device. Take a therapeutic implantable pump for cancer patients which was installed surgically and injected drugs regularly to obviate the need for chemotherapy. It was expensive in the short run but over the long run saved money. Under HCFA rules, a hospital would have to pay for this product initially. If the pump became accepted as a proven form of treatment, hospitals would report back that they were using the pump and that their costs were greater. "We would then increase the DRG payment accordingly," said Dr. Roper. "Generally it takes from 18 to 24 months for the billing information for a new device to be reflected in the DRG rates."

Dr. Roper's response to HIMA's contention that this procedure discourages innovation was that it "encourages innovation in cost saving." He added, however, "I am concerned at the margins. We look at things as they come along. It is hard for us to take a long view. Our accounting practices don't work that way. We need to have a better way of looking at long-run costs. Take bone growth stimulators, for example, which are costly to begin with but which speed up the healing of broken bones. We don't have a very good way of thinking about these kinds of things. We also need to think more about which technology works best for which kinds of patients. What works in one case may not in another."

Dr. Roper was generally not concerned about the competitiveness of the U.S. industry. "I've just come back from Europe. We are still the premier developer in health equipment. We devote 11 percent of our GNP to health care. That's more than any other country. So I think we're doing pretty well."

Both Dr. Roper and Streimer, spoke enthusiastically about Samuel's work: "He wants to deal in public policy issues instead of only those matters which directly affect his industry. He tries to help us do our job better. For example, the other day he was in here with executives from four of his member companies which make software for health information systems. He wasn't trying to sell us anything. He pointed out that these companies provide hospitals with information systems which are able to collect a lot of information that would be helpful to us in measuring the clinical outcomes of various technologies. He was suggesting that we talk to the hospital information systems people about getting data to help us contain costs better. In some instances, of course, this might alert us to inefficiencies—instances, for example, where some product might be overutilized—and this in turn might actually adversely affect one of HIMA's members."

Dr. Roper saw many areas where more cooperation would be desirable, however: "We have a major problem with decubitus ulcers (bed sores). These are very common among old people who are bedridden. They are painful, dangerous, and when they get infected, expensive. They are a primary reason for old people being forced into nursing homes, and thus account for a huge cost to us. But neither the government nor the industry had addressed the problem. Some companies I suppose make money out of bed sores. Then HIMA put together a coordinated industry approach. New products were developed, including beds which continually move the patient, and special pads. Samuel looks at health problems systemically, from our point of view. He's helped us to find common ground with the industry."

The interactive approach with Samuel, described by Dr. Roper, was less well accepted by the lower levels of the HCFA bureaucracy where analysts and rulemakers tended to regard themselves as the enemies of business, perceived to be reaping huge profits at the taxpayers' expense. Furthermore, the company people with whom bureaucrats dealt were invariably rigid and legalistic, often reporting to the general counsel in the firm, who had little technical knowledge or concern.

OTHER GOVERNMENT AGENCIES

Another important interface between HIMA and government related to world competition and trade. U.S. medical device and diagnostic products historically were strong competitors in the world marketplace; in fact, the United States exported more medical technology than any other nation. But the $1 billion trade surplus which the industry enjoyed in 1981 had been cut in half by 1987, and 1988 brought continued substantial deficits with both Germany and Japan in spite of the lowered value of the dollar.[7]

Japan presented a special problem to HIMA. Although Japanese imports into the United States in 1987 were only 3.1 percent of the market, they were double what they had been six years earlier. At the same time, a web of regulation effectively prevented access for U.S. medical equipment makers to Japanese markets. For example, until 1985 and partially even thereafter, Japan required that all test data submitted in support of product approval applications be generated from clinical trials in Japan on Japanese citizens. HIMA has sought and received help from the United States Trade Representative's office (USTR) in pressing Japan to open up.

HIMA staff were also increasingly involved in Europe. In Germany most health equipment was purchased by cities and towns for their hospitals. "They are loyal to Mother Siemens," said Bob Moliter of GE. "It would be unpatriotic to be otherwise." The French government was also extremely reluctant to buy any health equipment not made in France. And as Europe headed towards unity in 1992, the harmonization of health regulations was important to HIMA.

Association staff also worked closely with the Congress and the Department of Commerce to get relief from crippling export controls imposed by the United States for security reasons on many high-technology products such as ultrasound fetal monitors, blood flow detectors, heart monitors, blood analyzers and computerized tomography (CT) scanners. While most applications for relief eventually received approval, the industry's foreign competitors used the delay to get a substantial competitive edge.

THE MEDICAL DEVICE IMPROVEMENT ACT OF 1988

As 1988 came to a close, there was reason to believe that the close and cooperative relationships which Samuel had sought to create, especially with the Congress, were in jeopardy. Some key House members and particularly their staff assistants felt a sense of betrayal. Following months of negotiations with HIMA staff, the House passed a bill tightening and expanding FDA regulation of the medical equipment industry and sent it to the Senate for approval. It was endorsed in a letter from Frank Samuel to Sen. Edward M. Kennedy (D., Mass.), chairman of the Committee on Labor and Human Resources, which handled health matters in the Senate, and Sen. Orrin Hatch (R., Utah), ranking Republican on the committee. At the same time, however, three of HIMA's most powerful members, Pfizer, Eli Lilly, and Bristol-Myers, lobbied against the bill, and it was defeated.

The bill, called the Medical Device Improvement Act of 1988, was introduced in 1987 by Congressmen John B. Dingell (D., Mich.), chairman of the House Committee on Energy and Commerce, and Henry A. Waxman (D., Calif.), chairman of the committee's Subcommittee on Health and the Environment. It grew out of long-standing congressional dissatisfaction with the FDA's regulation of the health equipment industry, in particular its enforcement of the Medical Device Amendments of 1976.

In a 1983 report on the FDA's implementation of the 1976 amendments, Congressman Dingell's Subcommittee on Oversight and Investigations, found "a picture of bureaucratic neglect for public health and safety that shocks the conscience."[8] Further the report said: "Reflecting what the subcommittee can only regard as a cavalier disregard for the potential consequences, the FDA has barely begun to implement the provisions of the law."

The report was particularly critical of what it called the 510(k) "loophole" under which risk-laden Class III products were exempted from a full premarket review because they were not held to be new under the language of the act or were substantially equivalent to products which had existed before the 1976 amendments were enacted. The result, said the report, was that many of the riskiest devices, such as pacemakers, were essentially unregulated.

"Perhaps the agency's most disturbing default of all," the report continued, "is its failure to move forward with a requirement that manufacturers inform FDA when their devices kill, injure or lead to some other adverse experience. As a result, neither the FDA nor the public knows today how dangerous medical devices are, and we as legislators lack an adequate basis to decide whether the device amendments...are adequate."[9]

"We really beat up on the agency in that report," said Patrick M. McLain, oversight committee counsel, in 1988. "Today things are greatly improved. I have the greatest respect for the people at FDA. We work very closely together now."

Regarding HIMA, he said, "In the early 1980s we never heard from HIMA or the industry. When Frank Samuel came, all that changed. I have the greatest respect for him and what he's doing. We work very closely together also."

The 1988 act was designed to tighten up on industry reporting and expand regulation. The 1976 bill required firms to report equipment failures to the FDA.

The 1988 bill would require that hospitals report on any serious problems. It also mandated "an orderly timetable under which FDA either reviews old and new devices for safety and effectiveness or reclassifies them so that they no longer require such approvals." It further would give new authority to the FDA "to take action against products that pose an unreasonable risk of harm to the public health."[10] The bill followed hearings held in 1987 before Congressman Waxman's subcommittee.

"We found that more than 90 percent of the 5,000 or so new products going on to the market each year employ the 510(k) loophole," said Dr. Peter Budetti, counsel to the subcommittee. "That is, they are found to be 'substantially equivalent' to old products. They are reviewed by FDA but they do not get the thorough treatment which they should get."

Dr. Budetti continued:

> Manufacturers are required to report device failures but they don't always know about them because hospitals don't tell them. Some companies never report. Others report everything.
>
> We spent a year and a half negotiating this bill with HIMA. They repeated the FDA claims that it would deplete FDA resources and thus diminish what was available for inspections and enforcement. But the General Accounting Office could find no basis for that contention. Relations between the industry and the regulators are entirely too close.
>
> In June (1988) we finally had agreement. We bent over backward to be cooperative. And it wasn't easy because we have many groups watching us; we have to be fair to everyone.

The Waxman committee staff had a reputation in Washington for being particularly hostile to business. "Staff members compete with each other to see whose witnesses attract the most TV cameras," said one observer. Indeed, in the 1987 hearings, one witness testified he had received five defective artificial knees, which made a special impact on some committee members who suffered from arthritis. A couple told of how their baby had been "roasted to death" in a defective incubator. The media crowded the hearing room.

"We agreed to call off more hearings we had planned at HIMA's request in return for their promise to cooperate," said Budetti. "Next time we're going to give it all we've got."

Budetti was clearly angry that "HIMA's efforts to counteract lobbying by its maverick members against the bill in the Senate were ineffectual."

At its March 1988 board meeting all agreed that HIMA should support the House bill if some changes could be made in it. These changes were negotiated to the satisfaction of all except the three who opposed the bill in the Senate.

Gerald R. Connor,[11] vice president, legislation, of HIMA, pointed out, however,

> It was only three out of 300 after all. When we started with the 1988 bill our people were all over the map. We pulled things together and limited the dissenters. We convinced our members that there was going to be a bill, if not in 1988, then in 1989, and we would get a better bill if we cooperated. But you can't get everybody to agree on something this close to their hearts.

There were three camps among our members: those who said no way, those who said we've got to take it but if nothing happens that's O.K., and the vast majority who didn't care.

The bill's failure in the Senate was apparently due to a variety of factors, according to congressional insiders. The three companies persuaded Senator Hatch, to put "a hold" on it. This alerted the Senate leadership that the bill's passage would be difficult and time consuming, so it went to the bottom of their list.

Senator Kennedy's staff on the Labor Committee were not enthusiastic about the bill. It did not arrive from the House until July, which was late in a busy session. For Dr. Steven Keith of Kennedy's staff the bill did not go far enough. Furthermore, if there was to be a bill, they wanted it to be a Kennedy bill, not a Waxman one.

By the second week of October it was clear the bill was dead in the Senate. Said one observer, "Hatch refused to negotiate with Waxman and Dingell. He wouldn't even return their phone calls."

"There's no doubt at all that the 1989 bill will be much worse for the industry," said Gerry Connor. "I'd be very surprised if next time the TV cameras don't focus it on products of Pfizer, Lilly, and Bristol-Meyers," added Bob Moliter of GE.

Pfizer Hospital Products Group was generally regarded as among the HIMA members who have been most active in presenting its viewpoints on recent congressional proposals to modify the FDA's regulation on medical devices.

A key sticking point in the Waxman bill for Pfizer was a provision that would allow FDA to use the innovator's scientific data as a basis for approving an imitator's device as safe and effective. Pfizer, and other research-oriented sponsors of new devices, would have spent millions of dollars and years of time to develop such data, and would treat them as proprietary. Edward C. Bessey, HIMA director and president of Pfizer Hospital Products Group, observed, "The proposed legislation posed an unacceptable risk to the innovator, and amounts to appropriation of intellectual property." Pfizer, therefore, opposed allowing FDA to use an innovator's valuable data to approve the applications of other companies, and believed the proposed legislation would discourage innovation.

Apparently Waxman's intentions were to lower barriers to the introduction of new products and thus to increase competition and lower prices for consumers. Clearly some HIMA members would benefit from the waiver provisions, but other companies found it unfair.

Bessey acknowledged that the wide range of interests among HIMA members made it difficult for them to reach agreement on potentially divisive issues such as the legislative proposal. Recognizing this, Pfizer attempted to build consensus within HIMA, but at the same time preserved its rights as an independent corporation.

Ben Holmes of HP was with the majority of the board who felt that HIMA should endorse the Waxman bill. He valued close relations with FDA:

We train FDA inspectors—15 or 20 a year—in our plant. Our quality managers work closely with them. It's a dangerous game to be at loggerheads with government.

Generally they win. We're better off working with them, trying to understand their problems rather than trying to overpower them. In a political process you can never get the whole hog. You have to compromise. The House bill as it finally emerged was the best we could get.

I know that the pharmaceutical companies (which also make devices) were concerned about the PMA waiver business. They felt it would genericize equipment, but I don't think that's a real problem in practical terms. We had a big debate about it in the board. Indeed, we were still trying to get unanimity in August and we almost got it. There were only three holdouts. Feelings ran high. This was the first time that the HIMA board was divided on an issue. I've been wondering since then whether we should reorganize our committees in some way to assure continuing consensus.

Our committees now are set up around issues areas. Perhaps we should think about issues as they affect different kinds of companies: those who make equipment, for example, or implantables, or hospital supplies.

ISSUES FOR THE FUTURE

Burton Dole reflected on where HIMA was in the spring of 1989, on what had been accomplished and what lay ahead. He had before him an October 1988 report of HIMA's Science and Technology Section, composed of leading scientists from the larger member companies. The report identified a number of key technologies that would shape the future of the medical device and health care industry over the next decade. These included new sterilization techniques; new computer, communications, and manufacturing technology; and new materials, ceramics, for example.

There were, in addition, several issue areas in which Dole expected HIMA to be more active. The first was product liability. Almost 15 percent of the cost of medical devices was represented by insurance protection against product liability suits. Second was global markets. Although all HIMA members wanted to expand their exports, smaller companies were particularly eager to increase the proportion of their products that were sold abroad in 1988. They looked to HIMA to help keep world markets open, but realized that the big HIMA members might be reluctant to fund such activities since they already had large overseas staffs. A third issue involved the transfer of basic technologies—in materials science, for example—from government laboratories and the National Institutes of Health to the commercial industry. HIMA might be able to gather, screen, and distribute information about such technologies and also ensure industry access to it.

Finally, Dole wondered if HIMA could follow the practice of the American Business Conference (ABC) in which board member John Gilmartin was active. Composed of 100 high-growth, midsize companies, ABC made recommendations for United States policy which it felt would foster the national interest. These included a combination of lower government spending and higher taxes for the rich in order to reduce the federal deficit, and increased incentives for savings and productivity-improving investments to diminish the trade deficit. Gilmartin said of the ABC: "We try to come up with what's right for the United States as a whole. And when we decide, everybody must support the position. You can't grind your own axe. This makes for lobbying effectiveness."

ENDNOTES

1. Address to Food and Drug Law Institute Conference, Washington, D.C., December 15, 1987.
2. The function of oversight committees is set forth in Rule X2(b)(1) of the Rules of the House of Representatives: "Each standing committee...shall review and study, on a continuing basis, the application, administration, execution, and effectiveness of those laws...the subject matter of which is within the jurisdiction of that committee, and the organization and operation of the federal agencies and entities having responsibilities in or for the administration and execution thereof, in order to determine whether such laws and the programs thereunder are being implemented...in accordance with the intent of Congress and whether such programs should be continued, curtailed, or eliminated.
3. Medicare was the federal health insurance program that in 1988 served 30 million elderly Americans and some disabled; Medicaid was a federal-state health program for 22 million poor people. It cost $55.2 billion in 1988, 50 percent of which came from the federal government.
4. Association brochure, p. 2.
5. Experts expected medical costs to increase 21.5 percent in 1989 with 11.2 percent of that increase being due to "pressure on hospitals to purchase current technology." (Hewitt Associates, 1988, in *Medical Benefits*, November 30, 1988, p. 5).
6. OMB, Social Security trustee estimates.
7. Michael C. Fuchs, medical equipment industry analyst, International Trade Administration, U.S. Department of Commerce, "Economics of U.S. Trade in Medical Technology," unpublished report.
8. *Medical Device Regulation: The FDA's Neglected Child*, (Washington, D.C.: Government Printing Office, 1983), p. iii.
9. Ibid., p. 59. Since 1983, the FDA has required reporting by manufacturers of alleged device failures.
10. House of Representatives, Report 100-782, p. 10.
11. Before coming to HIMA, Connor was special assistant to the assistant secretary for legislation, Department of Health and Human Services.

Exhibit 1 HIMA Members

Abbott Laboratories
ABIOMED
Acme United Corporation
AcroMed Corporation
Adjustable Fixture Co.
Aequitron Medical, Inc.
Air-Shields Vickers
Alba-Waldensian, Inc.
Alcon Laboratories, Inc.
Allied Healthcare Products, Inc.
Alza Corporation
American Cyanamid Co.
American Medical International, Inc.
Americal Optical
American Sterilizer Company
Amersham Corporation
Amicon Division—W. R. Grace & Co.
H. W. Andersen Products Inc.
Angenics, Inc.
Ansell Incorporated
Applied ImmuneSciences, Inc.

Arbeka Webbing Co.
Arbor Technologies, Inc.
Arrow International, Inc.
Arvee Medical, Inc.
Ash Medical Systems, Inc.
Ashaway Line & Twine Mfg. Co.
AT&T
Arvery Laboratories Inc.
C. R. Bard, Inc.
Barnhardt Manufacturing Co.
W. A. Baum Co., Inc.
Bausch & Lomb
Baxter Healthcare Corporation
Becton Dickinson and Company
Behring Diagnostics
Beiersdorf, Inc.
Ben Venue Laboratories, Inc.
Bicarbolyte Corporation
Biochem International Inc.
Bioclinical Systems, Inc.
Bioelectron, Inc.
Bio-Metric Systems, Inc.

BioTechnica Diagnostics, Inc.
Biotechnology, Inc.
Bird Products Corporation
Blickman Health Industries
Boehringer Mannheim Corporation
Boston Scientific Corporation
Bristol-Myers Company
Buddy Systems, Inc.
Buffalo Medical Specialties Mfg., Inc.
Burdick Corporation
Burke, Inc.
Burron Medical, Inc.
Cabot Medical Corporation
Candela Laser Corp.
Carapace, Incorporated
Cardiac Control Systems, Inc.
Cardiovascular Devices, Inc.
Care Systems, Inc.
Carex Health Care Products
Carter-Wallace, Inc.
Cathlab Corporation
CD Medical, Inc.

Exhibit 1   (continued)

Cellular Products, Inc.
Centocor, Inc.
Central States Diversified
Cerner Corporation
Cetus Corporation
Chad Therapeutics, Inc.
Chattanooga Corporation
Chiron Ophthalmics Inc.
Ciba Corning Diagnostics
   Corp.
Cincinnati Sub-Zero
   Products
Circle Rubber U.S.A., Inc.
Clinical Connections, Inc.
CNS, Inc.
Cobe Laboratories, Inc.
Cochlear Corporation
Coherent, Inc.
Collagen Corporation
Concept, Inc.
Conco Medical Company
CONMED Corporation
The Copper Companies,
   Inc.
Cordis Corporation
Cox-Uphoff International
Criticare Systems, Inc.
Daig Corporation
Dale Medical Products, Inc.
Datascope Corp.
Delmed, Inc.
DeVilbiss Healthcare
   Worldwide
Devon Industries, Inc.
DHD Medical Products
Diagnostic Products
   Corporation
Diatex Corporation
Difco Laboratories, Inc.
DJ Medical Instrument
   Corp.
Domilens, Inc.
Dow Corning Corporation
Dravon Medical, Inc.
E. I. du Pont de Nemours &
   Co., Inc.
Dynamed Corporation
Eastman Kodak Company
E-Beam Services, Inc.
EdenTec Corporation
Electro-Biology, Inc.
Electromedics, Inc.
EM Diagnostic Systems, Inc.
Empi, Inc.

Entravision, Inc.
Enzo-Biochem
Erie Medical Products
Ethox Corp.
Everest & Jennings Int'l Ltd.
FCS Laboratories, Inc.
Ferno-Washington, Inc.
Fisher Scientific Group
Gambro, Inc.
Gaymar Industries, Inc.
Gelman Sciences, Inc.
GE Medical Systems
Genesis Labs, Inc.
Genex Corporation
Gerber Alley
Gish Biomedical, Inc.
W.L. Gore & Associates, Inc.
Graham Medical Products
Grandcor Medical Systems,
   Inc.
Grant Airmass Corporation
Graphic Controls
   Corporation
Grass Instrument Company
Griffith Micro-Science, Inc.
Haemonetics Corp.
Halbrand, Inc.
Harmac Industries, Inc.
Hausted
Hays Medical, Inc.
HBO & Company
Health Data Sciences Corp.
Healthdyne, Inc.
HemoTec, Inc.
Hewlett-Packard Company
Hill-Rom Company, Inc.
Hoffmann-La Roche, Inc.
Hollister Incorporated
Hudson Oxygen Therapy
   Sales Co.
IBM Corporation
Immunomedics, Inc.
Inmed Corporation
InTek Diagnostics, Inc.
Interpore International
Intertech Resources, Inc.
Invacare Corporation
IOPTEX Research, Inc.
IPCO Corporation
Irvine Scientific Sales Co.,
   Inc.
Isolab, Inc.
I-stat Corp.
ITW Deltar, Diamed

   Operations
James River Corporation
Jewett Refrigerator Co., Inc.
Johnson & Johnson
Kallestad Diagnostics
The Kendall Company
Kinetic Concepts, Inc.
Kirschner Medical
   Corporation
Kleen Test Products
The Larotex Company
Laserscope
Lawrence Medical Systems,
   Inc.
Liebel-Flarsheim Company
Lifecare
Eli Lilly & Company
Lionville Systems, Inc.
Look, Inc.
LTI Biomedical, Inc.
Lumex, Inc.
Lydall, Inc.
Mallinckrodt, Inc.
Marion Scientific
Marquette Electronics, Inc.
Mars White Knight
Meadox Medicals, Inc.
Medex, Inc.
Medical Concepts
   Incorporated
Medical Dynamics, Inc.
Medical Laboratory
   Automation
Medical Specialties, Inc.
Meditron Corporation
Medline Industries, Inc.
Medlon, Inc.
Medrad, Inc.
Medtronic, Inc.
Mennen Medical, Inc.
Mentor O & O, Inc.
Meridian Diagnostics, Inc.
Metrix Research
   Corporation
Mettler Electronics Corp.
Micortex Medical, Inc.
Midmark Corp.
Miles, Inc.
Millipore Corporation
Minnesota Mining & Mfg. Co.
Minnesota Valley
   Engineering
Molecular Devices
   Corporation

Monoclonal Antibodies, Inc.
Murex Corporation
Natvar Company
Newport Medical
 Instruments, Inc.
Nice-pak Products, Inc.
North American Drager
North American Instrument
 Corp.
Novametrix Medical
 Systems, Inc.
NYPRO, Inc.
Ohmeda
Olympic Medical Corp.
Optical Radiation
 Corporation
Organon Teknika
 Corporation
Pall Biomedical Products
 Corp.
Paper Manufacturers
 Company
Parker Hannifin
 Corporation
Patient Technology, Inc.
Pedicraft, Inc.
Pennsylvannia Engineering
 Co.
Pfizer, Inc.
Pharmaceutical Innovations
 Inc.
Pharmacia, Inc.
Philips Medical Systems, Inc.
Pilling Company
Plasco, Inc.
Plastron-Dalton, Inc.
Polaroid Corporation
Popper & Sons, Inc.
Porex Technologies Corp. of
 GA
J. T. Posey Company
PPG Industries, Inc.

Precision Dynamics
 Corporation
Professional Medical
 Products
Propper Mfg. Company, Inc.
Puritan-Bennett Corporation
PyMaH Corporation
Quantronix Corporation
Radiation Sterilizers, Inc.
Ranfac Corporation
Remel, Inc.
Respironics Incorporated
Richard-Allen Medical
 Industries, Inc.
A. H. Robins Company, Inc.
St. John Companies
St. Jude Medical, Inc.
Scan Detectronic
 Laboratories, Inc.
Schmid Laboratories, Inc.
SciMed Life Systems, Inc.
Semex Medical
SENMED, Inc.
Serono Diagnostics, Inc.
Sharpoint L.P.
Sheridan Catheter Corp.
Siemens Medical Systems,
 Inc.
Sigma-Aldrich Corp.
Sil-Med Corporation
Smith & Nephew, Inc.
SmithKline Beckman
 Corporation
Smiths Industries P.L.C.
Squibb Corporation
Staodynamics, Inc.
Sterile Concepts, Inc.
Stryker Corporation
Sunlite Plastics, Inc.
Surgical Dynamics, Inc.
Surgical Laser Technologies
Surgidev Corporation

Survival Technology, Inc.
Syntex Corporation
Tambrands, Inc.
Target Therapeutics, Inc.
Tecnol, Inc.
TeknaMed Corporation
Telectronics, Inc.
Terumo Medical
 Corporation
Therapeutic Technologies,
 Inc.
Thoratec Latoratories Corp.
Timeter Instrument
 Corporation
TOA Med. Electronics USA,
 Inc.
Tonometrics, Inc.
Toshiba Medical Systems
Tri-State Hospital Supply
 Corp.
Triton Biosciences, Inc.
Union Carbide Corporation
Unisys
United States Surgical Corp.
Vacudyne Incorporated
Van-Tec, Inc.
Versa Technologies, Inc.
Viscot Industries, Inc.
Vision Technologies Int'l.,
 Inc.
Vitek, Inc.
Vitek Systems, Inc.
Welch Allyn, Inc.
Welcon, Inc.
The West Company
Westmark International
Whittaker Bioproducts, Inc.
R. Wolf Medical Instrument
 Corp.
Wolf X-Ray Corporation
WR Medical Electronics Co.

Exhibit 2   WHAT HIMA DOES FOR MEMBERS

The basic issues affecting the medical devices diagnostics and health care information systems industry range from health care financing and international trade to technology assessment and the Medical Device Amendments. HIMA has established three sections to advise the association's board of directors and staff on policy and priorities. This is a brief description of the three sections and the work of each.

Science and Technology Section
Edward R. Duffie, M.D. (Becton Dickinson and Company), chairman
Noel L. Buterbaugh (Whittaker Bioproducts, Inc.), vice chairman
        This section through more that 30 committees and task forces, focuses on product safety, the manufacturing process, worker and environmental safety and health, standards, product specific technology, and international trade.
Topics currently being addressed include

- Good manufacturing practices
- Computer software in medical equipment
- Technology transfer
- Process and design validation
- Ethylene oxide emmissions and residues
- Ophthalmics
- FDA regulatory standards
- In vitro diagnostics inspection guidelines
- Reuse
- Worker/environmental safety
- Home care devices
- AIDS issues
- User education programs
- World trade issues
- Industry representatives to FDA advisory panels

Government and Public Affairs Section

Robert M. Moliter (GE Medical Systems), chairman
James R. Tobin (Becton Dickinson and Company), vice chairman

        The primary focus of the Government and Public Affairs Section is to bring the association's message on the appropriate role of legislation and government regulation as it affects our industry to government policy makers and the public. The association's congressional, executive branch, state affairs, and public affairs programs seek to affect public opinion and public policy in order to maintain a national commitment to high quality medical care and technology. Specific activities include

Federal legislation on

- Product liability
- FDA appropriations
- Medical device amendments
- Medicare budget and program characteristics
- Catastrophic and long-term care
- Clinical laboratory issues
- Technology assessment
- Export controls
- Reuse

Executive Branch issues at
- White House
- Office of Management and Budget
- Department of Health and Human Services, including the Food and Drug Administration and the Health Care Financing Administration
- Prospective Payment Assessment Commission
- Office of the U.S. Trade Representative
- Department of Commerce

Public affairs

- Guest editorials/letters to the editor
- Press conferences
- Other activities that share the industry's views with the media

State legislative activities

- Product liability
- Health cost containment
- Worker/environment safety
- Clinical laboratory issues

Legal and Regulatory Section

Raymond J. Dittrich (Medtronic, Inc.), chairman
Thomas A. Boardman (Minnesota Mining & Mfg. Co.), vice chairman

The Legal and Regulatory Section examines and analyzes those laws central to manufacturers' product development and sales. The section also provides ongoing communications with FDA and HCFA on industry concerns. The thrust of this section's committees and task forces is to streamline FDA's device approval process and to clarify HCFA's coverage and reimbursement procedures consistent with public health, safety, and fundamental due process. Section participants advocate regulatory policies which are responsive to technological innovation.

Specific issues include

- Changes to the medical device amendments
- Product approval process
- Premarket approval regulation
- 510(k) and IDE guidelines
- Product liability
- Medical device reporting rule
- FDA compliance issues
- Medicare coverage reform
- Clinical laboratory reimbursement
- Medicare fraud and abuse
- Device diversion
- Medicare coding

Exhibit 2 (continued)

Sector Specific Activities

In addition to the overall activities conducted by the sections, HIMA has established several committees to address the specialized needs of manufacturers. These groups look at issues affecting home care, health care information systems, IVDs, ophthalmics, and smaller businesses.

HIMA officers

Chairman, Daniel E. Gill—Bausch & Lomb
Chairman-Elect, Burton A. Dole, Jr.—Puritan-Bennett Corporation
President, Frank E. Samuel, Jr.—HIMA
Treasurer, Jerry E. Robertson, Ph.D.—Minnesota Mining & Mfg Co.
Assistant Treasurer, Kristen M. Bogenrief—HIMA
Secretary, Edwin H. Allen—HIMA
Assistant Secretarys, Gordon B. Schatz—HIMA

HIMA Board of Directors

Frank V. Atlee
American Cyanamid Company

Edward C. Bessey
Pfizer, Inc.

John W. Brown
Stryker Corporation

Jack Clawson
Hill-Rom Company, Inc.

E. Gary Cook, Jr., Ph.D.
E. I. du Pont de Nemours & Co., Inc.

Victor J. Dankis
Johnson & Johnson

George W. Ebright
SmithKline Beckman Corporation

Wilbur H. Gantz
Baxter Healthcare Corporation

Henry E. Gauthier
Coherent, Inc.

John A. Gilmartin
Millipore Corporation

Raymond V. Gilmartin
Becton Dickinson and Company

Ray E. Hannah
Porex Technologies Corp. of GA

Ben L. Holmes
Hewlett-Packard Company

John R. Hoover
W. L. Gore & Associates, Inc.

Irwin Lerner
Hoffmann-La Roche, Inc.

Robert H. McCaffrey
C. R. Bard, Inc.

R. James Macaleer
Sahred Medical Systems

A. Malachi Mixon, III
Invacare Corporation

Peter Riepenhausen
The Cooper Company

Robert T. Rylee, II
Dow Corning Corporation

Robert A. Schoellhorn
Abbott Laboratories

J. Dale Sherratt
The Kendall Company

Robert L. Stocking
GE Medical Systems

Roger G. Stoll, Ph.D.
Miles, Inc.

John L. Ufheil
Mallinckrodt, Inc.

Monty E. Vincent
Abor Technologies, Inc.

Winston R. Wallin
Medtronic, Inc.

Frank P. Wilton
Ethox Corp.

Richard W. Young, Ph.D.
Mentor O & O, Inc.

Exhibit 3   HIMA Staff and Issues

Frank E. Samuel, Jr., president
Richard G. Flaherty, vice president, Member Services and Administration
Betty Charles, office director
Mary Pat Triska, assistant office director
Laura Schweppe, systems administrator
Susan M. Moring, director, Meetings and Membership
Dolly A. Hanrahan, meetings manager
Kristen M. Bogenrief, controller
Norman F. Estrin, Ph.D., vice president, Science and Technology
George T. Willingmyre, P.E., vice president, Product Technology and International Projects Coordinator
Amiram Daniel, Ph.D., director, Diagnostic Manufacturing and Biotechnology Programs
James F. Jorkasky, director, Environmental, Occupational and Ophthalmic Programs
Robert T. Schwartz, MID, IDSA, director, Biomedical Technology Programs
Edwin H. Allen, vice president and general counsel
Gordon B. Schatz, associate general counsel
Stephen D. Terman, associate general counsel
Gerald R. Connor, vice president, Legislative Affairs
Leah Schroeder, vice president, Government Affairs
Bette Anne Starkey, director, Congressional Relations
Jill A. Eicher, manager, State Affairs
Ted R. Mannen, senior vice president, Policy and Communications
Ronald Geigle, vice president, Public Affairs
Donna J. Krupa, manager, Communications
Anne H. Oman, manager, Policy Information
Laura Washington, public affairs specialist
Paul M. Campbell, director, Health Policy
Gary S. Schneider, director, Policy Evaluation
Maggie Warnken, research assistant
Cass Foley, research assistant

4

MANAGING AT THE INTERFACE

MITI, MPT, and the Telecom Wars: How Japan Makes Policy

Chalmers Johnson

During the first half of the 1980s, the Japanese government initiated and pursued many important official policies for the nation. These included the decision to end the century-old governmental monopoly in telecommunications services by reorganizing the Nippon Telegraph and Telephone Company as a joint stock company. English-speaking observers like to refer to this development as "privatization" even though, in fact, all shares of the new NTT are under the control of the government and only a portion of them is being sold to the public (none to foreigners) over a five-year period.[1] The government also undertook to rewrite its laws regulating the newly demonopolized telecommunications business, tried to force the interest rates on postal savings accounts down to the level of those authorized by the Ministry of Finance (MOF) for the commercial banks, established new organizations to support research and development in telecommunications and other high-technology

This essay is excerpted from a working paper of the same title and published by the Berkeley Roundtable on International Economy, University of California, Berkeley, 1986, subsequently published in Chalmers Johnson, Laura Tyson, and John Zysman, eds., *Politics and Productivity: How Japan's Development Works* (New York: Harper & Row, Ballinger, 1989). Johnson is a professor of international relations and Pacific studies at the University of California, San Diego. Reprinted with permission of the author and Harper & Row.

industries, began to protect the property rights of authors and manufacturers of programs for computers, sheltered its domestic communications satellite industry from foreign competition so that it might one day become a viable exporter, negotiated with the Americans over what was euphemistically called "trade friction," and started to build digitalized telecommunications infrastructures for the eventual interconnection of "new media" equipment (video telephones, videotext terminals, two-way cable television, etc.). Each of these initiatives was the occasion for a major battle in what the Japanese called the telecom wars (1983–1985).

What were the interests and motives of actors within the Japanese governmental process and how did they conflict with each other?

The first group of actors is the official state bureaucracy. These are officials of the central government ministries and agencies who since Japan's emergence as a modern state in the late nineteenth century have been the planners, engineers, and supervisors of Japan's economic and social development. This group is an inherent meritocracy of talent, educated in the best schools and universities in the country, and it is very much aware of and jealously protects its high prestige within the social system. In the postwar from 1945 until approximately 1972, when Tanaka Kakuei became prime minister, the bureaucracy's monopoly of policy-making powers in Japan were virtually complete. The only areas where political rather than bureaucratic interests clearly prevailed were education, defense, and agricultural price supports.[2] Even after Tanaka began to change the system, most important policies still originate within a ministry or agency, not within the political or private sector, although these policies may be extensively modified once the bureaucracy makes them public....*

In the telecom wars, the two main bureaucratic actors were the Ministry of International Trade and Industry (MITI, Tsusho Sangyo-sho) and the Ministry of Posts and Telecommunications (MPT, Yusei-sho, literally, "Ministry of Postal Affairs" but since 1952, when NTT became a public corporation under MPT's jurisdiction, officially translated as "Ministry of Posts and Telecommunications"). Other agencies appeared on the battlefields as allies of one or the other side—the Ministry of Finance allied with MITI and the Agency of Cultural Affairs of the Ministry of Education allied with MPT—but generally speaking MITI and MPT were the chief protagonists and antagonists.

MITI SINCE THE "MIRACLE"

MITI's headquarters in Kasumigaseki, Tokyo, are located about 50 feet from the main office building of MPT, on the same city block, but the two are anything but friendly neighbors. After World War II, with the unification in 1949 of industrial development and trade administration, MITI emerged as the governmental sponsor and supervisor of high-speed economic growth. Given Japan's enormous success as a highly industrialized nation, MITI became what the press likes to call an "ultra-

---

*According to the Japanese Constitution, the Diet (Kokkai, the assembly of elected representatives of the people) is the "highest organ of state power and shall be the sole law-making organ of the state." The Diet, however, has never played a decisive role in policy-making; its most substantive power is in its ability, on occasion, to block passage of legislation.

first-class bureaucracy" (cho-ichiryu kancho), staffed with some of the finest minds and best managerial talents in the country.[3] MITI today is more or less in the same class as the Ministry of Finance—in recent years it has attracted even better talent from the universities than MOF—and it is without question one of the nation's most valuable institutional assets.

But MITI has a serious problem. It is losing jurisdiction. MITI's historic task of protecting and nurturing Japanese industries until they could compete in any market in the world is over. Japan's big businesses no longer need MITI. Moreover, the slower growth of the Japanese economy since the first oil crisis of 1973 has meant that MITI's usual methods—home market protection, preferential supply of capital, import of foreign technology, "excessive" domestic competition, cartelization according to market share, and so forth—are no longer appropriate.

Looking to the future, then, MITI sees two main prospects, one not very attractive but the other quite alluring. The unattractive option is that it might turn itself into a ministry of imports. This would require the ministry to lead the country from an almost totally supply-side–oriented economy to genuine demand stimulation. MITI could do this since it recognizes that anti-Japanese protectionism is probably the major potential threat to Japan's economic well-being.... However, becoming a governmental agent for importers would be a comedown for MITI; and such a posture would make it vulnerable to charges of betraying national interests and of toadying to foreigners, a point all too well understood at MPT.[4]

Therefore, although MITI continues to toy with the idea of becoming an agency of Keynesian domestic demand management, its real thrust is toward the promotion of the high-technology industries of the future.... MITI theorists and other Japanese futurologists note the increasing disconnections between modern manufacturing and the supplies of raw materials or labor. The raw materials of semiconductors and ceramic engines are virtually worthless in their natural state, and robots are not just *replacing* people on the production line, but they are often more effective than people....

The key industries for this future economy, identified over and over again in Japanese technical and popular literature will be telecommunications, new materials, and biotechnology.[5] In a world dominated by these industries Japan will no longer be a resource-poor, vulnerable trading nation living by its wits but one of the world's best endowed countries. It is on the basis of this vision that MITI vice-minister Konaga has sought to put his ministry almost totally in charge of administering research and development for high technology industries.[6]...

MITI's jurisdiction clearly includes the computer industry. The problem is, as MITI men like to say, "A computer without software is only a box, and a computer with software is still only a computer. But a computer connected to a telephone circuit is something else again: it is a telecommunications network."[7] Unfortunately for MITI, telecommunications circuits are clearly within MPT's jurisdiction. In order for MITI to usher in what it has identified as its "third golden age" (the first was the heavy and chemical industrialization of the 1950s and 1960s, followed by the global victories in international trade of the late 1960s and 1970s), it must overcome its rival and bring telecommunications under its jurisdiction. Given MITI's history, talents, and high esprit de corps, this should not have been too difficult a task. MITI may, however, have underestimated its rival.

For the elite bureaucrats of MITI and MOF, to the extent that they think at all about it, MPT has been considered a "third-rate business bureaucracy" (sanryu no gengyo kancho) utterly distinct from its own "policy ministries" (seisaku Rancho). What they overlook is that MPT always has been and still is a political powerhouse. As the balance of power between bureaucrats and politicians began to shift during and after the Tanaka era and as MPT bureaucrats began to imagine themselves recapturing some of the glory of their prewar stronghold, the old Ministry of Communications (Teishin-shō), MITI began to discover that it had taken on a tiger.

THE HISTORY OF MPT

It is important to recall that, in the wake of the Meiji Restoration of 1868, Japan's system of ministries and agencies came into being well before its political parties, constitution, or parliament. Differing from the United States, these ministries were not created to be "civil servants," or to provide regulation of private concerns, or to supply jobs for party loyalists, but rather to guide Japan's rapid forced development to forestall incipient colonization by Western imperialists.

From its beginning the Ministry of Communications controlled mail, the telegraph, maritime shipping, and lighthouses. In 1891 it added telephones and electric power generation to its purview. For exactly a century, from 1885 to 1985, the government supplied and monopolized all Japanese telecommunications. In 1892 the ministry also took charge of developing and administering the railroads, and in 1909 it was given supervision of hydroelectric power generation. In 1916 the ministry added postal life insurance; in 1925 civil aviation and the aircraft industry; and in 1926 the postal annuity system. An attempt today to put the Ministry of Communications back together would involve merging MPT, NTT, and the Ministry of Transportation, the Japanese National Railway, Japan Air Lines, MITI's Natural Resources and Energy Agency, and renationalizing the electric power industry.

The dismemberment of the Communications Ministry actually began during World War II and was completed by the occupation, but this "ancient" history is still relevant to the MITI-MPT rivalry 40 years later. During the war the Ministry of Munitions, in MITI's lineage, obtained jurisdiction over electric power and the aviation industry, sectors that are still securely in MITI's bailiwick. During the war Communications also lost all control over transportation, the railroads having been taken away years earlier and put into a separate Ministry of Railroads. The Occupation continued this arrangement except that it created a new Ministry of Transportation to regulate the industry and spun off the government-owned railroad lines into a public corporation, the Japanese National Railways.

On June 1, 1949,... the Japanese government in consultation with SACP (Supreme Commander for the Allied Powers) abolished the Ministry of Communications and replaced it with two new ministries: the Ministry of Postal Affairs (Yūsei-shō), in charge of the mail and postal savings systems, and the Ministry of Telecommunications (Denki Tsushin-sho), in charge of rebuilding the telegraph and telephone systems. Three years later, just as the occupation was coming to an end, the Ministry of Telecommunications was transformed into a wholly government-owned public corporation, NTT, under the supervision of the Ministry of Postal Affairs. The model for NTT was the Japanese National Railways (JNR) except that NTT was an absolute government monopoly whereas the JNR was allowed privately owned rivals. Over time this difference turned the JNR into the greatest source of red ink in the Japanese budget, whereas NTT has always remained profitable....

From 1952 to 1985 NTT perpetuated and strengthened the relationships that the Communications Ministry had established during the 1920s with preferred suppliers of equipment. NTT did research in its laboratories, set specifications for what it wanted to buy, and bought all of its equipment from a group of civilian firms that came to be known as the "NTT Family."

NTT's four largest suppliers were (1) NEC Corporation (Nippon Electric, founded in 1899, a member of the Sumitomo zaibatsu, and Japan's first joint-venture company (with Western Electric); (2) Fujitsu, established in 1915, derived from the Furukawa Electric Company of 1896, and allied with the Siemens Company of Germany; (3) Oki Electric, established in 1912 and associated for purposes of technology transfer with British General Electric; and (4) Hitachi, Ltd., founded in 1910, and independent of foreign connections. These firms maintained the most intimate personal, technical, research, and financial relationships with NTT.

Even though MPT was regarded as only a "third-rate business bureaucracy"—to this day its staffers refer to it as "our company" rather than as "our ministry"—politicians have always liked it....[8] The postal ministry is attractive to politicians for three reasons: it directly controls a large number of votes; each year it places large orders for equipment (uniforms, bicycles, and so forth); and it runs what is today the world's largest financial institution, the postal savings system, which is popular with the public because it pays higher rates of interest than the banks.

MPT's RISE IN STATUS

MPT's status...began to change in the early 1980s for a series of interrelated reasons. First was the KDD scandal of 1979. KDD, or Kokusai Denshin Denwa Company (International Telegraph and Telephone), is the overseas equivalent of NTT.... In October 1979, two KDD employees were arrested at Narita airport while attempting to smuggle some ¥10 million worth of jewelry and other luxury items into the country without paying customs duties. The ensuing investigation revealed that for at least four years they and other KDD employees had been smuggling valuable goods into the country for KDD president Itano Manabu. Itano in turn passed out these items as corporate gifts to KDD board members, clients in southest Asia, MPT minister Shirahama Nikichi (Ōhira cabinet, 1978–1980), and politicians of the LDP's postal caucus.

Paradoxically, the KDD case contributed to an upgrading of MPT's status because it alerted the political world to the danger of corruption in organizations such as KDD and NTT. It also raised numerous questions about the excessive independence of the public corporations, their poor financial accountability, and the lack of effective supervision by the ministries, which use them as *amakudari* ("descent from heaven") landing spots for recently retired bureaucrats. Some politicians concluded that MPT had to be raised in status and given more policy responsibilities in order to ensure that nothing like the KDD case would recur.

Another reason for the change of MPT's status was NTT's involvement during 1978–1980 in bitter trade friction with the United States. The issue was whether or not NTT's purchases of telecommunications equipment (worth over $3 billion per annum) were to be included in the liberalization of governmental procurements that Japan had agreed to in the so-called Tokyo Round of multilateral trade negotiations. The Americans did not target NTT from the start. All they asked was that Japan open up to international trade a share of its annual governmental purchases that was more or less equivalent to the share of American and Western European public procurements on which Japanese firms were free to bid. Whatever Japan's policy on this issue might have been, NTT quickly bungled the public relations aspect. After NTT president Akikusa was quoted to the effect that "the only thing NTT would buy from the United States was mops and buckets," many in the Japanese government recognized that NTT's engineers and "family" members could not be trusted with international negotiations.[9] MPT said that it could handle the matter better, but it needed new policy-making powers.

The third reason for the improvement in MPT's status was for the launching during 1981 of the Second Provisional Commission for Administrative Reform (Rinji Gyosei Chosa Kai, abbreviated Rinchō)...One of the things the Rinchō commission was determined to achieve was to get the government out of the railroad and telephone business by "privatizing" the JNR and NTT. As we shall see, it succeeded with NTT, at least on paper, but it required a major fight. Whatever its effect on governmental "reform," however, Rinchō had major unintended consequences for MPT. If the nation really intended to privatize NTT, then MPT would need new legal powers to regulate it and any other firms that might enter the telecommunications business in competition with it. Because of Rinchō, some farsighted bureaucrats at MPT began to envision a vast expansion of the ministry's jurisdiction and the real possibility of becoming a "policy agency."

Meanwhile, the winds of change began to blow in the summer of 1980. MPT minister Yamanouchi Ichirō, acting on the encouragement of his bureaucrats, proposed to the cabinet that the old two-person NTT supervisory office in the MPT secretariat be expanded and upgraded to a new "Communications Policy Bureau" (Tsūshin Seisaku Kyoku). The MITI minister, Tanaka Rokusuki (no relation to Tanaka Kakuei), one of the party's most powerful politicians, immediately objected. According to Tanaka, the idea was crazy. "Policy" was MITI's business, and it was unseemly to have a "policy bureau" in a ministry like MPT. Perhaps because

Yamanouchi and Tanaka are both members of the Suzuki faction,* Prime Minister Suzuki had to step in to settle the matter. He decided in favor of MPT. The new Communications Policy Bureau was charged with policy and supervision of legislation concerning new media, planning for the "advanced information society," research and development for telecommunications, space communications, and international technical exchange and cooperation. Being chief of this bureau immediately became an indispensable step for a postal bureaucrat on the road to the vice ministership (the highest nonpolitical post in the ministry).[10]

The telecom wars began in the autumn of 1981, when MITI successfully blocked an MPT-initiated bill that would have given MPT strong regulatory powers over computer-connected telecommunications circuits. They heated up during 1982 in the second VAN (Value-Added Network) campaign, spread to new fronts during 1983 over the issues of providing legal protection for the writers of computer programs and the building of regional infrastructures for the "informationized" society of the future, and during 1984 and 1985 became a general conflagration with at least seven different battles going on simultaneously.

Even though each of the seven battles is interconnected with the others, I have separated them here for discussion and analysis. The seven are (1) VANs and the fight over regulating the Japanese telecommunications industry, (2) the "privatization" of NTT, (3) product standards and certification procedures, (4) protecting computer programs, (5) foreign satellites and space communications policy, (6) Teletopias and New Media Communities, and (7) controlling research and development in the telecommunications field. Before we can understand these battles, however, we have to explore the ancient enmity between MPT and the Ministry of Finance. Because of it MOF became a MITI ally in 1985 in the battle over research funding.

MPT, MOF, AND THE POSTAL SAVINGS SYSTEM

In 1875 Japan established a system whereby its citizens could save their money at post offices. Since the creation of the Ministry of Communications a decade later, the postal bureaucracy has always administered the system, which is one of the reasons why prewar politicians wanted to be communications minister: it gave them control over the investment of people's savings, a trust that on occasion they abused. In the postwar era the postal savings system is much more strictly controlled than it was before the war....[It] has been fabulously successful and is the institutional linchpin of Japan's high savings rate, which has allowed the country to fund its industrialization more cheaply than virtually any of its competitors....The postal savings system is the primary source of funds for Japan's Fiscal Investment and Loan

*Shortly after the Liberal Democratic Party's (LDP) creation in 1955, it split into four or five internal "factions," which were actually miniparties that compete and combine with each other in order temporarily to dominate the LDP itself. These factions are not primarily ideological groupings but alliances among Diet members to advance their own interests within the party. The goal of a faction is, minimally, political self-preservation (i.e., reelection), and, maximally, to name the prime minister, who in turn has the power to name the members of his cabinet and the top party executive positions. The LDP has been in power continuously since 1955.

Program (FILP), a plan set up in 1953 for governmental investments in industrial development, research, public housing, and infrastructure. Because of the strength of the postal savings system, the FILP continues to be one of Japan's most powerful instruments of official industrial policy....

Postwar Japan created several programs to encourage saving as part of its overall industrial policy. One of these is the *maruyū yokin* system (tax exempt deposits), which makes the interest on the first ¥3 million in any savings account tax exempt. In addition, up to ¥3 million can be invested tax free in government bonds, and salaried workers can bank up to 5 million in a tax-free pension plan. Aside from this so-called *maruyū* system, any individual can deposit up to ¥3 million in a postal savings account without paying taxes on the earned interest; and another ¥500,000 can be deposited in a special post office account reserved for the purchase of a home. Many people in Japan open any number of different *maruyū* and postal savings accounts, often in the names of every member of the family and sometimes using invented names, at banks and post offices all over the country. (MPT had 23,000 post offices in Japan, which formed the organizational bedrock of the LDP.) During 1985 MOF declared that it had discovered an all-time high of ¥950 billion in illegal *maruyū* accounts, but it could not audit the post offices since MPT absolutely refused to give it access.[11]

Bitter clashes between MOF and MPT over this issue occurred in 1971–1972, 1975, 1977, 1980–1982, and 1984, with MPT always emerging victorious.... In March 1980 the Diet enacted a law that would have ended at least the tax fraud aspects of the problem by issuing to every saver a so-called Green Card for his or her identity when making deposits.... However, even though the law was passed, it was never implemented. This blockage of implementation is said to be one of the postal *zoku's** greatest victories.... MOF, however, has never forgiven MPT for its recourse to powerful zoku in order to protect its bureaucratic turf. Thus, when in 1985, MPT came up with a great new idea on how to spend the dividends from the shares of the newly privatized NTT, MOF allied with MITI to help frustrate MPT's plans.

THE VAN CAMPAIGNS

The Japanese break down the general concept of telecommunications into three broad types. First is direct, unprocessed communication, as in a telephone. Second is communication between a computer terminal and a data processing center, as in an automatic teller machine at a bank (what the Japanese call a CD, or "cash dispenser"). Third is a VAN, or "value-added network" (*fuka-kachi tsūshin*), which is a combination of the first and second types. A VAN is a network in which information

---

Zoku (roughly, caucus members) are pure politicians (as opposed to exbureaucrats) who have progressed in service through one or more stages of a particular ministry: parliamentary vice minister, Policy Affairs Research council section chairman or vice chairman, Diet standing committee chairman, and minister or director general. They are veteran Diet members who combine political influence with broad and accurate knowledge of the administrative fields in which they specialize. As Diet members, they belong to a faction, and factions try to have a range of *zoku;* but the interests of *zoku* sometimes differ from a faction's (or its leader) or, conversely, a faction might have several conflicting *zoku*.

from computers of one type is communicated to computers of another type, the data being processed in the transmission and becoming thereby "value-added." A VAN network is the electronic equivalent of a system of simultaneous translation from one language to another. The standard example is a Japanese travel agency's computer with its ability to communicate with the reservations computers of ten or more companies, including JAL, JNR, and the Japan Travel Bureau, private railroads, other airlines, and numerous hotel chains. Banking systems and supermarkets are heavy users of VANs. Until 1982 it was illegal in Japan to connect a computer to the telephone lines without the explicit permission of NTT.

During 1981 it became apparent to the new Communications Policy Bureau of MPT that demand for different kinds of VANs was outstripping NTT's ability to meet it. Therefore it proposed new legislation that would both legalize enhanced use of VANs and make absolutely clear MPT's responsibility for regulating this growing business. Entitled the Value-Added Data Communications Bill, it incorporated draconian licensing and approval requirements and put harsh limits on the degree to which foreign firms or domestic firms with high degrees of foreign capital (e.g., IBM Japan) could participate.[12]

MITI opposed the proposed law because MPT appeared to be infringing on its turf, both by seeking to regulate computer-based communications (computers are in MITI's bailiwick) and by presuming to regulate foreign commerce (which MITI also likes to think of as its exclusive preserve). MITI publicly and stridently opposed MPT's draft law, using as a pretext for its attack, the reports of the recently created Provisional Commission for Administrative Reform (Rincho), which called on the government to reduce, not add to, its required licenses and approvals. MITI won this battle and MPT withdrew its bill. In light of later events this contretemps became known as the first (there were two more) VAN campaigns.

During 1982 MPT renewed its efforts by arguing that as a matter of national security it had to regulate foreign VANs coming into Japan. The ministry successfully scared the political world with the specters of IBM and AT&T (the U.S. dismantling of which was imminent and which the Japanese wrongly interpreted as an act of American rationality and competitiveness) taking over Japan's entire telecommunications industry. In light of Rinchō's simultaneous advocacy of the privatization of NTT, which MPT and the postal *zoku* initially opposed, the possibility of an "invasion of foreign capital" was somewhat more plausible than usual. However, MITI countered MPT by arguing that the VAN business should be completely liberalized. It reasoned to itself that if VANs were opened up to competition, then MITI could advance into this terrain and bring it under control via its influence over the computer and microelectronic industries. Publicly MITI defended its position in terms of the threat of foreign protectionism if the Japanese domestic market remained closed.

In October 1982 the LDP intervened to try to settle this dispute. It took to the Diet and passed a revision of the Public Telecommunications Law of 1953 liberalizing VANs only for medium and smaller enterprises. The party was unable to resolve how much regulation large-scale VANs required or how much foreign penetration was acceptable. The LDP made clear that its revision to the country's basic electric communication law was an expedient to meet the needs of small businesses, and it asked the bureaucracy to undertake a total reform of the basic legislation in order to deal with the bigger issues. Reform was required if for no other reason than the fact that the government was also beginning to discuss the privatization of NTT.

The postal ministry spent 1983 drafting three new laws. These were, first, a new Telecommunications Business Bill to replace the old basic law of 1953 in order to deal with large-scale VANs, the regulation of foreigners, the setting of technical standards after NTT was privatized, and many other matters. Second was the Nippon Denshin Denwa Kabushiki Daisha Bill, transforming NTT into a private company under Japan's Civil Code; and third was an omnibus bill to revise and adjust all other laws made obsolete by the passage of the first two bills. A hint of the ministry's plans came in May, when it published the 1983 edition of its annual "Communications White Paper" or annual report. In it MPT identified as one of Japan's greatest needs the protection of the secrecy of communications, which in turn, it said required the "coordination" (*chosei*) and "stabilization" (*antei*) of all forms of telecommunications. (The terms *chosei* and *antei* when used by Japanese bureaucrats are invariably euphemisms for control.) MITI reacted with fury to this trial balloon, saying that white papers are places to report activities, not to advocate policies, and it demanded that MPT correct its own white paper. However, the *Nihon keizai* newspaper thought that MITI's manner on this issue was arrogant and high handed.[13]

In February 1984, MPT unveiled to the press the first drafts of its three new laws, and for the next year and a half the Japanese political, bureaucratic, and industrial worlds seemed to talk of nothing else. The heart of the Telecommunications Business Bill was its treatment of VANs. The original MPT draft divided the telecommunications business into two broad classes and then further subdivided the second class. Class I telecommunications businesses were defined as common carriers, like NTT, that installed their own circuits, either land lines or via satellite transmission. Under the new law, ownership of such Class I carriers is totally prohibited to foreigners or to Japanese firms that are more than one-third controlled by foreigners. The law also requires that such Class I firms be licensed by MPT and that the ministry approve their rates.

Class II telecommunications businesses are those that offer large-scale VAN services over circuits leased from a Class I carrier. They are further subdivided into special Class II firms and general Class II firms. Under the original draft, special Class IIs are firms that exceed certain narrow technical specifications that the ministry supplies through ministerial ordinances or that offer any form of international service between Japan and one or more foreign countries. Foreigners are prohibited from engaging in special Class II business, and all of them must be licensed by MPT. All other VANs are general Class IIs, which are open to foreign ownership and need only "register" with MPT. These complex distinctions were invented specifically to keep IBM and AT&T out of Japan.[14]

The American government was interested in this law. It had been deeply frustrated by its agreement of December 1980 with NTT to open up the Japanese market to American telecommunications sales; and it saw in MPT's definition of a special type II business a new Japanese nontarriff barrier to trade. MITI agreed, since it recognized that if the bill passed in its original form, MPT would dominate the telecommunications field through its licensing powers. Even the requirement that general type II businesses had only to register would not have deceived an experienced MITI official. An old Japanese bureaucratic trick is refusing to accept unsatisfactory reports, thereby making an activity that requires reporting illegal. In all formal written applications or notifications to Japanese ministries, filing of the report is the end of a complex process. The applicant or reporter is expected to negotiate in advance concerning how to fill out the forms. When the actual written report is filed, it is usually accepted. If a ministry intends to reject an applicant or a report, it will do so verbally during the preliminary negotiations.[15] On these and other grounds U.S. trade negotiators and MITI protested the terms of the new Telecommunications Business Law.

MPT's response was predictable. It accused MITI of selling out to the Americans, of using the issue of trade friction to advance its own bureaucratic interests, and of being agents of "national dishonor" (*kokujoku mono*).[16] It is useful to recognize that for both MITI and MPT, the United States was not so much an independent player as a counter to be used in their domestic struggle. American pressure on Japan was never decisive unless it happened to coincide with the interests of a major domestic player, in which case it could be quite effective. The Americans were usually ineffective because they typically did not know what was going on within the Japanese government and made their protests only to the foreign ministry or the prime minister. As one of the few Japanese linguists among the United States trade officials at the time of these negotiations said to Michael Berger, "The real battle isn't between the Americans and Japanese. This (telecommunications struggle) is a gigantic turf fight between the Ministry of Posts and Telecommunications and the Ministry of International Trade and Industry. We Americans are like a little terrier, yipping at the heels of two giants. Every once in a while we get their attention, and they toss us a bone."[17]

The Telecommunications Law was, of course, the kind of issue in which the LDP would have to get involved. Following MPT's announcement of its laws in February 1984, Keidanren endorsed them the following month. At the same time, the United States warned that restrictions on foreign participation of Class II businesses appeared to be a *prima facie* violation of the GATT code on capital liberalization. The prime minister said at a meeting of the lower house's budget committee that foreign participation in VANs would have to be liberalized, but NTT President Shintō vowed that "Even with the liberalization of VANs, we are confident of defeating foreign capital."[18] On March 16, the PARC* Communications section and its postal-*zoku*–dominated subcommittees approved the draft Telecommunications bill; but five days later, after a massive MITI counteroffensive, the PARC

*Keildanren is Japan's most powerful big business association.

*PARC (Policy Affairs Research Council) is the LDP's most important organ in the Diet; its chairman is one of the four most important positions in the party. The PARC is subdivided into an executive committee, which forwards to the party's Executive Council its recommendations on substantive issues, some 17 sections that correspond to the ministries and the standing committees in each house of the Diet, and a large number of less formal investigative and special committees.

Executive Committee made some major changes in the law. It opened all forms of Class II VANs to foreign participation; and it changed MPT's powers over special Class IIs from "license" to "report" and over general Class IIs from "report" to "notify."

On April 4, 1984, the four top leaders of the LDP met with MITI and MPT officials and endorsed the version advanced by the PARC Executive Committee. In the LDP's view it had given the MPT a victory, even though it had taken away a few things the ministry had wanted. MITI saw a victory of sorts in the weakening of MPT's licensing powers; and the Americans took the removal of restrictions against foreigners as a victory of their low key trade negotiations. Most external observers regarded the final outcome as a clear victory for MPT, which is also the way the ministry saw it....

The battle was not yet over, however. Because of delays by the opposition parties and the intervention of the PARC Chairman Fujio Masayuki...none of the three MPT bills had been passed when the Diet session ended on August 8, 1984. Fujio had sought a delay because he did not want Prime Minister Nakasone to take credit for passage in the forthcoming party presidential election campaign, and Nakasone himself was not too sorry to postpone the vote because some of the postal *zoku* were still not in favor of the NTT privatization bill....On October 30, 1984, Nakasone was reelected to a second term as LDP president, and the three laws were finally passed without fanfare on December 20, 1984. They came into effect on April 1, 1985.

THE "PRIVATIZATION" OF NTT

The Nippon Telegraph and Telephone Public Corporation had long had a reputation for low productivity, resembling more a typical government agency than a corporation, even a public one. With 1984 sales in the ¥2.3 trillion range ($23.8 billion at ¥200 to U.S. $1) and some 320,000 employees, each worker produced only ¥14.8 million for the company, compared with ¥40 million for Japan steel employees and around ¥20 million at the private railroads. Government auditors concluded that NTT had at least 100,000 surplus workers, and noted that they only worked a 37-hour week.[19] It was to deal with these and other problems that Dokō Toshio, the chairman of Rinchō, sent his trusted subordinate, Dr. Shintō Hisashi, to NTT as president.

Shintō was not popular at NTT. Internally the company had long been dominated by a group of technicians who much preferred that NTT remain a state-managed monopoly. Others opposed to Shinto and to privatization were the NTT "family" firms, led by NEC, and the LDP's postal *zoku*, who feared that if MPT and NTT were separated, they would lose control over one or both. In addition to members of Rinchō, the Americans and MITI favored privatization, the latter opportunistically (and erroneously) believing that privatization would weaken MPT.

U.S. pressure was an important background influence in this case. In mid-February 1983, U.S. Trade Representative William Brock complained in Tokyo that despite the three-year "NTT Procurement Procedures Agreement" of December 1980, during the previous year NTT bought only $11.6 million worth of U.S. products out of a total procurement of $2.9 billion. He threatened not to renew the agreement when it expired at the end of 1983. The Japanese got the message. Just before President Reagan's visit to Tokyo in November 1983, NTT placed orders in America for several one-time-only but big-ticket items (e.g., a supercomputer). The Americans were mollified and in January they renewed the agreement for another three years. Nonetheless, in 1984, U.S. telecommunications sales to NTT amounted to only $130 million, whereas Japanese sales in the United States spurred by the break-up of AT&T, surged to over $2 billion. For the Americans, a privatized NTT could not make things much worse than they already were, although there was concern over whether a private NTT would continue to honor the agreement of January 1984, which of course covered only purchases by governmental agencies.

The deadlock between those wanting privatization of NTT and those opposed was broken by a group of creative MPT bureaucrats. The more they thought about it, the more they saw in a privatized NTT a way of *expanding* the ministry's jurisdiction. Led by Telecommunications Bureau chief Koyama, these officials reasoned that they could write the law in such a way as to keep NTT under their jurisdiction while simultaneously expanding their coverage to include the new Class I carriers who were petitioning the ministry to go into business in competition with NTT. Similarly, privatizing NTT would mean that MPT would have to take over the functions that NTT had previously performed, including setting telephone rates, determining product standards and certification procedures, and supervising research in telecommunications. Old hands at MPT were also not sorry to turn the tables on NTT's proud engineers, who had long lorded it over the mere postal workers.

With this new conception of their task, Koyama and his colleagues set out to convince the LDP's *zoku*. They had several good arguments. As the country's largest single enterprise, a private NTT would be a much better source of political contributions than a public corporation. The actual sales of NTT's share would produce a bonanza of cash for the Japanese treasury. And competition might serve to strengthen NTT. Even more important to the eventual outcome of the NTT case was the involvement of Tanaka Kakuei himself. In its original draft of the NTT law, MPT proposed that the government hold 50 percent of the shares of a private NTT in perpetuity. Tanaka's concern was with the distribution of profits from the dividends and from the sales of NTT shares. The potential amounts of money were enormous. By selling some proportion of NTT shares and collecting dividends on those that it retained, the government might generate at least $8 billion in extra-budget funds. MPT wanted to control these funds, whereas MOF wanted to use them to reduce the national debt. Tanaka was the "don"* of the postal *zoku* but he

*Note all *zoku* are equal. Kawagushi Hiroyuki (see note 2) ranks them in five grades. "Don (as in don Corleone of *The Godfather*, a highly popular film in Japan); "boss (*bosu*), one who has passed through all the stages from parliamentary vice minister to the cabinet or senior party post; "elder" (*chōrō*), a politician who has served in most posts on the road to *zoku*hood but who will retire before making boss; "strongman" (*jitsuryokusha*), a Diet member who specializes in some subsection of a ministry's jurisdiction; and ordinary *zoku*.

was also first and foremost an expert in public finance. He favored the MOF's position on this issue, even though most of his followers supported MPT.[20]

Together with his close supporter and number-one postal *zoku* Kanemaru, Tanaka worked out a formula containing these points: (1) NTT would become a private company on April 1, 1985; (2) MOF would sell two-thirds of its shares to the public (but not to foreigners) and it would do so over a five-year period in order not to disrupt the securities markets, using the proceeds to help retire the national debt; and (3) the dividends on the remaining one-third would be used to fund a new telecommunications research facility. This last item was necessary to placate the NTT-family firms, which were worried about losing their research cartels under a privatized NTT.[21] Nonetheless, setting up this new research organ produced one of the most bitter battles between MITI and MPT.

The Tanaka-Kanemaru formula became the contents of the law passed in December 1984. In April 1985, NTT emerged as a new joint stock company. In January 1986, the private NTT even entered into a joint venture with IBM to create a new network service that can transmit and receive voice, character, and image messages. Deafening howls of outrage were heard from the old family firm, even though they continued to supply the majority of NTT's purchases.[22] MPT seemed unperturbed by these developments, knowing at last that NTT was not going to embarrass it by becoming a second JNR. Also, during March 1986, MOF announced its intention to sell the first batch of NTT shares, some 1.95 million of them. The ministry said that based on a net assets per share calculation of ¥213,210, the government stood to make ¥415.8 billion on this sale alone ($2.3 billion at ¥180 = U.S.$1). There is actually every reason to believe that MOF will eventually receive substantially more than the price based on net assets per share.[23] The Dai-Ichi Kangyo Bank was so interested in these lucrative goings on that it established a new department exclusively to handle NTT shares and said that it planned to hire a couple of NTT *amakudari* (descent from heaven) retirees to help advise it on the business.[24]

PRODUCT STANDARDS AND CERTIFICATION PROCEDURES

Michael Aho and Jonathan Aronson, in a study done for the Council on Foreign Relations, argue that "The Japanese government clearly devises rules that inhibit imports and promote exports....Japanese procedures and standards are often designed to exhaust all but the largest and most determined foreign firms wishing to sell in Japan. Today, on a percentage basis, Japan imports fewer manufactured products from industrial and developing countries than it did ten or twenty years ago."[25] The standards for telecommunications imports, which were set by NTT and its family firms until the Telecommunications Business Law of 1984 transferred them to MPT, seem an apt illustration of this point.

The new law requires that MPT use a "designated approval agency" to certify the acceptability of what NTT calls "consumer provided equipment" and what the Americans call "interconnect equipment" (everything from PBX to computers). According to the new law, this "designated approval agency" must be a not-for-profit foundation as defined under article 34 of the Japanese Civil Code (i.e., a *zaidan hojin*). This requirement alone makes it structurally impossible for laboratories outside of Japan to be designated as approval agencies by MPT. Moreover, on March 30, 1984, several months before the Telecommunications Business Law was even passed, NE, Fujitsū, Hitachi, Oki, and other companies set up the "Telecommunications Terminal Equipment Inspection Association" (a *zaidan hojin*), capitalized at 150 million, to serve as the "designated approval agency" whenever MPT got around to designating it. There are no other such agencies. The foundation itself had no staff, only a board of directors, since it borrowed its technical personnel and testing equipment from NTT's Engineering Bureau.[26]

The officers of this new approval agency are Akiyama Toru, a former official of the old Ministry of Communications and a former vice minister of transportation; Kashiwagi Teruhiko, a former employee of the Ministry of Communications and of NTT from 1942 to 1970; and Asanuma Isao, a former NTT director of engineering for Kanagawa prefecture (capital, Yokohama). Director Asanuma was quoted by the press as saying that "the association does not intend to accept U.S.-generated technical data." He also indicated that he had no plans to include foreign companies as contributors to the foundation and that technical standards would be distributed only to "friendly companies."[27] The foundation opened its offices for business in October 1984 in preparation for NTT's privatization the following April.

According to the Telecommunications Business Law, the technical standards themselves are to be set by the Telecommunications Deliberation Council, appointed by and attached to MPT. This council was created on October 1, 1982, by cabinet order and is composed of some 20 prominent citizens appointed for two-year terms by the Minister of Posts and Telecommunications. Prior to 1985 there were no foreign members nor any with a foreign institutional connection.[28]

Needless to say, the few alert Americans charged with watching such developments were not pleased by what they saw. MITI, too, thought that maybe MPT was being a little unsubtle in these arrangements and believed that it might embarrass its rival politically. MPT seemed determined to humiliate Prime Minister Nakasone, who in his January 1985 meeting with President Reagan had specifically promised to get rid of these kinds of nontariff barriers to trade in the telecommunications field. The Americans charged the Japanese with violating the GATT code of standards, which Japan signed in 1979 and which came into effect on January 1, 1980. This code states (Art. 2.1) that the "parties shall ensure that technical regulations and standards are not prepared, adopted, or applied with a view to creating obstacles to international trade."[29] Since the law setting up Japan's new system for telecommunications had already been passed, MPT claimed that it could not do anything about that. Interest therefore turned to how MPT would implement the law through its ministerial ordinances. Reagan sent his aide Gaston Sigur to Tokyo to plead with Nakasone for some improvement in Japanese-American trade in telecommunications products, which then stood at 10 to 1 in Japan's favor. MPT's answer to this pressure was to produce petitions from consumers' groups saying that the Americans were trying to sell Japan television sets one could not see and telephones one could not properly hear.[30]

A part of the problem is that in Japan standards settings and product certification are a governmental responsibility, whereas in American they are largely left to the insurance companies and their Underwriters' Laboratories. Japanese consumers by no means believe that in enforcing high standards their government is acting to restrict trade or violate international agreements. They think that foreigners should meet Japanese standards of quality and performance, just as Japanese must meet America's admittedly less stringent standards. Nonetheless, MPT determined that it could not win this battle, and while retaining its apparatus of a foundation and a deliberation council, began to compromise. In negotiations between vice minister Koyama and undersecretary of commerce Lionel Ulmer, Koyama started progressively to lower the number and stringency of MPT-set standards. He also agreed to add two members to the Telecommunications Deliberation Council from foreign-connected firms in Japan and to appoint experts from AT&T International, Nippon Philips, IBM Japan, Nippon UNIVAC, Fuji Xerox, and Nippon Motorola to its board of technical advisers.[31] The Americans declared themselves to be satisfied even though MITI charged, probably accurately, that these MPT concessions were only cosmetic.

PROTECTING COMPUTER PROGRAMS

The battle over protecting computer programs was confusing to foreigners because MITI, which they had begun to think of as "liberal," came down hard on the protectionist side, and MPT advocated what might appear at first glance as the free trade solution. Of course neither ministry is protectionist or liberal; each of their positions changes in accordance with the dictates of the bureaucratic struggle for survival. Computer software was probably MITI's best opportunity to make real inroads against MPT, and the fact that it lost this battle was probably its most bitter defeat. MITI was also highly self-righteous about software, believing that NTT engineers did not understand how important it was to the future of the Japanese computer industry.[32] It is true that not until April 1985 did NTT's Telecommunication Laboratory set up a unit devoted exclusively to software production—the Software Production Technical Research Laboratory (Sofutouea Seisan Gijutsu Kenkyūjo), located in Yokosuka.

As background to the software battle, one must recall the 1982 industrial espionage scandal in which Hitachi was caught red-handed in California trying to steal the operating secrets of a new IBM computer. As details of the case unfolded, MITI and the Japanese public became painfully aware that the software and operating systems in Hitachi and Fujitsū computers were basically copies of IBM products, for which Hitachi and Fujitsū subsequently agreed to pay IBM millions of dollars. The scandal revealed Japan's weakness in software, compared with the United States, and it also made clear that building IBM-compatible machines, Japanese firms were being tempted into industrial espionage against IBM. Far too much time was spent in Japanese laboratories on "reverse engineering," that is, taking apart someone else's product to find out how it works, instead of on independent development of new products. MITI's position on software thus reflected its concern to acquire legally the software that Japan needed from abroad and to avoid a repetition of Hitachi's humiliation.

Until January 1, 1986, there was no protection in Japan for computer software, and foreign programs were routinely pirated and rented or sold to personal computer owners. In early 1983, the Cultural Affairs Agency (Bunka-cho) of the Ministry of Education, which is legally responsible for administering Japan's copyright law, asked its Copyright Deliberation Council (Chosakuken Shingikai), an advisory body of 20 leaders from the book, film, recording, and university worlds, to look into the matter. The council proposed that Japan protect computer software by copyrighting it, meaning that for some 50 years the authors of computer programs could take legal action against unauthorized copying. Such protection is powerful but also rather narrow.

The opposite of copyright is protection through a patent, which covers both the form and the concepts involved in a work but which, being more comprehensive, is offered for a much shorter period of time. MITI, which viewed the protection issue from the point of view of Japan's computer makers, advocated patent protection (at first for 10 years but extended to 15 in the ministry's draft law).[33] This approach was itself controversial, since the United States protects computer programs under the copyright laws, but it was what MITI further proposed that set off a storm of protests. MITI's bill stipulated that anyone could use a program so long as a fee was paid, and in cases where the parties could not agree on the fee, a MITI-appointed panel of experts would arbitrate and set one. Most important, MITI's proposed law further required that the holders of software patents license their operating systems to Japanese computer manufacturers, again for an arbitrated fee if the two parties failed to agree.

In early 1984, MITI and the Cultural Affairs Agency unveiled their respective draft laws, setting off what was probably the nastiest fire fight in the telecom wars. The United States and IBM backed the Cultural Affairs Agency, although IBM-Japan did so more quietly since it would still have to work in Japan however this issue was decided. Fujitsū and the other makers of IBM-compatible computers strongly favored MITI's position. They feared that under copyright IBM would gain exceptional rights in Japan, whereas IBM feared that MITI was trying to continue it old policy of the early 1960s of forcing IBM to license its patent rights to Japanese as the price of being allowed to do business in Japan. Some press observers, who remembered the IBM sting operation against Hitachi in California, thought that MITI was merely trying to get even. In February 1984, while locked in battle with MITI over the VAN law, MPT also entered the fray, strongly endorsing the Cultural Affairs Agency's bill.

MITI was eventually defeated. American pressure helped the Cultural Affairs Agency and MPT. The U.S. Congress introduced reciprocity legislation to stop sales in the American market of the products of countries that failed to protect American intellectual property rights. The Americans also pointed out that in UNESCO the Japanese have always strongly opposed all requests by Third World nations for the compulsory licensing of patents. In April 1985, the LDP finally took the Cultural Affairs Agency's draft, modified somewhat to reflect MITI's concerns, to the Diet, where it was passed on June 7 and came into effect on January 1, 1986. The law gives copyright protection to computer programs, defined as "arrangements of commands to make computers function and to obtain functioning results," for 50 years.

SATELLITES AND SPACE COMMUNICATIONS POLICY

On February 4, 1983, Japan launched its first commercial communications satellite at a cost some three times greater than similar more effective satellites that could be purchased in the United States. The project was under the direction of the Science and Technology Agency, attached to the prime minister's office, and strongly backed by Keidanren. As the single most powerful association in the country for expressing the views of big business, Keidanren mirrored the divisions within the telecommunications industry over satellites. Its two main leaders, known as the "two Kobayashis," were the chairmen of the two leading NTT "family" firms. First was Kobayashi Taiyu, chairman of Fujitsu, who headed Keidanren's committee on data processing and favored buying Japan's satellites abroad. Second was Kobayashi Kōji, chairman of NEC, who headed Keidanren's Space Activities Promotion Council and favored the national production of communications satellites. When in July 1983, Kobayashi Kōji's committee recommended the national development of large (two or four ton) communications satellites rather than buying them from the United States, Japan's satellite program became a serious issue in Japanese-American trade friction and a skirmish in the telecom wars.

There is no doubt that Japan's decision to build communications satellites with public money is an unambiguous example of targeting and of industrial policy. The Japanese government refused even to discuss with the United States the possibility of buying better and cheaper satellites from abroad, saying that it was a matter of national security, even though Keidanren had already made clear that Japan intended to start exporting them to North America and Western Europe by the 1990s. Given that Japan's share of imports in the U.S. domestic market for telecommunications products had grown from 3 percent in 1978 to 11 percent in 1983 and that fully a third of Japan's total production was exported, the Americans were outraged. American pressure on Japan and on Keidanren ultimately forced the government to modify its position. It continues to prohibit sales of foreign satellites to government agencies but no longer prohibits Japanese civilians from buying them. Nontheless, when in 1985 two consortia of big trading companies, Mitsui Trading and Ito Chu on the one hand and Mitsubishi Trading and Mitsubishi Electric on the other, applied to become Class I telecommunications carriers, MPT refused to allocate frequencies to Hughes Aircraft or any other American satellites that they proposed to buy. The ministry ultimately backed down only when Keidanren reversed itself and decided to join one of the satellite consortia that were being formed.

Meanwhile, MITI was being made nervous by these goings on. It criticized MPT and the Science and Technology Agency for contributing to trade friction, but it also set up its own internal advisory organ, called the "Space Utilization Research and Examination Committee." The purpose of the committee is to help MITI try to take over space development from the Science and Technology Agency and to shift the emphasis in Japan's space program from science to industry. The Japanese government continues to work to develop a national communications satellite capacity, and one suspects that MITI is merely getting ready to assume jurisdiction when the nation starts exporting.

TELETOPIAS AND NEW MEDIA COMMUNITIES

Nobody of course really knows what the "informationized" society of the future will look like, but the Japanese are taking no chances. It is possible that telecommunications will require an investment in facilities and infrastructure equal to the investment in railroads in the late nineteenth century. During 1984, NTT was already using figures of from ¥30 to ¥100 trillion for the INS (Information Network System) alone. Towns and prefectures certainly wanted to make sure that their localities were included in which ever ministry's plan became national policy. For this reason the Diet Members' League for New Media, created in the autumn of 1983 by Kanemaru Shin and Satō Moriyoshi (both belong to the Tanaka faction) immediately attracted some 220 members.[34]

MITI was the first to air its proposal. On July 26, 1983, it unveiled a plan to build some 11 (later cut to 8) "new media communities," that is, towns around the country designated as test sites for digitalized, multimedia networks and new equipment. (Note that both MITI and MPT use English to market their offerings—*nyu media komyuniti* is MITI's term and *teletopia* is MPT's. Japanese commonly use English as the language of fashion and advertising, just as French is used in English-speaking countries.) MITI justified its choice of specific communities in terms of their diversity—textile regions, high-tech areas, resorts, and so forth—but it also took care to include Nagaoka, the capital city of Tanaka Kakuei's district in Niigata prefecture.[35]

MPT was astounded by this MITI announcement, and Telecommunications bureau chief Koyama scurried to the postal *zoku* to complain that MITI was infringing on its turf. The *zoku* told him to speed up his own announcement, and in August MPT duly published its list of some 20 cities it planned to designate as Teletopias. This meant that NTT would install in them its advanced INS system and supply them with its new CAPTAIN ("character and pattern telephone access information network") videotext telephones. Neither INS nor CAPTAIN was as yet available in the summer of 1983—full-scale testing began only in November 1984 at Mitaka, a suburb of Tokyo adjacent to the main NTT laboratory—and many thought that MPT's first announcement was merely designed to head off MITI. Nonetheless, since MPT has NTT on its side, it could probably deliver on its plans sooner than MITI, and cities all over the country began petitioning their Diet members to get themselves included as future Teletopias.[36]

In late 1984, MITI and MPT both sent to the LDP bills that would provide funds to build the new media communities and teletopias. They also flooded the press with propaganda about the wonders of the informationized society of the future. The party, however, scrapped both bills simply because they were too expensive (MITI's actually passed but in a watered-down version that provided only small-scale funding to test the collaborative use of computers in industries). Meanwhile, the Ministry of Construction decided that both MITI and MPT were infringing on *its* jurisdiction and produced its own bill to build new telecommunications networks along the national highways. Not to be outdone, in November 1984, the Ministry of Transportation got interested in laying optical fiber cables along the JNR rights-of-way and going into business as a Class I common carrier in competition with NTT and other new entries.

As a result of this bureaucratic free-for-all, the party hedged for more than a year. During this time MOF made clear to the politicians that they certainly could not afford all four ministries' proposals and very probably could not afford any of them. Finally, on February 28, 1986, the Nakasone cabinet approved a compromise bill, one that incorporated the LDP's newly discovered concept of "vitality." *Baitaritei*, an example of Japanese-created English that does not exist in English (so called *wasei eigo*), does not mean "vitality" in Japanese but rather governmental incentives for private sector initiatives. This is a code word for leaving a public matter to the private sector, as for example in the LDP Executive Council report of July 16, 1985: "The stimulation of domestic demand by actively promoting private vitality which is not dependent on government spending is the best policy to be adopted."[37]

The cabinet proposal of February 1986 combines the infrastructure plans of all four ministries. It offers a 13 percent special investment tax credit in the first year to private firms that come in on designated projects, and it also exempts them from property and land sales taxes. Additional funding is provided by concessionary loans from the Japan Development Bank, a government agency that invests postal savings through the Fiscal Investment and Loan Program. The areas designated for investment are: (1) facilities for high-tech research and development and for training technicians, (2) telecommunications infrastructure (MPT), (3) information-oriented society infrastructure (MITI), (4) facilities for telecommunications R&D for joint use by public and private enterprises, (5) facilities for international fairs and conferences, and (6) projects to upgrade harbors and port terminals.[38] Thus, in the teletopias case, the party seems temporarily to have solved interministerial conflict through an omnibus pork barrel bill that gives something to everybody.

PROMOTING TELECOMMUNICATIONS RESEARCH

The centerpiece of MITI's policy for fiscal 1985 was a new agency under its control to promote and help finance the high-technology industries of the future—specifically, telecommunications, new ceramics, biotechnology, and microelectronics. If MITI could occupy the high ground of high-tech R&D, it had a good chance of ushering in its until then elusive "third golden age." To get such a new agency approved by the Budget Bureau of the Ministry of Finance and the General Affairs Agency of the prime minister's office, however, it had to do two things. It had to find an agency under its control to abolish before the General Affairs agency would allow a new one to be created; and it had to find an off-budget way of financing its new project, given the generally flat budgets of the mid-1980s imposed by MOF and Prime Minister Nakasone. To meet the first requirement, MITI offered up for sacrifice its old Foreign Trade Training Institute (this being one area in which Japanese assuredly did not need further education), and it proposed to fund the new agency through low-interest loans from the Japanese Development Bank "private vitality."

As it turned out, MPT also wanted to fund a new organ to facilitate telecommunications research. With the privatization of NTT, the government's major telecom research institutes had passed into private industry, and MPT needed some kind of public agency to fund and keep alive the research cartels of the NTT "family" firms. MPT did not have the required agency to sacrifice to create a new one, but it had something just as valuable—lots of money. MPT believed that it controlled the dividends on one-third of NTT's shares, and it now proposed to use these funds to finance joint public-private telecommunications research.

Unhappily for MPT, the Ministry of Finance took the view that "At a time of great stress in national finance, to leave a third of the NTT shares—which is the joint property of the people—under the monopoly of a single ministry is scandalous."[39] Instead, MOF proposed, in cooperation with MITI, to revive the almost moribund Industrial Investment Special Account with NTT dividends, plus funds derived from the privatization of the government's tobacco monopoly. The Industrial Investment Special Account was an unconsolidated, earmarked account dating from the 1950s and early 1960s, when it was used as an instrument of industrial policy. Its funds had not been replenished for many years, however, when MOF and MITI urged reviving it to fund high-tech research. Needless to say, this proposal would have removed MPT from having any control over the NTT dividends, since all special accounts are under MOF's jurisdiction.

This three-ministry dispute went to the LDP for arbitration. Party secretary general Kanemaru devised a solution and then sold it to his own faction (i.e., Tanaka's), which ensured its passage in the Diet. Kanemaru accepted MOF's financing formula. He proposed that the new Basic Technological Research Promotion Center (Kiban Gijutsu Kenkyū Sokushin Sentā) be supplied with start-up capital from three sources. First, it would receive ¥6 billion from the Industrial Investment Special Account, which would itself be restored to life in the manner MOF had proposed. Second, it would accept a ¥3 billion loan from the Japanese Development Bank. Third, the private sector would contribute some ¥4.5 to ¥5 billion. In addition, Kanemaru authorized the new center to create joint research projects with two or more private companies, for which an additional ¥2 billion of working capital would be supplied from the Industrial Investment Special Account. Finally, he gave the center still another ¥2 billion from the Industrial Investment Special Account for research loans to private firms for risky projects (they do not have to repay the loans if the projects fail). NTT dividends should amount to at least ¥20 billion per annum, which is more than enough to fund all of these subaccounts and still build up the special account for the future.

Since MITI was supplying the sacrificial agency and MPT (indirectly) the money, Kanemaru gave them both jurisdiction over and responsibility for administering the new center. This decision produced one of the classic encounters of the telecom wars. On December 18, 1984, in MOF's press club room on the second floor of the MOF building, MITI Minister Murata and MPT Minister Satō gathered for a press conference. They had just completed final negotiations over the fiscal 1985 budget with Finance Minister Takeshita, in which the main issue was MOF's approval of the Basic Technological Research Promotion Center. Murata opened: "With regard to the center, it has been decided that both the Ministry of International Trade and Industry and the Ministry of Posts and Telecommunications will be involved, but MITI will take the upper hand." Satō then stepped forward, interrupted, and said, "This project is absolutely under the joint jurisdiction of both MITI and MPT. MITI is not playing any leading role."[40] The next day every newspaper in the country reported the "blood feud" between MITI and MPT. Incidentally, Murata and Satō are close friends.

The Basic Technology Research Facilitation Law, setting up and funding the center, passed the Diet on June 15, 1985. Because the center was partly funded by the private sector and was thus an example of "vitality," the government insisted that its chairman had to be a civilian. It asked the venerable president of Keidanren, Inayama Yoshihiro, 81 years old in 1985 and an official in MITI's predecessor ministry during the 1930s to find one. He first asked Iwata Jazuo, the former chairman of Tōshiba, but MPT rejected him for being "too close to MITI." Inayama then tried Shindō Sadakazu, chairman of Mitsubishi Electric, but MITI turned him down as a "member of the NTT family." Inayama finally went to Hiraiwa Gaishi, the respected chairman of Tokyo Electric Power, and when he declined, decided to take the post himself.[41] Serving under Inayama are the chosen agents from the three concerned ministries (MITI, MPT, MOF)....

So was launched Japan's largest bureaucratic effort to achieve scientific and technological preeminence in the industries of the future. The new center was given a big send-off on July 29, 1985, at the New Otani Hotel, Tokyo. Chairman Inayama brought out some 55 "*zaikai* (the world of big business) all stars" to pledge their support, including NTT president Shintō, Ishihara Takashi of the Japan Automobile Industry Association, Hagura Nobuya of the National Banking Association, and Morita Akio of the Japan Electronic Machinery Association (and head of Sony). The center is a typical Japanese hybrid: the product of bureaucratic competition, funded from public but not tax monies, and incorporating private sector supervision and participation....

Exhibit 1 Key Organizations and Individuals Listed in Order of Appearance in the Case

GOVERNMENT ORGANIZATIONS

Liberal Democratic Party (LDP)
Ministry of Finance (MOF)
Ministry of International Trade and Industry (MITI)
Ministry of Posts and Telecommunications (MPT)
Agency of Cultural Affairs, attached to Ministry of Education

Fiscal Investment and Loan Program (FILP), source of investment funds, (see
p. 9)
Zoku, groups of veteran Diet members specializing in different fields, that is,
postal, finance, communications
Rinchō, Commission for Administrative Reform
PARC, Policy Affairs Research Council, LDP's most important organ in the
Diet
Science and Technology Agency, attached to prime minister's office

COMPANIES

Nippon Telegraph and Telephone Co. (NTT)
Nippon Electric (NEC)
Fujitsu   MPT's "family"
Oki Electric
Hitachi
Japan National Railroad (JNR)
IBM
AT&T

INDIVIDUALS

Tanaka Kakuei, former prime minister, powerful leader of LDP and postal
zoku
Konaga Keiichi, vice minister of MITI
Yamanounchi Ichirō, MPT minister, succeeded by Satō
Tanaka Rokusuke, MITI minister, succeeded by Murata, powerful LDP
politician
Shintō Hisashi, NTT president
Fujio Masayuki, PARC chairman
Nakasone Yasuhiro, president of LDP and prime minister
Suzuki Zenko, former prime minister
Kanemura Shin, leader of postal *zoku*, member of Tanaka faction
Koyama Moriya, chief of MPT's Telecommunications Bureau, former chief of
Communications Policy Bureau
William Brock, U.S. trade representative
Lionel Ulmer, U.S. undersecretary of commerce

Exhibit 2 The Japanese Legislative Process

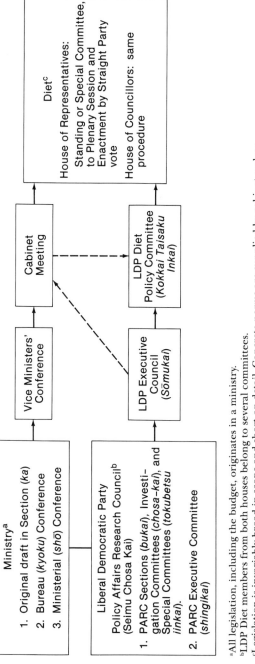

Ministry[a]

1. Original draft in Section (*ka*)
2. Bureau (*kyoku*) Conference
3. Ministerial (*shō*) Conference

Vice Ministers' Conference

Cabinet Meeting

Diet[c]

House of Representatives:
Standing or Special Committee, to Plenary Session and Enactment by Straight Party vote

House of Councillors: same procedure

Liberal Democratic Party
Policy Affairs Research Council[b]
(Seimu Chosa Kai)

1. PARC Sections (*bukai*), Investigation Committees (*chosa-kai*), and Special Committees (*tokubetsu iinkai*).

2. PARC Executive Committee (*shingikai*)

LDP Executive Council (*Sōmukai*)

LDP Diet Policy Committee (*Kokkai Taisaku Inkai*)

[a]All legislation, including the budget, originates in a ministry.

[b]LDP Diet members from both houses belong to several committees.

[c]Legislation is invariably broad in scope and short on detail. Concrete norms are supplied by cabinet orders, ministerial orders, and administrative guidance.

Sources: Murakawa Ichirō, *Seisaku kettei katei* (The Policy-Making Process) (Tokyo: Kyōiku Sha, 1979), pp. 192–193, and Kawakita Takao, *Tsusan-Yusei sensō* (The MITI-MPT Wars) (Tokyo: Kyōiku Sha, 1985), p. 87.

ENDNOTES

1. On "privatization," see *The Economist* (London), December 21, 1985, pp. 71–74.

2. Kawaguchi Hiroyuki, "Jimintō habatsu to kanryō: 'zoku' no rankingu" (LDP factions and the Bureaucracy: Rankings of *Zoku*), *Gekkan kankai*, Vol. 9 (November 1983), p. 95.

3. Kawakita Takao, *Tsūsan-Yūsei sensō* (The MITI-MPT Wars) (Tokyo: Kyoiku Sha, 1985), pp. 56–57. On the idea that MOF is also a "super-elite bureaucracy," see Jin Ikko, *Okura kanryō: chō-eritō shūdan no jinmyaku to yabo* (MOF Bureaucrats: The Cliques and Intrigues of a Super-elite Group) (Tokyo: Kōdansha, 1982), p. 19 et passim.

4. In early 1986, after All Nippon Airways, Japan's leading domestic airline decided to buy Boeing 767-300s as its next mainstay aircraft, the *Nihon keizai shimbun* reported charges that MITI had become "America's good friend" and "America's lackey." However, some analysts recognized in MITI's pro-import drive "a façade for expanding the ministry's influence over domestic firms." The *Nihon keizai* wrote: "The drive to cut the surplus is a good opportunity for MITI to recover its old iron grip on domestic industries which it lost in the process of Japan's trade liberalization. MITI plans to intervene in domestic industries as 'an emergency measure' and maintain that intervention for a long time" (*Japan Economic Journal*, January 25, 1986, pp. 1, 5). In the summer of 1985, MITI also discussed and then shelved as too controversial a draft "Overseas Investment Facilitation Law." This bill stipulated that firms whose exports exceeded MITI-set limits would be obligated to shift some of their production offshore. The draft law would have given MITI strong powers of control over export-oriented industries, particularly the electronics and telecommunications industries that do not have MITI-administered quantitative controls over exports such as exist in the automobile industry.

5. See, for example, Kawakita, *Tsusan-Yūsei sensō*, pp. 60–61. Compare National Research Council, National Academy of Sciences, *High-Technology Ceramics in Japan* (Washington, D.C.: National Academy Press, 1984).

6. Konaga Keiichi, "Tsūsan-shō no shin senryaku: tekunoraibaru Beikoku to no kyōsō" (MITI's New Strategy: Competition with Our Technorival, America), *Next* (December 1984), pp. 48–53. (Note that many new Japanese magazines use English words or phrases for their titles, including *Focus, This Is, Trigger, Voice,* and several others. *Next* is such a magazine.)

7. Kawakita, *Tsūsan-Yūsei sensō*, pp. 61–62.

8. "The Business-Minded Ministry: MPT, "*Journal of Japanese Trade and Industry*, Vol. 5, no. 2 (March–April 1986), p. 30. (Note that this magazine is published by a MITI-affiliated organization.)

9. Timothy J. Curran, "Politics and High Technology: The NTT Case," in I. M. Destler and Sato Hideo, eds., *Coping with U.S.-Japanese Economic Conflicts* (Lexington, Mass.: D. C. Heath, 1982), p. 201.

10. Gotoda Teruo, "Nihon ni okeru kōdo gijutsu hatten no kanryō kitō no taitō to sangyō seisaku no saihensei" (The Emergence of a Bureaucratic Apparatus for the Development of High-Technology in Japan and the Reorganization of Industrial Policy), *Himeji Gakuin kiyō* (Himeji University Bulletin), no. 13 (1985), p. 142.

11. Michael Korver, "Developments in Japanese Finance," *Japan Economic Journal*, May 17, 1986, p. 5, and Jin Ikkō, *Ōkura Kanryo*, pp. 189–201.

12. Kawakita, *Tsūsan-Yūsei sensō*, pp. 136–137.

13. *Nihon keizai shimbun*, May 10, 1983, and *Gekkan kankai*, November 1983, pp. 135–136.

14. Ouchi Takao, "Yūsei vs. Tsūsan: hateshi-naki arasoi" (MPT vs. MITI: A Struggle Without End), *Gekkan kankai*, vol. 10 (June 1984), p. 140; *NTTopics*, no. 11 (Summer 1985), p. 2; and *Zaikai tembo*, August 1984 (trans. FBIS, *Japan Report*, JPRS-JAR-84-017, November 14, 1984), pp. 32–35. For the text of the Telecommunications Business Law in English, see *Japan Law Letter*, February 1985, pp. 19–30, and March 1985, pp. 14–23.

15. See Mark E. Foster, "Telecommunications Equipment Standards and Certification Procedures for Japan" (unpublished paper), Foreign Commercial Service, U.S. Department of Commerce, Tokyo, October 1984, p. 12 (permission to cite obtained from the author). Also see Foster, "A Guide to Mandatory Technical Standards and Product Certification Procedures Under Japan's Electrical Appliance Law" (unpublished paper, ibid.).

16. Ōuchi, "Yūsei vs. Tsūsan," p. 138.

17. *Business Week*, March 11, 1985, p. 67.

18. *Zaikai Tembō*, August 1984 (trans. FBIS, *Japan Report*, JPRS-JAR-84-017, November 14, 1984), p. 34.

19. Kawakita, *Tsūsan-Yūsei sensō*, p. 75; Ohashi Ikuo (MPT official), "The Effects of Telecommunications Deregulation," in Program on U.S.-Japan Relations, ed., *U.S.-Japan: Towards a New Equilibrium* (Cambridge, Mass.: Center for International Affairs, Harvard University, 1983), p. 91; and *Zaikai tembō*, August 1984 (trans. FBIS, *Japan Report*, JPRS-JAR-84-017, November 14, 1984), p. 24.

20. Gotoda, "Nihon ni okeru kōdo gijutsu hatten no kanryō kito no taitō to sangyō seisaku no saihensei," pp. 146–147; Kawakami, in *Summaries of Selected Japanese Magazines*, April 1985, p. 6; Kawakita, *Tsūsan-Yūsei sensō*, pp. 78–82; and Takahashi Yoshiyuki, "Jimintō habatsu to kanryō: 'Tanaka shihai' no nouhou" (LDP Factions and the Bureaucracy: The Know-How of the "Tanaka Domination"), *Gekkan kankai*, Vol. 9 (June 1983), pp. 121–122.
21. Journalists' Roundtable, *Ekonomisuto*, April 17, 1984, p. 26.
22. *NTTopics*, No. 14 (Spring 1986), p. 3; *Journal of Japanese Trade and Industry*, Vol. 5, no. 2, (March–April 1986), p. 29; *Japan Times Weekly*, October 19, 1985, and January 11, 1986.
23. *Japan Law Letter*, March 1986, p. 13.
24. Ouchi, "Yusei vs. Tsusan," p. 145.
25. C. Michael Aho and Jonathan David Aronson, *Trade Talks: America Better Listen* (New York: Council on Foreign Relations, 1985), p. 85.
26. Foster, "Telecommunications," p. 25 and appendix.
27. *Denkei shimbun*, April 16, 1984 (quoted in ibid.).
28. General Affairs Agency (Sōmu-chō), ed., *Shingikai sōran* (General Survey of Deliberation Councils) (Tokyo: Ōkura-shō Insatsu-kyoku, 1984), pp. 402–403, s.v. Denki Tsūshin Shingikai.
29. Foster, "A Guide to Mandatory Technical Standards," Appendix O.
30. Kawakita, *Tsūsan-Yūsei sensō*, pp. 42–44.
31. Japanese Telecommunications Association, *New Era of Telecommunications in Japan* No. 1, (1985), pp. 3–4; Sam Jameson, "Japan: Rules Eased on Telecommunications," *Los Angeles Times*, April 4, 1985; Sam Jameson, "Japan Moves to Keep Its Promises to U.S.," *Los Angeles Times*, April 9, 1985; and William C. Rempel and Sam Jameson, "Japan Phone Market: Patience vs. Pressure," *Los Angeles Times*, April 21, 1985.
32. *Gekkan kankai*, November 1983, p. 140.
33. For an outline of the MITI draft law, see *Japan Law Letter*, April 1984, pp. 74–77.
34. "Shin Denden: Nihon ichi no kyodai kigyō" (New NTT: Japan's Biggest Enterprise), *Za 21* (PHP Kenkyūjo), March 1985, pp. 42–43, and *Nihon keizai shimbun*, October 22, 1984.
35. See the map of all new media communities and teletopias in Kawakita, pp. 148–149.
36. For the networks, capabilities, and vast array of equipment involved in the INS experiment at Mitaka, see the issue devoted to the launching of INS of *Denki tsūshin gyōmu (Telecommunications Business)*, no. 416 (November 1984), pp. 4–34. This is the monthly journal of NTT.
37. "Report on Concrete Measures for Activation of Private Vitality," *Seisaku tokuhō*, August 10, 1985 (trans. FBIS *Japan Report*, JPRS-JAR-85-024, December 1, 1985, pp. 34–64). For further explanation of "vitality," see "MITI's Six Important Projects for 1986," *Jihyo*, December 1985 (trans. FBIS, *Japan Report*, JPRS-JAR-86-002, January 24, 1986), pp. 79–85, and *Tsūsan-shō-kōhō* (MITI Gazette), August 1, 1985, pp. 1–2.
38. *Japan Economic Journal*, March 8, 1986, pp. 3, 8.
39. Kawakita, *Tsūsan-Yūsei sensō*, p. 157.
40. "Shōten: Kiban Gijutsu Kenkyū Sokushin Sentā ga hassoku" (Focus: Start of the Basic Technological Research Promotion Center), *Trigger*, December 1985, p. 10, and Kawakita, *Tsūsan-Yūsei sensō*, p. 153.
41. *Trigger*, December 1985, p. 10.

French Telecommunications in the 1980s (A)

In the spring of 1984, the Socialist government of France decided to sell Compagnie Générale des Constructions Téléphoniques (CGCT) to a foreign company. Past efforts to sell this small nationalized telecommunications company to another French firm had failed due to its dim future. With cumulative operating losses of approximately Fr 1 billion between 1976 and 1983 and no competitive central office switch of its own,[1] CGCT was hardly an attractive purchase. However, by the fall of 1986, the newly elected government of Prime Minister Jacques Chirac found itself in the midst of a diplomatic imbroglio as telecommunications companies from around the world fought over who was to acquire CGCT.

The companies involved—APT (a joint venture between AT&T of the United States and Philips of the Netherlands), L. M. Ericsson (of Sweden), and Siemens (of West Germany)—saw CGCT as the key to entering the relatively closed French telecommunications market. AT&T and Siemens had appealed to their respective governments to plead their case with France. The West German Post Minister, Christian Schwarz-Schilling, and Economics Minister, Martin Bangemann, had intervened personally to further Siemens' cause. For AT&T, U.S. Secretary of Commerce Malcolm Baldrige and Trade Representative Clayton Yeutter had argued forcefully that free-market principles required the French government to make its decision strictly on a commercial basis. Politics should not be allowed to taint the deal.

Because the sale of CGCT involved the privatization of a state-owned company, responsibility for the decision was moved from France's Minister of Industry Alain Madelin to the powerful Finance Minister Edouard Balladur who in turn reported to Prime Minister Jacques Chirac. Politically, Balladur faced an extremely delicate situation. He had a variety of domestic considerations to bear in mind. At the same time, he was anxious not to alienate either the West German or U.S. governments, because closer economic ties with both countries were desired. Yet companies from both countries were determined to acquire the troubled French firm. Tiny CGCT (with 16 percent of the French switching market) had become one of the most sought-after companies in Europe.

The sudden appeal of CGCT and the complexity of Balladur's problem can be understood only in the context of the rapidly changing global telecommunications industry.

This case was prepared by Postdoctoral Fellow Barbara Jenkins, in collaboration with Professor George C. Lodge, as the basis for class discussion rather than to illustrate either effective or ineffective handling of an administrative situation.

Changes in the Global Telecommunications Industry

Technological innovation has extended telecommunications applications far beyond their traditional use for voice transmission. With the development of "broadband" cable and satellite technologies and fully electronic digital switching equipment, several new services have become available to private and public users. The combination of computing and telecommunications technology has permitted the transmission of data, voice, and visual images in the form of telematics (audiovisual services). In the next few years, Integrated Services Digital Networks (ISDN) would make possible a combination of telephony, telematics, radio, and television in a single communications system. Private networks for such services had already emerged alongside public ones as large corporate users established their own systems for data transmission. Whether public or private, new applications such as electronic mail, videotex, and videoconferencing were fast becoming integral parts of new telecommunications systems.

The development of these new technologies promised enormous profits for firms able to provide a broad array of telecommunications services. However, it also meant that firms in this sector not only needed to conduct research into the upgrading of current or "first-generation equipment" but had to be prepared to expand into new second- or third-generation services such as videotelephones, videoconferencing, and bulk data transmission as well. Research into so many new applications, costly and risky, could easily stretch the resources of even the largest firms.

Many of these new products represented forays into previously uncharted territory, and demand was growing rapidly. Exhibit 1 shows the 1985 and potential world market for telecommunications and computer goods and services. It is important to note that although the relevant market for such goods was traditionally domestic, demand was becoming increasingly global. Firms had to expand abroad into new markets to amortize high R&D costs through larger volumes of sales. Combined with the high costs of R&D, the need to operate on an international scale led to partnerships between firms with complementary skills. Firms with technological expertise but inadequate access to foreign markets formed "strategic alliances" with companies that could provide them market entry. Similarly, alliances between computer companies and telecommunications firms increased as the two technologies overlapped. Partnerships between IBM and STET (Italy), AT&T and Olivetti (Italy), ITT and CGE (France), GTE and Siemens (West Germany), Honeywell and Ericsson (Sweden), Honeywell and NEC (Japan), IBM and NTT (Japan), and AT&T and Philips (Netherlands) were the best known examples.

Technological changes in the industry also presented a conundrum for governments. In the past, telecommunications in all countries had been highly regulated, reflecting the importance of the industry for national economic and security interests as well as a general desire by governments to provide universal access to users. However, the merging of computer and telecommunications technologies confused past distinctions between data processing (which usually was unregulated and competitive) and communication (which was regulated and generally monopolistic). Digital technologies were making data and voice transmission indistinguishable. Thus, most new services required access to the same networks. As a result, governments everywhere were forced to revise regulatory standards and to consider the possibilities offered by allowing new competitors with new products into the market.

Deregulation had already begun in the United States, Great Britain, and Japan in response to these pressures and, in 1986, was being debated in France and Germany. Whereas the approach to deregulation differed in each country, its implications were the same everywhere: higher levels of uncertainty, competition, and entry by foreign companies into previously closed national markets. In theory, foreign entry is a desirable side effect of deregulation; it should increase competition, lower prices, and improve efficiency. In practice, it presented some major issues for the state: how much foreign ownership of such an important industry is too much, and how much should be tolerated without reciprocal access to the telecommunications markets of others?

The Global Market in Central Office Switches

Within the telecommunications market, one of the most competitive "zones of contestability" was the market for central office switches. These machines, with a capacity for 10,000 to 100,000 lines, represented 80 percent of the world switching market.[2] Switch sales were particularly important to telecommunications firms because they generally meant future downstream sales as equipment was modernized, capacity increased, and software added to enhance capabilities. Furthermore, because many switches were incompatible, the sale of a particular brand could set standards for many years to come.[3]

In 1986, there were about 12 firms in the central office switch market. Exhibit 2 shows the worldwide, American and European market shares of the largest of these companies that year. However, given the market prospects, it was estimated that by the year 2000, only four or five of the competitors would remain. Because production costs were so high and competition so intense, further concentration (similar to that which occurred in the jet engine industry) was envisioned.[4] For this reason, the stakes in the market for local switches were particularly high, as each company tried to ensure its place as one of the few competitors of the future. This was particularly true in the market for digital switches. In many countries, telecommunications authorities were in the process of moving from analog switches to more economic and more versatile digital equipment.[5] Exhibit 3 shows the percentage of digital lines installed by the top companies in 1986.

Because the cost of developing such advanced equipment was so high, firms had to have a large share of the market to recoup R&D costs (Exhibit 4 shows the development costs of several companies' switches). It was estimated that to make a profit, switching firms had to have 7 percent to 10 percent of the global market. Therefore, expansion abroad was a high priority. With the exception of U.S. market producers, most manufacturers relied on foreign markets for at least 40 percent of their sales.[6] Along with the growing need for access to foreign markets came the realization that if domestic companies wished to expand abroad, traditionally protected domestic switch markets must be opened to foreign competitors. Reciprocal access was a major concern for both telecommunications firms and governments.

The French Telecommunications Industry

From the time it was nationalized, in 1889, until the mid-1970s, the most distinctive characteristic of French telecommunications was its poor quality. The network was expensive, inefficient, and undersubscribed, lagging far behind national networks elsewhere. In 1921, this backwardness prompted a debate over whether or not the system should be "denationalized," meaning that the operation and the network supply would be delegated to private, presumably French, companies. The American firm, ITT, offered a proposal to run the network as well as meet the industry's research and equipment needs, but the government declined. Under pressure from labor unions, which were opposed to private (especially foreign) ownership of the network, the government yielded, saying that complete privatization was "contrary to the republican customs of the country."[7] However, in 1923–1924, the government reneged and allowed foreign firms to bid for the Carnot Exchange in Paris. The companies that made offers evoke a true sense of déjà vu in the 1980s: Western Electric (AT&T), Siemens, Ericsson, and ITT.

ITT won the contract and used the opportunity to settle comfortably into the French marketplace. Having already conquered the Belgian and Spanish markets, ITT was familiar with the process of adapting itself to European industries. It acquired two French firms, began to manufacture equipment in France, established a research laboratory (Laboratoire Centrale des Télécommunications, or LCT), and adapted its switches to the unique French network. The opening of the Carnot Exchange in Paris in 1924 was followed by another ITT contract, a decade later, for the license of a rotary switch to serve the countryside.[8]

Although the government stipulated that customers' orders had to be shared with other French manufacturers, ITT's dominance in the French marketplace soon became apparent. This dominance provided ITT with a rather comfortable place in the market; however, it also cultivated a genuine sense of resentment among young French telecommunications engineers and managers in the 1930s. At the end of World War II, policy in this sector focused on promoting research and development of French industrial potential to compensate for the U.S. company dominance.[9]

In the postwar period, growing attention to the inadequacy of the French telecommunications network prompted a concerted effort to improve it. However, due to underfunding, little progress was made. Density was low, with fewer than five million telephone subscribers in France, three to four times fewer than in other countries of comparable size.[10] Prices were three times higher than those in Switzerland, Great Britain, and Scandinavia. Waiting lists for connections were huge, with 442,000 users waiting in 1966. While in the United States, 99 percent of requests at that time were met within three days, in France 10 percent of requests went unmet for three years or more. In addition, quality was extremely poor. In 1966, callers from Paris to the provinces had only a 50 percent chance of making a connection the same day. Hence the verity of the old saying that in France the population was divided in two: half of it was waiting for a telephone, and the other half was waiting for a dial tone.[11]

In the 1970s, the government attempted to rectify this situation, placing special priority on telecommunications. A thorough restructuring of the industry was implemented, directed by the government's telecommunications authority: The Direction Générale des Télécommunications (DGT) and the Centre Nationale d'Etude des Télécommunications (CNET), its research affiliate. The DGT oversees the equipping and operation of the telecommunications sector for the Ministère des Postes, Télégraphes, et Téléphones (PTT). French law stipulates that "no telecommunications installation can be established or used in the transmission of correspondence except with the authorization of the minister."[12] This stipulation did not mean that the PTT (through the DGT) performed all functions, only that all functions had to be overseen by it. (See Exhibit 5.)

In 1983, the DGT had 165,000 employees, 4,000 of whom were at CNET. Although it operated the telecommunications network alone, the manufacture of equipment and operation of specialized services were relegated to privately owned companies or to its subsidiaries.[13] In switching, the DGT relied on private companies for all its equipment needs. However, as the restructuring of the 1970s ensued, it relied more on CNET to increase the research and development capacities of private suppliers. It is estimated that 70 percent of French expenditures on switching R&D between 1970 and 1975 was funded by the DGT.[14]

In addition to its research efforts, the DGT implemented an extensive restructuring of the industry, beginning in 1976 under its new director, Gérard Théry. Théry was convinced that one of the reasons for the system's backwardness was a suppliers' cartel among ITT, Ericsson, and CGE. Despite efforts to divert some orders away from ITT in the 1960s, real competition in the industry was not evident. Théry sought to create a strong French competitor that would share the market with telecommunications. To accomplish this, he arranged the acquisition of ITT's subsidiary, LMT, and Ericsson's French subsidiary by the French company Thomson in 1976. As a result of these acquisitions, Thomson Télécommunications became the largest telecommunications firm in France.

The DGT's R&D and restructuring efforts soon began to show results. Through CNET Paris' concentrated efforts, CIT-Alcatel became one of the world's first producers of a completely electronic switch, the E10. Equipment prices decreased rapidly, telephone density increased at a rapid pace, and telecommunications value-added grew faster than the gross domestic product. (Exhibits 6, 7, and 8 show these trends.) By 1986, digital switches represented 45 percent of lines subscribed and 50 percent of usage. On a global scale, the French industry had more digital switches in service than any other country in 1984. Regarding exports, 35 countries adopted CGE's E10 switch, and 14 placed orders for Thomson's MT switch[15].

French Telecommunications in the 1980s

Despite the DGT's successes in restructuring the telecommunications sector, significant problems developed. Production capacity increased 570 percent between 1968 and 1977. Employment in the sector also rose dramatically, doubling in the same time period. But, as the backlog of unmet demand was filled, orders for French switches declined. Between 1981 and 1985, the DGT's orders for central office switches dropped 7 percent per year. This fall in orders was accompanied by employment redundancies caused by technological changes. Whereas it took 8.8 person-years to assemble one thousand-line electromechanical switch, a digital switch of the same size required 2.6 person-years.[16] Combined with falling demand, these productivity improvements resulted in a decrease of employment in the French equipment industry from 94,000 in 1977 to 70,500 in 1983.

The DGT undertook to resolve these problems in two ways. It attempted to create new domestic markets in videotex, facsimile, private exchanges, and "cabling" the country for television. It also tried to penetrate foreign markets, with a major export drive commencing in 1978. When the Socialist Party gained power in 1981, it believed the extra measure of nationalizing the major industry firms was needed to ensure control over restructuring. Thus, in 1982, the Socialists nationalized both CGE and Thomson, as well as CGCT and the large defense firm matra, under its *Filière Électronique* policy. The new government was concerned with the health of the electronics sector as a whole, which had a chronic and growing trade deficit that had grown from fr 2.5 billion in 1981 to fr 11 billion in 1982. Because telecommunications was an area in which France could have a strong international advantage, its health became an important part of industrial policy for the electronics industry generally. Exports in switching could help reduce the growing electronics trade gap.

Despite France's technological advantages in switch manufacturing, entering markets abroad would be extremely difficult. Thomson's MT digital switch, still in the development stage, had not yet entered full production. As a result, the company was sustaining large losses. Even CGE's highly successful E10 digital switch faced problems. As one of the first companies to develop and market a fully electronic switch, CGE had a major advantage over many of its international competitors (with the notable exception of other companies strong in digital switching, such as Northern Telecom, AT&T, and Ericsson). However, many of CGE's competitors had now developed digital switches of their own and were encroaching on its lead. ITT of the United States, ICL and Plessey of Great Britain, and Siemens of Germany were in the process of bringing on-line switches comparable to CGE's E10.

Consequently, competition intensified and overcapacity in switching was emerging worldwide. An OECD report estimated that there were

> Some 16 major systems developed at a total R&D cost which almost certainly exceeds U.S. $6 billion, all competing for annual world sales of U.S. $12 billion, of which only U.S. $2–3 billion are open to international competition. Even with substantial and growing home market sales, it is doubtful whether many of these systems will yield a positive return on investment.[17]

Given this emerging overcapacity, firms placed a premium on acquiring scarce market shares. Expanding abroad through exports put French companies in the middle of this intense battle.

The situation in the global industry became even more turbulent with the deregulation of the American telecommunications sector on January 1, 1984. The opening up of U.S. telecommunications provided a major opportunity for foreign companies eager to penetrate the lucrative American market, which constituted 40 percent of global demand for switches. After deregulation, the share of foreign company sales in the United States increased rapidly. Exhibit 9 shows foreign sales in the American telecommunications market as a whole, and Exhibit 10 shows the trade balances for the United States and others in telecommunications.

However, deregulation also created opportunities for the U.S. telecommunications giant, AT&T, to move abroad. Like other American companies, AT&T was anxious to expand its overseas markets, especially given the challenge foreign companies were presenting in its domestic market. To compensate for its lack of expertise in manufacturing in foreign markets, AT&T moved abroad in the form of alliances with Philips of the Netherlands, Olivetti of Italy, and KDD Telecom of Japan. GTE and ITT entered similar alliances. The progress of these firms in foreign markets was watched carefully by the U.S. Congress, which was becoming increasingly wary of the growing international presence in the U.S. market while many foreign markets remained closed to American companies. With its trade balance in telecommunications deteriorating, the United States increasingly demanded equal access to telecommunications markets abroad.

In the 1980s, U.S. government actions in retaliation for "unfair treatment" of American firms abroad increased. Under Section 301 of the 1974 Trade Act, as amended by the Trade and Tariff Act of 1984, the president was allowed to take action against foreign government policies that denied "fair and equitable market opportunities" to U.S. companies. Some of the first cases to be brought under the law were in the semiconductor industry, where Section 301 petitions were used in conjunction with dumping charges against Japanese semiconductor producers. Like all governments desiring access to U.S. markets, the French were concerned about what they perceived to be an increasingly protectionist environment.

In the context of the changing economic and political environment in telecommunications, it was clear to the French Socialists that a second round of restructuring for the domestic industry was necessary. However, the situation they faced in the 1980s was much more complex than that of the 1970s. First, the DGT was not in a position to intervene as effectively as it had in the past since its control of public procurement could not be used as effectively. Because the DGT's purchases were declining and increased markets abroad were sought, foreign buyers had formed an increasing proportion of the French suppliers' customers. Similarly, the growth of the private market for telecommunications goods and services in relation to the public one in France took even more purchasing power away from the DGT. In the future, companies would have to make more sales in private goods and services—such as private branch exchanges, cellular phones, office automation, and data transmission—than they had in the past.

Furthermore, the DGT's resources were being severely strained by the Socialists' policy of using them as a "cash cow" to finance other sectors of the French electronics industry. Compared with other areas (such as computers and semiconductors), the French telecommunications sector was highly profitable. Instead of financing more troubled sectors through government funding, the Socialists diverted funds from the thriving telecommunications authority, further reducing the DGT's capacity to restructure its own sector.[18]

A second complication resulted from disagreements among the various parties involved on how to handle the difficulties of CGE and Thomson. Some believed that the French market was simply too small to support two manufacturers of a product as expensive as digital switches and that the two companies therefore should be merged. To the CEOs of these companies, this was the most attractive option. Thomson's CEO, Alain Gomez, was anxious to be rid of the company's debt-ridden telecommunications division and concentrate on other products more central to the firm's welfare, such as semiconductors and consumer goods. Georges Pébereau, the CEO of CGE, was anxious to acquire Thomson Télécommunications. Such an acquisition would leave CGE in an extremely powerful market position, with 84 percent of the French market in central office switches.

Naturally the DGT opposed this option. It was the telecommunications authority that had orchestrated Thomson's entry into the telecommunications in the first place. In its view, the result had been lower equipment prices and a healthier telecommunications industry overall. With its previous power already waning, the DGT was loath to see its influence further diminish by the creation of a single, almost monopolistic seller in the French market. However, despite this opposition, the merger of CGE's CIT-Alcatel and Thomson Télécommunications was carried out under the auspices of the Ministry of Industry in 1983.

Further disagreements arose regarding the appropriate government response to the internationalization of the industry. In general, the Socialists wanted to develop a strong European counterweight to meet the challenge of American and Japanese companies. This position was associated particularly with the left wing CERES faction of the party, of which former Minister of Research and Industry Jean-Pierre Chevènement was a member. At the same time, there was a growing realization that as access to export markets became more central to the profitability of French firms, the French market had to be more open to *all* foreign companies to avoid accusations of unfair treatment.

The "Europeanists" argued that the French marketplace should be opened to other European firms and that Thomson and CGE should each find themselves a European partner. Others, such as Georges Pébereau, looked longingly at the lucrative U.S. market. With 40 percent of the world telecommunications market, the United States was an exceptionally attractive alternative to expansion in smaller, more segmented European markets. However, entry to the U.S. market was difficult, requiring the assistance of an American partner. Pébereau began negotiations with AT&T for this purpose in 1984. Exhibit 11 shows current and potential market growth in Europe and the United States.

These negotiations collapsed in May 1986 when it was discovered that the adaptation of CGE's E10 switch to U.S. standards would be difficult and expensive. With this option no longer available, Pébereau turned to another American firm, ITT. In July 1986, CGE bought 56 percent of ITT's worldwide telecommunications operations, establishing a new joint venture with ITT called Alcatel N.V. CGE thus gained substantial access to new European markets in West Germany, Norway, Belgium, Italy, and Spain. The signing of the joint venture agreement between CGE and ITT in July 1986 left the question of American market access unresolved.

The French government was aware that the large market shares CGE gained in Europe through its joint venture with ITT left it vulnerable to accusations of

French "imperialism." For this reason, it was paramount that European firms interested in selling or producing telecommunications equipment in France be given appropriate opportunities. This was the challenge facing Balladur: how could he assuage European interests without jeopardizing future options in the American market? Could he ensure the continued vibrancy of the industry in terms of technology, jobs, and growing exports and at the same time avoid political conflict with the Americans or Germans or both? Finally, could he provide the DGT with a strong second supplier and deal with concerns about maintaining the "Frenchness" of the industry?

Underlying these upheavals in the French telecommunications industry was the growth of a deregulation faction within France, particularly within the opposition party, Rassemblement pour la République (RPR). The deregulation of the British telecommunications market in 1984 further intensified the deregulators' demands. Falling long-distance prices in the British markets meant that many large companies operating in France were bypassing the public network and moving their long-distance needs to Britain. With the use of cable TV, microwave, and satellite technologies, large private users also could bypass the local network and connect to British Telecom's facilities. In a well-publicized move, 22 Japanese firms with operations in France transferred their long-distance systems to Britain as a result of lower costs there.[19] Unless they wanted to lose more business to the British, French companies had to be more competitive and lower their rates.

The RPR gained power from the Socialists in the March 1986 elections in March 1986 through a coalition with the center-right UDF (Union pour la Démocratie Française). PTT Minister Gérard Longuet and Directeur Général des Télécommunications Marcel Roulet argued forcefully that if the French industry were to continue its strong position, increasing competition and deregulation were necessary. Longuet submitted Prime Minister Jacques Chirac's review for a proposal for limited deregulation; however, progress was stalled due to major opposition from the industry's labor unions. Since 1984, through often unruly public protests, labor had objected to telecommunications job losses and lack of job security. It was in this context of change and uncertainty that the decision of what to do with CGCT had to be made.

The Problem of CGCT

Although CGCT's problems began in the mid-1970s, the question of what to do with it surfaced during the restructuring of the industry by the Socialists. Jacques Dondoux, the Directeur Général des Télécommunications under the Socialists had urged the government not to nationalize the firm. A subsidiary of ITT, CGCT manufactured ITT's Metaconda switch, a semielectronic switch that the PTT refused to purchase. Although ITT's fully electronic System 12 switch was in the process of development, it had many problems and future sales were questionable. The company's high losses and poor prospects meant that layoffs were inevitable. Let ITT take responsibility for the job cuts among CGCT's 9,200 employees, Dondoux argued.

Table A　CGCT 1981–1986

	Employees	Sales (in millions of francs)	Profits (in millions of francs)
1981	9,117	2,260	− 23
1982	8,852	2,047	− 345
1983	8,656	2,165	− 555
1984	8,389	2,721	− 557
1985	7,030	2,768	− 200
1986[a]	2,500	1,500	NA

Source: "CGCT: le Dallas du téléphone," *Le Monde*, March 14, 1987.

[a]CGCT's private switching business, sold to Matra in 1986, is not included.

In the end, however, politics triumphed over economics. ITT's reputation as an imperialist multinational corporation (symbolized by its role in the overthrow of Chile's Socialist president, Salvador Allende, in 1973) meant that its participation in the French economy could not be tolerated by the Socialists. The government purchased the company in 1982 for a sum of U.S. $215 million, acquiring CGCT's financial problems at the same time (See Table A).[20]

As CGCT's losses mounted, four options appeared available to the Socialist government. The first was to let either Thomson or CGE buy the company. Jean-Pierre Chevènement, then minister of research and industry, supported CGE as the buyer. Added to CGE's 45 percent market share, CGCT's 16 percent would provide the economies of scale necessary to make production of CGE's E10 switch more efficient. Furthermore, CGCT's expertise in private switching would help CGE's sales. Conversely, Thomson's MT switch was still in trouble, and it was in no position to acquire an even more troubled company.[21]

The minister of PTT, Louis Mexandeau, opposed this plan. He argued that if CGE and CGCT merged into a single large firm, the weakened Thomson would have no alternative but to merge with CGE, creating a monopolistic supplier to the PTT. Many believed this was the only option available in France, arguing that Thomson's financial problems were due to the French market's being simply too small for two large suppliers. However, the result of such a merger would be an inevitable shift in bargaining power away from the PTT and DGT to the single large supplier. This was intolerable to the telecommunications authority. Mexandeau thus proposed a second option of giving state assistance to Thomson to help its already burdened telecommunications division merge with CGCT.[22]

However, neither Thomson nor CGE was prepared to acquire CGCT, claiming that its huge losses would be an unbearable burden on either firm's resources. At this time, a third solution was presented by DGT's former director général, Gérard Théry. He proposed that given the convergence of telecommunications and computer technology, a merger with the French computer firm Bull would be more appropriate. Théry believed that if he, with his expertise in telecommunications, were appointed Bull's new president, the CGCT/Bull combination would resolve CGCT's problems[23].

A fourth solution—leaving CGCT as an independent competitor with state support—became the only option suitable to all parties involved after the merger of CGE's CIT-Alcatel and Thomson Télécommunications in 1983. As mentioned, the merger was carried out against the wishes of the DGT and PTT, but it had the support of the Ministry of Research and Industry. The ministry had been concerned about the security of the troubled French industry with the news of Philips' and AT&T's alliance, APT. It believed a larger French firm could better resist the potential for market encroachment from APT. For Thomson, it meant relief from the losses of its telecommunications subsidiary, and for CGE, it meant a powerful position in the French telecommunications market.

But DGT officials were irate. Dondoux argued that the restructuring required by the merger would not only lead to more job losses and problems in combining research teams, but it would leave CGE with 84 percent of the French switching market, its only competitors being the weakened CGCT. Publicly, the PTT and DGT argued that the enormous strides the French government had made in developing the telecommunications industry had been due to the breakup of the telecommunications cartel in the 1970s. However, the DGT privately worried about what would happen to the bargaining power of the telecommunications authority if it were faced with the near monopoly of a powerful supplier. In its view, a competent competitor to the new telecommunications company had to be found.

The question of what to do with CGCT thus became the industry's focal point of policy. The DGT was desperate to revive the failing company somehow, particularly after the 7,000 layoffs resulting from the CGE/Thomson merger led to large-scale labor protests. The prospect of a French buyer was shattered by the CGE/Thomson merger. Unless it wanted a single supplier of switches, the government had no choice but to seek a foreign buyer for the firm.

With the encouragement of Georges Pébereau, AT&T made a bid for the company. AT&T felt particularly fortunate to have Pébereau's assistance. He was a distinguished—if flamboyant—figure in French business and the CEO of the country's government-owned telecommunications company. For a year and a half, AT&T negotiated a comprehensive telecommunications package with CGE. In July 1985, it signed a protocol of intention with CGE to buy 70 percent for CGCT, begin a joint venture in microwave transmission between CGE and AT&T/Philips (APT) in France, and market CGE's E10 switch in the United States. There were two problems with this scenario, however. First, because AT&T was negotiating a joint venture to market CGE's switch in the United States, it was questionable whether it could compete with CGE in the French market when the firms were cooperating so closely in the United States. Second, and more important, an alliance with an American firm contravened the Socialists' principle of cooperating with European firms to provide a counterweight to the dominance of American and Japanese firms in the European electronics market. Mitterrand recently had strongly condemned Philips' and Olivetti's alliances with AT&T for this very reason. How could he then reverse his position and allow AT&T into the French market? In fact, the minister of research and industry in the Mitterrand cabinet was reported to be outraged by

Pébereau's presuming to offer CGCT to AT&T when it was not really his to give. Furthermore, the French perceived Philips as a poor partner for AT&T; it was a company that made televisions and household appliances, not an advanced telecommunications company.

The first problem was alleviated when AT&T's agreement to market CGE's switch in the United States collapsed, leaving only the smaller scale joint venture in microwave transmission and two new deals in satellite earth stations and light-weight submarine cables. However, the European cooperation barrier still existed. Prime Minister Laurent Fabius notified AT&T that a decision on this sensitive matter would not be made until after the upcoming March 1986 elections.

The question of what to do with CGCT soon became the problem of the newly elected Chirac government after its victory in the 1986 elections. As economic liberals (in the classical sense) determined to break away from the interventionist techniques of the Socialists, the new government decided to start again in the CGCT affair and open the bidding to other companies. The sale of CGCT provided an opportunity for those who advocated the deregulation and privatization of the industry to bring in fresh competition from abroad. For the new government, the opening of the telecommunications market signified an ideological commitment to less government intervention and a more open economy. Given the preoccupation of telecommunications firms with acquiring new markets, new offers flooded in. With $371 million worth of disbursements in 1984, the DGT was the largest purchaser of digital switches in the world.[24] In the end, the contest was between Ericsson of Sweden, Siemens of West Germany, and APT of the Netherlands and the United States.

Domestic Divisions

Different factions within the government quickly lined up behind each of these firms. Promoting Ericsson's case were certain groups within the DGT as well as those that favored a solution involving European cooperation, such as the unions and the Communist party. Ericsson supporters argued that allowing a large American company in the French market was to invite domination and would certainly not enhance the creation of a European "counterweight" to American and Japanese pressure. Communist economist Philippe Herzog warned that large American multinationals would soon begin to "fight like dogs" over the European market, claiming that allowing a large firm like AT&T into the French market was like allowing a wolf into the *bergerie* (sheepfold). Others agreed, noting that given AT&T's enormous resources, it would have no problem becoming a formidable force in the French economy. Combined with IBM, which was pressuring the Chirac government for entry into the value-added network market in France, American companies would once again dominate the French telecommunications market. On the other hand, Ericsson was more the size of French firms, and its technology was excellent.[25] DGT technicians, who had worked with Ericsson technology for years, worried about their job security should new equipment from AT&T be introduced.

Furthermore, they argued that admitting AT&T to the industry would do little to advance the government's stated desire of moving into the increasingly lucrative market for private switches and office equipment. Many believed sales in this sector were the only hope for future growth, but because AT&T already had a European alliance in this area with Olivetti, it was unlikely to be willing to accept a French partner.[26]

Perhaps more important, however, these groups feared that AT&T's capacity as a network operator, as well as an equipment manufacturer, would soon lead it to challenge the DGT itself. Given AT&T's expertise in network operation, it was not unrealistic to assume that once in the market, its next demand would be for a role in running the French network. Such a move would challenge the traditionally strong position the DGT had held in the industry, diminishing its ability to restructure or aid the industry as it had in the past.

This possibility bothered neither DGT Chief Marcel Roulet nor PTT Minister Gérard Longuet. AT&T's versatility was a clear advantage in their view. That AT&T was a network operator as well as an equipment manufacturer meant that it could play a critical role in the deregulated market that Roulet and Longuet aspired to.[27] In addition, AT&T could provide enhanced switching features that would enable the PTT to increase revenues from private networks.

Other groups supporting AT&T included Industry Minister Alain Madelin and factions within the DGT. Within the telecommunications authority, there was tremendous admiration for AT&T. The CNET research laboratories had been modeled after Bell Labs, which many engineers respected as the finest telecommunications laboratory in the world. Many regarded AT&T's switch—the 5ESS—as unquestionably superior to the other switches available. Allowing AT&T into the markets would enhance opportunities for cooperation and improve the overall quality of the system.

Advocates of AT&T dismissed warnings that the firm could eventually dominate the French market. On the contrary, granting it entry and then restricting it to CGCT's 16 percent market share was a way of controlling AT&T. Opponents cited this argument as misleading, noting that a 16 percent share now need not remain that size in the future, especially in a deregulated market. However, AT&T advocates countered that French companies had more to fear from a company like Ericsson. Given its familiarity with the French market (Ericsson had a subsidiary in France until 1976, when Thomson acquired it) and its experience dealing with small switches and small markets, Ericsson would become a formidable challenger to CGE in one or two years. However, it would take AT&T five years to become a real competitor.[28]

Furthermore, those who opposed Ericsson argued that it was incomptabile with CGE in terms of export markets. Expanding exports was a high priority for the government, yet there was not a single market CGE and Ericsson were not in together. This meant that rather than helping to increase export markets, Ericsson could end up competing with CGE abroad, depriving the French company of sales.

Finally, in political terms, allowing AT&T into the marketplace would be more expedient than allowing Siemens or Ericsson in. First, it would provide reciprocal access for an American company, an advantage that would blunt U.S. criticism if CGE desired to increase its presence in the United States. Second, if a decision against Siemens were to be made, advocates argued it would have to be in favor of AT&T. If the West German government were to demand reciprocal access to the French market, the U.S. government could threaten to monitor Siemens' sales in the United States, where the West German firm had a considerable presence. Such leverage was not available to Ericsson; therefore, a pro-Ericsson decision would do little to assuage the West Germans' demands.[29]

Siemens' bid was supported primarily by Prime Minister Jacques Chirac. He had placed a high priority on a more cooperative economic and political relationship with West Germany, and it was his office that approached Siemens when the bidding was opened. Economic relations between the two countries had been somewhat hostile in the past, and Chirac desired greater access to West Germany's healthy economy. Finance Minister Balladur also leaned in this direction. Although Balladur never publicly stated his support for Siemens, it was clear that in opposition to the ultraliberal wing of the party he favored a European solution to the problem.

Chirac thus not only wanted to make conciliatory moves toward the West Germans, but he wanted to avoid doing anything that might displease them. To Siemens advocates, a decision in favor of the West German company made good economic and political sense. Although Siemens' EWSD switch had problems in the past, they had largely been overcome. A Siemens solution would also mollify the pro-European forces. Furthermore, it would assuage the German government's concern that AT&T would use the French market as a launching pad into other European markets. Finally, it would provide the Germans with reciprocal access to the French market. Through its joint venture with ITT, CGE had gained a share of ITT's German subsidiary, Standard Electrik Lorenz (SEL) which had 40 percent of the German central-office switching market. Allowing Siemens access to CGCT would remove potential conflict over unequal access to markets.

Because of these conflicting concerns, the government in the summer of 1986 made a technological test of each company's switch. AT&T's switch ranked number one, considerably ahead of second place finisher Ericsson. Siemens' switch was ranked third. AT&T was confident of success, even though its supporter, Pérebeau, was fired from his post at CGE in July 1986 after Alcatel's acquisition of ITT. Some felt that the new finance minister, Balladur, who had been president of several CGE subsidiaries before taking office, was happy to see him go. Industry Minister Madelin said: "An empire builder is not always the best manager."[30]

The Tension Mounts

The French government had promised a decision on the sale of CGCT by September 1986, but no decision came. As the government continued to delay, impatience began to show, and tension mounted. In October 1986, the West German government notified the French government that unless Siemens was allowed to buy CGCT, it would cut procurement from CGE's newly acquired West German subsidiary, SEL. Because CGE had gained SEL's 40 percent share of the West German central-office switching market through its joint venture with ITT, the West Germans argued that it was only fair that reciprocal access to the French market be granted to Siemens.

The French government took the West German threat very seriously for reasons related largely to the status of the CGE/ITT joint venture, Alcatel N.V. In the beginning, Alcatel N.V., was designed to be a pan-European project, with ITT holding 37 percent of the shares and a European holding company named Eurotel holding the other 63 percent. Originally, CGE had planned to include partners from Belgium, Spain, Italy, and West Germany in the holding company. When the Italian telecommunications company Italtel decided against the venture and negotiations with the West German firm Bosch collapsed, only Société Générale de Belgique and Spain's Telefonica remained in the deal.

Telefonica eventually withdrew from the venture, saying it had wanted to be a part of a pan-European company, not a junior partner to a French-dominated project. This move left Alcatel N.V. in a fragile position on two counts. First, because it had allowed CGE a significant presence in several European markets, it was open to accusations of French imperialism. Second, Alcatel N.V. was in a delicate financial position, with CGE holding 56 percent of the shares. As a result, the French government was anxious to protect the health of the new venture by assuming a presence in the lucrative West German market. For this reason, it could not ignore the West Germans' threat to cut procurement from Alcatel N.V.'s West German subsidiary. As one French official noted, the West Germans "were cleverly exploiting an opportunity we left open. By trying to play the free market, we left the door open to politics, and in Europe, politics easily dominates things."[31]

When AT&T learned of the West German ultimatum, it immediately protested to the Commerce Department and to the U.S. Trade Representative. Given its growing concern with the issue of foreign market access, the American government believed it had to react strongly. Through its assorted subsidiaries, Siemens had $2.2 billion worth of sales in the U.S. market; in this context, AT&T argued that the West German attempt to exclude it from the French market constituted an unfair trade practice. When FCC chairperson Mark Fowler heard of the West German move, he wrote to the seven regional Bell companies and to GTE to learn how much equipment they had bought or planned to buy from Siemens and then threatened to cut Siemens' sales if it continued to pressure the French (Exhibit 12). In December, the FCC, prompted by the "inappropriate" actions of the West German government, announced it would launch an inquiry into the international regulations governing telecommunications. Fowler proposed introducing a rule that would bar U.S. telephone companies from buying West German or other foreign switching equipment. While on an official visit to the United States, West German Chancellor Helmut Kohl was approached by cabinet-level officials about his government's ultimatum. (AT&T CEO James Olsen had appealed unsuccessfully to President Reagan and Secretary of the Treasury James Baker to intervene on AT&T's behalf.) In November, the United States Trade Representative called in both the West German and the French envoys for consultation. Both the Dutch and American governments made strong official protests to the French government.

In December 1986, the companies involved were told by Finance Minister Edouard Balladur that French privatization law governing the sale of nationalized companies (such as CGCT) decreed that only 20 percent of such companies' shares could be sold to foreign owners. The bidders would have to find French partners if they wanted to enter the market.

The foreign companies duly found French partners. Siemens joined forces with the French electronics firm Jeumont-Schneider, Ericsson with Matra, and APT with Société Anonyme des Télécommunications (SAT). Ericsson's astute choice of Matra meant it had access to Matra chairman Jean-Luc Lagardère, a Chirac confidant who had recently failed in his effort to acquire France's government-owned television station, TF1. APT's choice provided yet another source of controversy. In addition to SAT, APT's French partners included Compagnie du Midi group and five French union trusts owned by the Dutch-controlled Neuflize-Schlumberger-Mallet bank and by Morgan Guaranty. Doubts over the "Frenchness" of the unit trusts arose immediately, causing embarrassment for APT and SAT. APT pointed out that it had also agreed on lucrative microwave and earth-station deals with CGE if it was allowed to acquire CGCT, and moved to change it financial partners.

In March 1987, the French government announced it would make a second "test" of each company's switch package. By April, the test was completed. It found that the switches of all bidders were excellent, although it ranked Ericsson's package first. AT&T was ranked slightly below, with high praise for technological superiority. Siemens' switch was ranked third, with a few minor technological flaws.

The companies involved expected a decision from Balladur once the test was completed. Although he had sought to diffuse the political tension by attempting to make a decision on technological grounds, the Finance Minister still faced a potentially explosive diplomatic situation. With the Germans threatening to cut procurement from SEL, the Americans complaining of unfair trade practices, and the DGT demanding a strong second supplier, Balladur had to make his decision carefully.

Appendix   *Chronology of Events, 1983–1987*

1983	Merger between CGE's CIT–Alcatel and Thomson Telecommunications.
1984	
January	Deregulation of the U.S. telecommunications market.
Spring	Socialist Government of France decided to sell the nationalized telecommunications company CGCT.
Summer	Negotiations between AT&T and Georges Pébereau of CGE on the purchase of CGCT, a microwave joint venture between APT and Alcatel, and the marketing of Alcatel's E10 switch by AT&T in the United States began.
1985	
July	AT&T signed protocol of intention to buy CGCT.
Fall	Decision on AT&T's purchase of CGCT postponed by the Socialist government until after the March 1986 elections.

1986

March	Prime Minister Jacques Chirac elected.
May	Deal between AT&T and Alcatel to market Alcatel's E10 switch in the United States fell through.
Spring/ Summer	New bids for the purchase of CGCT solicited by Prime Minister Chirac.
July	Alcatel announced the acquisition of ITT's Telecommunications operations, forming a new company, Alcatel, N.V. Péberau is fired.
Summer/ Fall	The first technical test on the switches of companies bidding for CGCT was conducted. AT&T was rated first.
October	The German Government notified the French government that unless Siemens is granted access to the French central office switching market, procurement from Alcatel N.V.'s subsidiary Standard Electrik Lorenz will be cut.
	West German Chancellor Hemnut Kohl visited the United States.
	FCC Chair Mark Fowler sent a letter to the Regional Bell Operating Companies and GTE requesting information on the amount of equipment purchased from Siemens.
	Secretary of Commerce Malcolm Baldrige and U.S. Trade Representative Clayton Yeutter made official protests to the French government.
December	Bidders for CGCT informed by Finance Minister Balladur that they must find French partners.

1987

March	The second technical test of each company's switch was conducted.

Exhibit 1   *World Market for Telecommunications and Computer Goods and Services, 1985 versus 1990 Est.* ($ billions)

	1985 Worldwide	United States	1990 Est. Worldwide	United States	Annual Growth Rate 1985
Telecom equipment (SIC 3661, 3662)	65	26	96	36	8%
Computer equipment (SIC 3573)	93	50	195	105	16
Telecom services (SIC 4811, 4821)	290	118	446	165	9
Computer services (SIC 737)	50	30	147	394	24
Total	498	224	884	394	12

Source: National Telecommunications and Information Administration, trade report (Washington, D.C.: U.S. Department of Commerce, 1987). *Assessing the Effects of Changing the AT&T Antitrust Consent Decree.*

Exhibit 2   *Total Local Lines Placed in Service, by Supplier, by Region, October 1986* (percent market shares)

Supplier	North America	Western Europe	Eastern Europe	Japan	Other	Total
AT&T	49.7%	0.0%	0.0%	0.0%	9.0%	21.5%
Alcatel	0.3	20.9	15.8	0.0	2.9	7.2
GEC	0.0	5.5	0.0	0.0	0.0	1.4
GTE	11.6	0.0	0.0	0.0	0.0	4.5
Plessey	1.7	5.5	0.0	0.0	0.0	2.1
Fujitsu	0.0	0.0	0.0	36.4	5.4	3.0
Hitachi	0.0	0.0	0.0	18.2	0.6	1.0
ITT	0.4	23.4	1.7	0.0	12.4	9.1
Oki	0.0	0.0	0.0	23.3	0.4	1.2
NEC	0.3	0.0	0.0	22.1	17.1	5.2
NTL	35.8	0.0	0.0	0.0	2.4	14.5
LME	0.0	15.1	0.4	0.0	28.8	11.4
Philips	0.0	5.5	0.0	0.0	2.5	1.9
Siemens	0.0[a]	12.6	0.0	0.0	7.3	4.9
Other	0.1	11.4	72.1	0.0	11.2	11.1
Total	100.0%	100.0%	100.0%	100.0%	100.0%	100.0%

Source: Northern Business Information, *World Public Switching Market*, 1987 Edition.

Exhibit 2 (continued)   Sales and Market Share by Supplier in United States, 1986 (thousands of lines)

	Market Total	Alcatel	AT&T	Ericsson	GTE	NEC	Northern Telecom	Stromberg	Siemens
Digital lines placed in service	12,004	134	6,078	0	1,867	8	3,592	325	0
Digital local line installed base	30,091	1,020	10,628	0	5,411	408	11,586	1,638	0
Analog lines placed in service	1,385	0	1,300	0	85	0	0	0	0
Total lines placed in service	13,389	134	7,378	0	1,952	8	3,592	325	0[a]

Source: Northen Business Information, *Central Office Equipment Market*, 1987 Edition.

[a] All of Siemens' central office switch sales were made subsequent to October 1986.

Exhibit 2 (continued) Market Share by Supplier in Europe (%), 1986

	France	West Germany	Great Britain	Italy	Belgium	Switzerland	Ireland	Spain	Sweden	Austria	Denmark	Finland	Norway
ITT	0	35	20	30	80	33	15	70	0	25	10	0	100
CGE	84[a]	0	0	0	0	0	35	0	0	0	0	50[b]	0
Ericsson	0	0	15	21	0	33	30	30	100	0	90	35	0
Siemens[c]	0	65	0	0	0	34	0	0	0	25	0	15	0
Italtel	0	0	0	49	0	0	0	0	0	0	0	0	0
Plessey	0	0	35	0	0	0	0	0	0	0	0	0	0
GEC	0	0	30	0	0	0	0	0	0	0	0	0	0
Northern Telecom	0	0	0	0	20	0	0	0	0	50	0	0	0
GTE	0	0	0	0	0	0	0	0	0	0	0	0	0

Source: *01 Informatique.*

Others: CGE, licenses in USSR, Poland, Czechoslovakia; AT&T-Philips: contracts in Great Britain and the Netherlands (70 percent); Ericsson 30: percent of Netherlands, negotiations in Norway and Great Britain; ITT: 20 percent of Netherlands starting 1989, contract in Finland.

[a]The other 16 percent to CGCT.
[b]License given to Telenokia.
[c]Fifty percent of Portuguese market.

Exhibit 3   Digital Local Lines Placed in Service, by Supplier, by Region, 1986

Percent Market Shares

Supplier	North America	Western Europe	Eastern Europe	Japan	Other	Total
AT&T	45.4%	0.0%	0.0%	0.0	10.3%	24.7%
Alcatel	0.3	34.0	88.6	0.0	4.7	10.2
GEC	0.0	9.0	0.0	0.0	0.0	2.0
GTE	12.1	0.0	0.0	0.0	0.0	6.0
Plessey	1.9	9.0	0.0	0.0	0.0	2.9
Fujitsu	0.0	0.0	0.0	40.0	8.4	4.0
Hitachi	0.0	0.0	0.0	19.2	0.6	1.2
ITT	0.4	12.0	0.0	0.0	4.2	3.7
Oki	0.0	0.0	0.0	16.6	0.6	1.1
NEC	0.3	0.0	0.0	24.3	26.7	7.2
NTL	39.4	0.0	0.0	0.0	2.8	20.1
LME	0.0	19.7	11.4	0.0	30.7	11.0
Philips	0.0	1.5	0.0	0.0	2.0	0.7
Siemens	0.0[a]	6.1	0.0	0.0	5.2	2.4
Other	0.1	8.8	0.0	0.0	3.9	2.8
Total	100.0%	100.0%	100.0%	100.0%	100.0%	100.0%

Source: Northern Business Information, *World Public Switching Market*, 1987 Edition.

[a]October 1986 view; all of Siemens' central office switch sales were made subsequent to this date.

Exhibit 4   R&D Costs of Digital Switching Systems, 1985 ($ billions)

System 12 (ITT)	1.0
Axe (Ericsson)	0.5
E10 and E12 (CIT-Alcatel)	1.0
DMS (Northern Telecom)	0.7
System X (GEC/Plessey/BT)	1.4
ESS 5 (Western Electric)	0.75
EWSD (Siemens)	0.7

Source: Dang Nguyen, "Telecoms: A Challenge to the Old Order," in *Europe and the New Technologies*, Margaret Sharpe, ed. (London: Frances Pinter, 1985), p. 108.

Exhibit 5   Industrial Policy Making in the Executive Branch, 1985 Agencies and Areas of Competence

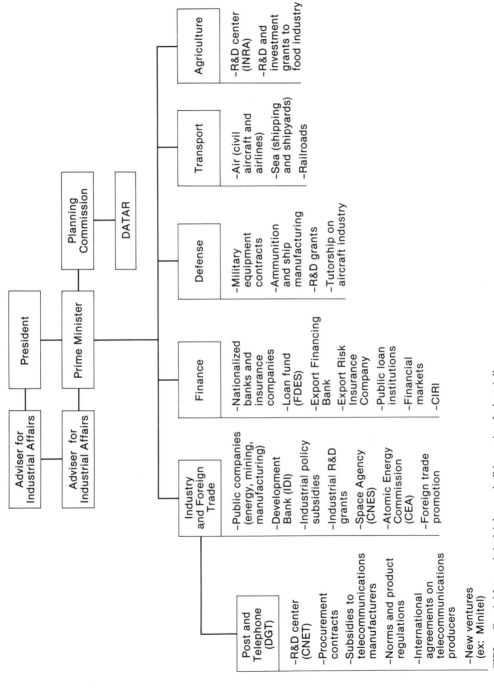

CIRI — Comité Interministérial pour la Rénovation Industrielle.
DATAR — Délegation à l'Aménagement du Territoire et à l'Action Régionale.
IDI — Institut pour le Développement Industriel.
FDES — Fonds de Développement Economique et Social.

Source: Policy Studies Institute, *Competing for Property: Business Strategy and Industrial Policies in Modern France.*

Exhibit 6   Telecommunications Value Added, 1974–1984

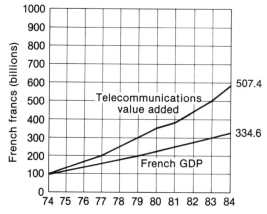

Source: Catherine Bertho, ed., *Histoire des Télécommunications en France* (Paris: Éditions Erès, 1984).

Exhibit 7   Lines per Inhabitants (international comparison)

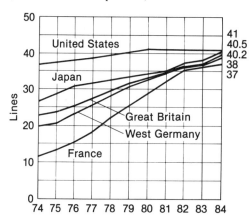

Source: Catherine Bertho, ed. *Histoire des Télécommunications en France* (Paris: Éditions Erès, 1984).

Exhibit 8   French Telecommunications Prices over Time, 1977–1980
(prices in constant francs)

	1977	1978	1979	1980
Digital	100	96	60	52
Analog	100	97	72	64
Electromechanical analog	100	99	126	104
DGT purchases (amount)	100	103	88	70

Source: Henry Ergas, "Industrial Policy in France: The Case of
Telecommunications," paper for Seminar on Industrial Policy and Structural
Adjustment, Naples, April 1983.

Exhibit 9   Bell Company Network Products Procurement Percentage
from Foreign-based and Affiliated Firms, 1983–1985

Procurement	1983	1984	1985
Switching equipment	6	18	29
Fiber optics	35	23	40
Transmission equipment	5	3	23

Source: National Telecommunications and Information Adminstrations.

Exhibit 10   Imports and Exports for
Telecommunications in 1985 ($
millions)

	Imports	Exports
United States	3,218	1,781
France	92	472
West Germany	161	757
United Kingdom	398	300
Sweden	150	959
Japan	123	1,839

Source: *International Telecommunications*, Stockton
Press, as published in *Financial Times*, October 19,
1987.

Exhibit 11   Telecommunications Market Potential, United States and Europe, 1986–1991

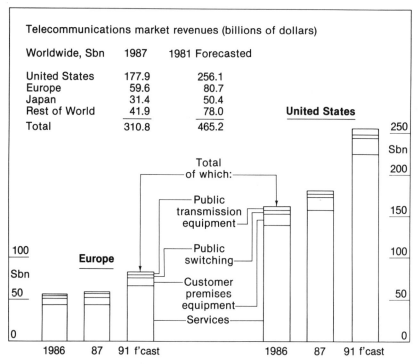

Source: *Dataquest*, as published in *The Economist*, October 17, 1987.

Exhibit 12   Federal Communications Commission Washington

William L. Weiss   October 21, 1986
Chairman and Chief Executive Officer
Ameritech Corporation
30 S. Wacker Dr., Suite 3400
Chicago, IL 60606

Dear Mr. Weiss:

There has been substantial concern in the U.S. government for some time over the large U.S. trade deficit. As a result of discussions I have had with the Secretary of Commerce and the United States Trade Representative, it has become clear that we also share an increasing concern about fair and reciprocal treatment of U.S. telecommunications equipment manufacturers and service providers.

In order to assist us in considering whether to initiate any action to further the public interest in this regard, I am requesting that your company provide the Commission with information concerning any purchases made from Siemens, A.G., its subsidiaries, or other affiliated companies over the last twenty-four months, as well as your company's plans to make any purchases from Siemens in the future. I recognize that you may view such information as proprietary. We are prepared to afford your submission confidential treatment as provided for in the Commission's rules.

Thank you for your cooperation in this matter. I look forward to hearing from you in the near future.

Sincerely,

Mark S. Fowler
Chairman

Key Names and Abbreviations

Alcatel N.V.	Joint venture between Compagnie Générale d'Electricité (France) and ITT (United States)
APT	Joint venture bewteen AT&T (United States) and Philips (Netherlands)
Balladur, Edouard	Minister of Finance in Chirac government, 1986–1988
CGE	Compagnie Générale d'Électricité
CGCT	Compagnie Générale des Constructions Téléphoniques
CIT-Alcatel	CGE's telecommunications subsidiary before merger with Thomson Télécommunications
Chevènement, Jean-Pierre	Minister of Research and Industry, 1982–1983 in Socialist government
Chirac, Jacques	Prime Minster of France, 1986–1988
CNET	Centre Nationale d'Études des Télécommunications, research division of DGT
DGT	Direction Générale des Télécommunications, telecommunications authority
Dondoux, Jacques	Directeur Général des Télécommunications, 1981–1986
L. M. Ericsson	Swedish telecommunications firm
Gomez, Alain	Président-Directeur générale, Thomson Télécommunications
Longuet, Gérard	Minister of Postes, Télégraphs, et Téléphones (PTTs), Chirac government
Madelin, Alain	Minister of Industry, Chirac government
Mexandeau, Louis	Minister of PTTs, Socialist government
Mitterrand, François	President of France, 1981–
PDG	Président-Directeur Générale (counterpart to CEO)
Pébereau, Georges	Président-Directeur Générale, CGE
PTTs	Postes, Télégraphes, et Téléphones
RPR	Rassemblement pour la République (Party of Jacques Chirac)
Roulet, Marcel	Directeur Générale de Télécommunications, Chirac government
SEL	Standard Electrik Lorenz, West German subsidiary of Alcatel N.V.
Siemens	West German electronics firm
Théry, Gérard	Directeur Générale des Télécommunications, 1976–1981
Thomson Télécommunications	Merged with CIT-Alcatel of CGE in 1984
UDF	Union pour la Démocratie Francaise

ENDNOTES

1. Central office switches "provide the intelligent interface between subscriber lines and interswitch trunks" (Peter Huber, *The Geodesic Network*, 1987 Report on Competition in the Telephone Industry, prepared for the U.S. Department of Justice, p. 14.1). The switches to be discussed are actually huge computerized machines that represent the first point for routing a call as it enters the public network. On average, these switches handle about 70,000 local access lines.
2. National Telecommunications and Information Administration (NTIA), *Assessing the Effects of Changing the AT&T Antitrust Consent Decree,* trade report, (Washington, D.C.: U. S. Department of Commerce, 1987), p. 30.
3. Ibid., p. 30.
4. In jet engines, three companies in 1988 produced almost all jet engines sold in the market economies.
5. A digital switch is a fully electronic piece of equipment that involves the representation of information through pulses of electricity or light using timing routines. For this reason, it is sometimes referred to as "time division" switching. In a digital network, a signal is converted into codes of binary digits for transmission. In contrast, semielectronic analog switches use frequency modulation to transmit information. A continuous circuit is established for each message, in effect reserving a space for each piece of information. Analog switching is sometimes referred to as "space division" equipment.
6. Peter Huber, *The Geodesic Network*, 1987 Report on Competition in the Telephone Industry, prepared for the U.S. Department of Justice, pp. 14–15.
7. Catherine Bertho, ed., *Histoire des Télécommunications en France* (Paris: Editions Erès, 1984), p. 130.
8. Ibid., pp. 137–138.
9. Ibid., p. 138.
10. David Encaoua and Phillippe Koebel, "Réglementation et dérégulation des télécommunications: Leçons Anglo-Saxonnes et perspectives d'évolution en France," *Revue Economique*, March 1987.
11. Henry Ergas, "Industrial Policy in France: The Case of Telecommunications," paper for the seminar on Industrial Policy and Structural Adjustment, Naples, April 1983, p. 9.
12. Bertho, *Histoire des Télécommunications en France*, p. 236.
13. The DGT's subsidiaries are companies of mixed ownership, under private law, of which most of the capital is owned by the state. Some of them (20 in 1980) operate abroad: in particular, France Télécom, Inc., in the United States. Others include the group France Cables, Enterprise Générale des Télécommunications (which provides, installs, and interconnects various equipment), and Télésystems (for computer services). Some of these subsidiaries are not entirely controlled by the DGT; for example, it owns only 67 percent of the data transmission company Transpac and 33 percent of Sofrecom (which provides engineering assistance to foreign countries).
14. Ergas, "Industrial Policy in France," p. 13.
15. Bertho, *Histoire des Télécommunications en France*, p. 222.
16. Ergas, "Industrial Policy in France," p. 17.
17. OECD, *Telecoms: Pressures and Policies for Change* (Paris: OECD, 1983), p. 83.
18. Kevin Morgan and Douglas Webber, "Divergent Paths: Political Strategies for Telecommunications in Britain, France, and West Germany," *West European Politics*, October 1986, p. 65.
19. *L'Usine Nouvelles*, No. 38, September 7, 1987, p. 5.
20. Jean-Michel Quatrepoint, *Histoire Secrète des Dossiers Noirs de la Gauche*, (Paris: Alain Moreau, 1986), p. 276.
21. Ibid., p. 277.
22. Ibid., p. 280.
23. Ibid., p. 277.
24. Huber, *The Geodesic Network*, p. 14.3a.
25. Interviews at DGT, June–July 1987.
26. Interviews.
27. Interviews.
28. Interviews at OECD, June 1987, and at CNET, July 1987.
29. Interview at the Institut des Recherches Economiques et Sociales sur les Télécommunications (IREST), July 1987.
30. Quatrepoint, *Histoire Secrète des Dossiers Noirs de la Gauche*, p. 367.
31. Quoted in *The Wall Street Journal*, October 16, 1986.

French Telecommunications in the 1980s (B)

The French government announced on April 23, 1987, that the acquisition of CGCT would be awarded to Ericsson and its French partner Matra. Many were surprised by the decision, assuming that because of its excellent technology, AT&T was destined to get the contract in spite of the politics surrounding the deal. Others felt that if politics had dominated, CGCT should have gone to Siemens to assuage the German government's demands for reciprocal market access.[1] Several observers postulated that given the controversy caused by the sale, the government had no choice but to opt for Ericsson. As one French official noted, "Because it became so horribly political, the choice of either AT&T or Siemens would have created a major problem. The only choice was to put it off again or go with Ericsson."[2]

Perhaps most shocked by the outcome was AT&T. Company officials argued that given AT&T's technical superiority and the advantages of the package for their French partners, CGE, SAT, and SAGEM, the decision was clearly made on a purely political basis. French government sources admitted that AT&T had better technology, but that when the overall package was considered, Ericsson's offer was better than AT&T's. They said Ericsson had offered its partner, Matra, access to its mobile telephone technology. Also, it had priced its switches lower. Furthermore, technicians were surprised to find that in the second test, Ericsson's switch actually outperformed AT&T's in some functions. In the first test, conducted in the summer and fall of 1986, AT&T's switch was ranked first. Overall, the testers still preferred AT&T's bid since it included some high capacity switches Ericsson did not offer. However, they concluded that Ericsson's technology was perfectly acceptable.

AT&T countered that the French had notified them of no shortcomings in their package. They complained that after the bids were submitted Ericsson's had somehow come "unsealed" and that Ericsson had won the offer because it had been unfairly allowed to sweeten its bid at the last minute. Ericsson's president, Bjorn Svedberg, denied this claim, stating that Ericsson had merely clarified its offer, not changed it. Ericsson officials argued that given the overall package, French authorities were clear that Ericsson's system was technically and financially the best alternative. In terms of switch price, acquisition price, and minimal layoffs, Ericsson's package was considered superior to AT&T's.

Whatever the reasons for the decision, AT&T was clearly angered by what it perceived as blatantly unfair treatment. Company officials felt they had been unjustly placed in the middle of a political battle. "We're convinced," said one company official responsible for the project, "that once the Germans made their bid, the case was closed. The French were not going to favor Germany over the United States or vice versa. At the end, partners didn't matter; technology didn't matter. What mattered was to make the right *political* decision to minimize losses."

Postdoctoral Fellow Barbara Jenkins and Professor George C. Lodge prepared this case as a basis for classroom discussion rather than to illustrate either effective or ineffective handling of an administrative situation.

Although not everyone agreed with this assessment, clearly the loss of the French business was a costly one for AT&T. It had been counting on a position in the French market to enhance its position in Europe. The purchase of CGCT would have given AT&T 16 percent of the French central office switching market, or $100 million in sales. The loss of potential sales, however, was minor compared to the setback this posed for AT&T's international strategy. CEO James Olson had pinpointed expansion into international markets as one of three goals in AT&T's business strategy in the 1980s, noting that international interests had become "an integral part of our product and market planning."[3] AT&T had been relying on a French presence to establish credentials to attract other European customers. The acceptance of their offer for CGCT would provide implicit evidence that the highly respected French PTT approved AT&T's technology and market presence.

Furthermore, AT&T's failure to achieve a position in the French market had major implications for the jousting among global competitors in the industry. In the zero-sum battles being waged in the international central-office switching market, the French market represented a substantial gain for the up-and-coming Ericsson— already the second largest switch producer in Europe after Alcatel, the telecommunications subsidiary of the giant government-owned French company Compagnie Générale d'Electricité (CGE). For all switch producers, this was a concern. (Figure 1 shows the relative positions of each of the major players before the CGCT purchase.) Although Siemens was relieved that it had stymied AT&T's second major effort to enter the European market, the Ericsson victory represented a clear challenge to its international expansion. For AT&T, the loss spelled trouble for its fledgling alliance with Philips (APT). After four years of effort, APT had no major European presence outside of Holland and had yet to record a profit.

Figure 1   The Biggest Players: World Market Share for
Telecommunications Equipment in 1986

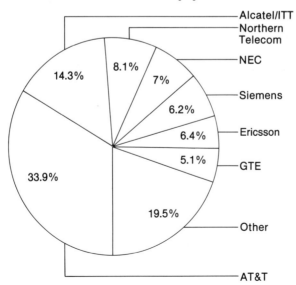

Source: *The Wall Street Journal*, April 24, 1987, p. 8.

Cognizant of the implications of the CGCT outcome for AT&T, U.S. government officials also were angered by what they perceived as a decision based on political rather than commercial criteria. The French government's move represented a major setback for the American effort to encourage foreign governments to open up their telecommunications markets in the same manner as, they claimed, the United States had. A Commerce Department official noted that, "If we are to find that this decision further restricts U.S. companies' access to the European telecommunications market, we might have to carefully consider what actions could best defend U.S. interests."[4] Wishing to avoid a further conflagration, the U.S. government took no counteraction in this case. However, in May and June 1987 the House of Representatives' Committee on Energy and Commerce conducted an investigation into the matter, equating the stature of the problem with the U.S./European battles being waged in the aircraft industry over Airbus.[5] The study concluded that there was no clear evidence that the French decision was protectionist. However, the controversy surrounding the event further supported the efforts of senators such as John Danforth (R., Mo.) and Lloyd Bensten (D., Tex.) to secure legislation that would penalize countries discriminating against U.S. telecommunications companies.

Resentment, frustration, and anger dominated the attitudes of the American players involved in the dispute. There were a number of theories about what had happened; the European and American perspectives on the course of events differed considerably.

PERSPECTIVE ON EVENTS

AT&T Public Affairs, Washington, D.C.

AT&T's Washington office had three vice presidents—one was in charge of government lobbying at the federal, state, and local levels, while the other two each handled an issue area, either U.S. communications policy or a miscellaneous group of functions such as taxation, human resources, international trade, and procurement. The Washington office became involved in the CGCT affair in the summer of 1986; prior to that date there seemed to be little need for their involvement. Until Jacques Chirac was elected prime minister of France in March 1986, AT&T's acquisition of CGCT was considered a *fait accompli*. "Everyone thought it was going to happen momentarily."

For this reason, AT&T did not involve the U.S. government in the process until the fall of 1986, although the American Ambassador to France, Joe Rogers, had been informed from the beginning. A vice president in the Washington office recalled, "AT&T France was advising us that our chances were good, and justifiably so. Chirac had run on a platform emphasizing the privatization of nationalized industries, making it likely that he would not oppose the sale of CGCT. There was some goodwill left for us in the Ministry of Industry and the Ministry of Postes, Téléphones and Télégraphes (PTT) from the days of negotiations under the Socialists."

Negotiations in France were being handled through APT, who worked closely with Philips and with AT&T's Network Systems, the division which provided AT&T's senior management for the joint venture. APT was put in charge of negotiating the deal, a fact that became politically important further on in the game. Certain French government officials had advised AT&T to keep a low profile to make the deal appear more European. However, the DGT later argued that they would have rather dealt directly with AT&T because they wanted a more direct route to Bell Labs. Two members of the Philips management board and a high-level AT&T executive were involved in discussions with the DGT, the Ministry of Finance, and the Ministry of Industry during negotiations.   APT opposed any U.S. government involvement in that deal, believing that American pressure on the French government would be counter-productive. Their view changed in the fall of 1986: "When the Germans got involved in the fall of 1986, we asked for help from USTR," the public affairs vice president noted.

APT believed that a letter sent by FCC chair Mark Fowler to the Regional Bell Operating Companies (RBOCs) in October 1986 prejudiced the French government against them. In response to threats from the German government that procurement would be cut from Alcatel's German subsidiary, SEL, if Siemens did not get CGCT, Fowler circulated a letter asking the RBOCs and GTE how much equipment they had purchased from Siemens in the past, threatening to curtail future purchases. This was regarded as highly aggressive behavior by the French, who resented being caught in the middle of the feuding between the United States and West Germany.

APT agreed with AT&T Public Affairs' assessment that until mid-1986, everything was going smoothly, although they considered the turning point to be Alcatel's acquisition of ITT in July 1986. To the end, they believed that they had the strong support of Alcatel, CGCT, and the PTT and that the powerful Finance Minister Balladur was neutral in his preferences. Even after the West German threats in the fall of 1986, APT did not regard Siemens as a serious competitor because its switch was inferior.[6]

In December 1986, AT&T Public Affairs received a telephone call from a middle-level official of the French Ministry of Foreign Affairs, who we shall call Pierre Rousseau. Rousseau said he had been sent by his Ministry, and advised AT&T that if it wanted CGCT, it should change the French partner it had chosen. Instead of its current partner, SAT, it should go with the large French defense firm Matra. While he could not guarantee that it would ensure Balladur's agreement on an AT&T acquisition of CGCT, it would help immeasurably. Matra had already been informally approached by a French government representative about a partnership with AT&T and was interested. Because Matra had previously purchased CGCT's customer premises equipment business the company made good sense as a partner. Matra had a lot of experience with large open government bids and could have helped AT&T in negotiations. Also, Matra was larger than SAT, so the partnership would have been better balanced. This meant that Matra would have more control, making technology transfer more likely—a fact that would please the French government. Finally, and perhaps most important, Chirac was good friends with Matra's CEO Jean-Luc Lagardère. Because he had recently denied Matra an opportunity to buy the privatized French television station TF1, Chirac owed Lagardère a favor. Rousseau urged AT&T to contact a senior vice president at Matra soon, since both Ericsson and Siemens were also interested in approaching Matra.

Public Affairs passed on this information, but after review by senior officers of AT&T, Philips, and APT, it was decided not to follow up on this option. Those involved in the project were puzzled. What exactly was Rousseau's role and what authority did he have? Why did Balladur not approach them directly on this issue, and what did this communication mean?

"Pierre Rousseau"*

"They should have known who I was!" exclaimed an exasperated Pierre Rousseau. "They should have known that I was a back-channel operation with a precise delegation from the French administration. They should have know that when the Reagan administration became involved, the Ministry of Foreign Affairs had to be involved too. This had to be a decision reached by consensus in the French government."

AT&T Europe echoed Rousseau's frustration on the question of APT's partners. It believed that APT had erred seriously in its choice of partners. Its first set of partners turned out to be unacceptable to the French government. While it approved of APT's choice of SAT, the financial partners involved were unacceptable because they were not French and because they were not telecommunications related.[7] AT&T Europe claimed that when APT was allowed by the French government to change its partners, its second choices were little better—a financial institution and a small, financially insecure telecommunications firm. In contrast, Matra was a powerful, profitable, more equal partner with a CEO who had excellent connections to high-level government officials.[8]

In Rousseau's view, refusing to go with Matra was only one of the mistakes AT&T made, however. Their second mistake was to take Philips on as a partner. Not only was it perceived as a consumer electronics company, the French believed that Philips wanted out of the central office switching market, he said. While they remained in the private branch exchange business, Rousseau believed that the alliance with AT&T was a way for Philips to exit public switching gradually and gracefully, without alienating customers.

Third, AT&T did not provide a good global package around the CGCT purchase. "There was more to this deal than switches," said Rousseau. "The French government was concerned about exports, employment, layoffs, joint R&D, and technology transfer." Furthermore, he claimed, AT&T changed its package between the two technical tests performed, not including some of the software that had been included in the first test in the second one.

Finally, Rousseau contrasted AT&T's behavior with that of Siemens and Ericsson. The president of Siemens came to France several times during the summer and fall of 1986, and high-level people were in Paris regularly. Similarly, the president of Ericsson was there a couple of times a month. In contrast, Olson never

*Ministry of Foreign Affairs, Paris, France.

came at all during the critical stages of the negotiations. Rousseau had stressed to AT&T that the French did not like dealing with APT and that someone from corporate headquarters in New Jersey should have been sent. "They (the French government) regarded APT as nothing more than a holding company."

AT&T Network Systems, Morristown, New Jersey

AT&T Network Systems had the lead role within AT&T for what became known as "Project France" from its inception in 1985 to its closure in 1987. The Corporate Strategic Group within the chairman's office was also deeply and continuously involved, but had no responsibility for day-to-day negotiations. APT, the European 50–50 joint venture of Philips and AT&T, was given the lead negotiating role.

Until January 1987, AT&T International had usually assumed responsibility for the development of international markets and sales but because of the special complexity and importance of Project France, International played a relatively minor role. In January 1987, the role of International was changed by an AT&T policy decision that gave each of the Lines of Business within AT&T the direct responsibility for the development and ongoing management of their global activities. International became AT&T's "in-country" presence, coordinating the corporation's activities abroad and supplying information about local political and economic situations. It also reported to the chairman's office on the collective global strategies of the various AT&T Lines of Business. It had no responsibility, however, for coordinating strategic activities; AT&T Europe was not represented at the bargaining table for the CGCT deal.

As far as negotiations were concerned, a company official said, "APT was given full autonomy but not full authority. Strategic and tactical issues were closely analyzed and coordinated by the parent companies." APT's president reported to both Network Systems (of which he was vice president) and to Philips. Figure 2 shows what the organizational structure looked like at the beginning of negotiations in 1985 and after the 1987 reorganization.

Network Systems pointed out that AT&T's and Philips' attempt to enter the French telecommunications market initially consisted of a total package containing three elements:

1. The purchase of CGCT to gain a 16 percent switching market share in France.
2. The establishment of a Microwave Radio Joint Venture with Alcatel that would market its products worldwide and would include $200 million of radio exports from France into the United States.
3. Development advice to Alcatel on its E10 Five switch and marketing support for its sale in the United States.

Network Systems discounted the importance of APT's failure to drop SAT and take on Matra as a partner in France. Both the finance and industry ministries had recommended SAT as APT's partner from the beginning. They believed SAT needed support from the APT alliance to stay viable in the marketplace. When Network Systems received the Rousseau input via AT&T Public Affairs, it went back to its ministerial contacts in Paris, along with Philips executives, and received affirmation that SAT should remain in the APT offer package.

Figure 2   Organizational Structure in 1985 and 1987

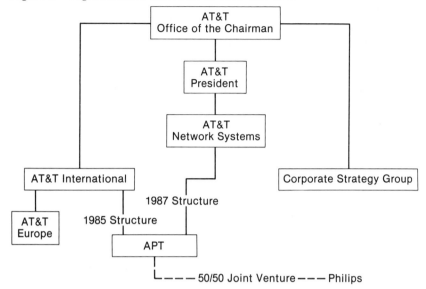

Network Systems felt the French administration did not give credit to what AT&T was offering Alcatel. At the point of final submission, it maintained that the APT package included virtually the same financial and technical offer as Siemens and Ericsson for the acquisition of CGCT, and equivalent contributions with its partnerships with SAT and SAGEM. In addition, AT&T was contributing its highly advanced radio technology to the radio joint venture with Alcatel plus a satellite earth station agreement.

Network Systems pinpointed another event as the key turning point in the story—Alcatel's acquisition of ITT. AT&T began to sense trouble when the E10 switch deal fell through in May 1986. Georges Pébereau, then CEO of Alcatel's parent company CGE, was getting pressure from the French government. The government was skeptical that AT&T and Alcatel could collaborate openly in switches in the United States and compete in switches in France. For this reason, the E10 part of the package was dropped, leaving the microwave deal and two new projects in satellite earth stations and light wave submarine cables. Although Alcatel retained interest in the project, it had lost a key opportunity to market its switches more broadly, and would have to look elsewhere for broader market access.

In July 1986, Pébereau announced the acquisition of ITT's telecommunications division. Soon after he was fired by the French government. For AT&T, this spelled trouble. It had relied heavily on Alcatel and Pébereau to help ease the way into the French market. With this important ally out of the deal, it would be on its own. Furthermore, as mentioned, through this deal, Alcatel gained access to 40 percent of the West German switching market through ITT's German subsidiary, SEL. Because of this, the German government insisted upon reciprocal access to the French central office switching market. It was around this time that Chirac wrote letters to other prospective bidders, inviting them to make offers for CGCT.

Network Systems denied that there had been any change in the package APT offered between the first (summer/fall 1986) and second (spring 1987) technical tests. They downplayed the technical importance of the second test, noting that the first one (which AT&T passed with flying colors) took six to seven months, while the second one took a few weeks. It further argued that the APT package was a great deal for Alcatel. The final package offered two excellent export opportunities—in microwave radio and satellite earth station equipment. "We looked at the Alcatel compensation as a real give. We were giving great microwave technology and an excellent U.S. marketing opportunity for Alcatel's satellite earth station products," said a Network Systems official.

He also countered Rousseau's claims that AT&T had mishandled the government contacts necessary to make the deal go through. In the beginning there was no need for government intervention—AT&T seemed destined to get CGCT and even as late as December 1986, Ericsson was seen as the least likely candidate. First, its switch technology did not receive high ratings in the first technical test performed. Second, by January or February 1987, it still did not have a French partner confirmed. Third, because of the political pressure from Germany, if AT&T were to lose out to anyone, it would appear to be Siemens. Even this was not considered a serious threat because of the DGT/PTT's disdain for Siemens' technology. As the 1987 CEO of CGE, Pierre Suard, noted, "If you can find one person at the PTT who wants to buy Siemens over AT&T, I'd like to meet him."[9]

Once Pébereau announced the ITT acquisition in July 1986, however, AT&T pulled out all stops. "When this deal was sprung, it floored everybody. Had we known it was coming we would have totally rethought our strategy in having Alcatel as our partner in the deal. This wouldn't have stopped the German pressure, but we would have taken another tack in getting the deal." By the fall of 1986, the Germans became politically active, and so did AT&T. It was decided that U.S. government involvement was necessary, and executives from Network Systems visited both U.S. Trade Representative Clayton Yeutter and Secretary of Commerce Malcolm Baldrige in October 1986. Both Yeutter and Baldrige made protests in response. "If we hadn't done anything, Siemens would be in France now," Network Systems argued.

Prior to this time, it had not been clear to AT&T that any U.S. government involvement was necessary, however. In fact, as early as 1985, AT&T had signed a main features agreement with CGE's Pébereau, including the package of three deals mentioned. Although CGCT did not belong to CGE, Pébereau explained that he had been given a "directed award" for CGCT's 16 percent share of the French central office switching market. By this, Pébereau meant that he had been authorized to sell CGCT's market share as part of a larger package involving CGE's Alcatel.

"Bertrand Tessier"*

"They should not have relied so completely on CGE and Pébereau," said former Alcatel executive Bertrand Tessier. "First, Pébereau was giving away something that

*Former high-level executive with Alcatel.

was not his to give. The new government said CGE/Alcatel wasn't going to give 16 percent of the switching market to AT&T—to give an Alcatel partner 16 percent was too dangerous. Second, Balladur hated Pébereau from his (Balladur's) days as chairman of two CGE subsidiaries, CEAC and GSI. When Balladur came in, AT&T was through. Everybody in the new government was furious with Pébereau and Pébereau couldn't stand Balladur. When Balladur discovered the ITT deal he fired Pébereau in July. That was the day AT&T was through."

AT&T Europe confirmed Tessier's view of the lack of French government support for APT. They argued that APT was mistaken to think that Chirac would be in favor of APT and that Balladur was in any way neutral. Chirac had cautioned against selling CGCT to "foreigners" during the 1986 elections campaign, and was a good friend of Matra CEO Lagardère. Balladur also was close to Lagardère, but more important he questioned the wisdom of allowing AT&T to have a role in France. In this sense, AT&T Europe believed that APT had completely misread the political situation. Despite its emphasis on privatization and market-led economic policy, the government elected in March 1986 contained a number of officials who were unsympathetic to APT.[10]

Tessier also emphasized that Ericsson had been in France for a long time. It had about a million lines in service already, and at the operating level the DGT was perfectly happy with Ericsson technology. "AT&T was new and many features of their switch were unfamiliar to the French technicians. They were not suited to French norms even though the higher ups in the PTT liked and respected AT&T technology." A former DGT official corroborated Tessier's point: "The DGT chief favored AT&T but the engineers favored Ericsson because they knew the equipment. They were afraid of losing their jobs." Tessier further mused, "Matra would certainly have been a much better partner for AT&T. You have to wonder whether the Ministries of Industry and Finance were really in favor of AT&T when they recommended going with SAT." Rousseau confirmed this argument: "The government was interested in solving SAT's financial problems—and they did not want AT&T to get the nod."

The DGT official argued that once the ITT deal was made it was difficult to also approve AT&T. Even though Siemens was completely incompatible with the French system, Balladur didn't want to make the Germans angry. "The DGT was highly opposed to Siemens. However, it was Balladur who was making the decision."

Neither he nor Tessier was impressed with AT&T's negotiating style. "AT&T didn't even know we were trying to take over ITT until it was too late. They didn't seem to give a damn," said Tessier. The DGT official admitted "AT&T is not the best negotiator. They are not Latin enough. I respect them but they have big boots." Tessier also remarked that the second test of the switches was more a test of the packages of each company rather than just their switch technology.

Office of the United States Trade Representative, European Division, Washington, D.C.

USTR officials were even less impressed with AT&T's ability to use the U.S. government to forward its cause. While stressing that they were reluctant to argue in favor of a particular company or of a particular sector, they pointed out that they were willing to help ensure that the decision concerning CGCT was made on a commercial rather than on a political basis. However, it was difficult to determine precisely what AT&T wanted the government to do for it in this case. One USTR official noted that in contrast to a company like IBM, "AT&T is terrible at using the government for its purposes. I call them up and ask them for their position on something and it takes them a week to call back. When they do, they often say that there is disagreement within the company."

They further observed that top executives at AT&T did not spend enough time with people at the top level of government, either in France or in the United States. "For them, it's a new game. The CEO of AT&T has to move in different circles. Take, for example, when Chancellor Kohl was here in the Fall of 1986. AT&T contacted Deputy Secretary of State John C. Whitehead and White House Chief of Staff Howard Baker to try to get the President to say something to Kohl. But you can't make cold calls when you're in trouble and expect results. If cabinet-level officials are not kept up-to-date, how can they judge how important an issue is? We're willing to help companies, but with AT&T there's no on-going, continuing relationship—no partnership."

AT&T Public Affairs explained: "After all the dealings we've had with government in the past, going to them to ask for help is slightly counter-intuitive. It's just not in our normal day-to-day thinking to ask the government for help. Compare that with the thinking of British, German or French firms." When asked why Olson did not travel to Paris as frequently as the CEOs of Siemens and Ericsson did, an AT&T official replied, "We were advised not to be a heavy-handed AT&T—to keep a relatively low profile. It was a judgment call."

The USTR official further commented on the implications of U.S. telecommunications policy in general—or the lack of it—for American firms such as AT&T who were trying to move abroad. "Deregulation was carried out by lawyers in the FCC and the Justice Department and was purely oriented to the domestic scene—international trade issues were completely ignored." In reference to Fowler's October 1986 letter to the German government, he remarked, "Fowler doesn't speak for the government, at least not for this administration. But I guess there were some folks in the administration who secretly cheered. There was also animosity, however, because nobody on the trade side wants to see the FCC getting its foot in the door of trade policy."

The decision in January 1984 to deregulate the telecommunications sector had significant implications for AT&T's efforts at home and abroad. Judge Greene's Consent Decree stipulated that the RBOCs should be split off from AT&T, leaving the company with four divisions: Long Lines (long distance), Western Electric (equipment manufacturing), Bell Labs (R&D), and American Bell (communications services). The Consent Decree also allowed companies desiring to compete against AT&T in long distance equal access to local lines. It had two major implications for AT&T on an international scale. First, it weakened AT&T at the same time that the American trade deficit in telecommunications (estimated to be $1.9 billion in 1986) was rising. Second, it unilaterally opened the American telecommunications market to competition from both American and foreign companies.

Despite the challenge from abroad, for more than 20 years the Justice Department had zealously pursued AT&T to break its monopoly in telecommunications. As one Justice official vowed, "We're going to have severed limbs, AT&T's limbs, on the table dripping blood."[11]

A USTR official pointed out, for the past 14 years, U.S. policy in the sector has been dictated by the FCC and the Justice Department. "This hasn't helped the competitiveness of AT&T in the industry." USTR's concern about the lack of a U.S. telecommunications policy was echoed by former AT&T CEO Charles Brown:

> The crucial question is, What is the long-run interest in telecommunications which we (AT&T) are dedicated to serve? It is not our job to define interest, and certainly it will not emerge from the kind of contest between plaintiff and defendant which we have had for so long in the courts. Surely it is not the job of the assistant attorney general to make that policy. Will it emerge naturally from marketplace competition? I have my doubts....It seems to me that there must be some way that government can identify those things which are truly of national importance in telecommunications.[12]

The American approach to telecommunications policy can be contrasted to that of the French government in particular and European governments in general. In the French case, the government supported research efforts by the DGT's research affiliate CNET, which in turn worked closely with, and heavily subsidized, private French companies. The government monitored closely the entry and exit of all companies to the French telecommunications market, exercising control through its procurement policies. Until recently, the DGT had been able to provide French suppliers with guaranteed market sales; in the past, it had used this power over purchases to urge foreign companies such as Ericsson and ITT to license their technology or to sell subsidiaries to French producers.

This high degree of government supervision in telecommunications was prevalent throughout Europe. Although the European Community (EC) was moving to remove the barriers to telecommunications and other trade posed by government procurement, it was concerned that non-EC companies would benefit disproportionately from this opening if they were allowed into Community markets without providing greater foreign access to their own domestic markets. The EC was planning to handle this situation by negotiating reciprocal liberalization with third countries before they were allowed into EC markets. As USTR noted, demanding market access after the domestic market had already been opened is more difficult. "When we asked (German post minister) Schwartz-Schilling about American access to the German market he basically said, 'You were foolish enough to open your own market unilaterally—why would we do the same thing?'"

Appendix

Key Dates, 1981–1987

1981

March   Socialist Party wins general elections.

1982   CGE, Thomson, CGCT, and Matra—among other companies—nationalized.

     French government purchases CGCT from ITT for $215 million.

1983   French government approves merger of CGE's CIT-Alcatel and Thomson Télécommunications; 7,000 people laid off.

1984

January   U.S. telecommunications sector deregulated.

Spring   British telecommunications market deregulated; 22 Japanese firms with operations in France transfer long-distance systems to Britain.

     French government decides to sell CGCT to a foreign company.

     Pébereau of CGE begins negotiation with AT&T as partner in entering U.S. market.

1985

July   AT&T signs protocol of intention with CGE to buy 70 percent of CGCT, begin a microwave transmission joint venture between CGE and AT&T/Philips (APT) in France, and market CGE's E10 switch in the United States.

1986

March   Socialists lose legislative elections; Jacques Chirac becomes prime minister.

May   Negotiations between Pérebeau and AT&T to market switch in U.S. collapse.

July   CGE buys 56 percent of ITT's worldwide telecommunications operations, establishing new joint venture with ITT: Alcatel NV; questions of U.S. market left unresolved.

     Pébereau fired as CEO of CGE; Chirac invites other CGCT prospective bidders.

     AT&T's Washington office becomes involved in CGCT purchase attempt.

September   Date French government established for CGCT decision passes.

Fall	First test of switches complete: AT&T first, Ericsson second, Siemens third.

1986

October	West German government notifies France that unless Siemens allowed to buy CGCT, it will cut procurement from CGE's newly acquired West German subsidiary, SEL; AT&T, learning of this, protests to the Commerce Department and USTR about unfair trade practices.
	FCC Chairman Fowler writes to RBOCs and GTE asking how much equipment they have purchased from Siemens and threatens to curtail future purchases.
December	The FCC announces an inquiry into international regulations regarding telecommunications.
	Finance Minister Balladur announces that foreign companies cannot own more than 20 percent of newly privatized companies (e.g., CGCT); three companies must find French partners if wish to enter market: Siemens joins with Jeumont-Schneider, Ericsson with Matra, APT with SAT.
	"Pierre Rousseau" calls AT&T Public Affairs office advising AT&T to change its French partner if it wants CGCT: should select Matra; AT&T decides against change.

1987

January	AT&T changes role of AT&T International; AT&T Europe not present at the CGCT "bargaining table."
March	Second switch test: Ericsson comes in slightly ahead of AT&T.
April 23	French government chooses Ericsson/Matra for CGCT acquisition.
May/June	U.S. House Committee on Energy and Commerce investigates decision, finding no evidence of French protectionism.

ENDNOTES

1. Through its acquisition of ITT's telecommunications division in July 1986, the French telecommunications firm Alcatel gained access to ITT's West German subsidiary SEL, which held 40 percent of that country's central office switching market. In response, the German government demanded reciprocal access to the French market in the fall of 1986.
2. Quoted in *The Wall Street Journal*, April 24, 1987.
3. Speech made by former AT&T CEO James Olson at Security Analysts' Luncheon, San Francisco, September 18, 1987.
4. Quoted in *The Wall Street Journal*, April 24, 1987.
5. See "Major Issues in United States–European Community Trade," Staff Report prepared for the use of the Subcommittee on Oversight and Investigations of the Committee on Energy and Commerce, U.S. House of Representatives, July 1987. The Airbus dispute centers around contentions by the

U.S. government that European governments have subsidized participants in the international Airbus consortium, resulting in an unfair advantage relative to the company's U.S. competitors—Boeing and McDonnell-Douglas.

6. "Major Issues in United States–European Community Trade," p. 3.
7. APT's first set of partners included SAT and five French unit trusts owned by the Dutch-controlled Neuflize-Schlumbergr-Mallet bank and Morgan Guaranty. It was the Frenchness of the unit trusts that was doubted. Its second set of partners included Sagem, SAT's majority shareholder and Omnium Financier de Paris, a financial company owned by the French Total Oil Group.
8. "Major Issues," p. 4.
9. Quoted in *Business Week*, May 4, 1987.
10. Major Issues," p. 4.
11. Quoted in Steve Coll, *The Deal of the Century: The Breakup of AT&T* (New York: Atheneum, 1986).
12. Quoted in George Lodge, *The American Disease*, (New York: Alfred A. Knopf, 1984), pp. 109–110.

JESSI

SEMATECH confirms that we are witnessing a battle between national economies rather than between semiconductor companies.
Pasquale Pistorio, CEO of STET[1]

In December 1988 Robert Hamersma, managing director of integrated circuits at Philips, in Eindhoven, Holland, contemplated his trip to the JESSI planning group in Itzehoe, West Germany. The Joint European Submicron Silicon Initiative (JESSI) was the next step in the Megabit Project—the joint venture between Philips and archrival Siemens. Whereas Mega was aimed at advancing the semiconductor capabilities of the two partners, JESSI was intended to improve the European semiconductor "food chain": the equipment and materials vendors, the chip manufacturers, and the end users of semiconductors. Philips hoped that with a proposed budget of 4 billion ecus[2] over the next eight years, JESSI would enable Europe to match U.S. and Japanese efforts.

The planning group, formed earlier in 1988, included representatives of more than 30 companies and research institutes from six European countries (see Exhibit 1).[3] Its job was to define JESSI's scope, identify and recruit participants, and work out funding, the technical agenda, and organizational issues. Once approved by JESSI participants, the plan would be presented to the governments involved and the European Commission (EC) in Brussels in early 1989. JESSI planners hoped that the Commission and the member states would cover 50 percent of JESSI's costs. Consequently, the upcoming negotiations over funding and governance would be a formidable barrier. Hamersma was heading to Itzehoe to devise industry's strategy for these talks.

As potential JESSI partners, the European Economic Community (EEC) and some or all of the 12 member countries would wield a great deal of influence. However, since the 12 countries were at different stages of industrial development, determining their roles in and contribution to JESSI would be difficult (see Exhibit 2). Community funds came from all 12 countries, and the possibility of pleasing all was small. Since countries like Germany and the Netherlands, who had supported Mega, stood to benefit more from JESSI than did Spain or Greece, JESSI expected those member states with large electronics interests to supplement EEC funds to make the country contributions more equitable. What returns member states and the EEC would expect was an important factor in preparing for the upcoming negotiations.

Since JESSI was designed to address the needs of the entire food chain, it would involve a variety of companies. Hamersma and the planning group had to design membership rules that allowed firms to participate at a level that fit with

*This case was written by Associates Fellow Robert S. Williams under the supervision of Professor George Lodge as the basis for class discussion rather than to illustrate either effective or ineffective handling of an administrative situation.

their scope, balancing the needs of each part in the food chain so that each received an appropriate share of JESSI projects.

JESSI planning coincided with Europe's drive to achieve unprecedented unity by 1992. Although most Europeans were optimistic about rivaling the United States and Japan in world economic power, it was uncertain how the Community would deal with many fundamental issues. The risks of uneven distribution of benefits, income, jobs, and technological development threatened to block legislation that would enable completion of the internal market. Social and economic cohesion were important, but how much convergence was desirable, how much decentralization, how much harmonization of taxes, standards, regulation, and government procurement was really necessary to realize the potential of 1992? To ease the legislative process, the Single European Act (SEA) was passed in 1986, enabling laws governing the internal market to be approved by a qualified majority of the Council of Ministers instead of requiring unanimity as before (see Exhibit 3 for more on the European Community).[4] Nevertheless, there were many obstacles to unity. Some felt, for example, it would strengthen the strong countries and weaken the weak, while others argued all would benefit.

Eurounity also raised serious external problems, concerning especially relations with the United States and Japan. Europe was not only the world's largest market, it was also the world's largest trader, accounting for 40 percent of world trade. JESSI participants, however, wanted to rectify Europe's high-tech trade deficit of $10 billion (compared with surpluses in 1987 of $1.3 billion for the United States and $8.6 billion for Japan). Some argued that to be corrected, trade policy should provide at least temporary protection in critical areas. But this would conflict with the free traders in Europe who emphasized a strategic trade policy geared to achieving high-tech strength using the notion of "reciprocity." The situation became more complex with the announcement that Japanese chip firms planned to build plants in Europe to avoid being locked out of the market. The Community responded by strengthening the rules defining what constituted a European product. This was to ensure that a set level of local added value was maintained to be considered "made in Europe."

Philips was interested in JESSI for several reasons. It had recently placed a new emphasis on core businesses. However, there were several weak links in the European chain that directly affected three of these four core businesses—components, information technology, and consumer electronics.

In 1988 Europe imported 80 percent of its semiconductor manufacturing equipment and materials (E&M). The weakness of the European E&M industry and Philips' exclusion from America's Sematech had made Philips increasingly dependent on its Japanese competitors. To purchase E&M, Philips was forced to share proprietary information with competitors (to customize the equipment) while also having to rely on them for the latest technological advances. Philips hoped JESSI would help it break this dependence by strengthening the European E&M industries.

The European food chain also had weak links between chip manufacturers and their customers. Philips produced chips for its own use as well as for sale to other companies in a wide range of industries—autos, consumer electronics, and computers. Part of JESSI's purpose was to design and develop application projects in order to stimulate the application of advanced ICs and create new markets so that ties between European chip producers and users would be closer and more reliable. It also sought to increase the use of chips throughout Europe.[5] In addition, JESSI's planners hoped to expand funding for product development and manufacturing in the chip industry itself.

While Hamersma and Philips were attempting to ready JESSI for its negotiations with the EEC and the member states, the Americans were setting up Sematech with a $1 billion budget for five years and the Japanese were fortifying their dominant position in commodity memory chips, consumer electronics, and key E&M industries. In spite of its operations and alliances all over the world, Philips felt it had no choice but to rely on an enhanced European effort to keep it competitive. Although Philips was one of Europe's most active participants in cooperative R&D with other companies, its world market share in chips was falling and its overall profitability decreasing. Philips needed JESSI to leverage its own R&D and to coordinate and improve the efficacy of the overall European R&D effort.

PHILIPS: HISTORY AND STRATEGY

Philips was founded in 1891 by Gerard Philips, a Dutch engineer who had developed an inexpensive process to manufacture incandescent lamps. In 1987, N.V. Philips' Gloeilampenfabrieken was the fourth largest industrial company outside the United States and was among the world's most widely known manufacturers of household appliances, televisions and radios, professional electronic equipment, lighting, and related products. The company had several hundred subsidiaries in 60 countries and operated more than 300 plants in some 40 countries, manufacturing thousands of different products. It employed approximately 336,000 persons in 1987.[6] Exhibit 4 shows the company's product deliveries, geographic sales, and value added for 1987. Exhibit 5 presents group financial data for 1978 and 1987.

With over 60 percent of its sales and three quarters of its assets in Europe, Philips' global strategy focused on core businesses—consumer electronics, information technology, components, and lighting. Decision making had moved away from national organizations (NOs) toward product divisions, whose task was to develop global alliances to exploit global markets. Philips was seeking, however, to achieve efficiency, responsiveness, and global learning in a manner that protected and built upon the formidable strengths of its NOs.[7] At home, the Netherlands and Philips had a relationship similar to that of the lion and the mouse in Aesop's fable—Philips the corporate lion, dependent on the tiny state of Holland.

The Netherlands: Government and Politics

The Netherlands is about the size of New Jersey, with a population of 14 million. Philips was the largest private employer with 70,100 people in 1988, and the largest exporter. Corporate headquarters and 30 percent of its total investment were in

Eindhoven. Although only 6 percent of its sales was in the Netherlands, about 30 percent of its profits were generated there (this included export profits). Sixty percent of its total $2 billion R&D budget in 1987 was spent in Holland. Its employment needs were so great that at times it took almost the entire class of Dutch engineering and electronics graduates. Although Philips actively promoted managers from around the world, the top management levels were almost exclusively Dutch.

According to Dick Snijders, director, corporate finance, "In the sixties and early seventies we didn't pay much attention to the Dutch government. But in 1974, a Socialist government took control, led by the PvdA party. It was clear we had to do something to communicate with the new political power. We established regular patterns of communication with the government. As far as they were concerned, all business was bad."

The socialist coalition survived until March 1977, when it collapsed in the wake of a bitter dispute between Labor and the Christian Democrats (CDA). A CDA–Liberal party (VVD), relatively pro-business coalition emerged. This center-right coalition lost its legislative majority in 1981, but regained its position in 1982 and strengthened it in 1986. Snijders was confident that the Dutch government's attitude toward business would remain favorable at least for the time being.

In 1978, to ensure it would not be blind sided again by political change, Philips set up an office in The Hague. Hans Moelikcr, its director, identified four government offices with which Philips had developed close relations: Social Affairs, Economic Affairs, Finance, and the Prime Minister's office.

Extensive social services, including complete medical coverage, resulted in Dutch government expenditures being among the highest in the world, 60 percent of GNP. Moeliker said, "Corporate tax in Holland is high—about 40 percent, and it is difficult to retain managers here because marginal income taxes range from 60 percent to 70 percent.[8] Stringent government constraints make firing and layoffs difficult and expensive. So while our roots are here and we attempt to keep the high value-added parts of our business here, we have exported mass production. Since 1972, we've cut back our work force in Holland 40 percent, while reducing worldwide employment 18 percent."[9]

"The Unions consider Philips to be a good employer," Moeliker continued, "even though only 15 percent of our employees are organized. This is because we provide lifetime employment, good training and education programs, competitive medical insurance, and pension rights. As a consequence, we have very high labor costs."

Philips was also dissatisfied with the educational system in Holland. Moeliker said, "When we employ a graduate we have to send him or her to school in the company for a year or more. We said to the government, 'you should make the system more pragmatic.' The government responded, 'fine, give us more money.'"

Another problem was that the university labs, under the jurisdiction of the Dutch Ministry of Education, had no relationship with the Ministry of Economic Affairs, which was responsible for industrial R&D. There also appeared to be few formal links between the universities and Philips. Historically academics had shunned industry and researchers prided themselves on keeping a healthy distance from commercial applications. Even at Philips this was a problem. Its labs, often compared with Bell Labs in the United States, were a main source of corporate pride, and yet Philips researchers had often bragged about their contribution to pure research which did not lead to a commercial product.[10] In 1987, Philips sought to change this approach. A reorganization was planned to increase the speed of product development and to bring design closer to marketing and manufacturing.

The Ministry of Economic Affairs and Finance

The goal of the Ministry of Economic Affairs was to create an environment in which business could thrive. It had power to grant subsidies, give R&D tax credits, and issue loans. The ministry had identified four areas for government support: biotechnology, medical equipment, new materials, and information technology (the ministry had spent in 1988: biotech HFL 33.9 million, information technology 99.8 million, materials 57.4 million, and medical 4.5 million).*

A ministry spokesperson said it was difficult for a small country to support such a large entity as Philips, when so many smaller companies were seeking help. Bill Ledeboer, head of cooperative research at Philips, responded, "The world is increasingly competitive. You have to produce truly outstanding work. In our industry, Philips is the only Dutch player who can do it. The Netherlands needs to leverage Philips in order to boost its economy, infrastructure, universities and prestige in the world." The ministry found this argument persuasive and saw subsidies as a way to encourage Philips to stay in Holland. In pursuit of European unity in 1992, however, the European Commission was discouraging national subsidies.

The Ministry of Finance, on the other hand, believed in only limited intervention: government should not "pick winners"; subsidies and bailouts were to be avoided. In fact, the ministry believed that Holland was basically a country of traders, not manufacturers. It was interested in creating a good business environment by keeping inflation and interest rates low and the Dutch guilder strong; not by industrial targeting.

Philips' Management of Governmental Affairs

Each Philips country manager was responsible for governmental affairs in his or her respective country. Frequent contact among country managers and with corporate headquarters kept Philips current on political trends, and regional managers tied together the different country perspectives.

Dr. Walter Grünsteidl, chief of Philips' Brussels office, was the corporate channel to the various European organizations, including the Commission and Parliament. Grünsteidl brought company experts to the Commission to provide information, which helped to establish Philips' credibility.

On Philips-Europe and Philips-Holland, Grünsteidl commented, "There are serious tensions between the two over such matters as plant closings, incentives for

*HFL was the Dutch guilder. One guilder was equal to $0.49 in November 1988.

plant openings, and the preservation of national identity in the face of diminishing national power. Country managers were once emperors; things have changed."

"It may be desirable to concentrate in one or two countries," Grünsteidl added, "but we have to balance our needs against those of other nations. We must prepare ourselves for the changes in Europe. We are for European strength, but we also need strategic alliances with U.S. and Japanese companies."

Philips evaluated the effectiveness of this information network by the degree to which it anticipated political change, and whether Philips people had established credible relationships with local politicians. Another way to judge effectiveness was by the number of European R&D projects awarded to Philips through ESPRIT (described shortly). To date Philips was leading all companies in projects received.

EUROPE'S CHANGING GOVERNMENTAL LANDSCAPE: 1992

The Treaty of Rome, signed in 1957, established the European Economic Community to achieve a harmonious development of economic activities through continuous and balanced expansion, a rising standard of living and closer relations among member states (see Exhibit 3 for more on the EEC). These goals were to be accomplished by establishing a common market and a more convergent economic policy of the member states. But after 30 years, many barriers remained. Duplication of effort, inefficient investment, high-priced social programs, and a quagmire of different national laws and technical standards resulted in competitive disadvantage for European firms.

Paulo Cecchini, special adviser to the Commission of the European Communities, chaired a task force in 1987 charged with quantifying the benefits of real unity. Estimates were that a total of 170–250 billion ecus could be saved from reducing red tape and border related controls (8–9 billion ecus), lifting government protection in procurement markets (46 billion ecus), harmonizing technical regulations and standards (61 billion ecus), and eliminating barriers to transborder business activity and production efficiencies (57–71 billion ecus).

Industry played a leading role in moving Europe toward achieving the promise of the Treaty of Rome. Trade barriers, lack of technical standards and norms, country currency fluctuations, and protected government procurement markets directly affected Philips' performance, especially since 60 percent of its sales were in Europe. Dr. Wisse Dekker, chairman of Philips, presented a blueprint for action to the Commission in 1985. This became the foundation for the 300 directives contained in Lord Cockfield's white paper on Eurounity, issued in June 1985.[11] This historic document defined the 1992 program and set the timetable. Under the leadership of the Commission's president, Jacques Delors, one-third of the directives had been approved by the end of 1988. Although half the directives were supposed to have been adopted by this date, most observers were optimistic that the situation would improve. However, such directives as VAT harmonization and a common European currency were expected to be difficult because the implications for each country varied greatly.

EUROPEAN SEMICONDUCTOR INDUSTRY

Philips was the largest chip producer on the continent with sales of $1.36 billion in 1986. The 1992 process would help JESSI legitimize a European effort. A Philips insider said, "It has already helped executives see the necessity of pooling resources, coordinating efforts and restructuring industry."

Although European companies had 19 percent of the world semiconductor market (down from the 1979 high of 27 percent), most firms in all parts of the food chain underperformed either their American or Japanese counterparts. European chip makers relied heavily on U.S. and Japanese equipment and materials suppliers, a strategy that worked as long as there was healthy competition between them for European business. This assured Europe of getting immediate access to state-of-the-art technology at competitive prices. When the Americans suddenly dropped out of commodity chip markets (DRAMs), Europe found itself dependent on one country (Japan) for some equipment, materials, and commodity chips. For Philips this was especially threatening because Japanese E&M firms were closely associated with direct competitors of Philips in computers, components, and consumer electronics.

The success of the Japanese and increased U.S. government support of its chip industry had forced Philips and other Europeans to increase cooperative R&D efforts among business, government, and universities. Although several cooperative programs were in place, complications beyond cultural difference made efforts difficult. With European unemployment averaging 11 percent, the unions and their political parties focused on job displacement, not job creation. They feared that emphasis on high technology would raise the unemployment rate. European unity supporters claimed a more competitive Europe would improve employment conditions and increase the region's standard of living. Opponents claimed that jobs would be taken overseas and that wages would be driven down.

In spite of these difficulties, several European government-sponsored R&D programs had been launched. Industry analysts felt, however, they were less effective than U.S. and Japanese efforts because many governments were making the allocation decisions resulting in too many small sums spread over too many small projects and over too many countries. Unlike the United States, the military role in R&D was minimal; most projects were funded by ministries concerned with the economy or with scientific and technical development.

One of the early private collaborations in Europe, Unidata, was a 1973 joint venture between Siemens, Philips, and the French firms Thomson and CII. Unidata's goal was to develop and manufacture mainframe "Eurocomputers." The project ended after two years in disarray with ill feelings among the partners who were never able to narrow the compatibility gap between their products.[12] As of 1988, European firms had still not penetrated the mainframe market. JESSI proponents used the Unidata debacle as an example of why Euro standards and compatibility were so important—to achieve scale and build a European infrastructure.

Several European governments were funding their own technology programs, but efforts varied widely. For example, government support in the United Kingdom was less than one-third of what it was in Germany and France; and all governments were finding it increasingly difficult to supply the huge amounts of capital necessary to be effective. Furthermore, national governments were interested in local jobs and skills, whereas multinationals found it increasingly difficult to guarantee local production in exchange for R&D subsidies.

European Strategic Programme for Research and Development in Information Technology (ESPRIT)

In 1980, Etienne D'Avignon, the EEC commissioner for industrial affairs, requested the 12 largest European-owned information technology companies to define the R&D needs of the industry, to draw up objectives, and to suggest how they could be achieved.[13] In 1984, this led to the establishment of ESPRIT, to coordinate and improve the European basic research in information technology. ESPRIT rules required a sharing of intellectual property within the community. Some industrialists thought such rules made companies less aggressive than they would be if the rights to intellectual property were safeguarded.

The total ESPRIT budget was set at 1.5 billion ecus—half to come out of the EEC research budget and half to be covered by industry on a project basis. ESPRIT concentrated on microelectronics, information processing systems, and information technology applications.

All proposals were approved centrally by the ESPRIT management committee, composed of government-designated representatives from each member country. Members had standard voting rights weighted by population size. Criteria for approval included technical merit and fit with other EEC efforts in high-technology R&D. The committee also attempted to ensure that each member country got a reasonable representation of projects.

Any company that conducted information technology R&D in the EEC and that demonstrated intention to remain in the community was eligible to participate in ESPRIT. By late 1986, a total of 1,016 proposals had been received, and 201 projects were underway involving 240 partners and 2,900 researchers. In 1988, a new emphasis was placed on ensuring that research results were used in applications.

EUREKA

Launched in 1985, EUREKA was a decentralized approach to obtaining cross-border cooperation. Nineteen countries were participating. Its activities were closer to market and broader in scope than ESPRIT projects. Examples included innovations in transportation, environmental protection, new materials, and information technology. EUREKA was more of a framework for cooperation than a program with a fixed budget. Some termed EUREKA a political declaration of will to increase cross-border cooperation.

A minimum of two companies and two national governments or institutes had to participate to qualify as a EUREKA project. Proposals were initiated by the participants. Funding was split between industry and the national governments participating—government financial support, however, was not guaranteed. EU-

REKA also served as a matchmaker among companies looking for partners and provided some antitrust protection.

Philips aggressively pursued cooperative R&D ventures. Between 1983 and 1987 Philips had obtained 157 million ecus of EEC subsidies and had partnered with over 600 companies.

One frequent R&D partner was West German rival Siemens. Their most recent effort, the Megabit project, in 1985, set out to counter Japan's domination of the microchip memory business by leapfrogging into megabit devices.[14] The goal was to make 1-megabit SRAMs and 4-megabit DRAMs.[15] The two partners joined with their governments to finance the project—HFL 1.5 billion coming from Philips, HFL 200 million from the Dutch government, HFL 1.5 billion from Siemens, and HFL 300–400 million from the German government (total $1.75 billion).

Although Siemens and Philips each had its own reasons for joining forces, both companies wanted to use the volume production knowledge from Mega for their more profitable application-specific products. Philips was committed to strength in components and key end-user markets.[16] To stay competitive it needed to leverage R&D dollars. Philips had two major disadvantages compared to Siemens: the Dutch government could not match the German government in terms of money to compete in the technology race, and the Dutch market was too small to rely on as a cash cow.

Siemens, on the other hand, had wanted to escape its reputation as "a prosperous but ponderous master of yesterday's electrical wizardry."[17] The German giant, controlled by the von Siemens family, had vacillated for years over whether to join the international front rank in semiconductor technology or simply buy from Japan. In 1984, its board decided to develop its in-house expertise, and it did not want to be forced to share information on its computers or PABXs to purchase chips from Japanese vendors, who were also its competitors. Siemens decided to commit $1.6 billion to acquire from scratch the sophisticated technologies needed to develop these chips in only five years.

Holland was willing to support Mega because the Dutch wanted state-of-the-art technology to remain in the country. Jans Huijbregts of the Dutch economic ministry said, "It is important for Philips to catch up to the Japanese and U.S. Its success will filter down to other companies and industries in Holland."

In West Germany, five semiconductor-related industries contributed one-third of its GNP. The government realized that for its companies to stay competitive, it had to have indigenous sources for chips. Teaming up with the Dutch enabled them to share the risk and obtain access to the famed Philips labs.

In 1985, as Siemens was negotiating the setup of Mega with Philips, it cut a deal with Toshiba to acquire miniaturization technology instead of developing the expertise in-house. Philips disapproved of the move, because it thought strategically developing the technology in Europe was preferable even if that meant delaying the project. Dr. Heinz Riesenhuber, the West German technology minister, was so angry at Siemens that he came close to withdrawing government backing of Mega.[18] Others in the German government felt this was proof that industry giants should not receive subsidies; they could not be trusted.

In January 1988, however, with a new Siemens factory in Regensburg, West Germany, producing 1-megabit DRAM chips, the move looked brilliant. It turned out that Toshiba's technology had been the best in the world. Philips also expected to benefit from Siemens' gamble with a new 1-megabit plant in the Netherlands coming on line in early 1989.

According to Dr. Arjen Ronner of Philips, "Mega has been a great success. We both wanted to speed up our knowledge in submicron technology and it has worked. We have now caught up to the U.S. and Japan. We proved that a decentralized approach can produce results."

Although some industry analysts agreed with Ronner's assessment, the project still had its problems. Due to exchange rate losses from the declining dollar, and disappointing overall performance, Siemens' earnings had dropped 13 percent. Siemens was also receiving flak for making big investments without immediate return. Yet, many analysts felt this was unfair, for in the long term it appeared Siemens would be in great position to exploit the burgeoning European PC market that would need scarce 1-megabit DRAM chips.[19]

The Philips/Siemens relationship appeared to be working; however, an industry insider stated that culturally there had been some clashes. "I saw Siemens give a presentation of Mega and they spoke about it as if they were the only ones involved." Other observers had mentioned the German "smugness" as difficult to deal with. Cor Vreven, company spokesman for Philips replied, "I don't think we would be exploring JESSI with Siemens if we weren't satisfied with the current cooperation."[20]

Thomson and some of the other 12 from the original ESPRIT group had pressured Philips and Siemens to open up participation in Mega. Bill Ledeboer, European affairs coordinator for R&D in Philips, said, "Neither we nor Siemens wanted to share our knowledge with the rest of Europe.

To avoid being left out, Thomson, owned by the French government, formed a joint venture in the spring of 1987 with STET, a division of SGS Microelectronica, the state-owned Italian electronics giant. SGS/Thomson became the second largest semiconductor firm in Europe after Philips, with a combined world market share of 3.2 percent.

JOINT EUROPEAN SUBMICRON SILICON INITIATIVE

Philips and Siemens had actually initiated JESSI discussions in 1986. A working group with the French should have one or multiple labs. (Germany wanted one lab, the French multiple labs, and the Dutch were noncommittal.)

In early 1987, Philips and Siemens became aware that companies were growing concerned about what their role in JESSI would be. Thomson stated publicly in 1987 that it resented being relegated to what it considered a junior role.[21] It was clear that some of the animosity between Thomson and Siemens dating back to Unidata still lingered.

Philips and Siemens had also experienced difficulty communicating with other potential partners. An official from the U.K.'s Department of Trade and

Industry (DTI) felt JESSI was an enigma. "We first heard about JESSI in 1986. We weren't sure what it was. All we knew was that the Germans and Dutch were putting something together. We though it was rather curious, here we go again, 'son of Mega.' The name 'Joint European' seemed peculiar. Where was broader Euro participation?"

The British gathered their industry together and discussed JESSI, but realized they needed more information. Dr. Melvyn Larkin from Plessey undertook the job to discover more. Although it took him several months to get an appointment with JESSI, U.K. firms agreed to participate in the planning phase. Larkin was supportive of the project but had reservations, "I think Philips and Siemens realized this thing was too expensive to do on their own. The commission told them to get more countries involved if they wanted EEC money."

In 1988, a JESSI planning group was organized in Itzehoe, West Germany (near Hamburg), headed by Professor Dr. Anton Heuberger, Director of Fraunhofer-Institut für Mikrostrukturtechnik (FhG), a leading research institute in Berlin.* The group was being financed by the German government (with some Dutch government assistance). This time, JESSI planners hoped to involve many companies, countries, and institutes. By the summer of 1988, 30 companies and institutes from six countries set out to develop a plan by the end of 1988. Planners hoped JESSI projects would begin by mid-1989.

The JESSI planning group formed four section teams to look at technology, equipment and materials, applications, and research (see Exhibits 1 and 6). A company like Plessey, for example, with interests solely in applications, would only participate in that section, whereas, Philips, with interests across the food chain, would be involved in each section. A core team had been formed to supervise the section teams and the JESSI council was formed to approve the plans before they were presented to the participating companies. The planning group was also to examine company and government participation, roles, and organizational relationships between partners, links with institutes and universities, and foreign participation.

Getting the Food Chain Involved: E&M

Since Philips did not want to become more involved in the E&M business, it had to ensure that broad European E&M participation took place. However, it was questionable whether the European industry was strong enough to have exclusive access to JESSI. Some thought this was not possible because Europe relied so heavily on foreign suppliers. One strategy was to concentrate on a couple of E&M areas and use that expertise as a tool to assure access to other equipment and materials.

U.S. equipment and materials companies had good relations with the Europeans and could bring sorely needed technology to JESSI. However, it was difficult to say what the U.S. role would be because Philips and other key European

---

*Dr. Heuberger, Mr. Weinerth from Valvo (Philips' German subsidiary), and Mr. Dudenhausen from BMFT (the German Ministry of Science and Technology) were credited with being the founders of the JESSI concept.

semiconductor firms were still stinging from the Sematech rebuke, made worse by U.S. firms' participation in ESPRIT and EUREKA projects (see Exhibits 7 and 8).

Dr. Theo Holtwijk, head of IC strategic planning at Philips, claimed, "The United States screamed about the Japanese taking its market share, but the same thing could be said about the Americans in Europe. We only have 7.7 percent of their market while they have over 43 percent of ours. Is that fair?* As long as a company is contributing to the local R&D infrastructure, participation should be allowed. However, now that we have been excluded from Sematech, I would keep the United States out of JESSI."

Craig Fields, the deputy director of the Defense Advanced Research Projects Agency (DARPA) within the American Department of Defense and pointman for Sematech, said, "If the Europeans think it is in their best interest to let us participate, they aren't doing us any favors. At this time, we just don't feel it's in our best interest to let them in SEMATECH."

A Philips insider said, "Without healthy interaction between the U.S. and European semiconductor industries, the Japanese are going to run away with the world's chip equipment business."[22] Hamersma said, "We've told the Americans, if you don't want to work with us, we'll go to the Japanese."

Another unanswered question was how an exclusively European effort would affect Philips' subsidiaries and labs from around the world. Would JESSI cut learning off from Philips' non-European NOs? It had two labs in the United States and good relations with several Japanese firms, including Matsushita. Would there be a role for them? Ronner from Philips said, "Signetics, with labs in the United States, is very important to us. Because of these American interests, we'd like to see cooperation between JESSI and SEMATECH."

Allocation of projects was complicated because of European vertical integration. Would, for example, Philips' ASM, a lithography manufacturer, be guaranteed JESSI contracts, or would it be forced to compete with other vendors for JESSI projects?

The end-user markets were also important for JESSI. New applications like high-definition television (HDTV) would be critical to the overall success of JESSI because HDTV was predicted to be a multibillion-dollar market and would require large amounts of advanced DRAM chips. A thriving HDTV industry in Europe would force links between chip makers and users and provide both with large volume production. Holtwijk said, "Philips would certainly stand to benefit because we are strong in both areas."

Holtwijk also thought management of the food chain was essential. "In Japan it seems to happen naturally. The culture and MITI seem to guide the process. In Europe discipline is terrible. There is no loyalty. Users will buy from anyone if its cheaper. Everyone is out for themselves." Heuberger of the Berlin research institute FhG said he would like to see the Europeans copy what IBM was doing. "They have a

---

*According to *Dataquest*, excluding IBM captive production, over 24 percent of European-made chips came from U.S.-owned plants. Chips sold in Europe that were made in America received a 14 percent duty. Duties on European chips sold in America were eliminated in 1987. During the 1987 Tokyo Round of trade negotiations, the Europeans refused to eliminate the 14 percent chip duty.

great relationship with Perkin-Elmer. They give them money to develop a product specifically for their needs and then IBM gets first access; long-term contracts would also help."

Another issue was restructuring. Did each European nation need its own chip makers, or could they rely on a couple of European firms? Many Europeans felt it would be a waste of resources for each country to develop its own champion. Would protection laws be needed? The new DG-IV commissioner for competition, Sir Leon Brittan of the United Kingdom, said he would oppose any attempt to get the EEC to subsidize or protect so-called key industries. "It doesn't seem to me that the community is in a position to chose winners or consider the future of European industry."[23] DG-IV was also taking a sharp look at JESSI for possible antitrust violations. It appeared, however, that JESSI would fall within existing EEC regulations (see Exhibits 3 and 9).

On the other hand, some in Europe thought JESSI was a waste of time. Ledeboer of Philips said, "We've had heated discussions on what was needed. Nixdorf, a German computer company, thought we should buy our ICs from Japan. They think we should be looking only at software projects. Certain niche European companies were also against JESSI. They felt it wasn't important to have a European technology base."

Sources of Funding

If JESSI's scope remained large, EEC financial support would be a necessity. EEC participation was, however, important for more than just money. Holtwijk of Philips said, "Using the EEC forum will give us legitimacy and the opportunity to leverage off of existing European level R&D programs. European support will heighten the awareness of the issues and keep us strategically focused." Dr. Heuberger added, "EEC involvement would help overcome the multiple political and market barriers. It could also help with the macro perspective of infrastructure problems and education."

Why should the Community contribute to JESSI? According to Julio Grata, Division Head of the Commission's DG-XIII's Microelectronics Area (see Exhibit 3).

> The community believes that semiconductors have a fundamental value for an economy. Europe needs to be assured of timely access to key technologies. At the moment Europe is heavily dependent on foreign suppliers in critical areas. Do we want Tokyo determining Olivetti's PC market share? Although there is no clear indication that this would happen, we cannot afford to take that risk. The community's job is to help provide the capability within Europe for important technologies. This means helping with basic research, infrastructure and education. We don't, however, get involved in building production facilities. That's industry's role. We have expressed an interest in JESSI and agree with what it is attempting to accomplish. However, we have not determined whether we would contribute funding. We have declared a willingness to examine options for participation. We must first see where we can add value to JESSI. If we can, we will participate.

JESSI planners and the Community were evaluating several options for providing JESSI with the proposed 2 billion ecus required from governments over the next eight years. The easiest way would be through ESPRIT. Each year ESPRIT issued a call for projects; JESSI proposals could be presented through the normal ESPRIT process, with a qualified majority of national votes required for approval. Additional funds had been made available for R&D in 1988 (for use between 1989 and 1992) following settlement of budget problems. JESSI would certainly apply for some of this money. The Community also could delay prior commitments to ESPRIT projects and shift those funds to JESSI projects. However, all of these options could only provide a part of the public funds needed by JESSI. Some at Philips thought that the Commission needed to support the entire JESSI concept, as a symbolic gesture to the importance of a holistic approach.

A second possibility for Community funding would be through an amendment to the Single European Act, clause 130L (see Exhibit 3). This clause allowed supplemental funding to occur with a qualified majority vote. If DG-XIII agreed to using this approach, it would forward a proposal to the Council of Ministers for approval. This process could take from a couple of months to a year. It would also require those member states which were heavily involved, at the moment—Germany, Netherlands, France, Italy, and possibly the United Kingdom—to supply additional funds beyond those provided by the community.

What would the EEC want for its money? Varying degrees of economic development among the 12 member countries made prediction of an EEC position difficult. Would specific levels of country participation be required or local production and employment guarantees mandated? Many of the Southern European countries were not developed enough to take advantage of a massive program. Why would they support it?

Grata thought the Community could help in getting those countries involved that were currently not big in electronics. "Ensuring that Spain would have access to JESSI developments is one way," Grata said, "but mandating production levels in Spain is not likely." But a JESSI planner said, "Grata is pushing us on sharing JESSI property rights. He wants ESPRIT rules. We think that means socializing the results. We want strong companies in Europe not a strong Community. The chip companies in Europe aren't strong enough to give structural help to Spain."

Some had concerns that Brussels would dictate the research agenda. Dr. Heuberger did not think so; "I anticipate that they'll play a large role in helping us develop the framework and the organizational tasks. But it will be industry's role to work out the details and set the research agenda."

Grata said, "We want to be assured that a winning strategy is devised and executed. We want to see the benefits materialize. We will certainly be asking tough questions but we don't expect to burden JESSI with many formal requirements. We will, of course, closely monitor the process if we participate."

One JESSI insider said, "Grata is in a tough position. If the EEC doesn't support JESSI, and we carry on with only member state funding, Grata stands to lose his entire budget for microelectronics R&D because member states will say DG-XIII is not relevant anymore, we want our money in JESSI." Larkin of Plessey, for example, said, "We already receive ESPRIT funding for ASIC-type projects, we don't want to be left out of JESSI—if JESSI replaces those funds. We hope Philips and

Siemens don't say to the EEC, 'funnel all money into memory, because that's the key tech driver, let us control everything.' That would really hurt us."

In addition to EEC funds, individual country subsidies would be required. The EUREKA framework was the most likely means of getting member states involved. Country support would be linked, however, to the potential payback for each country: jobs, skills, exports, learning, local value added, worker training, and contributions to local infrastructure. Whether JESSI could provide these things was unclear, but, most believed that benefits would filter through to the countries that had a place in the semiconductor food chain.

Clearly countries like Germany, Holland, and France were in a better position than were Spain or Portugal to exploit the opportunities. Ledeboer of Philips said, "Countries without a chip industry still could benefit. For example, Greece has an outstanding research institute." But, he admitted, "Trying to get everyone involved will be cumbersome."

A working group composed of senior policymakers from Holland, Germany, France, Italy, the United Kingdom, and the EEC had met regularly throughout 1988 to deal with some of these issues. Huijbregts from the Dutch government said, "We're attempting to forge consensus on JESSI rules. It makes no sense to have six sets of guidelines. We're also trying to work out the power structure so that all have an equal say. Most of us want to see a mechanism that works quickly, ensures close cooperation among all members, and provides some guarantees that certain goals will be met."

Some of the challenges of getting member states to work together, however, were formidable. For example, it was well known how U.K. Prime Minister Margaret Thatcher felt about government subsidies. In January 1988, Britain had overhauled its subsidy program terminating £120 million of annual support to the British microelectronics industry. Thatcher, in a recent caustic speech in Bruges about 1992, had said: "We have not successfully rolled back the frontiers of the state in Britain only to see them reimposed at a European level."[24]

Another difficulty in coordinating European research was that each country funded technology projects out of different ministries. Philips and Siemens experienced this with the Mega project because the Dutch funded the program out of the Ministry of Economic Affairs and the Germans funded it from the Ministry of Research and Development (BMFT). The orientations of the two ministries were quite different. The Dutch were more interested in the economic implications (GNP and jobs), while the Germans were more concerned with the technical issues. The U.K.'s Alvey project, designed to enhance Britain's chip manufacturing ability was partially funded by the Defense Ministry. Would JESSI's goals be compromised by having to tailor specific projects to national needs even if they did not fit with overall European goals?

Could the Dutch government afford to support another large R&D effort? Jans Huijbregts from the Ministry of Economic Affairs replied, "Politically it is much easier to support companies that are growing; then we can point to the number of jobs our money has helped create. JESSI, on the other hand, is a long-term endeavor. Although most people in the government support the concept, it is unclear how that will translate into money. We could easily channel to JESSI some of the money that has been going to Philips, but will Philips want to do that? It will be much harder to go to the Finance Ministry and ask for additional funds. But, Japan and the U.S. provide support for their industry, so we must follow, if we want to see that expertise in our country."

Huijbregts wanted to see JESSI enable Philips to produce chips in Holland competitively. He also wanted to see the Dutch Science Institute involved: "If we see JESSI as a way to get many of our Dutch companies involved, we will support it. We have been working with Philips to see how we can get our small and medium sized companies involved. At the moment, most of them don't use information technology as well as they should. They know about JESSI, but don't understand how it could benefit them. We want Philips to help us with this."

Ronner from Philips responded, "Industrial policy is not our role. We certainly will be supportive of the Dutch government's objectives, but we don't have the resources to conduct that type of effort." Heuberger said, "The German government is asking JESSI the same question. Politically it is important to appear to be supporting the smaller firms, but in reality they only compose 5 percent of the market. We have no small firms in the JESSI planning phase. We know this is a problem, and we plan to address it, but we don't think it has to be dealt with immediately."

Another difficulty all JESSI participants faced was the nature of the budget process. Although JESSI was planned as an eight-year program, most potential members (government and industry) budgeted annually. None of the participants could actually commit funding to the entire project. Would this slow it down? Also, would all the JESSI rules have to be written now, or could they create a living contract that was amended over time?

Dr. Heuberger felt in the final analysis all countries would unite. "The bottom line is that each country realizes that alone they cannot compete. It's that simple. We have to figure out how to work together." (See Exhibits 10, 11, and 12).

Centralized or Decentralized Approach

Because many countries were involved, politically JESSI had to be decentralized, but would this compromise the R&D? Dr. Ronner of Philips felt it would. "By having one facility we could increase communication and decrease our costs. Can we afford to set JESSI up in multiple locations?" Holtwijk, head of IC strategic planning at Philips, disagreed. "With one lab you put all your eggs in one basket. It takes time and money to set it up, plus you have to relocate your people. Using existing labs is much faster and less expensive. I'd like to see us use existing facilities all over Europe. We could create a management team advisory board that judged proposals from all over Europe. If approved, it would receive a JESSI label. It would then be up to those companies involved to apply for funding in their own countries, similar to EUREKA."

The Germans were pushing for one central JESSI lab, similar to Sematech's. And since they were probably going to be the largest single country contributor, they carried a lot of clout even though most of the other governments were opposed to one lab. Some JESSI insiders felt that one lab was being pushed by German politicians as a way to provide employment in Northern Germany, an economically depressed area. He said, "That's the problem, we all have our own motives for doing this and sometimes it creates conflicts."

Links to Universities and National Institutes

It was important for JESSI to make the best use of knowledge from throughout Europe, but research centers were highly fragmented and were governed by a variety of different bureaucracies. For example, Germany suffered similar difficulties to the Dutch in attempting to coordinate universities and national labs with industry. Heuberger exclaimed, "If anything it's worse in Germany because the labs are under centralized control of the BMFT and the universities fall under Länder control.* But we must overcome these problems because Europe is substantially behind Japan and the U.S. in attempting to forge bridges between the two."

DECISIONS FOR HAMERSMA

Although JESSI was still only on paper, Hamersma and the planning group had to bring it to reality. Funding and JESSI's governance were the two areas that had to be resolved. To understand how best to set JESSI up, the complex political landscape of Europe, the European food chain, and the dynamics of the world's electronic industry all had to be appreciated. Although Hamersma and the planning group did not have complete information on all areas that had to be sorted out, they had to prioritize and then define positions. Hamersma knew what Philips' goals were, but, now he had to anticipate what other JESSI members would want, and what positions the EEC and national governments would take in exchange for their support. Unfortunately, the Europeans were not setting the time schedule. Events around the globe were forcing JESSI to move quickly.

Principal characters in the case are:

Philips	**Robert Hamersma,** managing director of integrated circuits
	Walter Grünsteidl, chief of Brussels office
	Dr. Wisse Dekker, chairman
	Bill Ledeboer, European coordinator for R&D
	Dr. Arjen Ronner, liaison with Dutch Ministry of Economic Affairs
	Dick Snijders, corporate finance
	Hans Moeliker, director, Hague office
	Dr. Theo Holtwijk, integrated circuit strategic planning
Dutch Government	**Jans Huijbregts,** Ministry of Economics
Germany	**Dr. Anton Heuberger,** director of FhG research institute and head of JESSI planning group
European Commission	**Julio Grata,** head, DG-XIII microelectronics area
	Sir Leon Brittan, head of DG-IV
Plessey (U.K.)	**Dr. Melvyn Larkin**

*After World War II, Germany was divided into 11 Länder, similar to provinces or states, because the Allies wanted to dismantle centralized decision making in the country.

Exhibit 1 JESSI Planning Group Participants

JESSI Council

Philips C-N
Siemens C-G
SGS-Thomson C-I-F
FhG I-G
LETI/CNR I-F-I
Delegates of Equipment and Materials
Application Industry

Section Team One: Technology: Process/Memory

FhG I-G
LETI/CNR I-F-I
Philips C-N
Siemens C-G
SGS-Thomson C-I-F
STW I-N

Section Team Two: Equipment and Materials

Alcatel C-F
ASMI-AMTC C-N
BOC C
Convac C
DSM C-N
FhG I-G
Hoechst C-G
LETI/CNR I-F-I
Leybold C-G
Matra Harris C-F
Philips C-N
Siemens C-N
SGS-Thomson C-I-F
STW I-N
TNO-TU Delft I-N
Süss KG
Telefunken C-G
Valvo (Philips' subsidiary in Germany)
Wacker Chemitronic C-G

JESSI Core Team

Philips C-N
Siemens C-G
SGS-Thomson C-I-F
FhG I-G
STW I-N
LETI/CNR I-F-I
Chairperson for section teams: FOM,
    Leybold C-G, Nixdorf C-G

Section Team Three: Applications/CAD

AEG C-G
Alcatel C-F
BMW C-G
Bosch C-G
Bull C-F
FhG I-G
CMD IMEC Leuven I-B
Krupp Atlas Elektronik C-G
Nixdorf C-G
Philips C-N
Plessey C-U
Siemens C-G
SGS-Thomson C-I-F
STW/SCME Delft I-N
Valvo C-G

Section Team Four: Basic Research

CNET Grenoble I-S
CNR Italy I-I
FhG I-G
FOM Utrecht I-N
IMEC Leuven I-B
LETI Grenoble I-F
Philips C-N
Rutherford
Siemens C-G
SGS-Thomson C-I-F
STW/TU Delft I-N
TU Twent I-N
Uni Hannover I-G

Key
First letter denotes company = C or institute = I; second letter denotes country: Germany = G,
    France = F, United Kingdom = U, Netherland = N, Italy = I, Belgium = B, Switzerland = S.

Exhibit 2 A Possible Financing Scheme[a]

Total JESSI budget	4 billion ecu
Industry	2 billion (Philips, 0.6, Siemens 0.6, STET 0.3, Thomson 0.3, Plessey 0.015, others 0.185)
EEC	1 billion
Member states	1 billion (Germany 0.35, Netherlands 0.25, France 0.175, Italy 0.175, United Kingdom 0.1)

Another scheme also was being discussed: one-third industry, one-third EEC, one-third member states.

[a]These figures are only estimates. No companies, countries, or EEC agencies have agreed to this proposal.

Exhibit 3 The European Landscape[a]

TREATY OF ROME

On March 25, 1957, the two Treaties of Rome were signed setting up the European Economic Community (EEC) and the European Atomic Energy Community (Euratom). The period since 1957 had seen a doubling in the number of member states. The six founding member states—Belgium, Germany, France, Italy, Luxembourg, and the Netherlands—were joined by Denmark, Ireland, and the United Kingdom in 1973, Greece in 1981, and Spain and Portugal in 1986. With a population of 320 million, the potential market was tremendous; however, separated by language and custom, the barriers to success were many.

Responsibility for achieving the aims of the European Community rested principally with four institutions:

The Commission was the guardian of the treaties. It was responsible for their correct and full implementation. It proposed policy and provided administration for the Community. The Commission was composed of 17 commissioners (appointed for four-year terms), and 10,000 permanent staff in 22 directorates general (DGs).

The Council of Ministers established the priorities for the Community. It was the only place where the governments of each country were directly represented. The council was composed of 12 ministers, each with 25–30 staff. The council presidency was taken by each member of state for a period of six months (Germany first half 1988, then Greece, Spain).

Parliament reviewed and debated proposed legislation and could require amendments by commission or council. There were 518 directly elected members distributed among eight political groups.

The Court of Justice ensured member states' treaty obligations.

[a]Parts of this exhibit were adapted from information provided by European Community and EC Committee of the American Chamber of Commerce.

Exhibit 3 (continued)

> The European Commission was broken down into 22 directorates. The JESSI planning group dealt with DG IV and DG XIII, Competition and Technology, respectively.
>
> *DG IV—Competition.* This directorate dealt with the community's general competition policy and its coordination. It examined the competitive effects of mergers and acquisitions, joint ventures, and cooperative research. It also had jurisdiction over state subsidies and their compatibility with the EEC treaty.
>
> *DG XIII—Telecommunications, Information Industries, and Innovation.* This directorate was responsible for the community's overall strategic vision in technology. It dealt with intellectual property, technology transfer, standards, and integration. It performed analysis and coordination of a variety of research programs including ESPRIT.
>
> *The Single European Act.* Enacted in 1987, this piece of legislation was heralded as the most important European act since the treaty itself. Whereas in the past any member state had the power to halt community legislation, now only a qualified majority would be required for areas governing completion of the internal market.[b]
>
> The SEA was also designed to strengthen the community's institutions, to have a positive impact on the decision-making process, and to set new objectives for community policies.
>
> The SEA would speed decision making and add new priorities for the 1980s. It added environment and social policy to the treaty base. It also strengthened the role of the European parliament and gave procedural and psychological boost to the legislative process.
>
> Industry expected the SEA to enable increased legislation in the areas or harmonization of technical regulations, modifications of customers duties and social, research, and environmental policy.
>
> JESSI hoped the 130L clause in the SEA amendment would enable supplemental funds to flow. This would require a qualified majority to be approved, instead of unanimity among the member states.[c]

[b]Qualified majority meant that 54 out of the total 76 votes were required.

[c]Standard voting rights for the EEC were 10 votes for France, United Kingdom, Italy, and Germany; 8 votes for Spain; 5 votes for the Netherlands, Belgium, Greece, and Portugal; 3 votes for Ireland and Denmark; and 2 votes for Luxembourg.

Exhibit 3 (continued)   The European Institutions

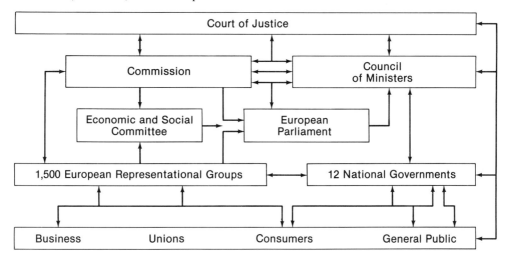

Exhibit 4 Philips' 1987 Commercial Activities

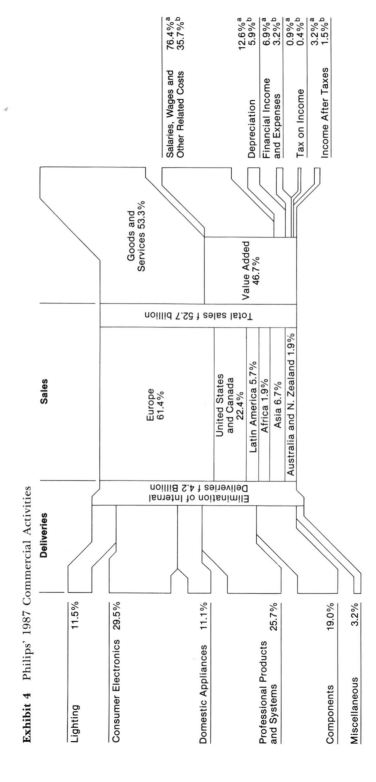

Source: Philips 1987 annual report.

f = Dutch guilders
1f = U.S. $0.49

[a] As a percentage of value added.
[b] As a percentage of sales.

Exhibit 5 Financial[a] and Related Information, 1978–1987

	1987	1986	1985	1984	1983	1982	1981	1980	1979	1978
Net sales	52,715	55,037	60,045	53,804	46,183	42,991	42,411	36,536	33,238	32,658
Income from operations	2,445	2,194	3,075	3,473	2,755	2,130	2,193	1,577	1,796	2,210
Net income	818	1,015	919	1,113	647	433	357	328	564	651
as percentage of stockholders' equity	5.2	6.3	5.6	6.9	4.9	3.4	3.0	2.7	5.0	6.0
Inventories	12,092	12,851	13,942	15,547	13,615	12,199	12,374	11,974	10,468	9,362
Accounts receivable	13,823	13,992	15,094	14,825	12,963	11,258	11,081	10,370	9,636	9,370
Current assets	27,757	28,167	30,770	31,964	28,266	24,879	24,748	23,687	21,417	20,009
Total assets	49,939	50,630	52,883	54,535	47,758	43,295	42,730	39,647	35,150	31,967
Current liabilities	18,594	18,453	19,693	19,781	17,601	15,747	15,198	14,204	12,121	11,229
Long-term liabilities	13,533	13,840	14,609	15,108	12,503	11,395	11,755	11,028	10,192	8,719
Equity	17,812	18,337	18,581	19,646	17,654	16,153	15,777	14,415	12,837	12,019
Employees (thousands)	337	344	346	344	343	336	348	373	379	388
Wages, salaries	19,126	19,755	21,491	20,240	18,364	17,488	17,369	15,399	14,159	13,471

1987 Percentage of Total

Product Sector	Sales	Operating Income
Lighting	11.5%	25%
Consumer Electronics	29.5	28
Domestic Appliances	11.1	13
Professional Products	25.7	25
Components	19.0	4
Miscellaneous	3.2	6

Source: Philips financial statements, 1987.

[a]All amounts are expressed in millions of guilders unless otherwise stated. (The exchange rate on October 1, 1987 was 2.07 guilders per U.S. dollar.) Due to factors such as consolidation and divestments, the stated amounts are not directly comparable over time.

Exhibit 6   JESSI Objectives

The JESSI planning group presented its detailed plans at year end 1988 to the participating companies for approval. More than 60 experts from over 30 institutes and companies from six European countries took part in drafting the 800 page document.

The plan provided for some 21,000 person-years of work divided into four subprograms:

Technology: Process/Memory. A proven semiconductor technology that can be easily adapted to the demands of all IC application areas, and, in spite of the high complexity, will allow competitive, economic, and flexible IC production (29 percent of the funds to be spent here).

Equipment and Material. The European microelectronics industry can only be competitive on an international level and less dependent on the United States and Japan, if the development of equipment keeps pace with the advance technology. This requires very close R&D cooperation between IC manufacturers and the IC equipment and material industry (15 percent).

Applications/CAD. The computer-aided development tools of the future must allow the realization of highly complex systems from widely varying application areas in the shortest possible time...from the idea, right up to the finished product. Such tools require a standardized, open architecture, portability to existing computer operating systems, and trained personnel (34 percent).

Basic Research. The present trend shows a gradual increase in the number of switching functions on a chip and at the same time a reduction in the size of the structure. For physical reasons, this reduction in size will come to an end. Therefore, one of the strategic tasks for JESSI's basic research is to overcome these physical barriers (22 percent).

All these concentrated efforts will secure Europe a place in the world market...even after the termination of the JESSI program.

Source: JESSI brochure.

Exhibit 8   The European Semiconductor Market
U.S., Japanese, and European Market
Share, 1988

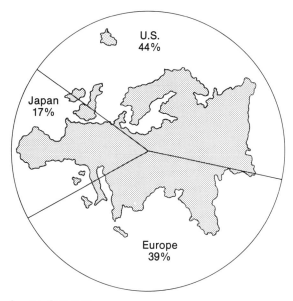

Source: *Dataquest.*

Exhibit 9   EEC Regulation on Cooperative Research

COMMISSION REGULATION NUMBER 418/85 OF DECEMBER 19, 1984

On the application of Article 85(3) of the treaty to categories of research and development agreements.

Cooperation in R&D and in the exploitation of the results generally promotes technical and economic progress by increasing the dissemination of technical knowledge between the parties and avoiding duplication of R&D work, by stimulating new advances through the exchange of complementary technical knowledge, and by rationalizing the manufacture of the products or application of the processes arising out of the R&D. These aims can be achieved only where the R&D program and its objectives are clearly defined and each of the parties is given the opportunity of exploiting any of the results of the program.

In general, cooperative R&D was permitted in the European Community if the following four conditions were met:

- The Community had to benefit economically from the activity.
- These benefits had to be shared fairly by the community.
- Consumers had to generally expect benefit.
- There had to exist no possibility of elimination of competition.

Exhibit 10   Collective Sector in 1986 as Percentage of GNP

	Expenditures	**Revenue**	**Deficit**
Netherlands	62.5%	55.5%	7.0%
Belgium	54.9	46.8	8.1
West Germany	45.9	45.0	1.0
France	50.7	47.8	2.9
Italy	57.1	44.6	12.6
United Kingdom	44.3	41.2	3.1
Denmark	58.3	61.3	-3.0
Sweden	63.1	62.2	0.9
United States	37.4	34.0	3.4
Japan	32.1	30.6	1.5

Source: Philips.

Exhibit 11   Industrial Labor Costs per Hour,
Selected Years 1980–1986 (U.S. = 100)

	1980	**1984**	**1986**
United States	100	100	100
Japan	57	51	73
Korea	11	11	12
Belgium	134	70	98
West Germany	126	76	92
Netherlands	123	70	92
United Kingdom	75	47	57

Source: Philips.

Exhibit 12   International Comparison of Average Number of Work Hours per Year, 1988

Country	**Hours**
Japan	2,104
United States	1,920
Switzerland	1,889
Sweden	1,824
Spain	1,804
Italy	1,792
United Kingdom	1,778
Finland	1,776
Netherlands	1,768
France	1,756
Denmark	1,749
Norway	1,740
Austria	1,733
Luxembourg	1,712
Belgium	1,709
West Germany	1,669

Source: Philips.

ENDNOTES

1. STET was the Italian state-owned electronics firm. It had recently joined the JESSI project. Quoted from Jack Gee, "Europe's Chipmakers Speak Out About Sematech," *Semiconductor International* (September 1988), p. 52.
2. An ecu in January 1989 was $1.13.
3. The planning group had received $40 million from the Dutch and German governments for planning and feasibility activities.
4. The Council of Ministers had 76 votes. A qualified majority was 54 votes. Standard voting rights for each member state were 10 votes for France, United Kingdom, Italy, and Germany; 8 votes for Spain; 5 votes for the Netherlands, Belgium, Greece, and Portugal; 3 votes for Ireland and Denmark; and 2 votes for Luxembourg.
5. Per capita consumption of chips in Europe was much less than that in Japan or in the United States.
6. Francis J. Aguilar and Michael Y. Yoshino, "The Philips Group: 1987," Harvard Business School, Case N9-388-050, p. 2.
7. Christopher Bartlett and Sumantra Ghoshal, *Beyond Global Management: The Transnational Solution*, (Boston: Harvard Business School Press, 1989), Chap. 4, p. 6.
8. There were two proposals being considered in Parliament to reduce taxes in 1988.
9. In Europe, Philips had eliminated 10,000 jobs in 1988—6,000 of those in Holland.
10. "Enough with the Theory, Where's the Thingamajig?" *Business Week*, March 21, 1988, p. 154.
11. Lord Cockfield was vice president of the Commission of the European Communities and a representative of the United Kingdom. In 1989, Margaret Thatcher recalled Cockfield, stating he had become "too European."
12. Some industry insiders felt Siemens was still upset with Thomson over the Unidata failure and that this could cause problems in JESSI.
13. The 12 firms were Holland's Philips; West Germany's AEG, Siemens, and Nixdorf; France's Bull, Thomson, and Alcatel; Britain's GEC, Plessey, and ICL/STC; and Italy's Olivetti and STET.
14. Mega had been formed prior to the creation of EUREKA; therefore, it was not affiliated with that program.
15. DRAMs stored data that could be erased from memory by interruption of flow of electrical current. SRAMs performed similar functions more quickly but did not lose data when electrical current was stopped. SRAMs, however, cost more and had less memory than similar-sized DRAMs; both were considered commodity products. ASICs were customized chips for specific application uses and were also considered commodity chips.
16. Components were electrical parts such as resistors, diodes, transistors, and integrated circuits.
17. "Megabucks for Megachips," *International Management* (May 1988), p. 37.
18. Gee, "Europe's Chipmakers Speak Out About Sematech," p. 53.
19. "Megabucks for Megachips," p. 37.
20. Ibid., p. 40.
21. Gee, "Europe's Chipmakers Speak Out About Sematech," p. 53.
22. Ibid., p. 53.
23. Mark N. Nelson, "EC's Competition Czar," *The Wall Street Journal*, February 9, 1989, p. A18.
24. "Whoa Europe," *The Economist*, November 5, 1988, p. 11.

Sensing the Earth from Space

Obtaining, processing, and selling information about what is on or beneath the earth's surface, using images recorded by satellites in space, was a $90 million industry in 1988. Beyond their obvious value to military planners and intelligence agencies, the images had many commercial uses, including mapping, weather prediction, water and crop management, oil and mineral discovery, and urban planning. Annual sales were estimated to range from $200 million to $600 million within the next decade.

Since the early 1970s, the U.S. government had spent more than $1.5 billion to promote the development of remote sensing from space.[1] Until the early 1980s, the United States had a virtual monopoly in the industry. In 1986, the French space agency, CNES (Centre National d'Études Spatiales), entered the field with the world's first strictly commercial remote sensing venture, establishing a quasi-private company, SPOT (Satellite Pour l'Observation de la Terre) Image, to distribute and market earth images. SPOT was a collaborative venture of the French, Swedish, and Belgian governments and private investors, most notably France's big defense company, Matra; as of 1988, the French government's investment was $500 million.

In 1985, the U.S. government system also went private; the Department of Commerce contracted with a new company, EOSAT, allowing it to sell images coming from the government's Landsat satellites. In 1987 the Japanese government entered the field, and others were in the wings.

During congressional hearings on the industry in 1987, U.S. Rep. James H. Scheuer (D., N.Y.), chairman of a subcommittee of the House Committee on Science, Space and Technology, warned that unless action were taken, "the U.S. earth remote sensing satellite program, with all of its benefits to our government and to the private sector, will simply cease to exist and we will have abandoned the field...to our international competitors, the French and the Japanese."[2]

By 1988, the two largest commercial remote-sensing ventures were EOSAT and SPOT. SPOT's worldwide market share had climbed to over 30 percent, with more than half of its sales coming from U.S. customers. Other countries were operating or planning remote-sensing systems, including Japan, India, and the Soviet Union; Brazil, the European Space Agency, Canada, and Pakistan had also announced plans to establish systems during the next several years (see Exhibit 1).

EOSAT

The Earth Observation Satellite Company (EOSAT) was formed in 1983 as a joint venture between Hughes and RCA, to bid for commercialization of the U.S. government's remote satellite sensing system (RSS), known as Landsat (Hughes and

Associates Fellow Robert S. Williams prepared this case under the supervision of Professor George C. Lodge as the basis for class discussion rather than to illustrate either effective or ineffective handling of an administrative situation.

RCA's space division were later acquired by General Motors and General Electric, respectively). EOSAT won the bidding contest in 1985. Under the contract, EOSAT became responsible for worldwide marketing of the images of earth sent from the two satellites which were then operating, Landsats 4 and 5. It could keep the revenue earned for investment in future satellites, and the Commerce Department agreed to cover the corresponding operating costs.[3] The government also promised to fund EOSAT's development of two new satellites, Landsats 6 and 7, and their respective launches. EOSAT would assume full operating costs for 6 and 7 and all future research, development, and construction beyond 6 and 7.

Within a few months of signing the contract, however, the Commerce Department reneged on it, and ever since, EOSAT had been mired in legislative inquests, inadequate funding, and confusion. Consequently, EOSAT was forced to delay the development of Landsat 6. Although negotiations with the government in 1987 resulted in full authorization to complete 6 and partial appropriation of the funds in 1988, its launch would be delayed until 1991.

Since Landsats 4 and 5 were approaching the end of their engineering life limit (the exact day of death was unknown), this delay could leave EOSAT without a satellite for up to two years. Funding for the last installment of Landsat 6 construction also had to be included in the incipient fiscal year 1990 budget and somehow the upcoming data gap had to be resolved. As 1988 ended, EOSAT's most immediate problem, however, was money to pay for the operating costs of Landsats 4 and 5. In March 1989, government funds would stop. Quick resolution of this issue was needed to assure EOSAT customers of continued data.

In addition, feuding between EOSAT and the government had put Landsat 7 in jeopardy. Although the 1985 contract had included the promise to pay for the design and construction of 7, in January 1989 the government was examining other options. Some thought it should invite new bids; however, recently released studies conducted by the Commerce Department concluded that Landsat could not be commercialized without federal support.

EOSAT had to convince Washington that it was best equipped to handle Landsat 7 and then secure favorable terms for its funding. At the same time, the government had to reevaluate its approach to commercialization in remote sensing. America's space leadership, national security, and technological capabilities were at stake.

THE FOOD CHAIN AND THE INDUSTRY

The remote-sensing industry had two main components: (1) the space and ground system and (2) the data collection and interpretation system. The space and ground system consisted of the satellite and its corresponding ground stations. The satellite provided a platform for sensors, communications, and operational support equipment. Sensors recorded the images, which were not photographs but digitized bits of information that revealed specific characteristics of sensed objects. Depending on the type of sensor used, these characteristics varied according to two broad categories: the degree of magnification of the earth's surface ("spatial resolution") and the "spectral band," which determined the area covered and the attributes sensed, such as heat, moisture, or particular substances.

U.S. defense and intelligence satellites had two-inch spatial resolution, for example, which was so good that they could read a car's license plate from space.[4] Commercial resolution capability was more limited. EOSAT sensors had 30-meter resolution, while the French system, SPOT, had 10 meter. Spectral bands enabled forest service officials in Yellowstone to determine where the hot spots were in the summer blaze of 1988. Farmers used them to determine crop growth and mining companies to analyze areas for development. Utility companies purchased images to determine growth patterns and changes in land use to help with planning; local governments could monitor urban sprawl; Ducks Unlimited, a conservation group, could keep track of wetland habitats in the world; and some progressive farmers used the data to monitor the growth of their competitors' crops.

Besides resolution size and spectral analysis, RSS attributes included global reach, frequency of visits to an area,[5] total turnaround time (the difference between when the image was taken and when delivery was made to the end user), infrared sensing, stereo imaging, and an accumulated database.

Because of the large up-front costs, remote sensing required substantial government support. A satellite took four years to design and build. In year 5, the satellite could be launched and revenues start to come in. "All in all, it takes about 15 years to earn the initial investment back," said EOSAT's president, Charles Williams.

Ground Stations

The communication system provided a path for command and control signals from the ground to the satellite and for the return of data from the satellite to the ground station, which controlled it.[6] The Landsat system included 15 operating foreign ground stations around the globe that were owned by the local government. Each station paid EOSAT $600,000 annually for the right to receive, distribute, and sell data from the satellite. The average cost of a ground station was $20 million to build plus $3 million a year to operate; these costs were generally paid by the host country. Most of the stations were being equipped to receive data from other systems besides Landsat.

Value-Added Providers

Nonenhanced raw data had dominated end-user market sales until 1988, when increased opportunities for data interpretation services developed. Services of value-added firms included specialized information processing hardware and software for analyzing remote sensing data; actual analysis of such data; and the integration of data from space with other databases to produce analytical and predictive products. For example, one could take images of specific crops around the world, analyze yield and volume, and then predict supplies based on these analyses. Many of the established value-added firms had activities outside of RSS. Autometric, for example, an imaging technology company, enhanced both Landsat and SPOT data. It also offered services in such areas as artificial intelligence, mapping, telecommunications, and intelligence data handling.

Companies like EOSAT and SPOT, however, sold only nonenhanced data. According to Williams, "We aren't forward integrating. Our emphasis is on developing the infrastructure of the industry by encouraging entrepreneurial firms to become our customers and use our data in creative ways. Commercially, this helps us expand our reach and, it is hoped, sparks innovation. Politically, it helps our cause in Washington. Having a couple of hundred companies in the industry food chain gets political attention." There were over 50 U.S. firms producing information processing hardware and software for remote sensing applications and more than 125 value-added firms. Both groups were growing rapidly.

Although 1988 worldwide sales for sensing data, including value-added services, was $90 million, the Commerce Department projected that the cumulative sales through 1997 would range from $0.7 to $1.5 billion for nonenhanced and $6.5 to $7.5 billion for value-added products and services (see Exhibit 2). The U.S. government accounted for about 56 percent of worldwide user demand;[7] U.S. private firms for 15 percent; and foreign entities, governments, and companies for the rest. The U.S. government percentage of total purchases was projected to drop to 40 percent by the year 2000.

Peggy Harwood, Landsat administrator for the National Oceanic and Atmospheric Administration (NOAA), part of the Commerce Department, felt the market would grow faster as the technology improved:

> At the moment the data isn't user friendly. You have to be sophisticated to use Landsat images. The value-added community can do a lot to help in this area. At the moment the turnaround time isn't fast enough for many applications. Take a state official in a drought-stricken area. If she could order a series of images over time depicting the effects of the drought, write up a report and get it on her supervisor's desk in a couple of weeks, RSS images would be extremely useful, but we can't do that yet.

HISTORY OF THE U.S. REMOTE SENSING INDUSTRY

The launch of *Discoverer XIV* on August 18, 1959, provided the United States with spy satellite ability to produce regular images of the Soviet Union from space. Earlier, in 1955, a summit meeting in Geneva established the first U.S. policy on spy satellites, the Eisenhower "open-skies, open-access" policy. Whereas air space could have nationalistic boundaries, outer space, the policy said, should not: Any country could take images of any others from space and the United States would make its images available to anyone.

Although it took the Soviets until 1962 to develop its Cosmos reconnaissance satellites, whose technology was similar to *Discoverer's*, Eisenhower's "open-skies, open-access" policy was being questioned by the U.S. military even in the late 1950s. General James Gavin said, "It is inconceivable to me that we would indefinitely tolerate Soviet reconnaissance of the U.S. without protest."[8]

In the 1970s, superpower ability to "sense" one another gave both countries the confidence to verify compliance with arms control treaties. According to Colleen Sullivan, an industry expert at Villanova University, "As a result of this confidence, the Salt I Treaty and the unratified Salt II agreement had been created."[9] Nevertheless the defense and intelligence communities on both sides kept reconnaissance satellites shrouded in secrecy.

Thus, within the United States, there was a conflict between the open-skies policy and defense interests. While the weather satellites and Landsat adhered to the Eisenhower guidelines, Department of Defense (DoD) activities were not bound by them.

NASA (National Aeronautics and Space Administration) was assigned responsibility for the development of the civilian aspects of remote sensing. Its weather satellite, TIROS, launched in 1960, was the first civilian bird in the sky. From 1972 to 1984, NASA had spent over $1 billion on the Landsat program.

Although the military had resolution of less than a meter in the seventies, an agreement between DoD and NASA prevented Landsat from using that technology. The U.S. intelligence community wanted total control of high-resolution technology, fearing that if it were freely distributed under the U.S. open-skies policy, it would restrict the options available to the president.[10] Governments without satellites were also concerned. Their countries were vulnerable not only to spying but also to the RSS capability to find valuable minerals within their borders.

By 1978, the sensors of Landsat 3 had improved to 40 meters, from 80 on Landsat 1. The same year, President Carter signed a secret National Security Directive that restricted the resolution of commercial satellites to 10 meters. "This resulted in inhibition of serious development by companies which might have been interested in building remote sensing satellites."[11]

Landsats 4 and 5, developed by NASA, marked a new generation of U.S. satellites. Launched in 1982 and 1984, respectively, both were equipped with a thematic mapper (TM) sensor which provided 30-meter resolution in six visible and infrared bands and a thermal infrared band with 120-meter resolution with the uses mentioned earlier.

Commercializing the Landsat System

Although commercializing Landsat had been discussed throughout the 1970s, legislation was not passed until 1984 to get the process moving. Peggy Harwood of NOAA said, "NASA enjoyed tinkering with Landsat, but didn't want to be burdened with the customer demands of operating the system. Besides, NASA is only a R&D agency. The ground stations were never designed with throughput in mind. The system was for scientific purposes only."

The Carter administration recognized NASA's legal limitations, and since the Commerce Department already operated the weather satellites through NOAA, it seemed logical to place the responsibility for commercialization there. NOAA focused on the science of the oceans and the atmosphere using weather satellites, environmental monitoring, and ocean charting. NESDIS (National Environmental Satellite, Data, and Information Service), the group within NOAA that operated the weather satellites, was excited about the possibility of getting Landsat. According to Harwood, "It gave them the opportunity to expand their mission to earth observation. But NESDIS was only interested if LANDSAT came with more dollars. NOAA did not want to spend its own money, because it didn't really fit in NOAA."

The Carter plan intended to commercialize Landsat in phases. According to Harwood, "In 1980, NOAA conducted an analysis of the RSS market and concluded that it was not big enough to support the high capital investments required. Government had to play a role." Consequently, in Carter's five-year budget plan, starting in 1981, the NOAA budget included money not only to complete Landsat 4 and 5, but to develop and construct Landsat 6 and 7 (a total of $743 million through 1986, see Exhibit 3).

The Reagan administration wanted to cut back discretionary spending to decrease the federal deficit, while keeping defense spending high and lowering taxes. Many programs were reexamined including Landsat. Reagan agreed with Carter's intention to commercialize Landsat, but wanted to speed the process up. David Stockman, Office of Management and Budget (OMB) director, suggested cutting Landsat 6 and 7 from the budget (a savings of $597 million) and handing the program over immediately to the private sector.

In May 1983, Secretary of Commerce Malcolm Baldrige appointed a task force, the Source Evaluation Board for Civil Space Remote Sensing, to examine how best to turn Landsat over to industry. Twenty companies eagerly followed the proceedings. In January 1984, Commerce issued a request for proposals (RFP). The RFP told the bidders to be specific on the amount of government support they required. Commerce received three solid bids: Kodak/Fairchild, EOSAT, and Space America, an entrepreneurial venture led by former astronaut, Deke Slayton.

Dr. Cary Gravatt, director of commercial space programs for the Department of Commerce and one of the leaders of Baldrige's task force, noted the government's vagueness regarding financial support for the transition to the private sector. The president had stated in a memorandum in February 1983 that the government might provide up to $150 million a year for several years. David Stockman, on the other hand, felt the program was a waste of government money (see Exhibit 4).* He was hoping someone would pick it up for free; if not, he wanted it abolished. Reagan disagreed but refused to be specific on how much the government would support. The task force wanted the RFP to assure industry of a maximum level of government financing. OMB, however, refused, expecting that all bidders would come in just under that number. OMB felt it was better not to give any guidance, to wait and see what the result was, and its position prevailed.

"It came down to Kodak or EOSAT," said Gravatt. "Kodak was stronger on the marketing side and EOSAT was stronger on the technology. But both bids were submitted expecting a total of about $500 million in government support over 10 years. They had independently come up with this number." Williams of EOSAT said, "Our initial proposal was based on four spacecraft beyond Landsat 5. We wanted

---

* Stockman polled each agency, and none said Landsat data was essential. Some felt the agencies were afraid to admit the need for the data in fear that OMB would want them to pay more for it. Agriculture, the largest government user of the data at the time, announced in late 1984 that it was cutting its purchases substantially.

one back-up for 6 and 7 in the event of a disaster. In addition, we intended to automate the ground facilities to improve response time and cut operating costs."

Baldrige started negotiations with both companies and went to OMB with the two bids. When Stockman heard about the $500 million, Gravatt said, "he blew his stack." Stockman had found $597 million in Landsat budget savings (see Exhibit 3), and now $500 million was coming back. He met with Baldrige several times in May 1984 to resolve the situation. Stockman's proposal was to provide $75 million a year for three years, to cover the operating costs of 4 and 5 (this was already in the budget), $250 million to cover construction of 6 and 7, plus the revenues from the sale of Landsat data (about $10 million a year). His plan would require the private sector to kick in a $250 million investment in 6 and 7. Stockman wanted the risk shared. Baldrige, however, said a minimum of $425 million was needed to construct 6 and 7, $175 million more than Stockman had proposed.

According to a former OMB official, "Baldrige was putting in requests for other Commerce programs at the same time. Stockman wanted Baldrige to set priorities, but Baldrige claimed that everything was important."

By July 1984 they were at an impasse. The next step was to present the issue to the Budget Review Board (see Exhibit 4). The board was composed of Stockman, Attorney General Edwin Meese, and White House Chief of Staff James Baker. The board looked at three options: $425 million, $250 million, and $0 worth of government support. The board voted 3 to 0 in favor of $0. Baldrige was furious and demanded to see the president. The president told Stockman and Baldrige to work it out themselves. Within a week Stockman and Baldrige cut a deal: $250 million for two satellites, 6 and 7.

Now Baldrige had to find out if the two bidders would still play at this level. Kodak said no; EOSAT replied that with modifications they could do it. "It meant higher operating costs," Williams said, "because we wouldn't be able to automate the ground stations. And without a back-up satellite, one catastrophe would wipe us out. But since the space program hadn't had many problems, we thought we could do it for $250 million."

In July 1984, Congress enacted the Land Remote Sensing Commercialization Act (see Exhibit 5), which allowed the government to privatize Landsat. According to a Senate staffer,

> As originally passed, the legislation was vague on what the government's role would be in the transition to the private sector. The bill only authorized $75 million because the Congress was not privy to negotiations with the bidders. Discussions and analysis on the subject were very weak. Also, at the time the Senate was under the Republicans control and they were committed to implementing the Reagan initiatives without much questioning of the details. The fact that Commerce had released a RFP and required enabling legislation to sign a contract to privatize Landsat expedited consideration of the bill. Furthermore, several major U.S. firms with significant marketing expertise had stated an interest in privatizing the system, and that convinced a lot of members that this could be a market-driven system, a commercially viable system. So we went with it.

In August 1984, Commerce officially stated it would provide $250 million for the transition. Kodak dropped out of the competition. A Senate staffer reflected,

"In hindsight, the final two proposals by EOSAT and Kodak were not really market driven, despite the fact that everybody agreed it would take a market-driven system to achieve commercial success."

Because of the 1984 election, not much happened until early 1985. EOSAT unsuccessfully attempted to push the government's $250 million number higher. According to Williams, "We had spent about $12 million before the contract was signed. We changed our proposal 19 times in 15 months." Gravatt said, "Already in late 1984 the relationship was souring. EOSAT was acting like a government contractor, not an entrepreneur. We had screwed them. We had asked them how much support they would need from the government and now we were cutting back their number. Maybe we should have stopped there, instead of trying to make it work at $250 million."

Although EOSAT had verbally agreed to two satellites for $250 million in the summer of 1984 (launch responsibility, however, had never been explicitly defined), its formal proposal presented to Commerce in early 1985, only included Landsat 6 and its launch. When Stockman heard this he again tried to wipe out the deal.

Four senators, Paul Laxalt, (R., Utah), Warren Rudman (R., N.H.), Slade Gordon (R., Wash.), and John Danforth (D., Mo.) who had witnessed the Baldrige/Stockman feud, got together with the two to try and resolve the impasse. They wrote a letter, known as the Laxalt letter, which helped smooth the way for the authorization by Congress of $297 million (the difference from $250 was the cost of the two launches) with an appropriation of $125 million for fiscal year 1986.* The funding came out of the Commerce Department, but was not included in its baseline budget.

When the contract was signed in September 1985, the government had agreed to support two new satellites, Landsats 6 and 7, and their launches. EOSAT would receive the revenues from the data marketed from Landsats 1–5, and would design, construct, and operate Landsats 6 and 7.† Additional investments beyond 6 and 7 would be EOSAT's responsibility.

At about this time Stockman left OMB. The new OMB director Jim Miller, armed with a new mandate from the Gramm-Rudman-Hollings legislation, enthusiastically reexamined government spending.‡ Landsat review resulted in OMB "zeroing out" the second round of funding, $62.5 million during the review of the fiscal year 1986 NOAA budget request in October 1985. Baldrige appealed and OMB replied if he wanted it badly enough, he should take it out of existing

---

*Some $90 million went to EOSAT for development costs and $35 million went to NASA as a down payment for shuttle launches. At the time, NASA and the Air Force were feuding over launch vehicles. The military thought NASA's shuttles were too expensive (because of the safety precautions required with astronauts). NASA was awarded the EOSAT business, even though it was more expensive than the Air Force's *Titan II*, because Congress needed to subsidize shuttle development. Nevertheless, NASA's quoted price of $45 million for two launches (6 and 7) was well below the going price for shuttle launches much to its chagrin.

†Although only Landsats 4 and 5 were operational in 1984, data accumulated from Landsats 1–3 were still marketable.

‡The Gramm-Rudman legislation passed in 1985 was an attempt to reduce the federal deficit. It forced the government to ratchet back expenditures. Volunteer cuts were encouraged, but if the deficit did not meet G-R targets, across-the-board cuts were mandated.

Commerce programs. Baldrige objected. According to Gravatt, "Baldrige tried everything, but nothing happened. All of a sudden Washington was saying Commerce was screwing up Landsat, but it simply wasn't true. I had pleaded with OMB in August 1985 that we were about to sign a contract, that if you're going to say no, say it now, before the train starts down the track. Yet what they did was to say no two months after the start of the contract."*

An OMB official said, "It was a difficult time. We had a new director, Gramm-Rudman-Hollings had been passed, and budgets were tight. We were trying to deal with the deficits. Landsat was relooked at and it was determined that we couldn't afford it. Neither OMB nor Commerce saw Landsat as a high priority, other programs seemed more important."

Gravatt of Commerce replied, "In August 1985 we had discussed with OMB the implications of Gramm-Rudman for Landsat funding. And yet, they had said yes to Congress's authorization twice in the summer of 1985. OMB had all the information they needed to say no in September."

A Senate staffer said, "We tried to save funding for Landsat, but Commerce didn't support it. Commerce could have taken it out of its budget if it thought it was so important. Congress even tried national security as a justification, but it didn't work.†

Donald C. Latham, assistant secretary of defense and a strong supporter of Landsat, testified at a 1987 hearing that Landat's spectral capability and coverage were important to the national security. However, he said, "It was Commerce's responsibility to fund...Defense will do all it can to support it, short of funding it."

Robert Palmer, of the House Subcommittee on Space, said, "Landsat never had a broad-based constituency and EOSAT has done nothing to expand it on the Hill. No agency has enough interest in it to put up money, so it just slips through the cracks." A Senate staffer added, "Since Landsat isn't a high priority issue in the congressional budget process, a handful of people influence the funding decisions in Congress. The Chair and ranking member of the Appropriations Subcommittee have a lot of power in these situations."

In November 1985, EOSAT approached NOAA about making a major design change. Instead of launching two short-lived, three- to five-year satellites, EOSAT wanted to create a space platform called OMNISTAR, that could hold not only Landsat sensors, but weather and other types, and could remain in orbit 10–15 years.

NOAA agreed to the change. Tony Calio, administrator of NOAA, testified at a House Space committee hearing in 1987 that, "NOAA experts thought the plan was sound and EOSAT assured us that it would not cost the government additional funding."‡ But an OMB official claimed, "NOAA didn't consult either the Congress

*Technically, the government did not violate the contract. There was a clause stating that the government could back out at any time for any reason.
†The international community had voiced concerns about DoD participation in Landsat. It felt that DoD could compromise the open-skies policy.
‡Dr. Gravatt chaired a task force charged with examining the technical and business aspects of the OMNISTAR proposal. In January 1986, the task force concluded that there was some additional risk, but not unreasonable, and that OMNISTAR looked good because it was flexible and serviceable and EOSAT could rent out space on it for other applications.

or us on this. We were shocked. In a session OMB had with RCA and NOAA, we discovered several technical flaws, and we aren't technologists!" A Senate staffer said, "RCA was a big proponent of the platform concept, and RCA was known as the preferred satellite vendor at NOAA (RCA Astro Division had $750 million a year in sales). The whole deal concerning EOSAT's use of the OMNISTAR platform just didn't look right, especially in light of the severe problems already facing the Landsat program."

In January 1986, the space shuttle *Challenger* exploded. EOSAT suddenly found itself lacking not only government money but also a launch vehicle, the space shuttle.* In addition, an important relay satellite that would have enabled Landsat 5 to cover 97 percent of the globe had been on *Challenger*. As a result, Landsat 5 could not provide coverage of the Pacific Basin. The shuttle disaster also caused the Air Force to stop California space shuttle launches, and OMNISTAR, if it was to fly, needed a West Coast launch to provide its required polar orbit. EOSAT now faced major delays. A congressional staffer added, "EOSAT and NOAA continued to spend money on OMNISTAR, long after the technical flaws and the lack of an available polar orbit launch were discovered."

Dr. Gravatt felt NOAA was getting a bad rap.

> The Landsat budget was cut in late 1985, the Challenger went in January 1986 and in spite of all that, NOAA approved the change to OMNISTAR in March 1986. However, because OMNISTAR was considered a way to combine missions [a single spacecraft to handle Landsat and weather], it was felt this was the only solution (in the short term) for the budget crunch. NOAA hoped that some of its funding for weather purposes could be used to offset the lack of Landsat funds. In addition, NASA was claiming, up until the summer of 1986, that the shuttle delay would not be long. A range of ideas was being generated, albeit with some technical flaws, but all designed to salvage the situation.

In January 1987, EOSAT ran out of government funds. It terminated hardware development and laid off some people. Williams said, "We were at the point of completely shutting down six times in 1987."

Finally, in October 1987, the administration and Congress reached an agreement: (1) $209 million to cover funds already expended and additional work to complete Landsat 6, (2) $50 million would go to the Air Force to provide one *Titan II* launch (for Landsat 6), and (3) $2 million would be spent on a study to evaluate government options for RSS beyond Landsat 6.†

A few months later (February 1988), President Reagan, in a directive on National Space Policy and Commercial Space Initiatives, stated that the U.S. government would "encourage the development of commercial systems, which

---

*To encourage the development of a domestic industry, American companies were prohibited from purchasing launch services from foreign competitors. Although launch vehicle manufacturers were pleased, the regulations infuriated satellite companies.

†EOSAT claimed they required an additional $11 million to complete Landsat 6. The government refused, but agreed to loan EOSAT the money. EOSAT agreed to pay back the money over four years out of Landsat revenues. Funding problems also forced design changes, resulting in projected Landsat 6 operating costs climbing to from $6 million to $12 million a year. EOSAT also lost legal rights to build Landsat 7.

image the Earth from space, competitive with or superior to foreign-operated civil or commercial systems." Gravatt of Commerce commented on what "encourage" meant. "It means there will be no preset limit to the satellite's resolution. It encourages companies to build anything as good as the Soviets or SPOT. It does not mean a subsidy." A Senate staffer said, "Reagan was famous for policy proclamations. The public remembers the directive, but forgets about the implementation. Reagan says we must have space leadership, but what does that mean and how much will it cost?"

In the spring of 1988, NOAA, which had responsibility for financing three satellite systems (Landsat, Polar Weather, and GEOS), was experiencing serious budget overruns on the GEOS (Geostationary Operational Environmental Satellite).* In an emergency meeting, Senators Fritz Hollings (D., S.C.) and Warren Rudman (R., N.H.), determined that terminating Landsat funding was the only way to ease NOAA's budget crunch. Informally, they polled the 11 members of the subcommittee on the idea: Canceling the funding was favored 6–5.

According to a Senate staffer,

> When Senator Frank Lautenberg (D., N.J.) [a subcommittee member who supported Landsat, had RCA in his state, and was up for reelection] heard these results, he appealed to the Senate Majority Leader, Robert Byrd (D., W.V.), to get the members of the subcommittee to reassess their votes before the final tally. After a few calls from Senator Byrd, the vote started to turn around, and, seven days later, the vote was 6–5 in favor of Landsat. No Republicans voted in favor of funding Landsat.

NOAA, however, at the same time was telling EOSAT that Landsat activity would be terminated because full-year funding for 4 and 5's operating costs had not been appropriated. EOSAT responded by quickly going to the Hill pleading for its life. Finally in March 1988, NOAA and EOSAT reached an agreement: EOSAT received $62.5 million and work on Landsat 6 began again.[12]

Because of the delays, however, Landsat 6 could not be launched until July 1991. An enhanced thematic mapper (ETM) developed by EOSAT would give Landsat 6 15-meter black and white resolution, and Sea-WiFS, a new wide-field sensor, would allow Landsat 6 to sense ocean surface properties. EOSAT claimed it had also cut Landsat 4 and 5 operating costs and turnaround time by 50 percent.

According to Richard P. Mroczynski, director of public affairs for EOSAT, "NOAA satellites are our biggest competitor. Its data compete especially in the agricultural markets. NOAA also provides coverage in some areas twice a day. We can't do that." Another EOSAT official said, "NOAA is supposed to be our government champion, but it has no incentive. We are a competitor and a budget drain."†

Foreign competitors had better spatial resolution, but Williams did not think this was a problem. "Thirty meter resolution is more than sufficient for many

---

*A geostationary satellite maintained a fixed position in space, enabling continual images of one area to be taken. The Landsat system orbited around the globe. The estimated budget overrun on GEOS was $250–500 million.

†By 1988, the two government champions that EOSAT had, Baldrige and Calio, were gone. Baldrige died in a horse riding accident, and Calio went to the private sector.

applications. Fires, environmental monitoring, and urban planning don't require five meter. We have seven spectral bands; SPOT only has three. That's our competitive advantage."

The business/government relationship in other countries, however, did give foreign systems an advantage. Williams said, "Since the French fund on a four-year basis, they can make long-range plans. In the U.S., it's one year at a time and the government can renege for any reason."

Williams added:

> Over 25% of my top executives' time is spent dealing with Congress and the administration. We are understaffed at the moment, but we are afraid to staff up again, because of inconsistent funding. We just can't cover all the bases in Washington as well as we should. We are frustrated. The government has already defaulted on our contract five times. The original deal would have cost taxpayers $297 million. They'd have gotten a fully integrated system, two satellites, 6 and 7, and two launches. Now they're going to get a limited data system, one satellite and launch for $256 million.

Many government officials, however, thought EOSAT had not adequately developed the market. Robert Palmer from the House Space Subcommittee said, "Based on Congressional hearings, customers of Landsat and industry experts, there appears to be consensus that SPOT is much more aggressive in its marketing." Another government official said, "At the Congressional hearings, SPOT made a spectacular presentation, and then EOSAT took the floor and put us to sleep." An EOSAT official responded, "Our biggest problem in marketing is explaining the inconsistent government position on Landsat funding."

In spite of its difficulties, EOSAT had revenues of $18 million in 1987, $11 million from nonenhanced image sales, and $7 million from ground station fees. The U.S. government represented 60 percent of EOSAT sales, foreign customers were 20 percent and 15 percent went to private U.S. firms. EOSAT had established 12 international distributors, had 8 of its own sales reps, and also used the ground stations as a vehicle for sales (see Exhibit 6).

EOSAT claimed it had spent $16.6 million of its own money from 1983 to 1988 and that 80 percent of Landsat revenues were reinvested in EOSAT ($40–45 million).* EOSAT's parent companies, General Electric and General Motors, were major suppliers to Landsat 6. EOSAT stated that bids went out to the public, but that RCA and Hughes were consistently better than their competition.

FRANCE

The French entered the commercial remote sensing market in February 1986 with the first SPOT satellite aboard an *Ariane* launch vehicle. The SPOT I satellite was capable of 10-meter panchromatic resolution and 20-meter resolution for the three-

---

*Several government officials thought these numbers were "awfully high."

band multispectral images. Comparison with Landsat 4 and 5 was difficult, even though SPOT's panchromatic images were nine times more detailed, because its scene sizes were much smaller and had limited spectral coverage. In fact, according to the Commerce Space Assessment Report, EOSAT and SPOT "actually were complementary data sources." A good example was the image from the Chernobyl nuclear power plant accident in the Soviet Union. SPOT's resolution combined with EOSAT's short-wave infrared band had enabled observers to determine the extent of the damage by the amount of heat the reactor was generating.

The SPOT program was begun by the French government in 1981 under the leadership of the French space agency, CNES. The program objective was to design and develop the first remote sensing satellite specifically for commercial use, and major investors included the French, Swedish, and Belgian governments and industrial concerns from each country. According to David Julyan, executive vice president of SPOT Imaging Corporation, the U.S. subsidiary of the Toulouse-based SPOT Image responsible for marketing and distribution of images in the United States, "France wanted to step up to the world space table. The French government wanted the international prestige and saw remote sensing as a complement to its current space efforts."*

SPOT's commercial objectives were to achieve financial self-sufficiency for data distribution and marketing as soon as possible. There were no plans to commercialize the satellite development or ground station segments. Because CNES in 1985 committed funding for four satellites, SPOT was assured of continuous service for over 12 years.

In 1988, SPOT had acquired over 30 percent of the world market share for remote sensing images, a market EOSAT had virtually to itself the year before. According to Julyan,

> We have been successful for many reasons, but the most important has been defining up-front what role the commercial entity, SPOT Image, would play, and what CNES would be responsible for. SPOT Image is completely responsible for the marketing and distribution of the data. We decide what images are taken and as soon as those images hit the ground, the private sector takes over. The operation and launch of the satellite is CNES's responsibility. By keeping the lines divided clearly, we keep politics out and allow business to thrive.

"We determined early that dependence on government contracts was no way to grow a market," Julyan added, "especially in the States, where we would always play second fiddle to EOSAT. So we set out to find new customers." Julyan did admit, however, that about 50 percent of his sales were to the public sector. "That figure should decrease to about 30 percent in the next five years."[13]

SPOT's 10-meter resolution (compared with EOSAT's 30 meters), and its rapid revisits to an area, stereo imaging, and data continuity were its most

*The French space effort included the successful *Ariane* launch vehicles. The launch site, Kourou, French Guyana, allowed a more favorable orbit, which extended the life of a satellite by 12–18 months. The French also subsidized its insurance system which provided industry with a $3 million insurance savings over the life of the satellite as compared to U.S. firms. NOAA provided key technological assistance to SPOT in 1986 as an international gesture. Without this assistance, SPOT's program would have been delayed.

important product offerings. Julyan said, "Urban planning and engineering and construction have been successful market segments for us. Media, on the other hand, has been a disappointment. The media want high resolution images, quickly and for little cost. Unfortunately, nobody can do that."

SPOT's distribution network was scattered across the globe. "We have over 50 distributors worldwide." Julyan said, "We expect this network, in conjunction with our image data base to be a formidable barrier to entry." (EOSAT on the other hand claimed to have 25 worldwide distribution outlets.)

Julyan did not see EOSAT as a significant competitor, "They are having too many problems right now to be a challenge for us. In fact, I'd like to see them get government funding. We need help in growing the market. If there were two solid sources for images, more companies would be willing to go with the new technology."

JAPAN

The Japanese government launched its first remote-sensing satellite, the Marine Observation Satellite 1 (MOS-1), in February 1987. MOS-1 was designed to sense the oceans and atmosphere. Although the system was for internal use, the government had not dismissed the idea of selling the data abroad. It was also developing a radar capability that would record images during cloudy conditions. Said a Senate staffer, "The Japanese will be a major contender in the 1990s. They've already sent signals that they want a major part of the market by the end of the next decade."

TRANSNATIONAL REGULATION

The opportunity for RSS abuse was great, and over the years Washington think tanks, governments, and private firms attempted to sort out the issues. In 1961, the United States asked the United Nations to ensure that all space activities would be regulated by international law with international registration of all space vehicles. DoD, however, was never enthusiastic about such actions.

Developing nations, fearing exploitation, wanted territorial jurisdiction over remote sensing. They wanted countries with satellites to obtain prior consent before sensing. Because Landsat was taking images all over the world and military observations were not publicly available, the requirement was not practical from a superpower perspective.

In 1986, the United Nations Legal Subcommittee agreed upon a set of remote-sensing principles. These represented a compromise that addressed the concerns of sensed states while legitimizing the rights of states to orbit and operate remote sensing systems and to collect, interpret, and distribute the data received from those systems:

> As soon as the primary data and the processed data concerning the territory under its jurisdiction are produced, the sensed State shall have access to them on a non-discriminatory basis and on reasonable cost terms.

To promote and intensify international cooperation, especially with regard to the needs of developing countries, a State carrying out remote sensing of the earth, upon request, will enter into consultations with a State whose territory is sensed in order to make available opportunities for participation and enhance the mutual benefits to be derived therefrom.

According to Leonard Spector of the Carnegie Endowment for International Peace, the issues were not so clear cut:

The timing in delivery of an image is a key issue in the non-discriminatory access policy, especially for governments using these images for intelligence and other military purposes. A country with a Landsat or SPOT ground station—like India or South Africa—can get its images, including images of neighboring states, almost instantaneously. In contrast, a rival state that lacks a ground station may have to wait weeks for images of the ground station country to be sent out from EOSAT or SPOT headquarters. What's more, in targeting the SPOT satellite, SPOT Image is starting to give preference to its larger customers, which can spell big delays for disfavored clients. With this discretionary power, SPOT Image could all too easily begin giving preference to foreign governments on political grounds.

COUNTDOWN FOR EOSAT

EOSAT faced several obstacles before it would reach a safe orbit. Operating funds for Landsats 4 and 5 would dry up in March 1989. The rest of Landsat 6 funding was still uncertain. A potentially devastating data gap loomed on the horizon, and Landsat 7 was slipping away from its domain.

Charles Williams gave several reasons why the government should support EOSAT.

If EOSAT fails, we will have broken many international commitments. We have signed understandings with 14 countries. We told them we would supply data if they built a ground station. What will that do to our image abroad? The U.S. uses Landsat as a vehicle to ensure that the Open Skies policy prevails around the world. What will our leverage be if we don't have a system? Over 100 countries use our data. Our images are used to fight drug activities, provide economic intelligence, and monitor environmental trends. What message will we be sending to the world? The U.S. needs RSS. Can we rely on the French and Japanese for data? In the long term we will lose control of the data, our end users will be subjected to higher costs and access problems, and in the long term our national security will be jeopardized. If we lose commercial RSS, then the U.S. value-added companies will go out of business, and then DoD will lose access to a valuable industry and be forced to rely on foreign firms.*

LANDSAT 4 AND 5's OPERATING COSTS

Although only $9.4 million was needed to continue operating Landsat 4 and 5 for the next six months, the implications were much more serious. Many experts

---

*There was debate as to what would happen to U.S. value-added firms if Landsat stopped operating. Many of the diversified established firms would survive; however, there was disagreement among industry experts on whether foreign RSS would use U.S. value-added vendors.

believed once the satellites were shut off, it would be difficult to turn them back on. And even if it were possible, many people would lose their jobs if 4 and 5 were shut off. Therefore, if the issue was not resolved by the end of March, the system would be out of business until the launch of Landsat 6.

The government had agreed to cover all operating costs for Landsats 4 and 5 when the original deal was struck with EOSAT. At the time, 4 and 5 were expected to cease operating by 1987, and, therefore, authorization of operating funds past 1987 had not occurred. With the delay of Landsat 6, and the extended lives of 4 and 5, fiscal year 1989 operating costs were now an issue, but who would provide these funds had not been resolved. Early in 1988 Congress had appropriated funds for the first six months of fiscal year 1989 operating costs. Then also the new Landsat 6 agreement with EOSAT had been reached. EOSAT claimed that this agreement clearly stated that the government was still responsible for the operating costs. NOAA officials disagreed. Thomas Pyke said, "We are in a bonus period, EOSAT should share some of the costs. They still get the revenues."

In February 1989, Vice President Dan Quayle was put in charge of a new National Space Council, a task force designed to set the vision and strategy for America's space policy. Washington observers thought resolution of Landsat 4 and 5's operating costs should be the first issue to tackle. Although the council's staff was not in place, Quayle's office publicly pledged to somehow get the funds for Landsat. He was trying to get some money from each of the government agencies that used Landsat data. His office wanted to buy time to evaluate the situation before deciding Landsat's fate (see Exhibit 7).

EOSAT, on the other hand, had the option of lobbying Congress for the funding, supplying the money itself, finding a third party or negotiating a combination of these options. EOSAT was also asking foreign-ground stations and the value-added community to voice their concerns. Dick Mroczynski of EOSAT said, "We are exploring all options, but as a matter of principle the government should pay for it. There has never been an argument about this. They're supposed to cover all operating costs for 4 and 5."

THE DATA GAP

Because Landsats 4 and 5 were both past their engineering life span, at any time EOSAT could find itself without a satellite. EOSAT claimed that not all users demanded current data. Such applications as cartography and geology could use data that were a couple of years old. EOSAT could also continue to provide images from its 2 million image library begun in 1972.[14] But that would not seem to satisfy the Defense Department, which some years bought as much as $4 million worth of images from EOSAT. As Assistant Secretary Latham told the Congress, "Landsat (EOSAT) has great value in being able to search very large areas very rapidly....For example, we can tell whether there's an airfield being constructed in some part of the world or not, or if highways have been changed."

EOSAT could perhaps become a reseller of data generated from RSS of other nations. An EOSAT official said, "We could sell Japanese or Indian images, for example. Neither one is marketing data at the moment. Another concept we are working on is one stop data shopping, where we would offer many types of data, including even NOAA's or the Soviet's. A venture with the French is possible, but since we both have marketing in the U.S., dividing that territory would be difficult."

LANDSAT 6 FUNDING

To complete Landsat 6, $37 million from the government was required. If 6 was going to launch in 1991, EOSAT would need fiscal year 1990 money. The government process was already underway. NOAA had submitted its budget request to Commerce, but NOAA was not saying what funds it had requested for Landsat. Commerce would consider NOAA's recommendations, finalize its entire budget, and then present it to Congress in February 1989. Williams would not know anything until then. At that point, he would garner support on the Hill to help his cause. "We have no influence at Commerce," Williams claimed.

LANDSAT 7

According to Williams, for 7 to be launched in 1995, "We need to start work on it by 1990. That means getting funding approved now." Commerce commissioned three studies looking into Landsat 7 options and had concluded the market was still not large enough for a complete private sector effort (see Exhibit 8). EOSAT had to formulate a proposal that would convince Commerce that it was the best company to produce 7.

NOAA was known to be looking at a couple of alternatives for Landsat 7. One option was to reopen the bidding. Several companies had expressed interest, including earlier bidder Space America and value-added vendors GeoSpectra and Terra-Mar.

GeoSpectra President Robert K. Vincent said, "The government pays for the satellite and then turns around and pays for the data, how can taxpayers stand for that? The government should let Landsat/EOSAT die a natural death and then let private firms compete. There will be a gold rush."[15] Harwood of NOAA said, "If you examine GeoSpectra's proposal carefully, you'll see that it depends on guaranteed government purchases to offset no direct government support."

Thomas Pyke, NOAA assistant administrator for satellites, was examining the possibility of a joint venture with SPOT and CNES. Some felt that NOAA was growing tired of its relationship with EOSAT and the budget and time drain Landsat had put on NOAA. In January 1989, *Aviation Week* reported that NOAA was discussing with CNES a possible merger of SPOT and Landsat after Landsat 6 was launched.

The House hearings on Landsat in 1987 had explored foreign relationships in RSS. Donald Latham of DoD when asked about a joint venture with a foreign nation, replied, "I'd rather go it alone. We have to continue our leadership in space....Third World nations look to the United States for imagery, we generate a lot of intangibles—political good will and international relations. We should not abrogate our position in RSS to the Japanese, the French, or anybody else."[16] Several congressmen were upset with NOAA for talking with the French. Many on the Hill had favored Landsat because of national security, U.S. leadership, and other geopolitical goals. EOSAT officials were upset because they were left out of the negotiations and were not even notified of NOAA's intentions. One executive said, "How can NOAA represent the commercial RSS in this country alone? They don't have any money. What do they bring to SPOT?" NOAA responded: "We couldn't include EOSAT, because that would jeopardize its position to bid on Landsat 7. Furthermore, nothing has been decided."

LANDSAT's FINAL ORBIT?

Landsats 4 and 5 continued to orbit the globe, faithfully sending images back to earth. Meanwhile, its parents, EOSAT and the U.S. government, were squabbling over who was responsible for their care.

EOSAT had several immediate issues to deal with. Most important was how to convince the government that a consistent commitment to Landsat was imperative. Perhaps it could mobilize the industry. By uniting the food chain, it could form a coalition and forge a long-term political strategy. There were some problems with this option, however: most important, some value-added firms wanted EOSAT to fail. EOSAT could, however, leverage the power of its parents. Both GE and GM had impressive lobbying capability. Was EOSAT willing to forget the past and look to the future? Was this a good business deal for it? Did it matter one way or the other?

LOST IN SPACE

Could the U.S. government, under the new administration, devise a coherent space policy? Besides the pressing problem of Landsat 4 and 5's operating costs, the government had to answer some fundamental questions. What did it want out of a civilian remote-sensing industry? Was it really necessary? Were the benefits greater than the costs? And, who should be responsible for these costs?

Exhibit 1   International Remote-Sensing Systems Time Line, 1972–1999

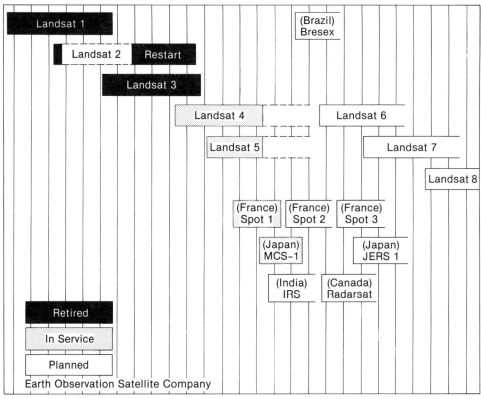

Source: EOSAT.

Exhibit 2   Market for Remote-Sensing Data Products and Services, Projected Total Demand, 1987–1997

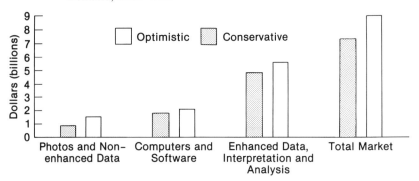

Source: Commerce Department.

Exhibit 3 Carter and Reagan Budgets for Landsat, 1982–1986 ($ in millions)

	1982	1983	1984	1985	1986	Total
Carter budget plan	124	174	165	149	131	743
Reagan changes	-122	-138	-129	-113	-95	-597

Source: Office of management and budget.
Note: The money left in the budget covered operating costs of Landsats 4 and 5.

Exhibit 4 OMB 1984 Position on Landsat

Lack of viable market, no significant federal market

No use of data by Commerce/NOAA.
Total federal purchases estimated at $8 million in 1985 budget.
USDA (Agriculture) decided to discontinue data purchases.
No agency would commit to data purchases.

Insignificant private market. Landsat subsidizes special industries at general taxpayers' expense

Oil and gas industry and crop forecasting firms major beneficiaries. Total nonfederal revenues only $6 million in 1984. System doesn't recover a fraction of its operating costs.

United States has archived reams of data

Existing data files should meet needs.adequately.

United States allies will fly land sensing satellites

The French and Japanese will be flying subsidized RSS. Let's let them subsidize us for a change.

United States continues to maintain its technology leadership role through basic R&D in NASA

From 1985 to 1989 the NASA budget contains $130 million for RSS R&D.

RECOMMENDATION

Recommend getting out of the business. RSS is not an inherent or important federal responsibility. If there is a market, RCA, Hughes, GE, or whomever should be able to develop it without federal subsidies.

Source: Adapted from OMB position papers.

Exhibit 5 Land Remote-Sensing Commercialization Act of 1984

To establish a system to promote the use of land remote-sensing satellite data, and for other purposes.

SEC. 101. *THE CONGRESS FINDS AND DECLARES THAT—*

(1) the continuous civilian collection and utilization of land remote-sensing data from space are of major benefit in managing the Earth's natural resources and in planning and conducting many other activities of economic importance;

(2) the Federal Government's experimental Landsat system has established the United States as the world leader in land remote-sensing technology;

(3) the national interest of the United States lies in maintaining international leadership in civil remote sensing and in broadly promoting the beneficial use of remote-sensing data;

(4) land remote sensing by the Government or private parties of the United States affects international commitments and policies and national security concerns of the United States;

(5) the broadest and most beneficial use of land remote sensing data will result from maintaining a policy of nondiscriminatory access to data;

(6) competitive, market-driven private sector involvement in land remote sensing is in the national interest of the United States;

(7) use of land remote-sensing data has been inhibited by slow market development and by the lack of assurance of data continuity;

(8) the private sector, and in particular the "value-added" industry, is best suited to develop land remote-sensing data markets;

(9) there is doubt that the private sector alone can currently develop a total land remote-sensing system because of the high risk and large capital expenditure involved;

(10) cooperation between the Federal Government and private industry can help assure both data continuity and United States leadership;

(11) the time is now appropriate to initiate such cooperation with phased transition to a fully commercial system;

(12) such cooperation should be structured to involve the minimum practicable amount of support and regulation by the Federal Government and the maximum practicable amount of competition by the private sector, while assuring continuous availability to the Federal Government of land remote-sensing data;

(13) certain Government oversight must be maintained to assure that private sector activities are in the national interest and that the international commitments and policies of the United States are honored; and

(14) there is no compelling reason to commercialize meterological satellites at this time.

Exhibit 5   (Continued)

CONDITIONS OF COMPETITION FOR CONTRACT

Sec. 203. (a) The Secretary shall, as part of the advertisement for the competition for the contract authorized by Section 202, identify and publish the international obligations, national security concerns (with appropriate protection of sensitive information), domestic legal considerations, and any other standards or conditions which a private contractor shall be required to meet.

(b) In selecting a contractor under this title, the Secretary shall consider—
(1) ability to market aggressively unenhanced data;
(2) the best overall financial return to the Government, including the potential cost savings to the Government that are likely to result from the contract;
(3) ability to meet the obligations, concerns, considerations, standards, and conditions identified under subsection (a);
(4) technical competence, including the ability to assure continuous and timely delivery of data from the Landsat system;
(5) ability to effect a smooth transition with the contractor selected under Title III; and
(6) such other factors as the Secretary deems appropriate and relevant.

DATA CONTINUITY AND AVAILABILITY

Sec. 302. The Secretary shall solicit proposals from United States private sector parties (as defined by the Secretary pursuant to Section 202) for a contract for the development and operation of a remote-sensing space system capable of providing data continuity for a period of six years and for marketing unenhanced data in accordance with the provisions of Sections 601 and 602. Such proposals at a minimum, shall specify—

(1) the quantities and qualities of unenhanced data expected from the system;
(2) the projected date upon which operations could begin;
(3) the number of satellites to be constructed and their expected lifetimes;
(4) any need for Federal funding to develop the system;
(5) any percentage of sales receipts or other returns offered to the Federal Government;
(6) plans for expanding the market for land remote-sensing data; and
(7) the proposed procedures for meeting the national security concerns and international obligations of the United States in accordance with Section 607.

AWARDING OF THE CONTRACT

Sec. 303. (a) (1) In accordance with the requirements of this title, the Secretary shall evaluate the proposals described in Section 302 and, by means of a competitive process and to the extent provided in advance by appropriation Acts, shall contract with the United States private sector party for the capability of providing data continuity for a period of six years and for marketing unenhanced data.

(2) Before commencing space operations the contractor shall obtain a license under Title IV.

Exhibit 5   (Continued)

(b) As part of the evaluation described in subsection (a), the Secretary shall analyze the expected outcome of each proposal in terms of—

(1) the net cost to the Federal Government of developing the recommended system;

(2) the technical competence and financial condition of the contractor;

(3) the availability of such data after the expected termination of the Landsat system;

(4) the quantities and qualities of data to be generated by the recommended system;

(5) the contractor's ability to supplement the requirement for data continuity by adding, at the contractor's expense, remote-sensing capabilities which maintain United States leadership in remote sensing;

(6) the potential to expand the market for data;

(7) expected returns to the Federal Government based on any percentage of data sales or other such financial consideration offered to the Federal Government in accordance with Section 305;

(8) the commercial viability of the proposal;

(9) the proposed procedures for satisfying the national security concerns and international obligations of the United States;

(10) the contractor's ability to effect a smooth transition with any contractor selected under Title II; and

(11) such other factors as the Secretary deems appropriate and relevant.

Source: U.S. Congress.

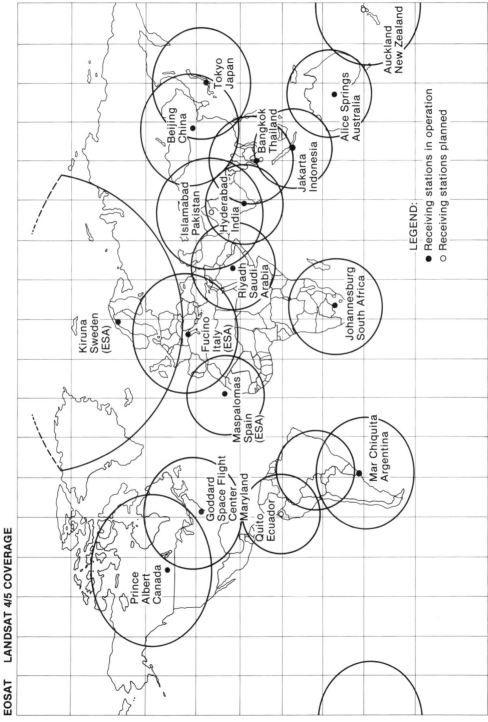

Exhibit 6

EOSAT   LANDSAT 4/5 COVERAGE

LEGEND:
● Receiving stations in operation
○ Receiving stations planned

Tokyo
Japan

Beijing
China

Bangkok
Thailand

Jakarta
Indonesia

Alice Springs
Australia

Auckland
New Zealand

Islamabad
Pakistan

Hyderabad,
India

Kiruna
Sweden
(ESA)

Riyadh,
Saudi
Arabia

Fucino
Italy
(ESA)

Johannesburg
South Africa

Maspalomas
Spain
(ESA)

Goddard
Space Flight
Center
Maryland

Quito,
Ecuador

Mar Chiquita
Argentina

Prince
Albert
Canada

Exhibit 7 Petition from 100 Members of Congress

February 24, 1989

Vice President Dan Quayle

The White House
Washington, D.C. 20500

Dear Mr. Vice President:

We are pleased to learn that the Administration has developed a plan to prevent the shutdown of the Landsat 4 and Landsat 5 remote sensing satellites at the end of this month. We felt you should be aware of the strong congressional support for our civilian remote sensing program.

Sincerely,

U.S. Rep. Robert A. Roe   U.S. Rep. George E. Brown, Jr.
(D., N.J.)   (D., Calif.)

Dear Mr. President (Vice President):

We are writing to urge your prompt assistance in helping prevent the shutdown of the nation's only operational civilian land remote-sensing satellites: Landsat 4 and Landsat 5.

On February 15, the Department of Commerce directed the Earth Observation Satellite Company (EOSAT) to cease operations of Landsat 4 and Landsat 5 as of March 31. The "Landsat Shut Down Plan" began on March 1.

We believe that Landsat has been one of the greatest triumphs of the nation's civilian space effort. The technology for remote sensing was pioneered by the United States, and is now being successfully operated by France, Japan, the Soviet Union, and India—with other nations soon to follow. Although construction is underway on Landsat 6, that satellite will not be launched until June 1991. The Landsat Shut Down Plan would thus cause a two-year break in data collection. This would impair the prospects for successfully commercializing remote sensing technology, and it would be a serious setback for the nation's civilian space program.

We respectfully request that you help develop a plan to find the $9.4 million necessary to keep Landsat 4 and Landsat 5 operational for the remainder of this Fiscal Year. We urge you to convene a meeting to instruct the National Aeronautics and Space Agency and the Departments of Defense, Commerce, Interior, and Agriculture, in conjunction with EOSAT, to mutually agree on a formula that raises the necessary $9.4 million. It would be a tragic mistake if this relatively small amount of money could not be found in order to preserve an enormously important program.

We appreciate your attention to this request.

Exhibit 8   Study for an Advanced Civil Earth Remote Sensing System
Space and ground segments of an advanced civil earth remote sensing system (ACERSS). The owner/operator of the space segment bears all costs of domestic ground stations and collects access fees from foreign ground stations.

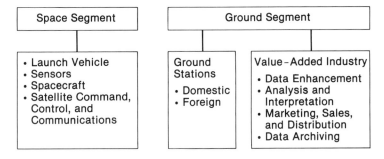

Exhibit 8   (Continued)

Space segment revenue shortfall: typical annual space
segment cost compared with projected total annual
revenues from raw data sales and foreign ground
station fees in three market growth scenarios.
Projected space segment revenues cannot cover space
segment costs during the 1990s, even assuming a 100
percent market share of such revenues in the
high-growth scenario.

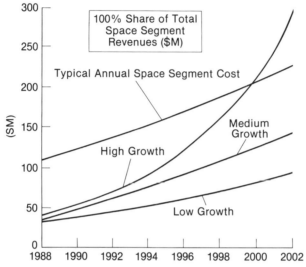

Typical annual cost of Landsat–type space segment,
assuming 3–year mission lifetime and 5%/year inflation.

Table 1. Projected total revenues from raw data sales, foreign ground station fees, and
value added products during the late 1990s in three market growth scenarios. By the
year 2000, in the high-growth scenario, total annual revenue is approximately $0.6
billion.

Low Growth ($M)	1988	1996	1997	1998	1999	2000
Raw data sales	$27.2	$ 44.0	$ 46.3	$ 48.6	$ 51.0	$ 53.5
Ground station fees	12.0	21.6	22.8	24.0	2.2	26.4
Space segment revenue	**$39.2**	**$ 65.6**	**$ 69.1**	**$ 72.6**	**$ 76.2**	**$ 79.9**
Value-added products	51.8	82.8	86.8	90.9	95.3	99.9
Total Revenue	**$91.0**	**$148.4**	**$155.9**	**$163.5**	**$171.5**	**$179.8**

Medium Growth ($M)						
Raw data sales	$27.2	$ 69.4	$ 77.3	$ 86.3	$ 96.3	$107.5
Ground station fees	12.0	21.6	22.8	24.0	25.2	26.4
Space segment revenue	**$39.2**	**$ 91.0**	**$100.1**	**$110.3**	**$121.5**	**$133.9**
Value-added products	51.8	120.9	133.3	146.8	161.9	178.7
Total revenue	**$91.0**	**$211.9**	**$233.4**	**$257.1**	**$283.4**	**$312.6**

High Growth ($M)						
Raw data sales	$27.2	$105.7	$124.1	$144.9	$168.9	$196.7
Ground station fees	12.0	21.6	22.8	24.0	25.2	26.4
Space segment revenue	**$39.2**	**$127.3**	**$146.9**	**$168.9**	**$194.1**	**$223.1**
Value-added products	51.8	190.4	227.0	268.4	317.3	374.0
Total revenue	**$91.0**	**$317.7**	**$373.9**	**$437.3**	**$511.4**	**$597.1**

Table 4. Case for international ownership of the space segment. International partnerships lower U.S. investment and increase the likelihood of grammar market share.

Ownership Option	Advantages	Disadvantages
100% U.S. ownership	•Best guarantees of data continuity to U.S. users •Best means for assuring "open skies" and "non-discriminatory access" •Maximum flexibility and control in setting system specifications •Demonstration of continued U.S. leadership	•Highest U.S. investment •Possible loss of revenue because of reduced market share
Bilateral ownership	•Lower U.S. investment •Likelihood of greater market share for the space segment[a] •Talent pooling •Conservation of capital	•Time-consuming negotiations required
International consortium	•Lowest U.S. investment •Likelihood of greatest market share for the space segment[1] •Maximum talent pooling •Maximum conservation of capital	•More difficult and lengthy negotiations required •Risk of interruption of data to U.S. users if United States does not have a controlling share •Difficulty in establishing government/industry partnership for managing the U.S. share

[a]Market share and revenue increase if the cooperating nations would otherwise have been competitors.

Table 6. Projected growth in civil markets.

Market ($M)	1988 (Estimated)			2000 (High growth scenario)		
	Raw Data Sales	Value Added Products	Total	Raw Data Sales	Value Added Products	Total
Private industry	5	7	12	68	147	215
U.S. government	5	5	10	33	17	50
Foreign	17	39	56	87	203	290
State and local	—	—	1	4	8	12
Academia	—	—	—	3	1	4
Nonprofit	—	—	—	—	—	1
Total data sales	**27**	**52**	**79**	**197**	**374**	**572**
Ground station fees	12	—	12	26	—	26
Total revenues	**39**	**52**	**91**	**223**	**374**	**598**

Exhibit 9

EOSAT GOVERNMENT FUNDING

September 1985 $90 million
April 1988 $62.5
October 1988 $20.3 (second installment from the March 1988 renegotiated contract)
$10 (to be repaid in four installments)

OMB had requested $36 million for the final Landsat 6 payment in the Fiscal Year 1990 budget. The budget now went to Congress. The Air Force had agreed to launch Landsat 6 some time in 1991 or 1992. OMB officials felt confident that funding would be made available for the launch. One official said, "It wouldn't make sense to fund the entire satellite and then not launch it."

Source: EOSAT.

ENDNOTES

1. "The Future of the Landsat System," Hearings before the Subcommittee on Natural Resources, Agriculture Research and Environment, and the Subcommittee on International Scientific Cooperation, of the House Committee on Science, Space, and Technology, March 31 and April 2, 1987 (Washington, D.C.: Government Printing Office, 1987), p. 1.
2. Ibid., p. 2.
3. Approximate revenues for Landsats 4 and 5 in 1985 were $15 million. Annual operating costs were about $30 million.
4. House hearings, p. 93.
5. Satellites orbited the earth and could only image a percentage of the globe at any time. Different systems could provide an image of the same area as frequently as daily to once a month—the trade-off was total global coverage versus frequency to one area.
6. Department of Commerce, "Space Commerce: An Industry Assessment," May 1988, p. 66.
7. Large government users included the departments of Defense, Agriculture, Interior and Energy.
8. Colleen Driscoll Sullivan, "Commercial Observation Satellite Project," unpublished, March 10, 1988, p. 10.
9. Ibid.
10. Ibid.
11. Ibid.
12. Department of Commerce, "Space Commerce," p. 60.
13. David S. Meyer, "French SPOT and the U.S. LANDSAT," *Commercial Space Quarterly* (March 19, 1987), p. 64.
14. Rob Stoddard, "The Selling of Remote Sensing," *Satellite Communication*, (December 1988), p. 16
15. Carol Matlack, "Landsat's Slow Death," *National Journal*, (July 25, 1987), p. 1904.
16. Hearings, pp. 94 and 95.

5

ENSURING ECONOMIC JUSTICE

Bailout: A Comparative Study in Law and Industrial Structure
Robert B. Reich

Economies are like bicycles: the faster they move, the better they maintain their balance. Changes in consumer preferences, technologies, international competition, and the availability of natural resources all require economies to reallocate capital and labor to newer and more profitable uses. Societies that redeploy their capital and labor more quickly and efficiently than others are apt to experience faster growth and greater improvements in productivity.

In recent years the U.S. government has responded with increasing frequency to calls for aid to certain large, distressed businesses. Conrail, Lockheed, Chrysler, and Continental-Illinois Bank are only the most visible "bailouts." Tariffs, quotas, and tax and regulatory relief are examples of additional efforts also directed at failing enterprises. These responses have released a storm of criticism and debate. Some people, recoiling from the ad hoc nature of these government actions,

Mr. Reich teaches business, law, and public management at the John F. Kennedy School of Government, Harvard University. This case has been adapted from an article with the same title which appeared in the *Yale Journal on Regulation*, Vol. 2 (1985), p. 2. Reproduced by permission of the author.

have called for a new government institution to aid troubled industries and companies. They typically point to Japan's Ministry of International Trade and Industry (MITI) as a model. Opponents of this approach typically point to the failures of Britain's National Enterprise Board or similar institutions.

The four cases described here are not intended to be representations of how these political-economic systems typically redeploy people and capital within normal business reorganizations. To the contrary, the four cases are atypical; they depict systems under stress. These major business failures threatened, or were perceived to threaten, entire regions of the country and, to some extent, the entire national economy. Each case occurred during a particularly turbulent economic period. Each was perceived as exceptional and generated controversy, debate, complex negotiations, and a search for new solutions. Each case tested the system of normal political and economic arrangements among finance, labor, management, and government, and thereby illuminated the detailed rules and understandings that shape the relationships among these groups.

Typically, we see only the gross movements—the large deals, lawsuits, statutes, and economic aggregates—and mistake these for the social organization lying beneath them. It is only when the system is under stress, when the normal institutional relationships are stretched and tested, that we can see these underlying patterns more clearly, and understand what is unique about them and why their uniqueness matters.

AEG-TELEFUNKEN, A.G.

AEG-Telefunken was founded in Berlin in 1883. The company was dismembered after World War II, since 90 percent of its production facilities were in East Germany. But the company rode the consumer boom of the 1950s and 1960s, becoming a giant conglomerate in the process. It bought up small companies that made washing machines, ranges, and household appliances. By 1970 it was then the second largest electronics manufacturing company in West Germany, after Siemens, and the fifth largest in Western Europe. It also was responsible for approximately 1 percent of the nation's GNP.

By the mid-1970s Japanese manufacturers of consumer products began to invade the West German market, eating into AEG's sales. The deutschmark began to rise relative to foreign currencies, making imports even more attractive and AEG's foreign sales even less so. Moreover, the company never had fully digested its various acquisitions or imposed any coherent management structure upon them; as losses mounted, the firm seemed incapable of cutting costs. In addition, all the acquisitions had left the company deeply in debt. As costs mounted, the company dipped into pension reserves, creating a large deficit in the pension fund.

The crisis came in 1979. Losses had mushroomed to $580 million. In October, management presented to the supervisory board a plan to reduce costs still further, including a cut of 20,000 jobs, 13,000 to occur in 1980 alone. Labor representatives on the board were strongly opposed.

AEG's labor leaders met in Bonn with Count Lambsdorff, minister of economics in Helmut Schmidt's coalition government, and Hans Matthoefer, minister of finance. They argued that the government should invest in the firm, possibly taking over the company, and thereby saving jobs. Matthoefer, a union member and also leading member of the Social Democratic party, was sympathetic, but concerned about the government's mounting deficits. Lambsdorff, a Free Democrat and economic conservative, was against the plan. There was no agreement.

The banks then took the initiative. In December, Dr. Hans Friderichs, chief executive of the Dresdner Bank, hosted a meeting at the bank's headquarters in Frankfurt. Dresdner Bank, the second largest bank in West Germany, was AEG's lead bank; the firm was more indebted to Dresdner Bank than to any other creditor, and the bank managed a substantial share of the firm's stock. Friderichs himself served as director of AEG's supervisory board. He had preceded Lambsdorff as West German minister of economics. Friderichs had invited to the meeting 66 of West Germany's most powerful business and financial leaders. His message was clear: AEG needed financial help. If the help didn't come from the banks, insurance companies, and other industrial giants there assembled, then it would have to come from the government, but if help came from the government, it would come with strings, and the strings would be tied to organized labor. One managing director of the Dresdner Bank, Dr. Meier-Preschany, put the matter bluntly: "Let's face it, either we are going to provide the subsidy or the State will, and if the State does then the State will want control...and there are certain voices in our political system that will be happy to ease the way."

The assembled financiers and industrialists also were aware of mounting public concerns about the powerful role of the banks in the West German economy. The government was then considering legislation to limit the amount of equity any bank could hold in a given company. A government official described the situation to a reporter for *The Wall Street Journal*: "[our] bankers realize their own reputation is at stake. If they even admit that the State would step in, they raise serious questions about why they should enjoy such sweeping power in corporate boardrooms."

The group agreed to Friderichs' plan. A consortium of 24 banks would provide the company with the equivalent of $376.2 million in new equity, bringing the banks' combined holdings to around 65 percent of the firm's outstanding shares. The banks also would reschedule about $1.16 billion of the company's long-term debt and some $700 million in short and medium term. The insurance companies would subscribe to $90 million in unsecured bonds at a rate 1 percent below that on long-term government bonds; other large industrial firms would subscribe to about $125 million more. In addition, shareholders would be asked to approve a two-thirds reduction in the nominal value of the company's stock. The company, in turn, would reduce its West German work force by 10 percent in 1980, and its chief executive would be replaced by Heinz Duerr.

But the plan proved to be inadequate. Losses continued to mount: in 1981, $260 million on sales of $6.2 billion, nearly the same in 1982. Accumulated debt rose to $3.2 billion. Equity shrunk to 10 percent of that indebtedness. The 1981 recession, coupled with high interest rates, was partly to blame; the firm was still struggling to repay loans for its 1960s expansion.

Once again, the Dresdner Bank took the initiative. Once again it sought to get the group of lenders to reschedule the existing debt and provide new loans. But this time the government's help would be needed; the company's debt was now too large, and its future too precarious, to rely any longer on a private sector solution.

In the spring of 1982 Hans Friderichs and Heinz Duerr met with Count Lambsdorff and the new finance minister, Manfred Lahnstein. The recession had pushed unemployment up to over 7 percent, and prospective job losses were on everyone's mind. Friderichs and Duerr proposed that the government become involved in the company's plight: the banks would write off the firm's 1982 debt repayments of $105 million and would provide new loans up to $800 million. But the government must back up the loans with a guarantee to repay them if the firm went into bankruptcy. Labor leaders met separately with the government officials; they too asked for government assistance, but argued—as they had three years before—that in return the government should obtain an ownership stake in the company.

A few months later the government announced its decision. It immediately would provide AEG with loan guarantees amounting to the equivalent of $239 million for the purpose of financing export sales, on condition that the banks provide $100 million in new loans. Additional loan guarantees would be made available to the company on condition that an independent audit showed that the firm was still viable, and could live without aid in two or three years' time. Lambsdorff made it clear, however, that any solution to the company's problems was primarily the responsibility of the company and of West German industry, not of the state, and that the government would not take a financial stake in the company.

Then the Dresdner Bank dropped the other shoe. On August 9, 1982, after an emergency meeting of AEG's supervisory board, the firm announced that it had run out of cash and that its losses for the year could be as much as $200 million. It therefore would seek reorganization under a court proceeding known as Vergleich, a type of half-way house to bankruptcy under which 60 percent of a company's debt can be written off so long as the company's reorganization plan is approved by a majority of creditors holding among them at least 80 percent of the debt. If successful, the reorganization would wipe the company's slate clean of over $2 billion of debt. Reorganization would have the added advantage of eliminating $520 million of unfunded pension liabilities; those claims would be taken over by the Pension Security Association, a semipublic corporation established in the early 1970s to insure the pensions of employees from involvement companies. In addition to seeking reorganization, Duerr announced that 20,000 employees would be laid off.

The announcements shocked West Germany's financial community and its labor unions. Labor leaders again called upon the government to buy up the company to stop job losses. Helmut Schmidt's Social Democrats were about to face an important contest with the Christian Democrats in the state of Hesse, in which labor support was crucial, but the government held firm. The Free Democrats, on whom Schmidt depended to maintain his increasingly fragile coalition government, opposed state intervention. The unions were philosophical. "The times have changed," opined Eugene Loderer, a chief of IG Metall. "A cave-in has occurred that cannot be handled in the usual bombastic way. Union policy must accept the realities."

Several weeks later the government formally agreed to guarantee up to $440 million of new loans to the firm. The independent audit, commissioned by the government, had concluded that the firm had a good chance of survival so long as the court-supervised settlement of AEG's current debts was approved, the new loans were provided, and the company continued to slim down. Half the loan guarantees would be provided by individual state (lander) governments, in proportion to their share of AEG's work force. In addition, certain states agreed to provide low-interest loans; for example, the state of Hesse would grant loans of up to $400,000 at subsidized rates to any supplier of AEG's headquartered within the state.

AEG's creditors approved the reorganization plan. The banks came up with over $800 million of new loans, half of which were guaranteed by the government. The crisis seemed to be over. Indeed, AEG appeared to be back on a relatively even keel. The company celebrated its hundredth birthday in 1983 with losses of just under $333 million for the preceding year. For 1983 it reported an operating profit of $13.2 million. Its stock price had rebounded to around $47 a share, up from around $12 in 1979. Its worldwide payroll was down to 76,500 people—60,000 of them in West Germany. It had sold off most of its consumer products businesses and had begun to specialize in telecommunications and defense-related technologies.

BRITISH LEYLAND

British Leyland (BL) was created in 1968 when Harold Wilson's Labour government decided that the only way to preserve a strong British automobile industry that could compete worldwide was to merge the two remaining British-owned automobile companies—British Motor Company and Leyland Motor Company—into a larger-scale enterprise. The government offered funds to induce the change. But the merger occurred on paper only. The two companies, which themselves were products of more than 30 mergers over the years, remained fragmented. There were over 70 plants scattered over the English countryside, many of them too small to achieve adequate economies of scale. Over 200,000 employees were divided among 8 divisions, 17 different unions, and 246 bargaining units; there were more than 30 different contracts to be negotiated, each of which came up for renewal at a different time, and fierce interunion rivalries. In 1970, 5 million work-hours were lost to strikes and stoppages; by 1972 the loss had reached 10 million work-hours. Indeed, many of the companies that had been merged into the new giant had been bitter rivals for decades. Despite the merger, according to one industry executive, "[t]he people at Longbridge [where Austins were made] wouldn't talk to the people at Cowley [the Morris plant], and the snobs at Jaguar wouldn't speak to any of them."

Despite these problems, BL managed through the early 1970s to coast along on rising automobile sales generated largely by the government's decision to lift restrictive credit and tax measures. BL sold all the cars and commercial vehicles it could produce—1.2 million in 1973 alone, and the company made money (although profit margins were extraordinarily low)—in 1973 it earned the equivalent of $66 million on $3.8 billion of sales (a paltry 1.7 percent).

Then came the oil crisis and soaring inflation. BL's costs were so high relative to other auto companies like Ford and Vauxhall, and its quality so poor, that it could not compete. It tried to change its system of wage payments based on piece rates, but this meant increasing overall wages by about 15 percent. The Austin 1300 sedan became one of the few cars ever to be awarded a "silver lemon" by the West German Automobile Club, a dubious honor bestowed for "horrible" mechanical faults. BL's share of the British market tumbled from 45 percent, just prior to the 1968 merger, to 33 percent in 1974; its share of the continental European market declined from 10 percent to 7 percent. It began to lose money.

In July 1974 BL executives met with the firm's principal bankers—Barclays, Lloyds, Midland, and National Westminster—to get their agreement to lend the company the equivalent of $1.2 billion for new investment over the next six years; this was on top of the $315 million that the company already had borrowed. By September BL's cash position was deteriorating quickly. Losses for the fiscal year amounted to $46.2 million. With its share capital valued at only $360 million, the company had a worrisome debt-to-equity ratio of approximately 1:1. The banks were unwilling to extend any more loans.

The crisis deepened. In a few months BL would not be able to pay its bills. BL executives and their bankers met in late November with Anthony Wedgwood Benn, secretary of state for industry in the Wilson government. On December 6, 1974, Benn announced that the government would seek Parliament's approval of public aid to the company, perhaps including some degree of public ownership. He immediately appointed a team of business and labor leaders, under the direction of Sir Don Ryder, a noted industrialist, to assess "the present situation and future prospects" of the company, and report back to Parliament.

The Ryder Report blamed BL's troubles on inadequate capital investment, poor labor-management relations, and an inefficient organization of production. But the situation was not hopeless: "[vehicle] production is the kind of industry which ought to remain an essential part of the U.K.'s economic base. We believe, therefore, that BL should remain a major vehicle producer, although this means that urgent action must be taken to remedy the weaknesses which at present prevent it from competing effectively in world markets." The company could become profitable again with an infusion over the next seven years of the equivalent of $6.2 billion for new investment (half of which would come from the government, the other half to be generated internally). Through its purchase of old and new shares, the government would own a majority of the company. In addition, there should be a new structure of "industrial democracy" within the company, in order to take advantage of the ideas and enthusiasm of the work force and overcome hostilities; and the company should be reorganized into four separate profit centers with responsibility, respectively, for cars, trucks and buses, international sales, and various more special products.

On April 24, 1975, Prime Minister Harold Wilson, the leader of the Labour party, spelled out to a packed and somber House of Commons the government's plan to rescue BL. "Vast amounts of public money are involved, representing one of the greatest single investments in manufacturing industry, which any British government has ever contemplated," he said. But such an investment was made necessary by the company's importance to the national economy. After a bitter and acrimonious debate, Parliament agreed. BL announced in a letter to its shareholders that it had accepted the plan. The company's managing director resigned, and was replaced with a new chief executive; BL's aged and notorious chairman, Lord Stokes, was given the figurehead position of president, and a new chairman was installed.

The government immediately provided BL with the equivalent of $426 million of new equity capital; the rest would come in stages, as BL met certain performance benchmarks. The installments would be provided by the National Enterprise Board, a semi-independent government agency, now headed by Sir Don Ryder. The board soon began working with BL's new management, restructuring the company along the lines that had been suggested in the Ryder Report.

Labor disputes increased. Ryder's plan for industrial democracy involved a complex hierarchy of plant committees, divisional committees, and senior councils. But shop stewards, who had the most power under the old arrangement, feared that the new system would create a rival channel of communication. A compromise was reached, by which the shop stewards would be responsible for putting forth a slate of worker delegates to the committees and councils. Problems still remained: middle managers felt excluded from the process; senior managers had all they could do to attend the 760 weekly meetings of the various groups; confidential company information leaked out to the press. Rank-and-file workers continued to engage in wildcat strikes. Toolsetters wanted extra pay; electricians argued with transport workers over specific responsibilities; warehousemen protested overtime policies; there were stoppages at the Triumph works over track speed, at Bathgate over pay, at Coventry's Jaguar plant over management's decision to install a new paint shop at Castle Bromwich—fearing that this jeopardized the independence of Jaguar.

Overall, productivity in 1977 was lower than the crisis year of 1974. The company estimated that strikes and work stoppages cost it the production of 225,000 vehicles. Losses amounted to the equivalent of $110.5 million. The company sold 785,000 vehicles (down from 1.2 million in 1973), and BL's share of the British automobile market slipped to 23 percent (from 33 percent at the time of the Ryder Report), just behind Ford. The National Enterprise Board continued to hand out money, but the government threatened to review and revise the entire Ryder plan.

A turning point of sorts came in the fall of 1977, when Leslie Murphy took over from Don Ryder at the NEB. Among Murphy's first acts was to dismiss BL's chief executive and its chairman. (The chairman's departure was somewhat hastened by his assertion, tape recorded without his knowledge at a private dinner party, that it was "perfectly respectable" for BL to be gaining sales abroad by "bribing wogs.") The NEB appointed Michael Edwardes to both positions. As chief executive of Chloride Group, Britain's largest battery maker, Edwardes had earned something of a "whiz kid" reputation; he had also been one of the first members of the NEB.

Edwardes immediately set out to reduce BL to a profitable size. He revised the firm's production targets downward to 800,000 vehicles and 25 percent of the British market and announced that there would need to be a corresponding cut in employment. He offered workers bonuses of up to $3,000 if they would leave the company voluntarily. Simultaneously, Edwardes took a tough line with the unions. He closed the Speke plant in Liverpool, which had been plagued by work stoppages and poor workmanship, thereby laying off 3,000 workers; he promised them generous severance payments on condition that the shutdown was peaceful. When machinists at Scotland's Bathgate truck and tractor factory went out on strike, Edwardes announced a $70 million cut in planned investment at the plant. He also reorganized the company by giving his division heads more responsibility.

By late 1979, as Margaret Thatcher moved into Downing Street and the Conservatives took over the reins of government, BL's share of the British auto market had fallen for the first time to under 20 percent. Only 625,000 vehicles were manufactured (down from 785,000 in 1977, 1.2 million in 1973). With under 2 percent of the world automobile market, BL was the smallest full-range automobile manufacturer on the globe. Losses for the fiscal year ending in September were the equivalent of $242 million, double the losses for 1977 and almost four times the losses for the crisis year of 1974. But the poor performance could no longer be blamed entirely on the company: sales of North Sea oil had strengthened the pound, thereby making all British exports less attractive; at the same time, higher oil prices dampened demand for larger cars, on which BL made its highest profits. Indeed, the company had slimmed: it now employed 165,000 people (down from 211,000 in 1975). All told, the Labour government had invested more than $1 billion and lent the company more than $500 million.

It was now the Tories' turn. During the election campaign Mrs. Thatcher had pledged to provide BL with additional funds; now union leaders met with Keith Joseph, the new secretary of state for industry, and argued for more government assistance. Edwardes himself announced that substantial new public investment was needed both to launch new models and to encourage voluntary layoffs. He warned that without the funds, BL would be forced into bankruptcy and he would resign. He also unveiled a plan to scale back BL still further by closing 13 more plants and cutting an additional 25,000 workers from the payroll. Keith Joseph relented.* The Conservatives agreed to provide the equivalent of an additional $600 million in cash.

Even worse was 1980. Losses were $1.2 billion on sales of $6.5 billion. The world auto industry was in a slump. BL's new models were only months away from appearing in showrooms. But new cash was needed desperately. After a stormy

---

*Sir Keith estimated that liquidation of BL would increase U.K. unemployment by 150,000 people and thereby boost public welfare spending by approximately $7 billion a year. Count Lambsdorff had made a similar calculation regarding AEG.

meeting of the cabinet in February 1981, Sir Keith announced that the government would provide BL with another cash infusion—this one the equivalent of $1.2 billion. One ministerial colleague commented dryly: "There's a job waiting for Sir Keith Joseph in Oxford Street. He's been practicing the role of Father Christmas."

The rest of the story is more upbeat. Losses were slightly less in 1981 than the year before; by 1982 losses had been reduced to $275 million; in 1983 the company just about broke even. Certain divisions, like Land Rover and Jaguar, actually turned a profit. The new models were enormously successful. The Metro became Britain's most popular compact. The Maestro, a five-door hatchback, was introduced in early 1983 to much acclaim (news reports featured Mrs. Thatcher at the wheel, proudly motoring up and down Downing Street for the cameras). BL's share of the British market bounced back almost to 20 percent. Productivity was up. The company was now considerably leaner, to boot. Capacity was down to roughly a half million vehicles. Employment was down to 100,000. Pundits predicted a rosy future.

TOYO KOGYO

Toyo Kogyo, founded in 1920 in Hiroshima, began as a manufacturer of cork products. The company's first automobile, appearing in 1931, was little more than a wagon attached to a motorcycle. During World War II the company produced rifles, rock drills, and gauges to measure the accuracy of precision-engineering instruments; it still manufactures the latter two products. When the United States dropped the atomic bomb on Hiroshima on August 6, 1945, Toyo Kogyo's factory and its 10,000 workers were shielded by a small hill separating them from the rest of the city.

Tsuneji Matsuda, son of the company's founder, took over as president in 1951. The company soon became one of Japan's leading truck makers, under the brand name Mazda, a contraction of Matsuda. But Matsuda was intent on competing with the much larger Toyota and Nissan automobile companies, on the basis of Toyo Kogyo's expertise in engineering. In 1960 the firm produced a tiny 16-horsepower two-seater.

Soon thereafter Toyo Kogyo turned for help to the Sumitomo Bank, one of Japan's large-city banks located in Osaka. Up to that time Toyo Kogyo's lead bank had been the Hiroshima Bank, but the firm was now sufficiently large that it needed the backing of a larger financial institution. The new relationship proved auspicious. Shozo Hotta, the chairman of Sumitomo Bank, introduced Matsuda to West Germany's Konrad Adenauer, and Adenauer in turn arranged for Toyo Kogyo to obtain from Audi-Wankel a license to produce a rotary engine that Audi engineers had just designed.

By 1967 Toyo Kogyo was the world's only commercial manufacturer of cars equipped with rotary engines. The cars were wildly successful. Rotary engines were relatively free of pollution (an important advantage, as the Japanese government progressively tightened pollution-control standards in the early 1970s); they were snappy and responsive (they really did go "hmmm" as the company's advertising claimed); they were novel. The firm concentrated exclusively on the rotary engine. Before the rotary engine, Toyo Kogyo was producing about 150,000 cars and trucks a year; by 1973, the firm was up to 740,000 vehicles and had become Japan's third largest automaker. Its export sales, mostly to the United States, were booming. It was expanding its facilities to accommodate production of 1 million vehicles. Its work force also was expanding rapidly, reaching 37,000 by 1973—4.5 percent of the working population of Hiroshima prefecture. If component suppliers are included in the calculation, 7.4 percent of total jobs in the prefecture derived from TK, one quarter of the total manufacturing employment. Since Hiroshima's other major industry, shipbuilding, was in steep decline, the regional economy was growing even more dependent on TK.

Then came the oil shock. With all their advantages, rotary engines had one telling disadvantage; they were inefficient. A report of the U.S. Environmental Protection Agency revealed the awful truth: Mazdas with rotary engines got only 10 miles to a gallon in city driving. Rapidly rising oil prices therefore meant rapidly falling sales. In 1974, U.S. sales of Mazdas declined by over 43,000 cars; Japanese sales also plummeted. Inventories bulged.

Nevertheless, throughout the year Kohei Matsuda, the president and grandson of the founder, continued to make rosy projections. In late 1974 he called a press conference to announce that a new rotary engine with 40 percent better fuel efficiency would be in production before the end of 1975 (in fact, it took Toyo Kogyo engineers six more years to achieve this feat). Despite declining sales, he refused to cut production, with the result that by the end of the year the company was left with 126,000 unsold cars. Not surprisingly, the company's performance in 1974 was a disaster: it lost the equivalent of over $75 million on $2 billion of sales. The firm sank even more deeply into debt than normal for debt-laden Japanese firms. By the end of 1974, the firm's bank indebtedness had grown to $1.5 billion, and the debt-equity ratio had mushroomed to 4:1.

Sumitomo Bank officials were not standing idly by. They suggested to Kohei Matsuda that the firm cut production and stop its expansion program, but Matsuda would not listen. Meanwhile, Toyo Kogyo dealers from around Japan expressed to bank officials their concerns about the company. The dealers' lack of confidence, coupled with Matsuda's intransigence and the rapidly deteriorating position of the firm, forced the bank's hand.

In October 1974 the bank sent two of its senior officers to Toyo Kogyo to join the firm's management temporarily and "strengthen the company's financing operations [and] prepare for a possible deterioration in the company's business," in the words of a Toyo Kogyo spokesman. They took charge of the biggest trouble spots: financing the ballooning inventories of unsold Mazdas in the United States and projecting the firm's performance over the next year or two. These emissaries were followed by others. In all, over the next two years, Sumitomo Bank and Sumitomo Trust Company placed 11 of their top-level executives in key positions within Toyo Kogyo. These included Tsutomu Murai, managing director of the bank, who took over as executive vice president of the automaker. Murai described the changeover bluntly: "For now, we're an army of occupation. Active intervention is unavoidable."

The Sumitomo rescue team acted quickly. Kohei Matsuda, Toyo Kogyo's president, was made chairman of the company without any operating duties; he retired from the company at the end of 1977. Two-thirds of the company's section chiefs were shifted to new positions. Costs were slashed: production was cut back, the expansion plans were dropped, $54 million in stock and real estate was sold off, dividends were reduced by 20 percent for three years, hiring of new assembly workers was halted for four years, all managers at the rank of section chief or above (about 4 percent of the total payroll) went without pay raises, directors' salaries were cut and bonuses ended for three years, and the union accepted pay raises lower than those received by auto workers at other automobile companies.

One major cost remained. With all the production cuts, the company no longer needed one quarter of its work force. Ten thousand employees were now redundant. But rather than lay them off, the new Toyo Kogyo managers devised a scheme for training them as auto salesmen and sending them to Mazda dealers around Japan to sell the excess cars door to door. About 5,000 employees, mostly from the shop floor, took part in the plan between 1975 and 1980. (The other 5,000 employees gradually retired from the firm over the five years.) Each participating employee spent two years in sales work before returning to his factory job. Most were assigned to Tokyo and Osaka, 200 to 450 miles north of Hiroshima. The company paid each participant his incidental expenses, provided a supplemental wage to match his factory salary, and housed him in company-owned dormitories.

Mazda dealers were delighted to have the extra help; it is common in Japan to sell automobiles door to door, but the practice obviously is labor intensive, and a larger sales force means more sales. But the displaced workers were less enthusiastic. The two-year shift often meant absence from family and friends; many found the transition from production to sales to be difficult. Hayato Ichihara, who later became president of the company's union, explained why workers went along: "[W]e feared that if we didn't accept the proposal the company would demand we accept dismissals of workers in exchange for wage increases. And union members did understand that there were too many workers for the work that existed."

Simultaneously with their cost-cutting efforts, Toyo Kogyo's new managers shifted the firm's competitive strategy. Rather than compete on the basis of engineering alone, the company henceforth would compete on the strength of its sales organization and its low costs. But the new managers also knew that Toyo Kogyo's future would depend on new models. The company continued to hire engineers and pour money into developing cars both with conventional piston engines and rotaries. Between 1977 and 1980 Toyo Kogyo introduced five new models, including a fuel-efficient rotary.

Sumitomo Bank financed much of this transition, and arranged financing for the rest. By 1976, when Toyo Kogyo's accumulated debt reached the equivalent of $1.6 billion, the bank's share reached $256 million, 16 percent of the total. The following year it boosted its lending by $70.9 million, to a peak of $327 million. When the other 60 banks and insurance companies which had lent money to Toyo Kogyo threatened to cut off future credit, Ichiro Isoda (later president of Sumitomo Bank, then an executive in charge of the Toyo Kogyo account) called the other lenders into a meeting at Sumitomo's headquarters in Osaka and assured them that regardless of what happened to Toyo Kogyo in the future, the Sumitomo Bank would "stand by the company to the end" and would be making additional loans in the near future. Isoda then asked the other lenders not to desert Toyo Kogyo either and promised them that all creditors would share equally in repayment of any new loans. In the end, only a few of the lenders came forth with additional loans, but none called in the loans then outstanding.

Sumitomo Bank also twisted arms. Members of the Sumitomo *keiretsu*—the group of companies sharing stock ownership and financial support—provided additional loans. They bought most of the $54 million group stocks and real estate that Toyo Kogyo was forced to sell. They also purchased large numbers of Mazdas from Toyo Kogyo's bloated inventories. Sumitomo Bank branch offices around Japan steered bank customers to Mazda dealers. The bank also provided a large loan to C. Itoh, a major trading company which was not a member of the *keiretsu*, on condition that Itoh take over Toyo Kogyo's sales organization in the eastern United States and purchase its inventory of 10,000 unsold cars. Finally, in 1979 the bank arranged for Ford Motor Company to purchase 25 percent of the outstanding shares of Toyo Kogyo, a move which dramatically improved Toyo Kogyo's cash position.

Additional help came from the city of Hiroshima. Business leaders formed an association called Kyoshin Kai (the "Home Heart Group") to promote Toyo Kogyo sales in the region. The prefectural government cooperated by enacting a new and far stricter pollution-control law—with the purpose and effect of reducing by half the pollution tax on rotary-engine vehicles while increasing the tax on conventional engine models. These efforts served to raise Toyo Kogyo's share of the regional market from 20 percent to 35 percent and further reduce inventories.

The national government did not intervene directly, but its presence was felt. From the beginning Sumitomo Bank officials understood that the Ministry of Finance was vitally concerned about the future of the company, and the central bank would make every effort to cooperate. The Ministry of International Trade and Industry (MITI) at first considered merging TK with Mitsubishi or Honda. In a widely quoted speech Tomatsu Yugoro, vice minister of MITI, let it be known that MITI would not look favorably upon a merger between Toyo Kogyo and either Toyota or Nissan: "A two-keiretsu concentration of the automobile industry is not desirable," he said. "I hope that Toyo Kogyo will remain an independent number 3." MITI also encouraged TK's large suppliers (like Mitsubishi Steel) to continue their dealings on "normal terms." The Ministry of Finance encouraged major banking institutions, like the Industrial Bank of Japan and the Long-Term Credit Bank, to provide Toyo Kogyo with additional credit. And in 1979 MITI obligingly cleared away legal hurdles for Ford's purchase of one quarter of Toyo Kogyo.

Toyo Kogyo's new models were successful, and because they all could be produced on the same production line at the same time, Toyo Kogyo had the flexibility to vary its output while fully utilizing its plant and equipment. This new organization of production fueled productivity improvements from 19 cars a year per worker in 1973 to 43 cars in 1980.

By 1980 the company was profitable once again. Its debt had been reduced to the equivalent of $943.5 million, while the infusion of new equity from Ford had reduced its debt-to-equity ratio to under 2:1. It sold over 1 million vehicles, slipping past Chrysler to become the world's ninth largest automaker, once again the third largest in Japan.

Successes continued. Export sales ballooned. Ford also began to rely on Toyo Kogyo's supply of subcompacts and components. In 1983 Mazda's most popular export model was named U.S. "Import Car of the Year" by *Motor Trend Magazine*. That year the company sold 1.2 million vehicles, earning the equivalent of $91.4 million on $4.3 billion of sales. In the fall of 1983, looking back on the nine years of rebuilding the company, Satoshi Yamada, general manager of Sumitomo Bank's credit department and one of the bank executives who had spent time at Toyo Kogyo, said "it was a difficult period. Many people sacrificed. We didn't know how it would come out in the end. We are very pleased."*

CHRYSLER

Chrysler's story begins in 1922 when several bankers, worried about their outstanding loans to the faltering Maxwell Motor Company, persuaded Walter P. Chrysler to take over management of the auto company. Walter Chrysler already had turned around another failing auto company at the behest of the bankers— Willys-Overland. Both companies had expanded too rapidly and incoherently during World War I and the short boom following it and had been unprepared for intense competition from other upstart automakers and a decline in demand when the market returned to normal. Walter Chrysler persuaded the bankers to extend new loans to Maxwell and forgive much of the old debt in exchange for stock and stock options, and raised more funds by hurriedly redesigning Maxwell's old line of cars and slashing the price. In 1924 he unveiled a new car with a high-compression engine capable of extraordinarily quick starts; 32,000 Chryslers were sold that year at a profit of over $4 million, and the name of the company was changed to the Chrysler Corporation. The company continued to flourish, purchasing Dodge in 1928, then weathering the Depression better than most businesses.

Chrysler's performance after World War II was less impressive. Walter Chrysler was gone. The company was slow to ready new models to meet the postwar boom; its historic strength lay in engineering rather than in marketing and styling, which now were in demand. It captured 22 percent of the U.S. automobile market in 1951, but then entered a long downward trend that would take it below 10 percent in 1962. It bounced back a bit in the mid-1960s under the direction of Lynn Townsend, who emphasized design and sales, but Townsend also launched the firm on an ambitious expansion program which drained the firm of cash and made it vulnerable to sudden changes in demand.

Chrysler's first brush with bankruptcy came in 1970. The firm lost $27 million in the first quarter and was deeply in debt. The Penn Central bankruptcy that year made investors wary of any company with heavy debt and current losses. A rescue mission was mounted by John McGillicuddy, then a vice chairman of

---

*Toyo Kogyo's employment declined by only 27 percent during the crisis.

Manufacturers Hanover Bank, Chrysler's lead bank; he organized a syndicate of banks to pump an added $180 million into Chrysler's critical financial subsidiary, which in turn continued to provide loans to car buyers. The firm got a second wind.

Then came the oil shock and the 1974 recession. Auto sales plummeted. Chrysler went into a tailspin. Lynn Townsend was replaced by John Riccardo, whose strategy was basically to keep the company solvent by selling off the foreign subsidiaries that Townsend had created and closing marginal factories around the United States. But these cuts were insufficient; in 1978 the firm lost $204.6 million on under $13 billion in sales.

By the summer of 1979, Chrysler's lenders were getting worried. The firm by now owed over $1 billion to almost 400 separate financial institutions spread around the globe. Chrysler needed more loans, but its creditors were in no mood to accommodate. McGillicuddy, now chairman of Manufacturers Hanover, persuaded Chrysler to host a meeting of the major creditors to allay their fears. The meeting was held at Chrysler's headquarters; one participant described it as little more than a pep rally, in which no new information was forthcoming, but Chrysler executives expressed determination and confidence. The bankers agreed to keep available to Chrysler $750 million in short-term credit, but warned that they could not arrange additional funding. Their fears and warnings mounted after Riccardo announced in July Chrysler's performance for the second quarter: the company had suffered a loss of $207 million on sales of $3 billion; this was worse than all of 1978.

Politicians also were becoming worried. Chrysler's 1978 plant closing might be a harbinger of worse ahead. The firm directly employed 140,000 people, hundreds of thousands more as suppliers; most were concentrated around the Great Lakes. Over 81,000 Chrysler workers lived in the Detroit area alone. Since President Carter's election, Riccardo had made repeated trips to Washington, seeking relief from fuel efficiency and environmental regulations and financial assistance to modernize certain plants. His requests fell on deaf ears. But as the company's position deteriorated, senators and representatives from affected states became increasingly active. In June 1979 Riccardo met with administration officials, seeking legislation that would permit the company to convert its mounting tax losses into a $1 billion cash advance, but the Carter administration still was not receptive. The Treasury Department feared that any such plan would pervert the tax code and open the floodgates to other companies in dire straits. Nevertheless, Treasury officials organized a task force to gather information on Chrysler and devise alternatives.

By August the Carter administration had decided to help Chrysler. It was likely that Congress would act even if the administration did not. In addition, Doug Fraser, president of the United Auto Workers Union, and Coleman Young, mayor of Detroit, had impressed upon the president and his immediate staff the importance of maintaining Chrysler jobs. With an election just over one year away, their advice rang loud and clear. On August 9, G. William Miller, the newly appointed secretary of the treasury, met with Chrysler's board of directors. He told them that the administration would support neither the tax plan nor regulatory relief, but might be persuaded to introduce legislation guaranteeing up to $750 million of new loans if the company came up with an acceptable restructuring plan, including financial concessions from lenders, employees, dealers, and state governments. Another requirement—well understood, although unstated—was that John Riccardo would step down as chairman of the company.

Riccardo resigned. Lee Iacocca, who had come to Chrysler from Ford in 1978, took over. The firm hired an investment banking firm and a management consultant to help it devise the plan. It also shifted its public relations strategy: instead of claiming that government tax and regulatory policies were to blame for its poor performance and that relief therefore was warranted, it now blamed itself for its past failures and warned that a bankruptcy would force 600,000 people out of work. And it shifted its lobbying strategy from Congress's tax committees to the bank committees.

Chrysler and the Treasury negotiated throughout October. Secretary Miller continued to demand that the plan include larger financial concessions from the banks and employees and that the earnings projections on which the plan was based be better substantiated. Treasury commissioned several independent studies of Chrysler, the automobile industry, and the possible effects of a Chrysler bankruptcy. Meanwhile, Chrysler's cash situation continued to deteriorate. Its losses for the third quarter reached over $450 million. No company in history had lost so much money in so short a time. Chrysler was approaching default on its loans. Its share of the U.S. automobile market was now down to 8.9 percent.

Chrysler's congressional allies were growing impatient. Senator Don Riegle and Representative James Blanchard, both from Michigan and both members of their respective chambers' banking committees, introduced their own loan guarantee legislation. Both committees held hearings at which Lee Iacocca, Doug Fraser, and Coleman Young made the case for loan guarantees. John McGillicuddy explained that "a loan at this point on an unsecured basis to the Chrysler Corporation is not feasible...[W]e can act...only in a way that is appropriate to...our shareholders and depositors."

On November 1, 1979, Secretary Miller announced the administration's support for a $1.5 billion loan guarantee. He explained that the administration's original estimate of $750 million was far short of what was needed to put Chrysler back on sound footing.

Immediately Chrysler swung into action, seeking congressional action before the end of the year. Chrysler dealers, members of the United Auto Workers Union, and key suppliers all visited congressional offices, armed with printouts showing Chrysler and Chrysler-related jobs in each district. There was no organized opposition, save for relatively weak lobbying by the National Association of Manufacturers, the National Taxpayers Union, and Ralph Nader's Congress Watch. Nevertheless, certain members of Congress did press for specific provisions in the loan guarantee legislation: the proposal was amended to include an employee stock ownership plan at the behest of Senator Russell Long; Senators Richard Lugar and Paul Tsongas held out for greater concessions from the employees. Other members simply opposed the whole idea on the basis that the "free market" should be allowed to work its will. Said William Proxmire, chairman of the Senate Banking Committee, to G. William Miller: "You're asking Congress to play Santa Claus—and a deaf, dumb, and blind Santa Claus at that."

A conference committee worked out a compromise between the stiffer terms of the Senate bill and the more generous House version. The final bill was enacted on December 20 in the House and the following day in the Senate. It set out guidelines for $2 billion of financial concessions required of the banks, employees, dealers, suppliers, and states, to be matched by $1.5 billion of federal loan guarantees, and it established a loan guarantee board—comprised of the secretary of the treasury, chairman of the Federal Reserve Board, and administrator of the General Accounting Office—to monitor the company's compliance with the legislation and to authorize issuance of guarantees on finding that the company continued to be "viable."

A few weeks later, in a subdued White House ceremony, Jimmy Carter signed the Chrysler Loan Guarantee Act while Doug Fraser and Lee Iacocca looked on. Chrysler's losses for the year totaled $1.1 billion. Iacocca said "[t]he hard part starts now."

The hard part was getting the various groups to agree to come up with $2 billion worth of concessions. Chrysler's workers were the first to cooperate. Annual pay increases specified in the industrywide "pattern" contract (which Chrysler workers already had agreed to delay in their October contract round) would be postponed further, putting Chrysler workers six months behind Ford and GM employees that year and another five-and-one-half months behind the next year. The 250-member Chrysler Council approved the new contract on January 9, 1980; three weeks later it was approved by over 75 percent of the workers voting in 75 Chrysler locals. One UAW official explained the large margin of victory: "The debate in Congress over federal aid and all the publicity convinced them. They voted to save their jobs." In addition, the UAW leaders agreed that Chrysler could postpone its periodic payment to the union pension fund; Chrysler viewed this as a "contribution" worth $413 million, even though the government—as insurer of pensions under the Pension Benefit Guarantee Act—ultimately would pick up the tab should Chrysler fall into bankruptcy.

Creditors were more recalcitrant. The act required that creditors contribute $650 million. But by January Chrysler had stopped paying both principal and interest on its outstanding debt; it was now technically in default, and some lenders argued that their forbearance from seeking bankruptcy was a form of contribution. Many of the 400 lenders were convinced that Chrysler eventually was going to fail; they feared that the government loan guarantee, which had priority over their claims, would only drain away assets that might otherwise go to the banks at liquidation. And the banks fought among themselves: European banks, and some small U.S. banks, demanded payment in full from the larger U.S. lenders; some banks seized funds Chrysler had deposited with them and applied the funds against Chrysler's debt; the larger U.S. lenders insisted that every lender must sacrifice directly in proportion to its outstanding loans. Negotiations dragged on through March and April, with Chrysler and Manufacturers Hanover executives trying to strike a deal with the others. Eventually the lenders agreed to defer certain debt payments until after 1983, in exchange for $200 million in Chrysler preferred stock.

The new plan that Chrysler submitted to the Loan Board at the end of April did not meet the letter of the law. State and local governments had not yet committed funds, suppliers and dealers only had agreed to "softer" terms on purchases, the lenders' agreement to defer payments did not represent "new" money for Chrysler. Nevertheless, the Loan Board conditionally approved the plan. Chrysler would receive the first installment of $500 million in loan guarantees so long as the various parties actually came up with the sacrifices to which they had agreed.

Even then the deal almost fell through. A few small banks and several foreign banks still held out. Secretary Miller and his staff, now firmly committed to Chrysler's plan, applied pressure: they met with the bank officials, explained that with anything less than 100 percent participation the entire deal would unravel, and subtly threatened retaliation (legislation affecting bank regulation was pending in Congress; in addition, one member of the Loan Board was Paul Volcker, chairman of the Federal Reserve Board, which directly regulated many of the banks).

By June Chrysler was without cash. It stopped paying its suppliers. Had they then stopped supplying Chrysler, the company would have shut down.

Final agreement was reached on June 24. Chrysler received its $500 million loan guarantee. The Loan Board approved a second draw-down of $300 million on July 15, 1980. The transaction, said Lee Iacocca, represented "the most complex financial restructuring program in history...for one purpose—to protect the jobs of 600,000 American workers who build American cars for American buyers."

Throughout this period, Iacocca and other Chrysler executives reported monthly to Secretary Miller and daily to the Loan Board staff. "We were like a board of directors," said Miller. "I tried to convince them that they could no longer be a big car company, offering a full range of models. They had to downsize the firm. They resisted the notion at first." But only at first. Chrysler abandoned the full-size car business, cut its production, and concentrated on compacts and subcompacts, including the much-vaunted K-car. Plants were closed. Employment continued to drop. When in October 1980 a UAW official charged that the Loan Board was putting "undue pressure on Chrysler Corporation to strip down its operations," Secretary Miller insisted that the board's "sole objective" was to put Chrysler back on a "sound financial and operative plan."

Chrysler's plight did not improve. The K-car did not sell, in part because the Federal Reserve Board was drastically restricting the money supply, forcing interest rates to over 20 percent, and thereby drying up automobile sales. By the end of 1980 Chrysler was back to the Loan Board for a third installment. This time Secretary Miller and the other members of the board demanded even greater sacrifices from the constituent groups. The board held all the cards; if the board did not approve additional loan guarantees soon, responsibility would shift to the Reagan adminis-tration, which was not likely to be sympathetic.

Miller summoned Chrysler executives, bankers, and union officials to an eleventh hour meeting at the Treasury Department in early January 1981. There he met separately with representatives of each group, squeezing them for more concessions. In the end, the union agreed to cut wages by $1.15 an hour and freeze them at that level until September 1982; the banks agreed to convert $1 billion on

Chrysler's $2 billion debt into preferred stock and accept repayment on the other half at a rate of 30 cents on the dollar. None was happy with the deal. William Langley, an executive from Manufacturers Hanover, said that the banks had been forced to the wall and had borne the brunt of the sacrifice. Doug Fraser called it "the worst economic settlement we ever made. But the alternative is worse: no more jobs for Chrysler workers." The board approved a final installment of $400 million in loan guarantees.

Chrysler came back from the dead. It showed a small profit in 1982. Then, helped by the strong upturn in the U.S. car market in 1983, the company earned over $700 million, a swing of more than $1 billion from the same period two years before. Chrysler had cut its long-term debt from $2.15 billion in 1983 to $1.07 billion, paid $116.9 million in back dividends on preferred stock, strengthened its capital structure by exchanging $1.1 billion in preferred stock and warrants for common shares, and retired 14.4 million warrants held by the Treasury (the warrants had been an afterthought, required by the Treasury after several banks asked for them). Its share price billowed to $35 during the summer of 1983—more than seven times higher than its low in 1982. Lee Iacocca said "Chrysler had won its long battle for independence."

The company was now "lean and mean," in the words of Lee Iacocca. It was also much smaller than it had been. Its capacity had been slashed to around 750,000 cars, down from a peak of almost 1.6 million in 1968, and its total employment was down to around 70,000, from 160,000 just five years before (U.S. employment from 110,000 to 60,000). It produced far fewer models, had no foreign subsidiaries, except for a plant in Mexico, had a far smaller budget for developing new models and technological innovations, and was relying heavily on Japanese producers to fill out its product line and supply it with technology. And yet, it survived.

Exhibit 1   AEG-Telefunken Employment by Year, 1977–1983 (in thousands)

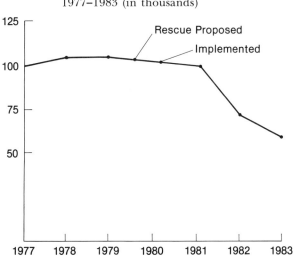

Exhibit 2   British Leyland British Employment by
Year, 1974–1982 (in thousands)

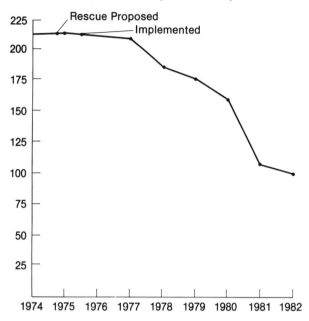

Exhibit 3   Toyo Kogyo Employment by Year,
1972–1978 (in thousands)

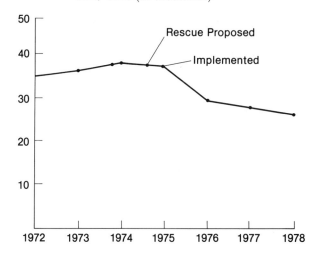

Exhibit 4   Chrysler Employment by Year, 1976–1982
(in thousands)

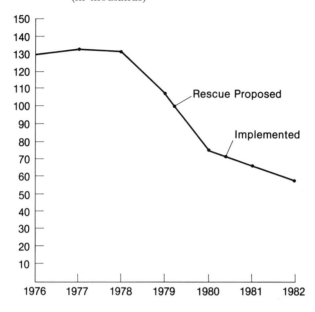

Exhibit 5   AEG-Telefunken Plant Locations and
Employment in West Germany
and West Berlin, 1979

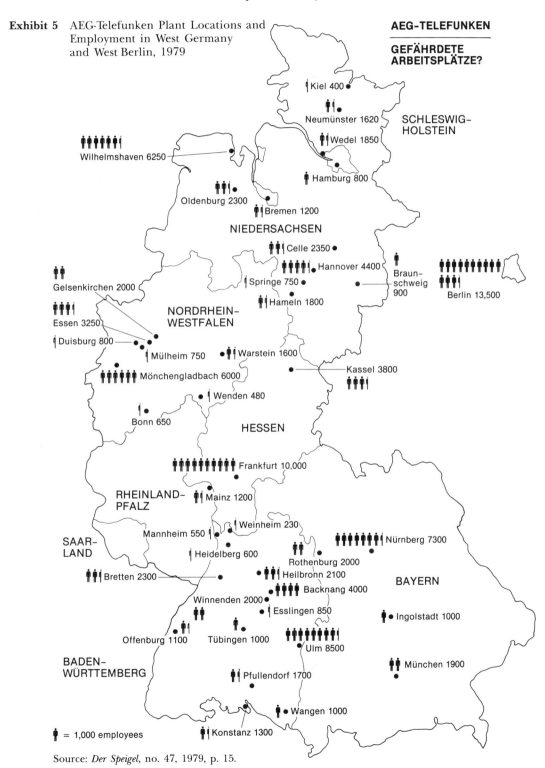

AEG-TELEFUNKEN
––––––––––––––
GEFÄHRDETE
ARBEITSPLÄTZE?

Kiel 400

Neumünster 1620

SCHLESWIG-
HOLSTEIN

Wedel 1850

Wilhelmshaven 6250

Hamburg 800

Oldenburg 2300

Bremen 1200

NIEDERSACHSEN

Celle 2350

Hannover 4400

Braun-
schweig
900

Berlin 13,500

Springe 750

Gelsenkirchen 2000

Hameln 1800

Essen 3250

NORDRHEIN-
WESTFALEN

Duisburg 800

Mülheim 750

Warstein 1600

Mönchengladbach 6000

Kassel 3800

Wenden 480

Bonn 650

HESSEN

Frankfurt 10,000

RHEINLAND-
PFALZ

Mainz 1200

Weinheim 230

SAAR-
LAND

Mannheim 550

Nürnberg 7300

Heidelberg 600

Rothenburg 2000

Bretten 2300

Heilbronn 2100

BAYERN

Backnang 4000

Winnenden 2000

Esslingen 850

Ingolstadt 1000

Offenburg 1100

Tübingen 1000

Ulm 8500

München 1900

BADEN-
WÜRTTEMBERG

Pfullendorf 1700

Wangen 1000

= 1,000 employees

Konstanz 1300

Source: *Der Spiegel*, no. 47, 1979, p. 15.

Exhibit 6 British Leyland Plant Locations and Employment in Great Britian, 1980

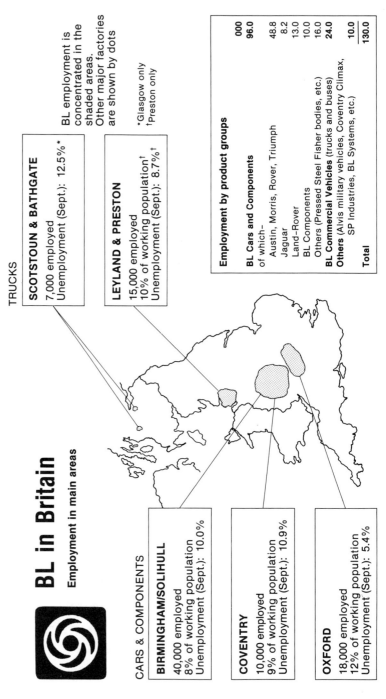

TRUCKS

SCOTSTOUN & BATHGATE
7,000 employed
Unemployment (Sept.): 12.5%*

LEYLAND & PRESTON
15,000 employed
10% of working population†
Unemployment (Sept.): 8.7%†

BL employment is
concentrated in the
shaded areas.
Other major factories
are shown by dots

*Glasgow only
†Preston only

BL in Britain
Employment in main areas

CARS & COMPONENTS

BIRMINGHAM/SOLIHULL
40,000 employed
8% of working population
Unemployment (Sept.): 10.0%

COVENTRY
10,000 employed
9% of working population
Unemployment (Sept.): 10.9%

OXFORD
18,000 employed
12% of working population
Unemployment (Sept.): 5.4%

Employment by product groups	
	000
BL Cars and Components	**96.0**
of which–	
Austin, Morris, Rover, Triumph	48.8
Jaguar	8.2
Land–Rover	13.0
BL Components	10.0
Others (Pressed Steel Fisher bodies, etc.)	16.0
BL Commercial Vehicles (trucks and buses)	**24.0**
Others (Alvis military vehicles, Coventry Climax, SP Industries, BL Systems, etc.)	10.0
Total	**130.0**

Source: *The Economist,* November 8, 1980, p. 65.

Government Redress of Market Imperfections: Procurement from Minority Firms

Since World War II the U.S. government has initiated a series of programs to redress perceived racial and sexual discrimination through government intervention in the economy (Exhibits 1 and 2). One such initiative is the designation of a certain proportion of federal procurement contracts as "set-aside" for assignment, on a noncompetitive basis, to firms owned by economically or socially disadvantaged minority persons.

These contract set-asides were first mandated in Section 8(a) of the Small Business Act of 1968. The Section 8(a) program remained in effect throughout the Reagan years, despite the commitment of Candidate Reagan in the 1980 campaign to the early windup of the Small Business Administration (SBA), the agency responsible for administering the program. Indeed in November 1986 the Congress passed, without Administration opposition, new legislation directing the Department of Defense to expand very substantially the amount of its procurement budget awarded to minority suppliers. The potential for obligatory minority involvement in federal procurement contracts, on a noncompetitive, advantaged basis, was thus extended.

FEDERAL LEGISLATION AIMED AT PROMOTING MINORITY BUSINESSES

For at least 50 years the federal government has been concerned about the preservation of small business; in the 1960s and 1970s this concern was coupled with special efforts to assist minorities. The Depression of the 1930s had prompted the establishment of small business committees in both houses of Congress, and during the war years the Smaller War Plants Corporation was created to act on behalf of small concerns seeking war contracts or subcontracts. It was only with the establishment of the Small Business Administration in 1953, however, that a potentially effective vehicle for aiding minority small businesses became available. The Small Business Act of 1958 charged the SBA ("it is the duty of the Administration") with seeing that small businesses received its aid in pursuing government contracts. To fulfill this obligation the SBA was given the power to extend loans and surety bonds to small businesses. The administration could also simplify contract applications through its certification powers.

In 1969 the policy of explicitly aiding minority small businesses found full expression. Through the efforts of Representative Parren J. Mitchell (D., Md.), chairman of the House Small Business Committee, and others, the Small Business Act of 1968 explicitly included the principle of no-bid contract set-asides for small businesses whose management and ownership were minority controlled.

The Section 8(a) program of noncompetitive set-asides was thus born. The program was strengthened in a subsequent 1978 amendment of the Small Business Act, which added provisions designed to facilitate the financing of minority-owned businesses, particularly through minority enterprise small business investment companies, or MESBICS. The Supreme Court gave its stamp of approval in the 1980 Fullilove decision, which upheld a 10 percent set-aside for minority contractors in the $4 billion Public Works Employment Act of 1977. Partly as a result of this decision, similar programs have been adopted by numerous states and localities. For example, at least 16 states have set numerical goals for government purchases of goods and services from businesses owned by women or minorities.

THE SECTION 8(a) PROGRAM

Companies eligible to participate in the Section 8(a) program must satisfy a number of criteria. Since the program is administered by the SBA, its standards for size must first be met. While required size, measured by numbers of employees (or, in the case of service firms, by revenue), varies across industry groups, the general ceiling in the late 1980s was 500 employees. In addition, firms seeking participation cannot be dominant forces in their respective industries, and must be owned and operated as independent entities, not as part of larger publicly owned or nonminority groupings.

The guidelines defining eligibility for the Section 8(a) program also specify that any participant must be a "socially and economically disadvantaged small business concern" that is

1. At least 51 percent owned by one or more socially and economically disadvantaged individuals; or, in the case of any publicly owned business, at least 51 percent of the stock of which is owned by one or more socially and economically disadvantaged individuals.
2. Whose management and daily business operations are controlled by one or more such individuals.[1]

The key qualification criteria lie, of course, in the definitions of "socially disadvantaged" and "economically disadvantaged," for participation in the program requires having the status of both classifications. "Socially disadvantaged individuals" are defined as "those who have been subjected to racial or ethnic prejudice or cultural bias because of their identity as a member of a group without regard to their individual qualities." "Economically disadvantaged individuals" are defined as

those socially disadvantaged individuals whose ability to compete in the free enterprise system has been impaired due to diminished capital and credit opportunities as compared to others in the same business area who are not socially disadvantaged.   In determining the degree of diminished credit and capital opportunities the Administration shall consider, but not be limited to, the assets and net worth of such socially disadvantaged individual.[2]

(In 1987, the general ceiling for the net worth of an "economically disadvantaged individual" was $750,000.)

While no comprehensive listing of groups in which membership might qualify an individual as economically and socially disadvantaged was specified in the 1968 act or its 1978 amendment, it was "presumed" that "socially and economically disadvantaged individuals include Black Americans, Hispanic Americans, Native Americans, Asians, and other minorities"[3]

Firms satisfying the foregoing criteria are eligible to apply for contracts which have been set aside for companies participating in the Section 8(a) program. Firms which have qualified negotiate with the Small Business Administration how long they may remain in the program up to a maximum of seven years. During this time in the program, they must meet all the criteria just described. At the end of seven years, all participating companies must "graduate" to the open market, although some may still qualify for other SBA aid based strictly on size (i.e., smallness). When Congress amended the act in 1978, all firms already in a program were given another seven years or until 1985.

A 1986 study indicated that of the more than 4,000 companies that had participated in the Section 8(a) program, about 700 had graduated successfully. This was out of a total of 843,000 minority-owned businesses, 6 percent of the total business population in 1982.[4]

In 1985, the federal government purchased $200 billion of goods and services from the private sector, of which $33 billion came from small businesses. Minority-owned firms received contracts worth $2.6 billion with $2.5 billion, or 70 percent, awarded through the 8(a) program. The Department of Defense was by far the largest procurer, accounting for 69 percent of the 8(a) dollars.[5] In addition, 8(a) firms received another billion dollars or so in subcontracts (Exhibit 3).

Set-aside contracts are awarded by the Small Business Administration acting on behalf of a government agency or department such as Defense. Each year, SBA negotiates set-aside quotas with the major government buyers (Exhibit 4). The big spenders, like Defense, are under particular pressure from Congress to maintain or improve on their 8(a) quota. In all cases, competition for awards is on a nonbidding basis. Generally, the procuring officer of a department requests from the SBA the name of a properly certified 8(a) company capable of performing the work required. The department's SBA contract officer then searches the "portfolio" of eligible companies (there were 3,000 in 1987) and provides the procuring officer with the name of the most suitable company. As one Defense Department official put it: "When we make a decision to go with an 8(a) contract, the SBA picks the firm and produces the certificate of competence. We cannot challenge it." Occassionally, a firm which is in SBA's portfolio may sell itself directly to a particular department.

For a minority-owned firm to be included in the SBA portfolio of 8(a) eligibles, it must first apply to an SBA district office located in one of 70 cities around the country. If it is approved by the district director, it passes through a regional office and eventually to Washington for the final okay.

In addition to assistance in obtaining government contracts, the SBA also helps 8(a) firms through "business development expense" grants which enable companies to buy capital equipment necessary to fulfill the contract. It also may make "advance payments" to provide firms with the liquidity required to complete the contract.

Thus, the set-aside program has two objectives:

1. To provide minority-owned firms with opportunities they might not otherwise have.
2. To assist such firms to become viable concerns, able to stand on their own without government assistance.

MOTIVATIONS BEHIND THE CREATION OF THE SECTION 8(a) PROGRAM

The existence of discrimination, whether conscious or unconscious, was widely recognized, even in 1987. Those minority rights activists with memories of the struggles of the 1950s and 1960s justified the Section 8(a) program as a vital door opener. Before its enactment minority firms had little hope of obtaining government contracts. The need for such preferential initiatives was also evident in their very success, despite the short period of time in which they had been in effect. Benjamin L. Hooks, executive director of the National Association for the Advancement of Colored People, pointed to progress in a June 1987 *New York Times* article:

> What so few Americans recognize is how the system worked up to, say, fifteen years ago. Before then, it was virtually impossible for a black businessman or woman to be considered for a contract by any significant company or Government body. White companies dominated every aspect of the business—and in many respects still do. Blacks occasionally got the leavings—small corner food stores, mortuaries, taxis and other modest endeavors that it hardly paid the whites to covet.[6]

One reason for the failure of governments and mainstream companies to use minority suppliers was a lack of confidence in the ability of minority businesses to perform on time and deliver quality, particularly on large and sensitive contracts. As John F. Robinson, president of the National Minority Business Council, a New York-based group of 300 minority businessmen and women, opined: "Corporations are just not doing enough in terms of national contracts. They just don't trust minorities with large orders."[7] As such, Pentagon contracts, often large, time-sensitive, and sophisticated, were seen by many observers as constituting excellent opportunities for minority concerns to prove their reliability, and "get their foot in the door" for future private sector business.

Another difficulty small minority firms faced in obtaining government business was the labyrinthine nature of the contract application and bidding process. Many small firms lack administrative staff, especially minority firms, which are often newly founded and undercapitalized. Add the difficulty of navigating the federal bureaucracy, and it is easy to see why the unaided minority entrepreneur was likely to swamp before even submitting a bid. The administrative assistance offered by the SBA as part of the Section 8(a) program was thus perhaps even more important than the noncompetitive nature of the award process. Even under

Section 8(a) the process remained problematic. As Mr. Hooks explained, "for small minority entrepreneurs the bureaucratic system has long been an unmitigated nightmare. Many are artisans working long days with no white collar backup to help get contracts. Unlike giant corporations, they don't have large legal staffs on retainer or lobbyists to expedite the paperwork through the labyrinth."[8]

Perhaps most distressing was the continued perception of unbridled racial discrimination against minority businessmen and women, despite the legal victories of the Voting and Civil Rights acts and even after proven performance. Alphonso Whitfield, Jr., president of the National Minority Supplier Development Council, Inc., a consortium of major corporations that buy from minority companies, observed: "All other things being equal, the minority entrepreneur is still prejudged that he can't perform the minute he walks through the door."[9] The perceived existence of such unthinking discrimination over two decades after the promulgation of Section 8(a) and after the initial success of the minority rights movement suggests a more basic motivation for Section 8(a): a desire for direct and mandated government action to ensure that minority firms get a share of government contracts more in keeping with the percentage of minorities in the population, regardless of the effect on mainstream attitudes or behavior.

Finally, several passages within the Small Business Act shed light on the motivations and assumptions of congressional politicians in their development of the Section 8(a) legislation. In reviewing the work of the SBA, the Congress found

1. that the opportunity for full participation in our free enterprise system by socially and economically disadvantaged persons is essential if we are to obtain social and economic equality for such persons and improve the functioning of our national economy.
2. that many such persons are socially disadvantaged because of their identification as members of certain groups that have suffered the effects of discriminatory practices or similar invidious circumstances over which they have no control.
3. that such groups include, but are not limited to, Black Americans, Hispanic Americans, Native Americans, and other minorities.
4. that it is in the national interest to ameliorate expeditiously the conditions of socially and economically disadvantaged groups.
5. that such conditions can be improved by providing the maximum practicable opportunity for the development of small business concerns owned by members of socially and economically disadvantaged groups.
6. that such development can be materially advanced through the procurement by the United States of articles, equipment, supplies, services, materials, and construction work from such concerns.
7. that such procurements also benefit the United States by encouraging the expansion of suppliers for such procurements, thereby encouraging competition among such suppliers and promoting economy in such procurements.[10]

Through this legislative dialectic the Congress seemed to have neatly accommodated both the government's commitment to the free enterprise economy and its intention to intervene in that same economy.

TRACK RECORD OF THE SECTION 8(a) PROGRAM

The Section 8(a) initiative has had both failures and successes. A 1986 U.S. Senate study found that of the over 4,000 firms that had participated in the program since

1985 less than 50 were still in existence, despite the fact that over 700 had managed to remain solvent during the time that they enjoyed the benefits of 8(a) participation. Critics have seized upon these figures as evidence that participating firms are merely cosseted by the program, their failings sheltered from the cold blast of the free market—only to succumb to the chill once the collectivist cloak is removed. The result of the program, such free market zealots contend, is merely reverse discrimination, and ineffective at that, since the failure rates for the participating businesses are generally believed to exceed those of mainstream small businesses, or even of mainstream start-ups. In short the futile, and indeed counterproductive, nature of intervention in the market economy is manifested in practice as it is decried in theory.

On the other hand, advocates who embrace the principle of affirmative action—regardless of the results of its application in practice—dismiss such armchair Adam Smiths as apologists for a "free market" that is in fact circumscribed by racial, ethnocultural, and sexist obstructions. In and of itself, the principle is not only legitimate, but transcendent of the admittedly difficult issue of implementation. Other supporters of the program point to the practice itself, to the success stories: the businesses which have used their time in the 8(a) program to attain the "critical mass" of both size and skills needed to succeed in the rough and tumble of a free market made even rougher by the onus of prejudice and bigotry. In short, the results speak for themselves.

There are numerous examples of entrepreneurial success among participants in the 8(a) program. Maxima Corporation, a Maryland computer services company founded by Joshua I. Smith in 1978, had by 1987 both graduated from the program and become a multimillion-dollar concern. Mr. Smith does not ascribe his success entirely to Section 8(a), but acknowledges its beneficial effects:

> Would I have succeeded without the program? Probably. But I doubt I would be where I am today were it not for the program. No one is suggesting the program is perfect. But it serves a vital purpose.[11]

Thacker Organization Construction Company, a Decatur, Georgia-based builder, is one company which survived a tough initial period immediately after graduation from 8(a), only to persevere and thrive. Thacker suffered a 62 percent decline in sales in 1985 after graduation. During 1986, however, the company revived strongly and finished No. 8 on the *Black Enterprise Magazine* list of America's top black businesses, with sales of $57.1 million. At No. 7 on the list, dominated for many years by such firms as Motown Records and Johnson Publishing (publishers of *Ebony* magazine), was Systems Management American Corporation, a computer systems integration company headquartered in Norfolk, Virginia.

But perhaps the most oft-cited success story has been that of Accurate Tooling (a pseudonym), a Philadelphia-based machine shop that became a major government contractor during the 1980s. The story of Accurate provides a sense of the actual experience of a company in the 8(a) program and how that experience was manifested in the company's managerial policies.

ACCURATE TOOLING

Accurate Tooling was founded in 1965 in West Philadelphia by Joseph Marona, the son of two West Indian immigrants. Joseph himself was born and raised in West Philadelphia, a depressed area of the city characterized by high unemployment, welfare dependency, and crime rates. For the next decade Accurate remained an obscure, if well-managed, small machine shop. Mr. Marona incorporated his business in 1969, and expanded his management team in 1970 with the addition of Frank Newman, who joined as treasurer, secretary, and vice president for marketing.

In retrospect the real break for Accurate occurred in 1975, when the company entered the Section 8(a) program. Membership in the program did not "make" Accurate overnight, however. The firm had built a solid business in the manufacture of tools, dies, and other precision-machined parts. Marona ascribed much of this initial success to his ghetto-recruited labor. The enthusiasm of former dole recipients for working in a business owned by "one of their own" permitted the timely completion of machining orders demanding close tolerances.

It was this commitment to neighborhood renewal that attracted the attention of President Carter during his visit to the area in October 1977. The presidential visit prompted Marona to present his case more directly in Washington, since his efforts to obtain government contract work had yielded little. In 1978 he approached his local congressman, Martin Crane, and described his firm as a redevelopment role model deserving of a fair chance in the competition for federal government contracts. Marona, like many other minority small businessmen and women, had encountered difficulties in getting his contract submissions through the Beltway bureaucracy in an effective manner—despite Accurate's Section 8(a) eligibility, and the SBA administrative and procedural assistance that supposedly went with such status.

Mr. Crane responded to Marona's request for assistance in getting a proper hearing by contacting several senior members of the Carter administration. He wrote letters to both Harold Brown, then secretary of Defense, and Clifford L. Alexander, Jr., then secretary of the Army, asking that Accurate get a fair hearing for an Army contract which the company sought. Initially this more or less routine overture by a congressional representative on behalf of one of his constituents did not bear fruit. Prior to 1980 Accurate performed limited work for the military, producing relatively unsophisticated items such as tow bars for military vehicles and air filters for helicopters.

In 1980, however, Accurate received recognition of its pioneering role in depressed West Philadelphia through the receipt of $4.2 million in Economic Development Administration loans. This money was in turn used by Marona and Newman to upgrade Accurate's capabilities and expand its capacity. Accurate's small size and limited product capabilities appeared to be a stumbling block in its attempts to get government, and especially Defense Department, work, despite its favored status under Section 8(a). Federal contract officials, and particularly those at the Pentagon, lacked confidence in Accurate's ability to complete contracts on time, in quantity, and according to specification—the old Catch-22 of minority businesses seeking government contracts. The EDA loans represented the chance for Accurate to achieve a critical mass in terms of capacity and also reconfigure its product capabilities so as to be better able to produce items more in demand by the military.

The arrival of the Reagan administration coincided with additional recognition of Accurate's efforts. During the 1980 presidential campaign Candidate Reagan had visited the street on which Accurate was headquartered. In 1981 Accurate won, under competitive bidding (and as such, outside the Section 8(a) program), an Army contract to produce suspension subassembly kits used in the rehabilitation of armored personnel carriers. The initial contract totaled $7.2 million, a large sum but not completely satisfactory in view of the extensive capital investments made by the company using the EDA money and the debt service associated with those loans. More contracts would be needed to justify the heavy long-term expenditures on plant and equipment.

Fortunately, however, during 1982, the year in which Accurate was due to leave the Section 8(a) program, the company received a $32 million dollar contract for small engines from the U.S. Army. The contract had not come easily, once again mainly because of a lack of Army confidence in the ability of Accurate to fulfill the contract on the desired schedule and for the amount which the Army had budgeted. This official skepticism persisted, despite Accurate's successful 1981 competitive bid, because the engine contract was not only much larger but was considered to be much more sophisticated. However, mobilizing all Accurate's contacts in Washington—principally Crane and a law firm with which the representative was associated and which had represented Accurate before federal agencies since 1980—Marona succeeded.

The role of the SBA had been crucial. In February 1981 Crane's chief administrative aide had called the SBA on behalf of Accurate, expressing the congressman's support for the efforts of the SBA to hire a consultant to help Accurate prepare its proposal for the engine contract. Early in 1982 SBA officials, accompanied by the Crane aide, visited Accurate's headquarters to help coordinate the overall negotiating strategy for the engine contract. The contract was finally awarded to Accurate in September 1982. An extension of the personnel carrier contract, given this time under the Section 8(a) program, was also awarded in September 1982, strengthening Accurate's foundation for the future.

After seven years in the Section 8(a) program Accurate had achieved "critical mass" and soon became a defense contractor of substantial size. By 1987 the company had received over $250 million dollars worth of Pentagon business, more than 90 percent of which was awarded under Section 8(a). For the Army it continued to produce engines and personnel carrier suspension subassemblies; additional contracts were won for personnel carrier cooling systems, M-60 tank parts, smoke grenade launchers, and floating platforms. Navy contracts included floating platforms and powered barges, some of which were utilized in key national defense programs. Again, Accurate was greatly assisted by SBA officials in overcoming Navy complaints about delays and shoddy work.

Not all the company's work for government buyers was for military purposes, or for that matter for official or even American buyers. By 1987 Accurate had been awarded (under 8(a)) contracts totaling $8.6 million by the U.S. Postal Service, albeit for the comparatively pedestrian production of all-purpose metal containers. Outside the United States the company had won a number of contracts, including one for electric generator engines from a West German firm, and from a number of foreign governments for personnel carrier modification kits.

Over time the nature of Accurate's responsibilities on its contracts became increasingly sophisticated. Initially the contracts awarded called for Accurate to produce subcomponents of a larger project or kits for modification of existing equipment. Increasingly, however, the purview of the contracts extended to what is known in the procurement lexicon as "configuration management," in which the contractor has overall responsibility for project coordination and is often involved in the design process and in development of specifications. Thus on the later barge contracts Accurate was charged with the development of accompanying software packages. And on the two Postal Service contracts Accurate did not even perform the actual manufacture of the metal containers, instead subcontracting this while providing administration, quality control, and engineering services. The company thus initiated a move toward offering higher value-added competences and products.

The growth represented by all this business necessitated a commensurate expansion of Accurate's work force and physical plant. By 1986 Accurate employed 1500 workers—up from only a few hundred in the early 1980s—1200 of whom were drawn from the ranks of West Philadelphia's residents. Production and marketing imperatives required substantial expansion at locations other than Philadelphia, however—including outside the United States. By mid-1986 Accurate had almost a dozen subsidiaries, situated in Michigan, Georgia, Delaware, and New York in the continental United States and in the Virgin Islands, Switzerland, and Israel overseas.

Accurate was proud of its manufacturing technology. Throughout its plants the company's process technology utilized CNC tooling, CAD/CAM, and advanced QC regimens. The Accurate shipyard on Lake Superior in Michigan is considered one of the most advanced in the United States, with modular construction methodology and fully automated steel fabrication, including plasma steel-cutting machines. Other plants employed welding robots. The company's attention to process technology permitted it to obtain Pentagon contracts requiring adherence to MIL-Q standards, the most stringent standards applied by the Department of Defense for the production of military equipment.

Accurate also initiated a significant in-house research and development program. Starting in 1980 the company embarked on a program to find commercial applications for a proprietary coating process. This patented technology facilitated the microcoating of metals, ceramics, silicons, plastics, cloth, and paper while minimizing the effect on the composition of the material being coated. Potential applications were thought to exist in the manufacture of semiconductor wafers and prototypes of circuit boards and in the coating of ceramic substrates and thermocouples.

The company's growing international reputation was also evidenced by two joint venture research and development agreements concluded with West German and Japanese firms. In 1984 Accurate agreed to collaborate with Wankel GmbH, a West German automotive company, in the development of a multifuel version of the rotary engine and in the invention of innovative air conditioning compressors, air compressors, and heat pumps. In 1986 the company concluded a joint development and distribution agreement with Sumitomo Corporation, a Japanese trading house, to commercialize the coating process described, known as low-temperature arc-vapor deposition (LTAVD). A similar indicator of the company's growing prominence was its involvement in commercial research: in 1985 Accurate was engaged by the Gas Research Institute of America to perform a $1.6 million research contract for the manufacture of small rotary engines to be used in residential cogeneration systems.

This expansion of business required significant amounts of investment capital, and as such Accurate began to attain a profile in the public capital markets—the first minority firm to do so. The company went public in the over-the-counter market in 1983, switched to the American Stock Exchange in late 1984, and was listed on the New York Stock Exchange in early 1986 (the achievement of a Big Board listing for a company less than three years after its initial public offering is itself an extraordinary feat). In addition to numerous equity offerings Accurate had by early 1987 sold over $115 million in straight and convertible long-term debt securities—being the first minority firm to access the public credit markets in such a fashion. In addition Accurate was able to raise over $60 million in medium- and long-term bank financings by 1987.

Accurate had become a $100 million business in 1985—up from $21 million in 1982—and this sales level was destined to continue increasing. In 1984 the company had been named one of the country's 100 fastest-growing small companies by *Inc.* magazine, and was rated third among them in terms of profitability. The company's management acknowledged their debt to the Section 8(a) program, stating in a disclosure document for one of its public securities offerings that

> the company believes that its experience in obtaining and performing United States Government contracts and its investments for property, plant, and equipment in connection with its contracts under the Section 8(a) program have prepared it to compete for contracts after the termination of its participation in the 8(a) program.

However, management ascribed Accurate's success mainly to management basics. The 1984 annual report described the company's progress in the following words:

> This success comes from two sources: First Accurate continues to do what it has always done very well—manufacturing everything from precision-machined components to the most demanding high-performance systems for military and industrial use. Second, Accurate is now on the cutting edge of new technology—coordinating the manufacture of an innovative pontoon structure for the U.S. Navy, developing new models of and applications for the rotary (Wankel) engine, and researching and testing a revolutionary coating process which has significant growth potential.

Government Redress of Market Imperfections: Procurement from Minority Firms

Exhibit 1 Characteristics of Minority-Owned Businesses Compared to All Businesses, 1982

	All Businesses	Businesses Owned by			
		All Minorities	Asians	Blacks	Hispanics[a]
Business ownership as a percentage of population	6.4%	1.8%	5.5%	1.3%	1.7%
All firms (thousands of dollars)	$14,545.7	$843.0	$255.6	$339.2	$248.1
Sales per firm (thousands of dollars)	$473.5	$53.8	$70.1	$36.7	$60.4
Firms with employees (thousands)	N.A.	127.8	49.3	38.6	39.9
Employees per firm (thousands)	N.A.	4.6	4.7	4.3	4.8
Sales per firm (thousands of dollars)	N.A.	$252.2	$264.8	$220.8	$266.9

[a]About 2.7 percent of Hispanics are also black according to unpublished data from the Bureau of the Census. The population with Spanish surnames was used to derive the mailing list of Hispanic business owners for the 1982 *Survey of Minority-Owned Business Enterprises.* Spanish surnames are considered a primary characteristic and race secondary in categorizing the Census data. Therefore, there may be some double counting—a maximum of 2.7 percent of Hispanic-owned businesses could possibly be categorized as black-owned businesses—among the Hispanic and black business owners surveyed. However, these small distortions should not significantly affect the distribution of minority businesses by race.

N.A.—Not applicable.

Sources: U.S. Department of the Treasury, Internal Revenue Service, Statistics of Income, *1978—1982 Partnership Returns* (Washington, D.C.: Government Printing Office, June 1985), Table 5.5; idem, *1982 Corporation Income Tax Returns* (Washington, D.C.: Government Printing Office, July 1985), Table 6; idem, *SOJ Bulletin* (Washington, D.C.: Government Printing Office, July 1984), Table 1; U.S. Department of Commerce, Bureau of Census, *Survey of Minority-Owned Business Enterprises, 1982, Asians, American Indians, and Other Minorities* (Washington, D.C.: Government Printing Office, August 1985); and idem, *Hispanic* (Washington, D.C.: Government Printing Office, September 1986).

Exhibit 2   Industry Distribution of Minority-Owned Franchises, 1985 (percent)

| Franchised Businesses | Franchises Owned by | | | |
	All Minorities	Oriental and American Indians	Blacks	Hispanics
Number of franchised establishments	9,147	3,039	3,399	2,709
Automotive Products and Services	17.3%	7.5%	26.2%	17.1%
Business Aids and Services	10.3	5.3	11.3	14.8
Construction, Home Improvement, Maintenance, and Cleaning Services	8.0	2.7	11.7	9.2
Convenience Store	8.5	19.1	3.0	3.6
Educational Products and Services	0.5	0.9	0.2	0.3
Restaurants (all types)	28.2	35.0	22.7	27.3
Hotels, Motels, and Campgrounds	2.8	7.9	0.1	0.4
Laundry and Dry Cleaning Services	1.5	1.3	1.9	1.1
Recreation, Entertainment, and Travel	1.6	0.6	1.9	2.5
Rental Services (auto-truck)	1.1	0.4	1.4	1.6
Rental Services (equipment)	0.2	0.1	0.2	0.4
Retailing (nonfood)	6.3	6.9	4.9	7.3
Retailing (food other than convenience stores)	12.9	11.9	13.8	13.1
Miscellaneous	0.8	0.4	0.7	1.3

Note: The Commerce survey does not include automobile and truck dealers, gasoline service stations, and soft drink bottlers, for which data were not collected. There were 2,090 business format franchises surveyed, with 342,495 total franchised establishments.

Source: U.S. Department of Commerce, *Franchising in the Economy, 1985–1987* (Washington, D.C.: Government Printing Office, January 1987), p. 44.

Exhibit 3   Federal Contract Actions Reported Individually, Small and Minority-Owned Businesses, Fiscal Year 1984 and 1985

| Contract Actions | Total ($000s) | | 1984–1985 % Change | Small Business Share | |
	1984	1985		1984	1985
Small business awards	$25,423,112	$25,246,877	-0.7	100.0%	100.0%
Minority-owned business awards	4,001,337	3,628,379	-9.3	15.7	14.4
8(a) awards	2,506,498	2,535,270	1.1	9.9	10.0

Source: Federal Procurement Data Center, "Special Report 86362" (prepared for the U.S. Small Business Adminstration, Office of Advocacy, April 24, 1986).

Exhibit 4   Federal Contract Actions Reported Individually, Minority-Owned and All Small Firms, by Federal Agency, Fiscal Year 1985 (percent)

Agency	Small Firm Awards	Minority Firm Awards	8(a) Awards
Department of Defense	81.7	74.0%	69.1%
Department of Energy	1.5	3.1	3.8
Department of Transportation	1.6	4.2	5.4
NASA	2.2	4.7	5.0
Veterans Administration	2.5	2.4	2.1
Other[a]	10.5	11.6	14.6
Total	100.0%	100.0%	100.0%

[a]For a list of agencies included, see Table A6.26.
Note: Date excluded for the Department of Defense for Fiscal Year 1984 and Fiscal Year 1985 are for prime contract actions over $25,000 rather than over $10,000.
Source: Federal Procurement Data Center, "Special Report 86361A" (prepared for the U.S. Small Business Administration, Office of Advocacy, April 25, 1986.)

ENDNOTES

1. *United States Code Congressional and Administrative News* (95th Congress, 2nd sess.), Vol. 1 (Washington, D.C.: Government Printing Office, 1978), 92 STAT 1762.
2. Ibid., 92 STAT 1762-63.
3. Ibid., 92 STAT 1767.
4. *The State of Small Business: A Report of the President,* transmitted to the Congress, 1987 (Washington, D.C.: Government Printing Office, 1987), p. 223.
5. Ibid., pp. xx, 242.
6. *The New York Times,* June 16, 1987, p. A35.
7. Ibid., July 5, 1987, Section 3, p. 6.
8. Ibid., June 16, 1987, p. A35.
9. Ibid., July 5, 1987, Section 3, p. 6.
10. *United States Code Congressional and Administrative News,* 92 STAT 1760.
11. *The New York Times,* May 12, 1987, p. A20.

Wedtech Corporation

It is fitting that as Wedtech enters its 22nd year it reaches a new level of maturity as a company. In the last two decades, Wedtech has passed through all the phases of corporate growth, weathering all the trials and tests of entrepreneurship to emerge as a seasoned defense contractor recognized for its product excellence and fully capable of holding its own in the competitive marketplace.

The Small Business Administration's 8(a) Program was, from the very beginning, more a financial vehicle for the Company than a marketing one. The Program entitled the Company to pursue grants, interest free loans, and government contracts in a favorable environment; however, the awarding of actual contracts was based on Wedtech's record of manufacturing excellence and success in competitive bidding....

Wedtech Corporation 1985 Annual Report, published May 1986

People like John Mariotta are heroes for the Eighties.

Ronald Reagan while campaigning in the South Bronx for the 1984 presidential election

If Wedtech was the proverbial American success story, these charges raise serious questions about the way we practice politics and conduct business in this city, state, and nation.

Rudolph W. Giuliani, the United States Attorney in Manhattan, announcing indictments in the Wedtech prosecution, June 1987

The story of Accurate Tooling related in the case "Government Redress of Market Imperfections: Procurement from Minority Firms" closely resembles the experience of the Wedtech Corporation while in the Section 8(a) Program. Wedtech was a defense contractor, founded in 1965 by an American of Puerto Rican parentage, John Mariotta—President Reagan's "hero for the Eighties." Its headquarters and principal operations were in the depressed South Bronx area of New York City. With the exception of the firm's name and location, and the names of two key figures—Frank Newman (really Fred Neuberger), and Martin Crane (really former U.S. Representative Mario Biaggi)—the story of Accurate Tooling is the story of Wedtech Corporation. The company entered receivership in late 1986 amid a welter of lawsuits and indictments. In early 1987 four top executives in the company agreed to comply fully with federal and New York State authorities in describing the real reasons for Wedtech's apparent success in the 8(a) program. The revelations of this "Gang of Four" described influence buying among politicians and bureaucrats in New York and Washington, including the White House, so extensive as to rival the

This case was prepared in 1988 from published sources by Andrew D. Regan, MBA 1988, and Professor George C. Lodge, as the basis for class discussion rather than to illustrate either effective or ineffective handling of an administrative situation.

ignominy of Tammany Hall and Teapot Dome. Another result of the alleged abuses was the compromise of U.S. and NATO security due to the award of contracts to Wedtech for which the company was inadequately equipped.

WEDTECH/ACCURATE TOOLING: THE REAL SECRET OF SUCCESS

In June 1987 a federal grand jury in Manhattan returned indictments against seven key figures associated with Wedtech. The indictments, which listed bribery, racketeering, fraud, and other charges, described the creation of a "racketeering enterprise" in which Wedtech gave millions of dollars in bribes to politicians and government officials, who in return helped the company to obtain hundreds of millions of dollars in government contracts. These alleged disbursements, difficult to value precisely as some were in the form of Wedtech stock and options and warrants to buy stock in Wedtech (the value of which fluctuated), included cash payments in excess of $5 million. The various stock, option, and warrant payments aggregated, at the times of their respective disbursements, an additional amount in excess of $5 million.

Among those indicted for allegedly receiving illegal payments were Mario Biaggi, a congressman from the Bronx; Stanley Simon, the former Bronx Borough president (a senior elected position in the New York City government); Peter P. Neglia, the former New York regional director of the Small Business Administration; the commander and deputy commander of the New York State National Guard; the partner responsible for Wedtech's account at the company's public accounting firm; and two "consultants" hired by Wedtech, seemingly through the intervention of E. Robert Wallach, a long-time confidant of Reagan aide and U.S. Attorney General Edwin Meese, III. Mr. Wallach had himself been hired as a consultant by Wedtech in 1981 and had at that time peppered Mr. Meese with memos, mailed to both home and office, urging him to aid Wedtech in getting a "fair hearing" before SBA and Department of Defense officials. (Warming to his work, Mr. Wallach presided at an "access lunch" for San Francisco area businessmen in 1983, at which he presented himself as one who could "communicate" their ideas and concerns to the White House.)[1] The indicted men were accused of exerting influence on behalf of Wedtech among federal officials with impact or potential impact on the process of contract assignment, in return for payment.

Ironically, a separate but related investigation in Maryland centered on two brothers who might have been expected to have had more regard for the proprieties of Section 8(a). The U.S. attorney's office in Maryland in 1987 accused Michael Mitchell, a Maryland state senator, and his brother, Clarence Mitchell III, a former state senator, of accepting $200,000 in 1984 and 1985 from Wedtech in return for using their influence on the company's behalf. A prime target of their efforts was their uncle, former Representative Parren Mitchell, a Maryland Democrat who headed the House Small Business Committee before retiring from the Congress in 1986 to become chairman of the Minority Business Enterprise Legal Defense and Education Fund. According to the Maryland Attorney General's office, the two brothers were paid to dissuade their uncle from spearheading an investigation into Wedtech. Parren Mitchell had repeatedly asked the SBA to conduct such an investigation, beginning in July 1984. It was largely through Parren Mitchell's efforts on the House Small Business Committee in the 1960s that the Section 8(a) program became law. Moreover, Clarence Mitchell II, brother of Parren and father of the two indicted brothers, was himself a prominent civil rights activist in the 1960s.

A further investigation conducted by a special federal prosecutor in Washington examined the relationships of Mr. Meese and Lyn C. Nofziger, another former Reagan White House aide, to Wedtech. Mr. Nofziger served as assistant to the president for Political Affairs from January 1981 to January 1982, directed the Reagan transition team preceding the first Reagan term, and had advised Mr. Reagan while he was governor of California. Mr. Nofziger was indicted in August 1987 on charges of violating the 1978 Ethics in Government Act by lobbying the White House on behalf of Wedtech within one year after leaving the Reagan administration in January 1982. During his employ as a consultant to Wedtech, Mr. Nofziger received cash and stock in Wedtech with a value in excess of $1 million. He was found guilty on February 11, 1988.

Finally yet another investigation connected with Wedtech's pursuit of federal contracts was brought to trial in the summer of 1987. A former U.S. Postal Service contract inspector, Jerrydoe E. Smith, pleaded guilty in August 1987 to charges of accepting a total of $20,000 in bribes on two occasions in 1985 and 1986 in connection with two contracts ($5.7 million and $2.9 million, respectively) for all-purpose metal containers. Wedtech won both contracts, only to subcontract the actual manufacture—an action in violation of guidelines governing Defense Department contracts, which require winning concerns to be the primary subcontractors on their respective contracts. Mr. Smith said he was actually paid the money by John Gnau, a former Reagan campaign aide and principal of a politically connected consulting firm who was given a three-year prison term for bribing Postal Service officials. The consulting firm of Gnau, Carter and Jacobsen arranged for Wedtech to gain control of a bankrupt shipyard on Michigan's Upper Peninsula. Gnau, Carter and Jacobsen then hired a key Navy official who had previously negotiated a pontoon contract with Wedtech.[2] This contract, awarded under Section 8(a), was initially assigned in late 1983 and expanded on subsequent occasions through July 1985 to a final total of $135 million—despite delayed and substandard performance by Wedtech in the interim.

Arguably the story of Wedtech's success is captured by an old Washington maxim: "you are who you know"—or in this case, pay. One measure of Wedtech's strength in this regard was the composition of its management team and board of directors—and their backgrounds before coming to Wedtech. In 1986 the board counted among its number the following luminaries: General Richard E. Cavazos, who retired in July 1984 as Commander of the U.S. Army Forces Command (and who described himself as a "self-employed management consultant," including among his clients the Wedtech Corporation); Verne Orr, secretary of the Air Force from 1981 until his retirement in 1985 and deputy director of the Reagan transition team; Bernard G. Ehrlich, deputy commander of the New York State National Guard and senior partner, with Mario Biaggi's son, in the law firm of Biaggi & Ehrlich, which represented Wedtech to federal agencies starting in 1980; and another major figure in New York state politics, Vito J. Castellano, who served Governor Mario Cuomo as chief of staff.

Also on the Wedtech board was W. Franklyn Chinn, a war refugee from Shanghai and former encyclopedia salesman. Mr. Chinn, along with another Wedtech "consultant," R. Kent London—himself a one-time executive of a waterbed manufacturer and a noted professional blackjack player who had changed his name twice—were sued in 1987 by Wedtech's new management. The company accused the two men of defrauding the company out of $1.14 million for "marketing" and "promotional" services in connection with the proprietary coating process, which was never successfully commercialized.[3] During 1985–1986 Mr. Chinn, introduced to Mr. Meese by Mr. Wallach, also administered a "limited blind partnership" on behalf of Mr. and Mrs. Meese which the Office of Government Ethics later judged was not in compliance with the guidelines laid out in the 1978 Ethics in Government Act.

In December 1987 the grand jury also indicted both Mr. Wallach and Mr. Chin on charges of racketeering, fraud, and conspiracy. The court-appointed prosecutor, James McKay, said he didn't have evidence "as of this date" to conclude that Mr. Meese "knowingly participated in criminal activity" involving Wedtech, adding that he was "actively investigating" other "issues and questions" involving Mr. Meese, "which do not lend themselves to immediate resolution."[4]

The Wedtech management team included other notable persons. James O. Aspin, brother of Congressman Les Aspin, chairman of the House Armed Services Committee, was appointed senior vice president for marketing in June 1986, having finished a long stint as an executive of an airport ground service and commuter airline company which went bankrupt midway through his period with the company. Howard Kegley, who joined the company in October 1984 as a vice president, rose to senior vice president of marketing in May 1985, and eventually became a director. Mr. Kegley had spent the decade preceding his arrival at Wedtech as a special project officer for the Defense Department's M-113 Family of Vehicles Program—a program for which Wedtech received several no-bid contracts to produce suspension subassembly kits. Interestingly, Mr. Aspin assumed the key post of SVP-Marketing in June 1986 at a time when the crucial "marketing" work required to obtain the initial M-113 contracts had presumably been completed by his predecessor, Mr. Kegley, the former M-113 administrator. Alfred Rivera, another fast-tracker who had joined the company in 1982 as assistant controller only to become treasurer, senior vice president for finance, and a director by 1984, had spent the four years preceding his arrival at Wedtech as an auditor employed by the Defense Contract Audit Agency, a government office which works with the Defense Department in monitoring contract assignments and performance. Indeed, all told four auditors who had examined the company's operations for the government under the auspices of the DCAA were subsequently employed by Wedtech.

A final Wedtech employee was James E. Jenkins, deputy to Edwin Meese while the latter was counsel to the president. Mr. Jenkins was the convener of a critical May 1982 White House meeting called to allow Wedtech to make its pitch directly to Army and SBA officials in the most congenial atmosphere possible. This meeting had been arranged through the intervention of Mr. Nofziger and Mr. Wallach, both paid "consultants" to Wedtech and both long-time acquaintances of Mr. Meese. The meeting was attended by Wedtech executives, SBA staff, representatives from the Army, and by Mark Bragg, Nofziger's partner in his consulting firm. Members of the "Gang of Four" indicated that it was at this meeting—arranged largely through the efforts of Mr. Nofziger, efforts described as illegal under the Ethics in Government Act by the Washington special prosecutor—that the key $32 million Army engine contract, awarded in September 1982, was won, opening the door to the even larger Army and Navy barge contracts. A former SBA official testified: "Frankly, we would not have gone along with the contract had it not been for Mr. Jenkins's interest."[5] And Lyn Nofziger in a letter to Meese suggested that "even Reagan" could help persuade the Army to give Wedtech the contract.[6] [The reluctance of the Army to assign the contract to Wedtech had something to do with cost. Originally Wedtech had bid $99 million for the engine contract, for which the Army had budgeted what it thought was a generous $19 million(!).][7]

In addition to these allegations of influence buying, Wedtech was also alleged to have violated rules and procedures of the Section 8(a) program. By 1981 the founder, chairman and chief executive officer, John Mariotta, had lost effective control of daily management, and probably all important managerial policy, to Mr. Neuberger and others—a violation of the Section 8(a) guidelines. Mr. Mariotta was unceremoniously sacked in January 1986, shortly after Wedtech had received an additional $150 million in new 8(a) contracts, and shortly before Wedtech voluntarily left the 8(a) program in March 1986. The company remained in the 8(a) program after its August 1983 initial public offering (IPO), despite the fact that publicly held companies were ineligible to participate. The multimillion-dollar fortune which accrued to Mr. Mariotta as a result of the IPO—well in excess of the already generous $750,000 ceiling—was also grounds for Wedtech's removal from the program. The company argued that Mr. Mariotta remained "economically disadvantaged" when compared to such multibillion-dollar contractors as General Dynamics, Grumman, and Lockheed.[8] The SBA did not act, and Wedtech remained eligible for set-asides. (Wedtech's work force had long numbered more than 500, the SBA's program limitation, but had remained eligible for SBA aid nevertheless.)

Moreover at the time of the initial public offering Mr. Mariotta lost ownership control of the company, another requirement for 8(a) eligibility. When the SBA began proceedings to remove Wedtech on this ground, the company allegedly put its case for continued eligibility first to the SBA's regional administrator, Peter Neglia, and then to more senior SBA officials familiar with Wedtech.[9] In January 1984 the SBA approved a complicated transaction in which 31 percent of the company's stock was transferred to Mr. Mariotta's name by Mr. Neuberger and others—although the transfer was actually to an escrow fund, where the stock was supposed to remain until Mr. Mariotta could find the money to pay for it, even if that process took years.[10] Prosecutors claim this transaction was a ruse to retain the company's minority-owned status, and indeed one member of the Gang of Four described it as "a sham arrangement."[11]

And Wedtech management demonstrated an ability to abuse the government entirely on its own. Over $6 million in false invoices were submitted during a cash crunch under 8(a)'s "advanced payments" initiative, which constitutes essentially an interest-free loan program. This maneuver was concealed for a time through the good offices of a partner in Wedtech's auditing firm—whose departure from accepted accounting practice was allegedly motivated by a multi-million bribe. Wedtech management allegedly also arranged "sweetheart" deals with the company's prinicpal unions, including the Teamsters, distributing bribes in return for labor peace and speed in the construction of its Bronx plants.

In the end, Wedtech remained in the Section 8(a) program long after the normal seven-year limitation expired in 1982 (and well after the "grandfather" period granted in 1978 expired in 1985). The company's ability to do so depended on the acquiescence of the highest SBA officials, including SBA head James C. Sanders, who in December 1983 had assisted Wedtech in getting its first Navy pontoon contract. The lion's share of the contracts Wedtech received under Section 8(a)—well over $200 million of the aggregate $251 million awarded—was assigned between 1983 and 1986. These contracts accounted for 90–95 percent of Wedtech's net revenues in this time period.

By year-end 1985 Wedtech was a publicly held company, the only one ever to be included in the 8(a) program—for which, indeed, publicly held companies were ineligible—with a market capitalization exceeding $100 million, borrowings and assets approaching $200 million, and sales approximating $120 million. And yet Wedtech not only retained its 8(a) eligibility, but continued to be awarded very sizable contracts despite a demonstrated record of nonperformance which eventually compromised national security.

THE NAVY CONTRACT

In 1983, the first slice of what by the 1990s would be a $700–800 million U.S. Navy contract was awarded to Wedtech for the construction of more than 700 different types of lighters, floating piers and causeways. This equipment was urgently needed to make operational the Navy's contribution to the Rapid Deployment Force, a fast-attack group capable of deploying U.S. troops anywhere in the world on short notice. The Navy was responsible for providing 18 ships equipped with sophisticated gear to provide oil, water, ammunition, aircraft parts, weapons, and other supplies to troops on shore. These were called Maritime Preposition Ships (MPS).

Admiral T. J. Hughes, deputy chief of naval operations (Logistics), had the staff responsibility for overseeing the assembling and equipping of the MPS squadrons. Responsibility for selecting the firm to build the lighters, piers, and causeways to allow the MPS ships to perform their mission lay with Everett Pyatt, assistant secretary of the Navy (Shipbuilding and Logistics). Mr. Pyatt had decided to use an 8(a) firm for the task, and the Small Business Administration had selected Wedtech. From the beginning, Admiral Hughes was doubtful that Wedtech had the capability to do the job, and he said so, but to no avail.

By January 1984, Wedtech was substantially behind in its obligations; Hughes objected to an additional $24.5 million contract to be awarded that April. He was overruled.

On November 21, 1984, Admiral J. P. Jones, commander, Naval Facilities and Engineering Command, in charge of the technical development of lighterage, wrote Pyatt's deputy of his concerns about Wedtech, citing "many weaknesses in the contractor's performance of cost and price analysis," and urged him to "reconsider" the contract (Exhibit 1). Three weeks later, on December 11, the chief of naval matériel, R. A. Miller, wrote Pyatt himself concerning a $26 million difference between Wedtech's proposal for continued work and the Navy's cost estimate (Exhibit 2). And on December 24, in a handwritten memorandum, Admiral Hughes wrote Pyatt, noting Wedtech's excessive pricing and informing him that the company's "first powered causeway has failed its first article test" (Exhibit 3).

The situation got progressively more serious; in February 1985, Admiral Hughes, deeply concerned about providing his MPS squadrons with critical lighterage elements, urged Pyatt to "take immediate action to move causeway procurement out of the SBA arena . . ., open our program to the benefits of competition, send a clear message to Wedtech of the seriousness of the situation, and limit exposure to a complete default." He said that estimates of the company's "ability to deliver were dismal at best" (Exhibit 4).

When Pyatt refused to act, Hughes again wrote on May 5, less than a month later: "We are past the point of simple schedule slippages and are now dealing with a very real degradation of our sealift offload capability. . . . We have had to make several decisions that effectively reduced overall readiness." Delays of up to one year and shoddy work were, he said, "reducing the Navy's amphibious assault capability" (Exhibit 5). Pyatt remained steadfast. When in October he sent word to Hughes approving competitive bidding on the project, it was too late to make a difference.

Pyatt explained his actions in approving the April 1984 contract in testimony before the Senate Subcommittee on Oversight of Government Management of the Committee on Governmental Affairs on September 30, 1987. Pyatt had a long and respected career as a civil servant in the Navy shipbuilding program (Exhibit 6). From June 1981 to August 1984 he had been principal deputy and acting assistant secretary in charge of shipbuilding. In August his nomination to be assistant secretary was sent from the president to Congress for approval. For some nine months prior to that time his nomination had been held in the White House.

In the summer of 1983, Pyatt testified, he had opposed including the pontoon causeway project in the 8(a) set-aside program because it was too big and complex. In November James Sanders, SBA administrator, officially requested that the project be placed under 8(a). The Navy rejected the request. Sanders appealed the rejection to the secretary of the Navy (Exhibit 7). In December Pyatt reconsidered and on January 6, 1984, finally agreed to the work being done under 8(a). Pressed by the senators as to why he changed his mind Pyatt would only say that it was the force of Sanders's argument. "I knew that in many places in the country, minorities do this work, and there was no reason why a minority business could not do this work."

On January 30, 1984 Sanders designated Wedtech as the firm to do the work.

Senator Carl Levin asked: "Your agency did have the right to refuse the selection of the SBA if it wanted to, did it not?"

Pyatt: "Yes, sir."

He said he did not refuse, however, because the Navy Facilities report on Wedtech stated: "The contractor can technically and physically do the job. However, he cannot meet the schedule." Acknowledging that the schedule was important to the Navy, Pyatt decided to go ahead with Wedtech anyway. At the same time, he testified that Admiral Hughes's objections were "totally legitimate."

"Tom and I have had a very long and professional working relationship; we air our views about various topics to each other as they go on, and we try to sort them out and do what seems to be the best at the time."

As Wedtech's performance deteriorated, Pyatt said that he called Lyn Nofziger and Mark Bragg to "try to get their help to get their client moving." He steadfastly denied that he had received political pressure from the White House or any other source.

In December 1986 the contract was terminated for default. Wedtech had delivered approximately two-thirds of the items for which the Navy had contracted.

THE ACHILLES' HEEL: PRINCIPLE OR PRACTICE?

In spite of Wedtech's infamous record, the larger questions raised by the company's actions are likely to remain a matter of controversy. Should the federal govenrment attempt the redress of perceived discrimination, both past and present, through active intervention in the market economy, and if it should, how—or can—such involvement be managed efficiently and without abuse? Or should Wedtech rightfully be the Waterloo of such governmental efforts?

In the immediate aftermath of the scandal the federal government seemed to be of two minds on the issue. In March 1987 a bipartisan group of congressmen introduced a bill (passed later in the year) to reform the 8(a) program which would increase the fine for defrauding the SBA from $50,000 to $300,000, introduce limits to the size of govenrment contracts that can be set aside for minority businesses, require reporting of consulting fees, and restrict the number of political appointees administering the program. As the House Small Business Committee Chairman John LaFalce, said at the time, "I'm not interested in making minority companies into *Fortune* 500 businesses."[12] At the same time legislation passed in November 1986 significantly increasing the amount of budgeted defense dollars to be awarded to minority contractors remained in effect. The Reagan administration favored the continuation of the program throughout the controversy, its vocal free market orientation notwithstanding.

Principle and Practice

Critics of the 8(a) program typically base their opposition either on a rejection of the principle of affirmative action or on despair of its realization in practice. Thus there are those who perceive discrimination and believe government action appropriate in principle, but unimplementable in action, and there are those who perceive discrimination but believe government intervention, of any kind, in the economy to be both inappropriate in principle and self-defeating, if not counter-productive, in practice. (There are no doubt others who, out of myopia or conscious choice, perceive no discrimination and thus consider the issue to be moot.)

Many who adhere to the principle of government redress of the imperfections and excesses of an essentially market-oriented economy had in the years since the 1960s grown increasingly dubious about the efficacy of government intervention. This concern focused not on questions of efficiency—the sacrifice of which was deemed acceptable in the service of equity—but rather on the actual *administration* of such programs, which seemed almost inevitably haunted by abuses. Hence the question of managing the 8(a) program is all-important.

Principle   While the March 1987 reform bill was aimed at eliminating abuses—and thus at the practice of the program—the same period witnessed several attacks on the underlying principle of preferential action to redress discrimination. Two such assaults came within a week of each other in April 1987. Both were within the judicial system, where the landmark Fullilove decision of 1980, sanctioning set-asides, was disputed. In the U.S. Court of Appeals for the Ninth Circuit in San Francisco, a San Francisco city ordinance conferring a 10 percent set-aside and a 5 percent bidding preference on minority-owned business seeking city contracts was struck down. In the first major rejection of a set-aside plan, the court concluded that the city had not demonstrated adequately that discrimination was the cause of the historically low level of city contract awards to minority firms.

The majority opinion maintained that "the city is not like the Federal Government" in that congressional action reflects the input of the wide spectrum of interests internalized in the federal structure, and as such it is only through its mediation that individual rights are adequately protected from political expediency. Moreover, the court asserted that "Unlike Congress, state or local governments do not have the power to discriminate on the basis of race simply to dispel the lingering effects of societal discrimination." This conclusion appeared to contradict the recent emphasis in Washington and elsewhere on the rights and abilities of states to administer official programs, especially social and economic initiatives, formerly implemented directly by the federal government.[13]

While the San Francisco decision seemed merely to locate the responsibility for redress with the federal government, the second decision, also in April 1987, found that a set-aside clause in a bid solicitation prospectus was unconstitutional. The prospectus, prepared to attract bids for construction work at the Fulton County–Brown Field airport near Atlanta, had specified that the contract would be awarded to the lowest bidder also complying with Fulton County's set-aside goals, or demonstrating good faith efforts to do so. The lowest bidders, contending that they had also made good faith efforts to comply with the goals, sued when the contract was awarded to another contractor. The federal district judge presiding ruled the set-aside program was unconstitutional, concluding that "no such discrimination was ever established." Going further the judge asserted that the operation of subtle forces—such as a lack of equity capital, difficulty in securing financing, inability to obtain bonding, lack of adequate management and operational skills, and the state of the economy—is, at most, a form of societal discrimination beyond a governmental agency's competence or authority to address.[14]

Practice   Rejections of the principles underlying the Section 8(a) program, such as that embodied by the Atlanta decision, have not been as common as the identification of problems of managing an initiative like 8(a). After all, approximately one-half of all military contracts are awarded as a matter of course without competitive bidding. Perhaps more surprising, this method has not been effectively challenged, despite the Reagan administration's much-touted efforts to introduce competition in big-ticket procurement, and recurring scandals, bringing only minimal disciplinary action, beside which those of Wedtech seem immaterial. Or as Parren Mitchell, a critic of Wedtech but not of 8(a)-like initiatives, expressed it, "We have cases where defense contractors have overcharged the Government by some $5 billion. But no one is telling them that they can no longer do business with the Government."[15]

Some of those who recognized problems nevertheless thought the program fundamentally sound as it was presently constituted, with only minimal reform needed. In the words of Congressman Nicholas Mavroules (D., Mass.), an architect of the March 1987 reform legislation, "We have worked out a reform bill that is aimed at restoring integrity to this program so that the minority community does not suffer from the greed of a few people and a faulty administrative system it had no hand in shaping."[16] Others were not so certain that limited reform was sufficient. The United States Commission on Civil Rights had expressed serious reservations when it had called for a one-year suspension of the program in 1986, before the Wedtech scandal had come to light, concluding that the program had not proven to be effective. And still others asserted that such initiatives are inevitably plagued by abuse and thus not manageable. John W. Sroka, executive director of the occupational division of the Associated General Contractors of America, which is opposed to all preferential programs, opined: "They're classic examples of a system that has been irrevocably corrupted."[17]

The problems of administration are legion. One very basic issue is eligibility, the definition of the person or persons to be assisted. As Senator Daniel Patrick Moynihan, the New York Democrat who has been involved in minority issues for a generation, observed: "This is an issue that troubles me. After all, there were slave-owning families in Puerto Rico in the 19th century. Do individuals from those families, too, qualify as disadvantaged minority group members?"[18] The legislation admonishes the SBA that in its determination of a person's eligibility it "shall consider, but not be limited to, the assets and net worth of such socially disadvantaged individual." This elastic language, abused in the case of Wedtech, could result, for example, in the son of a prosperous fourth-generation doctor of Hispanic ancestry benefiting from Section 8(a), while the accent-burdened, ill-educated, first-generation son of Welsh coal miner immigrants to remote Appalachia probably would not. Others have no problem with this basic issue. Commenting on the continued eligibility of John Mariotta after he became a multimillionaire in Wedtech's IPO, Henry Wilfong, who headed the 8(a) program in 1984, explained: "We ought to say to poor Hispanics and blacks this is the American dream."[19]

Another obstacle to effective administration is the almost inevitable politicization and subjectivity of the program. The March 1987 reform bill targeted this danger with provisions specifically prohibiting any action based on political affiliation or political activity, and limiting the number of political appointees participating in the management of the program. But the role of purely political influences has been strong in the past, with decisions made on the basis of merit at lower levels in the SBA being reversed higher up the chain of command. Charles Heatherly, acting administrator of the SBA during the initial period after the disclosure of Wedtech's abuses, perceived the tension of politics and merit upon his arrival at the SBA: "The front-line staff did not know whether they [were] supposed to be sensitive to political whims or the standards in front of them."[20] The lack of competitive bidding suggests that this tension will remain despite the provisions contained in the reform bill.

Another management issue is the development of dependency among program participants. John F. Robinson, president of the National Minority Business Council, a New York–based group of about 300 minority businesspersons, described this phenomenon: "I've seen minority firms go from $20 million in business to zero overnight because they graduated from 8(a)."[21] There is some evidence suggesting that this tendency is as unavoidable as politicization. The 1986 study of companies participating in the 8(a) program in the years since 1975 found that less than 50 out of more than 4,000 were still in existence in 1986. Is the Section 8(a) environment inherently too cozy, with the vast majority of participants becoming hopeless junkies of "reverse discrimination"? Indeed the addiction may be supported by forces other than Washington, with similar ill-effects. Joe E. Harris, the manager of minority business development for Polaroid, recalled one incident: "I saw one company accept shipments of bad diodes from a black supplier for years, without ever telling him they were bad. White buyers are sometimes too sensitized, too afraid of being called a bigot if they deliver bad news."[22]

An allied concern is the military orientation of the contracts often targeted by 8(a) companies as the most lucrative. As the program was itself designed to help young minority companies gain the "critical mass" which would enable them to compete in the private economy, it is arguably inconsistent logically to wean those companies on military contracts. Such early experience with defense work, by definition performed for the federal government, might ensure that 8(a) participants would keep coming back to the public sector once mature. Norma B. Leftwich, director of the Pentagon's office of small and disadvantaged business utilization, expressed concern about the result of this concentration on defense work, and the allied issue of dependency:

> Should we really focus the minority business community on government work? In the 8(a) set-aside programs, we've seen firms enjoy very rapid growth in a very sheltered market, growth they could not hold onto in the world at large. I'm not sure these programs are in the best interests of minority business.[23]

Most serious, however, are the peculiarities of processing noncompetitive bids in a large political bureaucracy. Care must be exercised to ensure that ineligible firms do not abuse the noncompetitive privilege. At the same time, however, if this process is overly cautious, it almost forces potential participants, who are ignorant of—or perhaps daunted by—the procedures, to circumvent them, often illegally. Wilfredo J. Gonzalez, the SBA's associate administrator for minority small business and capital ownership development, described how his agency's scrutiny intensified over time: "When 8(a) started, certification was done with a handshake. We got duped by fronts, companies that were not really minority-owned. So we have no choice but to be comprehensive."[24]

The solution was thus seen to be an exhaustive program of authentication centering on the completion of numerous forms and the provision of reams of documentation. Moreover, applications are reviewed at three levels of the SBA apparatus: district authorities, regional authorities, and the SBA headquarters in Washington. Obviously the process is time-consuming—a minimum of two months, SBA officials confirm, and typically much longer. The process is an anguishing one for harried and often unsophisticated minority entrepreneurs, consumed already, as are most small businesspersons, with simply running their businesses. Ralph C. Thomas III, the executive director of the National Association of Minority Contractors, explained that

> By the time many minority-owned companies figure out how the system works, it's time to go. Some of these firms don't get their first government contract under the 8(a) program for three years. Unfortunately, the program awards contracts on a random basis with no clear guidelines for which 8(a) firms should be given priority over others.[25]

Over time the enormity and caprice of the process has had a sinister effect, one which is at the heart of both the Wedtech episode and the administrative conundrum represented by the 8(a) program. Faced first with the strain of the application, and then with delay or failure apparently due to a lack of knowledge of the realities of the federal bureaucracy, minority businessmen, even honest ones, begin to seek help from former and current politicians and officials who offer themselves as "consultants," with knowledge of "the system" and appropriate contacts. Benjamin L. Hooks, the executive director of the National Association for the Advancement of Colored People, sees this recourse to the "consulting" fraternity as both inevitable and the source of the 8(a)'s problems:

> First, successfully obtaining a contract involves long accumulated experience and a network of contacts in both the private and public sectors. Blacks long possessed neither. History is not undone by fiat overnight....After a few years butting heads against walls, some potential minority contractors began to get the word: In government, it is who you know that makes the difference. This became translated into the utilization of the middleman, the power broker—elected and appointed officials and their friends. And so we have Wedtech.[26]

Indeed the malicious effects of the process are such as to render the very identification of actual abuses difficult. The absence of competitive bidding

virtually ensures that resourceful minority businesses will prevail on local politicians and others with influence upon those in control of federal contracts to do
whatever can be done "subjectively." As long as these efforts are made without
compensation, they are legal, part and parcel of of representative politics in a
pluralist democracy. They may also be legal if, although indeed compensated, they
can be represented to authorities as not having been compensated, with the
compensation having been paid for services rendered other than the exertion of
influence. This is often the case with fees for consulting and legal work. Gerard
Lynch, a professor at Columbia Law School and a former Manhattan prosecutor,
speculated at the time of the June 1987 indictments in the Wedtech case that the
lawyers for the defendants would probably follow this tack: "The defense is likely to
be that the payments were entirely separate from whatever influence was
exercised."[27]

CONCLUSION

On balance the principle of preferential treatment of minority small businesses, in
the case of the Section 8(a) program through set-asides, withstood the storm of
criticism which descended in the aftermath of Wedtech. The implementation of
legislation passed in November 1986 directing the Pentagon to increase the
involvement of minority contractors in its procurement to 5, and ultimately 10,
percent of total budgeted spending was not blocked. (The Defense Department will
itself administer this new initiative using a "self-certification" process for interested
firms.)

The issue of practice, however, remained as vexing as before. Indeed,
administration is if anything more problematic than before, in view of the huge
increase in minority participation which must be managed—and managed by a new
player, the Defense Department—if the expansion mandated in November 1986 is
to be achieved. Perhaps all that can be recommended is flexibility in developing
managerial and administrative methods as the program itself develops. As Ms.
Leftwich, the Defense Department official responsible for small and disadvantaged
business, speculated about the prospects of attaining the new goals:

> It will take at least a year before we know whether the goal is obtainable.... We see it
> as a program that will evolve as we determine what works. There are no answers yet
> to the questions of whether we can get there or how fast we can get there.[28]

However others, such as William Safire, a columnist for *The New York Times*,
saw only the prospect of more abuse, believing this particular intersection of
government and business to be unmanageable:

> Favoritism tends to corrupt; racial favoritism in procurement corrupts both
> government and corporation.[29]

ENDNOTES

1. *The New York Times*, June 22, 1987, p. B6.
2. *Business Week*, June 22, 1987, p. 46.
3. *The New York Times*, June 22, 1987, p. B6.
4. *The Wall Street Journal*, December 23, 1987, pp. 2 and 5.
5. *The New York Times*, January 31, 1988, p. 28.
6. Ibid., January 22, 1988, p. A15.
7. *The Wall Street Journal*, January 19, 1987, p. 1B.
8. *The New York Times,* January 19, 1987, p. 1B.
9. Ibid.
10. Ibid.
11. *Business Week,* October 5, 1987, p. 34.
12. *The Wall Street Journal,* June 25, 1987, p. 60
13. *The New York Times,* May 18, 1987, p. B2.
14. Ibid.
15. Ibid., May 12, 1987, p. A20.
16. Ibid.
17. Ibid.
18. Ibid., June 7, 1987, Section 4, p. 8.
19. Ibid., December 14, 1987, Section 4, p. 6.
20. Ibid.
21. Ibid., July 5, 1987, Section 3, p. 6.
22. *The New York Times,* July 5, 1987, Section 3, p. 6.
23. Ibid.
24. Ibid.
25. Ibid., May 12, 1987, p. A20.
26. *The New York Times,* June 16, 1987, p. A25.
27. Ibid., June 7, 1987, Section 4, p. 8.
28. Ibid., July 5, 1987, Section 3, p. 7.
29. Ibid., April 30, 1987, p. A31.

Exhibit 1

DEPARTMENT OF THE NAVY
Naval Facilities Engineering Command
200 Stovall Street
Alexandria, VA 22332

21 November 1984

MEMORANDUM FOR THE PRINCIPAL DEPUTY, ASSISTANT
SECRETARY OF THE NAVY
(Shipbuilding and Logistics)

Via: Chief of Naval Material (MAT 02)
Subj: POWERED CAUSEWAYS

1.   Your direction of November 19, 1984 to proceed with the exercise of the fiscal year 1985 contracts with Wedtech, the prime contractor, has been received. It is respectfully requested that you reconsider your direction to initiate the option procurement by means of a start work order with a minimum fund obligation of 50% of the estimated cost for the following reasons:

Exhibit 1 (Continued)

a. The preliminary business clearance for the Government prenegotiation position is presently being finalized at a Government estimate of $42 million for the entire FY 85 procurement. The contractor's position for the option is currently at $68 million.

b. The Defense Contract Administration Service Region for New York has recently conducted a contractor system review of Wedtech's purchase policies and is withholding approval of the system. Specifically DCASMA, New York has highlighted many weaknesses in the contractor's performance of cost and price analysis, single/sole ordering, documentation of procurement files, review and negotiations of vendors' quotations and competitive practices.

c. Issuance of letter contract in a not-to-exceed amount prior to formalization of firm fixed price will result in the need for distinct contract or controls to isolate costs incurred on the letter contract vice cost incurred under prior firm fixed price basic contract, an almost impossible administrative requirement. In addition, the Government will find it necessary to apply additional resources to verify, if not in fact control subcontractor and vendor orders and awards for material required for the option quantities.

d. Issuance of letter contract at this time will minimize contractor desire to reach full and final agreement on firm fixed price in an expeditious matter as it is to his advantage to accumulate actual cost vice forward pricing.

e. Award of the entire option by means of a letter contract will foreclose any realistic Government option to seek other means of production in the event negotiations of firms fixed price fail, except by a termination for convenience and its associated unnecessary additional costs.

2. Once again I request that you reconsider the direction given concerning the award of a letter contract. Should you desire additional discussion on this point, please be assured that I or my Assistant Commander for Contracts, Mr. Joe Cowden, am available to amplify on the points raised.

> J. P. Jones, Jr.
> Rear Admiral, CEC, U.S. Navy
> Commander

Exhibit 2

DEPARTMENT OF THE NAVY
Headquarters Naval Material Command
Washington, D.C. 20360

In Reply Refer to
Ser. 09/1326
11 Dec. 1984

FIRST ENDORSEMENT on NAVFAC MEMORANDUM FOR THE PRINCIPAL
DEPUTY, ASSISTANT SECRETARY OF THE NAVY
(SHIPBUILDING LOGISTICS) of 21 NOV 84

From: Chief of Naval Material
To: Assistant Secretary of the Navy (Shipbuilding and Logistics)
Subj: POWERED CAUSEWAYS
Ref: (a) Phone Conversation ASSTSECNAV SL and VCNM 26 Nov 1984

1. During reference (a) you rescinded your direction to initiate the option
procurement by means of a start work order with a minimum fund
obligation of 50 percent of the estimated cost. In its place you directed
that we should proceed toward contract award in an expeditious manner
in consonance with good practices. To this end, Wedtech's proposal has
been evaluated by NAVFAC and a pre-negotiation business clearance has
been approved by my staff. There is now a $26 million difference between
the Wedtech proposal of $68M and the NAVFAC pre-negotiation position
of $42M. I have directed that negotiations proceed on an expedited basis
and while difficult negotiations are anticipated, I am hopeful that a
mutually satisfactory business arrangement can be negotiated within the
next thirty days. I have requested NAVFAC to provide an update on their
negotiations by 10 December 1984. Hopefully, Wedtech will approach these
negotiations with the same degree of concern and desire to expeditiously
reach an agreement.

2. I will keep you apprised of our progress.

R. A. Miller, VCNM

Copy to:
COMNAVFACENGCOM

Exhibit 3

DEPARTMENT OF THE NAVY
Office of the Chief of Naval Operations

Date: 12/24/84

MEMORANDUM

FROM: DEPUTY CHIEF OF NAVAL OPERATIONS (LOGISTICS)
TO: ASSISTANT SECRETARY OF THE NAVY (Shipbuilding and Logistics)
SUBJ: WEDTECH Causeway Contract FY 85

NAVFAC PM still negotiating hard. The Government offered a labor rate and mfr overhead rate for Michigan; Wedtech reply received 21 Dec. and is being analyzed. Agreement reached on these rates for the New York yard.

The Wedtech price has come down from $68M to $59.5 (still at significant odds with government estimate of fair market value $42M). Problem still being worked. We could not afford $59.5M even if the price was right.

The first powered causeway has *FAILED* its first article test—68 outstanding items; 66 are minor and easily rectified, and two are more serious, but correctable.

  a. Undersized steering hydraulic pump shaft was jury-rigged and gave under load.

  b. Failed to weld both flanges of a stiffener. Anticipate another 10-day ship.

The PM (project manager) has requested permission to stop further negotiation of the FY 85 contract to put the pressure on the contractor. Since his assembly line is starting to produce components for the FY 85 option, this will impact him. However, we're at a point that delays could impact timeliness of delivery for MPS-2.

I would ask your concurrence to continue negotiations but threaten to break off at some point (perhaps about mid-January) if no success in further negotiation. We should then consider competitive bid and accept delay in causeways for MPS-2.

Very truly,

T. J. Hughes

copy to
0/42
Capt DEVICQ

Exhibit 4

DEPARTMENT OF THE NAVY
Office of the Chief of Naval Operations
Washington, D.C. 20350

In Reply Refer to
4020
Ser. 424/5U392819
20 Feb. 85

From: Deputy Chief of Naval Operations (Logistics)
To: Assistant Secretary of the Navy (Shipbuilding and Logistics)
Subj: PROCUREMENT OF CAUSEWAY SYSTEMS UNDER
SBA 8(a) SET-ASIDE

1. On 13 February I met with NAVFAC, MSC, and Mr. Saldivar from your staff to discuss the current status of causeway procurements to outfit Maritime Prepositioning Ships. We reviewed the current status as well as WEDTECH's efforts to get well. Estimates of their ability to deliver were dismal at best. As it now stands, it is optimistic to expect the final delivery of MPS-1 lighterage before October 1985. This is a full year after the original delivery date of the first powered causeway sections (29 October 84).

2. As you know, we were ready to start fielding MPS-1T late last year. All the Marine Corps equipment and Navy Support Element equipment have been ready to load when the ships were available, except for critical lighterage elements provided by WEDTECH. This puts the navy in the uncomfortable position of having a large investment in equipment at sea to respond to crises which cannot offload in the stream in the required five days. After careful review of WEDTECH's progress to date, the problems they are still experiencing and the prognosis for recovery, I now consider it imperative that we take what action we can to limit the exposure to their inability to perform.

3. I strongly recommend, in the interest of limiting risk, that we take immediate action to move causeway procurement out of the SBA arena with our FY 86 procurement. This action would open our program to the benefits of competition, send a clear message to WEDTECH of the seriousness of the situation, and limit exposure to a complete default. This action, as I explained to Mr. Saldivar, would not eliminate WEDTECH from competing if they should get on their feet. In our deliberations we determined that not giving the FY-85 option to WEDTECH would probably result in a further five-month delay. I have no doubt that WEDTECH will offer us many proposals that would seemingly meet our

Exhibit 4   (Continued)

schedule. Their past performance, however, has not supported their optimistic projections.

4.   My recommended course of action, then, is to offer the Army FY85 procurement with the Navy FY86 procurement as a competitively bidded contract.

T. J. HUGHES
Deputy Chief of Naval Operations (Logistics)

Exhibit 5

DEPARTMENT OF THE NAVY
Office of the Chief of Naval Operations
Washington, D.C. 20350

In Reply Refer to
4020
Ser. 424C/5U393830
08 May 85

From:	Chief of Naval Operations (OP-04)
To:	Assistant Secretary of the Navy (Shipbuilding and Logistics)
Subj:	PROCUREMENT OF CAUSEWAY SYSTEMS UNDER SMALL BUSINESS ADMINISTRATION 8(a) SET-ASIDE
Ref:	(a) OP-04 memo Ser 424/5U392819 of 20 Feb. 85

1.   In reference (a), I summarized the recurring problems with WEDTECH and their inability to deliver powered causeway sections (CSP) in support of Maritime Prepositioning Ships (MPS). I concluded by recommending that we offer the Army FY85 procurement and Navy FY86 procurement as a competitively bid contract. Since that time we have yet to receive the first CSP. We are past the point of simple schedule slippages and are now dealing with a very real degradation of our sealift offload capability.

2.   As a result of schedule changes thus far, we have had to make several decisions that effectively reduced overall readiness. In the first quarter of FY85, MPS-1T did not receive sufficient lighterage and, consequently, was not deployed as planned. In February, as deadlines continued to pass, we were forced to shift the priority of CSP loadouts from MPS-1 to MPS-2, in order that units of the MTPF might be relieved on schedule. Even so, units of MPS-2 will receive lighterage up to 257 days late and lighterage delays for MPS-1 will exceed one year. As a part of this same action, MPS

was given a higher priority than the assault echelon (AE), thus reducing the Navy's amphibious assault capability. We are providing MPS with a newer class asset before providing the active forces with equal assets for training or deployments. Finally, the FY84 SLWT deliveries to the Amphibious Construction Battalions would have supported the demonstration of the Offshore Petroleum Discharge System in September 1985. In order to demonstrate that system, we are now forced to further delay delivery of one SLWT to MPS-1.

3. Delivery of the first ten CSPs was required by 29 October 1984. At best, I anticipate delivery of the first CSP in June with the tenth CSP delivery in early August. With the exception of minor delays experienced in delivery of the initial GFE propulsion pumps and correction of a debris contamination problem in the GFE pumps, responsibility for delay in lighterage delivery rests with the contractor. WEDTECH's problems include a multitude of items such as: (1) inadequate production and assembly facilities, (2) improper tooling procedures, (3) absence of necessary production and assembly work procedures, (4) inadequate quality control measures and (5) inexperience in building small craft/ships. These are all contributing factors to delivery schedule slippage and also to the dimensional and tolerance problem WEDTECH is currently addressing. To expedite delivery of the first ten CSPs, we are granting rework waivers, however, all other lighterage must be built in accordance with plans and specifications. I am not confident, more than a year after contract award, that they have resolved their facilities, quality, or management problems to the extent necessary to preclude further delivery delays. Assuming no further schedule slippage, WEDTECH currently has a full year of production and assembly remaining.

4. I do not see satisfactory progress, and the delays experienced have severely impacted the fielding of MPS shipping and the capabilities of our amphibious assault force. I must reiterate my strong recommendation that we act now to cut our losses by issuing an unrestricted IFB for the Army FY85 and Navy FY86 procurements.

T. J. HUGHES
Deputy Chief of Naval Operations (Logistics)

Exhibit 6   Biography

EVERETT PYATT
ASSISTANT SECRETARY OF THE NAVY
(SHIPBUILDING AND LOGISTICS)

On 16 April 1984, President Reagan announced the nomination of Everett A. Pyatt to be the Assistant Secretary of the Navy for Shipbuilding and Logistics. He was confirmed by the Senate on 2 August 1984 and took the Oath of Office on 3 August 1984.

Mr. Pyatt graduated from Yale University in 1962 with a Bachelor of Engineering in Electrical Engineering and a Bachelor of Science in Industrial Administration. He also holds a Master's Degree in Business Administration from the University of Pennsylvania, Wharton School.

Mr. Pyatt entered Civil Service under the Management Intern Program. From 1969 to 1972, he participated in efforts supporting Vietnam activities and the U.S. Middle East Task Group, evaluations of Soviet technology, and U.S. weapon development planning processes as a member of special working groups. He worked in a variety of roles in the Office of the Secretary of Defense from 1973 to 1977 and served as Principal Deputy Assistant Secretary of the Navy for Logistics from June 1977 until January 1980. During this period, he was awarded the Navy Distinguished Service Award. He then served as Deputy Chief Financial Officer for Project and Business Management at the Department of Energy.

Prior to his confirmation as Assistant Secretary of the Navy, Mr. Pyatt served as the Principal Deputy Assistant Secretary of the Navy for Shipbuilding and Logistics, for which he was awarded the Meritorious Senior Executive Award in 1982.

Mr. Pyatt was born on 22 July 1939, in Kansas City, Missouri. He resides in Arlington, Virginia, with his wife, two daughters, and son.

16 January 1986

Exhibit 7

NEWS CLIPS

Date: Wednesday, February 3, 1988, P.M.

The Navy Office Of Information

PHONE: 697-5342

C 12   DAILY NEWS

Wedtech 'squeeze'

By KEVIN McCOY
Daily News Staff Writer

Navy job 'traded' for pact approval

A former White House aide to Attorney General Edwin Meese stalled the job promotion of a top Navy official in an arm-twisting bid to help Wedtech Corp. win a $24.5 million Navy contract, investigators have been told.

The 1984 maneuver, detailed in an FBI memo obtained by the Daily News, involves James Jenkins, chief deputy to then White House counsel Meese: John Lehman, then secretary of the Navy, and the lobbying firm of former White House political adviser Lyn Nofziger.

The memo indicates Jenkins "refrained from authorising" Lehman's appointment of Everett Pyatt as an assistant Navy secretary at the behest of Nofziger's partner, Mark Bragg. Bragg is identified in the memo as Wedtech's "middleman between (the) Navy and White House."

Based on an interview with former Wedtech vice president Mario Moreno, the FBI memo says Jenkins would authorize Pyatt's promotion "if Lehman dropped his opposition" to Wedtech's bid for the Navy pontoon contract.

Lehman later abandoned his objections, and the Bronx-based defense contractor won the contract in April 1984. Four months later, Pyatt got the promotion.

Bragg's attorney, Richard Ben-Veniste, and the office of Washington special counsel James McKay, now prosecuting Nofziger and Bragg on ethics violation charges in lobbying for Wedtech, declined comment.

Jenkins, now retired from the Wedtech job he took after leaving the White House in 1984, could not be reached. His attorney, Fritz Korth, said, "It would be inappropriate to comment" during the Nofziger-Bragg trial.

Lehman, now an investment banker, did not return calls.

Navy spokeswoman Lt. Kippy Burns said, "Mr. Pyatt had no knowledge of a connection between his nomination being forwarded by the White House and the awarding of the Wedtech contract."

The Navy contract allegation has not surfaced in the Nofziger-Bragg trial because the case hinges solely on alleged ethics violations in the year after Nofziger's January 1982 departure as President Reagan's top political aide.

The News reported Sunday that Moreno also told investigators that Nofziger & Bragg secretly squeezed Wedtech to help the firm win a $51.5 million extension of the initial pontoon contract.

The payment, which Moreno said "everyone knew would be illegal," was detailed in secret notes of a separate Moreno interview by McKay's staff.

BOOKS RECOMMENDED FOR FURTHER STUDY

I. GENERAL COMPARISONS: EUROPE, ASIA, THE UNITED STATES

The following are among the best studies of comparative business-government relations by historians, political scientists, and political economists:

Aberbach, Joel D., Robert D. Putnam, and Bert A. Rockman, *Bureaucrats and Politicians in Western Democracies* (Cambridge, Mass.: Harvard University Press, 1981). See especially Chapter 1 for a summary of the authors' findings from a survey of roles and relationships of bureaucrats and politicians in seven western countries.

Badaracco, Joseph L., *Loading the Dice: A Five-Country Study of Vinyl Chloride Regulation* (Boston: Harvard Business School Press, 1985). In 1974, the industrial world discovered that vinyl chloride, a gas widely used in the production of plastic, was a deadly carcinogen. This is a study of how business and government in five countries—the United States, Japan, Britain, France, and Germany—responded to the regulatory challenge. It raises the question of when a cooperative approach to governmental relations is more effective than an adversarial one, and of what some of the prerequisites to cooperation are.

Berhman, Jack N., *Industrial Policies: International Restructuring and Transnationals* (Lexington, Mass.: D.C. Heath, 1984). Berhman is Luther Hodges Distinguished Professor at the University of North Carolina Graduate School of Business Administration. From 1961 to 1964 he served as assistant secretary of commerce for domestic and international business in the Kennedy and Johnson administrations. He has written over 20 books on comparative business-government relations, of which this is the most recent. It has three parts: the first is a handy primer on industrial policies of government in Japan, France, Germany, Brazil, South Korea, Taiwan, and the United States. Part II examines pressures toward international industrial integration, and Part III focuses on various international organizations, like the OECD, that play a role in industrial restructuring and cooperation.

Chandler, Alfred D., Jr., and Herman Daems, eds., *Managerial Hierarchies: Comparative Pespectives on the Rise of the Modern Industrial Enterprise* (Cambridge, Mass.: Harvard University Press, 1980). This is a short (237 pages), up-to-date (1970s) description and analysis of the rise of managerial hierarchies in the four leading Western economies—the United States, Britain, Germany, and France. Chandler's chapter on the United States is a particularly useful summary of his work. Although the book does not focus directly on government relations, it reveals how the historical evolution of corporations was affected by the particular roles and policies of different governments.

Katzenstein, Peter J., ed., *Between Power and Plenty: Foreign Economic Policies of Advanced Industrial States* (Madison: The University of Wisconsin Press, 1978). This is a collection of essays by eminent professors of history, government, and political economy analyzing and comparing the foreign economic policies of the United States, four European countries, and Japan. The authors argue that the domestic structure of a country—its business and government bureaucracies and their relationships to each other—is a critical variable shaping the country's political strategy as well as its international relationships. The book has a theoretical orientation, focusing in part on how and why nations gain or lose control in the international economy.

Lindblom, Charles E., *Politics and Market: The World's Political-Economic Systems* (New York: Basic Books, 1977). This remains a useful analysis of the logic of the market as a device for controlling

and of its opposite—state planning. It also contains an interesting contrast between
ning of industrial activity in the USSR (pre-*perestroika*) and China (pre-Deng).

Ezra F. Vogel, eds., *Ideology and National Competitiveness, An Analysis of Nine Countries*
ness School Press, 1987). Seven authors from different academic disciplines
ideology as a way of comparing national systems. The authors find that
requires that certain ideological characteristics be present, and that there
of ideologies toward some version of communitarianism.

eds., *Comparative Government-Industry Relations: Western Europe, the*
Clarendon Press, Oxford, 1987). This collection of essays by
sts focuses on such industries as chemicals, pharmaceuticals,
legal cultures, methods of coping with industrial decline,
containment.

wth: Financial Systems and the Politics of Industrial Change (Ithaca,
political economist assesses what makes different govern-
ndustrial leadership. He looks at the role of the state in the
rial countries during the late 1970s and early 1980s.

business relations in the United States.

nerican Approach to Leadership in Business and Politics
is of the peculiar forces that keep business and
concludes that both "technocratic" and "political"
ey understand how differently they view their tasks.

olicy," *Harvard Business Review,* (November–December,
w of the relationship between business and public policy
om other countries. See also Thomas K. McCraw, ed., *The*
Business School Press, 1988), for a useful collection of
the evolution of "managerial capitalism" in America, and
other countries.

le: Dealing with the World as It Is," *Harvard Business Review*
discussion of how and why America differs from her
ains some useful figures and maps.

How Washington Works: The Executive's Guide to Washington
he best of many how-to-do-it handbooks on Washington
orks in clear and simple terms.

e Promise of Disharmony (Cambridge, Mass.: Harvard University
ican political history exploring the roots of the adversarial
business.

g Sweden: A Comparative Study of Occupational Safety and Health
981). Similar to Badaracco's broader comparative study of
ollution, this is a two-country study of government policies

nomic Perspectives, Vol. I, no. 2 (Fall 1987), p. 136. A landmark
that traditional American economics may need to adjust to
ting works—at least for them.

(New York: New York University Press, 1986), and *The New*
Knopf, 1980). The concept of ideology is defined and used to

Zysman, John, *Governments, Markets, and Gro*
N.Y.: Cornell University Press, 1983). A
ments more or less capable of exercising
marketplace, comparing the major indus

Wilks, Stephen, and Maurice Wright,
United States, and Japan (New York:
European and American social scient
and telecommunications. It compares
industrial policy formulation, and cos

odge, George C., and
(Boston: Harvard Bus
demonstrate the use o
national competitiveness
appears to be a convergence

unities a
ernment plan

describe the evolution of government and business in the United State
restraint on behavior by both sets of institutions. The author calls for
more effectively with the problems of the 1980s.

Lowi, Theodore, J., *The End of Liberalism: The Second Republic of the U*
Norton and Company,   ). A classic analysis of how interest
policies and priorities in the United States.

Scott, Bruce R., and Goerge C. Lodge, eds., *U.S. Competiti*
Business School Press, 1984). A collection of essays in
the relationship between government and busin
decline of the United States in the world eco
automobiles, and textiles.

Smith, Hedrick, *The Power Game: How Washington Wo*
Washington in 1987 by a veteran reporter for *T*
as well as a good many useful facts and figur

Vietor, Richard H. K., *Energy Policy in Ameri*
(Cambridge: Cambridge University Press,
business-government relations in industrie

Vogel, David, *National Styles of Regulation: Envi*
N.Y.: Cornell University Press, 1986). Voge
Britain and the United States and expla
approaches to controlling the externali

Weinberg, Martha Wagner, "The Political F
June 1988). This is an insightful study
legislation to provide federal product

Yoffie, David B., "How an Industry Builds P
Yoffie describes how the Semiconductor
Japan as a means of opening the Japanes

Zysman, John, and Laura Tyson, *American In*
University Press, 1983). A political scientist a
clearest assessments of how and why U.S. go
erosion of the nations competitiveness. They
nations is no longer static. It can be created

III. JAPAN

The following focus on Japanese government-bus

Hirschmier, J., and T. Yui, *The Development of Japanes*
and Unwin, 1982.) A good history of Japanes

Johnson, Chalmers, *MITI and the Japanese Mirac*
Calif.: Stanford University Press, 1982). A Be
working of Japanese government and busi
understanding of modern Japan.

McGraw, Thomas K., ed., *America Versus Japan* (B
comparative analysis of government-business
Harvard professors, headed by Professor McG
and banking; policy areas analyzed include tra
mental regulation, and government finance.

Prestowitz, Clyde, V., Jr., *Trading Places* (New York: Basic Books, 1988). After serving five years as the U.S. government's chief negotiator with Japan, Prestowitz, a former Department of Commerce official, tells what it was really like. He exposes the incoherence and conflict of interest among Washington executive departments, the confused nature of American goals, and the continuing failure of U.S. negotiations against better prepared, better organized and more unified Japanese rivals.

Yoshino, Michael Y., and Thomas B. Lifson, *The Invisible Link: Japan's Sogo Shosha and the Organization of Trade* (Cambridge, Mass.: MIT Press, 1986). A useful description and analysis of how Japan's trading companies work, including an exploration of their relations to the Japanese government.

IV. THE CORPORATE VIEWPOINT

The following approach government-business relations more explicitly from the corporate viewpoint.

Bower, Joseph L., *When Markets Quake* (Boston: Harvard Business School Press, 1987). Bower examines the restructuring of the world chemical industry during the early 1980s in response to worldwide overcapacity. He considers also the general problem of coping with overcapacity in other industries, such as automobiles, steel, and semiconductors. In many countries, government is a major player in reshaping markets as well as suppliers to those markets.

Encarnation, Dennis, and Louis T. Wells, Jr., "Sovereignty En Garde: Negotiating with Foreign Investors," *International Organization*, Vol. I (Winter 1985), p. 47. This article reports on the authors' research concerning government policies in a variety of countries concerning foreign investment. They examine both constraints on such investment as well as incentives to do more of it.

Gomes-Casseres, Benjamin, "MNC Ownership Preferences and Host Government Regulations: An Integrated Approach" (Boston: Harvard Business School Working Paper #89-023, August 1988). Gomes-Casseres reviews government policies in a variety of countries concerning the ownership of multinational corporations operating in those countries.

Porter, Michael E., ed., *Competition in Global Industries* (Boston: Harvard Business School Press, 1986). A collection of essays about the strategies of global industries; of special interest are Porter's "Introduction and Summary" and Chapter 1, which sets forth his conceptual framework; and chapters 7–9: "Government Policies and Global Industries" by Yves L. Doz, "Competitive Strategies in Global Industries: A View from Host Governments" by Dennis J. Encarnation and Louis T. Wells, Jr., and "Government Relations in the Global Firm" by Amir Mahini and Louis T. Wells, Jr.

Vernon, Raymond, *Sovereignty at Bay: The Multinational Spread of U.S. Enterprises* (New York: Basic Books, 1971). Vernon's classic explores the tension between the policies and interests of governments, especially in developing countries, and multinational corporations operating in their domain.